Library of
Davidson College

Ocean at the Window

Ocean at the Window

~~~~~~~~~~~~~~~~~~~~~~~~~~~~~~~~

Hungarian Prose and Poetry since 1945

Albert Tezla, *Editor*

UNIVERSITY OF MINNESOTA PRESS □ MINNEAPOLIS

Copyright © 1980 by the University of Minnesota.
All rights reserved.
Published by the University of Minnesota Press,
2037 University Avenue Southeast, Minneapolis MN 55414
Printed in the United States of America.

Library of Congress Cataloging in Publication Data
Main entry under title:

Ocean at the window.

Bibliography: p.
1. Hungarian literature—20th century.
I. Tezla, Albert.
PH3136.023   894'.511'08003   80-39770
ISBN 0-8166-0992-6

The following selections are reprinted by permission of the publisher or translator:

"The Boy Changed into a Stag," "Firelily in the Night," and excerpt from "Images of the Night," translated by Kenneth McRobbie and Ilona Duczynska, from *Ferenc Juhász: The Boy Changed Into a Stag, Selected Poems 1949-1967*, copyright © 1970 by Oxford University Press.

"Lovers," "Carrying Love," "Squared by Walls," "Without Mercy," translated by Tony Connor and George Gömöri, excerpts from "Wedding," translated by Kenneth McRobbie and George Gömöri, from *László Nagy: Love of the Scorching Wind: Selected Poems 1953-1971*, copyright © 1973 by Oxford University Press.

László Nagy's "The Bliss of Sunday," © 1970 Edwin Morgan and *New Hungarian Quarterly*.

László Nagy's "Elegy of the Green Tent" and "House," Ferenc Juhász's "Béla Bartók and the Tree Frog," and excerpts from "The Coffin of Zoltán Latinovits" and from "Notes for an Epic," © 1979 Kenneth McRobbie.

Artisjus granted permission to translate works especially for this book, to use the Miklós Borsos graphics, published in *Mai Magyar Rajzművészet*, and to include selections previously published in *Arion, Bulletin: Hungarian P.E.N.*, and *The New Hungarian Quarterly:* Sándor Csoóri's "Approaching Words," translated by Carl R. Erickson; István Csurka's "The Passengers," translated by Mari Kuttna; László Nagy's "The Martyred Arabian Mare" and "Evocation of the City" and Dezső Tandori's "The Belated Halt," translated by Tony Connor; and Ferenc Sánta's "The Initiation," translated by Albert Tezla.

The University of Minnesota
is an equal-opportunity
educator and employer.

"The ocean would come up to my window
in vain if I, its host, no longer knew
anything about myself."

      Sándor Csoóri,
      in a letter to the editor,
      August 1976.

Contents

Preface xv
Major Developments in the Imaginative
   Literature of Hungary since 1945   *Albert Tezla* . . .xix
How to Pronounce Hungarian Words   *László Országh* . . .xli

       PART ONE
  Authors from 1945 to 1965

István Örkény   *Translated by Carl R. Erickson* . . .3
Selections of One-Minute Stories
How to Use One-Minute Stories (Használati utasítás, 1968) 8
Honeymooners on Flypaper
   (Nászutasok a légypapíron, 1968) 9
Immortality (Halhalatlanság, 1969). 10
How Long Will a Tree Live? (Meddig él egy fa?, 1968) 11
In Memoriam Professor G.H.K. (In memoriam K.H.G., 1968). . .15
Two Cupolas in a Snow-Covered Landscape
   (Havas tájban két hagymakupola, 1968) 15
The Savior (A Megváltó, 1968) 16
Satan at Lake Balaton (A Sátán Füreden, 1968) 17

A Brief Course in Foreign Affairs
  (Néhány perc külpolitika, 1968) 20
Public Opinion Research (Közvéleménykutatás, 1969) 21
The Niagara Café (Niagara Nagykávéház, 1971) 22
The Old Traditions (Egy szoba, vályogfal zsúpfedél, 1968).....28
170-100 (170-100, 1969).....................................29
The Hungarian Hall of Fame (Magyar Pantheon, 1968)........31
The Last Cherry Stone (Az utolsó meggymag, 1969) 34

Iván Mándy   *Translated by Albert Tezla* . . .37
  The Watermelon Eaters (Dinnyeevők, 1957)................41
  A Summer Holiday (Nyaralás, 1957).......................46
  King Kong (King Kong, 1967).............................49
  The Death of Zoro (Zoro halála, 1967)...................50
  In the Spotlight (A siker fényében, 1972)...............59
  What Can a Writer Want? (Mit akarhat egy író, 1966).........70

Miklós Mészöly   *Translated by Albert Tezla* . . .73
  Encounter (Találkozás, 1959)............................77
  Shade (Az árnyék, 1959).................................86
  The Three Potato Bugs (A három burgonyabogár, 1962) 90
  A Map with Lacerations (Térkép, repedésekkel, 1971) 102
  Sunt Lacrimae Rerum (Sunt lacrimae rerum, 1971) 111

János Pilinszky   *Translated by Peter Sherwood* . . .115
  Fish in the Net (Halak a hálóban, 1942) 120
  Autumn Sketch (Őszi vázlat, 1946).......................121
  Passion of Ravensbrück (Ravensbrücki passió, 1959) 121
  The Desert of Love (A szerelem sivataga, 1959) 122
  Apocrypha (Apokrif, 1959) 123
  Quatrain (Négysoros, 1959) 126
  Agonia Christiana (Agonia Christiana, 1959).............126
  A Cold Wind (Hideg szél, 1959) 126
  The Imperfect Tense (Félmúlt, 1959).....................127
  KZ-Oratorio (KZ-oratórium, 1971)........................127
  Van Gogh (Van Gogh, 1971)...............................133
  Eine Kleine Nachtmusik (Kis éjizene, 1971) 134
  One Fine Day (Egy szép napon, 1972) 135

The Nadir Celebrated (A mélypont ünnepélye, 1972)........136
Cattle-Brand (Marhabélyeg, 1972).........................137
Self-Portrait 1974 (Önarckép 1974, 1974)................137
Tableaux Vivants (Élőképek, 1974) 138
"Creative Imagination" in Our Time
  (A 'teremtő képzelet' sorsa korunkban, 1970) 143
"An Autobiography" (Invented title for an extract
  from *Conversations with Sheryl Sutton*
  [*Beszélgetés Sheryl Suttonal*, 1977])..................147

Ágnes Nemes Nagy 151
  Trees (Fák, 1969) 158
  Night Oak (Éjszakai tölgyfa, 1969).....................159
  The Horses and the Angels (A lovak és az angyalok, 1967)....160
  Fig Trees (Fügefák, 1967)..............................162
  Breath (Lélegzet, 1967)................................163
  Formerly (Azelőtt, 1967) 163
  Akhenaton (Ekhnáton, 1967)............................164
  Dusk (Alkony, 1967) 169
  Landscape: At Home (Tájkép: otthon, 1957)..............170
  Combat (Viadal, 1957)..................................171
    Translated by Enikő Molnár Basa and Maxim Tabory
  Transformation of a Railroad
    Station (Egy pályaudvar átalakítása, 1974)...........171
  The Proportions of the Street (Az utca arányai, 1974).......173
  "Elusive Apple" ("Tünékeny alma," 1975)...............174
  From: Interview, 1967 177
    Translated by Enikő Molnár Basa

László Nagy..181
  Lovers (Szeretők, 1954) 187
    Translated by Tony Connor and George Gömöri
  The Bliss of Sunday (Vasárnap gyönyöre, **1956**)..........188
    Translated by Edwin Morgan
  Carrying Love (Ki viszi át a Szerelmet, 1965).............195
  Squared by Walls (A falak négyszögében, 1965) 195
  Without Mercy (Amikor nincs kegyelem, 1965) 196
    Translated by Tony Connor and George Gömöri

From: Wedding (Menyegző, 1965) 197
   Translated by Kenneth McRobbie and George Gömöri
The Martyred Arabian Mare (Vértanú arabs kanca, 1973).....201
Evocation of the City (A város idézése, 1973)..............203
Hiding in Poetry (Versben bujdosó, 1973) 204
   Translated by Tony Connor
Elegy of the Green Tent (A zöld sátor elégiája, 1977)........206
House (Ház, 1978) 208
   Translated by Kenneth McRobbie
From: Interview, 1965 210
From: Cognition, Language, and Poetry (Megismerés,
   nyelv és vers, 1975)..................................213
   Translated by Georgia Lenart Greist

Ferenc Sánta   *Translated by Albert Tezla* . . .215
Little Bird (Kicsi madár, 1954)...........................219
Fairyland (Tündérkert, 1955)............................225
The Initiation (Emberavatás, 1955)........................229
No More Dying Then (Halálnak halála, 1963)...............235
From: Interview, 1967 245

Ferenc Juhász 247
The Boy Changed into a Stag Cries Out at the Gate
   of Secrets (A szarvassá változott
   fiú kiáltozása a titkok kapujában, 1955)..................252
Firelily in the Night (Tűzliliom az éjszakában, 1961) 263
From: Images of the Night (Az éjszaka képei, 1961).........265
   Translated by Kenneth McRobbie and Ilona Duczynska
Béla Bartók and the Tree Frog (Bartók Béla a zöld
   levelibékával, 1970)...................................269
From: The Coffin of Zoltán Latinovits Written All Over
   Inside and Out Like an Egyptian Mummy Dummy
   (Latinovits Zoltán koporsója kívül-belül teleírva
   mint az egyiptomi múmia-bábok, 1976) 272
From: Notes For an Epic (Egy éposz
   jegyzetlapjai, 1977)...................................275
   Translated by Kenneth McRobbie

Sándor Csoóri 277
   Interrogating Ode to Women (Faggatodzó óda
     a nőkhöz, 1967) 282
   Farewell to Cuba (Búcsú Kubától, 1967) 283
   When I Touch You (Ha megérintlek, 1967) 284
   Just Nowhere (Csak sehol, 1967) 285
     Translated by Daniel Abondolo
   But That Water Is Still Flowing Here (De a víz
     még itt folyik, 1973) 286
     Translated by Robert Austerlitz
   On the Third Day Snow Began to Fall
     (A harmadik nap esni kezdett a hó, 1973) 287
   And to Step toward the Door (és lépni az ajtó felé, 1973) 288
   The Other (A másik, 1973) 289
     Translated by Peter Sherwood
   Mumbling (Dünnyögő, 1973) 289
   Meditative Inventory (Leltár, tűnődve, 1973) 290
   Eyes (Szemek, 1977) 291
   It's Not I Who Sit There Now (Már nem én ülök ott, 1977) ... 292
     Translated by Daniel Abondolo
   Self-Portrait in a Misty Mirror (Önarckép,
     párás tükörben, 1977) 292
     Translated by Robert Austerlitz
   Manhood (Férfikor, 1977) 293
   In Floodlit Night (Kivilágított éjszakában, 1977) 294
     Translated by Daniel Abondolo
   Approaching Words (Közeledés a szavakhoz, 1967) 295
     Translated by Carl R. Erickson

István Csurka 301
   The Two Rheumatics (Két reumás, 1968) 306
   The Main Wall (Főfal, 1972) 312
     Translated by Georgia Lenart Greist
   LSD (LSD, 1972) 319
   The Passengers (Utasok, 197?) 324
     Translated by Mari Kuttna

PART TWO
Authors since 1965

Anna Jókai Translated by *Georgia Lenart Greist* ...337
  The Angel at Reims (A reimsi angyal, 1975)...............339

László Marsall..345
  River and Sun (Folyó és nap, 1970).....................347
  The Depths of Silence (A csönd mélységei, 1970)..........348
    Translated by Daniel Abondolo
  Striptease (Sztriptíz, 1970)............................349
    Translated by Peter Sherwood

István Császár Translated by *John Freeman* ...353
  A Break in the Film (Elszakadt a film, 1971).............355

Dezső Tandori..361
  Irreducibility (A levezethetetlen, 1976).................363
  The Interview (Az interjú, 1976).........................364
  Cerebral Inions (Az agy-érzések V-je, 1976)..............364
    Translated by Robert Austerlitz
  The Belated Halt, or Dr. Jekyll's Dream (A feltételes
    megálló avagy: Dr. Jekyll álma, 1978)..................365
  For the Klee-Milne Sketchbook (A Klee-Milne
    vázlatkönyvbe, 1978)...................................366
    Translated by Tony Connor

Anna Kiss..367
  The Birth of the Tale (A mese születése, 1971)............369
  In the Vineyard (Szölőhegyen, 1971).....................370
  Silence (Csend, 1971)...................................370
    Translated by Enikő Molnár Basa
  Gentian, full-grown, everywhere (és mindenütt a magas
    encián, 1976)..371
  Two Little Snakes (Jár nyomomban, 1976)..................372
    Translated by Robert Austerlitz

József Utassy Translated by *Daniel Abondolo* ...373
  Illegal Honeymoon (Illegális nászéjszaka, 1969)..........375
  Envious (Irigykedő, 1969)................................376

After Harvest (Szüret után, 1969)......................377
Your Pennies (Filléreitek, 1969).........................377

Gábor Czakó *Translated by Georgia Lenart Greist* ...379
The Cat (A macska, 1971).............................381

Miklós Veress *Translated by Daniel Abondolo* ...385
Mothers (Anyák, 1964)................................387
Death of Planets (Bolygóhalál, 1975)....................388
Ballad (Ballada, 1975).................................388

Benedek Kiss *Translated by Timothy Kachinske* ...391
White Field (Fehér mező, 1973)........................393
The Winter Moon (A téli hold, 1973)....................394
An Old Stag (Régi szarvas, 1973) 394
What Do I Want? (Mit akarok?, 1973)...................395

György Petri...397
Once Again (Most újból, 1971).........................399
Only a Person (Csak egy személy, 1971).................400
Xenia (Xenia, 1971) 401
  Translated by Robert Austerlitz
Meeting (Találkozás, 197?)............................401
Lovers (Szeretők, 1974) 402
Inscription (Felirat, 1974)............................402
Grace (Kegy, 1974)...................................403
  Translated by Tony Connor

Géza Bereményi *Translated by Georgia Lenart Greist* ...405
Last Spin on the Water (Utolsó kör a vízen, 1970) 407

Vilmos Csaplár *Translated by John Freeman* ...415
Our Customers' Attention Is Drawn to the Model 968
  Zaporozsec Automobile (Vásárlóink figyelmébe
  ajánljuk a Zaporozsec 968-as típusú gépkocsit, 1975)......416

Szilveszter Ördögh *Translated by John Freeman* ...423
The Elephant (Az elefánt, 1973).........................425

Miklós Vámos *Translated by Albert Tezla* ...431
Keresztes (Keresztes, 1972)............................433
Little Boys and Big Boys (Kisfiúk és nagyfiúk, 1972)........435

Anthologies of Twentieth-Century Hungarian Literature and
  Writings of the Authors in the Present Work in English, French,
  and German Translation
        Compiled by Kathy Elaine Tezla and Ilona Kovács . . .441
Contributors 477

Preface

This anthology of short works of poetry and prose joins the increasing but still insufficient number of translations that attempt to acquaint general readers in the English-speaking world with significant aspects of Hungarian literature. The present volume, which contains works by authors who now reside in Hungary, seeks to deepen the nonspecialist's knowledge of the literature appearing after World War II, not by offering an overview through the contributions of numerous authors, but by giving most attention to the works of ten major figures chosen from among the many who established their place during the first two decades after 1945 and by presenting a few works of fourteen writers selected from those who first published in book form between 1965 and 1975. More space is devoted to prose works than to poems, so that readers can note some of the recent experiments in prose fiction and the sharp growth in treatises on literature, developments that deserve much more attention in English translation than they have received to the present. Almost all the selections are complete; the only excerpts are taken from two long poems by Ferenc Juhász and a long poem by László Nagy, from three literary treatises, and from the interviews.

It was difficult to choose authors from a period so torn by historical events and tested by radical social changes, and so rich in literary activity—and particularly difficult to select the ten major figures whose work would appear in Part One. To give unity to this section and, at the same time, to draw attention to some significant trends, I used specific guidelines in making my decisions. For example, I did not consider authors whose lifework could not be represented adequately by their short writings. More important, those chosen had to be among the writers who are widely read by intellectuals in Hungary, who exert considerable influence on current literary developments, and who measure up to the critical standards of world literature. Finally, their lifework had to treat themes that I thought would be of interest to general readers and not narrowly developed in detail. Although in Part Two I could not proceed as methodically, I tried to give a taste of the most recent work that I thought would appeal to the general reader and that promises to influence writing after 1975.

The selections are usually presented chronologically, as determined by the earliest date of publication that I was able to validate. The writings of the poets are grouped under poetry and prose, respectively, in both categories either by date of publication or, when necessary, by their place in the most recent collections supervised by the author. An exception is the work of Ágnes Nemes Nagy, which follows the reverse chronology that she adopts in the second and enlarged edition of her poems, *The Horses and the Angels* (*A lovak és az angyalok*, 1969). Her more recent poetry, however, follows chronologically after the selections from this collected edition. The selections by prosewriters also follow these principles of organization, except for the work of István Örkény and István Csurka, whose stories are arranged by themes. Also, wherever literary treatises and interviews are included, they close the selections from the author's works. In all instances, the Hungarian title of a selection appears in the Table of Contents, along with its date of publication, which is in italics if I traced it to a periodical, in regular type if to an edition of the author's works.

As editor, I express my deepest gratitude to all who have contributed their creative energies so generously to the venture since its formal inception in 1974: to those translators whose new translations in the text open fresh paths to the literature; to Kathy Tezla and Ilona Kovács for the practical bibliography designed for readers who want to extend their knowledge of twentieth-century Hungarian literature beyond the boundary of the present book; to László Országh, a close associate and friend of three decades, for the guide helping nonspecialists with the pronunciation of Hungarian words; and to Kent Bales, Joseph Duncan, and Joseph Maiolo, colleagues at the University of Minnesota, to the first two for their valuable comments on the editorial matter and to the last for his helpful counsel in choosing the fiction. I also owe a great debt to the staffs of the National Széchényi Library and the Library of the Institute of Literary Studies, Hungarian Academy of Sciences, for making available to me so promptly and efficiently the large amount of materials my reading and research required during three short stays in Budapest and also to the funding agencies that made these indispensable visits possible: the International Research and Exchanges Board, the Hungarian Institute for Cultural Relations, and the University of Minnesota's Office of International Programs.

The preparation of this anthology was an exciting adventure, often a very moving experience for me. I hope that readers will enjoy what they find here and that their knowledge of life and understanding of themselves will be enriched by the individual insights of these authors from a little-known literary heritage.

Albert Tezla

Major Developments in the Imaginative Literature of Hungary since 1945

Albert Tezla

More formidable impediments to the development of the literature of a small European nation can hardly be found than those present in Hungary during the postwar period. During these thirty years many historical events rent the intellectual and social fabric of the country. Hungarians had to bear the moral onus of the long alliance with Germany and of the savage acts of the native fascists, the Szálasi Arrow-Cross Party, in the closing months of the war. They had to restore the economic life of a land devastated by war and burdened by Soviet occupation. Their early attempts to revive national life occurred amid crucial struggles among political parties vying for popular support. When this discord ended with the sudden assumption of power by the Communist Party in 1948, Hungarians experienced radical upheavals in all parts of their lives. After eight years of the new social order, smoldering discontent with Party measures erupted in the Revolution of 1956, leaving Hungarians to face the consequences of the horrible blood-letting and the failure to reestablish a democratic government. The twenty years since that spontaneous uprising have witnessed the consolidation of a single-party socialist state, producing a profound impact not only on the economic and social life of the nation but also on the cultural policies that govern all the arts.

Even this brief summary of the chaotic and complex realities of postwar Hungary suggests that the circumstances in which creative writers had to work would pose grave barriers to the revival of literature and its evolution into a valuable interpreter of the human scene, as it had clearly shown signs of doing between the two world wars. In spite of the turmoil and uncertainty often attending these years, however, Hungarian authors developed a rich and varied imaginative literature, which, to a remarkable degree, eventually measured up to the enthusiasms and expectations that so many of them had expressed at the beginning of the post-war period.

The Early Post-War Period, 1945-48

At the end of the war, the atmosphere of freedom, unknown to Hungarian authors since the nation had been linked to Hitler's Germany in the mid-1930s, produced an outburst of literary activity. With censorship lifted and intellectual horizons unobstructed, all kinds of writing, including socialist, were published. There was much experimentation, and before long, many views of life and forms of expression existed side by side, particularly in poetry and fiction. This great surge of creativity was energized by many new journals that zealously advocated certain literary approaches, as well as partisan political viewpoints, and, for a time, found common ground in supporting humanistic principles. Although the struggle for power among the several political parties often interfered with literary activities, writers were vigorous enough to withstand the paralyzing effects of the worsening political atmosphere and to set in motion various trends so firmly that many outlasted the cultural policies put into effect in 1948, when the Communist Party took control of the nation.

Understandably, much of the imaginative literature appearing from 1945 to 1948 critically examined the events and social order of the previous twenty-five years that had culminated in the disaster of war. But, more significantly for the restoration of literature, authors probed issues ranging from current conditions in Hungary to the purpose of human existence and the nature of the universe. Certain poets among those who had established their reputations before the war stood out in this regard. There was Lőrinc Szabó, long an experimenter in verse forms, with his pessimistic view of humankind's struggle in an indifferent cosmos, and Milán Füst, a pioneer of free verse in Hungary, who rebelled against fate and felt deep compassion for humanity. Lajos Kassák, an early advocate of the avant-garde in both poetry and the visual arts, abandoned social themes to express his most intimate thoughts and feelings. Above the scene towered Gyula Illyés, the populist and poet of lyrical realism, who explored the issue of responsibility in the relationship between the individual and society, weighed thoughtfully the question of human efficacy, and viewed the problems of humankind from a historical perspective. István Vas, like Illyés a major inspiration for many young poets, was distressed by the anxieties pervading the times and offered the inherent strength of human reason and individual freedom as the best defense against calamity. Among the Communists, Zoltán Zelk pressed forward the need for revolutionary changes in the social and economic fabric, and László Benjámin, who published a volume of poems in 1939, urged radical reforms, based on his personal ideas, that would prepare the way for a socialist state. At the opposite pole, Sándor Weöres, divorcing himself from reality, searched for a private vision of a universal force that only a turning inward to the self could attain. These experienced poets were soon joined by those who would establish their place under conditions already looming on the political horizon. They fell into two groups. There were those who, as avowed Communists, dedicated themselves to the revolutionary transformation of their society: Ferenc Juhász, László Nagy, and István Simon, all of them from the poor social classes living in the villages. And there were those who, shocked by the moral implications of the war and Hungarian fascism, searched for new ethical and spiritual foundations on which to rebuild a relationship with life: Magda Szabó, who later wrote successful novels, János Pilinszky, Ágnes Nemes Nagy, László Kálnoky, and György Rába. The responses of these two groups and of prose writers who emerged at the same time to the stress and strain of impending historical events largely determined future trends in the post-war literature.

Prose fiction also manifested vitality at this time, although its themes and styles were not as various as those of poetry. For the most part, novelists and short-story writers preferred the values and attitudes of realism, and to arrive at a moral reckoning with their past, mainly re-examined Hungarian society since the end of World War I, analyzing sociologically and psychologically the semi-feudal social structure that lasted until 1945. This tradition, so firmly entrenched by the prolific and long career of Zsigmond Móricz, was best represented by several pre-war writers who were still active. Pál Szabó, another populist from the 1930s, portrayed peasant life and the conflicts between peasants and the intelligentsia. Péter Veres, then fifty years old, looked at peasant life in a satirical and humorous, though realistic manner. László Németh, more inventive than both, wrote his best novel, *Revulsion* (*Iszony*), in 1947. It depicts the problems of a family and life in a village through the confessions of wife whose marriage is falling apart. Also appearing at this time was fiction with a strong socialist theme, some of it written before the end of the war but not publishable until now. Probably the best example is Tibor Déry's *The Unfinished Sentence* (*A befejezetlen mondat*, 1947), which traces the gradual involvement of a middle-class intellectual in the cause of the working class between the two world wars, a narrative based on the author's past relationship with the proletariat. Another new current, one that soon caused serious problems for originality, was socialist realism. Béla Illés, an experienced writer just returned from Moscow with the Russian army, published a representative example, *Carpathian Rhapsody* (*Kárpáti rapszódia*), an affectionate portrait of Ukrainian life in the Carpathian Mountains, which appeared in thirteen editions between 1945 and 1960.

During these three years, other kinds of narrative representation did not develop significantly. They were present and had the potential to modify the realism that became such a fixture of the literary tradition. Unfortunately, the pressures of the times and social forces meant there was little opportunity to reconsider the purposes of prose fiction. To be sure, in the war years novelists were already experimenting with some elements of surrealism. Among the most accomplished were Emil Kolozsvári Grandpierre, György Rónay, István Sőtér, and Géza Ottlik, who were familiar with pre-war developments in the European novel and were associated with the progressive but short-lived literary periodical *Silver Age* (*Ezüstkor*). Some of the more promising authors among those making their debut immediately after the war vacillated between alternative styles and literary purposes. Imre Sarkadi turned to socialist realism for a time, believing that it served the needs of his country more productively than the realism of Zsigmond Móricz, which he had previously adopted; István Örkény, Ferenc Karinthy, and Lajos Mesterházi—who later became influential figures under changed historical conditions—first experimented with surrealism and then, for the same reason as Sarkadi, held up the mirror of socialist realism to their society—a mirror soon to be obligatory. Iván Mándy and Miklós Mészöly were also on the scene. Mándy was presenting an everyday world with an almost surrealistic mingling of the actual and the dream; Mészöly, who had quickly mastered the use of atmosphere in the short story to convey meaning, was experimenting with narrative techniques and style in search of new paths for Hungarian fiction. In 1948, amid these mixed trends and searchings, László Németh pointed the way that not only novelists but all writers must henceforth travel to foster a viable imaginative literature. In his view, the end of the war had brought a wider horizon to a literature that had just begun to mature between two world wars. "Now there is," he proclaimed, "no longer a national destiny; all humanity is now one nation, and the fate of everyone will be settled together: it is my right, indeed my duty to think about the whole human race." In the summer of that very year, the establishment of Communist control over national life abruptly arrested stylistic experimentation and the pursuit of Németh's concept of the writer's universal role.

The Effect of Schematism, 1949-52

The Communist Party's coming to power began the gravest period of literary creativity that Hungary had ever known. The Party's cultural policy seriously hobbled developments in imaginative literature for many years. Besides instituting radical economic and social changes and nationalizing all theaters and publishing houses, the government declared socialist realism, as promulgated in 1946 by Andrey Zhdanov in Russia, to be the sole course for the arts. In order to publish, writers were expected to adopt a schematic approach that interpreted reality in accord with socialist principles as the Party hierarchy defined them. Essentially, schematism, or socialist realism carried to an extreme, demanded that the writer abandon the right to select themes, surrender a personal interpretation of issues, and forsake a distinctive style. Writers had to subordinate individual views and conform strictly to prevailing Party ideology. Accordingly, imaginative literature was to achieve victory in the class struggle against bourgeois elements, to glorify heroes of the socialist revolution and vilify its enemies at home and abroad, and to sing about five-year plans, agricultural cooperatives, common people enjoying the fruits of socialist policies, the imminence of the earthly paradise that socialism would inevitably create, and the battle against capitalists for world peace. Moreover, to attain its strictly didactic aim, the style of a work had to be democratized, made simple and clear, so that uneducated workers and peasants could grasp and pursue the objectives of socialism. Failure to comply with these dictates did not necessarily shut every door to publication, especially in periodicals. The slightest departure from them, however, brought published accusations that the author had abandoned the nation, betrayed the proletariat, become apolitical, or turned to romantic self-indulgence. The rigid enforcement of this cultural policy by severely party-minded critics in an atmosphere charged with political threat and insecurity left open only two paths to writers who did not espouse the values of socialist realism out of personal conviction but who chose to remain in Hungary. Neither boded well for the acceleration of the vital trends that had emerged between 1945 and 1948. Writers could carry out the official policy if they were willing to act against the grain of their individuality and work below the level of their true gifts—the path chosen by such important authors as György Somlyó, Gábor Devecseri, Imre Sarkadi, Ferenc Karinthy, and István Örkény. Or like Sándor Weöres, István Vas, János Pilinszky, Ágnes Nemes Nagy, Iván Mándy, Géza Ottlik, Miklós Mészöly, and others, they could leave the literary scene if they were not willing to compromise the integrity of their convictions and style.

This is not to say that all literature of high quality vanished from public view. However, the aggressive enforcement of schematism nearly brought the evolution of a diverse literature to a standstill, particularly during the early 1950s, an effect openly acknowledged today by Hungarian critics and literary historians. The drama, its revival hardly begun, was made ridiculous by the dogmatic presentation of social issues from everyday life. Lyric poetry, the most highly developed genre in Hungarian literature, became platitudinous, its imagery commonplace, its forms repetitious, and its thought impoverished. Given the circumstances, it is not surprising that even among those supporting socialism only the more accomplished poets were able to write lyrics worth reading. Illyés, his prestige as a revolutionary populist ensuring his authority, continued to treat a wide range of themes; and Benjámin, his convictions deeply rooted in revolutionary traditions, infused his endorsements of the social changes taking place with enthusiasm and intense feeling. Among the new poets, Ferenc Juhász, László Nagy, and István Simon also managed to convey genuine emotions because they envisioned a better future for the social classes who had only recently begun to enjoy economic and social benefits. Prose fiction, with Móricz and the recent socialist realists in the Soviet Union serving as its exemplars, suffered even more severely than poetry. Even such eminent older writers of realism as Déry, Pál Szabó, and Veres, who successfully adapted their works to socialist realism, could not always erase every trace of disharmony between the official style and their convictions. Many established novelists chose to write autobiographies, autobiographical novels, and novel cycles presenting broad pictures of recent times. And often the heaviest burden of schematism fell on such authors as Karinthy, Sarkadi, and Örkény, who were striving to discover their individuality under the self-censorship that their attempt to weld literary purpose with political ends inflicted on them.

But in the long run the regime was not able to force writers into a single mold. Resistance to schematism as administered chiefly by the doctrinaire József Révai surfaced early, often publicly. György Lukács, the renowned Marxist philosopher, aesthetician, and literary historian, took issue with Révai and gave legitimacy to the reality created by the imagination. In the spring of 1951 authors strongly protested its injurious effect on originality at the First Congress of Hungarian Writers, which was summoned to evaluate the literary developments of the previous three decades and to fix the role of literature in a socialist society. Its proceedings were reported in the periodical *The Star* (*Csillag*) and then were expanded into a book published in the same year. During the sessions Benjámin and Juhász objected to policies affecting literary creativity and pointed to their inevitable consequences. Benjámin criticized the poetry being published for flatness and lack of inspiration. The youthful Juhász complained about editors who accepted only works that slavishly adhered to the standards of schematism and attacked certain colleagues, including Benjámin, for their dull depictions of reality. And addressing the heart of the problem, he insisted that poets had the right to express their beliefs in a style natural to them. The next year Révai challenged the prestigious Déry for "misusing" socialist realism in *Answer* (*Felelet*, 1952), an attack that underlined the widening gap between official critics and the most important members of the writing community. Révai charged Déry with falling short of Party expectations because his youthful hero did not join the Communist Party. In reply Déry protested that he could not realistically make his bourgeois protagonist a member of a political group that in the 1920s, the time of the story, was merely an obscure "sect" in Hungary. During these years such clashes between official critics and writers were regularly reported in Budapest by two periodicals, *The Star* and *Literary News* (*Irodalmi Újság*) and in the provinces by literary and cultural journals like *Transdanubia* (*Dunántúl*).

The Thaw, 1953-56

The year 1953 saw a crucial stage in this conflict. The period known as the Thaw began when, as a result of massive economic disarray and Stalin's death, the liberal-minded Imre Nagy replaced Mátyás Rákosi. In this less oppressive atmosphere, writers increasingly ignored the demands of schematism. For example, Benjámin took a firm stand against Stalinism, and Illyés responded not only to domestic matters but to large philosophical questions and, at a more personal level, to the sad fact of aging and the inevitability of death. In the pages of *New Voice* (*Új Hang*), the vehicle of young writers, Juhász and Nagy freely divulged their gloom at what they found in the world around them. Juhász, whose "The Boy Changed into a Stag" W. H. Auden called one of the greatest poems of this century, shared with readers his agony at the sight of human suffering; Nagy, dismayed by the limited satisfactions that human toil brings, yearned for simple pleasures to enrich life, in "The Bliss of Sunday," one of his more compassionate poems. In a series of poems published in *The Star* and *Literary News* in August 1953, a new poet, soon widely read, Sándor Csoóri, cried out at the disastrous disruption of peasant life that collectivization had wrought. It was also significant that the poems of Weöres and Vas appeared again, first in journals and then as editions, and more slowly, also those of János Pilinszky and Ágnes Nemes Nagy; and the fiction of Imre Sarkadi and Ferenc Karinthy, now critical of their society, was also published again. In an article appearing in *Literary News* in November 1953, István Örkény, who had suffered some of the severest treatment at the hands of official arbiters, captured the essence of the change that seemed to be taking place. He asserted that in the new climate a socialist writer no longer needed to embellish reality, that the truth as the writer saw it could be told without the guidance of official directives, and that, as always, the writer alone was responsible for what he or she wrote. This statement did not necessarily sound the death knell of schematism, but its wide acceptance by other Communist writers, even one as orthodox as the poet Lajos Kónya, augered well for fresh directions in literature.

At this time two developments in policy governing translations indicated that the literature of the West might again become more abundantly available than in recent years. Several publishing houses had, since 1950, been issuing translations of writings from all ages and literatures only as a secondary responsibility. Moreover, they published a narrow selection of twentieth-century works, preferring those of Russian writers and of western authors critical of their political and economic systems, such as John Steinbeck and Howard Fast. The unhappy consequence of this policy was that Hungarian writers, though not completely cut off from foreign literatures, were isolated from most of the more recent imaginative works in the West. This unfortunate situation was alleviated by the founding of two agencies that, unlike existing presses, were to publish translations only. The earliest of these is significant because of a change in its original scope. Created in 1954 to publish only translations of Russian literature, Új Magyar Kiadó (Európa since 1957) broadened its mission to include more recent examples of world literature. The importance of the second lies in its emphasis on immediacy.

In 1956 a journal called *The World* (*Nagyvilág*) was founded to keep Hungarians informed of trends through translations of more recent works from all parts of the world. These two vehicles, still functioning, opened ways to current writings that had a substantial impact on literary developments after the uprising in October of 1956.

The Time of Consolidation, 1957-62

The month of internecine bloodshed during the revolution and the Russian army's eventual crushing of all resistance left the Hungarian people with the tremendous task of restoring normalcy to their daily lives. During the period of consolidating the nation in compliance with socialist principles, writers, quickly recovering the momentum built up under the relaxed policies of the Thaw, advanced markedly toward a variety in imaginative literature not seen since the years immediately after the war. From 1957 to 1962 writers who supported the ideals of socialism abandoned schematism, and those who did not espouse socialism or strict didacticism in imaginative literature were again published in growing numbers.

Not unexpectedly, poetry resurged first. The many poets with various views and styles who were frequently published in the early 1950s soon appeared in anthologies. Those who were already familiar to readers before the revolution were included in a 1957 anthology entitled *105 Poems of 15 Young Poets* (*15 fiatal költő 105 verse*), which contained several selections by the promising Margit Szécsi and the brash Sándor Csoóri. This anthology is considered a milestone in the history of literary developments because not one poem evinced a trace of schematism. Quite different but equally important historically is another anthology, *Fire Dance* (*Tűztánc*), which was published the following year. The poets in this volume rose to the defense of the embattled socialist cause in distinctive ways. Among them were Mihály Váci and Mihály Ladányi, thirty-four and twenty-four respectively, the first furthering the interests of the proletariat and the liberation of all colonial peoples from imperialism, and the second lashing out against any middle-class weaknesses still present in Hungarian society. Also included was Gábor Garai, whose ethical view of revolutionary communism and its extension to all humanity placed him in the forefront of post-1956 socialist poetry. To these two groups must be added two poets who, like Sándor Weöres, returned after a long absence: Ágnes Nemes Nagy and János Pilinszky. Nemes Nagy returned with *Heat Lightning* (*Szárazvillám*) in 1957, her first book since 1946, and Pilinszky with *On the Third Day* (*Harmadnapon*) in 1959, his first book of poems in thirteen years. Unlike the preceding poets, they were not concerned with political or purely domestic issues; their vision embraced all humankind as they explored the ethical implications of their inner conflicts. Both bore the wounds of their times. To offer consolation, Nemes Nagy, tormented by the susceptibility of human emotions to the deceptions practiced by the world, searched for those invisible points where the transient and permanent meet. Pilinszky was seared by the moral debacle of contemporary civilization, especially as symbolized by the inhumanity of the concentration camp, and he suffered the Stations of the Cross that marked humanity's way. The many strands of thought and expression represented by all these poets tied into a warp that ensured their personal growth and led to major developments in Hungarian poetry in the altered circumstances of the 1960s.

In this six-year period, prose fiction showed signs of developing beyond its traditional commitment to a realism characterized by sociological and psychological analysis, careful articulation of plot, strict adherence to time sequence, and detailed description. As in poetry, schematism vanished, and the way opened to fresh viewpoints and techniques. The elevation of fiction to new artistic levels required contributions from authors determined to express their interpretations of life in their own way. Casting off schematism entirely, both Imre Sarkadi and Ferenc Karinthy now assumed their true character. Sarkadi, unfortunately a suicide in 1961, freely criticized socialism for its deception of the people. Perceiving that even successful social reform would leave untouched many grave problems, he offered in his narratives the ethical insights of humanism rather than those of socialism. Like Sarkadi, Karinthy registered his criticism of the course that socialism had pursued in Hungary, and turning his fertile imagination to themes found in the life of a big city, he revealed a playfulness and narrative skill that later matured in a novel, *EPEPE* (*EPEPE*, 1970), a remarkable allegory of alienation and limitations in communication between human beings set in an imaginary metropolis.

Developments in fiction were also greatly influenced by a group of writers who emerged from 1953 on, many of them becoming major figures in the 1960s. In 1957 the short stories of the more important of these authors were collected in an anthology called *Initiation* (*Emberavatás*), its title taken from a story by Ferenc Sánta about a youth encountering the double-edged experience of becoming an adult. Unaffected by schematism and not strictly bound to traditional modes of realistic fiction, yet committed to socialism, these authors made clear early that they were seeking new paths in realism. Many succeeded, adding to those followed in the writing of Sarkadi and Karinthy. Among them, Sánta, Erzsébet Galgóczi, István Szabó, György Moldova, and István Csurka particularly introduced new themes and fresh techniques that helped to enliven fiction. Ready to take issue with their society, they all focused on urgent matters. Sánta posed ethical issues, pondered the efficacy of revolution in producing constructive change, and extolled the role of the individual conscience, exalting the authority of the writer's conscience above everyone else's. Both Galgóczi and Szabó depicted the disruptions in peasant life resulting from collectivization, the former using nearly sociographical details lyrically and the latter applying psychological analysis. Moldova and Csurka, more oriented toward urban life, portrayed through penetrating satire and caricature the bizarre contradictions between socialist reality and its ethical ideal. Of course, many novelists and short-story writers then coming into their own, like the young poets included in the anthology *Fire Dance*, staunchly supported socialism. Noteworthy among them were Lajos Galambos, Károly Szakonyi, and István Gáll, who endorsed and defended the version of socialism that evolved after the Revolution of 1956.

These fundamental developments were importantly enhanced by the novels and short stories of two other groups of writers. Impetus was given to new trends by the long-delayed return of authors who had preferred silence to being stifled by schematism: Magda Szabó, Iván Mándy, Miklós Mészöly, and Géza Ottlik, who, like the poets János Pilinszky and Ágnes Nemes Nagy, were historically associated with the progressivism of the defunct periodical *New Moon (Újhold)*. Magda Szabó published two novels, *Fresco (Freskó*, 1958) and *The Fawn (Az őz*, 1959), launching a new career; in her works, often concerned with the clash between old and new values, she used the stream-of-consciousness technique with special skill. Mándy, whose last book, excluding his stories for children, had been published in 1949, returned in 1957 to chronicle with almost poetic means the lives of unsuccessful characters living on the fringes of society in Budapest, such as those in "The Watermelon Eaters" or the mother in "A Summer Holiday," who is out of place in the new socialist order. Mészöly, who had not been heard from since 1948, published in 1957 a collection of stories, written during his silence, that reached sensitively for the innermost human emotions, often disclosing them, as in "Shade," in an atmosphere of elemental eeriness. Of this group, Ottlik achieved the most immediate and dramatic impact on readers. After publishing a book of short stories in 1957, he caused a sensation in 1959 with a novel, *School on the Border (Iskola a határon)*, in which he symbolized the innateness of human savagery with a shocking picture of young military cadets discovering within themselves many subtle ways to torture one another, somewhat as William Golding does in *Lord of the Flies*.

The second group consisted of three similarly minded writers who launched their careers in the middle of the decade. Like the authors who returned after several years' absence, László Kamondy, Endre Fejes, and Gyula Hernádi disclosed an independence in their choice of themes and styles. Kamondy, never touched by schematism and not attracted by socialist realism, published an edition of short stories in 1957 and in 1960 a sparsely phrased novel, *Descendant of the Apostles (Apostolok utóda)*, that demonstrated his penchant for careful psychological analysis and thoughtful exploration of intellectual and moral problems. After Fejes put out a collection of short stories called *The Liar (A hazudos*, 1958), which often portrayed characters living on the boundary between dream and reality, he next produced *Generation of Rust (Rozsdatemető*, 1962), a widely acclaimed novel that used cinematic techniques to draw a painfully detailed portrait of the life of a postwar middle-class family functioning with mistaken values. Of the three members, Hernádi, whose first stories appeared in 1954 when he was twenty-eight, revealed the most dynamic tendencies for experimentation, a feature of his creativity that links his spirit with that of the older Mészöly. In 1959 a collection of his short stories and his novel *On the Steps of Friday* (*A péntek lépcsői*) appeared. Both works were rooted in the suffering experienced by his generation as they searched for the meaning of life in the difficult times in which they grew up, and they already displayed the surrealistic touches that later became typical of his style as he continued to confront the agonizing moral choices contemporary humans must make. The large variety of themes and the many techniques present in the contributions of these two groups and of the authors previously discussed indicate that fiction was mustering new strength and many adherents during these six years, in spite of the near paralysis of originality and inspiration it had endured from schematism and the shambles in which the 1956 Revolution had left the nation.

The 1960s and '70s

The more temperate climate of the early 1960s brought the richest growth of Hungarian literature since the years immediately following World War II. By this time the consolidation of the nation's political and economic life in accord with Marxist-Leninist socialism, a process proclaimed complete at the Eighth Party Congress in 1962, had undoubtedly produced greater stability in the daily lives of the people. The reduction of tensions between the government and members of the writing community cultivated an atmosphere in which literary creativity could prosper more easily. Several changes in cultural policy made it possible for the activity stirring since 1956 to increase. Opportunities for publication were expanded, although state control of publishing houses and the burden of self-censorship remained in force. Authors were less and less isolated from the world community, especially the West, and the quickening flow of translations of the latest literature helped them to evaluate their writings in the context of world literature and to react to the newest currents of thought and style. Ampler opportunities to travel abroad also enlarged their perspectives, although such travel was subject to strictest government control. Hungarian authors actively participated in writers' conferences in the West, and many of them visited the United States through a long-term program instituted in 1964 by the Ford Foundation, which included the translation workshop and writers' conferences at the University of Iowa. Still another change was the publication of literary criticism that once again applied sophisticated individualistic methods of analysis. Authors of imaginative literature published treatises that freely explored the nature and function of literature, and their distinct speculations sparked readers' expectations of new literary experiences.

But the most liberating factor was the official acceptance of a role for the writer different from the prevailing one, a role that had already evolved to a significant degree but was only then being acknowledged, often tacitly. Writers felt freer to exercise the right that Juhász had so passionately claimed at the First Hungarian Writers' Conference in 1951: t use the creative imagination, even confessionally, to explore universal questions of human existence as the writer responded to their unfolding within the recesses of his or her inner world, stirring reflections in readers that led them to deeper perceptions of life. This new latitude and other signs of growing liberalization represented significant gains for writers determined to speak in their own voices, to discover what they are through self-realization. Of course, if they were to publish, they had to show moral purpose, and could not attack the regime, and always ran the risk that their works would be interpreted by established arbiters. But within these severe limits they secured the measure of freedom necessary to raise to new levels the literature that had been developing since the end of the war.

From this time on, literary activities became more vigorous and diverse. A new age seemed to dawn. Writers whose works were published before the war added to their achievements in climactic, often different ways. Among novelists Déry was, perhaps, the outstanding example of what the changed atmosphere made possible. Released in 1961 from prison and absolved in 1962 of all charges relating to his participation in the 1956 uprising, he disclosed new artistic tendencies. Exploring universal problems of life and the historical choices forced upon the human race, he wrote short stories and several novels that expressed a passionate concern about the destiny of twentieth-century civilization. Among them were *The Excommunicator* (*A kiközösítő*, 1966), a historical parable of the personality cult, and *Imaginary Report on an American Rock Festival* (*Képzelt riport egy amerikai popfesztiválról*, 1971), a terrifying account of human cruelty and barbarity drawing on the events of the 1969 Rolling Stones festival in California that culminated in a riot and the murder of a black youth by the Hell's Angels. Before his death at eighty-three in 1977, Déry added several other works to the body of his work: *Cher Beau-Père* (*Kedves bópeer*, 1973), an ironic and illusionless novel about an old man's infatuation with a young woman; *The One-Eared Man* (*A félfülű*, 1975), another ironic novel satirizing the absurdities of western life present in the kidnapping of Paul Getty, Jr.; *No Verdict* (*Ítélet nincs*, 1969), memoirs reflecting the adversities through which his generation had lived; and, in 1972 and 1975, editions of his meditations, which he called "flotsam," about daily life and the unique problems of the present century.

Poets well known before the war continued to contribute to developments, sometimes changing their views and feelings. Gyula Illyés, returning after a long absence, published seven books of poetry between 1961 and 1973, not to mention some plays, a philosophical novel on old age called *On Charon's Ferry* (*Kháron ladikája*, 1969), and several collections of essays. The lyrical realism of his poems remained, but their humanistic themes increased and focused on the transitoriness of life and the inevitability of death, becoming more philosophical and less engaged with domestic matters. István Vas, who still applied the rational faculty to human experience in precise verses that seldom used metaphorical language, now became a father figure to many of the younger poets. He faced life without illusion, and he viewed humanity somewhat skeptically. László Benjámin composed leaner lines, less adorned poetry than before, and although he remained a committed Socialist, he expressed some resignation and pessimism not present in his writings of the 1950s, and felt some doubt about the power of poetry to improve humans and society. And finally, Sándor Weöres particularly benefited from the more temperate climate, which gave a greater opportunity to share with readers the individuality of thought and style that he had always fostered. That course of development is made clear in a collection of his works published in 1970, augmented by a third volume in 1975. Magically versatile in devising form and selecting images, he widened and deepened his use of oriental and primitive myths, often in ways as arcane as those of William Blake, putting many of his best poems beyond the reach of translators. In such books of verse as *Fire Fountain* (*Tűzkút*, 1964), *Sinking Saturn* (*Merülő Saturnus*, 1968), and *Psyche* (*Psyché*, 1972), Weöres searched for humankind's place in the universe. These works created a cosmic and mythic world in which a passive inward-turning, made possible by oriental thought, mystically merged the self with a universal will of which all things in time are a manifestation, so that every aspect of conscious reality is transformed into ephemeral expressions of that universal will within the evermoving processes of time and nature.

Although these authors and others with long careers remained vital and influential, the literature of the 1960s and 1970s was chiefly in the hands of those new writers who had established their standing during the post-war years. Among the poets who had appeared in the historic anthology *Fire Dance*, Mihály Ladányi, Mihály Váci, and Gábor Garai were now well out in front. Convinced that poetry is an instrument of reform, Ladányi passionately opposed anything impeding socialism in Hungary. Váci defined the worth of his poetry solely by the extent to which it reached those who, in his view, had been trod upon by capitalism, seeking to embrace them with a love born of his sharing their suffering. Of the three, Garai grounded his revolutionary ideals most deeply on general philosophical and ethical principles. In time both Váci and Garai altered their attitudes to a degree. Before his death in 1970 at forty-six, Váci was troubled about the prospects of improving the human condition and unsure if the power of poetry could produce change; Garai did not modify his ideas, but his poems eventually evinced some dejection and feelings of isolation. With these poets must be included István Simon, whose career began at the same time as that of Juhász and László Nagy, and also Imre Csanádi, whose first book was published in 1953. The tone of these two poets' commitment to the post-1956 socialist order is more subdued than that of any of the preceding. Simon, who died in 1975, offered to readers as much joy and escape from human cares as he possibly could, trusting ultimately in the strength to be discovered in the world of nature. Csanádi, whose meditative bent became more philosophical in the 1960s, expanded his themes beyond the peasantry, and humor gradually permeated his work. Attracted by the language of folk poetry and blending it with twentieth century speech, he speculated about human fate, attempting to reconcile individual destiny and the events of history, an effort effectively represented by a cycle of poems capturing in words the ancient Hungarian world of visual art.

But during these two decades, it was the poetry of Juhász and László Nagy that gained the largest following. Still avowed Communists, they suffered greatly from the painful paradoxes of events occurring since the revolution, and they experienced deep internal crises as they strove to bring their vision to their people. They wrestled with some of the most perplexing themes, Juhász reaching into the sciences for imagery and Nagy, though also using scientific images, always preferring natural and mythical imagery. The theme of death's inevitability is central to their thought, but each searched for consolation in different directions. Determinedly, sometimes desperately optimistic, Juhász sought the union of the self with the eternal universe. At first Nagy was confident that poetry had the power to create a valid relationship with reality for humankind, but he turned brooding and contemplative, seeking escape in poetry and finding solace in the supportive strength of love and, at times, relief in playful poetic moods. Experimenting freely with verse forms, as had the older Illyés and Vas, both poets contributed importantly to the variety of forms that became a prominent characteristic of the poetry of the 1960s and '70s, especially to the open and intricate long poem and the prose poem, which enabled the poets of the time to convey the layers of complexities they found in the turmoil of the present century.

Equally essential as Juhász and Nagy to poetic developments were János Pilinszky and Ágnes Nemes Nagy, who became increasingly influential. Neither of them as prolific as Juhász and Nagy and many other contemporaries, and, like Emily Dickinson, favoring the short stanza and poem and the scrupulous crafting of images into almost aphoristic lines, they both sought an intellectually and emotionally acceptable reconciliation with the terrible moral violations of the self that pervade twentieth-century reality. Pilinszky, to whom the tragic collapse of morality during the war remained a permanent part of reality, struggled with his conviction that human beings can only passively register what is taking place in the world, that they do not shape it, that every experience simply happens to them. His sense of human tragedy is poignantly imparted throughout his career, in a poem as early as "Fish in the Net" ("Halak a hálóban," 1942) and as recently as "Self-Portrait 1974" ("Önarckép 1974"). Nemes Nagy, sharing this personally desolating view of the moral malaise of the world, nevertheless trusted that manifestations of a better existence for humanity could be experienced in the emotions stemming from the intellect under the disciplined expression of lyric poetry, a belief strikingly developed in the magnificent "Akhenaton" ("Ekhnáton").

Prose fiction prospered even more dramatically than poetry in the relaxed atmosphere. Freer to select and examine issues critically and to cultivate an individual style, novelists and short-story writers laid the foundations of a modern fiction that may achieve the stature of Hungarian poetry. In the fifteen or twenty years since the revolution, the post-war authors of fiction, like the poets who came to the forefront in the same period, searched persistently for life's meaning amid the turbulence of the contemporary world. Provokingly analyzing situations, they explored such overriding problems of twentieth-century civilization as the autonomy of the individual, the ethical nature of the human personality, and the clashes between the individual conscience and the demands of society. These key dilemmas were treated chiefly and most effectively by some of the authors who had appeared in *Initiation* back in 1957 and those present earlier who had refused to adopt the modes of schematism. On the whole these authors yielded less to the authority of the social system, and their narratives used their own motifs and problems to stimulate the readers' thought rather than to impose solutions on them. István Szabó, who died in 1976 at age forty-five, improved his narrative skills in short stories about peasant life, drawn, as before, from his personal experiences, and Erzsébet Galgóczi enlarged her perspective by creating peasant protagonists endowed with attributes that transcended the simple particularity of village life. It is Ferenc Sánta, however, who, not limiting his narrative sources to his early years in a village, cultivated a wide spectrum of human experience. The life of a village youth depicted in his early stories like "Little Bird" ("Kicsi madár") and "Fairyland" ("Tündérkert") was followed by portrayals of humans making ethical decisions in situations that historical circumstances visited upon them, as in "No More Dying Then" ("Halálnak halála"). Moral dilemmas dominated his explorations of the authority of the individual conscience, his seeking to account for the way Hungarians cruelly turned on one another during the revolution, and his raising the issue of the worth of revolutionary activity itself. It was also during this time that György Moldova and István Csurka, casting a critical eye at their society even more than before, satirized the contradictions they observed between principles and realities. Moldova, who also made major contributions to sociographic literature, wittily portrayed the foibles of Hungarians and the shortcomings of their society. After several novels about Hungarian life in the troubled 1950s, he published in 1972 a historical novel, narrated in the manner of old chronicles, about forty Hungarian Protestant preachers sentenced to the galleys in the seventeenth century for refusing to renounce their faith. In 1975 he completed the first part of a trilogy describing, through the life of a twelve-year-old Jewish boy, the tragic history of his people in Hungary from 1944 to 1945, when they fell victim to the vicious fascism of Szálasi and the notorious Arrow-Cross Party. Csurka also directed his biting satire at Hungarian society, at its political absurdities and the shortcomings of life under the new social order, as in works like in "The Two Rheumatics" ("Két reumás") and "The Passengers" ("Utasok"). His short stories, novels, and plays presented a bleak view of the human condition, an existence controlled by chance, despite humankind's confidence in the efficacy of planning and action. He often found in the life of gamblers and the race track the symbols for his interpretation of existence.

Perhaps the novelists who published again after a long silence evinced an even more distinctive choice of themes and techniques than did the preceding authors. Magda Szabó's frequent novels were soon translated into many languages. Using the unsettled history of twentieth-century Hungary and the responding flow of thoughts and emotions within her characters, she depicted the conflict between old and new concepts with warmth and psychological insight. From the mid-1960s on, Gyula Hernádi extended the scope of his themes to the problems of the Hungarian professional classes and, chiefly in the 1970s, to the intellectual and moral choices that history has imposed on contemporary humans. In 1971 his *The Fortress* (*Az erdőd*) appeared, a horrifying novel about successful businessmen paying for the opportunity to play at real war within a fortress in Greece staffed by mercenaries. He experimented with a mixture of real and surreal images, sometimes to intentional excess, as the title of the novel *The Dry Baroque* (*Száraz barokk*, 1967) implies. He often used nearly every style found in twentieth-century literature, including science fiction, the absurd, and the grotesque, as shown in a selection of short stories, *Gates of Logic* (*Logikai kapuk*), published in 1975.

Three other writers had a most significant bearing on improvements in prose fiction: Iván Mándy, Miklós Mészöly, and István Örkény, who died in 1979. Mándy and Mészöly were building on careers that they had resumed shortly after the revolution, and Örkény, long silent after that upheaval, began publishing again in the mid-1960s. Mándy, whose novel *On the Touch-Lines* (*A pálya szélén*, 1963) was praised by Heinrich Böll, wrote with poetical concreteness about the world of the coffeehouse, the shabby side of the big city, and, later, the life of journalists, old-time movie stars like Greta Garbo, Harold Lloyd, the Danish comedians Zoro and Huru, and King Kong, and various activities connected with the cinema. His short stories and novels were influenced by surrealist modes and existential viewpoints, and they were unrelievedly pessimistic about the prospects of the human race. Mészöly, always in the vanguard of writers experimenting with narrative techniques and still arousing controversy, sought factual objectivity. Particularly effective was his portrayal of the inner states of characters, even their most irrational moments, through concrete details and facts, a mode typified by a novel, *Accurate Stories on a Journey* (*Pontos történetek, útközben*, 1970), in which he used the techniques of the *cinéma direct* to recount a woman's visit to the place of her youth. Earlier novels explored contemporary issues.

Death of an Athlete (*Az atléta halála*, 1966), his first novel and first published book since 1957, related the tragic story of a man who, unable to find inner peace, drove himself to death seeking even greater achievements as a middle-distance runner; *Saul* (*Saulus*, 1968) chose the story of Saul from *Acts 8-9* to delve into the moral implications of power. Mészöly, who is inclined, as in "A Map with Lacerations" ("Térkép, repedésekkel"), to present characters in transit without much regard for time sequence, was constantly concerned with the psychological conflicts of individuals who are incapable of making anything of themselves in the place they occupy, of establishing a constructive balance between themselves and that world. Örkény, the third of these major novelists, after a long and painful re-examination of his style and attitude toward civilization, decided that the grotesque was most compatible with his temperament. Returning with two books in 1967, he quickly took a commanding place in Hungarian literature with bold and absurd short novels—some adapted as plays —and many "one-minute stories" (*egypercesek*), a new grotesque-absurd genre pinpointing with amazing brevity, yet with deep meaning and often with affection, the problems plaguing human beings caught in the paradoxes of today's technological world.

The efforts of such writers as these produced radical changes in Hungarian fiction that continue today. Fiction, particularly the novel, has discarded, in the main, the episodic and descriptive techniques of realism and the panoramic mode in vogue for the more condensed and dramatic forms of the short novel. Rejecting the older modes that had developed as means of "reflecting" social reality, they chose the more startling and demanding forms of narration to impel the imagination to grasp the complexities of twentieth-century civilization: many-layered symbolic suggestion or exaggeration, the distortions of the grotesque and the absurd, the shaft of satire, and the shadings of irony. These experiments and the domestication of foreign literary influences promised the development of a prose fiction increasingly deserving of attention outside Hungary.

The appearance of many new authors primarily after the mid-1960s confirmed the creative vitality of poetry and fiction. The new poets generally fell into two categories: those who linked themselves with the works of Illyés, Juhász, and László Nagy, the last being especially influential, and those who were inspired by the poems of Weöres, Pilinszky, and Nemes Nagy. Among those in the first group were István Ágh, István Bella, Ferenc Buda, László Kalász, Sarolta Raffai, József Ratkó, and Simon Serfőző, who were called the Seven (*Hetek*) because they appeared together in an anthology. Often associated with them were Márton Kalász and Anna Kiss, who wrote differently and began their careers independently of them. These poets tended toward the autobiographical, often describing their struggles with poverty and declaring their devotion to those who had suffered economic hardship, and their support of the social order. Of the original Seven, three matured the most. Ágh began writing more intellectual and abstract verse than he had earlier, even though he was still commenting on the changes in his society, especially in the life of the peasant. Bella, influenced by László Nagy and Sándor Csoóri and partial to fixed poetic forms, called loneliness the major human experience, but frequently accepted the authority of ethical behavior in the relations between human beings. Ratkó, whose extensive use of detail gave his poems a sociographic character, made death the major theme of his poetry, devoting a large share of his more recent verse to struggles against senseless and premature death.

Belonging to the same poetic tradition were the Nine (*Kilencek*), who also appeared together in an anthology, *Unattainable Earth* (*Elérhetetlen föld*, 1969), a publication made possible by László Nagy, who also wrote the introduction and was their chief poetic inspiration. These young poets were László Győri, Benedek Kiss, József Konc, István Kovács, Katalin Mezey, Imre Molnár (later Péntek), János Oláh, Endre Rózsa, and József Utassy. In the beginning they wrote about their personal difficulties in life and voiced their protests. Their views reflected the sufferings endured by their parents' generation: the daily difficulty of making a living and the horrors of the war. Endre Rózsa and József Utassy became the most outspoken pleaders for justice, the former contemplative and philosophical, the latter energetic and dynamic. With the outstanding representatives of the Seven and the Nine must be mentioned Miklós Veress, who shared their desire to face life instead of retreating into a private world. By the mid-1970s Veress loomed large among the young poets holding this attitude. His successful blending of old and new themes, belief and skepticism, and seriousness and playfulness, combined with a mastery of a wide range of verse forms, revealed a poetic rigor that the bad health from which he had always suffered could not diminish.

Essential to the varied development of poetry were those young poets who chose Weöres, Pilinszky, and Nemes Nagy as their models. Like the older poets, they avoided the problems of national welfare in their works, preferring to unfold the innermost life of the human personality from highly distinctive viewpoints. They were greatly drawn to pessimistic philosophies, and their outlook on life was disillusioned and ironic. The earliest of these young poets were István Csukás, Tibor Gyurkovics, and Ottó Orbán. Csukás, whose first works drew on his boyhood years on the Great Plain, developed a style fusing folk and avantgarde poetry; Gyurkovics, whose style is highly condensed, composed love and confessional poetry and was deeply absorbed in his personal feelings and anxieties. Of the three, Orbán achieved the most dramatic evolution in theme and style, his technique and imagery substantially influenced by Weöres and by knowledge gained as a prolific translator of world poetry. Orbán mixed the ironic and the grotesque, and occasionally introduced obscenities. To this group of young poets must be added Imre Oravecz, György Petri, and Dezső Tandori. Both Oravecz and Petri cultivated the short lyric poem as their major art form, and Petri,

Major Developments in Imaginative Literature   xxxvii

whose disenchantment with existence often plunged him into deep pessimism, imbued his poems with the tones of self-mockery. Tandori, who also translated widely from world poetry, was the most versatile member of this group. Boldly, playfully experimental and inventive, he created unusual, even odd verse forms and altered the structure of long-established ones like the sonnet to express dramatically his pessimism about humanity's being able to escape finitude, to break out of the eternal limitation of time and space. In his view, human existence is completely determined; it is beyond the reach of assessment and improvement.

The future of prose fiction also remained auspicious. As is customary in Hungary, short stories and novels by new writers were published more slowly than works by new poets. But with the publication of their writings in growing numbers after 1965, the prosewriters gave clear evidence of following and modifying paths created by authors during the climactic stage of development in the first half of the 1960s. Three of the novelists who began publishing after 1965 were, like László Marsall among the new poets, in their later years. Two of them had been known as essayists, G. György Kardos and György Konrád. In 1968 Kardos published *The Seven Days of Avraham Bogatir* (*Ávrahám Bogatir hét napja*), a story about terroristic activities in Palestine experienced by the author himself after World War II, which was followed in 1972 by *Where Have All the Soldiers Gone?* (*Hová tüntek a katonák?*), another story about Palestine, this time about Polish soldiers who are aliens in their present world and the one they left behind. Both novels demonstrate the author's sensitivity to dramatic situations and his power to create atmosphere and develop characters. In 1969 Konrád, whose works immediately influenced young writers, brought out *The Caseworker* (*A látogató*), a novel about the inefficacy of bureaucratic attempts to deal with social problems, which he followed with another novel, *The City Founder* (*A városalapító*), in 1977. Both works were translated into English. The third author was Anna Jókai, whose first book, *4447*, a novel, appeared in 1968, when she was thirty-six years old. Since then she has regularly published short stories and novels looking mainly at the difficulties of children and families and the life of women from a psychological viewpoint, though, as in "The Angel at Reims" ("A reimsi angyal"), she has treated other motifs effectively.

Unlike these three novelists, all the young prosewriters making their first appearance were born into the new socialistic society. This historical fact had a strong effect on their views of the times, perhaps even a surprising one. Unlike most of their predecessors and many young poets of their own generation, they did not, on the whole, look upon themselves as representing a particular social class or sociological background; thus they did not engage in the class struggle or use sociographic materials to the degree so common in earlier Hungarian fiction. Not burdened by programmatic commitments or by a sense of responsibility for the social system, they examined their world as independent minds relying on personal experiences, and they approached problems from a fundamentally humanistic stance. In general, they presented a picture of young people striving to gain control over their lives but, failing to achieve that autonomy, turning to a life of dislocation, of aimlessness. Among their most frequently used motifs were those of the generation gap—often symbolizing the protagonist's clash with society—of the search for employment, of trying to participate in a social order that seemed to push the young to its periphery. Amid dissatisfaction, disillusionment, and alienation, these new writers fixed their sights on the integrity of the individual personality and the means of achieving it. As they looked at the world and the internal distress of characters, they used mainly the representational modes of realism. Both Gyula Marosi and István Császár were concerned with the role of the individual in society. Marosi concluded that life does not provide opportunities for humans to accomplish great deeds, or nurture convictions able to move humanity to noble achievements. Császár often portrayed characters hopelessly trapped in tensions between themselves and the role society forced upon them, wearing masks to survive. Other writers using similar themes were Szilveszter Ördögh, Péter Módos, and István Csörsz. Ördögh delineated peasant life and the strain existing between peasants and their intellectually advanced children; Módos, whose first book, *The Run (A futás)*, came out in 1967, depicted the crises of adolescents and university students; and Csörsz successfully analyzed the mental states of members of the hippy generation.

Also among these young writers were those who, influenced by such authors as Mándy, Mészöly, and Örkény, took even greater care in choosing themes and stylistic techniques. Vilmos Csaplár, tending toward the grotesque, portrayed anxiety-ridden protagonists who were prevented by society from acting genuinely. Péter Lengyel turned to a different source of tension, the divided personality which is seeking to uncover some continuity between adulthood and childhood. Miklós Vámos was unhesitatingly critical of contemporary Hungarian life in his depictions of loneliness and isolation. Géza Bereményi also emphasized the tension between the individual and society, the frustration of personal dreams and desires, creating grotesque effects with blendings of reality and fantasy and frequently using historical materials. Gábor Czakó stood alone in his uncompromising ethical attitude toward human conduct. Exploring the inner stresses of characters whose personalities are being stifled by circumstances over which they have no control, Czakó nevertheless held them fully responsible for what happened, no matter how tragic the consequences to them. Most recently, Péter Esterházy, a descendant of the famous family, sparked a controversy among Hungarian critics and readers. Having published his first collection of short stories in 1976 and another in 1977, he revealed structural inventiveness in his latest and most successful major work, *Productional Novel (Ssshort* [sic] *Novel) (Temelésiregény [kisssregény]* 1979). It mercilessly satirizes the learned institutes and work-places in Hungary dealing with problems of industrial and agricultural production and, in a set of notes longer than the novel to which it is appended, pre-

Major Developments in Imaginative Literature xxxix

sented a picture of Esterházy's life and an exposition of the novel's genesis.

During the 1960s the Hungarian drama, still the least developed of the major literary genres, also responded to the relaxed atmosphere in ways that held promise for its future. After 1957, established authors like Tibor Déry, Gyula Illyés, and László Németh continued to write for the stage, often presenting domestic issues through past historical situations, with Déry occasionally examining contemporary problems satirically. And new post-war writers like Imre Sarkadi and Ferenc Karinthy pressed upon audiences, not so much political as moral issues, often in experimental theaters. The influence of Brecht was, of course, very strong, but as the cultural policy governing translations grew more liberal, other dramatists pointed to innovations for Hungarian playwrights to adapt. Their increasing familiarity with the works of O'Neill, Miller, Dürrenmatt, Tennessee Williams, Albee, who visited Budapest in fall 1963, and Pinter spurred them to consider new techniques and to widen the scope of ideas for dramatic representation. To these influences were added those of the Theater of the Absurd through the writings of Beckett, Ionesco, and Genet, not only their technique of imagistic patterns but also their concept of a bewildered humanity abiding in a universe without purpose and past comprehension. Under the impact of these influences and the greater opportunity to stage plays, drama began in the mid-1960s to lose the provincialism from which it had long suffered.

At this time the work of István Örkény was especially important. His plays, particularly *The Tóth Family* (*Tóték*, 1967) and *Catsplay* (*Macskajáték*, 1970), which was adapted from his novel of the same name, were influenced by the absurdists and brought to the stage characters desperately trying to realize themselves in a world that always eluded their grasp. János Pilinszky's recent experiments with poetic drama also have injected new possibilities for the theater. Even more affected by the directorial techniques of Robert Wilson than by the dramatic modes of Beckett, he seemed to be abandoning the linear development of plot and character for unrelated scenes of states of mind in which past, present, and future frequently coalesce, as most recently in *Children and the Soldiers* (*A gyerekek és a katonák*, 1978), a three-part play that presents images of the horrors of war as if in a dream. The plays of István Csurka added liveliness to the drama. They are concerned with the absurdities of the Hungarian scene and the unhappy spectacle of humans completely controlled by chance, the latter concept being effectively portrayed in *Who Will Pay the Piper?*(*Ki lesz a bálanya?* 1970), which consists entirely of a dialogue at a poker session between players completely out of step with life and unwittingly revealing themselves to one another. The achievements of these writers, added to by the distinctive contributions of Ferenc Karinthy, Gyula Hernádi, Géza Páskándi, and the younger Géza Bereményi, indicate that the Hungarian drama may be moving toward a fertile age.

Since the early 1960s Hungarian poetry and fiction have developed ever

xl   Major Developments in Imaginative Literature

broader scope and refinement in the forms of expression. In the atmosphere of greater social stability and the acceptance of a more personal function for literature, growing numbers of Hungarian authors now offer their distinctive voices to world literature in its continuous effort at helping humankind deal with the conditions of life. Further enrichment of this literary experience is, as everywhere, largely dependent on leaving the creative spirit free to steer its own course and to share its vision with readers, a view openly endorsed by many critics in Hungary today. Clearly, the early challenges to schematism by many writers and their perseverance through the most trying historical circumstances have produced a diverse literature of high artistic quality, serving a centuries-old culture that has always given the literary imagination a paramount role in forming an understanding of the human condition.

How to Pronounce Hungarian Words

László Országh

What follows is not a learned discussion for linguistic experts but a highly simplified guide for general readers who wonder how the Hungarian words in the text are pronounced.

To indicate the pronunciation of a language with the letters of another tongue is by no means an easy undertaking, because a considerable number of the letters of any alphabet represent different sounds in different languages. Therefore, this method can never yield more than a somewhat primitive imitation of the foreign pronunciation. That is why professional linguists have devised a very precise but highly complicated system of phonetic transcription that for obvious reasons cannot be used here.

Fortunately, the relationship between Hungarian spelling and Hungarian pronunciation is relatively consistent and, on the whole, free from such absurdities as the five different English pronunciations of the *-ough* cluster (though, cough, tough, plough, through) that are likely to frustrate most beginning students of the language in almost any country.

There are, of course, a sufficient number of difficulties in Hungarian pronunciation. For example, there are the vowels written with various accent marks over them and some invariable consonant clusters; but the "marked" vowels and the consonant clusters are always pronounced in exactly the same way and do not play tricks on the unwary non-Hungarian.

Another, but one may say natural, difficulty is that in any language in the

xlii How to Pronounce Hungarian Words

world a few sounds exist that are completely missing from a great number of other languages. In such instances, an approximation is of very little help. Thus the English vowel of *but, cut, shut,* or the English *th* sound (*this, both*) and *w* (*we, where*) simply do not exist in Hungarian and can be only very inadequately approximated. Similarly the Hungarian letters *ö* and *ű* have no equivalent in English and can be approximated only with German or French sounds.

In the pronunciation key appearing below, each of the Hungarian letters is followed by an English word in which the Hungarian sound of the Hungarian letter, or often only the nearest approximation of the sound, occurs. Those letters of the English sample-word that are the nearest equivalents of the sound of the Hungarian letter are printed in italics.

At the end of the alphabetical list is a very short list of exceptions and curiosities.

a	= h*a*ll
á	= f*a*r
b	= *b*ook
c	= i*ts*
cs	= *ch*urch
d	= *d*og
dz	= hea*ds*
e	= h*a*t
é	= m*ay*
f	= *f*it
g	= *g*et
gy	= *d*uke (British pronunciation)
h	= *h*it
i	= b*i*t
í	= m*ee*t
j	= *y*et
k	= *k*ill
l	= *l*ook
ly	= *y*et
m	= *m*an
n	= *n*o
ny	= *n*ew (British pronunciation)
o	= d*o*g
ó	= st*o*re
ö	= th*i*rst, or in the French word l*e*
ő	= the long vowel in the French word d*eu*x
p	= *p*ot
r	= *r*ed (Scottish pronunciation)

s	= *sh*ip
sz	= *s*it
t	= *t*ip
ty	= *t*ube (British pronunciation)
u	= p*u*t
ú	= f*oo*l
ü	= the short vowel in the French word d*u*c
ű	= the long vowel in the French word r*ue*
v	= *v*ote
w	= *v*ote (the same as *v*)
x	= fi*x*
y	= s*i*t (but if preceded by g, l, n or t see under gy, ly, ny, ty)
z	= *z*ip
zs	= mea*s*ure

In archaic spelling (especially in a few surnames) one occasionally finds clusters that have long since been simplified in current Hungarian. Thus *th* = t, *gh* = g, *cz* = c, *tz* = c, *ts* = cs, *ch* = cs, *eö* = ő, *oó* = ó.

PART ONE
Authors from 1945 to 1965

István Örkény

Örkény was born on April 5, 1912 in Budapest, for which he felt a deep affection based not only on its beauty but also on its "abundance of creative energy." He died on June 24, 1979. His father was the proprietor of a noted pharmacy in the capital; his grandfather operated a small vinegar factory in Verbély (now Vráble, Czechoslovakia), a little village where Örkény regularly spent his summer vacations until he turned twenty. Belonging to such a well-to-do family, he traveled abroad frequently before World War II, and lived in France for two years, in England for one. To please his father, he first obtained a pharmaceutical certificate and then earned a university degree in chemical engineering. Eventually, however, against strong opposition from the members of his family, he chose to follow a writing career. His short stories soon appeared in *Belles-lettres* (*Szép Szó*), a progressive literary journal edited by Attila József, the ill-fated poetic genius of the 1930s. His first book, *Dance of the Ocean* (*Tengertánc*), showing initial traces of the grotesque outlook to which he returned nearly twenty-five years later, appeared in 1941. Unfortunately, his budding career was cut short by a call into army service. Reporting for duty in an officer's uniform to which he was entitled by earlier service, he was upbraided and ordered to return in civilian clothes; then, as a Jew, he was assigned to a labor battalion and sent to the Russian front. Captured after six months, he spent four and one half years in a Russian prisoner-of-war camp. His experiences during these years had, he says, a powerful impact on his outlook on life and his literary creations. The insight he derived from close observations of human capacity for good and evil, which was so theatrically compressed and polarized by war, made him very cautious about passing moral judgment on individuals: he came to understand, he says, that circumstances determine the morality that human behavior reflects. More important, his living with captives from many nations and all social levels helped him to perceive for the first time that all human beings are members of a single community because each of them has "individual memories, passions, longings, and sufferings." This understanding gave him, he reports, that sense of solidarity with humanity from which all his writings stem.

Shortly after his return to Budapest at Christmas 1946, he published the two accounts of his imprisonment that he had written on wrapping paper between 1942 and 1946 in the camp. He entered into the literary life fully and energetically, sharing the enthusiasms and hopes that pervaded the efforts of authors to revive and advance the country's literature and to lift the defeated nation out of its most recent historical tragedy. In 1949 he was dramaturge for the Young People's Theater, and from 1951 to 1953 co-dramaturge for the Hungarian People's Army Theater. His writings showed tendencies toward realism long before he had, he notes, even heard of Zhdanov, Stalin's arbiter of cultural policy; and he accepted the official doctrine of schematism in the belief that the schizophrenia it imposed on his literary perceptions was the necessary price to be paid for hastening national recovery. Nevertheless, he was, in 1952, publicly attacked, particularly by József Révai, the party-line doctrinaire literary critic, for bourgeois sympathy and for misrepresenting a party official in "Purple Ink" ("Lila tinta"). He acknowledged his error as a flaw in artistic technique. His literary career continued to flourish, and by 1956, in addition to reports and sketches, he had published several collections of short stories, a novel, and some plays. These successes, however, concealed Örkény's growing dissatisfaction with all forms of realism as adequate means of portraying his specific relationship with present reality.

Accordingly, he viewed the post-1956 setting as one in which, slowly at first but ever more quickly, certain possibilities for literary expression were once again developing as they had after the end of the war. "Self-abandon, literary experimentation, and artistic playfulness," he remarks, "were again enfranchised after a time during which terribly and increasingly severe deliberateness had already grown so conscious that in the end it completely erased the author's soul from his written work." In spite of this welcome release from the schizophrenic state in which he had felt compelled to write, Örkény entered upon a period of public silence that, except for a story published in 1963, remained unbroken until 1966. Working long hours as a chemist in a factory, he used this ten-year period to "look myself in the eye, to evaluate what was inside me: my strengths, talents, propensities, and delights." He ultimately discovered that he had to cultivate anew that playfulness, that grotesque outlook which had been present in his earliest short stories and had occasionally resurfaced in his writings even while he was centering his imagination on realism. This insight initiated a new phase in his development, one that eventually gave him a unique and influential place in the literature of his nation.

In 1966 he gathered the choice fruits of his ten years of labor and published under the title *The Princess of Jerusalem* (*Jeruzsálem hercegnője*) some short stories and a short novel called *Catsplay* (*Macskajáték*), the last adapted as a play in 1969. In his succeeding publications, he viewed the contemporary scene ever more strictly through the grotesque, leaning toward the absurd, among them: *Honeymooners on Flypaper* (*Nászutasok légypapíron*), grotesque stories, which also contained *The Tóth Family* (*Tóték*), a short novel, an experimental attempt to express the grotesque view in longer form, 1967; *The Tóth Family*, adapted as a tragi-comedy from the short novel, 1967; *One-Minute Stories* (*Egyperces novellák*), 1968, followed by enlarged editions in 1969 and 1974; and *Blood Relations* (*Vérrokonok*), a play, 1975. A four-volume edition of selected writings appeared in 1971-73. Since 1966, his writings have solidly established his reputation at home, and he has gained a wide audience abroad through his plays, which have been staged in many countries, including the United States, where *Catsplay* was the hit of the 1977-78 season of the Guthrie Theatre in Minneapolis, Minnesota. He has also received several literary awards: The Attila József Prize in 1953 and again in 1963, the Grand Prize for Black Humor in France in 1970 for *The Tóth Family*, which had been performed in Paris in the fall of 1968, and the Kossuth Prize in 1972.

Although Örkény continues to experiment, the grotesque outlook and its wide-ranging forms of expression are undoubtedly compatible with his individuality, serving, as he claims, quite possibly as an autobiography of his humor. Time being the home of all human beings, the twentieth century banished him, he says, from "the solitude" of his cell "apparently to follow more faithfully the inconstant and unassuagable feverishness" of the present age. To him, the grotesque cries out against the horrors of the twentieth century resulting directly from the unvigilant confidence and easy optimism that western civilization has inherited from the nineteenth century. In his view, the grotesque is a flowering of a prophetically dreamed, imaginary world reacting against the monster abiding in humanism, the monster tragically symbolized by the carnage of two World Wars, the holocaust of Auschwitz and Treblinka, and the moral horror of Hiroshima. Through the grotesque he is able, he asserts, to grasp the essence and terifying contradictions of contemporary times. By looking at life through its light-shattering prism he can use absurd suppositions to create new coordinates for a sovereign world in which, for example, obedience to "the law of gravity" means that a dropped object necessarily falls up, not down. This imaginary sovereign world—its creation, he suggests, demanding from the author the "gesture" of a kamikaze pilot—offends the readers' sense of symmetry, turns their world upside down. Nevertheless, this cosmic disruption is believable because the new proportions of the imagined world are both complete and logical. In the end they make readers laugh or laugh and cry at the same time, but they always compel them to shudder, like a spectator at a tragic play.

Among his works, the one-minute stories provide an extraordinary experience of the world whose dimness he seeks to penetrate. These stories are, he states, the first of his writings in which he probably has not compromised himself or his art, though only time can really tell. The antecedents of these sometimes absurdly humorous, sometimes grim, sometimes shocking stories lie in a few works by two early twentieth-century Hungarian authors, Frigyes Karinthy and Dezső Kosztolányi, and particularly in the six-word and one-line stories of Jules Renard, some of which were translated into Hungarian in the first part of this century. At some time during the period of his silence from 1957 to 1966, Örkény became convinced that the classical modes of description and plot were worthless; thus he deliberately kept "whittling away" at any narrative elements that seemed to serve primarily as ends in themselves. In every way he tried to record only those "notes," those resonances to which readers respond jointly, instead of details of description or action. The impact of these efforts on his style is dramatic. In addition, though he draws his materials from the Hungarian scene and aims his stories solely at Hungarians, Örkény's vision of the absurdities in contemporary life very often rises above domestic particulars to strike responsive chords in non-Hungarian readers as well. In keeping with his intent, these vibrations are produced not by abstract analysis of the tragic human condition but by the presentation of an imaginary world that forces readers to shudder at the senselessness and horror of life—at utter absence of hope for the existence or eventual creation of a moral world by humankind.

This bleak outlook, Örkény insists, does not lead him to Samuel Beckett's conclusion about the human prospect. He cannot, in the end, accept the notion that life is hopeless and unendurable. Since his concept of existence arises, he notes, not from theoretical speculations but from personal experiences with absurd, hopeless, and unendurable situations, he always finds, in his desperation, a glimmer of light that makes life worth continuing. Surrender to overwhelming grotesqueries and absurdities must be avoided, even in face of the certain knowledge that all will necessarily end in the tragedy of death. Örkény offers action as the only hope, "the only egress" for humans; he has an almost existential faith in "the saving character of action," even in "the futile action because it still gives us something subjectively." Ultimately human beings must, Örkény claims, agree with Camus's conviction that the moment must come when, despite the futility so painfully portrayed, they "imagine that Sisyphus is happy."

In the light of this endorsement of human action, as well as his personal triumph over adversities, it is hardly possible to accept totally the severe limitation that Örkény imposes on the ability of an author to contribute anything of value to humanity. Humans, he says, cannot learn anything from an author because they do not need this help; humans, he insists, have created what they possess solely on their own, though, he feels compelled to add, that has been little enough. Some exception must be taken to this earnestly expressed viewpoint. Both Örkény's own life and the actions of characters like the heroine of *Catsplay* and the disillusioned bride of "Honeymooners on Flypaper" offer a glimmer of light to sustain human hopes. At a time when the dismal effects of the first Industrial Revolution are being acutely felt, when dread at the progress in the atomic and electronic technology of the second Industrial Revolution keeps mounting, when the incineration of the human race can be avoided only through a balance of terror—at a time such as this, Örkény extends solace and encouragement to mankind. Stripping reality of every illusion, he offers a sense of solidarity with all humanity and the assurance of salvation through futile action.

How to Use One-Minute Stories

The enclosed stories may be short, but they offer full value.

Their advantage lies in the fact that they save time, since they do not require weeks or months of prolonged attention.

A one-minute story may be read in the time it takes to cook a soft-boiled egg or to wait for the operator to take you off hold.

Depression and shattered nerves are no obstacle. A one-minute story may be read either standing or sitting, in the wind or the rain, or even while riding a crowded bus. Most of them can be enjoyed while walking from one place to another.

It is important to pay close attention to the titles. The author has endeavored to be brief and has therefore not permitted himself the luxury of meaningless titles. Before boarding a streetcar, one naturally looks first to see where it is going. The titles of these stories are just as significant.

Mind you, this does not mean that one should read only the titles. The title should be read first, then the story that follows. Other procedures for using these stories are not advised.

A word of caution, however. What you don't understand, read again. If you still don't understand, then the failure lies with the story.

There are no stupid people. There are, however, faulty one-minute stories.

Honeymooners on Flypaper

They had decided not to go anywhere. Why, after all, should they? As the bridegroom explained, they had theaters, films, concerts—everything they could want—right there in Budapest.

So they stayed home. The first few weeks went by smoothly, and were filled with love.

Then, one evening at about 6:30, they got stuck on a piece of flypaper hanging from the lamp.

Now, how in the world could that have happened?

* * *

He: Love me, sweetheart?
She: Sure I do.
He: Well, come on over.
She: What, again?
He: Come on over.
She: You're never satisfied, are you?
He: Come on. Hurry!
She: Wait a second. My heel is stuck in something.
He: Kick your shoes off, darling. Quickly!
She: So we're staying home again. You know, there's a Tchaikovsky concert tonight at the Academy of Music.
He: I abhor Tchaikovsky.
She: Would you rather go and see a play?
He: I can't stand those preachy Hungarian directors. Say, does it seem to you that we're swaying?
She: You must be imagining things.
He: I'm convinced that we're hanging from something that's swinging back and forth.
She: Ignore it. Go see what's on at the opera.
He: Where's the paper?
She: On the kitchen table.
He: I can't. My foot's stuck.
She: Really. As I remember, they're performing "A Masked Ball."
He: Listen. The stuff you're caught in . . . is it shiny and sticky, like shellac?
She: Something like that.

He: Now my hands are stuck, too.
She: You do like to complain, don't you? By the time you're done, we'll end up staying home for sure.
He: What's that jerking motion?
She: I'm trying to pull myself loose.
He: Stop fooling around. You'll break the thread.
She: You give up so easily now. I fell in love with you because you were bold, because you made me laugh, because you were wild about music . . .
He: How can I be wild about music when I can't move my hands and feet?
She: Do you really think you're the first person who ever got stuck? What about cripples, who don't have legs? They get along fine. They have jobs. They even have fun once in a while.
He: We seem to be revolving.
She: So what if we are?
He: I've never seen anything like it.
She: Allow me to explain. There's a breeze coming in from the stairwell. The breeze is making this sticky thing move. Feel better now?
He: How can I, when I'm up to my navel in glue?
She: You sound like a broken record! It's twenty minutes to seven. The only way we can make the opera now is to call a taxi.
He: Do the realities of life mean so little to you?
She: We always said our marriage would be different. We swore not to run out of things to say, not to become bored, not to quarrel, not to end up divorced. I want to have fun. I want three children, and I want to send them to music school.
He: It's up to my mouth.
She: Will you please go and call a taxi?

Immortality[1]

Although no longer young, he was still in excellent shape. He was known and feared by the inhabitants of the marsh and by every four-footed creature for miles around. His vision was unimpaired. From half a mile up, he could still spot his prey and swoop down on it like a hammer driving a nail with a single blow.

Then, in the prime of his life, at the height of his powers, during one slow beat of his wings—his heart stopped. Yet the rabbits, the gophers, the chickens and the geese dared not come out, because he remained on high, wings outstretched, menacing in his stillness, surviving death until, a few moments later, the wind dropped.

[1] This story probably refers to Stalin.

How Long Will a Tree Live?

Although it was not quite evening, Mrs. Bán turned on the lights. With the war coming so close, she preferred to remain a step ahead of the darkness. Especially today, when she was at home alone, and the fog was so thick outside that the fence a few feet beyond the window could barely be seen.

She set out the lard tub and her pots and pans. Just as she was adding baking soda to the water boiling on the stove, someone knocked at the door. Mrs. Bán gave a start. Going to the window, she drew aside the curtain, expecting to see Germans. Instead, she saw a woman, alone.

"Is this the Sándor Bán residence?"

"Yes. I'm Mrs. Bán."

The caller's clothes had long been out of style. Pulled over her rapidly graying, flyaway hair was a felt cloche of the kind ordinarily seen only in films of the twenties. The handle of her old-fashioned parasol ended in a parrot's head, which had two tiny black eyes that stared fixedly in two different directions.

"It's about your advertisement."

"Advertisement?" Mrs. Bán asked. She and her husband advertised only in early spring and late fall, and it was now winter. Yet here was the woman rummaging through her purse, which contained so many trinkets, cosmetics, and souvenirs that she seemed to be carrying everything she owned. First she brought out a bundle of yellowed letters tied with a ribbon. These were followed by old engagement books, medicine vials, ticket stubs, and an empty atomizer of perfume that still retained some of its fragrance. There were also photographs of a young woman wearing a feathered hat and, in some cases, accompanied by an Alsatian dog. The young woman's face had faded, however, and the corners of the photographs were ragged.

To the sound of jingling coins, keys, and costume jewelry, the woman came up with a crumpled newspaper advertisement. The print had faded from all but the heading, which read, "Sándor Bán's Nursery in Tét."

"You've come to the right place," said Mrs. Bán, "but I'm afraid my husband's not at home."

"I had hoped to return on the five o'clock train."

"He won't be back until late," Mrs. Bán said. "He went to the village on business."

The visitor looked around wearily. The make-up was flaking from her face like plaster from a peeling wall. She gave no sign of emotion, yet precisely because of her mask-like appearance, there was something touching about her, as there is about a white-faced clown crying without tears.

Mrs. Bán knew very little about selling trees. She had been married less than eighteen months. Because her husband was somewhat overprotective, he took her with him to the nursery only on clear, sunny days. The most he allowed her to do, in any case, was to make an occasional graft.

Still, Mrs. Bán asked, "What can I do for you?"

"I'd like to buy something."

"I'm afraid we don't sell garden trees," Mrs. Bán said, "only very young fruit trees."

"It doesn't really matter," the customer said hesitantly, "as long as it's a nice tree."

"We have some four-year-old saplings."

"Well, I'm not sure." Still uncertain, the woman continued to look around. "I was thinking of something larger."

"My husband usually manages these things," said Mrs. Bán, "but if you'd care to wait a moment, I'll show you around."

Mrs. Bán rinsed the pans with scalding water, wiped them with a clean towel, then threw the water out into the yard. She was a small woman, plump and vigorous, who worked with such smooth, graceful movements that it was difficult not to watch her. The woman had no choice but to wait in silence until Mrs. Bán had finished drying her hands.

"You're expecting a child," the woman remarked.

"Yes."

"Shall we go?" The woman hooked her parasol, with its parrot's head handle, over her arm.

The path was muddy. The woman wobbled in her high-heeled shoes. They walked for about five minutes in the direction of a hill. The long rows of saplings, seen through the fog, were like soft pencil strokes.

"These are all Jonathans," said Mrs. Bán with a wave of her arm. "That's a Baldwin. This one's a russet. That's a London pippin. Those up ahead are apricot trees."

The visitor stopped. "I don't like them," she said. "I thought they'd be bigger. I expected big, solid trees, with a great deal of foliage."

"Over this way, then," Mrs. Bán said. "The almond trees bear fruit after only five years."

"The fruit doesn't interest me," said the gray-haired woman. "Besides, I don't have five years to wait."

Stopping, she prodded a tree with her parasol.

"I have a tumor in my womb," she said indifferently. "Cancer."

"How awful!" said Mrs. Bán. "Can't they operate?"

The woman shot her a sharp, sideways glance.

"When is it due?"

"Due?" asked Mrs. Bán, turning to look at her. "Oh. In March."

The woman started off again. As they approached the far edge of the nursery, the ground began to rise gently. The fog was as thick as a baby's diaper. They could barely see two steps ahead.

"What's that?"

The woman pointed her parasol at a gaunt weeping willow.

"Nothing special," said Mrs. Bán. "Just an ordinary tree."

"It's the first one I've liked."

Tottering, the gray-haired woman walked on ahead. The edge of the nursery was lined with a variety of trees, chiefly birch, willow, and ash. They had been planted by Mrs. Bán's father-in-law when he was a young man, probably in order to break the wind, or perhaps for no other reason than to mark the boundary between his own land and that of his neighbor. Beyond this line, the trees gradually thinned out until there remained only one, standing solitary on the crest of the hill.

"And what kind of tree is that?" the woman asked.

"A linden," said Mrs. Bán. "But it's well over fifteen years old."

"I'll buy it."

"That?" asked Mrs. Bán. "You mean, for firewood?"

"Of course not. I want it just as it is."

"I don't understand," Mrs. Bán said. "It's much too old to transplant."

"I have no intention of having it transplanted."

"What will you do with it, then?"

"Not a thing," said the gray-haired woman. "How much is it?"

"You're going to leave it here? Why, you can't be serious!"

"Let it stay right where it is," the woman said. "But remember, it belongs to me."

Mrs. Bán was bewildered. If only her husband were home! She looked at the linden tree. Though it was not especially tall, the top of it was shrouded in fog. With its straight, slender trunk it seemed healthy enough, like some strong, vigorous, but not particularly good-looking, adolescent.

"It's precisely what I had in mind," said the woman. "How much are you asking?"

"My husband usually manages these things," said Mrs. Bán hesitantly. "I'm sure he's never sold one of these before."

"I shan't be coming back," said the woman. "Whatever your price, I'll pay it."

There was a moment's silence. The nursery had done poorly that year, because of the war. The Báns were badly in need of money.

"A hundred pengős," said Mrs. Bán, taking the first figure that came to her mind. "Or would that be too much?"

"Whatever you say."

The visitor scanned the tree once more, then poked with her parasol at the ground near the roots. Then she and Mrs. Bán returned to the house. Emptying her handbag again, the woman placed a hundred-pengő note on the kitchen table.

"I want you to take good care of it."

"There's nothing to take care of," Mrs. Bán replied.

"I'll pay you for your trouble."

"It won't be any trouble at all."

"Keep it fertilized," the gray-haired woman said. "Will twenty pengős a year be sufficient?"

"Please, don't give me any more money," said Mrs. Bán. "The tree's going to be just fine."

Rummaging through her purse once more, the woman took out six ten-pengő notes and laid them on the table.

"I'm going to pay you enough for three years' maintenance. You must promise, however, that you'll take excellent care of it."

Mrs. Bán gave a little cough.

"I promise," she said.

The woman took out her mirror and powdered her face with a dirty puff. When she had finished, she turned her attention again to Mrs. Bán.

"Has it kicked yet?"

Mrs. Bán coughed again. "Yes."

The woman turned to go, then stopped.

"How long does a linden tree live?"

"Quite a while," said Mrs. Bán.

"How many years?" asked the gray-haired woman. "A hundred, perhaps?"

"Even longer."

Nodding, the gray-haired woman hooked her parasol on her arm and opened the door.

"You must water it, too," she said sternly. On the threshold, she looked back again.

"Good-bye," she said, and without so much as a handshake or a second glance, she was gone. The tip of her parasol could be heard tapping on the brick walk.

Mrs. Bán stood quietly for a moment, then put away the money and returned to her work. Her chief concern just now was the rumor that the Germans were requisitioning all available livestock. She performed her tasks with charm, grace, and no apparent effort, like a dancer moving to a rhythm sensed by the spirit alone.

In Memoriam Professor G. H. K.

Professor G. H. K. was digging a hole in which to bury the carcass of a horse.
"Hölderlin ist ihnen unbekannt?" he asked the German guard.
"Who's he?"
"The author of *Hyperion*," explained the professor, who dearly loved to explain. "The greatest figure in German Romanticism. How about Heine?"
"Who *are* these guys?" asked the guard.
"Poets," said the professor. "Surely you've heard of Schiller?"
"Sure I have," said the guard.
"How about Rilke?"
"Him too," said the guard. Reddening with rage, he shot the professor.

Two Cupolas in a Snow-Covered Landscape

The whole town of Davidovka should have been there. I mean, not just our battalion, but the local inhabitants, too. Somehow, it didn't work out that way. The Hungarians in our battalion were represented by only a few spineless brown-nosers, plus those who had something to lose if they didn't obey—chiefly the sick, the clerks, and the supplymen—about forty-five men in all. There were even fewer Russians. Those whom the sergeant major had managed to scare out of their homes drifted around the square for a while, then disappeared at the first opportune moment. Most conspicuous of all was the absence of our battalion commander, Major Holló, who had been present at all the earlier executions, and who had always been so careful to observe the formalities. During his brief appearance in front of headquarters, Holló had gloomily surveyed the church square, remarked that the weather was cold, then gone back inside to stay. Aside from the battalion surgeon and the sergeant major, the only men present with any authority were a German truck driver and a German NCO who had a Leica hanging around his neck. They had brought the offender to Davidovka, where the sentence of the German military court was to be carried out. And, of course, there was also Ecetes, a wagon driver who had volunteered to hang the woman in exchange for three liters of rum. The first liter was already gone, and Ecetes stood quite unsteadily on his feet.

The woman had been left standing under a tree. She stood there motionless, as though rooted to the ground. Her eyes were not even moist. From experience, we knew that it was the elderly who died with the least amount of fuss. They were alarmed, of course, as though unable to grasp what was happening to them, but they didn't beg, whimper, or scream. This, however, was an attractive, well-dressed young woman, who nevertheless uttered not a word of complaint. Instead, she was watching a little girl who had crawled under the truck, and who was now peeking out from beneath it. The child was about five years old. She was thin and dirty, but her clothes, like the woman's, were well made—a fur vest, quilted pants, thick woolen stockings, and galoshes. When the rope was tossed around the young woman's neck, the girl gave a bright little laugh, as though she'd been tickled.

A few minutes later, the battalion surgeon pronounced the woman dead. A cold wind had sprung up, and the body began to sway. The child crept out from beneath the truck. For a while she watched the corpse swing gently back and forth. Then, as though the whole affair were merely a game that had gone on too long, she cried up toward the tree:

"Mama!"

The Russians had gone. The only Hungarians remaining were Ecetes; Sergeant Major Elek Biró; Tibor Friedrich, the battalion surgeon; and Corporal István Koszta, formerly a bartender at the Golden Bull Hotel in Debrecen, who had repeatedly requested a transfer to a hospital somewhere behind the front lines to be treated for carbuncles. At the moment, Koszta was standing in such a way as to draw the surgeon's attention to the dark red swellings on his neck. The surgeon had turned away, however, and was looking in the direction of the Leica. The German NCO motioned to the little girl to get out of the picture. She remained where she was, however, her eyes wide and sparkling as she stared into the Leica. I suppose she had never seen a camera before.

The Savior

It was 10 a.m., and he had just finished his new play. The night before, he had had two difficult scenes yet to go. He had been working ever since, drinking endless cups of black coffee and pacing the narrow confines of his hotel room. At the moment, however, he felt light as a feather. He felt happy, as though life had suddenly become beautiful. He felt free, as though the world outside had ceased to exist.

He drank one last cup of coffee, then walked down to the edge of the lake to look for the boatman.

"Take me out for a while, Mr. Volentik?"

"Step in, sir."

Despite an overcast sky, the air was quite still. The smooth, gray lake shone like a broad sheet of isinglass. Mr. Volentik rowed with the short, rapid strokes of the experienced Balaton boatman.

When they had gone a short distance, the playwright asked, "Can they still see us from shore?"

"Yes, sir."

The boatman continued rowing. The red roof of the hotel vanished slowly among the trees. A line of smoke rose from an invisible train.

"Can they still see us?"

"Yes, sir."

The sounds from the lakeshore died out; nothing could be heard but the splash of the oars. Trees, houses and docks blended together. All one could see was a faint line marking the end of the lake.

"Can they see us now?"

The boatman glanced around. "No, sir, they can't."

The playwright kicked off his sandals and rose from his seat.

"Pull in the oars, Mr. Volentik," he said. "I believe I'll just walk on the water a while."

Satan at Lake Balaton

The traveler shook his host's hand over the garden gate, then set out on the road toward the railway station. Since his train wasn't scheduled to leave for another hour, he strolled nonchalantly along the hot asphalt in his white tennis shorts and shirt, swinging a white calfskin overnight bag and singing to himself.

Suddenly, he stopped short. Parked on the shoulder of the road was a huge tractor trailer with two flatbeds, each of which carried some kind of monstrous iron machine.

They were enormous green creatures, squat and round like a doughnut. The traveler had never seen anything like them. Were they pontoons? Arctic icebreakers? Or were they perhaps pedestals for some gigantic excavating machine? The bottoms were smooth and rounded like the bottom of a punt, while up above, a maze of pipes, valves, and cogs soared high into the air.

The traveler tapped the side of the nearest machine with his knuckle.

"Is this for sale?" he inquired.

"Is what for sale?" asked a member of the work crew, surveying the traveler. The workman was wearing denim overalls and no shirt. Beads of sweat glistened among the tufts of hair on his chest.

It was swelteringly hot.

"This thing here," the traveler said. He banged the machine with his fist and listened attentively to the hollow, metallic clang that came from inside.

"You want to buy *this*?" asked the workman, staring.

"Is the other one better, perhaps?"

"Nope," said the man, perspiring. "They're exactly alike."

The traveler drummed the machine lightly with his fingers.

"Then I'll take this one," he said.

"You really want to buy it, huh?"

"I might—yes."

"Who for?"

"I'd simply like to have it. Is it for sale?"

"Well, if this don't beat all."

The workman closed his eyes and wiped the sweat from his brow with the back of his hand. Casting a sharp glance at the traveler, he turned on his heel and walked toward the cab.

Under the cab, the driver lay on his back, while a maintenance man handed him tools. Three other workmen were standing around, waiting.

After a moment, the first workman returned with one of his companions, who had on a blue work shirt. Where it touched his skin, the shirt was dark blue with sweat.

"You the guy?" asked the second workman rudely.

"I beg your pardon?"

The workman stepped up and stared the traveler in the eye.

"Why are you so interested in this machine?" he asked. "Come on, out with it!"

"How dare you speak to me in that tone of voice?" said the traveler angrily. "If it isn't for sale, say so. There's no need to shout."

"Take it easy, Jóska," murmured the first man soothingly.

"Number one," said the man in the blue shirt, calming down somewhat, "I wasn't shouting. Number two, I never said it wasn't for sale. And number three, would you be so kind as to tell me just why you're so interested in this machine?"

"Look," answered the traveler. "I won't ask questions if you won't. However, to avoid another quarrel, I'll explain. I can use it."

The second workman pointed to the machine with his thumb.

"This thing?"

"Either this or the other one. I'd prefer this one, however."

"Wait here a second."

The two workmen walked off. The back of the second man's shirt was completely wet. They joined the other members of the crew near the front of the truck, where the cab provided a bit of shade. The maintenance man kicked the driver on the bottoms of his shoes, and he climbed out from under the truck. After a brief conversation, the driver and the first two workmen approached the traveler.

The driver went about it with a great deal more confidence than the other two had.

"So you want to buy this machine, do you?" he asked. Since his hands were greasy, he offered his wrist.

"Providing we can agree on a price."

"How much did you have in mind?"

"Make me an offer."

"You make me one."

"Well, I don't really know," the traveler said. "I'm still not quite sure what it does."

"It's a machine for pumping underground water," said the first workman helpfully.

"Excellent."

"It's well built, too," said the driver.

"It looks quite reliable," said the traveler, nodding.

Suddenly, the man in the blue shirt exploded once more. "You see what kind of guy you're dealing with?" he shouted, pushing his way forward. "He doesn't even know what it's for, but he wants to buy it!"

"Calm down, Jóska," the first workman said.

"Didn't I warn you not to talk to him?"

The traveler picked up his overnight bag.

"Just as you please," he said in a hurt voice. "I wouldn't dream of forcing you."

"Jóska!" snarled the first workman in exasperation.

"Good day," said the traveler.

"Just where do you think you're going?" the second workman shouted. "You come back here!"

"I have a train to catch," said the traveler. Nonetheless, he walked back a few steps and pointed to his host's garden.

"See that tree?" he asked, indicating a walnut tree standing deep within the garden on the right side of the house. "If you make up your minds to sell it, put it under that tree."

When the traveler had gone, the six workmen drifted slowly toward the fence. They stood motionless, looking at the tree and the deep, dark shade beneath it. Even out there on the road, they could feel through the shimmering heat the seductive coolness of that single dark spot.

A Brief Course in Foreign Affairs

I had been to every fuel dump in the district, including the coal yard—but no luck. Everything is so hard to come by these days. Then someone suggested a place in one of the outer districts. The dealer—a sharp, quick-witted fellow—could come up with any fuel you might want, in exchange for a mere bottle of rum.

I didn't even have to buy one; we already had a bottle at home. Real Cuban, at that. I located the place in question, which lay at the bottom of a short flight of stairs. I was just about halfway down, the rum in my briefcase, when a man's voice cried out from below:

"If it's those East German charcoal briquets you want, we don't have any!"

I went down, greeted the dealer, then opened my briefcase and put the bottle of rum on a small table covered with coal dust.

"I'm afraid that's not what I want at all," I said.

The coal dealer stole a glance at the rum. "What can I do for you?" he asked.

"I'd like to buy something fissionable."

Right away, the other dealers had said, "We don't have any." Not this one, however. Taking a step toward the bottle, he read the brand name, then gazed for a moment at the sugar cane on the label.

"Well," he replied, "I suppose we might scrape together a little pitchblende."

I couldn't help laughing. "Are you kidding?" I asked. "What do you expect me to do—process the stuff in my kitchen sink?"

Grabbing the bottle, I put it back in my briefcase. At once, the dealer began to back down.

"No need to rush, now," he said. "Just tell me precisely what you want, and I'll see what I can do."

You know perfectly well what I want, said I to myself. However, I explained to him that all I required was the standard atomic charge, namely, high-purity Uranium 233.

"If you don't have that," I continued, "Plutonium 239 will do just fine."

I took out the rum and put it back on the table. The dealer picked up the bottle and carried it to the rear of the cellar, where he placed it inside a rickety filing cabinet. Neither of us spoke; indeed, words were entirely unnecessary. By our gestures alone, we had communicated to each other that a deal had been made. From then on, the dealer's questions were merely *pro forma*.

"May I ask," he inquired, "if you have a carrier rocket?"

"Yes," I replied sharply.

I was not about to mention that small workers' cooperative in Buda where, in exchange for much more than a bottle of rum (an English player piano and eight bolts of linen, to be exact), they had agreed to swipe enough state-provided materials to assemble a medium-range rocket. By doing so, I might easily drive up the price of the isotope. My silence proved wise; the price asked by the dealer was remarkably low. I counted the money onto the table.

"Did you bring a container?" he asked.

"I'm afraid not."

"I'll need two forints bottle deposit."

I gave him the bottle deposit.

"No cork, either, I suppose?"

I didn't have a cork, either.

Heaving a sigh, the dealer tore a sheet of newspaper into strips, twisted them up, and stuffed them into the neck of a dirty milk bottle taken from the same filing cabinet in which he had placed the rum.

"Shall I wrap it?"

"That won't be necessary."

"Come again," said the dealer, escorting me to the top of the stairs. "You do intend to use it for peaceful purposes, I trust?"

"Why, of course!"

"I'm not so sure," said the dealer, wagging his finger at the end of my nose. "You certainly look like a troublemaker to me."

Public Opinion Research

Like other countries, Hungary now has a Public Opinion Research Center, where business is already in full swing.

Your enthusiastic support is hereby requested.

The following is a sample of the first Hungarian public opinion poll, which deals with the subject: "How do you feel about Hungary's past, present, and future?" To ensure validity, the questionnaire was mailed to 2,975 persons in all walks of life, regardless of rank, position, profession, or religious persuasion.

1. What is your opinion of the present political system?
    a. Good.
    b. Bad.

c. Neither good nor bad. Might be improved a bit, though.
d. I wish I were in Vienna.

2. Have you personally experienced the loneliness of twentieth-century man?
    a. Yes, I am completely alone.
    b. Yes, I am almost completely alone.
    c. Yes, I am virtually completely alone.
    d. I talk once in a while to my landlord.
3. What are your cultural activities?
    a. Films, soccer games, bars.
    b. I sometimes look out the window.
    c. I never even look out the window.
    d. I strongly disapprove of the views of Mao Tse Tung.
4. What is your philosophical background?
    a. Marxist.
    b. Antimarxist.
    c. I never read anything but detective novels.
    d. Alcoholic.

The results of the poll show that:
    1. Everything during the last twenty years has been fine.
    2. Things are fine now, except that the #19 bus doesn't run often enough.
    3. The future will be finer still, provided more buses are provided for Route #19.
             (Note: They're working on it.)

The Niagara Café

Mr. and Mrs. Nikolitch were going to be in Budapest for only two weeks, and they wanted to take full advantage of each and every day. They sat through a Wagnerian opera, which bored them to death, but which nonetheless sent them back to their hotel in a state of grand exaltation. The next night they went to an operetta called "The Queen of the Csárdás," which they thoroughly enjoyed, but which they described afterward as "terrible nonsense." They also attended a play by a Soviet author—not because they wanted to (they had already heard the play on the radio), but for fear of what the people back home might say if they didn't.

Finally, on the evening before their departure, Mrs. Nikolitch remembered the recently remodeled Niagara Café, which had been described to her as a very "in" place to go.

The desk clerk had never heard of the Niagara. Mr. and Mrs. Nikolitch weren't surprised. They had grown accustomed to this sort of thing. Although they were villagers from the middle of nowhere, they were always more familiar with the sights of a big city than the people who lived there. They searched for the address in the telephone directory, but could not find it. Nikolitch, whose stomach had been troubling him again, suggested that they go into the dining room, have a light dinner, and retire.

"We can sleep at home," said Mrs. Nikolitch. "Besides, the doctor ordered you to relax and enjoy yourself."

Two years before, hypertension had caused Nikolitch to have a gastric hemorrhage, which threatened continually to recur. Had there been any certainty that the Niagara would offer a bit of real relaxation, he would have been happy to go. His hopes were not high, however. In his opinion, this year's vacation had failed as miserably as the one last year.

"Something tells me we'd be smarter to turn in," he said.

His wife, however, wanted to see a bit of bohemian night life. In her youth, Mrs. Nikolitch had studied eurythmics. Under her maiden name, Melitta Ruprecht, she had performed several times with a group of amateur dancers, and, ever since, she had been wild about anything modern and artistic. She had no idea what she wanted that night, but she simply could not bear the idea of not going out.

As luck would have it, their taxi driver knew where the Niagara was. He drove them to a small, poorly lit square in Buda, where the letters of the café's neon sign were reflected on the slick surface of the cobblestones. Inside, illumination was provided by fluorescent lamps twisted around poles like corkscrews, coloring the patrons' complexions in a strange, sickly hue.

There was no dancing or music, not even a place to check your coat. When Nikolitch and his wife finally discovered a free table in a far corner, they threw their coats over the backs of their chairs like everyone else. The decor was rather sparse. Mr. Nikolitch described it as lousy; Mrs. Nikolitch praised it as ultramodern. The walls were divided up into squares of red, blue, green, and gold. The only embellishments were a few pieces of tulip-shaped porcelain stuck onto the poles. The air was thick with cigarette smoke.

They waited patiently for about half an hour. Finally, Nikolitch, who had been sitting with his back to the room, asked, "Where's our waiter?"

"I don't see any at all," said his wife.

Nikolitch moved his chair over beside hers. It was true . . . there wasn't a waiter in sight. Across the room was a bar, at one end of a which was a door concealed by curtains—no doubt the entrance to the kitchen. There was no one behind the bar serving drinks. The espresso coffeemaker was turned off, and there were no liqueur or cognac bottles on the glass shelves.

"You call this service?" grumbled Nikolitch. "I'm famished."

"Now, don't make a scene, Sándor. We've only just arrived."

"I've been trying to spot a waiter for over an hour."

"Do stop it. Perhaps they don't serve dinner until later. Maybe it's a new idea. I seem to recall hearing something about self-service cafés, I believe they're called . . ."

"Very well, then, I'll go and self-serve myself," said Nikolitch angrily.

"You're not going anywhere, Sándor. Look around you. Everyone else is quite calm."

Nikolitch had already noticed how patiently everyone seemed to be waiting. Only now, however, did he realize that the tables were quite bare. There wasn't a tablecloth, a knife or a fork, not even a glass of water or a demitasse on any of them. Everyone was blowing cigarette smoke and speaking in muted tones. From time to time, someone would cast a furtive glance toward the curtains.

Suddenly the curtains parted, and out stepped a stocky, red-necked man in a fishnet shirt. The man glanced around the room as though searching for someone. After a moment, he pointed to one of the patrons, who stood up and followed the red-necked man behind the curtains. Minutes later the curtains billowed, and the patron reappeared. Flushed, but wearing a satisfied smile, he returned to his table, where his friends seemed to find his brief absence so natural that they barely interrupted their conversation. Meanwhile, the stocky man signaled to someone else, and the two of them went out together.

"Melli, my dear," said Nikolitch, "where do you suppose those people are going?"

"To the rest room, I imagine."

"I know, but—on cue?"

"I couldn't say," his wife replied, powdering her nose. "I don't usually concern myself with such things."

She patted her elaborately styled hair, but her eyes were fixed on the man with the stocky neck, whose chest hair curled out from under his shirt. Another patron entered and came out, followed by yet another. Mrs. Nikolitch wondered if everyone got a turn, or whether you needed to be some sort of member. She turned her chair sideways so as to be more conspicuous from the curtain. The man's glance glided over her beautiful bouffant coiffure, but he pointed to someone at a neighboring table.

Unlike his wife, Nikolitch was intent upon removing himself from the man's line of vision. The fellow reminded him uncomfortably of a butcher. He watched uneasily as a gentleman from the neighboring table sprang from his chair and eagerly made his way toward the curtains. The man was evidently a prominent figure, not merely on the evidence of the red decoration on his lapel, but also because his eyes, his military bearing, and his white hair seemed to radiate dignity. Amazed, Nikolitch watched him go. He was forgetting his hunger and was feeling much less anxious. Had he not lacked the courage, he would have sneaked over to the door to see where the old man had gone. He shifted his chair so he could see the curtain directly.

He realized then that everyone else was facing in the same direction. The patrons were talking, all right, but their sentences were short and clipped. It seemed as though some fantastic, joyous event was about to occur, for which everyone wanted to be prepared. The tension began to affect Nikolitch as well. The moment the white-haired man returned from the kitchen, he sprang up and stood in his way.

"Pardon me for disturbing you, but we've been waiting for over an hour. How does one get served here?"

"Such impatience!" the old man said, shaking his head. "You're not a reporter, by any chance, are you?"

"No, sir. I'm an agronomist."

"Well, calm down, then." He patted Nikolitch on the shoulder. "We've been here four times, and the service tonight is better than ever."

The old man returned to his table. He had a slight limp, which he certainly hadn't had when he left.

Mrs. Nikolitch shot an angry glance at her husband.

"Was that really necessary?" she asked. "Just look at the quality of their clientele. Do you see Zoborhegyi making the kind of demands you are?"

Nikolitch looked around. Near the center of the room sat the famous actor-comedian, Zoborhegyi, whose picture had appeared in all the magazines. His small round eyes were riveted on the curtain, but otherwise, he sat at his table with exemplary patience, his arms folded like a schoolboy's. Nikolitch felt thoroughly ashamed. He sat up straight, like the white-haired man, and folded his arms the way Zoborhegyi had done. He watched each patron go, and waited eagerly for his return. Each time, he would search the person's face for some clue as to what might have happened behind the curtain. There was no telling. Everyone left with a tense expression, a vacant stare, and a dreamy smile, and returned with the same expression, and the same stare. Their smiles, on the other hand, now seemed somewhat forced, as though they were concealing some profound spiritual experience.

During the next few hours, nearly everyone else in the café made the journey between the main room and the kitchen. Nikolitch felt apprehensive. Whenever the man in the fishnet shirt appeared, he would try to attract his attention by means of some simple, childish trick such as jerking his head up, or pretending to sneeze. If the man noticed, he gave no sign. His searches grew longer, and often he would play a trick on a patron. On one occasion, he stared hard at a woman in a tulle hat, but when the woman leaped up, he motioned to someone else in a far corner of the room. Whenever he did such things, a murmur of appreciation swept through the café. The patrons would exchange glances and smile mischievously at the joke.

At long last, the man pointed toward the Nikolitch table. Both Mr. and Mrs. Nikolitch leaped up. The man beckoned to Melli with his right hand, while with his left, he motioned for Nikolitch to sit down. Mrs. Nikolitch rushed off, while her husband fell back wide-eyed in his chair and watched her go.

It was all he could do to sit still. Several times he ran out of patience and rose from his seat, but the wondering stares of the people around him brought him back to his senses, and he sat down again. Finally, the curtain was pushed aside, and Melli came out.

There was no time to ask questions, however, because the man was finally pointing at him. He did notice that Melli's eyes had a strange luster. Her face seemed flushed, and there was something not quite natural about the way she walked, as though she were drunk, pretending to be sober. When they passed each other, she did not look at him.

With a nod of greeting, the man in the fishnet shirt drew the curtain aside. From up close, his face seemed less threatening. His low forehead and his flattened, boxer's nose, with its two tiny nostrils, were not what you would call handsome, yet they suggested a kind of warm, animal tranquillity. Directly behind the curtain was a swinging glass door, which the man opened politely.

"Just walk straight ahead, sir."

At the end of a tiled corridor, Nikolitch came to a strikingly neat and well-ordered kitchen. The stoves were turned off, and the pots were lined up, untouched, along the shelves. A bright, round griddle for making crêpe suzettes hung on the wall like a full moon in a winter sky. There were no cooks and scullions. At least, the three men standing there in the kitchen certainly did not appear to be scullions. One of them was holding a blackjack. Another carried a bamboo stick. The third, who was standing empty-handed between them, walked up to Nikolitch and punched him in the mouth.

"Have you gone crazy, Somogyi?" shouted the man in the fishnet shirt. "How dare you attack a person that way?"

To apologize for this breach of manners, he turned with increased politeness to Nikolitch.

"It's overenthusiasm. He does it every time. What's your pleasure, sir? Will you be undressing or not?"

Nikolitch looked at the four men. He was not in the least afraid, nor was he at all surprised. He had always suspected—no, he had known—that something like this would happen one day. "Better now than later," he thought.

"If you don't mind," he stammered, "I'd prefer not to undress."

"Why, of course!" said the man with a friendly smile. "You must be from out of town. Would you like to be called names?"

"Whatever you think is right," said Nikolitch.

The man took a step backward.

"All right, men," he said. "Go to it! And no holding back!"

In obvious fear of their boss, the three men began to beat Nikolitch with great concentration, until their foreheads were beaded with sweat. They pounded him the way hot iron is pounded—quickly, before the metal cools. Occasionally, one of them would call him names.

"So our cotton's not good enough for you, eh?" said the man with the blackjack.

"Think you know everything, don't you?" shouted the man with the bamboo stick.

The third man, who had nothing to hit with, worked chiefly with punches and treated Nikolitch to more general abuses.

"Take that, twerp!" he shouted, as the rain of blows increased. "And that, snaggletooth! And that, you compost pile!"

The man in the net shirt did not participate. He stood aside, arms crossed, and waited, taking only an occasional opportunity to kick Nikolitch squarely in the pants. The man was plainly under no obligation to work and was merely trying to provide the others with a good example. As quickly as it had begun, the beating came to an end. The three men stepped back, and the one with the blackjack finally lit the cigarette which had been dangling from the corner of his mouth. Nikolitch had a headache and his knees were shaky, but otherwise he felt fine. Surprisingly, he felt light and free, as though he had just been given a massage, or had returned from a tiring but satisfying climb in the mountains. The secret anxiety which had tortured him was gone. He didn't dare move, however, until the man in the net shirt smiled and opened the door.

"This way, please."

Nikolitch stepped forward, then stopped. Was it customary to leave a tip? He placed a few coins cautiously on the edge of the table. The man with the blackjack bowed and put the coins in his pocket. Nikolitch walked back through the corridor and into the main room. His eyes were gleaming; his face was a rosy red. He tried to walk nimbly, like a soldier, for fear that he might have a bit of a limp. Licking his lips with satisfaction, he sat down beside his wife.

They remained at the Niagara for half an hour or so, then returned to their hotel. The next day they went back to their village in the middle of nowhere.

The Old Traditions

The old woman sat on the edge of the bed, her face a maze of wrinkles, furrows, and lines. The only thing youthful about her was the gleam of her brand-new teeth, a recent gift from the Union Health Center in Eger.

With a friendly smile, Mrs. Kászony held out the microphone.

"Tell us some more of your wonderful stories," she said. "Just speak in a normal tone of voice. This machine is here to preserve all those beautiful old stories you love to tell."

Wearing only the bottoms of a sweatsuit, the old woman's grandson lay on the bed opposite, reading a paperback novel by Balzac. "You don't have to explain," he put in. "Granny was on live television last spring."

"Well, then, shall we begin?" said Mrs. Kászony to the old woman. "Go ahead," she said to me.

I started the tape recorder. With a slight Palóc accent, the old woman immediately began to narrate the story of Bálint Puki Kiss, a rugged, hard-working blacksmith who had met his end under the bridge over the ice-bound River Hadik, hounded to death by a demon.

"A demon?" inquired Mrs. Kászony.

"That's correct, my dear."

"How very interesting. Can you tell us what a demon looks like?"

"I've seen quite a few demons, my dear. One was as thin as a whip and trailed fire, like a comet. Others were as small as a rat's tail, with lights in their heads the size of a match flame. There's all different kinds. Why, only the day before yesterday, a demon as big as a steeple ran right across our yard."

"You mean you actually saw it?" asked Mrs. Kászony.

In her amazement, the old woman's mouth closed so hard that her false teeth clicked.

"Why," she said after a moment, "have you never seen a demon, my dear?"

"As a matter of fact, no," said Mrs. Kászony with some trepidation. "Until a moment ago, I thought they existed only in folk tales."

"Tell me again, dear," said the old woman. "Where is it you work?"

"The Loránd Eötvös University in Budapest, ma'am."

"That's strange," said the old woman, shaking her head. "That's where my oldest grandson, Jóska, goes to school." She turned toward the other bed. "What is it Jóska is studying?" she asked. "I never can remember that word."

"Cybernetics," said her half-naked grandson, who went on reading his *Cousin Bette*.

170-100[1]

The telephone number above is that of the Special Information Service, which will answer your every question.

The Service is being used by more and more people, and the questions are becoming more and more difficult to answer. Did the Virgin Mary menstruate after the Immaculate Conception? Did composers miss the piano before the piano was invented? Did Marx and Engels meet by chance, or was the encounter predestined? Can a normal male and female zebra have checkered offspring? These are a few of the tamer examples.

Additional scholars and experts are being hired with each passing day. Out of this collection of great minds, the Service has formed about 120 information teams. Ties have been established with the Royal Academy and the Holy See. The Service is now able to answer even the weightiest questions, and although administration is becoming an ever-increasing burden, questions are still being answered with exemplary conscientiousness.

The following is just one example among many.

"Excuse me for bothering you, but we've got a little crocodile here that got hit by a ball."

"How little would you say he is?"

"About nine inches, maybe ten."

"Then he's only a lizard."

You'd think they would shrug off such trifles, wouldn't you? Not at all. The operator rang the first aid unit at once. The doctor who answered had won numerous awards for saving lives. His first question was:

"Are you yourselves lizards?"

"No, sir. We're students at Stephen I High School."

"I take it, then, that you are not related to the victim. We cannot release information to members of the family."

"We never saw him before. We were playing soccer and he got hit by the ball."

"Is he breathing?"

"Yes."

"How's his heartbeat?"

"His heartbeat is fine. The trouble is, he won't get off the field."

"Well, go and give him a poke."

The students went over and prodded the lizard with a blade of grass. It twitched a couple of times, but refused to move.

"It's a brain concussion," the doctor told them, "complicated by locomotor ataxia. I'll ring the neurology section."

You probably think the neurologist shrugged and suggested a swift kick to the head. Not so. After a moment's thought, he inquired:

"Would you prefer the classic treatment, or shall I call in a psychoanalyst?"

"We'd prefer not to have anything classic, sir."

Moments later, a bright, cheerful, encouraging female voice was heard. The difficulty, she said, was minor and easily solved. The patient suffered from a life-long inferiority complex, and this latest trauma—namely, being hit on the head by a ball—had given him amnesia. The reason he couldn't move was that he'd forgotten he was a lizard. This would have to be brought to his attention.

"What should we do?"

"Tell him that he's a lizard."

"But he can't understand human speech."

"I'm sorry, that's not my department."

"Whose is it?"

"Well, we do have a team of linguists who deal exclusively with the language of reptiles. Then again, I could connect you with the philosophy department . . . Would you prefer to speak to God?"

Of course, they said they would. The cheerful psychoanalyst explained that on Mondays, Wednesdays, and Fridays, the Divine Office was staffed by materialists; on the remaining four days the staff was composed of monotheists, polytheists, existentialists, or Zen Buddhists. Just getting through would be extremely difficult. After one ring, however, God Himself picked up the phone.

"What do you want me to do, kids? Bring your little lizard back to life?"

"That might be the easiest thing."

"Well, why not?" said God. "Go on back to your game."

The students returned to the field and looked around. The lizard had gone; the game could continue. (As a side benefit, the Service had also ended the centuries-old debate over the question of whether God does, or does not, exist.) You can see how reliable, how precise, how very conscientious they are. Or should I say . . . were.

We are, indeed, a most unfortunate nation. No sooner does something begin to go right, than out come the nitpickers, the hairsplitters, the troublemakers. One of these jokers recently called the Service and asked:

"Why is a raven like a writing desk?"

The operator gasped, and was at a loss what to do. Whom should she call? She rang this, that, and the other department, but no one could offer a satisfactory reply. In the end her confusion became so great that she could no longer speak, and the only sound at the end of the line was a pathetic crackle and sputter. Ever since, the Service has been a mere ghost of itself. It cannot answer even the simplest of questions.

If you ask what time it is, an intimidated voice replies, "We don't know." The poor devils have no self-confidence left at all.

[1] Like the remaining stories, this one is concerned with the author's view of shortcomings in Hungarian perspectives.

The Hungarian Hall of Fame

"It was announced in the papers," the museum custodian said over the phone. "We're closed for two weeks. 'Mementoes of the 1848 Revolution' is over, and 'The Loves of Franz Liszt' hasn't been set up yet."

"But what else can I do with them? We were planning to come down this afternoon."

"Take them to the Museum of Fine Arts."

"We've been there. Remember, these are country girls, only fifteen years old. A plain, simple object says more to them than all the beautiful paintings in the world."

"Well, I can't just conjure up an exhibit," the custodian said. "Besides, I'm here by myself."

The teacher sounded so disappointed, however, that the custodian asked for a moment to think. He might be able to throw something together before noon, although the exhibit would have to be small and somewhat improvised. There would not be a catalog, and they would have to make do with himself as guide.

As they entered the foyer, the girls noticed a piece of paper taped to the wall. The paper said, in typewritten letters: "The Sándor Hubauer Memorial Exhibit."

On display in the first room was the bayonet that Sándor Hubauer the elder had brought home from the First World War. The girls passed it by in silence. They barely glanced at the prayerbook once owned by Sándor Hubauer's grandmother, neé Mária Süle, despite the numerous interesting recipes scribbled on every page. The next showcase, however, containing a photo of Sándor Hubauer at the age of eight months, lying nude on his stomach, was a smashing success.

"Isn't he cute!" sighed one of the girls, as if in anticipation of the joys of motherhood.

The showcase also contained a battered tin pail, a shovel, and a wheelbarrow, all of which had belonged to little Sándor. There was a first tooth, a vaccination certificate, and a pair of eyeglass frames minus the glass. (As everyone knows,

Hubauer was myopic until the age of fifteen. His myopia was later corrected.)

"Let that be a lesson to you, girls," said the teacher. "You must have your eyes examined regularly."

The next showcase contained a beat-up old notebook.

"Even as a child," the custodian explained, "Sándor Hubauer kept track of all his expenses, down to the very last fillér. This over here is a sewing machine."

The girls were amazed, although in fact it was nothing more than a small, old-fashioned, foot-pedal sewing machine. It was over this machine, the custodian said, that Mrs. Hubauer had labored from dawn to dusk, while her husband was struggling to bring his great plans to fruition. Upon this poorly paid labor—the sewing of small monograms—had depended their entire existence. Blessings upon thee, O little sewing machine! Without you, how would Hubauer ever have fed his family of four on his meager custodian's salary?

"What kind of great plans did he have?" inquired one of the girls.

"All kinds," said the custodian. "Briefly, they can be divided into three groups—the economic, the political, and the scientific."

Unfortunately, considerations of time made it impossible to convey the variety of Hubauer's ideas except by a few brief examples. His scientific endeavors remained to be fully evaluated, although it was known that he had conceived the idea of a moon rocket much earlier than the Russians. He had also invented a device for storing solar energy, namely, a huge tinfoil bag similar to the bags in which roasted chestnuts are sold. Of his political views there was no written record, and his conversations with friends had nearly all been forgotten.

"How very unfortunate!" the teacher exclaimed. "And just what were his political views?" She turned around and scolded the girls, who had started to chatter.

"As you probably know, Hubauer was what we would now call a fighter for peace. To the utter dismay of his wife, he once shook his fist at a column of Nazi troops. He went AWOL from the army and went into hiding, using false papers. The travel permit there in case number seven is forged; the signature is the work of Hubauer's wife. His audacity would have made your hair stand on end. Toward the end of the war, while sitting in a Budapest beer garden that was under police surveillance, with false papers in his pocket, Hubauer cried out, 'The days of Hitler are numbered!' As you can imagine, several people glanced toward his table."

"Were they police informers?"

"No, they were all Hubauer's friends. But Hubauer was the kind of man who would say such things even to a Nazi informer."

The girls shuddered and walked on to the next case, which contained what appeared to be a toy railroad engine.

"This is the 'Be True To Thy Homeland' combination piggy bank," said the custodian. His pained smile seemed to say that nothing remained of this great spirit's plans but a trifle like this, which Hubauer had put together as a mere bagatelle. "And right next to it," he went on, "is another rejection slip from the patent office!"

"Why is it called a 'combination' piggy bank?" asked the teacher.

"When a coin is inserted, it plays 'Be True To Thy Homeland, O Hungarian!' "

One of the girls put in a coin. They waited expectantly, but nothing happened.

"It's out of order," the custodian explained.

"That's quite all right," the teacher said. "Obviously, the device teaches not only thrift, but also patriotic thinking."

"Didn't anyone ever give him any support?" asked one of the girls.

"No one. He was a lonely, misunderstood old man."

"And none of his plans ever worked out?"

"Here? In Hungary?" asked the custodian, with a wave of his hand. "You see before you a typical Hungarian life."

Not a word was spoken. All had been brushed by the wings of a nation's tragedy.

"This here," the custodian said, pointing to a color photograph, "is Major Yuri Gagarin!"

"Were they friends?"

"I'm afraid not."

"How come?"

"They just never met," said the custodian evasively.

There was one last showcase to go.

"This is the worker's weekly discount card which Hubauer used on the streetcar when he came to work . . . His was a modest, secluded life. He neither asked for, nor expected, privileges of any kind. His daily breakfast consisted of a half liter of milk, ten decagrams of sliced bologna, and bread."

The girls walked around the case that contained the milk, bologna, and bread. A few of the girls had tears in their eyes.

Finally, they all said good-bye, formed up in line, and marched out. A week later the girls were asked to write on the topic, "What I Saw on My Study Tour of Budapest." Now, young people prefer what is grand and spectacular. The girls turned out page after page about the Matthias Church, the self-service cafeterias, and the National Flag, but barely a word about the memorial exhibit for Sándor Hubauer. That's the way young people are these days. Just you wait, though. Some day, in twenty, thirty, perhaps forty years . . . *then* they'll remember Sándor Hubauer!

The Last Cherry Stone

There were only four Hungarians left. (In Hungary, that is. The rest were scattered all over the world.) These four had settled down under a cherry tree. It was an excellent tree, offering both shade and fruit—in the proper season, of course.

One of the four Hungarians was hard of hearing, and two others were under police surveillance. Neither of the latter two remembered just why he was under police surveillance, but occasionally one of them would say, for no apparent reason:

"*I'm* being watched by the police."

Only one of the four men had a name. That is to say, only the one named Sipos recalled what his name was. The other three had forgotten a great deal, including their names. Of course, when there are only four people, names aren't all that important.

One day Sipos said to the others, "We ought to leave something to remember us by."

"What in heaven's name for?" asked one of the men who were under police surveillance.

"So there'll be something left after we're gone."

The fourth Hungarian—whose name was not Sipos, and who was not under police surveillance—replied, "Who's going to care?"

Sipos persisted, however, until finally two of the others gave in. The fourth Hungarian kept pushing his own point of view, saying that he had never heard such a nonsensical idea in all his life. The others duly took offense.

"How can you talk like that?" they said. "Are you sure you're really a Hungarian?"

"Why?" the other replied. "What's so fantastic these days about being a Hungarian?"

He had a point. The four stopped their quibbling and sat down to figure out what sort of memorial to leave behind. They could carve a monument, but for that they would need a chisel. If only someone had brought a pin! With a pin, Sipos explained, they could scratch a message into the bark of a tree. The message would remain in the bark as long as the tree lived, the way a tattoo remains on human skin.

"Let's throw a big rock into the air," suggested one of those who were being watched by the police.

"You numbskull! It would only come back down."

The man didn't argue. After all, he'd never claimed to be brilliant.

"Well," he asked, "who's got a better idea? What can we leave that will last?"

The debate went on for a long time. Eventually, they decided to hide a cherry stone between two rocks. (That way, the rain couldn't beat it into the ground.) It wasn't terribly memorable, but it would do until someone came up with a better idea.

The question remained—where could they find a cherry stone? During the season, they ate the cherries. When the cherries were gone, they collected the stones, pulverized them, and ate them. At the moment, there wasn't a cherry stone to be found.

Suddenly, the fourth man, whose name was not Sipos and who had never been watched by the police, remembered that there was, in fact, one remaining cherry. (He was the one who had held out the longest, but now he fought for the project tooth and nail, his soul burning with the desire to perform a great deed.) The cherry in question grew at the very top of the tree, so high up that they had not been able to reach it. It was still there, although by this time it had dried up.

They thought and thought. At last it dawned on them that by standing one on the other's shoulders, they could probably reach the shriveled cherry. The procedure was carefully worked out. The first Hungarian to stand under the tree was one of those who were under police surveillance—the one who had more brawn than brains. Onto his shoulders climbed the one who was not named Sipos, and who had never been under police surveillance. Next came the second Hungarian who was under police surveillance. The last to begin the climb was the thin, bony Sipos.

After a great deal of clambering, Sipos reached the top and stood up straight on the column formed by his three companions. By the time he arrived, however, he no longer remembered just why he had made the climb to begin with. The others shouted to him to bring down the shriveled cherry, but there was no use shouting at Sipos, since he was the one who was hard of hearing. What could they do now? Occasionally all four of them would shout at once, but that didn't solve the problem either. And so they remained as they were, one Hungarian atop the other.

Iván Mándy

Mándy was born on December 23, 1918 in Budapest into a Protestant family, originally from Szatmár County, that experienced a continually unstable economic and social existence. His father, whose personality and bohemian life influenced him greatly, sometimes negatively, and who became a forceful symbol of much of the reality presented in his fiction, first worked at the city hall; then, after his assignment to see to the building of the new national theater was canceled, he became a journalist and worked on several periodicals but never as a regular member of the staff. During his boyhood, Mándy lived in numerous hotels in the suburbs of Budapest, in which he spent much time alone simply waiting—and observing. He attended as many as five secondary schools. The uncertainties caused by his father's lack of success in several publishing ventures and irregular income and the extraordinarily confusing world of his boyhood often led him and his father to seek out the dream world of the movies, a medium that was to influence the subject matter and style of his prose fiction tremendously. Eventually, with the help of his mother's earnings, the family established a home on Teleki Square, which became a rich source for many of the stories he later wrote, and in which he still lives more than thirty years later. His experiences in school made him wretched; he maintains that he wearied of the sour faces, and that he never enjoyed a good moment in the classroom, and hated even the recesses. At sixteen, while standing in front of a movie theater where he had just seen DeMille's production of *King of Kings* after classes, he decided never to enter a school corridor again. The increased loneliness and isolation resulting from this decision and his reading of Ibsen, Jens Peter Jacobsen, and Herman Bang deeply affected his outlook on life. He shortly turned to a writing career, a profession which had already begun to attract his attention while he was a student.

During the second World War, his father kept him from military service by placing him in a hospital, often with the cooperation of a physician friend, and reporting him ill whenever the summons came or threatened; on one occasion he went before the draft board, and, handing them one of Mándy's novels, he said: "This is what my son, Iván, sends to his country." In the 1940s, he worked for newspapers, for a time as a sports reporter, but, like his father, never on permanent assignment. From the end of the war to 1948, he contributed to several progressive literary journals. His first book, a novelette drawing on his life in hotels, was published in 1943. National recognition came to him in 1948, when he received the Baumgartner Prize, the most distinguished literary award, at the time, for a novel, *The Twenty-first Street* (*A huszonegyedik utca*), published that year. Although a significant collection of his short stories appeared in 1949 (*Guests in the Flagon* [*Vendégek a Palackban*]), and it was followed in 1955 and 1956 by three short works for young readers, the landmark year of his career was 1957, when a new collection of short stories (*Strange Rooms* [*Idegen szobák*]) and another novel for youth (*Csutak and the Gray Horse* [*Csutak és a szürke ló*]) both came out, showing striking development of lasting strands in his narrative art, particularly that of the short story. Since then, his writings have been published regularly, some being made into relatively successful films. They find a growing number of discriminating readers who themselves can meet the demands of a new, nontraditional style and technique that eventually influenced later authors, including Anna Jókai, Géza Bereményi, and Miklós Vámos to varying degrees.

Mándy's narrative sources lie entirely in the life and setting of Budapest, at whose streets and squares, sidestreets and doorways he marvels as if seeing them for the first time. The physical objects of that world, whether a kitchen wall, tobacco shop, door-latch, or wash basin, are, according to him, so vital to his creativity that he constantly uses them as a means of developing an understanding of the human condition. His short stories and novels project kaleidoscopically and at times grotesquely the world he has keenly observed from his boyhood—except for the period of the war years to which he is only now about to give substantial attention in a novel he is preparing. His portrayals of the decades of the twenties and thirties and the many changes that have taken place in Hungary since then provide, on the whole, a very gloomy montage of the human condition. Mándy writes about the suburbs, the hotels, the stalls of second-hand clothing, and fleamarket that once existed in Teleki Square and its environs, the coffeehouses, the soccer fields, and the world of the radio and journalism—places peopled mainly by drifters, derelicts, and social castoffs, and by unsuccessful professionals and intellectuals—all of them victims of vicissitudes that foredoom them to make their painful way as best they can. Regardless of their particular situations, his characters are typically suspended between the real and the unreal and are overwhelmed by circumstances; like Zsámboky and the secretary in "The Spotlight," they cannot hold on to anything firmly or nurture a satisfying relationship with a single human being. When their repression and frustration become stifling and their inner life, consequently, more distressing, his characters create a dream world to cushion themselves from reality, like the old projectionist in "The Death of Zoro." Mándy has also evoked the fantasy world of the films and stars of the twenties and thirties in two fictionalized accounts of the silents and the early talkies. His concerns with "insignificant human beings" led his critics in the 1950s to charge him with being exclusively interested in trivial subjects, wastrels, and useless humans, and with totally failing to recognize the successes of socialism and the new opportunities it presents to humankind. Mándy chose to remain with the world he knew so intimately and viewed as a microcosm of human society. Disclaiming any interest whatsoever in solving social problems, he believed that the worth of an individual is determined not by worldly success but by the quality of the soul, and that the success of a writer's work depends not on its breadth but on its depth. In 1969 he was awarded the prestigious Attila József Prize for his contributions to his country's literature, when Ágnes Nemes Nagy and István Csurka were similarly honored.

His narrative techniques are as distinctive in Hungarian literature as his subject matter. He is a deeply involved observer of the life about him who never permits himself to lapse into omniscience; he records, and then, in short, highly distilled sentences, he projects details of sight and sound that objectively convey the inner world of his characters, always realistically but often dimly, as if through a dark veil. His techniques reveal not merely a departure from conventional formulations of plot and character but also the influence of his life-long love of the cinema. Even the structure of most of his novels attests to his commitment to the genre of the short story and to his use of film techniques. They are, in effect, short stories strung together like "garlands" rather than structured by "logically advancing" plots. As his career developed, he took increasingly less trouble to shape characters fully and fashion plots clearly. Instead, as a painstaking craftsman he distilled and compressed details, conveying with lyrical symbolism the psychological states of his characters. Scenes roll as if flashed on the screen, sometimes affording only glimpses to be instantly absorbed in the flow of images by the reader. Individual scenes often evolve as if through the lens of a moving camera; sometimes, as in his description of the actress in "What Can a Writer Want?," two images are superimposed to enrich and deepen the reading experience. The frequent use of the dream technique of surrealism, though in a realistic manner, distinctly marks his break with conventional narrative modes and probably best displays the individuality of his style.

His stories supply no philosophical outlook, for such speculation is, according to him, alien to his temperament. Indeed, one of the reasons he prefers recent American novels to French is that he finds the latter too speculative. Certainly, his works reflect the influence of existentialism to an extent, but he is probably correct in stating that his concept of reality is closer to that of Dostoevsky than of Sartre or Camus. In 1971 he expressed profound pessimism about the prospect for human progress, and though he strives to believe otherwise, his gloom has increased since then. He emphasizes the need for individuals to discover their distinctive qualities and principles and then to abide by them as fully as possible, without creating insoluble dilemmas in facing life. His unrelenting, merciless observations of human beings in his writings have sometimes given rise to the opinion among critics that he has little love for mankind. On the contrary, his compassion for the troubled, the trapped, the abandoned, the lonely, however ignoble, often ironically conveyed, is omnipresent in the tone of his stories, binding his lifework into a harmonious whole.

The Watermelon Eaters

A face was ascending the stairs, a face very long and stony, as if borne on a platter. Its eyes closed, its mouth a straight, hard line. On this sightless face was visible the restaurant with cold mirrors, little tables, and guests, who failed to notice the face. The outstretched, dead hand then rose into view trailing an invisible veil. A blue-gray greatcoat closed at the neck held the entire man together like a sack. He passed by the booths and stopped in the middle under a chandelier. He raised his head in the glittering light; his face and hands glistened, but his tunic remained dark. He stood there, wordless, motionless, his face flung open to the light, his hands thrust out. Slowly, slowly, as if searching for someone, he turned to one of the booths.

Three persons were sitting in the booth: two women with a pimply faced youth. The woman with gray hair lifted her fork, then put it down, and said: poor thing. The girl ate and did not look up from her plate. She had thick blonde hair, and her arms were plump and darkly tanned as if she were sitting on the edge of a swimming pool.

The boy groped in his pocket.
The girl looked up.
"I will!"
The blind man caught the coin with a sweep of one hand, but by then he was being held by the arms. A waiter with a trimmed moustache was standing behind him; he pushed him forward slowly. The blind man opened his mouth wide and was now an astonished black hole.

"You know that's not permitted . . . " and the waiter pushed him down the stairs. The beggar tripped and banged a hand against the bannister. He remained there clinging to it, his head slumped forward lifelessly. The waiter grabbed his shoulders and stood him up on his feet like a rag doll. "Don't be such an ass!"

Half-risen, Károly, the pimply faced boy, was observing him. Now his head again slumps forward, and meantime his dark, gaping mouth seems to sneer. His sister touches his hand.

"What are you staring at?"

Ágnes's taut, impassive face, with two blue earrings, closed off everything in front of her. She lighted a cigarette with lazy, prolonged movements. Singing sounded from below. The blind man was already halfway out on the street; he was singing and meanwhile turned around.

He was surrounded by several persons acting as if they were snatching newspapers out from under his arms. For an instant his face rose above the crowd. "Let me go!" Then he disappeared from the door.

A woman with a bent back and wrapped in a shawl entered from the street.

"Why did you have to hit a blind man?"

"Beat it, old lady, beat it!"

The woman tottered at the door for a moment and then went out.

"Don't even mention Rudy Etlinger! That fortune-hunter, that vulgar fortune-hunter!" Ágnes's round, haughty shoulders jerked. "Shall I marry somebody who is interested only in my money? Of course, to you that makes no difference . . . "

The mother raised her sharp-featured face and seemed to be looking at the girl from an old picture frame.

"There are times when I simply don't understand you. Ágnes, you can say such terrible things. Etlinger is a distinguished lawyer, his name is on everybody's lips."

"Drop the subject!" Ágnes opened her mouth slightly and waved her hand. "Just getting married like you isn't really worth it."

"What is this 'like me'? Everybody knows your late lamented father courted me for years, and not for my money, absolutely not!"

They both were so remote from Károly that he did not receive as much as a word or glance from them. So this is his sister, this sparkling, blonde, deeply suntanned girl . . . "A cute gal," a classmate had said. One can feel the beach behind her as she lolls about on the sand in the torrential sunlight, then gets up, and enters the water with slothful, slack steps. Their mother is watching her from a bench in the shade; she does not go into the water with her skinny, dry body. "Now what does all this about Etlinger mean, this whole conversation?"

Downstairs shadows floated past the door. A bearded fluff of hair stuck his shapeless tuberous head inside as if into a shopping bag.

Someone said: "Of course, at a time like this there's never a policeman around."

"It is really easy to understand why nobody wants to take a pauper for a wife. After all, the man is making a start in life. When he is setting out, the foundation is very important. The financial foundation!" She sounded triumphant. "I can understand that very well!"

"Mother, don't strain at it!"

A spoon tapped the dish, then silence. The mother was quiet, Ágnes toyed with the salt shaker and smiled.

A waiter stood at the door, expounding toward the street.

"Nobody wanted to hit him, he is the one who created the rumpus. Mackó, I said to him, don't make a hullabaloo, don't make a row!"

Ágnes leaned her head back. She waited. Anticipation overspread her hair, face, arms; her cheeks glowed, her shoulders trembled as if a finger had touched her, her lips gaped strangely, dreamily, and her fan-like rows of teeth flashed. She looked at her mother, but no longer saw her. Expiring, crumbling, she sat like a martyr waiting to be captured and carried off, to be set on her feet and led away.

". . . and if you want to say your father married me for my money, then realize you are wrong, I say wrong!" The mother's voice faltered, and she jerked her head up suddenly. "What in the world is that sound?" She looked at Károly, but he disregarded her.

"We must phone the police." Downstairs a gray-haired man was drumming on the counter with two fingers; he blinked toward the street and then at a scrawny woman attired in yellow.

Károly pushed his chair aside and went down the stairs. A waiter galloped past him; he heard the lisping voice of the woman dressed in yellow.

"They all should be rounded up! All of them!"

Next he was standing out on the street in front of the restaurant in the cool evening breeze. He saw the watermelon eaters at the wall: the long row, the hands and faces stuck together, the outstretched blackened feet. Prickly mugs plunged into the plump watermelon, gobbled it, bit into it, and, already steeped in slush, fused with the watermelon. Half the sidewalk was filled with filthy, trampled rinds. A face parted from the row, a hand dropped from the wall. A little girl, with wrinkled face and clad in rags, ran forward brandishing a melon rind, behind her two howling children. And above them like a sharply cut line moving swiftly, came carts, hand-carts, enormous plump-bellied carts rumbling furiously.

Next to a poster kiosk the blind youth in the tunic shouted: "They kicked me!"

The row was moving as if the wall were going to collapse, the street to split open. A beggar rose up out of his beard and seized the blind youth's hand.

"Let's get going then!"

Behind Károly the restaurant vanished together with his mother and sister. He was standing all alone in front of the watermelon eaters who are now heading right for him. There's nothing else, only the living, moving wall with faces, hands, and beards . . . they are coming, he thinks, to call him to account for something.

He was yanked inside from behind, and a melon rind immediately whacked the restaurant's floor.

"Police!"

"We will have to wait for them a while."

A broad-shouldered, grinning character in the doorway, some kind of blanket around his shoulders as if he were walking about in his bed, his shapeless, worn coverall a night-robe. The blind youth appeared behind him, his two rigid arms came forward, leaving his face behind.

"They kicked me in the kidneys!"

"It's rotten to hurt a blind man."

Károly retreated to the counter. He heard a sickly, shivering voice. "I have already phoned, but who knows when they will arrive . . . this damned place, damned place. Lord, just this once . . . " The woman in yellow was praying behind him at the till. Above, however, as if a row of plates were sweeping forward, a small rag bundle slid down the stairway's bannister—into the arms of a waiter.

"You guttersnipe!"

"What do you want with my brother?"

The face in the blanket leaped at the waiter and grabbed his arm. A slap in the face, someone shrieked sharply.

Károly leaped behind the counter, the woman in yellow flew over his head.

The blind youth still stood alone, entirely by himself, two hands stretched out before him. All of a sudden, he reached into his pocket and lit a cigarette.

"It was your idea to come here!"

This his mother—to him it was strange that he really has Mother and Ágnes.

"Just lie still, my child," said the woman in yellow. "The police are bound to come. Oh, the cost! the cost!" She began weeping.

Károly looked up. A prophet emerged from the side door: wavy gray hair, emaciated red face. Meekly, piously, he carried a meat platter—he stuck it under his coat. A spoon fell out of his pocket.

"Pardon me," he said and reached for it.

The stone tiles of the restaurant swam with sticky watermelon juice, the scattered rinds just like scalps.

"What do you want?"

His mother again. The boy sprang from behind the counter, up the stairs. A woman wearing a shawl, smoking a pipe, long gray hairs hanging from her wrinkled face, appeared before him. She stood stooped over but still seemed very tall and immovable, like the arch of a gate. She began speaking from somewhere amid the dense wrinkles.

"What about the watch, you nice boy?"

"What watch?"

"The one you bought from me on Klauzál Square in the doorway. You know very well which one, and you forgot to pay me for it."

He looked and looked at her, and soon seemed to remember the watch, the doorway on Klauzál Square, the horribly hairy face he knew so well and he had cheated.

A man wearing pince-nez dashed past them in a torn vest, holding a crushed derby in his hand.

"Damn it! Damn it!"

Above, up high he spotted his mother, Ágnes, between them the stocky fellow with the blanket around his shoulders. The three were standing there. However, the boy was seeing them as in a mirror between opening doors, the mirror of a distant chamber and the depths of a dream. Every feature of his mother's bird face was leaping about separately; she was bending toward the man as if wanting to pluck him up.

"What do you want from me?"

The fellow did not want anything from her. He was looking at Ágnes, her jutting breasts, her muscular arms, her half-closed eyelashes, her curly hair-do—and he already possessed them all. With one movement he lifted up her breast. Ágnes's face was fixed as if she were rising above some waves.

The man in the blanket tore down the stairs whirling the woman with the pipe along with him. A fat man climbed out from behind an overturned table and dusted his trousers off.

"It's senseless, absolutely senseless!"

Ágnes still stood as if the man were there beside her—stood and waited. Her mother clutched her arm and shouted to Károly.

"Come, for god's sake!"

She practically flew with Ágnes. She almost slipped on a rind and hung on to the girl even more. Behind them, always behind them, Károly deserted them like someone who suddenly cuts into a sidestreet. He watched his mother, and he almost broke out roaring with laughter at the panic-stricken way she was waddling . . . afraid, she is still afraid. Bim, boom, budaboom.

Police were standing at the squad car, the blind youth between them.

"They beat me up," he said very clearly.

Then nothing remained of the entire affair. Just a dark street with the galloping mother, who suddenly stopped at a corner, raised her frightened little hand, and struck Ágnes in the face twice.

"Whore!"

A Summer Holiday

The mother leaned with her sharp-featured, pointed face into the lamp. She was mending a shirt collar with short, nervous movements. Next to her on the sofa were some shirts folded very neatly. Next to them some shorts and handkerchiefs.

Blinking her eyes, she looked up as if searching for something beyond the area of the lamplight.

"Bandi," she said. A chair creaked in the corner. "I think this shirt is in good shape too."

More creaking came from the darkness.

"Thank you, Mother."

She still stared straight ahead and spoke into the darkness.

"My son, I think we should still get a couple more things . . . a shirt and such." After a slight pause: "At least a couple of things."

"At least a couple of things," echoed the corner. Then a knee rose from the dimness, and a thin, swarthy face also leaned forward. "What more do you think we should buy?"

There wasn't the slightest drop of irony in the voice. Rather an expectation of: fine, please draw up a list, everything needed, Mother.

She lowered her head.

"I know you have lots of expenses. After all, besides me you are also helping Éva . . ."

"Let's drop that!" A creaking again. Then almost like a thick, dark cloud of smoke rolling in, the young man was standing there in front of his mother.

"I honestly don't understand why you insist on talking about it, Mother. Believe me, it is completely uncalled-for."

She looked up. Her hand started searching for his.

"Don't get angry."

"That's not the point."

Her hand touched his for an instant, then it fell back into her lap.

She fumbled around among the shirts, shorts, and handkerchiefs, and by the time she looked up again, a smile was on her face.

"You won't need a thing at Füred." Her eyes sparkled. "And you know, I won't either . . . I've put my gray dress into excellent condition, and yesterday . . . yes, it was yesterday . . . Giza lent me her sunglasses."

"I'm really delighted about that."

He fished out a paper from somewhere in the corner. Still standing, he began to read it.

His mother kept on talking.

"Of course, she didn't want to give them to me at first, and I really had to promise to take care of them. But you know I take good care of everything, and it will be good, after all, for me to sun myself a bit."

The newspaper crackled, then landed on the sofa. He took hold of his mother's shoulders.

"You can go in the water too."

"Oh no . . . no! But I can watch you swimming from the shore." She heaved a happy sigh. "It's nice we can vacation together . . . that they arranged accommodations for me too at the resort." She looked up at her son. "After all, that is so nice."

He bent down for the paper but didn't start reading it again. He walked about the room holding it in his hand. Occasionally he would move far into the darkness, then once again be beside the lamp. Suddenly he stopped.

"Mother . . ."

She flinched her shoulder. "If you think I'll be in your way, I honestly . . ."

"That's not it, you're no bother, why would you be?" He paused. "But I would like to ask a favor of you . . ."

She looked up at him. Her thin, parchment-colored skin tightened on her face. Something inside her could be expected to burst in the next instant.

He touched her shoulder. "Now . . . now . . ." He also smiled at her.

Her face obediently adopted the smile, but the smile immediately faded, congealing in the wrinkles.

"I would like to ask a favor of you," he repeated. He sat down next to her. He didn't look at her as he began. "You well know that this is a resort where there are different sorts of people, from factories and all sorts of places. In short, don't announce immediately on our arrival that your husband was a Justice of the Supreme Court."

"But Bandi . . ."

"I'd like it if you heard me out!" He looked at his mother sideways. "Forget father!" His hands swept the air. "Forget him! Forget him! I would also like it if you wouldn't mention that the two of you used to vacation in Fiume, and at times made trips down there for weekends."

"Sonny"—she bent forward—"you know your father had a railroad pass, and besides, the whole thing didn't cost very much."

He did not relent.

"Not a single word about Fiume. Or, I beg you, about how different things were. The meals, the service . . . and above all . . ."—his voice seemed to take on an imploring tone—"the people! Yes, the people you vacationed with."

His mother smiled at the lamp.

"Now, who was it that invited us to go sailing? Some Austrian count . . .

You know he was acquainted with your father. His books . . . yes . . . and he was the one who came over to our table . . ."

The young man's feathery hair began to tremble. His voice also trembled as he addressed his mother again.

"Not a word about the Austrian count! or the sailing! or the invitation! Please, please." He took hold of her hand.

"Why, that never even entered my mind!"

"I know," he retorted, "like the other day on the bus."

She shook her head.

"All I said was how rude people are . . ."—she glanced shyly at her son—"these days . . ." She stopped and then went on a little more boldly. "And it's true! They don't give you a seat, they elbow you, the ticket collector tells me to move forward, then asks what I am doing standing in the door if I'm not getting off."

"Then, Mother, you immediately started in. That you have known people other than the ticket collector . . ."

"But believe me, only so he won't abuse me!"

"In the end we had to get off the bus," he said. "And just recently the same thing happened on the streetcar."

"What happened on the streetcar?"

"Forget it, Mother!" The young man sighed. "And it isn't necessary to mention the fact that we had lots of servants."

"But they really seemed like members of our own family. Only their smell . . . You know, Bandi, I never said anything to them, but I think every single one of them has some kind of smell."

"I don't know about that, Mother. But forget the servants even if they were like members of our family. And don't call the women working there 'my child.' "

"What should I say instead?"

"Well . . . well . . . 'comrade.' Please say 'comrade.' "

"Comrade," his mother repeated.

"But not like that!" He made an impatient motion. "Not in that tone!"

"Well, what kind?"

He waved his arm and then went on.

"And in the dining room, don't rotate and look at the spoon as if you had got it from some infected patient."

"Oh no, no, Bandi."

"And when you make friends with someone . . ."

"I won't make friends with anybody."

"That's because you have such grand airs!"

"But son . . ."

"Understand that if you don't enter into conversations, they they will say . . ." He jumped up and started walking around and around the room again.

His mother, resting her hands in her lap, stared straight ahead of her. Suddenly she felt the sofa groan next to her. She heard the voice again.
"Please . . . Mother . . . !"

An enormous park with trees and shrubs. Red benches on the promenades. The brown building of the resort behind the trees. The mother was looking at it. She had just got up from a bench to speak to someone. That chubby-faced man who sits beside her in the little dining room. But for some reason she didn't know what to say. And so she simply smiled and let him leave with the woman dressed in blue. She should have greeted her too. But how? . . . Once a woman snapped at her privately: "Don't call me 'comrade'! " Then what is left to say? How should she address the girl who does the cleaning? The woman with black hair in the library? The one approaching her now? . . . If she stops and starts a conversation.

She took a couple of steps. Then she sank back on the bench and stared at the gravel. She remained that way until the steps receded. Then she stood up, and tottering uncertainly, she started out for the resort.

Then, like someone who has just remembered something, she sank back on the bench again. She just sat there, lost in the park like an old abandoned umbrella.

King Kong

". . . and if you really must know, King Kong is still alive today, and he is constantly walking about, but only at night, and he is lifting roof tops off and peering in everywhere because he won't rest until he finds the Blonde Wonder."
"Or Mrs. Rabnec."
"Mrs. Rabnec?"
"Mrs. Szecsey."
"Mrs. Szecsey?"
"Mrs. Tivadar Nagy."
"Mrs. Tivadar Nagy?"
"Mrs. Glemcsák."
"Mrs. Glemcsák?"
The usherette was lying in the cold, keen moonlight. She didn't know when

she had woken up. She heard her husband's heavy breathing far away in the distance, maybe not even coming from the same house.

Nothing was stirring in the moonlight. Nothing was stirring in the night.

Then in one swoop the roof top of the house across the street was pushed aside and King Kong appeared. The enormous apeman stands in front of the house like someone who has been searching for something a long time and finally found it.

"Oh!" said the usherette, and she sat up in bed.

King Kong was standing there in front of her bed. He gave a shove to the room with every movement. The room billowed around her like an accordian.

The usherette was already lying in the palm of King Kong's hand.

"But you are hunting for the Blonde Wonder."

The apeman shifted her to his other palm.

The usherette trembled and closed her eyes. "You have the wrong house. Everybody knows you have smashed several skyscrapers because you can't find the Blonde Wonder anywhere."

The apeman put her from one palm into the other palm.

"You have the wrong house!"

The usherette became speechless. King Kong strode over the window with her. Above the houses—out into the night.

The Death of Zoro

Two jolly fellows in the movie foyer. Zoro and Huru,[1] the two staunch companions who never so much as take a step anywhere without each other.

A boy stopped in front of them. He put his hand out as if he wanted to pat the "cardboard cutout" Zoro and the "cardboard cutout" Huru.

He was alone in the foyer. Around him on the walls were photos of film actors and actresses and scenes from next week's attractions. But all these disappeared beside the life-sized Zoro-Huru. They were standing at the cashier's window. Somewhat offended at being left all by themselves in the dim foyer.

Maybe the others are sitting in the dark theater this morning. Rudolph Valentino, Vilma Bánky, Barbara La Marre, Richard Dix . . . They are sitting there in front of the curtains drawn over the screen, staring straight ahead and staying silent. No noise of any kind reaches them, only the beating of a carpet from a distant courtyard. They are sitting there in the long rows of seats. Rudolph Valentino, Vilma Bánky, Barbara La Marre, Richard Dix . . .

Zoro and Huru in the foyer. The gangly, moustached Zoro and the merry, chubby Huru. The buttons had long ago torn off their coats, and string of some sort held them together. Little satchels were in their hands. What can there possibly be in those satchels?

The wall is covered with pictures from their film.

"Beach Photographers"

The two noble companions are in striped suits in one picture. Zoro's head was stuck under the camera's black cloth, while Huru posed women from the beach for a shot.

"I bet," the boy thought, "Zoro and Huru are playing tricks on the beach. Maybe Zoro won't even take his head out of the camera, and Huru is only interested in the girls. He positions the arm of one, the chin of another, meanwhile promising to marry them. It's quite possible that Huru will bamboozle the whole beach."

"Beach Photographers"

Photos from the film, captions next to the photos.

Zoro and Huru, who had already tried their hand at so many different things, decided to sally forth as photographers. They packed up their non-existent belongings and set off alongside the Northern Express.

Zoro and Huru were jogging between empty tracks. Huru was looking ahead confidently, Zoro with a vague distress in his eyes. His long moustache hung down droopily.

Zoro and Huru, the two inseparable great friends, arrived a couple of days later than the Northern Express at the bathing resort, where as beach photographers they again experienced funnier and funnier situations.

Huru's face so plump, but Zoro's stiff, as if numb with cold.

"The whole thing started with his eyes," spoke up someone behind the boy.

The boy didn't turn around. He knew it had to be the old projectionist. He had left the projection booth and climbed down. Once in a while he would climb into the booth early in the morning and inspect the projector and reels. Or he would start to show the film, just to himself.

Now he was standing in front of Zoro in his loose-fitting coveralls and round cap.

"One thing is sure, he'd stood before klieg lights for many more years than the other, this chubby one. He had already been a famous actor when this other one . . ."

"Didn't they begin as a team? Zoro and Huru?"

"How could they have!" The projectionist looked at Zoro as if wanting to ask his forgiveness. "Oh, we still remember very clearly when this pudgy here dropped in on Zoro to ask for some kind of work. Maybe not even in pictures, just so he has something. Meanwhile he told heart-breaking stories about his dear mother who is sick and must be provided for. Everybody knew about Zoro that that's exactly what he was a pushover for."

"You mean, somebody just starts in on his mother and Zoro . . . ?"

"The thing is, Zoro lost his own mother at a very early age. His house is full of portraits and statues of his mother."

Then he said that Huru got hold of this tip. He got hold of it and faked everything. It came out much later that Huru never gave so much as a fillér to his mother. Not even when he was a world-famous movie star.

They were standing in the foyer next to the cashier's window. Zoro who lost his mother at a very early age and Huru who never gave so much as a fillér to his mother.

"And the old lady died like that, in a poorhouse. Neighbors took up a collection to pay for her funeral. I don't have to tell you you would've looked in vain for Huru at the funeral."

Certainly, Huru got just bit parts beside Zoro at first, and nobody had confidence in him. But it is also true that Huru worked on the public diligently.

Huru visited schools and joked with the children. He even sat at a desk (in his sailor suit, of course) and acted awfully nervous about being called on to answer questions. And he was called on (prearranged, of course), and he hemmed and hawed at the blackboard so much they sent him to the corner.

Somehow Huru forgot to take Zoro along on these excursions. True, Zoro wouldn't even have gone with him. Zoro told him off. He said he also liked children but didn't care the least bit for tomfoolery. Huru just grinned and said nothing. Then newspapers began publishing reports that Zoro had contempt for his audience, especially children. And between the lines—yes, between the lines—was slipped the hint that Zoro was jealous of Huru's evergrowing popularity. At this point, Zoro stuck the item under Huru's nose: "What is this?" Huru protested he didn't know anything about it.

The boy leaned against the railing at the cashier's window. The window closed. A sign above it: balcony, stalls, easychair.

"There's no doubt Huru mounted a real campaign against Zoro . . . on the sly naturally. By then many were warning him to be on guard, but he still didn't want to believe the vague rumors. He didn't even think it strange that after several film previews school children marched ahead of Huru carrying their little pennants. Huru! Not Zoro and Huru together! Not even what the school children were shouting made him suspicious: 'Don't be afraid, Huru! We are with you!' Huru had sworn he didn't know anything about it, and that was enough for Zoro."

The boy swung himself over the railing.

"Meantime, Huru invaded Zoro's married life." The projectionist whipped his cap off and dug his fingers into his hair. "This is what nobody can figure out to this very day. Zoro married a Danish actress of astonishing beauty, Dalma Dagmarson. Their marriage was unclouded until . . . Yes, even now Zoro didn't want to believe the whispers. He threw the unsigned letters away."

Zoro was pacing in his room, wearing a lounging robe that reached his ankles. An unsigned letter was in his hand. Occasionally he would glance into it: " . . . your wife, dear artiste, and your own partner are seen together very frequently these days. I must note that lately they don't even care about keeping up appearances." Zoro took a step toward his wife's room, but he tore up the letter instead.

He didn't want to believe the gossip, slander, the whispers. He didn't want to believe his wife either, when one day she walked up to him. Dalma stood squarely in front of Zoro and looked into his eyes.

"We can't live together any longer."

She also told him the why of it, namely the who of it.

Zoro grasped the edge of the table, his head slumped forward.

The ravishing Dalma and Huru! . . . How was he able to sweep her off her feet?

The boy whirled on the railing at the cashier's window. Huru above him. "By hook or by crook I will sweep the ravishing Dalma off her feet."

"Zoro didn't stand in the way of the lovers. He let his wife go. He continued to make movies with Huru. It's true, he hardly spoke to him outside the studio. At this time he was being racked by terrible headaches. Headaches and insomnia. When he wasn't working, he lay behind closed shutters with a cold pack on his forehead. Or he walked about. With long, prolonged strides he walked from one room to another. But his eyes grew weaker, he was seeing with increasing difficulty. At the advice of friends he turned to a doctor."

Examination followed upon examination. They had him read letters from a chart, they stuck different kinds of lenses before his eyes. "Is this better? Do you see more clearly now?" They took him into a dark room where he had to lie for a long time. Robed figures moved around him. For an instant his wife seemed to stand beside him. Huru's round face seemed to pop into view. A lamp's small sphere in the dark. Closer and closer it came, like a klieg light. At the end of the examination, they announced: "Surgery is unavoidable."

The old projectionist walked back to the double-door through which the public is admitted. He opened it for a moment. The long passageway with its columns and buffet stand could be seen.

"They threw Zoro on the operating table."

The projectionist said this.

The boy slipped off the railing. He didn't get up immediately, he stayed on the tile floor for a while.

"A famous professor of ophthalmology operated on Zoro. Not quite free of charge. He touched him for quite a nice little sum. To this I must add that by that time Zoro wasn't exactly in the best situation. His wife didn't leave him in just the clothes she had on her back, you can be sure. The operation . . . ah yes. As they say, the operation was successful; only, Zoro couldn't see a bit better."

"Did they operate on both eyes?" The boy had hoisted himself onto the railing again.

The projectionist disappeared behind the double-door. When he reappeared, he was hitting an empty pipe against his palm.

"They kept Zoro confined for a long time after the operation. Did he have any visitors? Of course he did. But he was waiting for only a certain person."

Zoro lay with bandaged eyes in a darkened room. He waited for a particular voice, for a certain person to touch the covers and sit down beside his bed. He waited in vain. Not once did Dalma Dagmarson, who had left him for Huru, open the door and enter.

Huru, he was something else.

Huru really turned the hospital upside down. He came at the head of a merry group. In the corridor he pinched nurses, passed out autographs, opened bottles of champagne. Naturally, he was accompanied by a pack of reporters. Naturally, the newsreel was also with him. The Eye of the World.

As he entered Zoro's room, he stopped in the doorway. For a while he just stood there motionless. Then he spread his arms out wide and threw himself on Zoro's bed. "That we have to meet under such circumstances!"

The newsreel camera whirred, and during the following week, everybody could see there was no more faithful friend in the world than Huru. The Eye of the World also showed Huru weeping. "I won't leave until I can take Zoro along with me."

The Eye of the World didn't show Huru slipping out of the hospital that very same day . . .

Zoro stayed there.

The operation was successful, though, and the Prof decided to try his hand at newer surgery. They took a crack at it. They experimented with at least three different kinds of operations.

The projectionist was now poking his pipe with a little piece of wire. Then he kept hitting it against his palm again. He looked up at the boy, the pipe stayed in his hand.

"The result was that Zoro left the hospital with a glass eye."

Dark glasses, scarf, topcoat, small satchel. Zoro stood like that at the hospital entrance. The Eye of the World wasn't on him. Reporters didn't pay any attention to him either as a nurse took him by the arm and led him out of the hospital grounds. For some reason, even his friends forgot to come. The few friends who still remained from the old days.

Leaves circled listlessly on the hospital grounds. Zoro stopped and reached for a leaf hesitantly. He would have liked to linger in the yard a bit; perhaps he would even have sat under a tree. But the nurse led him on.

A small stubby-nosed taxi waited at the entrance. The hospital had hailed it. They still did that for Zoro.

The nurse straightened Zoro's scarf, gave the driver his address, and then squeezed Zoro into the taxi.

His housekeeper shrieked. She clapped her hands together, when from the window she saw her master with his little satchel. She rushed out to the gate.

"Dear sir! Oh, my dear, dear sir!"

Zoro allowed her to lead him in, he allowed her to set him down for some tea with her. He asked her to open the mail and read aloud the letters that had arrived during his absence.

She couldn't open any mail, for none had come. Not from the studio or anywhere else either. Later she finally brought forth a letter. Zoro's bank wrote that regretfully, unwelcome news must be sent, his shares had fallen, not just fallen but crashed, and the funds on deposit, which had already greatly declined anyway . . .

Zoro waved his hand to show it's enough, she should stop. He wanted to be left alone. He didn't want to do anything more than curl up in the corner of the sofa.

For that matter, he could curl up in the corner of the sofa to his heart's content.

If he had few visitors in the hospital, then now . . .

The boy was perched on the railing.

The projectionist was standing in front of him seeming to want to leap instantly on the railing too. But he merely shrugged his shoulders as he said:

"The day came when Zoro went to the studio. Don't think they sent a car for him. He had to tap his way to the studio, he who was one of its founding members. The porter greeted him but didn't leave his booth. He seemed to retreat even more into the corner. It was the same with the others he encountered in the courtyard or the corridors. They muttered confusedly, then stepped aside. He even came across some who wanted to stop him: 'We're shooting! You can't go in!' But Zoro continued on anyway among the cameramen, makeup people, and extras."

Sad was Zoro's passage through the cameramen, makeup people, and extras. Suddenly he did come upon someone, and then he really had to stop.

A long-legged fellow with a moustache hanging down the sides of his mouth and a sour countenance. On his head a sailor's cap unlike any other in the world, with a long ribbon hanging down.

They stood in the corridor, Zoro and the one with the sour countenance.

Suddenly only shouting was heard.

"We're starting to shoot! We're shooting!"

They didn't stir for a while. Then suddenly Huru appeared. He was also wearing sailor's cap.

"Don't you hear we are shooting?"
With that he pushed the sour-faced one onto the set.
Zoro drew himself into the collar of his topcoat and didn't say a word.
Huru caught his breath and straightened his sailor's cap.
"The fellow is working splendidly, and the public is already used to him."
"Used to him," nodded Zoro.
"Put more correctly, they didn't even notice that I had started a new Zoro on his way, that I had launched a new Zoro."
"Launched?"
Huru spread his arms out. "Old chap, we couldn't wait for you. The public—this thousand-headed monster of ours—is impatient. But you know that as well as I do. You really understand the public! In short, you still have to pull yourself together."
"I must pull myself together . . . "
"Besides"—Huru bent closer to him—"that glass eye . . . The public notices things like that. You know how it is. But come now, take a look at the new Zoro!"
"I am Zoro!"
Huru grinned and nodded. "You are . . . you are!" He seemed to sing it: "You are . . . or somebody else!"
Huru vanished. Zoro was alone in the corridor.
"I am Zoro!"
Suddenly he collapsed. A pain stabbed him in the head so hard that he fell against the wall. Someone took hold of him, led him into the courtyard, and sat him down on a chair.
He sat on a little chair in the courtyard. He pulled his shoulders up and spread his hands out. He could still hear the hubbub on the set, the horn as the clapboard slapped. Then he got up and started away. But he didn't go home. He went to the Film Cemetery.
The boy slid off the railing at the cashier's window. He is now going to hear something the old man has never related to anyone else. Something he will then relate to Gyuri Streig and the others in the evening on the square or in front of the street door.
"Lots of people think the Film Cemetery is in California, somewhere in the Film City. Well, they are completely mistaken! The Film Cemetery is up North, in Zoro's native land. From all parts of the world travel to this place those stars who can't keep up anywhere but still don't want to wind up in an old people's home. In greatest secrecy they travel to this place. In greatest secrecy they make their way across the suburb to the Woodland. The first stop is a shabby little movie theater. No picture is ever shown in this theater. Old posters cover its walls. Every movie star finds the poster on which his name appears in the biggest letters. He rolls this poster up and takes it with him."

Don't think you will find crosses and graves in this cemetery. Broken klieg lights, twisted cables, rusted derricks mark the route. Caved-in studios with discarded props.

A crumbled room from a baron's village house with split-legged tables and broken chairs. Rows of burned-out suburban streets, collapsed floors, abandoned arbors and promenades where nobody ever walks. Only an actor or actress grown too old. The actor walks the length of a promenade. He is in the studio again. He walks and walks until he reaches a room. On its walls are photos of the greatest roles. The room itself is the set of his most successful film. By then he has nothing more to do than sit down in an old easychair. Look at the photos on the wall, gaze into the air. Meanwhile he can even light up a cigar or a cigarette. And also find some beverage in one of the corners. There is still a bottle left behind from takes of *Hussars in Ingolstadt*.

Hither came Pearl White, the most elfish gamin, when they froze her out of the silver screen. Theda Bara, the real vamp, and Milton Sills, the pirates' captain, the old sea wolf. Pearl White found her old ball and jumping rope, Theda Bara her feather headdress and the divan which she could stretch out on full length, and Milton Sills the shipwreck with its torn pirate flag.

Hither came Zoro. He crossed the suburb, the Woodland. To the movie theater, the theater where he chose his poster. The one in which he is shown fighting the windmills with lance in hand. The poster of *Don Quixote*.

Zoro rolled it up and took it with him.

He carried the poster with him among shattered klieg lights, corroded cables, blinded lamps, burned-out searchlights. Torn ribbons of zigzagging streets, collapsed stairs of half-caved-in houses marked his route. Shattered statues, headless statues, undamaged statues, crushed heads, split foreheads. A hollow-ringing rail area with a broken glass roof, an unstocked department store, crumbling columns and balustrades.

The Cemetery for Sets was left behind.

He arrived at a barren, empty field. A kind of whinnying sounded. The outlines of a horse appeared. The outlines of a yellowish, impossibly scraggy horse. The slightest movement ran its bones one into the other. On the ground next to it were a lance and shield.

Zoro knelt down and bowed his head on his palm. He stayed like that for a time. He slowly straightened up. And then he was soon sitting on the horse with his lance and shield.

Windmills off in the distance.

Zoro's scarf became untied, the tails of his topcoat fluttered as the horse started out with him.

The windmills were turning. They were waiting to fly him into the air to pass him on from one vane to another, from one vane to the other . . .

Iván Mándy

The wind blew, the topcoat fluttered as Zoro headed for the windmills with his lance held up high.

The shadow of a horse, the shadow of a horseman on the broad, empty field as he rides toward the slowly receding windmills.

There was silence. One could not tell when the projectionist had fallen silent, but now silence reigned in the foyer at morningtime. Pictures of actors and actresses, pictures of the movie appearing next week. Zoro and Huru beside the cashier's window. The two staunch companions who never so much as take a step anywhere without each other.

It was silent in the theater at morningtime. Then the old projectionist spoke:

"It seized him while he was shaving. Yes, they found him like that, with his throat cut." He took hold of Zoro's shoulder. "They had been watching him for some time, he had already aroused suspicion at the studio, and then while shaving . . . They say he couldn't forget that day when the old Zoro, the real Zoro, stood in front of him in the corridor at the studio. They say that from that time on he practically begged them to give him something else, even if it is some worthless, tiny part. He would rather be an extra, just so he wouldn't be Zoro! As for the one who came after him, there was something with him too . . . something happened to him too."

The projectionist's hand slipped off Zoro's shoulder.

The boy hoisted himself onto the railing at the cashier's window.

"What is wrong with all the Zoros, that they always . . . ? Please tell me what is the matter with the Zoros. Please tell me!"

No reply came.

He flopped down from the railing. He looked up once more at the figure with the blank look and the long moustache, then the theater door slammed shut behind him.

[1] The Hungarian names of Danish comedians who achieved worldwide success, known as Fy and By in Denmark, Pat and Patachon in Italy and Germany, and Long and Short in England. Zoro (Carl Schenström, 1881-1942) made his stage debut about 1900 and began his movie career in 1909; Huru (Harald Madsen, 1890-1949), the member of a circus family, first made his living as a clown. They appeared as a team in forty-seven feature films between 1921 and 1940, their popularity peaking in the mid-1920s. Their humor was based on the differences in their looks and temperaments. Zoro was the suffering type, Huru the daydreamer who always dispelled his companion's gloom.

In the Spotlight

He stopped in the the doorway. Wearing a hat and coat, he looked back at the flat before leaving. At the two rooms opening on each other.

He went over to a chair, took hold of its back. He lowered the shutters a little more and adjusted a table cloth, looked out on the snow-covered square, passed by the sofa, then paused for a moment. The unstirring silence of the rooms. It enveloped him. He liked this silence. He enjoyed dawdling about the empty flat like this.

He pulled the chain in the w.c. He checked the soap in the lavatory. For a while he sat on the edge of the bathtub. He took his hat off. If he smoked, he would now light up a cigar. That is, if he smoked at all. His father had smoked cigars. Rather cheap ones: Fájintos, Cigarillos. Near the end, though, he smoked cigarettes, seeming to be ashamed of doing so. His mother had smoked cigarettes. She gave them up. She gave up many things.

And I? I never smoked.

He was strolling about in the hallway as if on a promenade. He stopped in front of the mirror.

Have I ever accomplished anything at all?

He turned the lights on everywhere. In the two rooms, the lavatory, and the kitchen. He rolled a lemon on the kitchen table. A hardened, grumpy lemon.

He turned the lights off. The flat plunged into darkness. He stood at the bedroom window and looked out on the square.

A meeting with the public.

A slip in his pocket. The Cultural Center's invitation. An open forum on the movie, on that particular movie. The leading lady has a performance to give, the director is abroad. "At least you must come." The girl at the Center appeared before him. "At least you mustn't leave us high and dry."

He turned around. He called over to the dining area.

"There's a discussion on my film." He waited a bit. "Do you hear, Father; I've written a film script."

He lingered in front of the dining area for a little while longer. Finally he set out. He locked the door to the flat, but he stood at the door pane and peered into the darkened hallway. Like a visitor who is just getting ready to ring the door bell. He thrust the key into his pocket and threw himself down the stairs.

The flat was left on its own. The brown dining table, with scattered empty ashtrays. Chairs around it. A studio couch over there, its cushions flattened. An easy chair beside it. A dark patch on the worn upholstery of its back. The outlines of a head. Exactly as if someone were sitting there leaning back in the darkness and silence.

After getting off the bus, he went past gardens, past little, tiny gardens covered with snow. In one a washbasin half-buried in the snow. Shutters and curtains closed.

A bleak gray building on the corner. As if it had just been pushed forward from somewhere. Dull glass sliding doors, a long empty corridor behind them. Two boys in gym shoes came running down the steps. When they spotted Zsámboky, they ran back up. They disappeared upstairs, on the second floor.

"Why don't you come in?" The young woman, a skinny brunette, pushed the glass doors aside. One of her shoulders dipped slightly as if someone had struck it. She smiled, but very hesitantly.

By now the two of them were standing in the corridor. A stamping sounded from the second floor; perhaps they were jumping on a footstool.

"The ballet," she said.

A small office with book shelves. In the corner a table with coffee maker and cups. The young woman took a bottle and glasses from one of the cabinets.

"A little cognac. You must be chilled. I always get chilled to the bone."

Later, as she was preparing the coffee: "Don't you want a poster? You can take it with you."

"What kind of poster?"

"The announcement about your forum." She tossed one rolled-up onto the table. "Not very many are going to show up."

"Klári Rotter!" Zsámboky stabbed a finger at a name. "Why, she herself said she has a performance tonight."

"We didn't know that when the posters were printed. Or that the director was going to be away."

"My director!" Zsámboky barked.

She looked out into the corridor.

"We'll wait a bit longer."

They drank a little cognac again. Zsámboky discovered a page from a notebook on the table. He began reading it in an undertone: "It was a big surprise to Julis that the men in the city adopted her so readily and did not send her away . . . "

"I have to translate it into English." The young woman peered out again.

". . . like a featherless crow, to soar if she could." He looked at the girl over the page. "Shall we continue to wait?"

Both were there. His mother was lying on the sofa covered with a greenish-gray blanket. His father was sitting in the chair next to the door in pajamas and high-crowned hat. His long white hands lay in his lap; he was stroking his fingers with long-drawn-out movements.

"You could take your hat off," said his mother from under the covers.

"I can't because of my hair-do."

"Hair-do! Now, what kind of hair-do do you have?"

His father didn't trouble to reply. He looked around. "He's on the run, always on the run."

"János receives countless invitations. Performances . . . forums . . . He is also invited abroad."

"He is not invited abroad." The father gestured. "He'd like to be, but nobody invites him."

"What about that society in Vienna?"

"Oh that, that was some kind of activity. They knitted sweaters, shawls, and such for the poor."

"What kind of shawls are you talking about?" She raised herself slightly.

"Well, if they weren't exactly shawls, in any case . . ." He stood up like someone preparing to go on a trip. "Books, let's say, books. They sent him some philosophical works. Philosophical works in German."

"Why shouldn't they have done that?"

He was still standing next to the chair. "Let's not mention that he never learned German. German or any other language whatsoever. If only he had taken a serious book into his hands somewhere along the way!" He slowly started away from the chair, from the furniture. "How I kept pounding into his ears that he should read Bölsche[1] at least!"

"Anyway, he's achieved a position in life."

The father turned around. "Just mention something worthwhile if you can."

The mother fell silent. She huddled herself up under the covers and said nothing.

On the other hand, he seemed to look back at her from some far away region. Some remote province. He shrugged his shoulders and moved on. Suddenly he stopped.

"What do you say to this, Ilonka?"

She stuck her head out from under the covers. "To what?"

"Television!" The father was circling around the set. "No matter what, this here is a television set. T.V."

Wrapped in a blanket, she sat up: "And why not?"

"But he never wanted anything like this." He pointed at the T.V. "It never even occurred to him."

"How do you know that?"

"He was perfectly satisfied with the little radio you bought for him. Television . . . T.V." He looked out on the square. He held the edge of the curtain. "It must have been that woman's idea."

"What woman?"
"That teacher, she is a frequent visitor these days."
"A teacher visited him often before as well."
"That one worked in an espresso."
"It couldn't have been a serious affair."
"It was quite serious. Only, the girl left him. She left Jancsi in the lurch."
"What do you mean she did!"

He left the window and walked over to the bedroom. "In any case, they threw out his little radio. And they also threw out that big bed."

"My son was never interested in such nobodies."
"They were the only kind. Espresso women, nurses, streetcar conductors."
"Streetcar conductors!"
"The armchair is still here." He took hold of the old torn arms and eased himself into the chair. "Fortunately, it is still here."

The girl stole a glance at Zsámboky over her shoulder. "Maybe we can have a look now."

Zsámboky felt as if he had been standing behind the girl like that a very long time. So familiar was the girl's neck with the fine dark fuzz. One movement and his hand will instantly close on it.

They were out in the corridor. They were standing next to each other as if pressed together. By then the piano no longer sounded from the second floor. The dark line of the street showed behind the large glass door.

"The posters were prepared far enough in advance." She was whispering as if afraid she might wake somebody up.

The lighted buffet counter in the depths of the corridor. A stocky man with gray hair was eating salami in a bun. "What's going on, Magda?" He gestured toward the girl. "Has Rakonczai arrived already?"

"Not yet."

The man turned away with his salami in a bun. Zsámboky asked her: "Who is this Rakonczai?"

The girl was staring at a pillar. Her shoulders shook now and then.

Can she be crying? It would be better to leave, to turn around nicely and leave. But he remained beside her. Unexpectedly there burst from him: "Do you always fall asleep on the bus?"

"Do I what?"

"A little while ago you said in there that you always fall asleep on the bus. You don't even know when you have arrived."

She continued looking at him with that frozen, unfamiliar face. Then very quietly, virtually syllable by syllable, she said:

"Anikó Láncos's night didn't come off either. What can I do? They don't come, they simply don't come."

"What about the hall?"

"What hall?"

"Well, where this would be held . . . this . . . " He fell silent.

They stood around among the gray-black pillars as if in some sort of waiting room. It was quiet. Then children on the stairs, children in gym shirts and satin pants. Strewn about like so many matchsticks.

"The ballet," Zsámboky said.

She nodded at him.

"You also said"—Zsámboky stepped a little closer to her—"that your shoe once got stuck in the asphalt. It was so hot your shoe got stuck." Since she remained quiet, he added: "You came barefoot with your shoes in your hand."

"Let's go." The girl broke into a smile of alarm. "Maybe somebody has come after all."

They started away.

"One time an older lady fell asleep in the w.c.," she related on the way. "We came upon her the next day."

"Then occasionally somebody does come after all."

"To get warm. And of course, when Béla Szente was here."

"Béla Szente?"

"He sings dance tunes. Don't you know him? He simply couldn't get into the Center. Crowds surrounded his car. We had to call the police."

"You don't have to now."

Flags in the corner. Furled flags. Dusty windowpane, blackened wall.

"Well . . . " She stopped at a door.

Zsámboky smiled uncertainly.

She pressed down on the latch. It bounced back.

"Why, it is locked." She looked at Zsámboky. "Shall I get the key?"

"Oh, why bother."

She was still holding onto the latch.

"Shall I show you our movie theater?"

"He is really earning good money these days." The father was again standing beside the television set.

"They appreciate his work," said the mother.

"They appreciate all kinds of things nowadays. But to buy a T.V. . . . Only a car is missing."

"And why shouldn't there be a car?"

"He will turn into an idiot, a complete idiot."

"You wretch!" she said in an angry, hurt voice. "Just because you never . . . "

"What do you know about it!" He moved away along the wall. He slid his hand along it. "This is what I read Anderson to him for . . . He spent the tuition money I scraped together out of my last fillérs. It's for this that I lugged his junk, those stories around. Nobody wanted to publish them anywhere, but I lugged them around until . . . He always kept his money if he got any."

"I started him on his way." He stopped. "Your picture is here. You are sitting in a straw hat in a spinach bush."

"That's not a spinach bush. It's a garden, the Valkays' garden."

"I know, where Gábor Valkay painted it. It's vomit."

"Gábor Valkay had a one-man exhibit, but he kicked you out when you went to him begging."

His hand was sliding along the wall. "Not a single picture is left, not an etching anywhere. General Görgey[2] has been tossed out. Well, he didn't appeal to somebody."

"They weren't even pictures. You cut them out of magazines, then you pasted them. You cut and pasted them."

"Even so, they were worth more than this spinach bush." He sat down on the sofa's corner.

"He'll be putting spoons away one by one."

"What kind of spoons, Gyula, if I may ask?"

"Silver spoons. By then he will own silver spoons, and he will shift them from one drawer to another, again and again. Silver spoons, knives, and forks. He will dump them all on the table and just look at them."

"You don't even know what you are saying anymore!"

"What do you mean!" A brief silence. "He handed over twenty forints a week. And things were then going really quite well for him. Twenty forints a week. True, he later did raise it a little."

"He acted badly enough!"

"He went regularly to the Mélyvíz,[3] to that part of the restaurant where writers . . . He strutted around down there among the other pompous blockheads. While I ate rice pudding above in the gallery."

"He used his own money."

"I could easily see from up there what he ordered. He would begin with consommé. Then would come all the rest. Last a deciliter of wine and demitasse. And when I wound up in the hospital . . . "

"Forget the hospital!" She sat up, the blanket slipped off her. "Don't talk about the hospital!"

"Why not? He brought you everything."

"Please, Gyula!"

"Nonsense!" She wrapped the blanket around her shoulders. "Sheer nonsense!"

They sat silently beside each other on the sofa.

They were in the little movie theater. Rows of empty seats beneath the screen. They were walking in the rows as if trying to find seats for themselves.

Zsámboky was right in the first row. He was staring at the screen. He sat down for a moment, then stood up again. The young woman was banging the seats somewhere behind him. She had been expounding about a boy for who knows how long.

"Never a concert! Never a play! Well, I wasn't that interested in the races."

"I can imagine."

"Besides, I couldn't even see any of the races. Somehow it always turned out that I couldn't see any of them either."

Zsámboky made a turn to the left. He swung into one of the rows. He unexpectedly encountered the girl. They smiled at each other somewhat wearily.

"Did your film get abroad?" she asked.

"Yes, I think so."

"What reaction did it get?"

"Reaction? What reaction?"

She sat down. Her face became taut. "After all, I couldn't go with a character like that cyclist."

Zsámboky sat down. For a time they just sat silently, like people waiting for the performance to begin.

"I was always completely covered with dust. As the motorcycles whizzed by me. I could see nothing, but I practically filled up with dust. My hair, my eyes, my skin."

She jumped up. She walked about in front of the screen. She shouted to Zsámboky from there.

"We were already on the motorcycle in the morning!"

"Did he also start in . . . ?"

"Like so much. Long before each race started we would cut along the track to wind up at the spot where we could see best. In his opinion! In the end we would find the side of a hill. We waited until ten, at least until ten, for the race to start. Then some faint rumbling din signaled the race had started. I sat there hanging onto a bush. Every half hour there was a beastly rumble. Huge clouds of dust."

"As the motorcycles whizzed by."

"You put it well: as they whizzed by. Even days afterward dust would just pour out of me." She stopped. She glanced up at the screen stealthily. "He was a nice fellow, I must say, and from a certain viewpoint . . ."

Zsámboky leaned forward, interested.

She sat down in one of the rows behind him.

"My girlfriend knows you."

"She does? Who?"

She did not reply. She leaned her head back and stretched her legs out.
"I kicked him out."
"The cyclist?"
"The cyclist."
She remained like that, head leaning back and legs extended.
Zsámboky gazed at the screen attentively. As if he were seeing the girl seated on the hillside clutching a bush.

Steps sounded outside. Coughing, hacking. The steps stopped right in front of the door.
Father: He will ring immediately.
Mother: No, he won't. It's Temunovich, the druggist. He is now going over to Mrs. Gyergyai.
Father: Oh, yes. But Mrs. Gyergyai once threw him out. Mrs. Gyergyai likes only directors of the Soldiers' Chorus. After all, a chorus director is really something else! Listen, somebody seems to be filing iron now.
Mother: That is Mrs. Somogyi's mother.
Father: Yes, of course. She puts paper on the railing and slides her hand down it that way. But she is unable to go out by now.
Mother: You see, occasionally she still . . .
Silence. Then the mother in a peculiar, girlish voice:
"One thing for sure, he always brought me something. If nothing else, a piece of chocolate. He never stayed long because he was terribly busy, but he always brought me something."
"Yes, he barely looked in. 'How are things, Father?' And he was gone."
"That shouldn't surprise you. Given the pressures of his work."
"The pressures of his work . . . !"
She took no notice. She didn't even hear the gloomy laughter. She merely spoke, spoke her own thoughts.
"He even brought me a banana once in a while, even though bananas are hard to get. An orange, a banana, and a piece of chocolate. He talked with the doctors, with the professor himself."
"If I only knew what you mean by that." His father stood up. He resumed his stroll.
"They really cleared the pictures out of here. At least they could have left the Görgey here."
"He brought me a nightgown and a robe, and he even saw to a fresh slip for the little pillow. Because they didn't provide any there. They provided bedding; it's just that for the little pillow . . ."
He was standing at the window. He was looking at the snowy, slushy balcony.
"How was it in your section? Did you get a slip for the little pillow?"

"Don't get angry, Ilonka, but somehow I don't recall that."
Suddenly she got up from the sofa and went over to him. "Did he view you?"
"View me? When?"
They were standing alongside each other. The mother sort of cuddled up to the father. "They displayed me to him."
"What bliss!" He left the window and made his way into the room.
"When he came down there into the basement, into the little chamber, they showed me to him." She also left the window and followed after him. "At first he didn't want to look at me, but then he did."
"Why don't you stop this? Don't you find this a bit in poor taste?"
"My, how finicky you've become, Gyula." She laughed mockingly. "How finicky you have suddenly become!"
The father sat down in a chair, he kept folding the brim of his hat. The mother stopped beside him.
"He was concerned about their dressing me properly . . . for that occasion."
"That occasion!"
"He brought in a dark blue dress, with a crocheted collar. He brought in a pair of black stockings."
"You don't say! Really?"
"He also brought in a little white handkerchief, but the person who dressed me sent it back."
"Don't talk to me about the dresser."
"What did he bring in for you?" She practically leaned into his face.
He was folding his hat brim even more furiously. "These pajamas, if you must know! Nothing was right, no suit, no shirt! Just these pajamas. They put them on me, that's what they dressed me in! For that occasion!" He choked up. He did not have a word to say, he just kept crumpling the hat brim.
She stood beside him. She would not move away from him.
"But you must have got a pair of stockings! Gyula, tell me, you did get some stockings, didn't you?"

The little office again.
The girl pushed an envelope in front of Zsámboky. He shrugged his shoulders: "But . . ."
"Never mind," she said. "You showed up."
"So what if I did!" He stuck the envelope into his pocket.
A form has to be filled out. Name, address, and the like. It seemed that meanwhile the room had shriveled up. Dark stains from leaks on the ceiling. The stains will slowly engulf the room.
"Well, that's that." Zsámboky looked at her. "They will certainly rake her over the coals for the program. The program that never came off."

"I am going too." She took her coat off the rack.

They started out. The girl turned in the key at the porter's cubicle. Then, as they got outside the building, she said:

"I am leaving. I am quitting this . . . "

"You are quitting?" Zsámboky also turned toward the Center.

Rows of dark windows. Among them a few lighted squares.

"You don't really think I would stay here, do you?"

They ambled toward the bus stop. The girl stuck her hands in her pockets.

Her thin face with its slightly pointed nose was barely visible from the coat collar, from the shawl. A long red shawl wound around her neck.

"This was also in style a long time ago." Zsámboky took hold of the edge of the shawl. "At the beginning of the twenties and earlier."

"I've been promised something, of course, but nothing's definite yet."

"Derby hats . . . lately derby hats can be seen again."

"It's possible I'll wind up in a film studio."

"A film studio?" He suddenly let go of the shawl. He looked askance at her. These words seemed to have transformed him.

"Assistants. Second assistants. I know that I will have to scurry around a lot, that they will foist everything on me from makeup to the extras, but even so . . . "

"And then?" Zsámboky's voice verged on exasperation. "What will come of it all? I know someone who has been a second assistant for thirty years, for thirty years he has scurried around with stupid scripts under his arm, for thirty years he has been yelling at the extras."

"Maybe it won't take thirty years in my case."

They were standing in front of the bus. The empty, darkened bus. Someone boarded it and immediately vanished into the darkness. Snow started falling. Not snow really, but tiny, stinging sleet. In an instant their faces were filled with it.

"It's certain I won't stay here. Either they fight and I have to call the police or there's nothing!" She began shouting. "I won't stay here, you understand?"

Zsámboky grabbed her by the arms and pushed her onto the bus.

The girl emerged from the shawl. "Where are you really going?"

"We still have time for a cup of coffee somewhere."

They sat on in the parked bus.

When Zsámboky stepped out of the elevator, he bumped into an elderly gentleman. The skinny man in a black coat apparently had been waiting for him a long time.

"You don't resemble your father at all, but there is something about your bearing."

Zsámboky nodded and sent the elevator down.

"Letters." The old man acted as if he wanted to descend after the elevator. "I have to get certain letters back."

"Certain letters?" He took out his key but did not unlock the door. The old man did not even expect that. He settled down quite completely in front of the door. "Your father and I carried on an extensive correspondence. You know, the Kossuth emigration. We both agreed that during his emigration Kossuth[4] matured into the role of . . . "

"But my father is . . . "

"We miss him terribly. The Monday Circle. You know, we meet every other Monday in the Simplon Coffeehouse." He broke into a smile. "Pardon me, the Szimpliczi! Your father expressed it like that: 'Let's go to the Szimpliczi! Onward: the Szimpliczi!' A certain gaiety distinguished your father . . . a liveliness." He headed for the stairs but immediately turned back. "The printer has got under way."

"Really?"

"They have detected that I am throwing light on the Kossuth emigration from an entirely new angle. The possibility of publication has presented itself."

"I understand, yes."

"That is precisely why I must have the letters."

"I don't even know if . . . " He looked at the old man and slowly turned numb. He could not conceive opening the door. Or the old man leaving. "Honestly, I don't know if my father . . . "

"My friend Gyula stowed everything away."

"Do you think so?"

"Oh absolutely! Undoubtedly these too in a special drawer, in a carton. If you will permit me, I shall help you, we shall search for them together."

"Together, yes." The key slipped into the lock. The old man stood behind him.

"Gyula didn't like Kossuth. He valued him but didn't like him." He started to wipe his feet, he practically scrubbed them. "I should have delivered a talk at the service."

"What kind of talk?" He looked at the old man as if he would as soon push him down the stairs.

"In the name of the Monday Circle. But the state of my health . . . " He stopped wiping his feet. When the door opened he asked:

"Was there a cremation?"

"Yes, a cremation."

He let the old man go ahead of him, and then he also entered.

---

[1] Wilhelm Bölsche (1861-1939), a German writer who tried to reform the world in accordance with the principles of the natural sciences, and viewed literature, particularly poetry,

from the vantage point of these disciplines. His works were very popular in Hungary between the two world wars.

[2] Artúr Görgey (1818-1916), a general in Hungary's War of Independence from Austria, 1848-49, who turned against Lajos Kossuth, the leader of the revolution.

[3] The sunken dining area of a restaurant, particularly the one at the famous Hungária in Budapest.

[4] Kossuth (1802-94) went into life-long exile in 1849, when Russian military intervention brought an end to Hungary's effort to gain independence from Austria.

What Can a Writer Want?

Above, in an upstairs room, is the head of the family. For years he hasn't come down to the rest of them, for years he hasn't wanted to see them. They have lived their own life downstairs. Meanwhile they keep hearing the old man walking around upstairs. At such times their eyes meet, but they don't speak a word.

I was reading Ibsen at the time, *John Gabriel Borkmann* among others. This was the one that was living within me quite vividly when I wanted to write a concluding episode on the grand old man of the family.

I was strolling on the back promenade of Kálmán Tisza Square. I was tormenting myself about how to bring the old man down on an occasion to his family in spite of everything. Then the great scene will take place. Some sort of squaring of accounts.

Weeks passed, months. Lilacs bloomed on the square's promenade, but the family's grand old man couldn't descend. The plot of the play didn't budge. Those living downstairs broke completely from the old man, who paced back and forth ever more solitarily, ever more savagely upstairs.

And he is still walking there to this very day. Until time eternal.

Because by then something had become clear. I can't plot the action. I can't even commence it. This I must admit.

I started a fairy play. This bogged down as well. My imagination simply wouldn't budge.

(Meanwhile, to fix the time: I had just then left the fifth form of the gymnasium. I had nothing else except a notebook with a double cover, the Ibsen volume, the Classical Collection of Fiction, and Kálmán Tisza Square.)

But already at the very onset I also had to realize that my imagination wasn't operative. Decisive matters emerge quickly.

The power of observation remained.

I heard something about Maupassant. Maybe it was actually Flaubert who gave the piece of advice to the young Maupassant. Observe a tree until it doesn't differ in any way from all the other trees in the world.

I took matters seriously. (I still take matters seriously today.)

I dropped anchor in front of a tree. It was an ordinary, sturdy little tree on the square. In no way did it want to be different from the others. I continued looking at it for a long time, I gradually began to hate it. I could no longer see anything at all, I just stared off into space.

At home I took out the double-covered notebook. I tried to describe the tree. I failed.

Then I saw someone once. A thoroughly drenched fellow. Then the tree appeared before me. This was worth more than every observation. From that I sensed something called inner reality.

I was that way with the street too. I wanted to describe the street on which the little hotel where I was living at the time was situated. Accurately, in detail. Therefore faithfully, I thought. I looked out the window, scrutinized the houses thoroughly. By the time I returned to the table from the window, everything had fallen out of me. It was as if I had never seen the street. Sometime afterward I stopped in front of an old store, and then I sensed the street.

No action, no imagination, no observation.

The inner world remained. And whatever flowed into it from experience.

The wonder of an old store, of a damaged fire wall, of a human face.

About the last. I once saw an actress's face during a rehearsal. She wasn't acting, she was left alone, her face was also left alone. A tired, lonely face. Across this face tottered sick, old parents who can no longer be forced out—they have died in vain, they wander about on that face forever.

Landscape . . .

Once out of duty I took a stab at description. I didn't get very far with that either. Some time passed before I realized that to me a cellar window, a puddle is landscape. At best, an empty meadow with discarded cheap wash basins.

A person discovers his own laws, and then he can attempt something.

The tone, that certain individuality of style, is a matter of luck. One has it or one doesn't.

Influence? Streets and squares exerted a great influence on me. And the movies. In them I felt something that is generally called condensed delineation. There are no evasions. Literary influences occur, of course. There is a trend in Hungarian literature. Krúdy, Gelléri[1] . . . A certain looser, more lyrical prose. It has absolutely no connection with foolish, festering "poetic" prose. So I feel I belong to this trend. This is not altered by the fact that at times Krúdy downright infuriates me. His heroes and female characters are, I feel, so false that they will make me sick and bedridden. But his minor characters, street scenes, eternally dripping faucets are unforgettable.

And Hemingway. Who is much more tender-hearted than is commonly thought. He isn't so much of a pugnacious fellow. Otherwise, I read Faulkner much more gladly, who is completely foreign to both Hemingway and me.

As for what I want?

Géza Ottlik[2] wrote in one of his studies: What does a novelist want? He hopes to write a novel.

With a modest alteration: What can a writer want? No matter how surprising, to write.

According to the laws of his talent.

[1] Gyula Krúdy (1878-1933), prolific novelist and short-story writer, noteworthy for evoking moods and sentiments in a dream world of his creation from which reality is viewed. Andor Endre Gelléri (1907-45), short-story writer and novelist, used autobiographical materials in fiction filled with sadness and expressed great compassion for the masses of humanity.

[2] Ottlik (1912–), novelist, short-story writer, and translator, often treats problems prevalent in today's chaotic world.

Miklós Mészöly

Mészöly was born on January 19, 1921 in Szekszárd, in a region of Hungary famous for its vineyards. His ancestors were Protestant ministers, lawyers, smallholders, and peasants. The thought of becoming a writer first occurred to him at the age of twelve, when, looking at photographs on a summer afternoon while alone at home, he suddenly realized that a picture could also be described in words, at which "every object, every phenomenon was immediately filled with hidden significance." He was ashamed of this decision for a long time, years during which he was a shotputter, discus thrower, tennis player, and a passionate hunter who shot game with a troubled conscience. At about eighteen, he was, he says, doing "more drinking and debauching than thinking, much more than can be forgiven"; however, he was, he trusts, the only one hurt by such behavior, and he is convinced that "those years of self-destruction" restored to him "the buried sensitivities of childhood." After completing high school in his hometown, and unable to fulfill his desire to attend the Sorbonne, he entered the University of Budapest. In 1943 he obtained a doctorate in law and political science, which he does not regret, for "I have always enjoyed immersing myself in waters into which I would never again dip my feet." While serving as a lawyer-candidate in Szekszárd early in 1944, he got a fifteen-year sentence instead of the death penalty for a gypsy convicted of murder, only to be, ironically, very shortly called into service himself and sent to the front.

While fighting with the German army against the Russians around Königsberg, he wrote up a false set of documents ordering himself and three companions to duty with a regiment in Hungary. They worked their way back, passing through an already heavily bombed Berlin, and deciding not to surrender themselves to American forces, continuing on to Hungary. When he arrived in the Szekszárd region, Mészöly was captured by an Arrow-Cross fascist, who knew that the regiment listed on the false orders never existed. Chance saved Mészöly from the firing squad, when the judge, secretly recognizing him, sent him back to the battlefield. He suffered shellshock and eventually became a Russian prisoner in Serbia. Fully expecting to be sent to Siberia, he was again saved by chance, this time by a Russian officer whose marriage to a Hungarian woman had been aided by one of Mészöly's relatives in the area. This officer, who was shortly afterward sent to Siberia for some undetermined reason, possibly because he had married more than once in Hungary, came to the camp and pretended to arrest Mészöly. Once outside the camp, he feasted him sumptuously and then sent him on his way home.

When he returned to Szekszárd in late 1945, Mészöly tried various ways of making a living. He first sought to establish a business manufacturing a cologne in his home but, at a time of great inflation, found no buyers. He then worked as a guard at a flour mill and a harvester of crops (or as a "potato bug," as the laborers called themselves). Then he became the editor-owner of a provincial newsweekly, only to find himself very shortly among the unemployed again. Fortunately, his writings began to appear in *Our Destiny* (*Sorsunk*), which had published a few of his stories in the early 1940s. This journal, published in Pécs, had had a pronounced anti-fascist leaning during World War II, and it was now the voice of writers who sought to sustain traditional trends in Hungarian literature during the postwar period. In Pécs, Mészöly joined the János Batsányi Society, a literary and cultural organization named after a writer of the Hungarian Enlightenment, which ceased in 1948 along with its official organ, *Our Destiny*. In 1948 he also published his first book, a slender volume of his short stories *Marshy Lands* (*Vadvizek*), under the society's imprimatur.

He moved to Budapest in 1949, where he became a contributor to the children's and young people's section of the periodical *Radio* (*Rádió*) and particularly to *Answer* (*Válasz*), the revived literary and social vehicle of the populists and democratic parties, which shut down in 1949 because of political conflicts among its staff members. From 1950 to 1951 he served as a dramaturge with the Budapest Puppet Theater; and although he had since 1949 been constantly at work on short stories and had completed several of them, he published only children's tales until 1956. His second collection of short stories, *Dark Signs* (*Sötét jelek*), containing works composed from 1945 to 1956, appeared in 1957, ten years after his first book, to unfriendly notices. Since that time he has made his livelihood solely by his writings, many of them, as always, appearing first in provincial journals. His diligent craftsmanship and experimentation with narrative techniques and style, together with the caution of publishers with an eye to the market, account for the long periods between major published works—excluding his fiction for children and young people, among the latter the novel *Black Stork* (*Fekete gólya*), which appeared in 1960. Nearly another ten years passed before his third major book, *The Death of an Athlete* (*Az atléta halála*), appeared, and then only after it had first been published almost a year earlier in French translation in Paris. This novel was soon followed, in 1967, by a third collection of short stories, *Report on Five Mice* (*Jelentés öt egérről*), which contained ten short stories written from 1957 to 1964, a short novel entitled *Perfect Example* (*Magasiskola*), which he had finished in 1956, as well as a revised version of an earlier story. The next year, *Saul* (*Saulus*), a parabolic historical novel, appeared, and in 1970 *Accurate Stories on a Journey* (*Pontos történetek, útközben*). Five years later *Evolvings* (*Alakulások*), a collection of short novels, stories and sketches —many previously published in book form—came out. This collection was quickly followed by *Film* (*Film*), his fourth novel, in 1976, and in the ensuing year by *The Discipline of Distance* (*Tágasság iskolája*), a collection of critical essays, most of them previously published, revealing his literary theories and aesthetics, his views on the visual arts and the film and his opinions of numerous foreign authors.

Mészöly, believing in the moral, though undogmatic role of the author, spares no effort to "contaminate the blissful simplemindedness" of human beings with "the undaunted anxiety" of the arts. To this end he fixes his eye on the tensions between his characters and the world into which time has thrust them, and attempts to seize the existential instant when they are straining to balance themselves on "a wire stretched tight between anxieties." In an effort to ferret out the link between apparently unrelated events, between seeing "doves taking wing" and soon after finding "the steeple of the inner-city church . . . in flames," he suggests obscurely—or at times does not even suggest—an insight into the impact of the outer world on the individual fate of his characters. Clearly a writers' writer in the vanguard of attempts to extend the range of prose in postwar Hungary, he constantly experiments with modes of achieving "psychic hygiene" for himself, a release from his anxieties that can occur only when his work is shared with readers. In his fledgling short stories of the 1950s, he sought to apprehend reality, sometimes in a quite parabolic manner, through the mysterious irrationality from another world menacing his characters—the fear caused by the killing of a butterfly on a balcony or the anxieties attending the quest for a just human.

Later, in the 1960s, Mészöly turned from interpreting reality, "the tableau of sorrow," in terms of this pervasive uncanny force to interpreting it through another kind of irrationality, the inner psychological states of human beings, in his search for harmony between the inner and outer worlds of humankind. In the stories of those years, he characteristically uses complex narrative means in order to "write down the obscure clearly." The stories continue to confound many critics and readers alike, for hardly anything seems to "happen" in many of them, if they have any meaning in the accepted sense of the word. In "Encounter" two friends meet by chance after many years; they walk, talk, and at the very end witness the accidental death of a truck driver. In another, "The Potato Bugs," the narrator, leaving his companions, wanders off with a stranger and then goes hunting. In a third, "Shade," the moral issue is presented with the strange reality of a vivid nightmare. Each of these examples is presented without the expected links between scenes, putting the burden of insight exclusively on the reader. In this same creative period another strain runs parallel to such writings, one that is objective, at times nearly sociographic. However, in the 1970s, a story like "A Map with Lacerations" and a novel like *Accurate Stories on a Journey* re-emphasize the central source of energy in Mészöly's art—the revelation of psychological states by means that are illogical, seemingly chaotic in their interweavings of time and space, or by deliberately providing an oppressive banality through the scrupulous recording of common details. Such writings show him reaching for meaning through subtle and demanding associations, the symbolic representations customarily found in poetry, without converting his writings into poetic prose.

This vital aspect of Mészöly's style is closely linked with what he thinks future Hungarian prose will be like. His turning to greater objectivity may well be an instance of "the backsliding" to which, he maintains, a writer is prone. The stronger strain, that of the irrational and subjective elements and his modes of presenting them, anticipates, in some ways, his own vision of future developments. The perceptions of that prose, he surmises, will be more intense, its questionings of reality more thoughtful than at present. Even more so than now, the *atmosphere* of a literary work will become integral to those perceptions. The essence of existence, he is convinced, is attainable, if it is at all, only through the atmosphere of a work. To him, atmosphere is "the uncertain coefficient" that gives validity to objective and concrete reality. It is not merely "the residue" of traditional modes of description; it is atmosphere that transmits the essence of reality to readers. Although it must necessarily be based on obscurity and suggestion, atmosphere, which he calls "the emanation of a single stylistic possibility," is the ultimate means of apprehending the meaning of a literary work.

Facing "the tableau of sorrow" with hope, Mészöly himself expresses a yearning "to exist without breathing in the atmosphere of imperishable transitoriness." Perhaps he experienced a faint glimpse of that inner peace within the mortal world in his remembrance of a cliff on a beach in Normandy. Ocean waves splashed high over it, and the cliff vanished time and time again. He then understood that "the timeless can manifest itself only through the transitory," and the timeless "will always have need for a single cliff, a single wave—for its remembrance undoubtedly."

Encounter

Ruddy leaves blanket the steep hillside. A lime-white serpentine road winds its way to the ridge between the trees, unconcealed yet deceptive at the same time; from the distance it looks like a streak of snow. Two women are strolling up the empty road, in their hands staffs they had broken off to use. They are slowly walking in the parallel grooves that cars hollow out in the roadway. One of them is slender, with stylish walking shoes on her feet and three pockmarks on her left cheek. The other is shorter. She is wearing a mannish-looking sportcoat, its stiff collar bent over her blonde hair.

"Look at all the buttercups!" says the woman with the pockmarks, pointing at the wayside slope.

"They're not buttercups."

"What are they?"

"Autumn crocuses. Purple-colored autumn crocuses."

"I thought they were autumn buttercups."

The blonde woman smiles at her indulgently.

"There are no such flowers as autumn buttercups. You have confused them with spring buttercups. And they are white."

"I have never had a flair for such things," the pock-faced woman says. "How beautiful they are. Aren't they beautiful? You always got excellent grades in botany."

"Your memory is incorrect. Only once, at mid-year, never at the end."

"Really?" She quickly tries to change the subject. "Come, let's climb over."

They help each other over the wayside barrier and sit down on their haunches among the autumn crocuses. One or two chilled bees are propelling themselves around above the blades of grass. The sun is warm on the back of their necks.

"Why did you take so long to have children? Didn't you want any?"

"Of course we did. It's just that, well, you know how things are. We planned for a time; we kept delaying. I didn't want to risk anything."

"You were still preparing for the conservatory, right?"

"Of course," replies the blonde-haired woman and, still on her haunches, she looks at the sun absent-mindedly as if the brightness were not blinding her at all.

"What are you doing?" her companion asks, taken aback.

"Once in a while I don't see very well, and then I do this. But the sun is no longer strong now anyway."

"Even so, don't do it; that will make things worse."

"I know. But it feels good while I am looking into it." She laughs. "Stupid, isn't it?"

"Yes, quite stupid," replies the pock-faced woman. Then she quickly raises her head. "I've changed a great deal since then. Don't you think so?"

"You?" The blonde woman glances toward the crest of the hill. "You have hardly changed at all."

"You are very kind," the woman with pockmarks says, and she bites her lip.

After a little while, the grinding of gears is heard at the crest, and the valley immediately fills with the barbarous noise.

"The bus?" begins the blonde woman.

"No, it can't be coming yet. It's early."

"The way we are crouching, the driver from the distance could think we are taking a pee."

"Oh, it's all right here," says the pockmarked woman. "Just so we don't hurt the crocuses."

They should actually be laughing now, but somehow they are late with it. And the droning dies away, too, like a tunnel sniffing a train in. The pockmarked woman waits until it grows completely still; only then does she reach under her dress and adjust her garter. Above them the sky is as cool and blue as a window thrown way open.

"What good luck to hit upon such a heavenly day," she says. "It hasn't been this nice since I've been here."

The blonde woman grabs her arms.

"Look out, you'll crush a buttercup."

"Crocus," the other docilely corrects her.

"No, that's a buttercup. Just look." With the movements of the near-sighted, she bends toward the brown, moldy flower. Somehow it has remained from the spring, if only in withered form.

"It's too bad you didn't come sooner," the pock-faced woman says.

The blonde woman purses her lips, then stands up slowly. She climbs back to the serpentine road. Reaching it, she throws her leg over the iron barrier and rocks a few times back and forth astride it, gazing down meanwhile into the valley. The iron is too hard and cold, so she doesn't press her legs together the way she has a sudden urge to.

"Come, stop now," she calls down to her companion.

"Shouldn't we pick a few more?"

"On the way back. This is the only way we can return. Or is there another road?"

"I don't think so. But I haven't been beyond the crest either. Shall we walk up there?"

"Fine, let's go. We are sure to see far from there. Isn't there a look-out nearby?"

"There's supposed to be a viaduct on the other side of the hill."

"Wonderful. Then we'll have a look at that."

They enter their wheel tracks again. They walk around two turns in the road without speaking a word.

Finally the blonde woman breaks the silence. "Were you still at home when they blew up the viaduct near our place?"

"No . . . my husband was being transferred just then."

"I remember that. They moved you very speedily."

"Don't talk about it. I don't even like to think about it."

"You didn't even say good-bye to us."

The pock-faced woman wrinkles her brow.

"What do you mean? I remember the day exactly. It was Saturday, at the end of October."

"You moved in November."

"Really?" She smells the bouquet of crocuses. "It was a horribly long time ago. And what about you?"

"A year later we moved away too . . . but exactly when? I simply don't know."

"The war was on."

"That too."

"So how long has it been since then? Is it seventeen years since we have seen each other?"

"Eighteen. We now have to count this year as well."

"You are right," the woman with pockmarks on her face sighs. She pries a stone out of her shoe.

The blonde woman watches her patiently.

"How long have you been at the resort?"

"Ten days, but I have to go home tomorrow. How long did you come for?"

"Three days."

"Is that all? Is it worth it?"

"Even that was hard enough to arrange. But at least we met. Can't you stay longer?"

"Sorry. You know I'd like to. But now we'll talk until night."

The blonde woman breaks into a smile.

"I thought about you a lot one day a couple of years ago. I came across one of your old letters. I remember nothing about what you wrote. If you're interested, I'll send it to you sometime."

"My husband burned up every one of my girlhood mementoes. Even snapshots. He wanted me to marry him without any memories."

There is still a half smile on the blonde woman's face.

"You were both terribly in love. Later I couldn't understand how we managed to stay on good terms."

"The two of us?"

"You were annoyingly pretty."

After a new turn in the road, they stop again and look back into the valley. The resort is a cold and precise miniature sketch down in its depths: the white walls and blue window frames, the pack-bearing donkey grazing in front of the terrace, the large stack of deck chairs. A colorful sun umbrella is left beside only one of the tables—the two women are the last guests.

"When did you get the smallpox?"

"Right after I had the baby."

"You weren't nursing it then?"

"Just for a week and a half."

"I had so much milk I could hardly rid myself of it."

"That's not good either."

"No it isn't. My breasts got ruined." She drew her finger across her companion's pockmarked face. "Put more makeup on it."

"What for? It doesn't bother me a bit."

"Couldn't you really stay on longer?"

"I don't know. I am expecting a letter today."

They slowly start up again.

"We may even meet him. He comes this way."

The blonde woman keeps tapping her staff rhythmically on the road surface.

"Actually, I can't complain either," she says. "I don't know what I could complain about. I left the conservatory of my own accord; it would be stupid of me to blame somebody else. In eighteen years one even forgets the reasons."

When she stops the tapping, she again fixes her look on the sun.

"Do you remember Csupi?"

"Of course . . . that little fat one? Whatever became of her?"

"I don't know."

"Do you know anything about Bea?"

"Teca?"

"No, Bea."

"Yes, I did hear something about her once. Just a second. What was it?" She can't remember. "Be careful, you'll lose some of the crocuses," she says. They go back a few steps and pick up the fallen flowers.

"Why do you think this road is so white?"

"It must be the lime. It's prettier this way, isn't it?"

"Much more. The green and the white . . . You know, it took me a half a year to get ready for these three days. Now I shall sleep myself out."

"Who did you leave the children with?"

"A neighbor. She is a very sweet person. She even likes my daughter more than I do. She has more time."

"And what about her father?"

"Oh, didn't I tell you?"

"You told me something. But I thought there was still somebody."

"You misunderstood." She repeats it: "You misunderstood."

"Don't you want to talk about it?"

"Of course I do, but there's time before night comes, isn't there? Or before morning? But it's heavenly that we hit upon such a lovely day . . . "

They now turn into the last hair-pin curve. Here the road slants down steeply like those courses of jointed flooring at fairs inside which the acrobat on the motorcycle tears around, first only down below and then ever upward on the wall of the two-story structure. From the curve two convex metal mirrors mounted on wooden posts shine into their eyes. They can see themselves as elongated and then in the next instant squashed fat as they pound their way up with their staffs. In the depths of one mirror the resort building appears faintly, in the other the row of fir trees on the crest of the hill.

"I think the mailman is coming," says the woman with the pockmarks, pointing her staff forward. "He just now rode out of the fir trees."

The two mirrors marking the road keep switching the image of the approaching youth. Finally one of them captures him and doesn't let him go: he is making clouds of dust in the hair-pin curve. He sticks his leg under the mudguard and brakes that way. He recognizes the pock-faced woman and stops beside her. He is wearing a coarsely woven white sweater and a black Swiss cap.

The woman puts her hand on the handle-bar.

"I've nabbed you now!" She takes pains to turn what she is doing into a joke. "I'm getting a letter today, aren't I?"

The youth rummages around in his bag hastily.

"I'm sorry; there isn't anything, madam. But maybe tomorrow . . . ." He purses his lips, his lips gleam. "You don't have to hurry home. If you wait another week, there's sure to be a letter."

The pock-faced woman is scraping the bicycle bell with her fingernails; the other woman is standing on the other side and doesn't come closer.

"Are you on the way to the resort now?"

"Yes."

"Tell the manager to set our supper aside."

"If it's something urgent, I can take one of you down," the youth offers. "If you don't mind riding the frame." He looks first at one, then the other.

They don't speak. The soft murmuring of the fir trees reaches them. The youth lifts his bicycle slightly and adjusts the pedal under his foot. Some drops of perspiration glisten, like soda bubbles, on the forehead of the pock-faced woman.

"All right, I'll tell him," the youth nods, and poking his forehead with his finger, he starts rolling downhill.

They watch the receding bicycle.

"A handsome kid," the blonde woman says and then turns away. "Do you really think we won't make it back in time for supper?"

"No, but that's not why I said that. I had to say something."

"You are right, though; there's no reason for us to hurry. And you won't miss anything either if you don't leave tomorrow. They'll tell you at home what they would've put in a letter. I'm happy when I don't get one."

"My son is eighteen."

"Those especially. They never write."

"He doesn't have the time for it," the pock-faced woman says sharply. "They always enjoy being alone at such a time. He and his father are real friends. Many times I don't even understand what they are talking about. Where is the father of your children?"

"In Algeria. He left back in fifty-six."

"Oh . . ."

Then later she adds: "Boys are on good terms with their fathers."

"I wouldn't know anything about that," says the blonde woman. "But it doesn't mean a thing that they haven't written. Tomorrow they'll send you a telegram to stay on."

"But I'd like to leave . . . ," the pock-faced woman says, and she is surprised that her eyes are getting moist. The air is now beginning to get nippy.

The crest is only a few steps away. When they reach it, a little wind runs toward them as if it has been waiting for them to arrive. Suddenly their eyes light upon the viaduct: down in the adjacent valley, it arches over a deep chasm, its balusters lost in the dense foliage. Dents and lianas cover its girders, clumps of grass reach out from its hollows, and the sun shines through its gridwork. An interconnecting road overgrown with weeds leads down to it, but it is blocked up by a pile of real rocks. A rusty sign hangs from a post: ROAD CLOSED.

"I'd hate to be in that," says the woman with pockmarks. "It looks as if they tried to blow it up."

The blonde woman is squatting at the edge of the road blinking as she takes stock of the viaduct.

"Quite a bungled job. They did it more carefully at our place. I remember I was at the hairdresser's at the time, but the explosion could be heard under the hair dryer even. All of us stuck our heads out of the dryers at the same time and glanced into the mirror."

"Then shall we go along the crest instead?"

"It makes no difference to me," the blonde woman says.

Confused, they patter about the rubble barrier, not knowing where to start out again. The road cuts straight as a bowstring along the length of the crest, like a white hemp-rope pulled taut. The pock-faced woman does not want to admit it, but she is shrinking from this straight-as-a-bowstring prospect. By then the valley is luring her more.

"We ought to look down from here," she says, pointing to the bottom of the slope, where the connecting road curves toward the viaduct.

"Good," the blonde woman agrees. "At least we can sun ourselves a bit there." She begins unbuttoning her blouse. First only to the embroidered edge of her slip, then finally she pulls the bottom of the blouse out of her skirt.

"My breasts were completely ruined," she notes again.

The pock-faced woman doesn't hear this, though. She is already sliding down into the tall grass.

"Remember how we used to roll and tumble about?"

For an instant the blonde woman looks at her petulantly, then suddenly she drops to her knees and begins to trundle herself rapidly downward. The other takes after her, bounding, and when she overtakes her, flops down beside her. The blonde woman is just then scratching a bit of sticky dirt off her palm. They discover the telltale scale from a pine cone under the dirt. They take turns smelling it.

"What a lovely smell it has!"

"Just fantastic!"

Only then does she take a closer look at the blonde woman's hand. A blue discoloration shows under the base of her fingernails and between her fingers, and the skin is peeling off her entire hand in dry flakes.

"From ink?"

The blonde woman nods.

"Won't it come off?"

"Three days aren't enough for it to wear off."

"But really with what . . . do you handle just fountain pens?"

"Mostly. Repairs, exchanges . . . And whatever else comes along. Gluing of synthetic material. I have a helper."

"What about your daughter? Can't she help?"

"Yes, she can. After all, two of us are teaching her," the blonde woman says scornfully, chewing blades of grass to shreds. "She will eventually leave and be on her own since she is such a good learner. Or she will have her own helper."

The pock-faced woman sits up suddenly.

"Listen . . . I am going to stay on after all."

"We'd already settled that. We still have so many things to talk about."

"And a letter may come tomorrow. They haven't written for ten days."

The pock-faced woman waits for some kind of answer, but the blonde woman forgets to reply. She is looking at the sun again. After a little while they get up and continue to ease their way downward.

The edge of the slope juts out in one spot like some craggy wharf pushed out into the air. They climb out to its end, and hanging onto the rocks, they look down into the depth. A little village is lying below them as if on the bottom of an aquarium where all kinds of objects have sunk. Toy houses, duck ponds, and silver-paper church steeples. Not a single sound, not even the barking of dogs. They are probably five or six hundred meters above the village.

"This makes our coming here worthwhile," says the blonde woman, rubbing her eyes. "The tower down there is red, isn't it?"

"No," says the pock-faced woman, seizing her arm. "Are you getting dizzy?"

"Not at all. But that steam at home . . . " She continues pressing her eyelids. "When we are gluing one of the synthetic materials."

"Why don't you go to the doctor?"

"What for? I should quit. My, how lovely it is here!" She looks down at the village again. "I'd just as soon stay here until night. I think we are really going to be late for supper today."

"Like on the day of flowers and trees. Remember?"

"Then we'd never get home on time. We always went on an outing with Auntie Ilonka during the last hour."

The blonde woman picks up a white stone and begins to sing softly to herself:

> The meadow is blooming
> With many roses,
> No, not with roses . . .

"Why are you crying?"

"Oh, it popped into my mind."

They make themselves comfortable on one of the rocky ledges, facing the sun, and pull their skirts up to their thighs. Soon they both begin to perspire. The blonde woman props her arms up so the sun can reach her underarms. Her companion takes out a bottle of cologne but doesn't open it; she forgets it in her lap. Meanwhile they steal glances at each other.

Neither speaks for a good ten minutes. Then suddenly a screeching sound strikes their ears. It is not exactly an unpleasant sound, but they would be happier without it. They raise their heads from the rocky ledge and look back.

"The bus?" asks the blonde woman.

"I don't think so. It is blue. It's some kind of truck."

As it comes closer on the road, it becomes more and more like a bulldog: fender ears pulled back, two bulging reflector eyes, the bumper horizontal— as if chewing the cubic meters up with that.

They look at it with interest for a while, then turn back to the valley again.

"Sing something again," the pockmarked woman says. "I never was able to sing."

"Do you think Auntie Ilonka could? She, too, wanted to talk me out of the conservatory. But actually, I left it of my own accord; I didn't have to leave."

And she sings absentmindedly.

In the meantime, the truck runs down the lower part of the crest with lime-white dust swirling behind it—like a fleecy cloud in the pictures of saints. To the extent that one can make out from its droning, it does not intend to stop at the fork in the road. There is still time for the two women to signal the driver, but it doesn't even occur to them to be driven down comfortably to the resort.

The blonde woman bends forward and keeps tapping the end of the rock ledge with her staff.

"Do you know the name of this village?"

"I haven't the foggiest."

"We should have asked the mailman."

"You're right. He would've been sure to know. Maybe telegrams are also forwarded from there."

"He was a handsome kid."

"Oh . . . my son is very handsome."

The blonde woman draws her hand through her friend's arm.

"Wait, I'll teach it to you. Sing . . . again . . . a little higher!" She begins the song all over again patiently.

> Oh, how red the meadow is,
> But not from the roses . . .

"That was fine!"

> Not from roses,
> From Mária's son . . .

The pock-faced woman smiles gratefully.

"Honestly now, wasn't it out of tune?"

When they snap their heads back at the unexpected crash, they have only time to see the truck loaded with cement conduits hit the barricade full speed, split it the width of the wheels, and tumble down the steep slope they have also lowered themselves on. It is heading right for them. For an instant they look at it paralyzed, then suddenly yank each other up: there isn't time for anything more. If they try to rush back on the rocky projection, the truck will sweep them away on its way down.

"Don't look!" exclaims the blonde woman, gripping her own arms.

"I just knew," the pockmarked woman mutters.

Trembling but very resolute, they turn back to the valley and the village. They don't see a body in gray coveralls swing out of the truck door, roll downhill a few meters, and then lie still. A few seconds later, the truck crashes into the first row of crags, its rear wheels fly up high, and it hurtles on that way, dumping the cement cylinders forward. It plunges into the depths a couple of meters away from them.

They remain standing there for quite a while, but they no longer have the strength to look down again and determine exactly where the truck has plunged. They can tell from the muffled rumbling that it is lying below them. Staggering, they crawl back on the rocky ledge, and stop short only when they spot the driver. He is lying on his back in the grass with his arms spread wide and his mouth open. He must be a bit older than the mailman. No serious bruises can be seen on his face, and the two women quickly get renewed strength from that. They kneel down, like two nurses, beside the young man, and without looking at each other, with calm identical movements they unbutton his coveralls, then his shirt down to his waist. The pock-faced woman takes out the bottle of cologne.

"It's a good thing I brought it along," she says.

"It's good at a time like this," nods the blonde woman. "So is vinegar. But we don't have any of that."

Then, pooling their strength, they begin massaging the young man's chest, one on his right, the other on his left; but the brisk massaging warms only their palms.

Shade

For years they believed there were three salt lakes in their vicinity. Strangers who came that way became aware of them only if they left the highway. From the distance they looked like three low hillocks, three shabby-looking tall fur caps. It was in their craters that the metallic motionless salt water glistened like a mirror. To them, the sick, barren women, and various persons expecting miracles came regularly every summer from town, even from distant provinces. Children especially enjoyed the fact that they scarcely had to swim and still did not sink. They shouted to each other: "Come on, we'll walk across the lake."

The house they lived in had been built by the former owner on an incline covered with acacia shrubbery. Every summer, bathers would clamber up the slope and knock on their door for milk. They quaffed it as if the salt water had sucked every drop of moisture out of them.

"How beautiful it is here!" they said rhapsodically. "You drink goat's milk instead of water, don't you?"

And after they had quenched their thirst, they praised the environs, the grazing goat with sudden extravagant appreciation. They even admired the thick nettles.

"Oh," they kept saying, "how wonderful it would be to live so simply!"

Toward fall, the number of bathers thinned out. The ampelopsis on the house turned red; blackbirds pecked at the withered berries.

In the evening they would go out for a walk to the salt lakes. In the dusk the water seemed like skin numbed with cold.

"Let's not look at it," the woman said, shuddering.

Nevertheless, they walked along the edges of all three craters. The man enjoyed courting horror; whenever the wind blew a gossamer at him, he would rend it asunder.

One fall morning they awoke to blazing sunshine, an unexpected and almost provoking gift. The highway shone between the brown plowlands. Snow-capped mountains outlined the horizon's rim like untouched wadding. The landscape, which one could not emerge from, grew fantastically but still remained clear-cut.

The wife ran out of the house gate and clambered up to the ridge of the hill. At first she mistrusted her eyes and the uncommonly piercing sunlight. On the other side of the hill where previously had stood a grassy meadow with purple-colored blooms, she now set her eyes on an enormous lake with an island in its center. The island barely emerged from the water. It was flat and small, as if only a shadow had fallen on the surface of the lake. There were no shrubs or trees anywhere, only the lake and the island.

Still it was a gift. It did not form a skin-like layer the way salt lakes did, and its small waves wrinkled the surface like pliant silver paper.

With deep joy, she ran back to the house and called her husband.

"Come, bring your bathing suit!" she said.

He had just started raking up and burning the autumn debris.

She showed him the lake.

"When did this happen?" her husband asked, losing his sense of security.

"I don't know. Maybe during the night?" Then she added, childishly: "I fell asleep late in the evening."

They changed into their bathing suits and stretched out on the beach. The water reached their feet. It was warm. The woman wet her hand and licked it.

"It's not salty," she laughed loudly.

They lolled about in the grass for hours. They took dips, then dried themselves again. The sun was blazing as if it were midsummer. Toward noon the woman began to grow faint from the unseasonably hot weather. She asked her husband to swim over to the island with her; there was a bit of shade there.

"How could there be; there's no shade there," he said.

"But I see there is. Sit up and take a look."

He sat up and, laughing, shook his head.

"I still don't see any there. Believe me, you are just imagining it. Isn't it fine right here?"

"Yes, it is." She quieted down. "I just wanted a little shade."

Suddenly she felt foolish and small. The lake turned inimical, the sun's rays lethal. She was standing at a large shining gate and thought she would go blind. Vanquished, she drew aside. She stood up and put her red dress over her arm.

"I am going in. Are you staying?" she asked quietly.

Her husband was lying on his back in the grass with his arms spread out.

"Just a little longer," he replied.

Later the desire to take another dip came over him. Running, he waded into the water, then dove into it full length. Then he ran farther, much farther than he had ventured before with his wife. But the water wasn't any deeper out there than near the bank.

He walked the rest of the way to the island without any difficulty.

To his surprise, he saw that a shadow actually did cut the island in two, even though there wasn't a cloud in the sky. He felt a slight confusion, but still he sat down in the shade and dozed off.

He awakened to a gentle puff of wind. He couldn't have slept very long because the sun still stood high in the sky. The lake, on the other hand, had lost its silver gleam. It looked as if its waves were covering great depths. He shivered because of this change. Nervously, he started rushing about and searching the sand dunes of the island. First he circled its beach, then he swept across it diagonally with unwarranted expectation. Finally he realized he was deceiving himself: he was examining a plundered island.

With resolute, irrevocable shame, he waded into the water. He slipped and stumbled about in his haste to get out of the lake as quickly as possible, but arriving on the shore, he continued to feel what he had on the island: that he could not behave any other way, that he was the only one who could mete out his punishment. He walked over to the iron archer pointing in the direction of the highway and, standing beneath it, looked back at their house once more. He did not fail to notice that blackbirds were swarming over the reddening ampelosis. He was sick at heart, but even that could not stop him.

His wife was waiting for him among the acacia shrubs. She had second thoughts along the way; she didn't want to return to the house alone after all. She put her shoes on and slipped into her dress, and she listened patiently for the sound of footsteps. The sun was shining into the shrubs only in a subdued way. The leaves rubbed softly together in the gentle puffs of wind, but in them she heard the little slapping sounds of the distant scaly surf. In this fragile silence she became conscious of the approaching herd.

She was sitting quite some distance from their yard; still, she could have easily escaped behind their fence, but she didn't even try. In the first instant she did jump up, but then she slowly kneeled down again and clasped her hands. Like someone not hiding that she is praying.

A large herd of black buffaloes rumbled toward her from the thicket. Their strange horns extending out were not only straight, they were twisted as well, like drills. These spiraling horns did not let her turn her eyes away. Hairless, small black pigs trailed the buffaloes. The buffaloes' gleaming yellow teeth kept snapping at the ground, but not a single one of them stopped. They streamed ahead in lumbering, uncontrollable flight, their heads bobbing up and down, their backs billowing as they ran.

The woman closed her eyes to make the struggle even more unequal, more submissive. For her husband as well.

A long time passed.

Occasionally she thought one of them would charge at her, the horns pierce her, wet noses knock her over. But the hooves pounded past her a hair-breadth away. They dashed past her red dress; she even felt the breath of some of them. Emboldened, she opened her eyes. At this, the animals avoided her even more cautiously, if possible, than before as they trotted past.

They feel good because they could hurt me but they don't, she thought, smiling hopefully. Suddenly she looked at her clasped hands as if they didn't belong to her alone.

When the herd had passed by, she did not dare to look after them. Exulting, she began running back to the lake to find her husband so that they could rejoice together and cross the water splashing like children during the summer— but by then, only puddles of seepage, instead of the lake, glistened in the grass.

She slowly put her hands to her face. She looked around.

"Where are you?" she mumbled. Then she shouted: "Where are you?"

She turned around.

Her husband was hanging from the arrow of the road marker, his head slumped forward and his legs stretched out grotesquely. His belt buckle glittered above his head in the blazing sunlight like some false, ostentatious star.

The Three Potato Bugs

I remember, everything suddenly came to a head in the fall of 1947. The wartime frostbite flared up again in my hands and feet, and my request for a boost in pay had been turned down for about the third time. It was also the time when I broke up with Böde—nastily, true, but, all the same, conscious of the justice of my case. All this was just too much. And so was the rain. At times it seems to me as if it rained constantly that fall. But on the day we had the flat tire outside Ireg, it was really bitter cold, almost winter. This happened about six o'clock at night. It turned dark early; we could see nothing in the area, so to speak, but a diamond-shaped fieldguard's shelter and some sort of deep ravine on the left side of the road. Shivering from the cold, we stamped our feet around the truck. Arany Ger had promised us a room by eight o'clock with spiced tea laced with brandy—and Janika, the Ireg county clerk's ninety-kilo wife, who supposedly always smells of almonds and has a tiny mouth. The belief among us was that a tiny mouth was another encouraging unit of measurement with women from which a definite conclusion could be drawn. In the same way, we took it for certain that open thighs are a circumstance to arouse suspicion, for actually, only women with closed thighs could be good wives and lovers.

Perplexed, we tinkered with the limp rubber tire as if it were a baby that had made a mess.

"What now?" asked Varga Kis, meanwhile slapping his pimply face that was blue from the cold.

"What else can we do? We'll go in on the rim," Arany Ger said, looking at Paja. "If they begrudged us a spare inner tube, they will now issue us a new one."

"That isn't possible," said the driver phlegmatically.

"What isn't?"

"To get in on the rim. The carburetor is also bad, completely shot."

"Yes," Arany Ger muttered. "Then everything's just perfect."

All this began when the control public address system of the Governmental Potato Committee ordered a work gang out and the choice fell on the three of us. A ten-ton truck was placed at our disposal, and Paja into the bargain. Paja was from a drivers' pool. He couldn't stay with any company, but we got along well with him. He even posted that crinkled nude picture above the steering wheel, something he did only if his buddies deserved it. We had been traveling around the province for the second week. During the summer I still believed naively that I would land a job in Pest; then, in the end, everything fell through. Only the rain came off well. And the potatoes. Laughing, the mayor in Bogdány said: "Comrades, we have triumphed. Thank God, the potato crop is an enormous success!" At the time I also felt that this was the utmost that could come off successfully. In fact, I could also conceive that from now on everything would always be like this, just sacks and potatoes, and drafty crop storehouses, and that all this would become as familiar to me as Böde, this utterly roving existence, the weighing sheds, the loaded wagons, and that unfamiliar station where I couldn't find the w.c. or that bar in Borjad where I sat next to a window and saw a ditch into which the clay-yellow liquid bubbled from three concrete pipes. Ever since I got shell-shocked, this kind of lame poeticalness has been inside me; ever since that happened, I have a better memory for things like that than for something useful. For example, for the naked light bulb in front of the pile of cylinders in Belac after every light in the village has gone out, except this one illuminating the loading yard with its puddles and the running motor of a Hoffer-Schraz tractor that all along kept a single word from being heard, it made such a din, and sank ever deeper into the mud.

It doesn't matter. Arany Ger still recounted to the two local potato inspectors the details of the flat he had just missed getting in Pest. We were already quite bored by these stories, but it was the proper thing for us to hear them out. He was the oldest among us, close to forty. His hair was pure white, his face apple-red and sensual, and his mouth amusingly small, but that did not have any significance in his case. We knew he was going to become an opera singer, but he didn't get a flat in Pest and so his career collapsed. This is funny? Maybe so. But a person can fail in much smaller ways than this; I know that for a fact. When Arany Ger asked me why I broke off with Böde, I said "from love." There was no need for me to explain more fully, we had all got so used to each other in the two weeks we'd been together. And yet, I walked out on them without so much as a word to them.

However, it is possible this began earlier; I have little signs in mind. At the front I was once sent back to battalion headquarters for an important letter. On the way back I got lost in a forest, and I lay down to sleep without any pangs of conscience. I slept for a day and a half from exhaustion. Only my company commander's feeling sorry for me saved me from a firing squad. "What did you do? Where have you been?" he shouted at me. "Don't you have any sense of responsibility?" I should have said I don't, but all I said was I don't feel guilty. He slapped me around, and that settled everything. Fortunately, he belonged among those who sensed the war would soon be over anyway.

As for Böde, that's a more complicated matter. A few weeks before our job with the potatoes, I shot up to Pest by car to redeem the yellow oxfords I had placed an order for back in the summer but never had enough money for. When I boarded the train, I felt a faint premonition inside me that in Pest or along the way something long due would befall me. And, I thought, perhaps, if I got a good night's sleep on the banks of the Danube, I'll forget the vast emptiness I felt I always saw no matter where I was, that void where we all commit some awful horror and we keep silent about it in vain. But I am not the intelligent type who can put this better.

To be brief, I entered the shoemaker's and saw a young woman bent over the counter looking at something—my shoes. It was Böde. I thought I would go through the floor. The day before, I had told her in a telegram . . . but then it makes no difference what I said. Some monstrous lie, so I could go to Pest alone. She turned red in her confusion. She asked what I was doing there, and I what she was doing there. The whole episode was terribly embarrassing. Böde had recommended this shoemaker to me (she knew him from some time back), and so the master suspected that what he saw and heard was a little family spat. Böde paid the amount due without saying a word, took the shoes, and said goodbye. I trailed after her. Neither of us spoke before we reached the Piarist Church. There's a little sidestreet there, a dark and narrow one. It has no stores, shop windows, or real entrances, just basement steps and large whitewashed storehouse windows. Shutters shredded by machine guns hang down rusted above the painted area. If true, I thought with tenacious obstinacy, this is one of those streets from which the bellies of sparkling-clear stores are stuffed every day. Why deny it? This perspective, this setting stifled me. Böde didn't speak either. Somehow everything suddenly turned wrong-side-out—as when one chances to glance into a dirty kitchen from which daintiest morsels are being fetched that we too had eaten with some relish a short time ago. I was looking at Böde. She was greenish-yellow in the rain; her chin was pimply. I then felt that it would be nearly a miracle if we could walk the length of this narrow little street without some particular tragedy occurring. But she started crying out only on the banks of the Danube. She wept silently with her lips compressed.

"I wanted to surprise you," she said, after we had both got soaking wet. "I wanted to take your shoes home."

That was heart-wrenching. Also past redemption. Nevertheless, the greatest difficulty was the fact that I didn't want to mince matters. Now I asserted that I loved her, then that I didn't know what my trouble was with her when she had given no cause for it. In the end, I can't even say I broke off with her intentionally; it simply befell me, like fate. I didn't even lose my head. My muscles remained just as relaxed, and my voice didn't change. Only, I was disgusted with myself for not having a greater sense of responsibility, and on considering the matter fundamentally, I wondered why I was blameless after all.

We were standing on the lower part of the embankment opposite the burned-out royal palace, and without intending to, I had nothing on my mind but what I had naively bolted from to come to Budapest: the office, the work orders, the potatoes.

Böde noticed I was looking at the palace.

"What a good place that would be to store potatoes in," I said with genuine bitterness. Böde clutched my shoes under her arm and walked out on me. When she heard my footsteps behind her, she began shrieking with surprising passion.

"If you come any closer I will jump in!" She ran to the edge of the river bank.

At that, I turned around so she wouldn't see my face. And so she wouldn't feel so humiliated by the scene. Just like out on the the highway, this was a perfect blow-out. Nothing could be done with the carburetor.

Paja voiced the opinion that he wasn't Christ and that the only thing we could do was to leave the truck on the side of the road and ask for a tractor from Ireg. Or that if we encountered a truck on the way, we'd wave it down.

It was past ten when we knocked on the county clerk's door. Paja had already left us back at the dairy products plant to try to scare up a tractor there. We agreed he would follow us to Janika's and we would move on in the morning.

Four dogs rushed at us from the depths of the spacious yard, but Arany Ger brought them under control with a single command. This alone was enough proof he wasn't telling tales; he was really at home here. The place had probably once been a peasant house, now remodeled into a home for the county clerkship. Several fruit trees and cedar shrubs in the yard, and a round flower bed with some stakes decorated with colored glass balls—these tell-tale marks in the dark gave evidence of Janika's finer tastes. Otherwise there was nothing to see, not even a chicken-pen; only the large, dull emptiness of the bleak house, and a useless yard thoroughly slashed into frozen wheeltracks.

A young servant girl pitter-pattered the length of the veranda in wooden shoes and stopped at the steps. Meanwhile a light was turned on from inside. The girl's legs were bare, and the cold nipped her husky arms red. Mute and grinning, she watched us enter and informed us that the lady of the house had already retired for the night. Arany Ger patted her bottom and said that was what we would like to do too. Later it turned out that Janika had observed the entire scene from the room. She greeted us in a negligée with its sash drawn tight at her waist and with unbelievably small slippers on her feet. Arany Ger hadn't exaggerated a bit: Janika was an extraordinary phenomenon, a well-proportioned giantess, an entirely uncommon mixture of physical strength and delicacy. Not only was her mouth tiny, her feet were as well. She had two dimples on her face left from the early part of the century, but her shape was like a weightlifter's. She seated us in the dining room, where the dinner-ware, the white tablecloth dotted with breadcrumbs, a large loaf of homemade bread rolled up in a cloth, and a French fashion magazine were still on the table. The room was stupefyingly hot, at least twenty-four degrees.

"Well, go ahead and eat." She looked at us from the head of the table. "I enjoy feeding the shipwrecked."

Varga Kis wanted to say something, but I saw Arany Ger kick him under the table. Apparently he wanted to set the style of the conversation and didn't want to flop with us. I couldn't imagine, though, why his style would be more polite than ours. But something else was at stake. He was fearing for certain rights he had acquired. And so we allowed him to sparkle. We deferred every reply to him as to a boyscout master responsible for us all—and because of this the atmosphere soon became vibrant. We laughed uproariously, even though the conversation turned mostly to the past two weeks—the sad potatoes. I sank completely into a green plush easy-chair and tried to picture in my mind what the county clerk was like. I supposed he was a small man who didn't even reach to Janika's shoulders but had a bushy black moustache and a copper-red face. And he undoubtedly had plans for the big barnyard that Janika neglected. It can be infuriating to such a plucky little fellow if his wife, with such a big body and such muscles, does nothing all day except wait around for something to fall due in the end. Even if the yard is all mud, she goes out in her little black slippers, stops, and then realizes she won't find what she went outside for. She is alone a lot, but she enjoys being alone, for that at least keeps her restlessness alive. In my opinion, she didn't go to bed with Arany Ger that night nor had she at any time before. Just so long as she doesn't go to bed with someone, she can always be expecting something soon.

Later the loud rumbling of a motor could be heard inside the house, and we instantly thought Paja had wrought a miracle and was arriving with the Csepel repaired. But only a strange truck entered the yard; we didn't know why it did. However, Janika said something about trucks entering their place at other times, parking there during the night, then continuing on at dawn, and often they don't even know what kind they were—various section trucks, transporters of construction materials. "Besides, the yard is quite large," she said. "You saw that yourself. It's at least 3600 square meters. It isn't right these days to padlock such a big yard."

The drab servant girl entered with another demijohn, put it down next to Arany Ger, and immediately turned to leave. Janika spoke after her.

"Where is he from?" She pointed toward the yard.

The girl was apparently innocent in the matter, but she still turned red.

"He wanted some water for his radiator," she said. "It had run out."

I thought to myself: "It's like a house with passageways. It's entirely a yard with passageways."

"Where is your husband? In Kiszállás?"

"Oh, no," she laughed. "He's gone hunting with the veterinarian. That may take even two days at a time like this."

"Don't you like to go along?"

"We can't leave the house alone," she replied. "You know, so many show up here. And I am also waiting for my lady friend. She's been promising since spring to visit me."

"From Pest?"

"Oh hardly," she laughed again. "From Paris."

The unknown driver raced the engine occasionally, and whenever he did so, the windows rattled. Arany Ger crossed over to the darkened parlor and rummaged around for something. Janika smiled at me, but I felt she intended her smile for Arany Ger: like one who knows exactly what her guest is doing in the other room and what will follow afterward. Meanwhile the heat had become more stupefying, and the promised scent of almonds struck my nostrils: Janika was perspiring this exquisitely. Varga Kis had sunk into his easy-chair and dozed off from all the wine. This eighteen-year-old kid had a pleasant fox-like face; his chin was pointed and white like wood that had been sanded down. I tried kicking him, but that didn't wake him up. Janika still smiled for a while; then only her blank look remained fixed on me. She completely paralyzed me with that look.

"You would have been asleep long ago if we hadn't barged in on you the way we did, wouldn't you?"

"Oh no"—she laughed for the third time—"I'm sure I would've gone out for a walk."

"In the village?"

She pouted with her moist little mouth.

"Heavens no . . . just here in the yard." She hefted the demijohn with her powerful, down-covered arm. "Why aren't you drinking?"

We were forced to pay attention to something else, however. Arany Ger had opened up the piano in the adjoining room, and he began playing it softly with one finger and then struck a few chords as well. Later he sang a Verdi aria in our honor with a tight throaty voice.

"He has a splendid voice." I praised him in the spirit of comradeship.

Janika put her hand on my knee and squeezed it.

"You are a wonderful little fellow."

A sudden anger toward every lie overcame me, however.

"You are wrong!" I replied. "I am absolutely not wonderful. First of all, I have no sense of responsibility at all. I could also have said this: he has a terrible voice. And tomorrow, if I am forced into it, I'll be ready to say something ugly about you. But what's really wonderful is that you go out and take walks in the yard. I like your yard."

I think I was drunk. I seized her hand and bowed by head. I would've liked to snuggle up to that enormous body and tell her about Böde, but it was simpler to remain quiet. Besides, whenever I have more to drink than I can handle, I have to constrict my throat and my eyes immediately fill with tears. I despise this capacity of mine because it always tempts me to misuse it; and even though I know I am being a fraud, I have to see that the joy I am causing is genuine. On that occasion, too, I raised my head after I felt the little warmth under my eyelids.

"You permit yourself too many liberties," Janika said sternly, and she squeezed my knee again. "Go outside and pull yourself together."

I spread my coat over my shoulders in the vestibule and stepped onto the veranda. The aroma of the air and the whiteness suddenly struck me: snow had fallen in the meantime, the first snow. It was barely a centimeter deep, but it made the yard even larger and the objects in it even more incidental. A twenty-five-ton dump truck purred in the middle of the yard. Its cab was empty. The light was no longer on in the veranda; light was filtering out only in the back, beyond the kitchen. I scooped up a little snow with my hand and began licking it. The four dogs were running about soundlessly on the opposite side of the yard and eyeing me from there. I heard soft footsteps. I took it for granted that the driver was on his way to Janika's servant, and I deliberately didn't greet the man wearing a leather jacket I saw passing behind the cedar shrubbery. I thought he was going back to the girl. But when he came into the shaft of light, his hair suddenly showed red. It was Paja. I was so surprised that the shout stuck in my throat. "The bastard! He kept quiet about this in our presence. In the morning he will turn up here with the truck the very picture of innocence." I had to laugh. Meanwhile Paja disappeared behind the door, and the dogs trooped out onto the highway. The truck was shaking in the snow like something bad or good about to come to pass. Still, when I think back on it, there was in me then for the first time in weeks a bit of confidence that I would find my way back to human beings.

I walked around the basement earth mound from propriety, so Janika wouldn't see me just in case she stepped outdoors—and there I unexpectedly stumbled into the unknown driver. He was just buttoning up. We stared at each other a little nervously. He was a tall, thin man with a pale face and thick black hair. He looked toward his truck, then back at me.

"I thought you were Paja," I said awkwardly.

"I am not he," he answered precisely, sticking his hands in his pockets. And from then on to the end, he helped me. I had only a very slight nausea, and that was caused more by the heat inside the house.

"Bend over; don't stand like a post," he said.

Then later: "What are you actually doing here?"

"Nothing really," I answered. "Our truck was on the way to Tropa, and we got stuck here."

"Your truck has been repaired already," he informed me, and that sobered me up very quickly. According to that, he knows Paja and our situation as well, I thought. Then there was nothing for me to explain; we might just as well be on familiar terms. All of a sudden I was flooded by that chummy good will from which women are forever locked away. We lighted up and strolled back to the truck.

"What a night!" I said, filling my lungs. "Do you come this way a lot?"

"Quite often. I'm really from Földvár, I'm now working here with a construction outfit."

"Do you park here at Janika's?"

"Not anymore," he replied with a mysterious smile and looked about the yard. "This snow is driving me wild."

"Why is that?"

"I am curious to find out if it fell elsewhere also. I think I will go home to Földvár. I'm home in two hours, then I'll come back in the morning. It's worth it. A man can sleep once in his own bed."

"If he has one," I said, laughing.

He looked at me sidelong; he swung his cigarette back and forth with his tongue.

"Do you have some job to do here?"

"I really don't know," I muttered. "I don't think so."

Still, I was sorry to leave that yard behind; I was beginning to feel friendly toward it. On the other hand, the snow lured me, and trees gliding by in the beams of the headlights; I boarded the truck impulsively. A few minutes later we were barreling along out on the highway.

*   *   *

I must add that my friend's name was Berci, some kind of Berci, but even to this day I don't know more because we didn't care to take our measure beyond our first names. On the way, he told me that they had butchered a little pig by way of "an introduction," and that he would be glad to treat me to some of it. "I hate eating alone," he reassured me, "and the wife won't get up to eat with me anyway. Then you'll put up for the night in the kitchen. You'll get two blankets; that'll be enough."

"That will be splendid," I said gratefully.

"Not really, but it will do," he replied. "Look, what a powdery snow!"

No one had gone before us. The highway was unmarked and almost without curves. I have noted that when one is rumbling along in a truck on a road like this, one's thoughts become childishly simple. That route running into the distance and closed in on both sides by trees stretches the very same thought like rubber. And the more swiftly one races along, the more stupid and vacuous one becomes. This is, however, a saintly stupidity and vacuity when snow is falling. No doubt Berci would have been grateful if I had talked about Böde, but I couldn't bring myself to say anything about her. Perhaps to Janika, yes, but not to him. I didn't much want to talk to him about anything. It just felt good knowing that we were going to eat some steamed bacon together and that I would get to know what their blankets smelled like. I think he must have felt the same, for he didn't grill me about my doings. And yet the feeling of complicity between us was perfect. When this night passed, I thought, and we go our separate ways, he too will remain silent because of bashfulness about what happened between us. Which will be made all the easier because there will be nothing to tell.

It was two o'clock when we reached Földvár. We had emerged from the snow belt about twenty minutes before. We were as vexed with this as though some famous brain could do something about it. Why couldn't it also be snowing in Földvár? Cursing, we reviled the mud we encountered. Berci didn't live in the village but past the marketplace in the new section where farmlands and meadows began. The new section itself was formerly the *Oncsa* settlement, and that had been expanded over a period of time. As best I could make out in the darkness, Berci's house was one of eight houses within a hair of looking exactly alike, in about the middle of the development. This calculation wasn't at all intentional on my part at the time. It was rather that after Berci applied the brakes abruptly —not even noting in advance, "Well, here's where we live"—I unintentionally recalled the pair of houses we had just passed and the several others that could be seen in the beams of the headlights. Only one lamp was burning in the settlement, the one at the artesian well.

Berci led me across the barren front garden; the house was in its far end. The open veranda was full of coal and wood. I lagged behind outside for a moment and stared at the coal without any reason whatsoever, at that even duller black in the darkness. Meantime light struck it, and Berci called out from the kitchen: "Should I get a fire going?" At this, I entered. It was a shabby little kitchen with rose-colored furniture. The tile floor was sparkling clean, but unwashed dishes stood in a pile on the table. Berci pushed the whole stack farther up on the oilcloth and made room at the end of the table. By then he had forgotten about starting a fire. An alarm clock was ticking loudly on a shelf, and both of us began yawning. It became evident that we had even less to say to each other now than in the truck. However, our trust in each other remained unchanged. We didn't even have the desire to eat. Berci produced on a blue tin-plate some pieces of blood sausage and bacon seasoned with pepper. Then we just sat in the cold and, as a matter of form, swallowed a couple of bites. He didn't have any wine or brandy. I drank about four glasses of water, Berci even more. Once he smiled at me and said that we had pulled a fast one on those in Ireg, and that it was something to snack peasant-style without a lot of bother. Then he stood up and opened a door, and I heard him talking softly with his wife about something. He returned with one blanket, not two.

"We'll fix ourselves a good breakfast with brandy tomorrow," he said. "The neighbor has some brandy, I just don't want to wake him up."

He made a sign for me to follow him. He entered some cubbyhole that opened from the veranda. By the time I reached it, half a couch was sticking out of the doorway, and he called out from the darkness for me to take hold of the other end. Apparently they stored it like that owing to lack of space, for when we set it up, it blocked half the room.

"Well, are you going to eat some more?" he asked, after which he added his leather coat to the blanket in a friendly way. "There's regular sausage, too, if you want some." He sat down at the table again.

Totally unexpectedly, I told him I'd decided never to get married. Partly because I lack the moral courage for it, partly because of what would happen if I did. Even then, one will stand alone in the yard, eventually.

"You are depressed now; that's why you are talking like that," he consoled me. "But it's good for you to express it. Problems must be voiced, or one's self-respect goes to pieces."

I didn't understand this completely, but it still felt very good. His was a human voice, and he didn't ask for anything in return. Then we began yawning again. He stood up, clasped my hand, wished us good rest, and went in to his wife.

I dropped into sleep like a rock. I have no recollection of anything about the night, not even the fragment of a dream. I woke up at early dawn to Berci's crawling over me. It was already growing light outdoors. Berci puttered about in the kitchen cabinet in long underwear and barefeet, then he went out. As I watched him go, my eyes landed on the coatrack at the entrance. Worn coats and a double-barreled shotgun hung from it. I hadn't noticed it was hanging there the night before. I immediately got up to take a closer look at it. It was quite an old gun with a famous trade name; it had been made by Paterlongo in Tyrol. I didn't think of anything at the time; I just felt an intense longing to take it into my hands. But I didn't touch it; instead, I went out through the kitchen door. It was marvelous. During the night snow had fallen in Földvár, and the coal on the veranda was covered with snow too. I could see out to the white meadows, and somehow nothing had any definition in the half-light of dawn. All this affected me like an unavoidable stage on which one must make an appearance.

In the meantime, Berci came around the house, and when he noticed me, he gave me a wink.

"Well, what do you have to say? I told you, didn't I?"

"A gorgeous day," I answered.

"We aren't going to start back in a hurry either," he replied. "We'll call in some trouble with the truck, and breakfast pleasantly. Until then, we'll get another hour's sleep."

I didn't say yes or no. But my first act in the kitchen was to take the shotgun down. I pointed it at Berci.

"Do you have a license for it?"

"Of course. I go hunting every weekend."

After this, the rest went easily. Berci immediately understood that I was struck by the desire to look around the meadows a little. In fact, if he had two guns, he would join me; that is to say, it is the greatest pleasure to wander about in search of game in fresh snow. But he said I should just go safely by myself; the whole area before our eyes is his own hunting ground. I should head back an hour and a half from now at the very latest.

I said good and put the five shells he gave me into my pocket.

When I last looked back at the settlement, I could definitely single out Berci's place among the numerous identical houses. I don't exactly know on what basis, perhaps from the direction and the distance still fresh in my limbs. Then the far-flung whiteness made me ever dizzier. For the first half hour I didn't really keep an eye out for wild animals. The setting and the roundness of the double barrels in my fist completely satisfied me. It seemed to me that after this roaming about, everything would be different with me thereafter: this snow-covered meadow would saturate me like mercy.

I had gone some distance when I saw the first rabbit. For some reason, it was running directly at me instead of retreating. But I missed it. The crack echoed in the distance—and I think it started with that. It's difficult for me to explain this. At one time I did a lot of hunting, but in spite of that, a sense of shame now flashed through me. Like dizziness from nicotine, to those familiar with it. It comes and suddenly passes, but the feeling still lingers that others had noticed it. It was as if the entire settlement and village had shuddered at the report. But I didn't concern myself about it very much. Soon another rabbit sprang up and ran sidling toward me. It might have been the same female as the previous one. Anyway, I didn't miss this time; it suddenly turned a somersault in a magnificent arc. This time the echo was fainter than with the first shot, but only later did I discover why. The bunny's abdomen was yellowish, like sulphur; some chemical could have stained it in the paint factory's dump. I held it up by the legs and looked back toward the settlement. Meanwhile such a fog had descended I couldn't see a thing: that was what had kept down the echo of the shot. Shortly the fog surrounded me as well. An uneasy, painful feeling seized me—as if I had fired a gun into my own good conscience. For a time I was able to retrace my steps, but shortly I couldn't find them either. From that point on, I struck steadfastly in a single direction, but I had apparently taken a poor bearing because I had not reached any houses after three-quarters of an hour had passed. When the fog lifted from a shorter sector, I caught a glimpse of a distant repair shed that I had absolutely no recollection of. At that, I immediately turned back. By this time I hated the rabbit. I didn't have the authorization to possess arms or a hunting license, and in those days we were still close enough to the war for such a matter to be observed to the letter. I stumbled around maybe for an hour totally blindly; not until then did the sun break through. Ten minutes later I was standing in the blinding light in the middle of the flatland, four kilometers from the settlement. Meanwhile life in the village had also begun. Dull tapping came from the paint factory, and men in water-proof coats were cutting across the field toward the factory, the settlement, and the repair shed. One of them made a turn rather close to me. Though he greeted me, I still didn't like the look of him—his eyes had turned anxiously to my weapon. I felt he was going to swing around after me. When he was quite some distance away, I got down on my haunches as if I were doing my business, hollowed out a hole quickly with my knife, and put the rabbit into it. At first I was ashamed to scrape earth over it, but I finally buried it. I knew unerringly that I had again bungled a good opportunity; in vain had the snow come to my assistance. Finally I dashed toward the settlement, and I stopped only on reaching the first row of houses. I searched all eighteen streets but didn't see Berci's dump truck anywhere. On the other hand, tire tracks were so numerous they only confused me all the more. I roved back and forth but was unable to detect which house was Berci's. And I didn't know his last name. I had begun to attract some attention roaming around with the shotgun. I couldn't do anything else; I had to speak to someone. I shouted to a woman in one of the yards, and I tried hard to describe every characteristic of Berci's that I could. But the woman didn't recognize them; they too had arrived there not very long ago. "What about your neighbor?" I asked. "They did too," the woman replied. It came to light that the settlement was more of a residential section for transients, with the prefecture renting the houses mostly to families of migrant workers.

By this time it was already past eight o'clock, and I could be certain that Berci hadn't waited for me, and it wasn't worth searching for the truck. And so, not very many options remained to me. For a while I sauntered along the streets, but when I saw a man in uniform appear, I quickly slunk away toward the meadow, holding the gun so my body concealed it. I put it down into the first ditch I came across and stamped mud and stones on it. This was a dreadful feeling for me who always enjoyed hunting so much. But it was a relief at the same time. It just didn't last very long.

When I straightened up I noticed a young woman in a sweat suit on the road about thirty meters away. She was observing my actions with interest. She had long black hair, but what struck me more about her was that she didn't resemble Böde at all. I started toward her slowly. She stepped inside a yard gate, which she had paused in front of. After a little thought, I opened the gate. The house was within a hair of looking like Berci's, with a big pile of wood and coal on the veranda. This completely confused me. I pressed down on the latch without knocking. The woman was standing in the heated kitchen unpacking. She was much prettier than I had thought; the polish was beginning to peel off her fingernails. Here, all the furniture was blue instead of pink.

"Is this my friend Berci's house?" I asked.

"Whose?" She was surprised, but I could tell from her eyes that she wasn't feeling unfriendly.

"My friend Berci's. A driver. He has a house exactly like this."

The woman burst out laughing.

"You are a real card. On that basis you could enter every house around here."
"But it's fortunate I came in here. You certainly won't report me," I said.
The woman laughed again.
"You didn't murder somebody, did you?"
"Yes, I did. A rabbit."
"Is that what you were burying in the ditch?"
When she said that, the tightness in my chest suddenly vanished: According to that, she hadn't clearly seen what I was doing. And this gave me courage again. Why bother with further details? I began courting her and I stayed there. Her husband was working in another province and came home only on weekends. I lived with her for four days and never left the house the whole time so the neighbors wouldn't become suspicious. I just lolled about and gazed out on the snow-covered meadow and the plowed fields and waited for her. She didn't resemble Böde in any way whatsoever. And she didn't want anything at all from me. In fact, when we parted she gave me an address where they then wangled me a job with the next campaign, one with the sugar beet workers.

A Map with Lacerations

Last night between ten-thirty and three in the morning. Five drunken young men in the seat facing me, two wearing red pullovers and the others identical checkered shirts. We have been standing on the open track for an hour. Inside, the singing of nightingales can be heard and soft quiverings in the rankly growing bushes clutching the slag heap. Trickling sewage at the latrine behind the watchman's hut, smoke-wisp cloud racks around the moon. A baby cries out in the compartment. They are sitting behind me. Until this instant I have not been aware of them; I thought I was alone with the five sleeping drunks. I get up and look out the window but at an angle allowing me to see the woman and the baby. The moonlight is bright. I look at them intently through the contracted apertures of my eyes. A young working woman, Mongol-shaped eyes, chapped lips. She takes out a tattered rag, wipes her face, undoes her bodice, and begins nursing the infant. She notices I am watching her. She returns my look with fixed eyes glinting metallically, immobile as a statue. I strive not to move; I shoulder her immobility. The car shakes with a powerful crack; it jerks back and forth. One of the drunks wakes up. "What the fuck!" he mutters, then snores on. The baby's head slides down and tumbles under the mother's arm. She transfers the baby to her other breast. By now both breasts are bare; the forced-down slip pushes up the mound of white flesh into a tower. We continue staring at each other. After a little while, she closes her eyes, leans her head back, and searches for support. Beyond the row of trees, a headlight from the highway illuminates the barren meadowland, but I don't hear the drone of the auto, and the shaft of light "recalls," "sucks" itself back. I am sampling the two words to determine which portrays more sensitively the moving, temporal disappearance of the light. Flocking nightingales keep adorning it. A cat appears on the slag heap, its tail curving symmetrically into an incomplete semicircle. In the sky, stars are shimmering sparsely in massive dispersion. It isn't August yet. I go out to the w.c. When I return, she is still leaning her head back with eyes closed. I sit down opposite her. Not immediately but a few minutes later, she looks at me. "What is the name?" I ask, but she remains uncertain whether I mean hers or the child's. "Emőke," she says hoarsely, as if I have ruined something irreparably with the accent. She slips her breast back into her slip, takes the baby into her arms, and stands up. She doesn't have any belongings. She leaves. I hear her stumbling across the gangway to the adjoining car. The train starts up with creaking bumps and jerks. Slag heaps and indistinct mounds pass by for many kilometers. The Danube gleams through leafy boughs. The young man wakes up again, he stirs, the burlap around his belongings comes undone under his head. Something metallic suddenly reflects light. I ask him what it is. "A prismatic hammer," he mutters and goes back to sleep. So they are rock-breakers, rock-breakers in the quarry on the prairie. Tentatively I look up high, but then that spectacle does not beguile me either. Shadows of Egyptian vultures glide over the rocks, despite the fact that the air is completely empty. Elephantiasis of the slag heaps—like some abortive, solitary revolution. At that moment I am surprised how exactly everything is oriented geographically toward *Bolivia*. It is a joint mission, a completely precarious one: I have to accomplish the dubious task together with a young man[1] I don't know and whose language I don't understand. We quickly become lost, and there is already no hope that anyone will find us. We hide in a sheltered cave; day dawns, the day passes, and another. Because of hunger, I see turquoise-blue spots at the half-moons of my fingernails; a hair-thin wire coils around my penis into a tautly ascending slope, from which all will become like a metamorphosed caterpillar, like a toy mummy. Parched, I can spit pellets of white foamy sponge into my palm; I pulverize them. A dust finer than flour—the sun scorches it into my skin like a glaze. I sense it would be proper to let the uncrazed gleam remain that way, but something keeps urging me, completely without reason, to clench my hand. Then it chips off, and I can start the process over again. Meanwhile, the young man and I feel an ever deeper attachment for each other. We try lighting a fire, but we quickly run out of something to feed it with. We burn our clothes up. From this point on, we converse even more convivially, each in his own language. Only days later do we notice that we are napping more than usual, sometimes even while standing, without having anything to lean against. These details are important, for they don't expect to account for anything; still, they are enormously vivid. I can still hear the nightingales in the distance. And this seems to reinforce my belief that duty lies somewhere else entirely. I think it ridiculous that I once wore a tuxedo in a magnificent hall and held my cigarette in a studied manner. What ridiculous arrogance, especially now when I think back on it. Afterward I carry my companion's corpse for a couple of days on the prairie quarry; then he carries my corpse for a couple of days. During these last days, the resemblance between us is so striking that it would be most righteous to take upon ourselves the fiasco of our assignment, to die together, but somehow it does not work out that way; we constantly have to spell each other: sometimes I carry him, sometimes he carries me. This way it is no longer determinable whether the language each of us is speaking is the same language, or one only the inversion of the other. As best I can remember, I perpetrated the betrayal by making known beforehand what I am preparing for. I shall wait for my turn, then lay his corpse down in a rocky gully. I am even careful to place a rock under his head; this way I can almost feel his eyes following me until I vanish from view. The air is immutably empty; only the shadows of Egyptian vultures keep following me. Eventually they make me rush along. I am unable to endure the irony of the silent shadows cast by the birds. Even in their incorporeality they are so sternly calling me to account that spittle and sweat shame me. The train stops again on open tracks, not far from the station I am supposedly heading for. For a moment or two, I am bewildered by the fact that every decision rests in my hands. What task can there still be that I am unfit for, that I can betray by outlasting it, by leaving it with indifference? And that nobody can call me to account for without hope! Here the prospect is different; there is no trace of slag heaps. The moonlight gleams coldly on the prismatic hammer. The drunk in the red pullover sitting to the side thrusts his clenched fist into his unbuttoned fly. The engine jerks the carriage a bit; this rouses him. A streak of white saliva protrudes from his mouth as he looks at me. He has a human smile, and this now almost touches me like some undeserved gift. I tell him I would like to examine his hammer. He lets me pull it out of his sack and swish it about in the air. Its slender head is astonishingly heavy for its flexible handle. "Do you know where we are?" he asks. "I am already at home," I answer, and I am enjoying how nicely the handle fits my palm. He does not inquire further. He gets up, goes to the window, and looks out at the landscape that I know with my eyes shut better than he. Here the stagnant channel broadens so widely that at dusk it deepens into a purple-red wasteland. The seasons do not affect its solitude. The village is four kilometers away; more accurately, not the village but that enormous garbage dump, that rubbish pit where diseased animals are also buried and layers of lime poured on them afterward. Burning them would be simpler, but an economical technology to do that has not been worked out yet. It's possible I am badly informed, though. Probably something else is at stake in the matter. One August morning, a little chaise with light springs from the *N . . . Governorship* turns into the village mainstreet, its passenger wearing a white dust-coat.[2] He puts up at the Calvinist minister's place. The guest room of the parish house is placed at his disposal, though he hasn't come on a religious assignment, but instead, on an administrative matter connected with the sphere of authority exercised by the local guardhouse and, according to others, with the health difficulties of the animals in the area. The window of the guest room looks out upon an inner yard with lilac bushes divided from the parish's large yard by a circular well and a woodpile several meters high. In some peculiar way, everything here is more transitory and perishable—the flower beds, the twisted plum trees, the log table and bench, the household linens hanging on the clothesline. Yes, even the linens. We might also express it like this: here the more spectacular life takes place, the bride and groom wait, people reporting baptisms and deaths, and voluntary blood donors. But all this is more likely to perish than is the desolation of the inner yard. The window of the aloof senior civil servant looks out on it, however. This hardly means that the civil servant does. The inner yard can also be approached from the adjacent plot through an iron gate secured with barbed wire, and the civil servant comes this way more often than not. Altogether he spends two days in the village, but this is enough to make hopefulness and uncertainty dominate the sailors who leave the island only during the winter months to seek occasional jobs elsewhere and the few intellectuals who have some insight into matters, though they never feel it to be sufficient. It must be said about the minister that he is obsessed in the most conventional sense of the word, whether the matter involves his chopping firewood for the cripples or old people in the village or his saving or threatening a soul with damnation. Below the gardens, he can express his views about stealthy Jehovists in fiery words. At this, the young man in the red pullover bends toward me. His face is close to mine, a half-crushed Kossuth cigarette in his mouth. My lighter illuminates his dark grainy skin. "Stone dust?" I inquire. I wait until the flame dies out in the wick. He nods and takes the hammer out of my hand. He strikes his palm with it lightly. His movement is exaggeratedly expert and flaunty. He shows me the iron's blunt shape and explains that a mere flick and the cranial bone goes crack! "Even a bull's," he says. "We can't test that," I reply, also laughing, and take the hammer back. He takes a deep and hard drag on his cigarette; the embers glow hotly. I sense that I have again ruined something irreparably. I wasn't enough of an accomplice. We are still standing on the open tracks. The door is open; we are sitting in a slight cross-draft. The cool smell of mud flows from the Danube; it is the sixth week without precipitation. Water is slimy in the wells. The young man juts forward at the doorway and starts urinating. Meanwhile, I hear a different stirring sound, and I step behind him. He points out that he has unintentionally urinated on a mole; we can still see it stumbling about with awkward haste in the moonlight on the weed-covered gravel piles. "Wait, I'll catch it," he says, and he snatches the hammer out of my hand and jumps down. I consider whether I should leap after him, but then I don't. For a while I observe him from the door as he keeps stooping, stopping, stiffening, and from time to time striking the stones. He is already down at the bottom of the railbed. Then, without any transition whatsoever, my interest wanes. I return to the compartment and lean out of the window on the other side, in the direction of the stagnant channel. Actually, I could have got off long ago; it isn't much farther from here even on foot. If I take a short cut across the edge of the dead channel to the place of the herd disaster, I shall arrive in the village directly at the burial pit. The civil servant inspects the pit on the afternoon of his second day. They proceed out there in the little chaise with springs—the civil servant, the chief officer of the guardhouse, and the director of the council office. They walk carefully around the fetid site on the edge of the earth mound encircling the depression fit for a gorge. The earth mound serves as a safeguard, for the danger of spontaneous combustion is always present. Apparently, an agreement regarding the burning of the sick and infected animals is to be arrived at after this inspection. I have been living in the village for a year and a half, but I have never once seen the animals incinerated. They continue to be slaughtered and buried. I notice a stag appear in the moonlight on the willow-covered prairie of the stagnant channel with the dream-like quality of slow-motion pictures. He is either wary or thoroughly engrossed in his own relaxed movement. I should be holding my old Winchester an inch to the left, with medium sight in line as well. The stubbornness of weapons—I'd like to say, instinctive stubbornness—is a match for our own. If I get off the train earlier, I can plot the map of the expanse that he has strayed into for a moment. I could shoulder his immobility when our eyes happen to meet. At a nervous twitching of his chest, he raises one of his legs, somehow without moving at all. Whether he brought it to pass is incalculable; that must now remain an open question. "He is very canny. Thus is failure built into every gain," I think like a pamphlet. I wait for some perverse noise, the silence being so pervasive. It's as if our engine has also died; it shows no sign of life. Meanwhile, the young man in the red pullover reenters through the door with soft steps (in gym shoes), carrying the mole with its head bashed to bits. My presence is made indistinct by the moonlight shining in. His black satin shorts show through his open fly; his four companions are snoring with jaws hanging loosely. He is surprised the seat behind us is unoccupied. "Did she get off?" "No, she went to the next car." "Should we pay her a visit?" He wipes his nose with the hand holding the mole. I nod, good, and I lead the way. He brings his hammer along and strikes the arms of the seats one after the other. She is sitting in the last empty compartment of the adjacent car. I don't know where she obtained it, but she now has a torn army blanket with her, and her baby is lying on it. Her bare legs are resting on the seat opposite her, and her breast is half-exposed again. Her abdomen still bulges after giving birth, and she still lays her hands on it with the movements of pregnant women. She isn't startled when we stop beside her; she just clutches the edge of the blanket and pulls it a couple of centimeters closer. The young man in the red pullover clicks his tongue with disappointment. "I thought he was bigger, and I wanted to show this to him." He flicks the mole with the handle of the hammer; it swings in his hand like a sluggish clock pendulum. The woman pushes her skirt between her knees with the edge of her hand and presses her thighs together. "Even a bigger one wouldn't play with such a thing," she says without mimicry. She closes the door without making a single concession, and it is impossible not to feel she is the stronger one. Somewhere, farther away, the nightingales start in anew but quite widely dispersed in the empty landscape. We leave the woman without saying good-bye. By now, I am not going back to our compartment. I stop at the door and step down on the stairs. "You want to get off here?" he asks in a sudden fury. "Then why the shit did you wait until now?" I tell him I can't give him an exact answer to that, especially so quickly. He bursts out laughing. He presses the mole into my hand and strikes me on the shoulder with the hammer handle. "Then go and get your ass in gear!" By the time the train starts up, I am well into the dead channel. The engine is puffing sparks thickly. The shifting membranous mud sounds as if I were stepping on dessicated vermin. Underneath, however, the mud is almost as hard as rock; the civil servant's chaise could travel over it safely. The sharp outline of the church steeple appears above the willow groves on the river bank; the sandy cattle pit is a deflated white streak. A *mark*, we once called it. A long-held aim of medium range. I am carrying the mole in my left hand, pinching its hide together with two fingers. Its head no longer drips; its blood has congealed on its pelt. Now even the scurrying sounds are impersonal. Only the hill above the village, north of the sandpit where the forest of planted fir trees stretches, only this hill is personal. "Taking everything into account, only from here is it possible to fire a shot into the dead channel with sufficient accuracy." And I am in it, one who is still moving. Now one must be careful, cautious. "One must not confuse caution with the incaution of cowardice!" In any case, nothing is more challenging than cowardice. And for the moment, duty can be tackled only on this mud-prairie, prismatic and lacerated with rents and mosaics. The meaning of duty is to be faced here only. The obsession of duty. The mole liquidated previously is now the specious, protruding mark—it is the bait, the bone, the tendered sacrifice. And so it is, not I. I am masked, secure with respect to duty. The mole is under medium sight. Yes, this is the most carefully weighed strategy now: the rekilling of the carcass. For a moment I clearly hear the nightingales settling themselves elsewhere in the forest of fir trees stretching along the height. I whirl the mole around twice and then hurl it away in a wide arc. It curves in a flawless trajectory in the moonlight. In its flight it is slightly lower, but even so, there are some moments when, from my sight line, the squat body ascends almost weightlessly above the strip of fir trees. It could also be put this way: I am alone again, I have no companion. I can't make allowance for my shadow, for on the one hand, the moonlight is very obliterating; on the other . . . I don't know. Suddenly my confidence in words abandons me. Probably this is what causes me to break into a run toward the site of the cattle disaster with all the strength I can muster. Meanwhile, only one thing flashes through me: not enough pits, not enough ditches . . . I don't get beyond that. In the winter, an enormous sandbed shaped like a dull wedge stretches northward from the tip of the island into the Danube; ice a couple of centimeters thick covers it, on which frost freezes. If I head directly toward the tip, I won't be able to determine when and where the frozen river channel starts underfoot. Theoretically, possibly, the ice could give way and I could sink into the pit of the river bed. The next time, I shall bring and iron-tipped stick along and poke and tap to find the end of the sandbed, the last solid point where I could still dig myself in, as in some advanced heroic observation post. But completely unarmed, which fittingly spoils the entire old-fashioned notion, the whole dubious venture. I sit crouching on the ice, and I can feel like somebody who has voluntarily remained behind as the last target rather ridiculously. Farther ahead, crows take flight at the cracking din. They circle in formations of six. Their shadows leave no more trace on the snow than my eyes on the clear, cold sky. I have sunk into the sand up to my ankles, when the unmelodious growling of the bass fiddle becomes audible from the tavern. At the dump, the strong smell of thick ashes and fumes strikes my nostrils. In the moonlight I can conclude that a spontaneous fire could have occurred during the two days of my absence. Or an experimental incineration of the animals has been carried out on the orders of the civil servant. In any case, the stench leads to this surmise. The stench is almost unbearable. There is no longer any trace of coals; I can only make out an odd-looking smut on the earth mound, as if the flame has burned its negative into the side of the bank. I sniff my hand to see if it still gives off the mole's acrid stench. It doesn't; it must have stayed somewhere in the dead channel. Is it possible that it will find its way back to the flung-away body? This would be much too rational. It is already two o'clock when I reach the main square, the feeding ground for geese. In the middle of the square is a scale for weighing animals, its wooden planks edged with iron clamps. The animal steps on it, and there are also iron posts on two sides to brace the animal with chains if it is restless. Mounds of gravel and lime are situated behind the scale. Beyond them is the recently completed Old Peoples Park, without benches and enclosed by a wire fence. Between its geometrical flower beds are paths parallel to them and a few young trees. A freshly painted lock secures the park's trellis gate. The statue of St. Christopher from the previous century shines with lacquer from the black and white enamel paint. A single lamp is burning on the square among the acacias; the bright bulb forms pellets of green light in the entangled leaves. The windows are dark. Light is streaming only from the outside room of the parish house. I turn in that direction. The scene almost meets possible expectations. Looking directly ahead from the street, I can see the minister standing on a pulpit-like platform with the Bible in his hand. Before him, two old peasants are sitting with their backs to me and their heads bent slightly forward. There are no pictures on the walls, not even the colored Biblical calendar of the Dutch Protestant Mission. There are only the lime-white walls and an unshaded bulb. The coat collars of the two peasants are turned up; even so, a narrow streak that hasn't tanned since their youth still shows on their necks. Propriety permits a mature man to work in the fields only if he wears a shirt. Their hair is freshly clipped up to the middle line at the back of their heads, in keeping with the taste of the village barbers. This technique especially accentuates the fasicled protuberance of the neck's trapezius muscle, which is somewhat similar to the neck contour of animals in poor health. The moment for all this is really odd, but it is all fact. The civil servant again spends the evening of the second day at the minister's place as official guest for supper, and anybody can verify this from the street. The diaphanous curtains do no more than mark the bounds of private property. The minister's son is living in Sweden; he is a dental technician and judo instructor. He lives with a frail girl, a ceramist. The color photographs may persuade the civil servant that the minister belongs to the progressive line of protestantism. Helga is playing naked with her baby and goes in naked to wish goodnight to the minister visiting them. This is natural with God's sanction and precious to the senses. But he cannot forgive the Jehovists who crept in furtively at the bottom of the garden. He weighs one hundred and ten kilos and can snap a cervicle vertebra with one hand. At the tavern I learn what I have missed while I was away. After seven o'clock in the evening, a fire blazed up in the refuse and burial pit from some inexplicable cause. The herd wending homeward turned savage because of the fire; the dogs driving the cattle also lost their heads. Eventually two steers and five heifers rushed headlong into the flames, willingly rather than inevitably. The minister rescued a calf on his own shoulder; all the rest perished. To shorten the agony of the animals, the incineration was accelerated—at the minister's recommendation—with gasoline stored in the guardhouse. I learn all this in front of the tavern entrance, where a larger gathering is discussing the event. The tavern is staying open so late because of the happenings piling up so suddenly. For a while, I survey the smoke-filled establishment from the doorway. Floor lamps stand around the walls shedding soft light through silk shades, most of them scorched by the oversized bulbs. The establishment is divided by an imitation embossed arch constructed of bronze-colored papier-maché, a piece from the agricultural and industrial club, with stylized simplification. I finally go in for a glass of beer. It is warm and watery; I can drink only half of it. B., the longshoreman, elbows his way over to me; he completed two years of law studies before the war. He insists on addressing me as a doctor; he squeezes my shoulder and unexpectedly kisses my hand. If anybody, I will understand, he explains; the Jews atoned for the curse of the seventh generation and the Germans lost the war for the curse of the seventh generation. His eyes are soggy, like the eyes of pursued game that is in no longer in need of pursuit. His neighbor is relating how, after the conflagration, the time came for the world-famous midget theater of Budapest to perform, but the promised great act—the dance of the world's two smallest midgets—turned out to be a fraud. It amounted to just one midget dancing with a midget doll. Meantime, vendors sold photographs of the grandfather of the dancing midget autographed by his grandchild. I try breaking through the crowd to the street door, but I am blocked after taking a couple of steps. I ask permission to go behind the bar to reach the yard through the back door. The large empty yard is almost like a stage with its unplanned outbuildings. A few drunks are scattered about in the darkness, and coal barrels are placed in a row on the weed-covered bowling green. The stench from the w.c. is pungent. On my way out, somebody grabs me by the shirt and mistakes me for the sculptor whose hair is also gray. "You know what we ought to do? Throw a quarter kilo of yeast into the latrine. That would push the shit out into the yard like dough. It couldn't be stopped, it would increase five times. Then we'd get a new latrine. You don't think so? We did this once in Constance." On the way home I again hear the nightingales. At home I look at myself in the mirror absentmindedly, and for a moment there are almost two of us. It is three o'clock by the time I go to bed. Before doing so, I go out into the yard and look at the empty street. It is possible the tavern was closed in the meantime; the silence is pervasive again. There is freshly mowed grass next to the fence; I feel out some firm buds on the rosebush with my fingers. I accidentally touch a thorn. There's a little blood in my mouth. Here, in the upper row, a four-year-old boy rounds up cattle at the break of day to drive them to the herd beside the Old Peoples Park. At the end of his whip is a tiny piece of lead sewn in a leather pouch. Once I said to him that this wasn't a good thing, that this way it didn't make a loud report. He knew this, he replied, but it stung more this way when it was needed. It is certain they will be out by five-thirty.

[1] Che Guevera.
[2] A temporary shift to the style of the opening of Gogol's *Dead Souls*.

Sunt Lacrimae Rerum[1]

To N.N.Á.[2]

Physical objects have always greatly affected me, their silence and stability—that self-realization darting to a stillpoint which we discern in their forms and which brings time to such a halt that they simultaneously step out of time.

I preserve two archaically distant memories from my childhood. One of them is a never-again-seen street lined with mulberry trees leading straight as an arrow in flight to a secluded house. The house is surrounded by a lush garden; inside is a long corridor with a tile floor and doors stained black opening off it. I open one of them and enter. I find nothing inside, only a pile of nuts reaching nearly to my knees, and atop it a stuffed eagle with its wings spread wide.

The other one. I am standing on a wide street; someone is holding my hand and trying to pull me forward, but I refuse to give in to the tugging, and I fix my eyes on crowded housetops in a narrow lane and see doves taking wing one after the other from them. I start crying, and I am taken home. By the time we get home, the steeple of the inner-city church stands in flames.

These two memories have permeated every single subsequent memory, and ever since I haven't encountered a more permanent sight. Everything that came thereafter was a repetition, and everything that comes hereafter is ever more recognizably of the past.

The superiority of objects is so pervasive that they are always capable of projecting the most permanent still picture behind variations. They are the enchanted of existence. Their expanse is the most endless dead-end street in which motion can lock itself. The restless, edgy light—the intellect—that "separates objects from night" is displaced compared to them: it races across sky and earth. Meanwhile, it strains at its effort to infuse its extraordinary superiority with the extraordinary composure of physical objects.

>to exist without breathing,
>to live famished, alone—
>the sky is pondering: it clouds over, clears up—
>no, I don't want to die, no.

No, not to die, but to have form, to be at a stillpoint, yes.

A tiny room piled high with nuts, a stuffed eagle, crowded roof structures in a narrow lane: is not this the setting in which the transitory does not pass away most lastingly?

Whatever can be held by the hand is also the gate of the timeless. To be a gate! With outstretched hand to clasp the object and what issues from it. Never to remove our eyes from the bristles formed on reeds in the marshes, the curve in the pathway, the post leaned against the wall, the absoluteness of rusted wire bales, the cars parked on deserted squares, the impersonal drudgery of pistons: never to forget anything.

A good remembrance will suffice for an eternity.

We mistake objects if we think they weep. The sorrow of objects can be likened only to our joy: each of them responds to the excesses of reality, only differently. The sorrow of objects is a congealed joy; our joy is a thawed sadness. It is more correct if we say our tears are held in common.

I remember a cliff on the ocean shore in Normandy. The waves splashed high over it; the cliff disappeared again and again. A banal remembrance, but at the time there was called forth from within me a certain "transcendental" malicious pleasure: the timeless can manifest itself only through the transitory. If for nothing more, it will always have need for a single cliff, a single wave—for its remembrance undoubtedly.

Aptitude is discontented without creativity. "Latent aptitude" is merely a metaphor: what can be always will be and what was always is. We and objects: we are such involuntary offspring of the timeless that alone we cannot overcome our state of non-becoming.

The yearning for the timeless: to wear everything down to the point where at least it will create the illusion of the tranquillity of its non-becoming; the yearning for the transitory down to the point where it will make itself believe in the everlasting. There is neither gain nor loss. The bondage of aptitude is not any more joyful than being at someone's mercy. One must think he hears in existence a weeping that treats all things equally.

The confident smile on the statues of gods is a mistake of our wisdom: it holds out the promise of such a nirvana that not even the gods have it in their power to create it. In *being* the irrevocable is inescapably present. It must continue to carry every possible past event, and it lives in the present of absolute remembrance.

When we imagine Nothing, we conceive *tension*: the ineradicability of things past and things that may come to pass. And likewise, every layer constructed upon it is *tension*: between the restless, edgy intellect—and the extraordinary composure of objects.

The Gate at which we would like to stand: a razor-sharp no-man's-land. To be incorporeal there in the heart of corporeality; *"to exist without breathing"* in the atmosphere of imperishable transitoriness.

Die? No. Deny the ocean, the cliffs, the snow-capped mountains? The trails of airplanes in the sky? The broken mechanical pencil I saw in the blind window of a village house five years ago and yesterday? Deny the rose-spout of a sprinkling can in the grass, then in the snow, and again in the grass? No.
Never to forget anything, and to be in harmony with everything. To die? No.

[1] From Virgil's *Aeneid*: "Here are tears for human sufferings."
[2] Ágnes Nemes Nagy, who also attaches great importance to physical objects in her aesthetics. See pp. 000-000 for her works.

János Pilinszky

Pilinszky was born on November 27, 1921 in Budapest. His family was well-educated and middle-class; his father was a lawyer, his maternal grandfather a master cooper in a village. After completing his studies at the Piarist High School, he studied law at the University of Budapest, but after a time, he turned to Hungarian literature and the history of art. He began a dissertation on Jenő Péterfy, the influential nineteenth-century essayist and critic but never completed it. In 1941 he became an assistant editor of *Life* (*Élet*), a weekly of the St. Stephen Society, and held this post until the fall of 1944, when he was called into military service. During this period, he wrote numerous articles, mostly unsigned reviews of books, films, and plays. More important, some of his poems appeared from 1941 to 1942, not only in *Life*, but in such prominent and prestigious journals as *Silver Age* (*Ezüstkor*), edited by the noted author and literary historian and critic István Sőtér, *Hungarian Star* (*Magyar Csillag*), a continuation of the influential *West* (*Nyugat*) under the editorship of Mihály Babits, one of Hungary's greatest poets, and *Vigil* (*Vigilia*), a highly regarded voice of Catholic intellectuals.

His army duty outside Hungary began in February of 1945, and after several weeks of travel, his corps arrived in Harbach, a little village in Germany and the title of one of his poems. The scenes of the concentration camps, the prisoners of war, and other horrors there and in Frankfurt and Wiesbaden left a permanent imprint on his relationship with reality and on the nature of his Catholic faith. He grew ill and was assigned to field work, which he carried on to the end of the war, putting aside any more writing until after his return to Hungary in November 1945.

116   János Pilinszky

He immediately became active in the literary life of Budapest, where the prevailing freedom encouraged his development until the political turn of events in 1948. He did some work for radio, mainly preparing translations for broadcast. He was selected a member of the Writers' Federation, which was just then being formed. He became an important editor, along with Iván Mándy, of *New Moon* (*Újhold*), which carried on its staff young writers who attempted to continue literary trends developed in Hungary between the two wars. In that short-lived periodical, Pilinszky published only one poem and an extract of Hofmannsthal's *Elektra*. His poems appeared frequently, however, in *Hungarians* (*Magyarok*), *Reply* (*Válasz*), and *Diary* (*Diárium*), and, in 1949, *Vigil*. The poem "Trapeze and Parallel Bars" ("Trapéz és korlát"), which appeared in *Silver Age* in May 1946, provided the title for his first book of poems, also published in 1946. Although containing only nineteen poems composed from 1940 to 1944, it won the Baumgartner Prize in 1947. Five of his poems were included in 1948 in *Four Generations* (*Négy nemzedék*), a landmark representative anthology of the time.

Cut off from literary life like so many of his contemporaries after 1948, Pilinszky has served since 1957 on the editorial staff of *New Man* (*Új Ember*), a Catholic weekly. His second book of poems did not appear until 1959, when he published *On the Third Day* (*Harmadnapon*), not counting *Golden Bird* (*Aranymadár*), a book of verse tales brought out in 1958. A volume including "Requiem" ("Rekvium"), a movie script, "Fish in a Net" ("Halak a hálóban"), some poems, and "Dark Paradise" ("Sötét mennyország"), an oratorio, appeared in 1963 with a 1964 copyright. *Big City Ikons* (*Nagyvárosi ikonok*), a collection of his writings from 1940 to 1970, was published in 1970. Since then his books, though always slender, have appeared more frequently: *Splinters* (*Szálkák*), poems, in 1972; *The Birth of the Sun* (*A nap születése*), children's verses illustrated by Endre Bálint, one of Hungary's greatest artists, in 1974; *Final Dénouement* (*Végigfejlett*), poems and plays, in 1974; *Crater* (*Kráter*), collected poems, in 1976; and *Conversations with Sheryl Sutton* (*Beszélgetések Sheryl Suttonnal*) in 1977.

Since the early 1960s, his reputation abroad has grown significantly, and he has traveled extensively. In 1963 he made his first visit to Paris, as the guest of Pierre Emmanuel, the poet, translator, and journalist. Five years later, on the one hundredth anniversary of Baudelaire's death, he gave a reading of his own poems at the little Odéon in Paris. In 1969 he participated in a festival of poets held in London, and in 1970 he spent six months in Paris at the invitation of Gabriel Marcel, the Catholic philosopher, dramatist and critic. He held a reading of his poems in Canada in 1972 and was named a corresponding member of the Bavarian Academy of Fine Arts in 1973. In his own country, he was awarded the Attila József Prize in 1971.

Despite the appeal of his poetry, the length of his career, and the increase in his productivity during the 1970s, the corpus of his poems is remarkably small relative to other poets of the times and lacks a wide-ranging vocabulary, a variety of form, and an experimental bent, except in the poetic drama. Concerning his limited productivity, he notes that the amount is not so little, after all, and that "it isn't the number of times a bird beats its wings that matters but its having the power to soar." In a 1978 radio interview, he explored the question of the long interruptions in his creativity, maintaining that often a person finds himself doubting everything he had learned and then asking himself what is to take its place. At such a time an individual must have the strength to surmount himself, "to see the world anew as if with the eyes of an infant," thereby ridding himself of "everything routine." His periods of silence are very likely, he believes, attributable to this, and so he "writes islands and meanwhile the ocean is there." Pilinszky attributes the relative paucity of his poetic vocabulary to his having learned his native language while mainly in the care of an aunt whose speech, because of a childhood accident, never advanced beyond a stammer and who thus was forced to choose words carefully and express them with uncommon intensity. He adds that since the beauty of a native language is precisely that it is a received phenomenon, he is reluctant to add anything to it, to "embellish our origins." Besides, he asserts, economy of language in art enables "the deaf to hear, the blind to see, the lame to walk"; insufficiency there "may transform itself into a creative and highly refined power." In the same interview, he also threw further light on this question when he said that, as is so often true with a long known, a, perhaps, accepted truth about life, he suddenly sees an old familiar word as if it were perfectly new, with the result that it is "fresher and more elemental than if I were seeking exotica."

The power of Pilinszky's poetry does not derive from an exotic language or from any variety of forms, indeed not even from a broad range of themes and motifs: it rests upon the relentless probing of the absurdly grim realities of twentieth-century life, made especially painful by the second world war and the character of existence since its conclusion; it rests upon the authentication of the despair in his poetic world and the intensity with which it is conveyed. Addressing these tragic times and his personal struggle against Nothingness without offering any belief in the capacity of the human race to alter the conditions, Pilinszky portrays, in an increasingly universal way, the loneliness of the individual, the futility of escaping from the pain of existence, the uselessness of any effort at expiation in this "dark paradise," and the pervading fears and horrors and anxieties marking the stations of life. The intellectual foundation and the most important motifs of his views are mostly laid down early in his career, for example, in such poems as "Trapeze and Parallel Bars" and "Fish in the Net," to be built upon throughout his life without any accomodation or resignation to existence as he perceives it to be. He does not respond directly to specific social and political events in his nation, but there is no question that his personal knowledge of the concentration and prisoner-of-war camps in Germany is the background against which his poems must be seen. According to him, the *silence* of Auschwitz, now that its gates are shut and it has become a museum, only increases the horror of the moral failure of contemporary civilization. The catastrophe of the war and fascism leads Pilinszky inevitably to an abstraction of himself from his surroundings, to a monk-like confrontation of his personal self, and then to a religious and philosophical attitude nearly always full of struggle and agony, with his belief in God and his intellectual Catholicism nearly always anguished and beset by doubt. Although many of his poems are not religious, his struggle with God is vital to his relationship with existence. In the 1978 interview, after quoting Rilke's view that "it is dreadful that we never reach reality from facts," he illuminates his position on God in the context of the artist:

> All of us now feel that we are living among facts that more or less transmit reality. If this were not the case, then what meaning would there be for Goya to paint portraits . . . , for Van Gogh to paint the shoemaker? Those were all more real as facts than what got on the canvas. They [the artists] were seeking the reality behind the facts. Perfectly unresponsive. Perfectly silent, really without a single weapon, purely good and present.

Pilinszky unmistakably considers himself, like all members of his generation, ordained to the universal, in his words to "self-effacement, truth, and humanity." Those of his compatriots who have thus lost their individual lives in living among the uprooted and to whom "the story of the Passion is once again an everyday reality" can never return to the mere personal as it was understood in the times before the war; moreover, even if the most beautiful future were lying before them, that prospect "would change into a moral wasteland if we did not feel a responsibility for what had already occurred." To Pilinszky the role of the artist is that of raising the tragic past to the level of the universal, of preventing the silence of historical relativity from prevailing over the horrors symbolized by the closed gates of Auschwitz. Thus the crying out against isolation, against this no-man's-land of existence, this nothingness of life, this absence of a governing moral order that challenges all the easy and comforting illusions of religious belief untested by the reality that always *is*.

Again not surprisingly, Pilinszky's poetry grows out of an aesthetic view that is fundamentally religious. He rests his concept of the creative imagination on the broadening effect of the sin of the first parents. Their fall not only dimmed the power of the human intellect and predisposed the human will to violent acts against all things; the original sin also infected the imagination, so that it cannot effectively carry out its natural function of ultimately consummating the incarnation of the reality of the world. Consequently, life is now no more than the irreality of merely existing. The creative imagination has not renounced its function, but, unhappily, it now desires "the certainty of science," hoping to find in "the certainty of style" what it can accomplish only with "the self-effacement of submission, 'with downcast eyes.' " But poetry—all art—is *imagination's mor-*

ality, and its labor is to restore the reality and incarnation of creation. In their agonizing vision, in their reliving of the Passion, Pilinszky's poems are themselves illusionless scriptures, like parts of Ecclesiastes. They are products of a creative imagination seeking to give readers a sense of the eternal, to reach for that God who, as he says, "bleeds through events at times." To confront the terrors of reality, he said in 1971, humankind turns to the artist:

> Art is the message of the Universal, and the artist is the messenger of the Universal, the Cosmic. Every work is a prototype of the world. A message derived from the Whole.

This is the consolation he extends, and given the continuing moral failures of the present century and the illusions of which civilization continues to base its concepts, Pilinszky gives human despair some glimmer of an attainable experience with a moral world.

Fish in the Net

We thrash about in a net of stars,
fish dragged to the shore;
our mouths gape into nothingness,
snapping dry void.
The lost element, whispering,
calls us in vain.
Among sharp-edged stones and pebbles
gasping for air
we must live and die against one another.
Our hearts tremble.
Our struggles wound
and strangle our brother.
Not even an echo answers
our voices, each outshouting the other;
we have no reason to fight and kill
yet do it we must.
We atone yet our atonement
is no punishment;
no suffering can redeem
us from our hells.
We thrash about in an enormous net
and at midnight perhaps
we shall be food on the table
of a mighty fisherman.

Autumn Sketch

Beneath the eavesdropping garden
the tree sniffs out into space,
the silence is fragile and empty,
the meadow seeks boundaries.

Startled, your heart constricts,
the road slinks past hurriedly,
even the rosebush searches
its soul with a nervous smile:

on distant, doubtful terrain
there gathers, slowly, pain.

Passion of Ravensbrück

He steps out from the others.
He stands in the square silence.
Prisoner's dress and convict's head
flicker as on a screen.

He is terrifyingly alone.
Even his pores are visible.
Everything about him is so huge,
everything about him so tiny.

And that is all. The rest,
well, the rest was simply
that he forgot to cry out
before slumping to the ground.

The Desert of Love

A bridge, a steaming highway:
daylight empties its pockets,
carefully laying out its all.
You are alone in the catatonic dusk.

The landscape like the bottom of a creased pit,
white-hot scabs in the shimmering haze.
Dusk. The glitter freezes,
the sun blinds. A summer I shall never forget.

Summer and lightning heat.
They stand, and I know not a wing moves,
the chickens stand, like burning cherubs,
in the boarded-up, splintered cages.

Do you still remember? First the wind,
then the earth, and afterwards the cage.
Fire and dung. And here and there
a few wing-beats, a few empty reflexes.

And thirst. I ask for water—
even today I hear the feverish gulps,
and tolerate them helplessly, like a rock,
and extinguish the mirages.

Years pass. And years. And hope—
is like a tin cup toppled in the straw.

Apocrypha

1

For then shall all things be forsaken.

There will be set apart the silence of the heavens
and forever apart the silence
of the fallen fields of the end of the world
and apart again the silence of the dog-kennels.
In the air a fleeing host of birds.
And we shall see the rising sun,
dumb as the demented pupil of an eye
and calm as a watchful beast.

But keeping vigil in banishment—
for then I cannot sleep at night—
I toss and turn as with its thousand leaves
the tree speaks at the dead of night:
Do you all know the procession of the years,
of the years on the creased fields?
And do you understand the wrinkle of transience,
do you know my care-worn hand?
And do you know the name of orphanhood?
And do you know the kind of pain
that treads here the eternal dark
on cracked hooves, on webbed feet?
The night, the cold, the pit,
the convict's head jived askew,
do you know the frozen troughs,
do you know the torture of the abyss?

The sun has risen. Sticks of trees dark
in the infra-red of the wrathful sky.

So I set off. Facing the desolation
a man walks without a sound.
He has nothing. He has his shadow.
And his stick. And his prison dress.

2

This is why I learned to walk! For these
belated, bitter steps.

And evening will come, and the night will petrify
around me with its mud, and under closed eyelids
I continue to guard this procession,
these fevered shrubs and their tiny twigs,
the little, hot forest, leaf by leaf.
Once Paradise stood here.
In half-sleep, the renewing pain:
hear its gigantic trees!

Home—I wanted to get home at last,
to arrive as he in the Bible arrived.
My terrific shadow in the courtyard.
Care-worn silence, aged parents in the house.
And already they are coming, calling me,
poor souls, already crying, stumblingly embracing me.
The ancient order welcomes me back.
I lean out on the windy stars—

If just this once I could speak with you,
whom I loved so much. Year after year
I never tired of saying what a small child
sobs into the gap between the palings,
the almost choking hope
that I come back and find you.
Your nearness throbs in my throat.
I am startled, like a wild beast.

I do not speak your words, human speech.
There are birds alive
who are fleeing now as fast as they can
beneath the sky, the fiery sky.
Forlorn poles stuck in the blazing fields,
and burning cages immobile.
I do not understand human speech
and I do not speak your language.
My words are more homeless than the word!
I have no words.

          Their terrible burden
tumbles down through the air,
the body of a tower utters sounds.

You are nowhere to be found. How empty is the world.
A garden chair, a deckchair left outside.
My shadow clatters among sharp stones.
I am tired. I jut out of the ground.

        3

God sees me standing in the sun.
He sees my shadow on stone and fence.
He sees my shadow standing
without a breath in the airless press.

By then I am already like stone;
a dead shutter, a drawing of a thousand grooves,
a good handful of rubble
are the faces of the creatures by then.

And instead of tears, the wrinkles on the faces,
trickling, the empty ditch trickling down.

Quatrain

Nails asleep in the ice-cold sand.
Nights asoak in poster-loneliness.
You left the light on in the corridor.
Today they shed my blood.

Agonia Christiana

How far still the dawn,
with its streams and cool breath!
I put on my shirt and coat.
I button up my death.

A Cold Wind

uninhabited rock, my back lolls,
without memories, without me.
in the dead ashes of millennia.

A cold wind blows.

The Imperfect Tense

for Ted Hughes

It arrives and it stiffens,
it sits on the ash-dumb wall:
the moon. One gigantic blow.
Dead silence its core.

It breaks up the roads,
the moonlight breaks them up.
And tears the wall in two.
White crashes upon black.

The black day flashes with lightning.
And flashes. And flashes.
White crashes, and black.
You comb your hair in the magnetic storm.

You comb your hair in the glittering silence,
in a mirror more watchful than the imperfect tense.

You comb your hair in the mirror,
silently, as in a coffin of glass.

KZ-Oratorio

(An empty stage or concert platform. The chorus occupies both sides of the stage in a semicircle, leaving a narrow passage in the middle. Spotlights above, in a horizontal row.)

Cast: LITTLE BOY; OLD WOMAN; R.M., a young girl. All three inhabitants of the concentration camp.

As the orchestra is tuning up, R.M. is the first to appear, the LITTLE BOY is next, and the OLD WOMAN last. R.M. wears striped prisoner's clothes; her hair is cut short. The OLD WOMAN is in black. The LITTLE BOY in a dust-coat. Bearing lighted candles in their hands, all three come to the front of the stage. Before them on a music stand is the text, whose pages they turn during the performance with their free hand. The LITTLE BOY stands in the middle, the girl on his right, the OLD WOMAN on his left. The orchestra falls silent. Pause.

R.M.: I come from Warsaw.
OLD WOMAN: I'm from Prague.
LITTLE BOY: I don't know where I'm from.
OLD WOMAN (cocking her head): It sounded as if they were rattling nails.
R.M.: As if I rattled nails!
LITTLE BOY: That was when I first saw night!
OLD WOMAN: The nails did not awaken.
R.M.: It was me screaming in the box!
OLD WOMAN: I never again awoke.
R.M.: I come from Warsaw.
OLD WOMAN: I'm from Prague.
LITTLE BOY: I don't know where I'm from.
OLD WOMAN: It was night when we left the city.
R.M.: All lit up, forgotten.
OLD WOMAN: The ice-empty stars were knocking.
R.M.: The ice-empty light bulbs were knocking.
OLD WOMAN: It sounded as if they were rattling nails.
R.M.: Faces, hands. Exhausted rubble.
   The open-stage mass came crashing down.
OLD WOMAN: Lights on a forgotten face.
R.M.: Wrinkles in a face never seen.
OLD WOMAN: Prague, were you no more than this?
R.M.: All lit up, forgotten.
LITTLE BOY: Don't speak to me anymore.
R.M.: Never in my life have I seen a house!
   It stood among the pines at the end of a row of trees.
   Its windows shone.
   I did not touch it with my hands.
   I am touching it very carefully.

   Forget me, forget me, my love!
   Who is interested in the beast leaning against a tree stump?
OLD WOMAN: Scribes in the moonlight.
R.M.: Churches and graveyards.

OLD WOMAN: Walnut-trees, jailer-peasants.
R.M.: Half-sleep files; needle and cotton.
OLD WOMAN: Dead silence.
R.M.: Gothic type.
OLD WOMAN: Germany.
LITTLE BOY: Very far and quite near
           someone lay on the stone table.
OLD WOMAN: It was just like a house of flowers,
           but there were no flowers in it.
           A single long corridor;
           wattle and daub but with the earth's warmth.
           The corridor widened at one end,
           and shone like a monstrance.
R.M. (As if in another tale, with heightened simplicity):
           Once upon a time
           there lived a lonely wolf.
           Lonelier than the angels.
           Once he came upon a village,
           and fell in love with the first house he saw.

           He had come to love even the walls,
           the masons' caresses,
           but the window stopped him.

           There were people sitting in the room.
           To none but God had they ever appeared
           as beautiful as they did to this pure-hearted beast.

           And then at night he went into the house,
           stopped in the middle of the room,
           and never moved from there again.

           He stood open-eyed all night
           and was still open-eyed in the morning
           when they beat him to death.

LITTLE BOY: We're dead, aren't we?
R.M.: It was just like a house of flowers,
           But there were no flowers in it.
           A single dark corridor;
           wattle and daub but with the earth's warmth.
           It was afternoon, about three o'clock.

János Pilinszky

> The corridor widened at one end,
> and shone like a monstrance.
>
> Its roof must have been of glass,
> for it caught the sunlight.
> Naked and definitively
> someone lay on the stone table.

OLD WOMAN: Scribes in the moonlight.
R.M.: Churches and graveyards.
OLD WOMAN: Walnut-trees, jailer-peasants.
R.M.: Half-sleep files; needle and cotton.
OLD WOMAN: A single gigantic blow!
R.M.: The dead in the magnesium flare.
OLD WOMAN: Dead silence.
R.M.: Gothic type.
OLD WOMAN: Germany.
R.M.: It is late. Only the fraying thread
> of the prisoner's dress remains with me.
> I tear off the thread and put it in my mouth.
> Here I lie, dead on the tip of my tongue.

OLD WOMAN: My dear ones, don't judge me!
LITTLE BOY: There are seven squares.
> I don't know the first.
> The second is roads and the distance.
> In the third: soldiers.
> We are in the fourth square.
> In the fifth: hunger and bread!
> In the sixth square there is silence.
> I don't know the seventh square.

R.M.: I'm dreaming that I'm waking up.
OLD WOMAN: Try it, my dear, what can you lose? Try!
R.M.: I'm so afraid that I could lose it. (Pause.)
> I hurry across the deserted courtyard.

OLD WOMAN: You are lost! You have nothing to lose!
R.M.: I can feel that it is here, quite close.
OLD WOMAN: Close, the way only we can love.
R.M.: It's here. My heartbeat stops.
OLD WOMAN: Break the door down! We're allowed to, now.
R.M.: I'm weeping. It's here on my face.
> Everything is here, what is mine and what isn't.

OLD WOMAN: Yes, but if we could just know one thing:
> can we in the end break, not our own,

                but the other's loneliness;
                the sacrifice's, who is afraid,
                the murderer's, who doesn't feel that he has killed!
                That of one who no longer dares even know of us.
R.M.: Here is everything, a river down my face.
LITTLE BOY: I don't know the first square.
                The second is roads and the distance!
                Dark roads and empty distance.
OLD WOMAN (supporting her hands on air): It's beginning to snow.
                It's winter in Prague.
                A little table stands under a glass roof.
                One of its legs is loose.
                The clockwork is turning inside.
                Once I thought I was here.
LITTLE BOY: We are in the fourth square.
R.M.: All lit up, forgotten.
OLD WOMAN: I hurry across St. Wenceslas Square. (Pause.)
                (As if talking to herself): People!
                Have mercy!
R.M.: Finally by myself.

            Only the fraying thread
of the prisoner's dress remains with me,
having donned the unwritten fate of a line.

There is nothing but the place and the time,
where it is all recorded in the end.

There is only me and them. (Pause.) Those still sleep.
OLD WOMAN: My dear ones! Don't judge me!
                We lived here like cattle.
                Like pigs we knelt in the dust,
                  and yet by the time the food reached our tongue
                  it was gentle, like the body of God.
LITTLE BOY: In the sixth square there is silence.
R.M.: I'm dreaming that I'm waking up.
            The night is unbelievably deep.
            I hardly exist.

            A single room,
only one window lit up: his.
and that, too, is empty.

János Pilinszky

>   His room tumbles
> Like a shattered mirror, and cannot reach the ground!
>
> I have to brush aside the soft forest
> leaf by leaf. Each a wound.
> I faint to unravel his beautiful head
> from the sodden, soaked leaves.
>
> More beautiful than the most beautiful young girl —
> The forest is no more.
>   What more do you want of us?
> No, our death, we won't give that.
> We cling to that and won't give it.

R.M.: How soft the air is.
    Dripping eaves, barracks-wall, distance.
    Destruction slowed down to happiness.
LITTLE BOY: In the sixth square there is silence.
R.M.: Improbably weak
    pulses strive;
    try hard to remain.
LITTLE BOY: In the sixth square there is dumbness.
R.M.: Everything stops. It is evening in Warsaw.
    A white blanket covered my bed!
OLD WOMAN: My sweet ones! My sweet ones!
R.M.: My dark heaven.
    (The lights also go out.)
OLD WOMAN: It was like a perforated palm.
        Its windows glittered.
        It shone at the end of the row of trees.
        There were people sitting in the room.
        We marched along the highway.
        The trees cover the house.
R.M.: It is late. Only the fraying thread
    of the prisoner's dress remains with me.
    I tear off the thread and put it in my mouth.
    Here is everything, a river down my face.
LITTLE BOY: I don't know the seventh square.
R.M.: There is only me and them, those still sleep.
OLD WOMAN: Scribes in the moonlight.
R.M.: Churches and graveyards.
OLD WOMAN: Walnut-trees; jailer-peasants.

R.M.: Half-sleep files, needle and cotton.
OLD WOMAN: A single gigantic blow!
R.M.: The dead in the magnesium flare.
OLD WOMAN: Light on a forgotten face.
R.M.: Wrinkles in a face never seen.
OLD WOMAN: It sounded as if they were rattling nails.
R.M.: As if I rattled nails.
LITTLE BOY: I'm seeing night for the first time!
R.M.: It was me screaming in the box!
OLD WOMAN: I shall never wake up again.
LITTLE BOY (Takes one or two steps forward. Slightly isolated and with both
    hands held inquisitively before him):
    Unhappy the moment
    the orphan discovers himself,
    and imagines that this hand,
    this crookedness, could be important
    for another, too, and thenceforth
    longs to be loved.
R.M.: I come from Warsaw.
OLD WOMAN: I'm from Prague.
LITTLE BOY: I don't know where I'm from.
                    (The lights go on.)

Van Gogh

1

They undressed in the dark,
embraced and slept,
while you in the radiance
pondered and wept.

2

Dusk gathered.
In the ramshackle heat
the sun came paper-close.
Everything stood still.
An iron ball stood there too.

3

"Lamb of the world, lupus in fabula,
I am ablaze in the glass cabinet of the present!"

Eine Kleine Nachtmusik

Bouquet
Oh, the smell of last places!

Dialogue
Let me in, I am here;
open the door, I have arrived.
There is no door that we can open.
There is no lock to lock you out.

Midnight
They roll away in the unknown silence,
deep beneath the stars;
they roll away
and come to a stop,
the unmoving billiard balls.

Mozart
A house, a yard. My dream and my death.
Southland silence, memory.
Spotlight on the walls.
Emptiness and marble veins.

"Dans cette maison habita Mozart"
Mozart lived here once.
A bouquet in a vase.

Oh, the smell of last places!

(Paris, 1963)

One Fine Day

Always have I sought
the discarded tin spoon,
the littered landscapes of misery,
hoping that one fine day
the tears would well up
and the old yard welcome me back
gently
with the ivy quiet
and whispers of our house.

Always,
always, I have longed for home.

The Nadir Celebrated

In the bloody heat of the sties
who dares read?
And in the splintered field
of the setting sun,
at earth's ebb
and sky's flow,
who dares set off—anywhere?

Who dares
stand still, eyes closed,
at the nadir,
at the point where
there will always be a last flailing wave,
a roof,
a beautiful face, or even
a single hand, nod, movement of the hand?

Who can
ease himself into sleep
with a satisfied heart,
into sleep that splashes beyond
the bitterness of childhood
and lifts the sea to his face
like a fistful of water?

Cattle-Brand

1

There is no cattle-brand
that I do not deserve.

It will be good for me to cross
the whitewashed threshold of death.

All that we have deserved is good.

2

A nail hammered into the palm of the world,
pale as death, streaming blood,
am I.

Self-Portrait 1974

for Endre Illés[1]

My shirt, like a mass-murderer's,
is white and well-ironed,
but my head, like a little boy's,
is a thousand years old and mute.

[1] Illés (1902—) is an eminent dramatist, short-story writer, and critic, whose imaginative works are based on his experiences as a medical student and on the life of intellectuals, and who views existence from a Catholic and strongly humanistic perspective.

Tableaux Vivants

A work for the stage in one act

CAST: Young Boy, Young Girl, Master Carpenter, Abbess, First Unknown Animal, Second Unknown Animal, Third Unknown Animal, Servant Girl, Little Boy, Little Girl, Old Bird, Gentleman in Wig, Fox, Bear, etc.

Preface

Young Boy and Young Girl in front of curtain. Eyes closed, in dream-time. The boy stretches out an arm and touches the girl's shoulder.

YOUNG BOY (After a long, dream-like pause): I have touched you.
YOUNG GIRL: You have touched me.
YOUNG BOY: The performance can begin.
YOUNG GIRL (Without moving): I am touching you.
YOUNG BOY: You are touching me.
YOUNG GIRL: The performance is drawing to a close.
YOUNG BOY: But at least until then.
YOUNG GIRL: Yes, even until then.
YOUNG BOY: The scene may come to a stop and may move.
YOUNG GIRL: We shall be listening and talking.
YOUNG BOY: We meet. We talk. We listen intently.
YOUNG GIRL: I have touched you.
YOUNG BOY: I can't feel it!
YOUNG GIRL: I have touched you.
YOUNG BOY: The war, I'm afraid, will reach us here.
YOUNG GIRL: Don't be afraid. By the time it gets here, it will be as gentle as a sunset.
YOUNG BOY: Yes. Now I know that there is hope.

The curtain rises. A stage within a stage. The *tableaux vivants* will be shown on the upper level; the audience is seated on the lower level. A bear; a fox; one or two unknown animals; an old woman; a gentleman in a wig, sitting in a chintz armchair; one or two children; an abbess and a few high-ranking officers from the army. Perhaps even an enormous old bird. They are all snoring loudly. The curtain of the inner stage rises: the first tableau. A carpenter's workshop full of shavings and sawdust. A diligent master carpenter at work, his saw in such a position that this could justly be called the apotheosis of all saws and their users. The snoring becomes even louder. The interior curtain falls. Bear, fox, everyone wakes up for a moment. Scattered but even applause registers the performances they have slept through.

Enter the servant girl. On a silver tray, she proffers name-cards to the abbess. Pause. Waiting. The owners of the name-cards enter. Two children, a boy and a girl. They blink in the light. Where have they come from? From a dream perhaps? Or have they themselves been asleep?

The old, big bird offers them two chintz armchairs, stiffly facing the audience. The two young people sit down.

The scene freezes.

General snoring. Another tableau. The curtain of the inner stage rises. A young girl at the piano. A broken chord. The man in the wig rests his elbows on the piano. The audience snores loudly. The tableau is still, motionless, when the ungainly servant girl rushes onto the motionless inner stage.

SERVANT GIRL (Awkwardly, screaming): War's broken out! We're done for! We're all done for!

The tableau moves. The girl at the piano and the man in the wig together drag back the unwelcome newcomer. Interior curtain. The audience startles awake. Scattered but even applause.

FIRST UNKNOWN ANIMAL (In the ensuing silence): My origins are obscure. My hide is that of a bear, my eyes those of a leopard. Yet my heart beats in the normal way, and my muscles have stood the test of time. When I drink, it is water, sun and mud that I drink. When I bathe, it is in water that I bathe; in water, sun and mud. As happens to all animals by the time dusk falls.

FOX: My father was a fox, and so is my mother. My pelt is that of a fox, and my eyes, too, are those of a fox. Yet I do not know who I am and why it is that I am sitting here. Had I the hide of a bear and the eyes of a leopard, perhaps I would be more inclined to protest against my having been born, but at all events I would accept with an easier heart the sunset we are all now awaiting.

ABBESS: It is perhaps surprising that I am the one who at this moment is thinking of the more everyday needs of human nature. There is no sense in my

trying to be secretive. After the manna of art, a glass of wine or even a good bean soup would, I think, do us all good.
SECOND UNKNOWN ANIMAL: My eyes are those of a fox. But I cannot name my pelt.
FIRST UNKNOWN ANIMAL: My pelt is that of a bear and my eyes those of a leopard, but as the sun goes down, my pelt and eyes tend increasingly to be my own. Mine alone. Can it be possible that by the time everything comes to an end and the world falls to pieces, I shall myself be *one*?
SECOND UNKNOWN ANIMAL: You, perhaps, will be. But I, who cannot even name my own fur?
ABBESS: My hunger lasted but a moment. I think we should continue to watch the tableaux, without red wine and bean soup.
THIRD UNKNOWN ANIMAL: I am waiting for darkness to fall. Together with the big old bird I await the sunset, the war's turning gentle by the time it reaches us here. (To the abbess) Mother, will you allow me to touch you? It is true, however, that you had already done me a great honor by inviting me to view the extraordinarily beautiful tableaux; even though we snored through them, the invitation is still an honor.
ABBESS: Do you not think you have strayed from the fold? (Pause.) Hurry with your touch!
THIRD UNKNOWN ANIMAL: Turn aside, Reverend Mother. You are not the one I am touching. It is not I who am touching you. It is the irregularity that is touching the rule. The slave touching the throne. The exile the king. The lump of an animal hoof the petals of a human hand.
LITTLE BOY (From the chintz armchair): How far he must have flown, that big old bird now sitting in the armchair!
ABBESS: Touch me!
THIRD UNKNOWN ANIMAL: It has happened. Forgive me!
ABBESS: There is nothing to forgive, my child.
THIRD UNKNOWN ANIMAL (Withdrawing its hoof): You forgive your child, Mother. But do the others, the world?
LITTLE GIRL (From the chintz armchair): Yes, they commit that which is forbidden. They will do unto you that which must never be done unto anyone.

The first stage darkens. The third tableau. A middle-aged dancing couple. Slow waltz. The pair begin to turn round. Curtain. No applause.

ABBESS: I think we should let human nature have its way after all!
GENTLEMAN IN WIG: We have already permitted more than enough.
OLD BIRD: We birds, too, have already permitted you more than enough!
ABBESS: Well, then let us fly a little! Straight into the sunset. Is this how you imagined it? The entire respected company . . .

LITTLE BOY (From the armchair): I have touched you.
LITTLE GIRL: You have touched me.
LITTLE BOY: This is what it is all about. The whole performance.
LITTLE GIRL: I am touching you.
LITTLE BOY: You are touching me.
LITTLE GIRL: The time of the world is drawing to its close.
LITTLE BOY: But at least until then.
LITTLE GIRL: Yes, even until then.
LITTLE BOY: How far has he flown, that big old bird now sitting in the big armchair!
LITTLE GIRL: I have touched you.
LITTLE BOY: I can't feel it!
LITTLE GIRL: I have touched you.
ABBESS: Yes, yes, the entire respected company! (Toward the big old bird) Straight into the sun. (Obsequiously) Is this how you imagined it? (Graciously) Or are you too tired to do it?

The interior curtain rises. Another tableau should be there, but the stage is bare.

SERVANT GIRL (With an enormous handkerchief covering her eyes and nose, awkwardly totters onto the lower stage, where for the first time no one is asleep. First unknown animal embraces her comfortingly.)
FIRST UNKNOWN ANIMAL: Don't cry, don't be afraid. By the time it gets here, the war will be as gentle as the sunset. What's more, as gentle as hope.

The big old bird goes up a little wooden staircase to the empty inner stage, where the tableaux have been performed.

OLD BIRD: Exercising my right to the last word, let me say only: "Lean ye bravely upon the air." (Exit.)
ABBESS (Following the bird onto the stage): Lean ye bravely upon nothingness. (Exit.)
FIRST UNKNOWN ANIMAL (Already from the inner stage): My eyes and my pelt are each other's enemies. Yet I manage to see with the one and I am kept warm by the other. It is the first time in my life that I have ever been a guest, and already the war is upon us. I ought in fact to be screaming, yet I am happy nonetheless. (Exit.)
SECOND UNKNOWN ANIMAL: Everything here has been as beautiful as in my childhood, when I did not yet know that nothing in creation resembles me. For as the sun goes down, and the enemy troops approach in the horizontal rays, I am beginning to believe, yes, increasingly I believe that there is hope. (Exit.)

ABBESS (Returning to the inner stage): Perhaps we should let human nature have its way after all. In a word: Before the last judgment reaches us here, let us accept our chef's suggestion.
THIRD UNKNOWN ANIMAL: Mother!
ABBESS: My child!

We must feel that this is truly a mother-child relationship. The sound of marching soldiers can be heard in the distance.

FIRST UNKNOWN ANIMAL: As the world falls gradually to pieces and the final noise of battle draws near, so I become increasingly entitled to my invitation, I, who have settled down at the round table which in earthly terms is called a celebration.
ABBESS (In fear caused by a sudden realization): Take the chairs and move up onto the stage! This stage, you see, does not exist. Only if you move up here can you escape the passing of time, the wrath of God, and the approaching war!

Some move up onto the inner stage, others remain below.

SECOND UNKNOWN ANIMAL (In the name of those who remained below): We, who have remained below, have a preference for obscurity, for the throes of death over life and death.
FIRST UNKNOWN ANIMAL (On behalf of those who have moved into the eternity of the stage): We, on the other hand, have a preference for the extraterritoriality of the stage and heaven.

Light on the inner stage, darkness on the lower level.

ABBESS (Letting herself down the staircase, in the half-light between the two levels): You have taken your decision. Some have chosen this, others that.
THIRD UNKNOWN ANIMAL: I am alone, Mother, though you have called me your child.
ABBESS: I, too, am perfectly alone, my child.

The sound of marching soldiers comes nearer and its blare extinguishes everything. Then a few chords on the piano.

CURTAIN

"Creative Imagination" in Our Time[1]

The task set by the title of this lecture surpasses my powers. I can but offer a series of reflections, without a knowledge of more profound interrelations.

If I understand him aright, Baudelaire draws a sharp distinction between fancy and imagination. Fancy wanders imprisoned in the more dilute medium of the surface, in the freer combinations of fantasy. By contrast the "creative imagination"—insofar as it is combinative—is known by the term analysis for its combinations and strives beyond the insights gained through analysis for that ultimate, unanalyzable simplicity whither the imagination can *find its way home* only at the cost of unconditional obedience. There is no such thing, in a literal sense, as artistic creation. But the obedient imagination may find it possible to establish contact with that absolute freedom, love, immanence, and familiarity with which God chose the world.

In short, what we call "creative imagination" is nothing else than the sacrifice of the imagination: it is *passive creation* (by comparison, fancy is imagination's venial sin, its chronic childhood disease).

As my choice of words has already revealed, for me art is fundamentally religious in origin, and this is perhaps why I feel that every expressly religious work—even a masterpiece—is in a sense a paraphrase. (More concretely: if it is recognized that all art is truly rooted in religion, religious art cannot really be said to exist, least of all religious literature, given the proximity of the sacred texts.)

But what, then, is the ineluctably religious core of art?

I believe that with our Fall not only did our intellect grow duller, not only did our will become disposed to evil-doing; our imagination, too, fell into sin with us, flawing as it were the reality of the world, its incarnation, that final fulfillment and consummation which in creation was originally and naturally entrusted to our imagination.

Our Fall reduced the reality of creation to the irreality of mere existence. *Since then*, art has been *imagination's morality*, its contribution, its arduous toiling toward the fulfillment and restitution of the reality and incarnation of creation. "Et incarnatus est"—*since then*, this could be the final sentence, the authenticating seal of every masterpiece.

The fulfillment of this incarnation is wholly spiritual in nature, and like prayer or love, freely permeates the most diverse stations of time. It has a distinct preference for the past and especially for that in the past which is tragic, irreparable, outrageous, and "insoluble." It prays for its dead by incarnating them.

Much has been written on the kinship of mysticism and art. In fact these two are one by being perfect opposites: they are perfectly coinciding branches of the same road, of the same love, ascending from and descending into the same world in the dynamic equilibrium and inscrutable peace of sacrificial obedience and liberated ecstasy. Jacob's ladder, with God's angels ascending and descending, is the shared, and only, means whereby imagination finds its way home.

If we now consider our own time, we find that the fate of our imagination is rather disquieting and tragic. I would not go so far as to say that it has renounced its arduous mission for good, but it has undoubtedly strayed onto heretical paths, taking the wrong turning. It succumbed to its original weakness when it began to covet the *certainty* of the sciences. Imagination has since then led a mirror-existence, striving to experience in the certainty of style that which should be attainable only in the self-forgetfulness of obedience, only "with eyes downcast."

Whether it meant to do so or not, scientific thought in art has in a curious way inaugurated a mirror-age, an age of narcissistic elements. It is since then that we speak of good stylists. A new epoch dawned, an epoch that places the stylistic certainty of appearances before the self-forgetful incarnating of the world. We have striven to remove into the mirror all the virtues of the great literatures, from carefully controlled beauty to carefully controlled ecstasy. We see all and know all, what's more we see and know better since then; but would that we were blind and alive—with our backs to the mirror.

When the soul—and with it, the imagination—grows tired, we objectify the world in a style somewhat as love grown tired objectifies the other person in sexuality. The always-creative readiness to shoulder the world's burden is overtaken by the spirit of worldliness, by corporeality, in a word by the spirit of materialism: the vain rule of our incarnation, superficially and temporarily secured —and aggravated—through the freedom of nothingness.

And yet it is paradoxically we, and we alone, who have become truly blind, just as jealousy's thirst for certainty ultimately sees nothing of the other person, corporeality nothing of the body, worldliness, in short, nothing of the world. We have lost sight not only of reality, but even of our chief ambition: the experience of our presence in the world. The modern theater provides a striking illustration of this.

One fine day we awoke to the realization that what happens on the stage is *nowhere present*. It is as if the action had lost its predicate. All mimicry—adjectives, nouns, participles—became useless with the disappearance of that which is capable of realizing and establishing the action vertically, with the strength of the *hic et nunc*. It was out of this totally horizontal drama that the theater of the absurd sought a way out. Its failure, however, is patent. If in a desacralized and deincarnated world I choose the verticality of the verb, this action becomes identical with the moment of suicide and assassination, with that moment's dimensionless chasm. In order to gain some sort of life the *adjectives* of the theater of the absurd have thus to be stolen—painfully and with much difficulty—from here and there, in the same way as the *verbs* of the theater of mimicry. They both suffocate in the same lack of air. The one wanders in the desert of its adjectives without ever really happening; the other, apart from happening, has really no other possibilities. The only difference between them is that one attempts to deceive "vertically," the other "horizontally."

We wanted to be present at all costs, and it is our very presence that we have chiefly destroyed.

It is certainly true that in the mirror everything is more intensely together. What falls outside it appears to be nothing, but it is just this "nothing" that is alone worthwhile. And since it is precisely this "alone worthwhile" that has turned into a desert, all the treasures and surprises of the mirror are as nothing to us.

The mirror does, however, have one great and disastrous advantage: it can be infinitely manipulated. Today, when art protests against the various kinds of manipulation, it fails to notice that it has itself been guilty of this much earlier, and that it is its mirror-existence that makes possible its unfortunate flexibility, its unhappy instability, its readiness for every kind of illusory rebirth.

The question thus remains: can we break the mirror by our strength alone? I do not know. Hardly. All I do know is that God from time to time bleeds through the fabric of history, and by the grace of the situation man once more becomes obedient. Today Auschwitz is a museum. The dents and scratches that can be seen on the objects piled up in the showcases are the hieroglyphics of our century, of life itself. An eternal lesson. Those who "wrote down" these signs perhaps never managed to compose their sentences: further evidence of how far real things fall outside the calculable bounds of personal achievement. Real value (beyond the chaos of publications, in the eternal peace and stillness of communication) is a table that is laid, where everyone is welcome and everyone can eat his fill without depriving anyone else of his share. In the context of the divine: it is usually one person who lives out the value and someone else who may write it up. Does it matter? It is God and God alone who writes, on the fabric of actions or on paper.

I am thinking aloud. Just as there is no individual salvation, so there is no collective salvation either. And yet the interpersonal nature of an act of kindness, universal in its directness, is always the concretization of everyone's presence in the "other person." Similarly, in the drama of the imagination there is no way out without the shouldering of the most extreme lapses. If it is at all possible to determine the rightful place of the "religious artist" today, it can only be in the position of infinite patience and brotherly sharing. And it is perhaps because we have all, without exception, reached the farthest possible point from here, that we have come closest to the realization of an "evangelical aesthetics." We cannot today confound God's incarnation in time with God's final coming. Our faith can in no way be unresponsive to that deathly infirmity for which the God of defeat alone can offer remedy, that public human defeat in which the unsurpassably intimate, divine counterpart of resurrection was from the beginning included.

For us it is not difficult to realize that in the last resort everyone at all times is working on the same harvest, even the literature of deincarnation and of the manipulators, and speeding up the drama—the drama of our imagination, of our incarnation—toward the *dénouement*, even if only by straying from the path of righteousness.

☆

In 1967 I happened to meet André Frenaud on the Boulevard Saint-Germain and we sat down to have an espresso. There we sat at the café table, both of us gray and neatly combed, like two inspectors of flour mills, while outside the unkempt masses just risen from their beds undulated by, half-naked and in fantastic garb. It was then that I truly understood that the literature of the mirror—to remain faithful to glass as the raw material of the metaphor—became ultimately and necessarily the literature of the test tube when it chose the assailing intensity of the moment and was irredeemably left behind the street's disproportionately more monstrous possibilities.

It is well known that on his deathbed Rilke dismissed with a single impatient wave of the hand all that his pen had created—his works and his letters. It is also well known that all his life (with a mortal presentiment and sense of justice, as it were) he was especially drawn to simple, unlettered folk, and the peasant girl, the only person he allowed near his sickbed, had not the slightest idea of who it was she was tending in his last agony. This beautiful and tragic document proves two things to me. First, that the role of our imagination far transcends the bounds of art, and second, that it is not enough to love and praise simplicity: we must ourselves find our way back into its self-forgetfulness. But this moving document, which exemplifies the constantly recurring trial and encounter of (in Rilke) consciousness and (in the peasant girl) unconsciousness, for me also somehow represents the two Europes.

While one half of our continent has for centuries been writing the drama of the individual, of freedom, and of complexity, the other half has been testifying through the ages to the hardships of community, of oppression, and of the simple human fate. I shall give but one example. Western art left behind the potential world of motionlessness in the thirteenth and fourteenth centuries and through the Renaissance and the Baroque's storm of movement painted canvases full of the problematics of freedom, while in the East the icons remained motionless, and only the ebb and flow of their intensity testified to all that they found inexpressible in time.

It would be easy to conclude just from this one example that for a long time the West has been preoccupied with the problems of freedom and the individual, while the East has been concerned with those of oppression and collectivism. But this is not true either, not in the past nor in the present. In the last century it was a Dostoevsky in the East and in the present century a Simone Weil in the West who wrote the most authentic accounts of the individual and of the human masses, respectively. The truly "obedient ones" knew and gave news of all things at all times. Only superficially are there two Europes (more precisely, three: I would say Central Europe is the third, it being the scene of the other two's dramatic confrontation). In reality the drama of the imagination is one and indivisible. And although on the surface—with the postponing of salvation—there is a welter of the most diverse variations and improvisations of errings and errors in the interplay of the mirror and our daily life, deep down the unity is unbroken, the burden is carried, justice is loved, the continuity of awe and obedience remains. It is true that this unity and continuity is only occasionally called art, only occasionally literature. Does it matter? In the true history of the imagination silence is sometimes more important than all the sentences that have ever been written.

And here—finally—I have in mind that imageless imagination, that ultimate and inexhaustible source, that brotherly stillness of imagination, which no sort of noise can silence.

[1] A speech delivered at the International Conference on Poetic Imagination held at Poigny in October 1970. The translation is based on the version in *Crater* (*Kráter*, 1976).

"An Autobiography"

I was born on the 27th of November 1921, under the sign of Sagittarius. My right palm, it seems, could readily be that of a common criminal, while the lines on my left indicate order and a talent of sorts.

Looking at childhood photographs, faithful to the faded reality, I see my sister holding sway over me with her mermaid beauty, while I grew up, ultimately, in the peace of subjection, under her auspices without the slightest ruffle, like some hothouse plant that might otherwise have died. It could hardly have been called living, but I felt everything that was done to me, and especially what happened around me, so intensely that I shuddered with cold.

I was looked after by a Mother Superior of a convent, so I spent most of my childhood among primitive nuns and half-institutionalized, half-imprisoned underage prostitutes. A dress that is too loose or too short—with its impersonality, by the wearer's arm, say, being too long for the sleeve—to this day still attracts me in unnameable ways. As I looked about, however, an element that could be called both personal and everyday was perhaps overly precocious. The nuns and institutionalized girls, who embraced me countless times and sometimes even burst into loud sobbing, obviously not on my account, marked me for life. Meanwhile I just looked at the trees, or simply at the sun, without feeling the slightest compulsion to understand.

Awakening with my adolescence, my bent for poetry was wholly different from the nature of my childhood. Here, on the piece of paper, I was preoccupied with the *solution*, at least for a time, and perhaps it is only now that I am beginning to suspect that Sister Pia and Sister Alexia, or Krecsa and Micsicsák, by being with me without beginning and embracing me, and then unexpectedly and finally disappearing, gave me almost the only Alpha and Omega in the growing chaos of my life.

For me poetry is not an ultra-linguistic phenomenon; it is, rather, infra-linguistic or sub-linguistic, just as life itself remains under the surface of the entirety of the universe. For me the poet inhabits a casemate; for him the bare act of touching is more important than what he has managed to put his finger on (one thinks of Hölderlin and Don Juan); he wishes to encounter the entirety of the world in such a way that he is increasingly content with what has been left at the bottom of the plate. I have been aware of only four such artists in recent times. One is Dostoevsky, another Simone Weil, the third Witold Gombrowicz,[1] and the fourth Robert Wilson, when he staged his "Le regard du sourd."

Before the war my timidity—which to an outsider may have seemed more like a disease—briefly attracted me to heresies. I did not regret this then and do not regret it now, nor am I ashamed of it. However, the war and the collective shock that followed impelled me without wanting it back into communality, into average life and thus into average humanity.

I did not live through, or endure, the war; it became mine. It gave back to me poverty's words and the anonymous poet's touch, and with it, of course, the corner of the floor, which was mostly not enough even to sleep on.

It is a peculiar scandal and resolution of my life that its most immediate shock was caused by Germans, while my mother was herself German. Even in civilian dress my father looked like a First World War officer. Every part of his body—

hands, feet, brow, and concave stomach—seemed so lonely, as only the backs of certain men can be when they are leaving home. Mother, however, was an arbor, a grove of trees until she died.

In the course of my life, at least for as long as they could stand it, I have been surrounded by many, many people. An old aunt, for example, who never really learned to speak because of a childhood accident. I, the child, tried to teach her, but it seemed to be of little use. Then once, weeks later, taking my face in her hands, she uttered for the first time the word we had practiced in vain for several days: "Tree."

My father was hewn out of a single block of stone, which explains both his goodliness and his occasional explosive brutality. He had, too, a few unfortunate principles. He never raised a finger to my sister after the age of ten because "one should never beat a girl." But he would beat me hard and indiscriminately. I have often since dreamed of his fist, as it was when it shattered me and also as it was when, clumsily open, it tried to put me together again, something that had even by then been impossible for many years.

---

[1] Gombrowicz (1904-70) is a Polish novelist and playwright, whose first play, *Yvonne, Princess of Burgundy*, written in 1938 and first performed in Kraców in 1957, is sometimes considered a significant precursor of the Theater of the Absurd. His works were influenced by existentialism and expressed the view that humans are never independent of their environment. The themes of his plays are developed in an allegorical, fairy-tale setting.

Ágnes Nemes Nagy

Nemes Nagy was born in Budapest on January 3, 1922, not long after her parents had left the family's traditional home in Transylvania because that region had been separated from Hungary and joined to Rumania by the Treaty of Trianon. Her ancestors were chiefly lawyers and ministers of the Reformed Church, and, according to family legend, one of the ministers was sentenced to the galleys in the seventeenth century for not renouncing his religious convictions. The legendary behavior of her grandfather during the nineteenth century was very real, however: rising suddenly from the family table, he would go off for months to Egypt or Jerusalem, Paris or London, and when asked why he was about to leave for Denmark, he replied: "Because I have never been there." A book on Egypt from his library gave Nemes Nagy, when an adolescent, an acquaintance with the Pharoah Akhenaton, who became a crucial symbol of human progress in her later poetry. Her father, like her grandfather, was a lawyer. Having been forced to leave all possessions behind, her parents arrived in Budapest impoverished. Like so many in those days after World War I, the family lived in a box car for a time, and, at first, found it difficult to adjust to the life of the big city.

Nemes Nagy's early years contributed in major ways to her literary development, though her poems are not autobiographical. Her mother played the piano expertly, and the home contained several other musical instruments, including an alpine horn. Her mother read avidly and randomly; books of all kinds, including detective novels and the works of Jules Verne, were stacked high on her nightstand, and copies of *The Bulletin of Natural Science* (*Természettudományi*

Közlöny) were always at hand. This environment gave the poet a sense of rhythm and an early consuming interest in reading and natural science. Her many visits to the provinces, especially to the Great Plain, left lasting impressions on her. She speaks of long summers, Easter holidays, and Christmases spent with relatives, and particularly remembers times with an uncle in Northeastern Hungary whose farm consisted purely of dunes "where by the time the horse had pulled the wagon up the hill, it was wading in sand over its pastern." She recalls vast forests that were not gloomy but "cheerful, full of sunshine, and filled with glades of daisies" and "where stags, deer, badgers, and boar leaped across forest trails." She enjoys similarly warm memories of "an aunt baking bread, a kerosene lamp, horses, dogs and cats, much playing, tree-climbing, and tending of geese." She vividly recollects the Tisza River, where she learned to swim and row, and where she observed "the flowering of the Tisza," a phenomenon occurring when large swarms of May flies soar above the river to blanket everything for just a single day; and she also remembers "scorching summers, outings on the prairie, a flood, and merry young relatives dancing." Later, the beauty of Lake Balaton and its environs, located not far from Budapest, reinforces these natural experiences; and the Budapest setting harmonizes warmly and tenderly with both natural settings, especially "its streets, each cast-iron lamppost, its doorways, and its churches," not to mention the neighborhood of Kristina Square, the Southern Railroad Station, and Castle Hill.

A student who enjoyed school from the beginning, she singles out with special fondness the years at an excellent high school conducted for girls by the Reformed Church and containing, as she notes, "something of the spirit of old Calvinist colleges"; and she speaks affectionately and gratefully about its director, the poet Lajos Áprily, who was the first to give critical and encouraging attention to her attempts at writing poetry. A day-boarder, she participated in what she calls the "good life" of the school: "the student pranks, the discussions, the absorbing adolescent conversations, gymnastics, sports, holidays, and language lessons," all of which led her to conclude that "everyone is gifted until the age of eighteen." Her "literary hobby," very strong by then, was accepted by those around her, and if she had any trouble with physics, the teachers "prompted" her. Playing Cyrano, she conscientiously obtained a large papier-mâché nose, but, persuaded by her schoolmates' furious protests that it made her look "inexpressibly ugly" and would reduce the audience to stitches, she performed in her own "tiny nose" to no one's distraction.

During her high school years, she wore her "own face for the most part," but during her years at the university, she was "incognito." Expecting the faculty to be intimately involved with literature, she found, instead, that it was, even in the best instances, interested only in literary scholarship, a factor that made her conclude that she learned much less there than in high school. She survived by reading and writing on her own. For her dissertation topic, she chose the poetic diction of Mihály Babits, who was still living then, but the outbreak of the war prevented her from completing the project.

Marrying during the war, she was with her husband at his army post in a small village in 1944, when the Hungarian Nazi Party, the Arrow-Cross, took power and "every loudspeaker in town boomed the horrible news." She and her husband then returned under authorization to Budapest, where he never reported for duty. The life about them soon turned into complete chaos and left an indelible mark on her: "hiding, aliases, police raids, the siege of Budapest, my husband's imprisonment—this is that 'war material' which ever since I have not been able to avoid in my poems." She adds: "I saw the war up close. I buried dead soldiers and horses. Tank battles, coal bins, snow, hunger. This is the most important and untimely experience of the writers of my generation. We—unfortunately—participated in history extensively." She obtained a teaching certificate in Hungarian and Latin at the University of Budapest in 1944, served on the staff of *Public Education* (*Köznevelés*), a pedagogical journal, from 1945 to 1953, and taught Hungarian and other subjects at the Petőfi High School from 1953 to 1957. After that she devoted herself entirely to writing.

Nemes Nagy participated fully and enthusiastically in literary life from 1945 to 1948. Along with other young writers of the time, she served on the staff of *New Moon* (*Újhold*), a journal concerned with the development of contemporary literary currents and edited by her husband, Béla Balázs. She published her first book of poems, *In Two Worlds* (*Kettős világban*), in 1946. Winning the Baumgartner Prize with this work enabled her and her husband to visit Rome and Paris, both cities offering invaluable artistic and scenic resources for her creativity. Of this period of exciting ferment in Hungarian literature, she says: "This literary spring lasted for three years, and then came '48, the year of change. The *New Moon* was terminated, for its anti-fascistic middle-class and humanistic tendency was no longer considered adequate." She was silent for about ten years, a period she used, however, to rigorously search for a fresh and true voice, and also to translate extensively from past and present lyric poetry of the world and from the works of French classical authors, Rilke, Brecht, and Dylan Thomas, among others; selections of these translations were published in a volume appropriately entitled *Journeyman Years* (*Vándorévek*) in 1964. The year 1956, the year of the Revolution, was another turning point in her career. After the fierce turmoil and the battles in the streets, there came, she reports, a slowly settling situation, and writers long silent began speaking up and expressing their own ideas in individualistic ways. In the context of these events, she says about herself:

> I really am not a political creature; existence concerns me first and foremost: life and death, man and nature, morality and ideas. But it cannot be denied that my literary career—like that of every other writer under the wide sky—is closely connected to turning-points of history. God forgive me, but I want much less of history for myself than has been my share up to now.

Faithful to this concept of herself and her creativity, during her long career she has constantly addressed crucial issues of human existence of her own choosing and in her distinctively uncompromising style. Her second volume of poetry, *Heat Lightning* (*Szárazvillám*), was published in 1957, and her third, *Solstice* (*Napforduló*), appeared in 1967, to be followed in 1969 by a collected edition of poems, *The Horses and the Angels* (*A lovak és az angyalok*), for which she was awarded the prestigious Attila József Prize. In addition, she has published several books of verses for children, including *Purple Swallow* (*Lila fecske*, 1965), which respect their intelligence. Lately she has undertaken the writing of essays, a genre that she found difficult until she "learned how to write prose sentences and to express ideas, not emotions," and at which she persisted because what she had to say "demanded it." They are essays, not studies, for she cannot understand "why it is necessary to speak about literature so boringly as the case is with us so very often." A selection of her essays was published in 1975 with the title *64 Swans* (*64 hattyú*), and in the fall of 1978 she was preparing a volume of recent essays for publication, including her thoughts on the subject of Rilke, the poetic image, and science fiction.

From the very first, her poetic style and aim, as critics quickly noted, have differed markedly from practices customarily followed in Hungarian literature. Despite their being deeply rooted in Hungary's culture, her poems lack a distinctly native diction, and they have a carefully wrought economy beyond that found in the works of any other Hungarian poet, even including those of János Pilinszky, whose poetry, she claims, influenced her considerably. And although her poems are ineradicably grounded on her experiences with the physical horrors and moral shock of the war and the political upheavals that overtook her people shortly thereafter, she does not explain her own views of national social problems or offer set solutions to philosophical or religious questions. Inevitably, her demanding mode of poetic expression and her unrelenting quest for an order rational enough to sustain new hope for the human prospect produced the ten-year gap between the publication of her first and second volumes.

The word *object* has always had a very special significance in her poetic projections of reality, for every object, she insists, contains a quality to be expressed, not merely "a message" but "a certain kind of joy." She maintains that like all poets, she is a materialist living in sensations and thinking and expressing herself in objects "imbued with a certain kind of spirit, a certain soul." Her increasing use of concrete objects, often descriptively, endows her verses with an impersonality and intellectuality suggestive of the metaphysical poets. Driven by the impulse to think and thus to fix her eye on a reality between anxiety and knowledge, she purposely reduces personal elements in her poems, choosing images of nature, urban life, and science with their own "spirit" instead of stating her thoughts and emotions abstractly. To such objective materials, she eventually adds, at first seemingly by chance, mythic resources to shape her grapplings with "man's extremest relations with life, death, and God." The most recent of these is the figure of Akhenaton, whose mythic attributes as the first perceiver of a visible monotheism, a social revolutionary, and a contributor to the origin of a living visual art as opposed to its static form, make him capable of carrying the most urgent problems of the twentieth century: "Morality and death, materialism and resurrection—his character can take all this upon itself. He offers us the outlook of man seeing for the first time." Not surprisingly, the achievement of such concreteness within the confines of the restricted verse forms she uses requires a highly deliberate process of composition. When she first sees the poem she is creating, it is, she says, half as wide as the Milky Way; then, over a long period of time, she casts away the inessential, selecting one simile out of eighty, selecting two memories out of one-hundred-twenty until only a "few lingering helium atoms" remain. This disciplined method brought to her, in the middle of her life, the additional awareness that in lyric poetry structure itself can be used to express thought and emotion, because a lyric poem has an inner imagistic structure "hovering on the edges of the consciousness which [the poet] seeks to approach with words, or rather between lines."

This disciplined application of the craft and the progressively impersonal and intellectual tone of her poems are related to an intense desire to limit the influence of emotion on her poetry, a desire founded on the conviction that, as she said in a 1978 radio interview, the members of her generation were fed on "emotional humbug" and had, in effect, thought with their emotions rather than their minds. Wishing to free herself from this bondage, she strove to eliminate "the heart" from her verses and permitted the words of emotion to re-enter her poems only after a long passage of time. Eventually she lessened this mistrust by learning to feel with the mind as she recognizes "the emotion of the intellect in the face of senselessness [in human existence]" as well as "the emotion of humanity in the face of inhumanity." Consequently, a lyric poem takes on the mood, the atmosphere of intellectualism, but seldom reasons; it suggests, instead, and to be successful, it can develop "no train of thought without a strong strain of emotion." The ultimate duty of poets, she claims, is "to enlarge the range of emotional knowledge" for humankind. To this end, poets, constantly concerned with the obscure parts of the consciousness, perceive names for the previously nameless, a view which she supports with a quotation from Rilke: "We plant our feet at our limits and snatch to ourselves the Nameless."

Her poems face the collapse of a world built on prewar value systems. The cruel coursing of events has estranged humankind from both itself and the surrounding order as it has steadily alienated humans from their ideals. In her poems she attempts to reconstruct ideals of "life, death, and God," which involve not just philosophical but "emotional questions." According to her, human reality consists of isolation, anxiety, and a distressing sense of the absurdities of existence. But instead of simply reflecting the relations between humans and their world, her verses reveal the deepest conflicts of the soul as it struggles to find new, unknown linkages between humankind and reality, a soul studying to learn

> that streak
> where the crystal begins to smoke,
> and the tree swims into the mist,
> as the body into memory.
>
> (Trees [Fák])

They search for the way to experience resurrection, an event that occurs "at the time man rediscovers perception." "I devoutly respect the human species for having climbed down from the trees," she says, and her poems confirm the fundamental importance she attaches to knowledge and the need to rely on the reasoning faculty in order to make the moment of that perception possible. At the very least, she persists in the hope that knowledge will help to reestablish moral order out of the prevailing chaos. And she conceives the emotional power and the demanding intricacy of poetic imagery to be a potentially major instrument in helping human beings to live with a moral sense and an awareness of the eternal in the cosmos.

The pursuit of her art has convinced her that even in light of the painful realities of existence, it is worth living.

> Between morality and terror
> In light and pitch-dark together . . .
>
> (To My Profession [Mesterségemhez])

Amid these tensions, she recognizes the need to be concerned with the direst human experiences, so that the bitterness of life can be faced in ways that uplift the human spirit. She has said that as a poet she would like to be "bitter, like the orange," which, though containing all the bitter flavors, so effectively disguises them that "they strengthen the sweetness." And often she becomes "this bitterest fruit of all" as she strives to reconcile harmoniously humans and their alien world, the human personality and the conditions under which it must define itself. An affecting instance offers consolation to all humanity amid profound bitterness:

> A bird sits on my shoulder
> that was with me born.
> Already it is so large, so heavy
> I stumble with every step.
>
> Weight, weight upon me, lameness;
> I would push it off, it clings to me;
> Like an oak tree its roots,
> it digs its claws into my shoulder.

I hear it, next to my ear
its bird heart beats frightfully;
Should it fly away some day,
By now I'd fall down without it.
                    (Bird [Madár])

Trees

One must learn. The winter trees.
Frost-covered to their feet.
Immovable curtains.

One must learn that streak
where the crystal begins to smoke,
and the tree swims into the mist,
as the body into memory.

And the river past the trees,
the wild duck's silent wings,
and the blind-white blue night
in which hooded objects stand.
One must learn the trees'
unutterable deeds.

Night Oak

It happened at night; the passer-by
heard something and turned around:
an oak tree was following him.

He stopped and waited. The oak came,
its roots freshly pulled,
still earth-covered, undulating on long snake-feet
onto the asphalt road,
like an ungainly mermaid, straining.
Its outsize head brushed
the silent shutters of the shops;
when it reached the passer-by
it leaned against the lamppost,
then it tossed aside its hair.
From behind the hair, an oak tree's face stared.

Large, mossy face. Perhaps. Or some other kind.
The passer-by then felt
his own contours slacken,
a fog floated over his liquid shores,
like someone suddenly
darkening into a forest lake,
because a face like that he could reflect.

And they both breathed.
There were a few birdnests in the oak's hair,
birds sleeping in them, as if heedlessly
forgotten there.
                For it was urging.
So urgingly, motionless it stood,
a message in oak form
growing weary undeciphered.

It let its curtain of hair drop into place.
Turned around. Started to move. Strange feet.
It carried its nests, its birds,

and before the hardening gaze
of the passer-by,
was sprinkled with sparkles from the row of neon lights.
Waiting is the abandoned pit
where it will heal again.

The Horses and the Angels

They Are Coming

Welcome, lovely angels.
I offer you apples stored for winter.
Who sent you here to comfort me?
Here's a Jonathan, here's a Batul.[1]
How I feared you might strike
your foreheads against the lintel,
and how could I nurse a broken angel?
What luck attended you on the way!
Like the flame of an oil lamp, you have
shrunk your angelhood.

They Are Going

Ariel arose first,
who sings in the choir.
Raphael arose next.
Don't go yet, please.—I must go.
Then Gabriel, the one with steps
billowy from youth and indolence
started.—Don't leave yet.—His face
was fuzzy like a pussy willow.
Michael was the last to leave,
His hair wiry and steel-gray,
an angel like the fathers.
—I'll grab the tip of your cowl;

the apple was mushy, I know,
but there is no other, none, none—stop!
Michael left anyway.

Road

Shoe a horse for me, smithy,
so it may take me home at last.
This milk-steed will do.

We'll stop at the pastry shop,
there for the last time I'll look in
as if through dusk's casement;
how the pastries glisten,
the many heavenly marzipans—

and then everything is drab,
and no one sees us.
Only the horses' pounding hooves, a dull drumming,
as if a heart were throbbing, grow distant.

Slowly we wade on,
some water, some trees,
some leafy muteness,
perhaps some rustling,
a runner under leaf-domes,
perhaps a river in the wilderness,
but I don't know—everything is nameless—
I bend down. So the branches won't reach me.
I hug the horse's neck.

The Horses and the Angels

Finally nothing remains,
only the angels and the horses.
The horses stand in the courtyard,
The angels are in my room;
they lounge around, sometimes seeming a hundred—
what does one do by himself?
Paws the ground and desists,
or flaps his wings at times
like a bird cooling itself.

They just stand; there is nothing more,
only the spectacle, only the vision,
only legs, only wings—the road, the sky.
The remote dwells within them,
they are so far, so near.
Perhaps they will not leave me.

[1] A wintering apple, like the Jonathan, but native to Transylvania.

Fig Trees

Scrubby
Fig trees
Motionless moonlight

Under the trees   under the moon
A tinkling herd of goats advances
The figs are ringing now
Their seeds jingling in their hollow hulls
Only the black-bronze
Clanging of the vast sky is silent

Silence
Vibrating
From the ore

Breath

Do not abandon me, air;
let me breathe deeply,
then angel's robes flutter
silvery in my chest,
like x-ray images.

Give me a silver poplar;
then, my face thrust into quivering boughs,
let me blow my breath on it,
and it blow back unceasingly
my new untainted life,
while between our faces hovers
the eternity of a breath.

Formerly

Formerly a tulip grew there.
It clashed with a foxglove;
a field of wild oats billowed,
then rippling, it calmed down at night
and like the glimmer of the buoy lamp
poppies gleamed above it.
A tulip was there formerly.
But now, secretly a tree grows
inside it; I didn't notice it before, no;

but now I feel the rough trunk
within the stalk, and rootlets
rooting in its capillaries,
its massive wave gathering
to form slowly the annual rings.
In the night I awake startled
at the swishing of the vast foliage.
Beside it, all else is mere weed.
But its name—that I do not know.

Akhenaton

*"You rise and you set,
living sun.
Dark you pass away and bright
you return.
You beat in my heart."*

*(From Akhenaton's Hymn
to the sun)*

From the Notes of Akhenaton

*I must do something still undone:
I must deal with pain.
I ought to make a god
to sit on high seeing all.*

*The desire is no longer enough,
I must build a solid sky.
So, Almighty, take my shoulder,
I'll help you rise, and as you limp
to your throne, lean on some cherubs.
Don't worry, I shall clothe you,
so the night won't see you naked.
I fasten suffering around your neck*

*like a circlet of blood appearing,
and make my love of plants your warm cape.
In your bejeweled heart I settle this:
I always strive for justice.*

*Enough. Find it good,
and perform your mighty offices;
sit and stare through all eternity.
I can no longer postpone you.*

Akhenaton's Night

When he went down to the square, the tents
were swimming in lantern-light,
candles stood in necks of bottles,
a summer All-Hallows-Day light,
on shelves dusty
pink crêpe-paper dolls.

He passed by mounds of olive-green melons,
on every rind a scarred heart
tattooed by knitting needles.
Above, the waving hair of neon lights.
Hot wind. Some straw.
It was dark that night.

He went imbedded
in his disguised presence,
he went motionless, an elevated train
sped by above.

*Wash your face,
Bend to your cupped hands,
Bend over a palmful of water,
the will is striated,
make it drink like a bird,
make it drink like a beast,
wash, wash your face, and the sun—
each beam ending in a tiny hand—
then the sun's hand
your face shall . . .*

Ágnes Nemes Nagy

Night. Its tents, grown heavy,
pitched themselves among the lights.
Counters gleaming like ribbon candy
or glow worms, candles
flickering at rush of wind.

In the old garden.
In the garden the unnumbered
under a sky Host-luminous—
make a feast of the other—The face,
the green flower, the elder branch
on which Judas hanged himself,
and the green glimmer of a single star.
In the garden was the immeasurable.
If only you were small, my love,
as God in the Host.

Then the tanks came.
                    The street fled
the cresting metal waves between stone banks,
soft bodies fled between metal and stone,
some still streaming balloons here and there,
canvas-tear of falling booths,
splash of bridge railings,
distant ashes, shower of glass
and between roarings another sound above,
another sound above,
up, up, above the whole planet.

He hurled himself over a parapet
along with the others,
jerking, jolting they tumbled down,
above distant volleys, they one upon the other
like an avalanche.

He woke up to fog.
He lay on a shore among the reeds.
Beside him, a body in the mud
Laid out so cool, so flat

it seemed a special snow had fallen on it.
He rose easily,
like smoke,
rose up from beside it, or from within it,
so transparent where he lay.
He rose and he lay down without effort.

And he carried the body on setting out,
carrying it dimly.
He went through the fog's sprawling horizontals.
His right hand
           holding his left.

When

When I carved a God
I chose hard stone.
Harder than my body,
that I may believe when he consoles me.

The Only-Good

Is the Only-Good neither fish nor fowl?
I am no Manichean.
I would never tire
of eternal bliss.

Akhenaton in the Sky

Everything is the same there. The mine,
The mountain split asunder, the tools.
He touches the limestone wall
and the dawn comes uncertainly
from within the thin surface of the cliffs;
the stone, the iron translucent
with final failure.

Through the forest
the fog drifts in patches.
Five fingers like lost hands stretch out
or reach upward sweepingly.
Not finding their meaning,
they wanly touch the earth;

they grow, they fall,
these long cloud trunks,
another forest moves among the trees,
eddying other foliage.

A tunnel under the trees.
Shaded grass, pebbles:
narrow gauge rail line in the dawn.
The sun rises steaming
cutting into the mist,
with the mute rumble coming nearer, nearer.
The metal sparkles under the grass;
Morning scintillates
but suddenly a wall of shrubs springs up,
for there the rails end.
Then only a few sleepers
stagger on—
the sun stops in the clearing.

It is forenoon. There tall plants grow.
There the vast meadow of camomile lies still,
a few metal fragments scattered in it,
a honey-comb denseness above it,
an unruffled Milky Way
with white-rayed plant-suns and no wind.
Always. Forever. High noon.

The Objects

High aloft, slabs of stone stand in the noon light.
In my heart happy are the objects.

Above the Object

Because there is light above every object.
Trees shimmer like Northern Lights.
And glimmering infinity, come
the ninety-two elements in caps of light
on each one's brow its own reflection—
I believe in the resurrection of the body.

Dusk

I love matter,
and often think of my bones.
The vein throbbing in my neck
easily drives the living blood.
I struggle with life each day,
but my strong lungs and heart triumph.
My tresses fall rich unbound: I can't
yet believe they will be thin.

The wondrous hours—I stretch out
on the large sofa, dangle my foot;
the days evaporate
like small puddles in summer.
One hand boldly reaches
the arch of the dusky sky,
the other opens wide
to these plump lilacs.

Only at such times is the skin smooth,
the throat's tightness eases.
Bones are more important than eyes;
they buttress order securely,
which recovers now, hesitantly, deep within,
measures time in syllables,
and feels the pillow by its face
responding to the throbbing vein.

Landscape: At Home

I can see far from my window,
although sunset brings the fog.
Down there glows the blacksmith's forge
under the frost-covered tin awning.

And there, now approaching, now retreating,
sniffing the smooth road
with its orange-red lamped nose
a streetcar roving in the fog.

*

Like a river, I'm resting in my bed,
in linen hills and valleys.
Slowly transformed from body into time,
I swim from day into night.

In the stillness of the night,
from my shores a bird soars
high, stirring the fog,
and soundlessly wheels above me.

*

Lock the door while you can,
let the wind bicker with the lock.
The silence is uneasy, it cowers—it fears
when it will be rent by sound.

The wall resounds. Someone is walking.
The plaster holds, still uncracked.
The silence cowers, the lock clinks,
The floor resounds. Stand fast.

Combat

What both hands can grip,
The enduring things—I have loved images:
The living yet unfleeting,
The vibrant yet unwavering.
Feet, horses, the gracefully moving,
Have ever throbbed in my life,
And with them I have tried each ascent
In the armor-glow of nocturnal fear.

But when fear turns inward
And his own fate rises against the warrior,
And after slaying dragons he cannot conquer worms,
Suddenly he flings away
The spear both hands had gripped,
Unties the coat of mail, straps fall away,
And he holds his naked body out
To stench and decay.

Transformation of a Railroad Station

It is uncertain
           that there is still earth below where the cobblestones seem xenolithic formations. But it seems that under the stones, under the cables, under the delicate lymphatic system (this pulsating apparatus) there is earth down here after all; in spite of all, there is earth.

Right now, it is a crater. Or an operation. That on a rare, huge zoo animal, with anesthesia, with oversize instruments. Towers of animal innards. Because they are taking this body apart layer by layer. They set the liver and the kidneys aside. Rough, exact movements between butchering and mending.

The wound's periphery is sensitive. Tortured houses—their scaling like a secondary symptom; the stumbling of weary streetcars in the clamped veins: the tacked together interchanges, the stoneless bogs, those bloated rail sutures. And the plants, the completely defenseless ones, whose stems are broken as they are thrown into the trashcan, virtually like the legs of Jesus after his removal from the cross: the plants in their dusty terror.

In the middle, however, the activity. The excavators, the fixed platforms. The engineer up above, like a pilot left suspended. Astronauts in lemon-yellow suits climbing into ditches. In the midst of unbearable noise barriers, the calm of catastrophes, panic-stricken unconcern. A plastic bag on a coil of wire. (The universal food-packages. Paper, plastic, and, here and there, canvas. The textures, the knots and fastenings. Yes, here and there my friends.) And what strange caps: the headgear of whalers or the masks of a ritual. And the gigantic work gloves, these abstract forms mimicking hands.

This is where the central edifice will be. This is where the concourse will be. Here apparatus, information. Here the . . . do you see? Up, where the air cubits are still empty, up, up, the non-existent. Still transparent, still contestable. Far too much wind blows through it. But a good lens would immobilize it. In the right light. After all, such a narrow layer keeps it out, such a narrow layer keeps it from being. So the edges can almost be seen up there, in the space between the certain and the uncertain; so it is almost recognizable, as it slides into the picture, this upside-down depression (huge, hazy hull) with its invisible stories preceding existence.

You still remember, don't you, the turntable in the roundhouse? The railway yard ended in a fieldstone ellipse; there, at the end of the ellipse, was the steel drum. The engine stood on it and turned with it, like a dancing elephant. The old yellow stationhouse is still there, with antiquated but still functioning nostalgia. Lamps behind the curling fog; dawn in the rain. And the night of rails and ties (look at this from above, from the bridge), these glimmering celestial ladders reaching into horizontal infinity.

But turn back. Look again at the construction site. (I mean: among the blocks of events, try to find again that which can be called the present.) Then look at the Vérmező. And above it, the Castle. The peace of practiced survivors. Study them closely (in their retroactive relations also); then scrutinize more explicitly the bend as the hollow nestles at the foot of the hill. So. Now the scene is sharp.

You remember, don't you, when it was completed? You were there when it was done? You were even there at the opening? It was spacious. Competitive. The escalator landings didn't quite . . . but no matter. The control of the tracks. Building blocks. Intersection.

You still remember the lemon-yellow rubber suit, don't you? The universal food-packages? The space between the uncertain and the uncertain? You still remember the Vérmező, don't you? The hollow at the foot of the hill? The retroactive relations? The reconstruction? The building blocks? And the transformation? The aerial port? Do you remember that city?

You were there at the opening?

The Proportions of the Street

But the details: the cats. Because it is clear that the streetcar leans into the curve like an old runner or the earth on the turn of its elliptical orbit, where the simile is not a comparison, purely another face of the same law. The relation of mass and movement—proportions, dependencies, coefficiencies. This can be seen on the street.

This can be seen, if I break down the incidental; the plane of the ellipse is visible, in the morning or at six in the evening, in cloudy weather or under sunlight. If I strip the house, if I uncover the bone, if I denude the district (the vegetation, the climate), then the lines remain, the curves, the network. But the network also is just a diagram, the curve also a hieroglyphic. The law is invisible. This is visible.

And the intersecting points. By these I mean, for example, the intersecting points of the living and the non-living. Two laws. Three laws. Sixteen. Their concurrences. If, therefore, I peel off the incidentals, the stars of the intersecting points and the trajectories streaming from them scintillate, like contrails on a blue-hued fancy.

But the details: as I say, the cats. Although, compared to laws, they are undoubtedly only curled bubbles. Fur balls meant to be blown away; pitching wigs in a flood. Under and behind them, the large basin, the valleys and reliefs, the crumpled mountain chains of watersheds, the geology of known planets. Under them, the comparisons and the measures: the cubic miles, the half-ounces, the large cone-mantle of the earth's shadow in space, the inches, the years, the celestial degrees: foot, dyne, decibel, Monday, Tuesday; consequences, abstractions.

This is clear. The world is so translucent. The house, the asphalt; behind them the metallic frame of the gauges is translucent. They are already coming into focus as in a fade-in on film, another face, another sky.

If I strip away the incidental, the black of celestial charts is behind them: the silver perceptions of a northern sky.

What is the foreground compared to these? The pauper's Bible, surely: image, image, again an image, shape and tendril. Painted in a neat line, displayed on the walls of the cathedral. First the two little naked ones and the apple; next the sweet wings of the angel, the musing sword in his small fist; then the flood, the ark, the peacock; then the grape cluster; then the lamb; further and further: Nehemiah. (And of course behind them the stone wall—lest we forget—the above-mentioned frame, the gauge-buttress, now and then protruding as it elbows into the pattern of the histories.)

Nevertheless . . .
                But I. Only one. Once. To tell a story, after all, of a cat; a cat almost without consequences as it cuts across the street, across, through, athwart the ridges of the gauge systems, as it goes on its four worn eraser-feet, as it moves with the rhythm of its small, protruding shoulder blades, and disappears (a silent cry of independence) between the side of a car and the trunk of a linden tree.

It is no more. It is nothing. Only from a distance—last gesture—do the leaves of its lilac-green eyes reach me.

"Elusive Apple"

How does one ever decide to write poetry? Of what use, after all, is that which we call poetry? In no way am I venturing to answer these fundamental questions here; all I wish—as a poet of sorts—is to raise my head now and then from the unending occupation with the poem and to follow, at least with my eyes, these questions which flash around me threateningly more than once.

Let me attempt an answer right away—even if not a straight answer. I have thought—for some time now—that actually everyone is a poet. Everyone is a poet, even he who has never written a poem, he who has never read or heard a poem, and he who immediately turns off the radio if the program is about poetry. All of us, without exception, are full of unexpressed consciousness, emotions and the tension of barely thought ideas, poem trunks and poem buds—what becomes of these? Generally, nothing more than an exclamation, a half-sentence, or a gesture. The gardener who points to a tree and says "mountain ash," the soccer fan after a goal, the old woman polishing a Jonathan apple, all recite a poem without being aware of it. If it were not so, I would surely say that this not very lucrative profession would have ceased long ago indeed, or, to speak in the idiom of the folk tale, all the poets of the world would have been sewn into a sack and thrown into the Danube. All the more so because until now not a single ambitious undertaking has succeeded in somehow explaining perfectly and understandably just what a good poem is. Still, it seems that there is in mankind a hidden quality which tolerates and sustains poetry. True, this hidden artistic instinct is more gracious to the other arts than to poetry. For example, there is music. I heartily envy the sect of musicians who encompass the earth with the lines of their scores, whose notes fly from Australia to the North Pole. This can hardly be said of the words of poetry. Yet—and God sees our soul—we cannot determine the purpose of music anymore than we can determine the utility of poetry.

But no matter. Let's not be jealous. Let us not envy the subconscious lightning bolts of the other arts. Rather, let's admit that poetry is something like a two-humped camel—like the one I once saw on Soroksári Road. A long line of cars stood and honked, while the camel—this mysterious and stray camel—changed lanes and, glancing with slight disdain at the nervous or petrified drivers, proceeded with calm steps toward the center of the city. Strikingly many associations occurred to me even then about the camel; its symbolism was so unavoidable. So let's use him, let's use the camel of Soroksár as a symbol of poetry. He had two humps, I have said. I came to know these two humps in sequence. What I mean is: over the course of years I had the opportunity to experience unmistakably the dual nature of poetry.

In the beginning was childhood. I have been writing poetry since childhood, like so many others; and, like so many others, completely unself-consciously. This childhood versification is good. No, let's not believe that each child-poet becomes a poet, because then, truly, everyone would be a poet. The child's feeling for poetry is well known. This is the age of rhythmical mumbling, of word-euphoria: the eternal image, source and advocate of one kind of versifying, or perhaps of the writing of poetry itself. Everyone was a poet, thus, at three or four, possibly even earlier. The jumping, singing reciter of meaningful and meaningless words, the prattler of sense and nonsense, the child lives through one of the greatest experiences of human life: the dawn of human speech. He experiences this partly unconsciously, and with an excellent sense of rhythm—in short, poetically. The rhythmic speech of childhood is the function of life, and I believe all later rhythmic speech must have such a function also.

Nor is there any problem until the second hump of the camel appears; none, as long as the second half of poetry does not appear on the horizon. This occurs when the pubescent content begins to interfere with the under-age rhythm, and one realizes with a shock that poetry is a mode of expression. Or rather, that poets should also say something, that words have meanings and are designed so we can express ourselves with them: all our emotions and at least the totality of human existence. This is the gushing moment of adolescent poetry, the moment of torrents of poetry. And who is unaware of this, when everyone is a poet, or has been a poet two or three times in his life?

And yet, the poetry of adolescence teaches too much. If we have truly been born for poetry, we soon realize the distance between word and subject, expression and emotion, the sign and the object. The word-euphoria of childhood is at an end, as is the undoubting self-expression of adolescence. We have grown up and can now carry the two humps of the camel, the eternal duality of the writer's craft: the joy of the word and the inadequacy of the word.

The writing of poetry—for me—is a balancing act between these two. It is a delicate balance: a narrow path between two cliffs. Or, put another way: it is the duel of the unequivocal word and the unarticulated general condition, the corraling of these "between" states, which is, for me, poetry. But how would poetry not be at least two-fold, when life itself is that? Our every moment and our entire existence is the crossroad of contrasts—as the philosopher of the Renaissance stated—or, if you wish, it is the intersection on the highway of facts and ideals, or the airport of the contrailed meetingplaces of earth and sky. It is a miracle that we live, a miracle that we write in such a whirlwind of impressions, amid the overcrowded cognizances and vicissitudes of the 20th century. Only slowly does it become clear to us, progressing on the stages of our adulthood, that writing is hard. How does János Arany,[1] the father of us all, put it, speaking of the mythological and the daily anguish of man and the poet?

> I am no Prometheus, but I feel his pain;
> Like Tantalus of old, thirsting, I hunger;
> The peace of my moments flees.
> Only now are the tales clear to me,
> The ever-consumed and ever-restored liver
> And the elusive apple.

Yes, the elusive apple, the tantalizing apple, which the poet wishes to pluck with his poetry. But then, what else can he do? To ever try again.

---

[1] Arany (1817-82) is Hungary's greatest narrative poet and one of the creators of realistic poetry grounded in native folk traditions. His literary criticism and studies in Hungarian literature, written in the best traditions of scholarship, are useful to the present day.

From: Interview, 1967[1]

Let's begin. What do you think of what is called "intelligibility" in poetry?

Clarity

Right away you pose one of the basic questions of modern poetry. An involved question deserving an intricate answer; but, as far as I am concerned, I will give a straight answer. In my whole life, I have never written so much as a single letter intending to be incomprehensible. It would be a fundamental mistake to confuse my kind of poet with movements that (now found almost universally) are characterized by either a planned or a constitutional obscurity—which, in their own place, naturally have a role. On the contrary, I believe in reason. I cling to this as steadfastly as possible. Though we know that a poem which has *only* a rational sphere isn't worth a rap—after all, the poet could then relate his message in prose, and why should he put himself to the trouble of composing verse?—yet, I still believe that poetry has a rational sphere *also*. It doesn't matter whether the logical sphere is tangible. This, unfortunately or not, is the result of the poet writing words. Words which are the common means of communication.

. . .

Taste . . . is a historical category. And the true daughter of taste is clarity, likewise? Thus the popularization of style is simply a matter of time?

Not simply. Only in part. Today we generally believe that poetry is one of the means of disseminating information. We are constantly preoccupied with the hazy realms of knowledge, so that we can give a name to that which until now was nameless. This is no easy task for the poet or for the reader. Let me cite Rilke: "We plant our feet at our limits, and we snatch to ourselves the Nameless." To broaden at least, if only by a hair's breadth, the area of emotional comprehension: this is what we consider the poet's task to be. Because our age is compulsively curious. The historical convulsions fractured our nineteenth-century concepts, and we are now trying to reformulate them. As the outstanding Polish poet Lec states, no one in the nineteenth century would have thought that it would be followed by the twentieth. Lec is supposedly a humorist. I take him seriously. I believe that self-knowledge that is willing to struggle with vagueness is more vital for the poet and the age than ever before.

Writing is Difficult

You write little. Why?

Because it is hard to write poems. It is a hard, bitter struggle to write what one has in mind. *Only* and *precisely* that. But I believe in this Golden Rule. After all, as I have already mentioned, I cherish reason. I devoutly respect the human species for having descended from the trees. I spend half my life explicating, condensing, chiseling. When I first glimpse the poem-to-be from a distance in its original state, it is as wide as half the galaxy. Then I leave out the superfluous. This takes a long time. From among eighty similes I select one. From a hundred-and-twenty memories, two. I unceasingly throw away the components of the substance, so that my muscles ache. Finally, perhaps nothing more remains of the whole thing than a few lingering helium atoms.

You don't believe, in spite of being an intellectual poet, in the direct elevation of scientific or generally conceptual content into a poem?

I both believe it and don't. Because, of course, that is intellectual. The poem, most often, only absorbs the intellectual mood, the atmosphere of reason. For instance, in a love poem, the poet would much rather give information about his feelings than the exact appearance and circumstances of the beloved lady. The poem rarely speculates: the poem suggests. But it pretends to be reflecting. This is the intellectual poem. But it is the poet who is thinking. Not on the subject of the poem. No. If that is what he is thinking about, he should write an essay on it. . . . One thing is certain: there is no mental process in poetry without an emotional process. Thought is rarely the content of a poem; for the most part it is its excuse. In the poetry of the 20th century, a word such as *helium-atom, concrete, carbon dioxide* or *matter, mind, society* is nothing more than a single loud yell in a huge, echoing cave. We all know this. Will the word bearing the exciting contents of our age thus be diminished? No, on the contrary. Not only our mind, but all of our emotions reverberate it.

Myth

In [your newest poetry] recurrent mythological motifs are conspicuous. Why does the modern poet turn to ancient symbols?

We could say that all modern poetry turns toward myths. You could hardly cite a significant contemporary poet whose works do not contain the fruits of either ancient or modern mythical creations. Which, of course, means nothing for one's own poetry. Each poet must discover his own distinctive aptitudes. For myself, I discovered it rather late. I did not even seek it. Myths began to infiltrate my poetry almost by mistake: a Tristan legend, a Garden of Eden motif, several angels, Easter Island statues, and most recently the Akhenaton story. . . . I have no desire to write about historical curiosities. . . . Myth to me is merely the sound-box of today's melody. New wine in old bottles. One of the levels of our associations. But Akhenaton—that is something different.

Why did you choose the Pharaoh Akhenaton as the hero of a cycle of poems?

He is an old friend. I first met him during adolescence among my grandfather's books. And most recently in Paris, at the Tutankhamen Exhibit. A larger than life statue with that disturbing, long head. A horse's head, no doubt. And from the restless, over-refined face, a calm, powerful Egyptian gaze stares over one's head. This is he, Akhenaton, or Pharaoh Amenhotep IV, religious leader and philosopher from the fourteenth century before Christ. The husband of Nefertiti; Nefertiti is beautiful because, among other things, the pharaoh also created a new artistic style. Akhenaton turned Egypt upside-down, introduced monotheism and raised human thinking to new abstract levels. He is sometimes called the first European intellectual. And then everything returned to the old ways. The statues of el-Amarna were covered by sand; polytheism was reestablished; Akhenaton's name was even scratched off the columns. For three thousand years he was silent. For three thousand years mankind was silent about him. And along with him, that brief, improbably beautiful moment which we call the el-Amarnan culture also fell silent. Recently this impossible historical interlude has begun to speak. A strange story. It pleases me.

From your verse cycle, characteristically, we learn nothing about Akhenaton's historical role. Why?

Because I don't wish to write a picture-book of cultural history.

Akhenaton . . . is only an excuse for prying into philosophical questions?

I believe it is a suitable excuse. His mythically restless disposition—that of the perturber and the creator—is appropriate for me to attach to it the metaphysics of our age without metaphysics. Morality and death, materialism and resurrection—his figure can absorb all of these. He lends us the countenance of the first visionary man.

Realism

Despite the philosophical restlessness of your poetry, the images are realistic.

Your angels are all massive, and even in heaven your Akhenaton strolls between the tracks of an industrial railroad.

This is self-explanatory. Where else would he be strolling? I couldn't possibly imagine it otherwise. My imagination is unusually earthbound.

In other words, it is very pictorial. As you yourself write: in your imagination spectacle and revelation go hand in hand.

The pictorial, I believe, is precisely the unalienable quality of Hungarian poetry. The French, for example, are not in the least pictorial. The cool, soaring abstraction which is one of the characteristics of modern verse is easier for them. The Hungarian poet would, I believe, be destroyed by this. How on earth could we exist without horses, oak trees, neon lights, fat ferns, crowded streetcars? Of course, I am speaking of poetic horses and poetic streetcars. We are, thus, considered "gaudy." Our images are too cluttered. This is true. But what can we do? We spoke considerably in this interview about philosophy and intellectual passion, namely, about one of my basic themes. But all this is worth nothing without power, muscle, sensation. Abstraction, in my view, has body.

"I love matter,/ and often think of my bones."

Yes, I love matter. Beyond the matter of nature, also the matter of language. As the carpenter loves the board and the plane. If I consider my love of objects, I should have been a carpenter; if my need for abstraction, a mathematician.

About the Orange

Yet, you still became a poet. "My profession, you beauty,/ that makes me believe: it is important for me to live." And shortly after the beginning of your career came the Baumgartner Prize.

No. Before anything else came the war. The war, this basic experience of my generation lasting even to this day. This is an inescapable memory, and one never fully capable of being digested. We must speak of it again and again to the end of our lives.

Perhaps the basic humane-poetic program of your verses, its moral commitment, comes from this. And perhaps the tone of struggle, and that bitter taste which is sometimes called pessimism comes from here. Do you consider yourself a pessimist?

Pessimism? That is like an orange. It is said that the orange is the bitterest fruit of all. Most of the flavors that evoke bitterness are hidden in it. But they are so cleverly disguised that they strengthen the sweetness.

I don't deny it: I'd like to be bitter, like the orange.

László Nagy

Nagy was born in Felsőiszkáz, a small village not far from the region of Lake Balaton, in 1925, on July 14 according to his mother or, more probably, on July 17 according to his birth certificate; he considered the former more appropriate to him since it was the day on which the Bastille was stormed. He died of a heart attack on January 30, 1978, in Budapest, which he had made his home since August 1946. His parents, often present in his poems, were peasants who barely managed to keep up with interest payments on the mortgage on the land they had purchased to support their family of four children. His life in the village and his experiences with its culture strongly affected both his views of life and his poetic development. During his boyhood, Nagy spent his time outside school hoeing in the fields and tending to livestock. Wet and cold weather sometimes made the latter painful, but mostly it gave him a specially intimate relationship with the natural world, teaching him to tell time without a clock and to identify all the grasses and flowers. Folk customs were an indispensable part of his family's celebration of all major holidays, such as Christmas, New Year's Eve, and Easter, which always included the singing of traditional folk songs. He was, as he said, raised "among tales and ballads, in the enchanting, commanding rhythms and in the Niagara of the songs of wintry festivity assailing the house." Magic, witchcraft, and superstition pervaded village life, without a clear line drawn between fairy tales and reality. The world of superstition often made him fearful. He instantly thought of the devil whenever the fire roared in the chimney, and he was afraid of the "child-devouring pig" and especially of death. At the age of six, he fell asleep while tending the cattle; waking up at dusk and suddenly thinking about the inevitability of his death, he sobbed so loud that the animals stared at him. Although he remained afraid of death, he never again, he once noted, responded so uncontrollably to it. The vigorous play of his half-tamed life in the fields, trees, and hills and in pursuit of wild animals ended abruptly at the age of ten, when osteomyelitis lamed his left leg permanently.

Only his wide-ranging curiosity gave him the strength to endure the strict discipline of his early schooling, and he gained distinction only in penmanship, spelling, and drawing. Later, he and his two sisters attended school in nearby Pápa, where they lived with their maternal grandmother, who had been persuaded by their mother to move there from Nyárad, so that a good education would help her children to a better future than their parents knew. Interested in the graphic arts, Nagy really wanted to become a painter. Yet he was, strictly on his own, studying and translating Heine, and, like many of his schoolmates, he was also versifying. In the fall of 1941, he entered the Business School of the 400-year-old Reformed College in Pápa, but he often neglected his studies, going to the outskirts of the city to paint. The school was closed early during the last fall of the war, and he spent the winter painting in the family's stable. After the Russian army arrived, he went back to the school, where he participated in student reforms, but in 1945 he returned home with his diploma and remained there for a year. The poems he wrote during this period revealed his love of nature and animals, particularly the horse, portrayed the hard life of the peasant, and expressed his early obsession with the paradox of life and death.

After the war he felt increasingly stifled by the life in his village and decided to escape. In the fall of 1946, he went to Budapest to study graphic arts at the College of Industrial Design, but because of the uncertain conditions of the time, he left it and entered a people's college then being established. Soon he was caught up in the optimism about the opportunity for social and economic justice that socialism could provide workers and peasants. The new world before him was to affect his entire life and career. He finally decided to become a poet because, he discovered, he could express more in writing than in painting. Seven of his poems, accompanied by a short autobiography and one of his graphics, were published in the Christmas 1947 issue of *Reality* (*Valóság*). At the college, he met Ferenc Juhász, with whom he had a warm relationship until serious differences developed between them with the 1970s, when Juhász assumed an ever more public role in society; the two of them vowed to create a new kind of poetry and poetic language for their nation. Nagy also formed a lasting friendship with the late István Kormos, who also was to become a distinguished and influential poet. After a time, Nagy and Juhász matriculated at the Attila József College to study Hungarian literature, philosophy, and sociology; but when their courses became meaningless to them, they abandoned them permanently.

In 1949 the first of his sixteen books appeared. Entitled *Vanish, Pain* (*Tünj el fájás*), it contained many poems that enthusiastically supported actions intended to give a radically new political, economic, and social character to the native land to which he was utterly devoted. Full of hope, they celebrated its growing industrialization, the first agricultural cooperatives, and the lives of workers and peasants. They also showed him adding to the verse forms of folk poetry the modes of versification from seventeenth-century Hungarian poetry and from twentieth-century European poetry. This deliberate experimentation produced in his later poems a fresh synthesis of the various verse techniques so successful that their rhythm became as essential as imagery to their meaning. Shortly after the publication of this volume, he spent eighteen months, with brief interruptions, in Bulgaria, learning the language and translating extensively from that country's folk poetry, which resulted not only in the publication of his translations in 1953, but, even more important, in the deepening of his knowledge and in the honing of his use of folklore and ballad measures in his later poetry.

On his return to Hungary in 1951, he was sickened by the conditions he found. Turning combative, he wrote the poems that expressed his deep disappointment at the betrayal, in his view, of the humane ideals of socialism by political leaders, in effect anticipating the 1956 Revolution in the causes already present. These poems of disillusionment were not published until 1953, when István Király, then managing editor of *Star (Csillag)* and later a distinguished literary historian, accepted them.

In the summer of 1952 he married Margit Szécsi, herself a gifted poet, and they celebrated the event by sharing a supper of red cherries and red wine. Together, they struggled against poverty in a sublet room, their dire situation only slightly eased, after a time, by income from the publication of his translations of Bulgarian folk poetry, which had been delayed for political reasons. Nagy joined the staff of *Drummer Boy (Kisdobos)*, a magazine for children. Soon the horrors of the 1956 Revolution and its consequences wrenched the nation. Not an actual participant in the events, Nagy contributed to the historic development through the critical issues he had already raised in his poems. Later, in "Squared by Walls" ("A falak négyszögében"), he voiced his regret at not having helped his people during the crisis. After that time, he was tied down by his wife's long illness. In 1959 he became picture editor of *Life and Literature (Élet és Irodalom)*, a post he held until his death.

New editions of his poems had appeared in 1951, 1954, 1956, and 1957, this last a collection of works from 1944 to 1956, but between 1957 and 1965 only books of his translations were published, and even as late as the early 1960s public recitations of his poems were being discouraged because they continued to voice his disillusionment and pessimism about the future of Hungarian society. After the publication of *Hymn at All Times (Himnusz minden időben)* in 1965, however, his poems, as he himself observed, "received their due, even though I did nothing in their behalf, did not campaign, did not abase or sell out anything or myself." This book of poems, which marked a dramatic point in his development, was followed by seven new editions of poems, including the last to be edited by him, *The Bells Are Coming For Me* (*Jönnek a harangok értem*), which appeared in 1978, after his death; and was then snatched up at bookstores by lovers of poetry. Recognition again came his way. To the Attila József Prizes of 1950, 1953, and 1955 were added the prestigious Kossuth Prize of 1966 and the Golden Laurel of the International Poets' Festival held in Struga, Yugoslavia, in 1968. Thousands of mourners—young and old, intellectuals, workers, and peasants—attended his interment in the Kerepesi Cemetery in Budapest. As the wintry air carried the sounds of folk music and his own lyrics set to song, they came to pay tribute to his humaneness, his artistic integrity, and his illusionless, courageous, and often joyous affirmation of human finitude.

A dramatic evolution in his thought and art occurring over a period of several years after his return from Sophia laid the groundwork for the poetry he wrote after 1957. One important modification was his abandoning the concept that poetry is obligated to serve the commitments of a particular society. Discussing poetry in 1972, he said that he and his fellow poets soon modified this view that had dominated the early 1950s. Poetry, Nagy now insisted, contains an inherent ideal purpose which the poet expresses as the voice of the entire human community. Unfortunately, although poetry contains and seeks the good and exerts influence on readers, he went on to say, it has not been able to prevent "the murderous twentieth century," and some persons, even some poets, like those in the school of art-for-art's-sake, deny that poetry involves any ideal purpose whatsoever. In this 1972 interview, Nagy made clear that poetry is not a bemoaning of private troubles; instead, it is always an expression of humanity, of the kind of human being the poet is.

At this time, another factor was impelling him in the same direction: his disillusionment with the conditions he encountered on his return. His thought and imagination turned from the immediate and particular problems of the national scene toward deeper involvement in "the burning issues" that absorbed him the rest of his life. Although an avowed socialist throughout his life, Nagy cast a combative and compassionate eye about him, as in "The bliss of Sunday" ("Vasárnap gyönyöre), and during his remaining years struggled between feelings of hope and despair at humankind's capacity to attain a world in which joy and kindness reign. More and more, he addressed himself to the ultimate questions of life and death, happiness and pain, love and loneliness, infinity and finitude. And as he reached out for the human community in his responses to these agonizing dilemmas, his poems, like "Wedding" ("Menyegző") for instance, rely ever more on mythical and folkloristic materials divorced of their traditional associations so as to convey archetypal patterns of behavior and situations, in the manner of other twentieth-century poets seeking similar objectives.

The paradoxes of life and death, growth and decay, hope and despair are central to his confrontation of existence. Death's shadow always falls on his joy in life and frustrates his passionate longing for it, for that joy which a human being needs even if "you get it from hell," for "how else bear the blood-stained/relay-race, without it you jackknife, stagger, sprain." His view of life makes it difficult for him to find this sustaining joy. According to him, humankind is frozen in finitude, and life is not a gift from a provident God but a product of indifferent natural laws that subject human beings to accidental forces. Nor does human nature bode well for the future. In a 1977 interview conducted by Kormos, he painted starkly the duality of human nature: " . . . we are selfish, arrogant, vain; we are gentle and brutish, born murderers, lechers, marauders. In short, we are good and bad, we are human beings, we are fallible." In spite of this bleak view, he persists in his search and frequently celebrates the triumph of life without resorting to illusions, even when mourning the death of those close to him. In the very finitude that torments him, he discovers, it seems, the inner force that gives human beings a sense of community, a feeling of responsibility for others, the capacity to love, and the need for artistic creativity, all of which are placed in the framework of a poet's existence in "Carrying Love" ("Ki viszi át a Szerelmet") by assigning to him the ideal function of rescuing love from destruction and transporting its grace to others in a future age.

Just past the middle of the nineteenth century, Imre Madách in his classic *The Tragedy of Man* (*Az ember tragédiája*), extends consolation to Adam, who is about to commit suicide in despair at the future of the human race which Lucifer has presented to him in a visionary journey that revealed the failure of all religious and political ideals in every age. As Adam is about to leap from a cliff to foreclose that future, God informs him that Eve is with child. To the despondent Adam, God says: "Strive on, strive on, and trust." A century later, Nagy, who had quickly stripped away the Christian beliefs of his forefathers, can accept only a part of Madach's solace. In the face of present-day reality, he can only exhort humankind: to struggle against every peril, against mortality, against every despair, for only through striving man can human beings sustain the hope held out by the vision of a free and happy humanity living in an unattainable earthly paradise. And so, too, must poets and humanists. In the 1977 interview, he urged them to "continue as the combatants, partisans, and secret advocates for a better human lot," and to hang on to hope, for "only hope helps us to break out of the greatest tragedies and catastrophes, the afflicted masses to rise from them." Characteristically, he insisted on the right of poets to exercise doubt, that "motor of creativity," to meet their inner ideal and to edge, however slightly, however temporarily, toward their never attainable objective. The synthesis of this dialectic was the primary need of his being and the essence of his poetry.

In his last years, he became more philosophical about the human condition, and, deciding that tragedy lay ahead if he considered himself overly important, he turned playful in his poems, sometimes even curt. But he continued his combat, awaiting every peril at the ready. His doubts kept tormenting him; he was always wary. To the end, he mustered all his knowledge and experience in search of joy,

> Spite of despondence, of the inhuman dearth
> Of noble natures, of the gloomy days,
> Of all the unhealthy and o'erdarkened ways
> Made for our searching. . . .

Lovers

Beside their temples a wrist watch ticks:
a metal flower dripping a deadly dew.
Falling stars score the black sky;
night soughs like a branch the wind shakes.

A man knows no peace once childhood's past;
his brain whirls, like the earth under fog.
He is flogged by minutes as meteors flog
the sea. He is nailed to the cross with Christ.

Nibbling his troubled thoughts, all he will say is:
'I can hear the stars being torn, can you?'
'Everything sinks in the end—do you believe that too?'
But his woman is silent; her love is at its zenith.

Her little slip is rucked and pushed back;
the pale, exposed flesh beneath
cannot be harmed by night and death.
Her wakened thighs gleam all night through the dark.

The Bliss of Sunday

Many worship you, Sunday, throw into you feverishly
six days and themselves: you the seventh, you the free.
In crowds we flock to you, you our good shaman who
need no consulting room yet heal us sweet and sure.
Our stifling rose-grove lungs groan for you to arrive,
dark stars of soot have burst in them like butterflies.
We come to you with heart tremors and chilled kidneys,
high blood pressure, toxins, rages, stitches.
Scare off these goblins, rout the microbe-gangsters,
organize peevish organs into peace with a mum's stare.
We come for our quietness to melt our raw nerves,
your dear cool hand to pillow half-crazed heads.
You are the best go-between, the brightest-minded,
you are the violin where dance and kiss are kindled.
You are also the goal, the nearest: the island where
fabulous clangor strikes from the loved workshops of pleasure . . .
The blue wheezing night-ship creaks against you—
what breaking radiance, what ruby hullabaloo!
The red gangway of dawn is lowered—but it's still
only the silent old folks who step ashore: the song, the din
lie sleeping in laborers' hearts, dead done like them;
wrestlers with iron and air stay to draw out their dreams.
Grannies trot about like toys, may they know long days!
they mutter anxiously, set the kettle on the gas,
the milk bubbles up, hop-pop, it's almost over,
the malt-coffee's boiling, fizz-frothing, golden,
the bread-cubes dance as they redden in the fat,
to drop their fragrance on the brown soup steaming in the pot.
A rainbow throbs on the vapory mist and falls on the heart,
it urges me to get up and wash, I whistle in good part.
The lather puffs out my face, the razor walks round
to show how sometimes suffering pares you down.
Oh, let fate keep that strange razor from your cheek:
you grow pale and thin, the stubble cringes, bunches up thick.
My ancient pair of shoes has filched the morning star,—
nylon socks on the line, two tiny shining sacks

flutter, and under fine soles will steal a fine day again,
the ironed shirt winks mother-of-pearl, teases your brain.
Clean shirt: your clean world, this is the bliss you want.
pray for it if the branch of your good smile is cut.
Mirrors, soften your truth for kindly vanity,
let them look and still say: I'm pretty, I'm happy.
If her face twisted up, oh, what would become of her!
Let the women dance, hawk-brown hair or starling-black or
blonde exploding with hydrogen peroxide
or long-dead Titian's dream of a redhead.
I love them all when I look through the window and admire
their earnest iron will — imprisoned in humming driers,
with tropical heat floating on the waves of their hair
and alpine-brilliant ice-white mirrors everywhere.
She drives me crazy, the girl who stands in the snow
against the wall in her lunchbreak to be burned by the glow;
eyes closed, tempting a sky of ice to tan her slowly,
she spellbinds sun-rays into kisses, ultraviolet only . . .
White-gold-handed Sunday, you scoop out small boys
with their bullet heads from bed like well-shelled peas,
they roll and tumble like mad, bump heads together,
they are pothooks like the letters in a jotter.
Bees drone in swarms, bells clang their songs at me,
the rushing windstream sets imagination free.
My villages, yellow, white, watchers along the road-dust.
I see you tip your roof-caps to disaster.
To number your names is music: Vid, Nagyalásony, Doba,
Egeralja, Káld and Berzseny, Kispirit, Csögle, Boba.[1]
A universe you were, now you are its mica-flash,
frighteningly huge this life, frightening to confess.
I was a millet-seed in you, now you are that seed,
the memory pushes out a tear and it mists all that scene.
Then memories peal like bells and ringing years leave sleep,
the boy I was is here, the pond-murmur, the day dream.
No desire to be Peter Pan but no desire to die,
the flash on the fine silver poplar-leaves his reverie.
The student I was is here, splitting skies are above,
Sunday, the bombs lash your light into blood,
butterflies panic and flap in his hair, his head
nettle-stung like his mind life-stung, he lies on his side.
Well, I throw down a horse-rug under the silent stars,
I throw my troubles open to the mercies of flowers.

László Nagy

You bud-bright peonies, cover me in pity,
tight baby bombs, blow up into flowers on my heart.
And let my whole being be irradiated with new colors, new rays,
let the frescoes of horror and tribulation be wiped away,
the terror-born figures smeared teeming on my soul's wall
be banished with Neros and popes, fell Crescent and yataghan, all
needles in fingernails, Haynau's icy pupils, heads awry
in living-death nid-nodding agony.
And blood-soaked earth, soot-sky lit by a skull,
let burning phantoms of sea and air go dead and dull.
What am I that I should endure what makes my flesh creep?
I can wait,—no moments of magic waken that bad sleep.
Many pleasures move me, yet cannot break the spell,
bringing only strength to defy, to bear a great shame well.
You who sink down on the horse-rug beside me, Hope
my edelweiss-eyed angel, you know I am no fool, I grip
you, whirl you about like a green branch, Jacob
was not more diligent in flooring God's angel.
Yet stay by me, don't cry; I have to stamp on the monsters;
whisper to me that the road I go is not monstrous.
I am desperate fighting for beauty. I want to know the sun
dazzling, the singing green-gold forests, bright winds that stun
the leaves, tall flower-stems shaking tiny dewdrop earrings,
petals and veins like girls in love, trembling even in breathing.
Being shouts out: no no! It doesn't want to be dead yet.
The wasp drones off at a tangent, spins out the moment.
Highest, deepest teats are sucked by emerald heads:
cherry and morello, emerald aching for red.
The golden oriole calls out its glorious Sunday,
and father brushes chaff from his hat, walks away
to see the world: silver-blue sea of rye,
copper-ruddy carrots, maize standing straight and high.
Blind love wraps the crop-gazer as he pads on his way,
a hundred disappointments dissolve in his love of this day,
sweet pea in his hat, even that makes him rich,
he flicks his boots with a flame-red willow-switch.
Oh, all those paunches to be taut as drums, the draught animal
champs and stuffs itself with grass after six days' toil,
the belly of the hill, the boneyard broods in hunger,
full now of nothing but sunlight and acacia-flower.
The blessed meadow, it wants happiness,
goodbye now to memories of pain and sharp distress.

The telegraph wire chirps half-asleep, no news or orders
whiz over it, the post-office girl writes a letter:
Come, I'm dying for you—and the wonder seizes her heart:
she is clasped from behind with a kiss by her soldier at last.
Bicycles, look: modern reindeers, lilac, yellow,
the wheels purr feverishly with a student and his girl to the valley,
motorbikes roar by, meteor lapping meteor,
zhee, zhoo, a woman's hair streams in comet-eaten air.
To vanish in the green night of the woods is marvelously good,
twin spheres of wild cherry suit the ear grown red.
For blood, like soul, goes thirsty for a storm,
a hot and forcing wind springs up, beats down the stems
of rose and lily thrown in each other's arms, love's way
is blessed, love's bed is blessed, and you, the day.
Sunday, you are here, we see the feast day of the workworn,
the bent backs straighten in your majestic dawn.
Children at a mother's apron: they play on your barn floor
after the bucking tractor seat and shouldered sacks galore.
The miner looks up at the sky, his crows'-feet glisten,
the grimy machinist marvels at a blackbird: listen!
The navvy who has pushed his squealing barrow countrywide
is at home, admires and makes much of his darling child.
The blacksmith's in fine fettle, the postman drops
the tiredness of a hundred stories down, laughs and can't stop.
The seamstress heals her heartache with gleams of pleasures,
a myriad tiny daggers glint on heart-shaped cushions.
The workshops are empty, the stitched jacket on the dummy
holds up in one arm the pain and point of creativity.
The blue dynamo squats stiff, cut off from savage energy,
the belt wilts, the transmission is silent and weary.
Nothing and nobody runs, the turning lathe is asleep,
a rainbow strip of peeled steel in its teeth.
Dour mouths of iron vices gape, the quietness is a sea,
rasps doze like fish, scales glimmering fitfully.
Beer froths in the brewery, matures, hums a wild dream,
horses' harness flashes its moons on pegs, they lean
to the manger, those magic beer-horses, rank with hops,
and stamp in happiness with tumbling bells of hoofs.
I swim past riveting images, I see the blood-spattered
abattoir and angels walking in white there, scattering
jasmine flowers,—my heart gambols and foals
something fantastic-impossible from what is truly-real;

the poleaxe forgets to degrade and lay low the gloomy bull,
or crack the star on the horse's trembling skull.
Blood for six days, but see the shrieks fly on the blade,
renew your smile, parables of blood.
You kill yourself too, to be reborn from death,
you are a Sunday phoenix, to drink and break bread.
Oh how often you have to die for one small Sunday,
how often for one far-off thought-out joy!
The victim, the dead, was always you, humanity,
no workshop, no workshop of delight this earth and sky.
Thunder? Uncouth belching, that's how they live up there,
hiding forever behind the law of the unsated banqueter.
What I sing again and again is not those loose-mouthed brutes
with their jovial riot, but all men's modest delights.
Oh it is frustratingly minute, no home for my heart,
Sunday: doused spark, dust of an imagined star.
Imagined ravishing star, that's where I'd be,
with gaiety ineradicable—oh never to see
that distant beauty!—entrance me, draw my heart out
of the dust, save me from Psalmus Hungaricus and jeremiad.
You are the goal, it is there life lies indivisible,
nothing else makes me cry out haunting the butcher's table.
It is for this that vision and holy rage are sizzling in me,
the melancholy temple of my sight falls down to make it be.
I have been gentle, it is time I was an activist,
even if you get it from hell you need joy, it is tonic, it
is rations for the voyage, how else bear the bloodstained
relay-race, without it you jackknife, stagger, sprain.
Come now, come now, set up the feast, unwind,
slice the fish, cast its scale-coins to the whistling wind,
close your eyes and wring the panting pigeon's neck,
laugh with the pot of horseflesh-soup all sweet with mignonette,
stew potted head, shred radish, and if there's nothing else
pluck at the sky, fry the red kestrel's eggs.
Eat from a striped cloth or on the grass, but sit
as an august great power, in the smile of space you are bright.
You should know that only you can kill pain and original sin,
only you have the right to feast; rifle the larder and bread-bin,
you may eat, there is no curse, drink too; drinking,
recharge your soul at the tumbled shadows of living.
Sunday today, Sunday, the sun is a frantic sultan,
his swordblade splits the earth, tears fences down.

How to hide from its fury, it extorts sharp sweat-tribute,
a dream of plunging in snow to escape the churning heat.
Softly rounded hips strip off at the water's edge,
they put on wavy green-cool skirts for dancing. Foliage
opens and beckons so fresh and cave-like below,
shades of the beer garden come to life, beer foams
as tap-copper turns, jugs clink weighty and cold,
hats and caps are cocked jaunty on every head.
The ice-cream freezes, its tent floats like another heaven,
the cones are tucked up in towers, high and even,
towers to be annihilated by an army of children,—
at last rebuilt no more as cold winds freshen.
The summer is a breast-pierced bull on the frost-pinched sand,
the leaves are blood-drenched, the gossamers fly around.
The hawthorn shivers, shakes its blood-red pearls,
and don't think it's the sunset-embers of the flames that fell.
The fevered stags begin to butt each other's brows,
they bell, the steam fans out like storm-blown boughs.
The setting sun paints fire on the windows of the city,
Sunday, your tempo quickens, drives us crazy for beauty.
Hundreds of thousands throng the streets, din fills the air,
they march with their furled flags of desire and power.
And the funfair bangs out, its daft delights come cheap,
a dream-orbit round the earth—we bucket and leap,
and shame on us, we monopolize the toys of our sons,
the scarlet-feathered whistle-cock crows smartly in our hands,
paper-trumpets blare,—vermilion-nosed horses
carrousel their sexy-seated women-riders forward . . .
The earth whirls with time and sky like a star-wheel,
this is beyond play, it roars round your head, you reel.
Insane fragrances invade you, the wine fizzes,
meteors plunge and plunge, hearts take their bruises.
The instincts flower, fear of mortality bids
revelry and bids it quick, sit in the midst of it!
Whisper and sigh: you, thin violins, weep it out,
and you, lumpish drums, take joy and beat it about.
Roll drums, cry violins, we must have a dance,
the spurs of your music make me rear and prance.
You can see through this intoxication everywhere,
your feet itch to trample king, president, emperor,
your sly fate too, which covers you with wing and claw
and lifts you up only to dash you like a griffin's prey.

László Nagy

You drink deep, clink your glass, you need this spirit, this fever,
this is for loosening your tongue and see how it sobs, how it reasons!
Your fingers spread into the skies, watch towers of your truth,
would that no tomorrow saw them shaken and ruined!
I sing and sing of the great joy of the many, now
darkness is theirs, furrowed by the star-plough.
The crop of dreams is murmuring, the ear of corn is harder,
men cut it now, the reaping-song strange pearly laughter.
Strange cables these, the cemetery telephones,
from the wisdom of death some send messages:
leave no stalk of delight uncut, someday you will be sorry,
enjoy yourselves my daughter, little son, little grandson, my orphans!
Huger the hunger, the thirst, wilder the music,
it rings and wrestles with the dear dead message.
Light-power, teeming current changes the muscle-springs
prone to dance, the bones with their live ball-bearings.
He who kisses today tastes lava, he himself breaks
into flame and his whispered words are crested flames.
A spark-shower hits the icefield, between damnation and salvation
even the border can be on fire, now the mind is in its passion.
Night: life in space, its obscure laws welling,
bodies: saturns rolling in their erotic rings . . .
Here comes the end of our star-being, the end is here, goodnight!
The heart is orphaned, Sunday's flowers—gone in what flight!
Cooled stones, snow-drifted stubble, alien and wind-song,
snow-curtain dances—and man sleeps deep and long.
Sky, like mind, must want again to lighten,
and soon on the unhidden breasts a dawn whitens.
The world that was all glow and flame's now white, my dear.
Wake up, wake up, it's morning, the winter is here.

[1] All villages in Transdanubia, within the area of the poet's birthplace.

Carrying Love

When my life has sunk beneath me
who will admire the cricket's cadenza?
Who will kindle the frosty bough?
Who will hang crucified from a rainbow?
Who will transform hips that are rocks
into a flowering field among hillocks?
Who will stroke the hairs in stones,
the pebble's blood, the wall's veins?
Who will build an immense cathedral
where tongues cursed and faith fell?
When my life has sunk for good
who will battle that deadly bird?
Whose mouth will be strong enough to bear
foundering Love to the farther shore?

Squared by Walls

Couldn't you have died,
or at least bled,
instead of pacing the floor
stunned with despair?
You kept clear of the trouble:—
bullets, armored tracks, emblazoned
girls' screams. Not for you broken
wheels, scattering rooftiles,
grim gangs of working lads,
and soot-brindled petals.
You did not spill one drop

of blood, and when it stopped,
you had only gone gray and mad.

In usual winter weather
you stand here; no other
but yourself, and wide awake,
squared by walls that echo
a cough like raking
gunfire. It's not merely
your flesh that's cold;
mind and heart are frozen—crowned
by knives of ice.
You are ashamed of your melting phrases;
as if it were a sin
to think of spring
and lilacs,—the lung-like trees blossoming.
What agony for a Lord of Life!
Yet, deep in the secret places
of your being, furtive with guilt,
you are breathing on the frosted pane,
that you may look out at the world again.

Without Mercy

You lay down under a blasting light,
a flower at your elbow,
over your inward head
my love's wild flags flew.

I sit alone in the luminous dark
of a room with closed shutters;
the scabby slats break—
drunken sunshine enters.

Raspberry twilight in a rose-glass;
fragrance of the clipped rose
drifting upward to enquire
my summer's scope and size.

In place of your waving-goodbye hand
vacant air vibrates;
memory is an enormous
butterfly on your bedsheets.

Splaying sparks, the summer's grindstone
is honing my dulled heart.
Let recognition wake you
under a blasting light.

Young blood soon tires of sacred love—
return to me, undress:
let's wrestle our lives away,
majestic and merciless.

From: Wedding

Faces to the sea, here as a couple we stand
in a blaze of trumpets in festive gold alarms
in whinnying whistling, stunned and numbed by drums
flinching in the stamping din, our backs
menaced by thrusting dancers like waves surging:
for this is our introduction to the sea
that it should acknowledge us, here as a couple standing
on this tongue of rock where land's reared beak
bites at infinity, two human stars in wedlock's
trajectory conspiring forever to do what's good and what's right
giving pleasure too, such a new order surpassing the most fevered

dreaming so that through us it surely would come to pass;
then let the sea in its incessant siege concede
the elders are wise, the elders in conclave so inclining
permit: Let The World If It Can Become Flesh
why should their solemn marble profilehoods
within such a cruel code press dry the flame-flower,
why bring down to dust the heart at its zenith
with their glance's comet of hunting hoarfrost,
why should their old gods' snot-matted beards smear the sky
wrapping this grassy satellite in germ-killing shadow
in black ribbon?—but be off, panicky awe
we are the majesties here, our crown is eternal flame
galaxy-circuits and superstitionless lamps of reason
towers of discoveries spiraling into the infinite;
. . .
we are the fire and the blood, the milk, the honey
we the cosmic mission against forefathers' stone scriptures
to crumble them to chaff like unleavened bread: this our struggle
we the peace, the sudden urge to create anew
we imagination's blossoming against the canon's barrenness
and the ball-less, ours the potent come-back of Greek heroes
because the stars urge us toward the greatest wedding ever
that our pollen-flecked faces should scare off eternal death
that May should be completed by our love's tranced scent,
night of our burst-off buttons cricket-loud and glow-wormy
emerald fields grow tall from our love's dew . . .
. . .
Oh the sea, the sea, so genuine a best man for us
out of the violet faraway wedding gifts bearing on its waves
babies' swaddling clothes, lacey white cylinders
praising with its dimensions of space our immeasurable yearning
and our law of the future which now even those who protest
are brought to respect, for they'll be contorted by salt
wounded by light—after all, something does happen;
let the sea rejoice: here as a couple we stand, blossoming
on this crag of quartz, here in the shop-window of the world
doing even as the chalk-white beards direct
hand-in-hand, waiting for the ceremony to end; . . .
. . .
hands at our backs, hands in the lightning flash
of clinked glasses, hands hoisted high for the new couple
Long Live The New Couple Long Live, here as a couple we stand, meekly
faces to the sea, and there are hands at our backs

hands turning loose murderous melodies, ravening rhythms
from the auriferous kennels of music,
panthers and eagles claw at others who have not moved
but we must stand regally very still hand in hand
fingers welded together, our bloods' circuits interconnected
within a halo of veins, bridal clothes smelling of lily-of-the-valley
faces to the sea; and we have to smile at the tricks,
swaddling clothes a vision of spun sea-foam,
we must suffer the tireless wheeling of albatross-couples
but must stand statue-still as dancers wind-devil around
just wait while feet stamp to the drum's beat
rapping on the fire-veined brain of mother earth . . .
. . .
—and the celebration's complete
ringed doves scatter skyward startled, sudden salvoes crackle
shakoes and hats lift in salute never to descend again
sword blades flash forth silvery glittering rosemary
Sunday-best headscarves and Veronica kerchiefs flutter
banners balloon high into the sky up above beyond
them floating age-worn chalk-white god-beards
and their admonitions unfruitful winds from icefields:
Long Live The New Couple Long Live But Who Now Must Stand Still
faces to the sea, here as a couple so beautiful we stand
by magic immobilized now being immortalized
by propeller-headed photographers clicking shutters
hovering above the fish on one knee kneeling in green air; . . .
. . .
faces to the sea, and the wedding goes on at our backs
and dear time flies more swiftly than falcons
but in front of us always the day, behind us is the night
behind us always the night, though making against its darkness
there's the apple orchard white with blossom, the blazing
flower tree, tulip tree, everywhere lamps of spring
the rainbow of blood and flame, the furnace of daydream
the ultra-world of brains; but still night is a power
and it is in vain this wedding, this wedding behind our backs . . .
. . .
the kitchen is ablaze, scullions sweat without a break
meat is gobbled up and bones swept into the sea
the wedding throws up, shits, pisses into the sea
yet again The *Weh Weh Weh Wedi Wedi* Wedding The Wedding
it elevates our wine, it breaks our bread, the wedding
it wolfs our heritage, it ruts on our bridal bed

László Nagy

it's shameless, it's drooping, it's jerking, it's kicking
its elbow sends our flower-candle flying and with caustic secretions
humiliates the earth, murders the roots, the wedding
frill infringing on frill, form foreclosing form
cart coupling with cart floor-bottoms jammed into one another
and interlocking worldwide trademarks' carapace-unions,
Oh night you bridal night of corruption, Oh Wedding
you Satan's sable sabbath, bitch ugly, you glowing in the night
mother-of-pearl nails, embers of scabby pox
of vermilion rose, black lacquer, Spanish fly green enamel
topaz on withered finger, porcelain teeth on a reeking palate
platinum bridging carious piers, opalescent liquid decay glowing
wilted treemoss glowing too, and loathsome bat-pendants on dry
            fungus ears . . .
                      . . .

and faces to the sea, here as a couple we stand, grown stiff
glasses and strings glowing, the dance and mother earth glowing
glowing the wedding, glowing this inextinguishable feast
it whirls up to the sky and bombs back to earth screeching
the orchestra strikes up for it again purring, madly yelling, it dances:
Here goes: Old Hag, Make Your Mare's Ass Move!
        Up And Over The Seed Of Love!
Call That A Dance? We'll Make You Prance!
        Step It Out, You Bag You!
Once It Was His Wedding Day. What If His
        Lungs Will Dry Away? Play!
When Gout Feels The Wet, It Sticks Out
        A Rooster's Head, Trumpet-Valve Way!
What's Here? Lice On The Tuberose! Below
        Iron Gloves, Today!
Here's Old Skin And Bones. She Foaled A Flogging Horse.
        It Came Out Piebald, Play!
Hey You Bastard! You're To See Stars, Not Watch The Bride's
        Behind! Play I Say!
White Lamb, White Ram! This Wedding Is Long
        And Will Last Longer. So Play!
The Bridal Pair Have Undressed. Waiting So Long
        Down To The Bare Bone. Yes!
This Is A Bone That'll Not Be Seen. We'll Cement
        It Over, Keep It Clean. Yes!
Let The Castle Of Buda Tumble. Hear Corsetted Captains
        Rumble, Take It!
See The Crow Dance. Its Gut A Crypt. In Its Beak
        Veils And Meat, Shake It!

                    Dance With The Song, The Notes Aren't Wrong. With A
                         Thousand Santa's Dance, And Go!
                    I've A Thousand Barrels Of Wine, Each On Tap, Each
                             Tastes Fine. Here's Your Chance!
                    You Intellectual Burrower, Drink! Don't Be Scared.
                             Your Health! Don't Think!
                    Others Toss It Down Like Me. While The Gullet
                             Holds Up, Feel Free! Hold Fast!
                    Bitch On Heat Dressed In Stoat's Fur, Here I'm
                             Not The Only Whore, To Play!
                    I Wish This Night Would Never End, But Last Forever
                             Without End. Play!
                    while, we, wreathed and ribbon-hung stand amid roaring time
                    faces to the sea, we stand tensed and cooled into a cast as one statue!

The Martyred Arabian Mare

White and stiff-necked she stood on the hillside, like the small Margaret-chapel on the basalt promontory. Inside the chapel, in a silver frame is a picture, and it is cold. But inside the horse is a foetus, in its unripe mouth's red glory, the placenta. The white Arabian mare stood and waited. At times she waved her parted silken mane. Her hide undulated, the many freckles jerked—goldcentered daisies. Still she waited, looking across the Besenyő woods toward the Iszkáz spire.

The early bird had already hidden when the drunken diggers —having exposed the vinestems to the spring—staggered from the oaktable. There they sat, stacked in the cart, their eye-windows clanging crimson in the dusk. Alcohol raved in those windows: heroic light ranted of a day unwilling to die. The horse looks back and sees the blazing city of eyes towering above, and she shakes her head: No. She does not move forward, though the whip's sweep strikes swearingly between her eyes where her forelock dances. The drunken diggers become medieval centurions. Like giants they rip the thatch from the roof of the wine cellar. They burn faggots under the little lady's belly. They question her by fire, would drag the road home out of her by fire, that white ribbon written all over with songs, such as: We have hoed our vineyard three times, and: I earn what is needed for the winter, what my sweetheart needs for silk panties.

László Nagy

My mother stood by the door in a shabby rose-patterned dress, chapel-white, with child. She lifted her head high lest her mane touch the ground. The stars in the sky likened themselves to her freckles, come out early. But she only stood and waited and looked at the distant basalt hill in the cold. And she shivered because she saw a flaming star run down the hill and collapse in the forest's night. That star was the little horse flaming in the wind with the burning cart.

Then my toys fell on their backs on the table. My dear maizestalk animals stiffened their legs toward the sky. And it was then that I finally put down the tiny cornfiddle tensed against my heart, because my mother came to meet me with the hurricane lamp, as if she took out of her belly that light-giving, smoke-hairy kid brother. Go, you brave boy, she said, and I went holding the tin-clamped, glass-swaddled baby against my breast. On the top of its navel the flame shook with laughter as though we were going to Bethlehem, but I suspected the infinity of the tragedy. I trotted before yelping dog-throats, before the mortal teeth of cemeteries. The fox-like red flags slapped my face on the battlements of gravel-pits. On either side murderous archers stood on the ramparts in the cold.

With an arrow-stitch in my side I reached the forest. The drunken diggers had tumbled there already and were flaying the horse in the starlight. Their incendiary fierceness had expired for good, had shriveled into embers in their chest baskets. They are sooty-cheeked, soot-masked like black doctors, as, stooping, they perform the operation. They skin the hide on both sides, and lift it from the trunk like large white wings. The cracking of the membranes can be heard clearly. The miscarried colt is flayed by my father, as if he were skinning my younger brother to come. Kneeling they are lamentably small, but their shadows on the violet ramparts show that huge he-demons are dealing the cards here, playing off my life. Now I ought to kill my father, I prayed—who was hardly bigger than the lamp. It would be fair to stab him as he does the pigs. Now. First my heel onto his throat, then the knife! In imagination I have finished with him. And suddenly I began to whimper because of my mortal sin. Neither earth nor heaven gave consolation. In the sky I saw the upturned cart in flames, and there too was the milk brook, which lifted the violet leaves below, pouring from the udder of the unhappy mother. And now I knew: we are there in the images of the world; our sins are there, and can never be erased from there.

Folding the infant coltskin my father put it round my neck as a black fur. He himself in catatonic silence put on the harness. He took the trappings on his back, the reins on his head. In his masquerade feelings of guilt glowed like starry-eyed altar candles. The others stood behind him with the martyr's hide. Nothing but breath poured from our O mouths. Silently we began to go, in the name of God and the horse. Clasps and metal rings clinked, jolting with each step. They glittered pure silver-light against our sooty, penitential procession. So we stumble on, down an eternal road. Onward through the night until the end of time. I am in front with the hurricane lamp, and the frost is as tall as a man.

Evocation of the City

The spires of fairyland were all I knew. I soared as I breathed—without a thought. My lampflower wheels walked high and creakless, ah! where were you then, Anxiety, you dead-weight born of devils? But there came a dawn of such excitement that I burst my glass bubble and stepped forth onto solid ground. I acquired a knife, a catapult, a shepherd's crook and a proper anger for the drought I found. Locusts and open razors sang in the pasture; flies were bundling into black baskets the spittle, tears and innocent blood of my young cattle. So I swatted the winged worm and I shot the sun with my catapult. When the water disappeared I climbed to the top of a poplar, throwing sparks from my heels, and there I placed my tears. Then I caught sight of the city, and straightaway the wheel of my imagination walked there jolting. It can't be all big buildings and different levels or how would horses and wheels walk? The answer was thrown up to me by a rum-sodden cattledriver with a head like a God: go there, my son—find out for yourself.

In time the hands of the city bless me. In time they slap my face. Reborn in the eternal ringing of her bells, I quivered in the open book, the savior's cradle. Lifting my head I saw the city with its millers flaming in flour and its dyers steaming. I saw soldiers and priests bearing the precious ores of being on all kinds of shop signs. I saw the spurs of cavalry captains scratching the windows, wounding the see-through souls of ladies. In my dream royal hunters shot me in the breast, and I witnessed the drama of the gift: the stag on his back in the cart offering saffron in his cloven nails to the high window where the most beautiful woman sits. Then, like damnation, the council of drunken doctors appeared above me. They would have chopped off my left leg for their swine had not a blessed hand torn me away from their breath.

I am blessed in time because a gipsy girl walked over me as I lay in the suburbs watching a fleecy cloud. I am drowning, too, because my butcher-brother brought into our bed the stink of the slaughterhouse mingled with lime and convent-scents. He always came at sunset, his flayed body astride a flayed steed. And then in the night his skin grew back, so that by dawn he slept recovered, ready to be flayed again. Now the gingerbread-maker's painted artifacts—the cake-cavalrymen—fought for us on the fabled plain, and in the autumn when, from the apoplectic hills, the caravan of wine approached the flesh, the processed blood, then this sentence came together in me: The world hath become aged. I made a proclamation to a window full of pocketwatches:—Hurry up! I pointed my finger at the public clocks:—Hurry up! My velvet school cap blossomed like the dawn. The oak tree on the badge swished in a roaring gale. O, the souls of old pupils, the muscles of galley-slaves awakened at this symbol! But where now is the graduation ceremony with its lovely flowers? Pale and resigned I chose ours from four ways. I walk it in an ashen cloak under thundering sieves.

Hiding in Poetry

You are a fugitive hiding in poetry,
distress is your dress, and prayers, and fate.
You lurk in a self-created night
of infamous forest and creeping thicket,
where even your bush-hung, silken shirt
is a fluttering nightmare phantom—
mere wind-wobbled flame of a drunken trance.
You are a fugitive hiding in poetry,
with an eye with an eye that is quickly fading
as it strives to focus through shifting leaves
on an open view forever closing:
a finding place that cannot be found.
Outside is wolfish fire and rigor;
inside—the playful beasts you love,
and inside, too, is the iron blood
where, seen through azure panes of membrane,
your burden and vice seem a dazzling world
lit by the real, the only sun.

You are a fugitive hiding in poetry:
a magus, miracle-man, a mother—
a partisan mother smothered in leaves,
so as to escape the feast of fighting,
so as to escape becoming a drum,
so as to escape the midwives of death
who would pummel on life till it miscarried,
then tease from your flesh with surgical fingers
the brilliant ghostly lightnings of your senses
to hang in a withered bunch on a mirror.
If all that inhabits your breathing shirt
is a stony pillar the world will freeze—
O stay where you are and remain yourself!
You are a fugitive hiding in poetry
as flames consume the heavens and earth,
the plummeting bird scatters in ashes,
and the maker of worlds and wheels
dervish-whirling goes made with loss.
See! The maple-seed spins and weeps,
deep in a nightmare of propellers,
and because the sky is not an Eden
for parachutes—death's daisies—to bloom in,
earthly existence comes to a close.
Explosives and manna mingled together
muddle and spoil all blessings:
the infant turning its new-born flesh
from searchlights scything the sky
bangs on the womb-gates to return,
and in their astonishment the immense
mountain ranges of protein-chain
slide back to hide in the primal cell
under skies shaken by burning moons.
You are a fugitive hiding in poetry,
at home with leaf-mold, beetles and moss.
Phosphorescent with restless poison
you make your judgments among sharp thorns—
those judgments of truth you must always make.
You are a fugitive hiding in poetry,
you throw your glove, five-fingered flower,
to the baying hounds in hot pursuit,
and look! as they pounce it trickles blood.

Elegy of the Green Tent

I used to be happy, too,
happy through to the bone in yon valley
in guiltless Wolf's Gorge,
in such a big-bad epoch happy the man
who as the marvels rain down upon his head can hope,
because I lost my shirt, a panic
symbol smothered beneath a bush,
because I've put on forest's and sun's
green-gold reflexes to be the sort who
pierces through and through with eyes of summer
the hearts of traffickers in burned-out embers,
and through thousanding teeth laughs down
the unrepenting infamous.
In yon valley, in Wolf's Gorge
I was not to be expendable, or suppressed
from among the world's made marks, nor to be set aside,
because my betrothed is the nomad god's own daughter
chinking though chainless leaf-wreathed
to whom as wedding present the eagle drifts down
his fairest feather that she should abhor dust,
our altar dry twigs aflame, beautiful the plighting
raising her little nicotined fingers
up toward the maddeningly vacant zenith above the epoch,
and fabricating the future, its fable
out of branches, their aliveness a tent for the two of us,
I bend it, patriarch to be, her
primogenital mama's hand already latent in the waters,
crayfish from her little sworn fingers
hanging on, mossy, obstinate,
vice-gripping nails' rose and moon,
but their stove-pot weeping pains the more
never, never again, this the newest vow,
just imagine, if we were in place of them
being boiled by centurions red,
nails grating on cauldron walls.
But glory be, loving in a green tent,

it lays us down kissing, fire our very own
painfuling us toward unspeakable ecstasy,
I don't stop to eat, mounted upon swarthy summits,
from my sun-dappled back out start showers,
rushing silver cymbalo, out and in,
until your sugary mouth's saliva runs dry
and we can lie stretched out beside each other
on swanning crossed bones swooning
in such make-believe death, but still I see
you soar up through the green arch branches
and your air split-apart legs sing
and in a rainbow bundle-bag on your little back
you bring a brat, star wide-eyed.

Now my roof and my heaven and my daylight are lime,
now of leaves cracked across with lime
and eyelids broken away from dream, that's
an appointment kept I've had to live to see, time.
Here lies upon tempered steel springs
my lacklusterness, but this isn't me,
the body here's not mine, somewhere far away
within a green arena, my own true self
you have pinned down, time, fenced in there,
misappropriated, leaving not even a glimpse
between the bars, ringmaster time.
In time, palace, dwelling-place, strong castle . . .
I intone the flowery line—but in time
hard tooth, full head of hair, fire too, waste away
solid balls of stallions, the genes, blood,
and non-delivery at the address on veins' postal-
route of what was dispatched or not sent at all,
thus salt, magnesium, phosphorus, like parceled up virgins
sift into slag and lose their way down
into ocean night's flower gardens, time.
I've no more words to waste on them, won't
whine after ultra-violet for myself.
Out in fire-center speckle space
no thoroughfares, flame-wheels or prospects'
magic can attract, because ambition drives
me no place at all, not even godward.
Whether its cosmic or divine, I'm the sort
who looks to no comfort of any kind. For why to make

myself a blade of grass or angel or plain cuckoo?
Is my end in my beginning? Well said, because
the other way round it's just as bad, O lord,
the laureate in top-hat who composed that
is just as tall and hollow and rounded.
Pain's flare does the talking here, not your pride
because my roof and my heaven and my daytime are lime
and my ears' fading greenness is not yet
so dulled that the lime-foliage music does not grate,
nor my heart so dulled that it doesn't hate
compromise with whatever's in prospect, no use
bleeding each time I open my mouth,
the white has not yet made me all through white.
But like the sickly being forcibly
fed, you have me pinned here, time,
stuffing me with lime fit to bursting, time,
you snap off green rustlings' arches inside
me, and grind them in your mortar.
No memory, no self. Now can you, time, in time
keep up the white pace you've set,
you're done in fit to drop, time,
destroyed by the nothing, the nothing I feel
and I am sorry, time, because I live within you,
sweetly I sing you, are you listening, time?
This is the elegy of the green tent.

House

Down upon it, the curse—go on, well go on
down with you, house—a woman of time past
hair-to-her-knees woman calling it down.
Curse coming to pass, already a mourning ribbon
frigging the frontage: tarry roadway.
Its door won't open, no one, no one.
The rambler rose falls from the wall onto its back,

and maize-corn peers over into the yard,
now sunflowers, tucking the roof-tree
under their chins, golden-cheeked
stare back at me, the stranger there.

Just idling, craning this weak neck of mine,
just standing there; for what should I, could I, do?
Try to do something about misery, yes,
a try turning into horseplay, as I holler:
Hallo there, got anything to grind today?
Any pots and pans for patching there?
Any calf or lamb to sell in there?
No naughty boys or girls to take away?
White chinaware for your old iron, rags, oakum!
Out quick with mum's shift, kids, a whistle for it!
Powder for those cheeks, ladies, from Ivan here!
For your bloomers and trousers, for both left legs
elastic here! It's Fancy Dan, dear, at the door!
Anyone for cream-wafers, oranges, a drop of rum?
I'll tell your future for cottage cheese,
just a right eyeful! I got hurt in a fire,
don't have nothing, what I'd give for a plate of soup!
How d'you see it, the government set-up?
G'morning, g'day, and don't fall asleep tonight,
plant the seed-corn good, there's grease in the well!
G'morning, g'day, g'night!
Oo, my head took such a crack, may I wash it?
Oo, my horse croaked under me, where'll I doss down?

Just standing there, craning this weak neck of mine,
yes I did cry out, to do something about misery,
a try turning into horseplay; it didn't come off.
Just senseless leaf-rustling. Just sunflowers in
gold-stupor amazement, like the urchins around Raphael
while he dreamed up most beautiful of mothers.
I pull down a plum, father's corpse-mouth cold.
A night's lodging, that's all, because I'm a wanderer,
fool public-scribbler, even the pheasants made it
inside, closing one eye in leafy hazel shelter.
Well, if this split-apart trough's to be my bed
I'll line it well. No one's home at all?
I'll mow the camomile patch, stretch out there and

> listen to wild boar grunt-grunting, one ear
> toward the fairy folk in my gold watch; I'll be poisoned
> by nicotine before dawn—but first, moon at the full,
> I snuff you out with rusty scythe. Good night.

From: Interview, 1965

On Clarity of Meaning

Your poems of the last few years are difficult to understand. Don't you think that restricts the effectiveness of your poetry?

I write for myself. It must be understood that I accept responsibility for the effects of my writings. I write for myself, and if I am able to voice one social desire, will, or outrage, then I am completely happy. I am certain that my poems speak to many. I also know that a few of my writings are, for some, difficult or almost impossible to understand. But the obscurity is not always in my poems; it is in those who are aesthetically unimaginative and sluggish. We cannot begin poetry anew at an elementary level. Let them learn also, let them be attentive, let them strive for understanding. I am always respectfully interested in the professions followed by others, and I scorn those who view my profession with contemptuous disrespect. I scorn those who consider their sole calling to be the unceasing examination of poets for simplicity. . . . They appoint themselves as the representatives of public opinion; they speak everywhere; they sprout more leaves than the swamp willow. They do not call the poet into productive service; they would rather shove him into vilest servitude.

Timeliness, Morality

In your poems there is often what appears to be a timeless, an abstract morality.

I believe I write for the present. Directly as well as indirectly. But I put into verse only that which is impossible to express in a novel, an editorial, a dissertation, or a philosophical essay. Otherwise there is no need for poetry. I am a living citizen of this country, not a miraculous creature or a Martian. If I speak I seek to express in every way modern man's woe, sensuality, struggle, or anger. I am not concerned with eternity, but I would like one thing—that my poems be instructive documents for future generations about one poet and this frequently mentioned present. My moral standards are clear. He who reads my poems will discover them; he may readily accept them, or be indignant at them. Socialism proclaims the standards of its morality as upholding the common interest. When socialism commands one not to steal, it also means one must not take from the community. When socialism dictates that one must not kill, then I also understand that the salvation planned for this earth may be achieved without bloodshed. To the masses socialism promises material and spiritual improvement. Can anyone call it middle-class moralizing if I am indignant at the refined glorification of common horse dealers? Usually I do not sing about moral themes, but I am sensitive about the ethical implications of my poems.

The Poet's Power

If given the power, what would someone who has such strict and specific standards of morality do?

The poet believes he has power. This is an inherent trait. At the beginning of history, the sorcerer was also a poet. He had power over the community, and, what is more, he believed he controlled nature. He insured the success of each undertaking because he hardened and prepared the community. If the hunt was unsuccessful, they could rightfully kill him. Thanks to the division of labor, I, who am today's "sorcerer," can be satisfied if I have power over words, over my message.

Today, if I had the power, I would summon brigades of angels to the fields. Because, it seems to me, it is more difficult to summon migrated manpower back from industry and other places. Let these angels hoe the sugar beets, let them reap, let them mix the slop for the pigs, carry in the frozen bales through the snow drifts, for the old men are dying off. If I had the power, I would give more independence to those who are entitled to it. If I had the power, I would not treat literature as an elite matter. If I had the power, I would tear up the lists of protocol, because even if I had the power, I could not tear up the real authorities. If I had the power, I would insure the modern aesthetic education of the citizenry from the nursery to the home for the aged. I would make young people love, not hate literature. I do not strive for personal power. If I had that kind of power, I would lose it. There is power in my poems.

Today Hungarian poetry is rich, meaningful, healthy, and aspiring. It is not inferior to foreign poetry. I do not long for the freedom of western poets. As far as my personal decisions and the fulfillment of my poetic aspirations are concerned, I am free up to now. I am free, and because of my difficult experiences, I am, in general, more so than my western contemporaries. These experiences are not for everyone, and I do not wish them either on the "free" who look askance at us nor on those who sympathize with us.

On Literary Criticism

What do you think of literary criticism?

I do not follow criticism continually. But I do have an opinion about it, and I do not think it is entirely without foundation. . . . With the exception of a few extraordinary individuals, critics have changed their views too often; so often that today they do not know which one is their own. Instead of striving to employ the one possible idea, one that will not need revision later—the extraction of literature's values and the education of readers—so far they do not so much examine the work as wonder what they could appropriately write about the poet's personality. . . . There is still another way to destroy the credibility of criticism: valueless writings are annointed as literature, their errors being "bravely" castigated, as if advertising them, whereas excellent works are lost in the jungle of ordinary criticism. . . . I am concerned . . . about the fate of our literature. Today it is a rare event when a contemporary work is appropriately analyzed as an aesthetic reality as well. I have a better opinion of literary historians. Does distance help them? Could it be that today's literature will only be properly judged by literary history?

Illusions, Shocks

We ask [László Nagy] to describe how he views his own development as a poet, as an individual, and his successes and failures.

I had illusions; for the most part, I destroyed them myself. I have been disappointed and shaken in the faith that sustained me since my youth. I am not ashamed of my perturbations. They are part of the condition of both man and poet. My loyalty has always bound me to the people whose child I am and in whose language I write. I wanted to be loyal to Hungarian poetry. To the main living thread that runs through out poetry from Balassi to Attila József (and later)—a thread that not only calls us to join the battle for our survival but also contains the belief that we must come closer to our already "atoned for" ideal future without unnecessary sacrifices. My answer only marks the difficulties of loyalty and commitment, and because I am not at the crossroads, I do not consider it appropriate to place my bitter extravagance in the balance.

No matter how I feel, I cannot, once and for all, ease my pain and my problems; they flare up again and again. For the rare joy, I constantly and painfully struggle with my social, personal, and creative problems. But I am also strong, and barring some natural disaster, I shall fight on for a long time.

From:
Cognition, Language, and Poetry

Bringing dishonor on the word is not a new discovery, but it is more evident and painful than formerly. We witness how language is being used for hoaxing and lying. It is not surprising that many turn away from vital questions: good if to play, painful if to silence. The philosophy of silence is not today's discovery either. . . . In my presence, silence seems like a comfortable state—the calm of the dead. Boasting is comfortable too, but it is also immoral. I want to be the true protagonist of the word. If the impossible is without hope, even our failure is a celebration.

I have grown old, and my very being knows I am one with the word. I know that every poet is indicted by his own language. (As man's work is, in general, a reflection on himself, even as his eating is.)

If there is an impartial judgment of the poet, it is his poetry. I am calmed by one certainty: I believe in the word. My duty is to heed the word. I care for the word: it is devotion and responsibility. I also believe that it will lead me behind the seals where secrets await me. It is leading me to something that does not exist in this world. It is leading me along the brim of chasms, ceaselessly on the lips of death.

Ferenc Sánta

Sánta was born on September 4, 1927 in Brassó, Transylvania, formerly a part of Hungary, for which he retains a deep emotional and cultural attachment. His family—he was the third child—often moved from place to place as his parents tried to establish a secure way of life. While still an adolescent Sánta left home to seek his future in Debrecen shortly after the Russians had driven the German forces out of Hungary. His first-hand experiences with direst poverty, the daily struggle of the poor, both peasants and workers, to obtain the meagerest necessities for subsistence, find touching expression in his short stories and novels, in the lasting affection and respect that he displays for the strength, courage, and integrity of ordinary people, no matter how flawed they may be. His own temperament, he says, developed between the opposite poles of his parents' personalities: his father was emotional, volatile; his mother rational, matter-of-fact. His independent spirit and sensitivity to injustice were early manifested by two actions against authority. He was expelled from the Unitarian High School in Kolozsvár for reciting on a school holiday a satirical poem by Mór Jókai, an important nineteenth-century romantic novelist, instead of a poem composed by his teacher. Later, anticipating dismissal for leading a month-long student strike to secure greater rights for his peers, he left the Debrecen Reformed College's High School voluntarily, thereby terminating his formal education. Both these experiences bore fruit. The first was an important influence in his consideration of a literary career. The second, as he records in a notebook at the time, gave him pride at not being "born to be a creature in a herd of cattle but a free and independent human being."

After the student strike, he married, and four sons were soon born to him and his wife. Before moving from Debrecen to Budapest, he supported his family as a laborer and miner and, for a short time, as a teacher in a people's college. He arrived in Budapest in 1951, where he worked as a lathe operator in a tractor factory before becoming a librarian at the Academy's Institute of Literary Studies in 1958. By that year his literary career was successfully launched, and eventually the publication of two collections of short stories and two novels wrought such interest among readers that he left this post in 1965 to devote himself entirely to writing. Two of his novels have been made into successful films: *Twenty Hours (Husz óra)*, concerned with the events of the 1956 Revolution, was awarded a prize at the 1964 Moscow Film Festival, and *The Fifth Seal (Az ötödik pecsét)*, portraying the major moral dilemmas prevailing among Hungarians in the closing months of World War II, enjoys frequent reruns and was also produced as a play in 1976 in Debrecen. *Night (Éjszaka)*, a play adapted from his third novel to date, *The Traitor (Az áruló)*, and an evaluation of contemporary revolution in the context of the Hussite wars in the fifteenth century, has also been presented on the stage in Budapest. Editions of his earlier works continue to appear regularly, but he has not published anything for many years, except for a third collection of short stories in 1970, which contained no new works, and two scenes from a projected play and parts of *Gray Stone (Szürke kő)*, a novel on which he has been working for some time. This period of silence is long even for an author who is deliberately not prolific. Perhaps some indication of his future course is apparent in a comment he made in 1976: because he has been involved with the genre of the novel for such a long time, he can no longer manage the formal demands made by the short story.

Sánta's style and thought have been significantly influenced by factors besides the poverty he knew so well: the rich folk culture of the Székely people among whom he grew up and the story-telling of his father, who related—indeed acted out—the folk tales of that culture in a vivid and lively manner to gatherings of family and friends. Another influence is the literature he has chosen to probe. Until fourteen or fifteen he confined his reading almost exclusively to the folk ballad; his first book purchase was a three-volume edition of folk poetry collected by a nineteenth-century Transylvanian bishop. This early absorption in folk literature, when added to the culture in which he was living and to the story-telling of his father, imbues his style with the measures and lyrical concreteness of the ballad which he does not abandon even when in his later stories and novels he turns to harsh ethical conflicts.

His eventual search for enlightenment in world literature more than demonstrates his hunger for knowledge; it also illuminates significant sources of the humanism that lies at the heart of all his writings. Among the authors he mentions are the Greek tragedians and philosophers as well as Dante, Montaigne, Pascal, Byron, and Verlaine. At sixteen he was mesmerized by Dostoevsky's

Brothers Karamazov, and he later judged Tolstoy to be the best writer of all, an almost perfect human being, and the one from whom he gained the most. His humanism is succinctly revealed in his comments on other writers. For example, the satire of Erasmus is deeper and truer than Voltaire's because it comes from "depths where eyes have been wept tearless and only laughter is possible" and because Erasmus loves humankind; and he is grateful to Rousseau for helping him to conclude that education can spare children the evils that civilization visits upon human beings. His emphasis on the inner needs of humans is further seen in his explorations of the literature of the French Revolution and also in his rejection of Engel's belief that human problems should be approached through a materialistic world, this latter evincing his ethical, more than political commitment, to the principles of socialism.

His first short story, "There Were Too Many of Us" ("Sokan voltunk"), which was immediately acclaimed when it appeared in 1954, signaled a new development in Hungarian fiction because of its symbolic use of realistic details not found in the critical realism of earlier prosewriters or in the socialist realism that the Rákosi government sought to impose on authors at the time. His first collection of short stories (1956) revealed his penchant for the parable. They are deceptively simple tales of peasant life based mainly on his own family experiences in Transylvania. His second collection showed a change in narrative direction; the stories are products of his realization that, instead of continuing to draw on his memories, he must invent characters and situations that best express his conception of existence. He, as a writer, has, he insists, the inborn prerogative, to a degree greater than others, to select and shape his interpretations as a judgment of the state of society and of the world—an act apparently with its perils, as the story "Little Bird" implies. This creative process and this inviolable right he continues to exercise, especially through the device of dialogue, in his three short novels, a genre especially well suited to didacticism. His clear intent is to force his readers to confront moral issues by experiencing vicariously the ethical struggles and dilemmas that history ineluctably imposes on common people, in whom he places so much hope for the future of humankind.

In Sánta's eyes, human salvation lies in humanistic ethics. Convinced that new criteria for behavior are required because the moral values founded on religious belief have decayed, he builds his *ars poetica* on the axiom that "whatever debases, harms, ravages a human being is sinful." Everyone must recognize that wrong means never serve right ends, and that the most perverting sin is fanaticism, the easy succumbing to the temptation of reducing the moral dialectic of life to black or white. To avoid this enticement to fanatic acts, human beings are born to make judgments, an act as natural to them as eating. Moreover, they can actually achieve ethical perfection by proper exercise of that judgment. Fortunately, nature has endowed every human being with a conscience that, like the Demon of Socrates, instantaneously distinguishes between right and wrong. The universal ethical laws embedded in human nature and voiced by the conscience are heard increasingly as the walls that the events of time raise between the individual and that moral guide are worn away by the arduous exercise of a balanced and impartial judgment. An author's function, he believes, is to give his readers the opportunity to carry out this exercise and so to move toward an ethical ideal. For even as an author's superior judgment is freely applied to reality, so too his conscience, purer than that of other human beings, comprehends within himself the moral order of humankind.

Sánta's optimism about human prospects is exemplified by the moral act of the two prisoners in "No More Dying Then." Steeped in humanistic values, they hear the Demon within and instantly obey its command; their judgments long having swept away the values humans normally live by, they rescue the guard conducting them to their execution, to the befuddlement of the guard and, perhaps, many readers as well. So clearly do they hear the voice of the conscience that their selfless act of mercy tolls the death of the old morality and hails the imperishability of the new.

Little Bird

My mother called me "little bird" because I sang so beautifully. People would stop me on the street, and if they had any small change, they would press something into my palm: "There's a penny, now sing." Whenever my mother sent me to the store for some little thing or another, the shopkeeper would put two pieces of candy on the counter: "Aren't you going to sing for me? If you do, I'll give you all this candy." Old people liked my singing best, and I liked them most because we exchanged songs like friends of the same age. When they let me go they always said: "You have a blessedly beautiful voice. God created you in his joy." I tended sheep, and when they were at rest, I would stretch out on my back in the beautiful hills and sing every song I knew, one right after the other. At times like that I too believed I was a little bird, because I wasn't singing for candy or money but only for my own joy.

When I took home the first money I received for singing and put it in my mother's hand, she kissed me and was happy as a child. I told her some people had given it to me for my singing. She hardly looked at me, took her scarf, quickly tied it around her head, and ran out the door like someone being chased. Only then did I understand how poor we really were. My mother went to the store and brought home a big bag of flour.

From then on, I walked only those streets where certain people lived and only when they were sitting in front of their gates. I didn't want the money, I wanted happiness for my mother. But happiness flew off as a bird from a hurled stone. The more often I brought money home, the farther away it flew. My mother no longer looked into my eyes. She took the money from my hand as if she were borrowing it and some stranger were giving it to her, not I.

At St. Nicholas time I took home a lot of money, more than five Sundays put together, and placed it all on the table before my mother.

"Look at all the money, Mama!"

She was lighting the fire then, and at my words she stood up. She came to the table but didn't look at me, only at the money, wiping her hands in her apron. Her eyes were fluttering so fast I thought she was going to burst into tears. She spoke to me in a strange voice:

"God is going to punish me, my son!"

I didn't understand why she said that. I urged her to take the money: we needed it and it's good there is so much; if the smaller amounts had been so welcome, how much more so the larger. She just stared at the money in a frightening way. Her face was as it had been the time my younger brother died. To look at her, you'd have thought she was again burying someone. That's exactly how she looked. My heart tightened so, I could feel it struggle and pound. I rushed to her, knocking over a chair and bucket that were in the way, watching only her face. I got to her and she clasped me in her arms. She pressed me to her as if someone were trying to take me from her. She kept kissing me, slowly lowering herself onto a chair. She pulled me into her lap, and as if she never wanted to stop, she kept repeating over and over again between moans: "God is going to punish me, my son—God is going to punish me!" I buried my face in the folds of her apron. My tears flowed like a suddenly swollen brook. I couldn't say a thing, but I wanted to express what I didn't understand: "My soul can't rest, it hurts very bad, Mama." When my brothers and sisters came home we were still sitting that way. I don't know who ate my supper, I went to bed without it. I didn't want anything.

After that, only the old people heard me sing. Never strangers. But only until Christmas. Two weeks after my mother's despair, my little sister, Katica, fell ill. There was no money in the house, my father was in the army, and we knew that if we didn't do something, she would die. We needed money for a doctor and medicine, and when there isn't any, not even God cares for a poor man. I learned early that when it comes to trouble, it never rains but it pours. And I now knew that was true. My mother became dizzy just then at the head of the sick child. She began holding her stomach, and asked for some water. I immediately knew God was punishing us—my mother was expecting again.

Katica, in her burning fever, always called for me. Her widened eyes followed me everywhere. She seemed to be only two large dark eyes. In the house I felt as if all the walls wanted to fall on me, to crush me.

The third day of her illness came right on a Sunday. I dashed out of the house and ran all the way to the tavern. I ran the length of the street. I only stopped at the entrance. I went up the steps on legs that seemed made of lead and were unable to manage themselves. I sneaked through the door like a thief. My forehead burned as if I too were sick in bed, and if crazily, yet I firmly felt, with absolute certainty, that my soul was exactly like my mother's face on that St. Nicholas night. I scurried through the noisy crowd to the farmers' room. At the door jamb I threw my back against the wall and waited for someone to speak to me. Oh, if only Katica's crying would leave my head, for I won't be able to sing! The men at the long table looked like a troubled dream in a restless night. They sounded like the voices of daytime passers-by heard from a deep, dark cave. The midwife's husband, the miller, Gáspár Rece, noticed me first. He called me over and jingled the money in his pocket. I stopped before him and he asked:

"Do you want some candy?"

I fought the lump in my throat. I knew I couldn't look into his face. And if I could have followed the dictate of my own heart, I would have grabbed the front of his white shirt at his chest and shouted into his nice pink face: I don't want any candy, my little sister is dying at home, give me money for medicine, you'd have plenty left anyway! Instead, I said what I had to :

"Yes, that's what I want, candy."

He snapped his fingers in rhythm and started the song for me. He hummed, and I picked it up:

> "My top-boots are made of pigskin,
> My father brought them from Régen . . . "

The others joined in, but softly so my voice could take wing above theirs. And it flew, for I drove it. It flew out of me as if someone were beating it and it were fleeing. Its wings were loaded with my sorrows, but couldn't bear them. It struggled and kept breaking under the heavy burden.

Whenever they wanted another song, the one who began it lured me over with a nod of his head and pressed money for candy into my hand. If there had been a clock in the room, I would have fixed my eyes on it, but there wasn't, so I kept them on the bare walls. I drove Katica's crying from my ears, and I worried the money in my clenched fists, I was counting it so hard. Every coin was damp and slippery, for sweat was pouring from my forehead and palms, my whole body.

It was getting late when András Kácsa called me over to him. My father had rented land from him in the fall. He pushed his ugly flat forehead against my face. He began the song between his sharp yellow teeth, and I sang it to him. I sang as if my lungs were about to burst, for he was hard of hearing and could understand it only that way. I was nearing the end of the song when the door flew open. I looked and saw Imre, his wagoner son, come in. All my strength ebbed from me. What voice I had, stuck in my throat. My blood rushed to my head. This was the man who drove my grandfather from their yard with his dog and had thrown a stake brace at my heels. We were cutting wood at their place and my grandfather had taken a handful of dried prunes from the porch and slipped them into my pocket.

Having turned my head away, I didn't see Imre, I only heard him greet everyone loudly. I could sense he sat down beside me because the bench creaked and the cold he brought with him struck my face. My voice faltered and trembled like a dying bird's. I ended the song so badly I didn't know if I would get anything or not. I don't know what my face was like, but when András Kácsa looked at me, he put some money into my hand without a word, though he had always before thrown it high into the air so I'd have to jump and catch it. I don't know where I got the strength to start for the door. But I can still hear Imre Kácsa's voice: "Hey you, stop!" Jani Botos, the beekeeper, stuck his leg in front of me, and I stopped. The door looked like the gate of heaven. I swallowed the tears that welled in my eyes. Imre Kácsa grabbed my arm and pulled me back to the bench. He squeezed my shoulder but addressed his father:

"You don't know what you are doing. You are just wasting your money. I wouldn't have given him anything for that song." He flipped my chin upwards with two big fingers and asked:

"Maybe you haven't eaten any dried prunes today and your throat has dried out, eh?"

I was looking at his black boots.

"Come on, you owe him another song for his money. Pay him with the one that goes . . . "

He raised his hand and beat time on my head and sang:

"Green is the pulp of the lemon . . . "

All the money in my hands fell to the floor. My voice tore out of me like something shouting for the first time:

"I won't!"

The silence was so great I could hear my heart beating. It sounded like a big cauldron being pounded for cracks. I felt as if my eyes would fall from their sockets, because I couldn't close them, and I didn't dare look up into Imre Kácsa's eyes. I saw his boots move and heard the floor creak. He was standing before me. I saw his large bony hands rise before me. He grabbed my hair and raised my face in line with his eyes. He looked the way he did when he had noticed my grandfather's hands that time. He drew his mouth to one side as if he were smiling. Maybe he really was. Oh, Grandfather, where are you? I thought. You aren't holding my hand now, and this man sicked his dog on you. Grandfather! My body strained upward, my blood began to race. My grandfather's hand was before me offering the dried prunes. "Put them away, you can eat them on the way home." I could feel the stake brace strike my heel as if it were happening this very instant. My heart was in my mouth. My hands felt like big hoes. Andras Kácsa's trousers danced before my eyes, their braids twisted like a forester's whip, as if they were not on his trousers but on my back. "I won't!" I cried. I remember even now, as if it had happened only yesterday, that the flame of the lamp hanging from the wire flickered. I would have shouted as long as my breath held, I would have yelled as long as my heart could stand it, but Imre Kácsa grabbed my throat. He didn't raise his voice, just said quietly under his breath:

"Sing, damn you, sing."

I could see his yellow gums, his mouth twitched so.

"Sing, you damn beggar, sing."

I lifted my head. I hadn't looked at a soul that night, but my eyes now glared into Imre Kácsa's face. I spoke as if making a declaration:

"I won't!"

The first blow in the face staggered me, the second knocked me down. I kicked all the money on the floor in every direction, and my whole body, my whole life became a large, powerful voice yelling up at the shiny boots:

"I won't! I won't!"

If my mother hadn't come in, they would have killed me. I later learned that the larger of my younger brothers had been standing in the doorway and had dashed home to call mother for help. Her scarf streamed behind her when she ran in. She seized Imre Kácsa's hand. She half covered me with her body.

"You godless one, how dare you raise your hand against my son!" She raised me to my feet and took my face into her hands. "Don't you fear God? Your mother will turn over in her grave. Hit *me*! Hit *me*!"

She took hold of me and we started for the door. We reached the threshold. The men made way for us. They had cleared the way to the street door when András Kácsa grabbed our arms, both mine and my mother's. He stood before us like God Himself.

"Stop, Anna, and come to your senses!"

He was exactly like his son, except that he kept his hand in his trouser pocket. It was worse this way. He was holding my soul directly, I felt, not my throat.

"Your son will sing or you'll have to get off my land. There are many kinds of agreements, and I'll keep ours only if I want to."

It was frightening the way he stood there.

It is good that mother is here. She will help me, I thought. She knows everything because she is a grown up, and she loves me. Maybe she loves me even more than herself. I pulled at her skirt to get us started. She didn't move. I looked up at her face. She looked as if a flame were burning in her body. But she didn't bat an eye. She was looking into András Kácsa's face, but as if past him into some vast empty darkness. Her heart was pounding next to my ear. They stood facing each other for an eternity. They were rigid, like two large stones that figures are carved out of. Then, as if the ceiling had fallen on her, or the bones had been ripped out of her body, my mother suddenly collapsed. I felt the weight of her body on my shoulders. She bent her head to my face and whispered so quietly I could hardly understand her:

"Sing, Ferike, sing."

The whole world spun. I reached for her dress and grabbed it above her breasts. I spoke, almost wailing:

"Mama!" I shook the dress on her bosom. I tore at it as if I wanted to strip her naked. I opened my throat and yelled into her face:

"Mama! Mama!"

Tears began flowing from her closed eyes. She pulled my head to her, and kneeling, she smoothed my hair with her hands.

"Sing, Ferike, my little bird, sing."

She turned me toward the men and almost shouted:

"My sweet little bird, sing! Sing because these are not humans. See how I am, and God gives me no help. Sing, my little bird, sing!"

I started to cry. I could feel my beautiful strength fly far away. I looked at my mother as if we were both dying . . . she hugged my shoulders and said:

"See, I am singing, too."

Her tears flowed into her open mouth and she began singing in a small, thin voice. I sang with her:

> Green is the pulp of the lemon,
> My lover's name is János,
> Bitter is the seed of the lemon,
> Sweet are the kisses of my lover.

I don't know if anyone understood what we sang, though I pronounced every word.

Something flared up before my eyes. András Kácsa was lighting his pipe. I tore my arm from my mother's hand and ran at him with my head. I didn't reach him. A boot heel leaped at my face and I ran into it. I fell at the feet of András Kácsa's son, and the last thing I felt was the warm blood on my face.

Fairyland

My father was away on a long trip, and we children were staying alone with mother. The smaller ones spent their days in whatever ways they could find, but I didn't move from my mother's side. I didn't know why, for she never told stories as my grandfather used to or my father did once in a while. She came and went, did this and that, and put up with me. I didn't help her a bit. After all, everything she did was merely woman's work. I just gazed about around her and daydreamed. She went about her tasks the way I had seen her do all her life. Once in a great while she would stop, and lean on the edge of the wash tub or rest where she stood. She'd take a deep breath and then work on. If lunchtime was near or supper, I couldn't resist speaking to her gruffly. Exactly the way my father did: "Isn't supper ready?" Then, deep inside me, I would silently add: "Now, Mother." If she noticed this or the passing of time, she would wipe her hands on the edge of her apron and go into the house and prepare supper. I just stood there, looking around until she called me in to eat.

Near the end of October my mother moved all her work into the house. I was sitting beside her, she was washing clothes. That day we hadn't eaten anything at all. What food we had was being saved for supper. I thought of my grandfather, and if I closed my eyes for a moment, I could hear his voice. I felt so sad I could barely stand it. My mother's hands were busy, the water splashed in the tub. I had become so used to the sound that I hardly noticed when it stopped. I looked up at her. I thought she was straightening her back again or bracing herself for a cough. She didn't do either. She was bending over the tub, her hands in the soapy water up to her wrists. She seemed to be resting, but her face and the look in her eyes made my heart throb. I didn't know if God was playing a trick on me or I wasn't seeing clearly, but at that moment her face looked again like my little sister's, whom we had buried and should never see again. I stared at my mother as if I were beholding some marvel. Her eyes were lost in the light of the window, and her lips parted as if she were smiling. Her scarf slipped to one side, and strands of her hair fell down over her forehead. She brushed them back the way a little child does. I couldn't take my eyes off her. She was more beautiful than I had ever seen her. I hardly recognized her voice when she spoke to me:

"Feri . . ."

She didn't turn toward me; her eyes were wide-open. She stared out the window into the distance. Across from us no house or fence blocked the view, and we could see all the way to the distant hills. I could barely speak from the astonishment that swept over me. Perhaps she didn't even hear me.

"Yes . . . Mama?"

She seemed to have forgotten she had spoken to me. She just stared into the distance. A small, frail smile moved over her lips. Her voice stirred and she began singing. She hummed a song I had never heard before. Then, as if following the rhythm of the melody, she slowly turned toward me. She had forgotten to wipe her hands, and as she raised them breast high, the water dripped from her wrists. She was smiling, but the dripping water made her look as if she were weeping. When she finished the song, she stood in the middle of the room, fixed in her place. She fastened her eyes on me, and tilting her head halfway to one side, she seemed to be listening after her own words, for the melodies echoing from afar. I didn't know what she wanted. She was acting as if someone had spoken softly to her but she didn't know from where. She looked around the room; then her eyes settled on the fire in the stove. A smile rose in the corners of her mouth and spread over her face. In a voice sounding as if a tiny bell were tinkling inside her, she began:

"After that, they all drew aside, all the lovely fairies, stepping as if they were dancing. Maybe their feet weren't even touching the ground . . ."

Holding the sides of her skirt, she went back to the wash tub as if strolling in a field of flowers.

I was so confused I couldn't say anything, but thoughts kept whirling around in my head. I didn't know if I was scared or what it was that flew into my heart. It was pounding so hard I could hear it. I stood up as if lifted by my mother's legs. Then she began dancing beside the tub as if she had been doing so all her life. Her arms waved and swam in the air, her feet skipped and stamped when she turned. And all the time she didn't speak a single word. I heard only her gasping for breath. Her feet didn't make the slightest sound. I thought it was a miracle, for every wrinkle had vanished from her face. Her face was wreathed in a smile and flushed with the stirrings of her blood. She stopped at the cupboard and glanced at me again. Her eyes glittered like brilliant stars. Or maybe more like red-hot embers burning my face. I'd never seen anything like them. Anyone else would have thought she was crazy, and fled from those eyes.

"And then the Princess entered, the Princess of the fairies. She was so beautiful, so very beautiful, that men's hearts would break. Too beautiful to be human . . . And before the young women, and before the men, all of them watching only her, she began to dance . . ."

My mother spread her arms like wings and began to twirl. Her dress swished and swirled, but heavy with all the splashed water, it clung to her body. Still she twirled and twirled. Her face burned like the red meadow flower. She'd bend her back and spread her fingers out as if she wanted to smooth the earth from end to end. Then she'd twirl on again and lift her face high as if she were looking at the clouds or wanted to hold it to the sun for a moment. And she kept on singing. In her rapid breathing her voice hardly came, but when it broke she always tried again. At last she stopped in front of the stove. She pressed her hands against her breast. Her shoulders were rising and falling so fast that they seemed to be tearing themselves from her body. I went to her, as if walking in a dream. I don't know how my legs carried me, and I couldn't take my eyes off her.

"Mama, what are you doing . . . "

I felt I was going to cry out, but my voice is stuck in my throat. I was just about to try and grab her arm, when she put her hand on my head. Her voice was like the one she used with us in church or like my grandfather's when he told us stories. But I didn't know if she was speaking to me or someone else. She was looking over my head, far off into the distance unaware of the furniture, the wall, or anything else around her—the way you look around from the hilltop and see the whole world.

"Then music sounded, all kinds of music. And voices, my little son, as many kinds as there were fairies. One voice sounded like a weeping child. No, not like that . . . but you feel it's like that. Another sounded as if he were laughing heartily, or more as if he were smiling a bit but felt like weeping at times."

She raised a finger, and her voice soared, sounding like a dove or a flute. Stopping, she listened as if awaiting an echo. Then she began to caress my head, and spoke on as if I were not there.

"The whole world seemed to come crashing down, and only these beautiful fairies and the music remained. It was so wonderful, as if you were left alone with them in the whole world . . . yet there were so many it was not possible to count them all . . . All the fairies and music seemed to lift you until you flew. And before all those eyes, the Princess, the fairy Princess, danced and danced and danced . . . "

Then my mother started to dance. As if there were no boots on her feet, as if she were weightless and the room were a broad meadow. She whirled, lifted her feet, sometimes closing her eyes for an instant. I walked around her, asking her to stop, not do it any more. I ran between the cupboard and the stove afraid she would hurt herself. I thought she had lost her mind. She doesn't know what she is doing, I thought, even though she is a grown up. My God, what would happen if my father should see her! What if anyone saw her! Nothing could ever wipe away the shame of my mother's madness, her bewitchment. She leaves her washing to dance across the room at her age as if she were at a ball. But my mother kept on whirling and whirling so fast she seemed to want to leave the earth. I started crying. Everything ran together as if the world were one big tear. House, tub, mother—everything melted into one. I kept calling: Mama! Mama!

A great silence brought me finally to my senses. My mother was leaning on the door jamb like someone who has lost all her strength. Her head forward, she was looking at the world beyond the window. Her lips trembled as if weeping welled within her. That's really how she looked. She slumped and pressed her hands so high against her breast that her fingers were at her throat crushing her blouse into a thousand little wrinkles. Slowly, like someone waking from a dream, she looked around the room. She looked first at the chair, then at the bed, the stove, and at last she fixed her eyes on me. She looked me over from head to foot. Then she fastened her eyes on the dirt floor. Her boots had dug it up. It looked as if large, strong fists had pounded it from one end to the other. As I glanced toward her, I saw that every little footprint was filled with water. Water that had spilled from the wash tub had settled into each of them, like dew, and now flashed like a mirror everywhere she had stepped. I couldn't move. I stood as if weights stacked on me had sunk me deep into the ground. My mother started toward me, calmly straightening her skirt and scarf. When she reached me she took hold of my chin.

"Come now . . . Feri."

As she raised my head slowly, I noticed she was crumpling the side of her skirt with her free hand. She was clutching it in her fingers, then letting go like a little child who is being scolded or has been caught at something shameful. I looked into her face. Beads glistened on her forehead and temples. Strands of hair had fallen from beneath her scarf to cling to her face like wrinkles, and here and there among the black wrinkles I could see gray ones. There were tears in her eyes, and pain showed in her face as if she had been tortured.

"Come, come, my son . . . are you all right?"

I didn't answer. She sighed and took her hand from me. She untied her scarf, snapped it in the air, and put it back on her head. Pushing me aside, she went back to her wash tub. But she hardly touched the water and went instead to the stove to pour boiling water on the clothes from the large pot. She ignored me. She touched her apron into her waist and bent over the unwashed clothes. I just stood there, unable to escape the great heat burning my body. I started to go out to the yard, expecting her to call me back. I heard only the sounds of her washing. While closing the door, I looked back at her. She stopped for a moment, looked straight ahead, stirring the water with her hand. Then she grabbed a shirt and began scrubbing it hard, as she always did. Not even a speck of dirt would remain.

I went out to the porch and lay down in my grandfather's place. I had been sleeping there ever since he'd gone away. I watched the sky, and perhaps would have stayed there until morning if my brothers and sisters hadn't returned and if I hadn't heard mother call us in for supper.

The Initiation

The sky had never been more splendid, the day more pleasant, the houses finer, and human beings seemed made of pure loving kindness—that was how I saw the world. I could barely keep from running. When people came directly toward me, I lowered my head so they wouldn't laugh at the big grin on my face. I was afraid they'd think I was crazy. I wasn't. I was simply full of joy, such a big, full feeling that my spine tingled. I wasn't walking, I was dancing along.

When I reached the beginning of our street, I slowed down, forcing every smile back to the center of my soul. Then soberly, like someone doing his chores, I entered the butcher shop on the corner. Some woman was the only one at the counter. I waited casually for her to give her order. Then I took her place and looked right at the butcher. I spoke as if I wanted to buy up his whole store:

"I'd like a half kilo of cracklings, a kilo of bread, and give me a package of butter, too."

"Butter?" asked the clerk.

"Butter," I said, and looked ready to fight him if he didn't believe me and didn't give me any. He was shaking cracklings into a bag and watching the pointer so he wouldn't make a mistake. Meanwhile he said brusquely:

"What did you do, hold up somebody?"

At some other time this would have rubbed me the wrong way, for no other reason than that the response would be justified. But I couldn't get too angry and then not be able to get credit from him when we needed it. Besides, he was the first one I could tell. Joy played in my face again. I deepened my voice and slowed it down a bit so it would sound older:

"It's payday, you know, and I'm taking something home for the family."

Someone behind me started laughing, a soft, silky laugh. The manager's wife was sitting at the cashier's desk, and when I turned around at the sound, she looked up at me from the paper money she was stacking at the time. She had a pretty, round face, thickly tumbling wavy hair, and firm, full breasts, which I always looked at. I blushed because she was laughing at me.

"Are you laughing at me?" I asked. I was immediately sorry for speaking so quickly. What could I say if she answered, yes, you, right to my face?

"How old are you?" she asked, all her laughter gathering and glowing in her eyes.

I glanced quickly at her round breasts, and by the time I answered I had added to my age.

"Sixteen." I looked at her just as I had at the clerk when he didn't want to believe I could afford butter if it struck my fancy. Maybe she noticed my first glance, for she pulled her white coat closer together. She didn't stop smiling, however.

"Well, take the packages," the clerk said.

He was holding them out to me and I took them in order—the bread, the cracklings, and the butter. I went to the desk to pay. I'd had a purse made for myself the day before, and now, as I arranged each of the packages under my arm, I took it out gracefully. I had enough small change to pay for everything, but I took out the ten pengő note. I put it down on the marble top and smoothed it with my palm. I didn't look up, I was afraid my eyes would wander to the wrong place.

"Change, please."

I waited for her to take it. I began cursing myself, thinking it would have been better to give her the change and take the bill home. Showing it would've been enough. She'll take it quickly, I thought. She didn't. She put her fingers on it and rested them there, right next to my own. Until I raised my head and looked at her.

Every hair on my head shivered. In the flash of an eye, my heart pounded, my forehead grew cold, and I gulped loudly. Then she looked me squarely in the eyes. She closed her eyes a little, and a tiny smile played hide-and-seek around her lips and her whole face. When she slowly pulled the money away and picked it up, she continued to look at me, and she kept looking at me while, without speaking a single word, she put the change in front of me. I didn't count it, I swept it into my purse. In my rush I left a coin on the counter and she reached for it. I wanted to take it out of her hand, but she nestled her fingers into my fist and pressed the coin into the middle of my palm.

"Thank you," she said, gazing into my eyes in such a way that I had a hard time finding the door on my way out.

I felt as if I'd gone from a searing fire into cool air. I went homeward, my head still dizzy, as if I'd been spun around. I thought: See, that's what the world is like and a woman too. I don't want to believe it, but that's what she is really like. She loses her head when she sees a man with money. As I snatched at this idea, my thoughts gathered and took flight. I closed my eyes and let them see. The way the butcher's wife had looked at me, her pretty neck white as a flower, and even more, whatever my eyes wanted to see, all the way until my thoughts strayed to my mother. My face suddenly grew hot. My mind returned to reality, and I walked faster. To restore myself even more to this world, I put each of the packages to my nose one after the other and kept smelling them. Good strong cracklings, fresh yellow butter, warm fresh bread. My mouth watered and my tongue moved as if I were already eating. I flitted from joy to joy. Suddenly I pulled out my purse and counted the money. I had taken money home to my mother before but never this much nor ever as wages.

When they called my name at the end of the job and I stepped up to the paymaster's table, I hadn't noticed it yet, but when I went back to my place with the money in my hand and put my fingers to my mouth to wet them for counting it, the thought flashed like a mirror through my mind—just like my father! I even walked just like him, and rubbed my finger tips together quickly and put them and wet them the way he did. And yet, outside of a few coins, there was only a single tenner. I felt ashamed again, as I had shortly before when I had thought of my mother, for I couldn't come close to stepping into my father's shoes.

I could see the fence around our house and picture my mother's hand and me slowly counting the money into it: the cracklings cost this much, the butter and bread that much, and here is the rest, and I saw the bread thickly spread with butter. Mainly, after all, I saw the bread, and I remembered that if I don't tear off a piece and instead sink my teeth into the bread, I can see my toothmarks in the butter and count them. I don't know why that came into my mind, but I kept on seeing that. It felt like night, not day, and I was sleeping in my bed and not walking in the street. I quickly threw the gate open and entered the yard. One of the front tenants—we lived in back of the yard—was sitting before his door. He didn't wait for me to say hello. He looked at me, resting his hands on his knees and blinking in the sunlight.

"It's over, eh?" he asked.

I felt like shaking my money in his face, but I couldn't. By this time I knew the rules and what follows what. Without stopping, I replied slowly, sighing a little occasionally:

"Yes, it's over . . . and tomorrow everything starts all over again."

He nodded in agreement.

"That's the way things are," he said.

Just two days ago, he had sent me for some tobacco. Now I reply:

"We'll get along somehow."

"Yes," he said, and he ignored me. Under the walnut tree, in the middle of the yard, I turned toward our door. I smoothed my hair down with the palm of my hand and went inside.

"Is that you, my son?" asked my mother when I put the packages on the corner of the table.

"Yes. Did we need any bread?"

She came to the front of the table, wiping her hands in her apron. I poured some water for myself. I pulled my shirt off and began washing up. I finished quickly, and my mother handed me the towel. She was grumbling but I didn't mind; she always behaved like that when my father went shopping without her.

"You shouldn't have bought so many things. For heaven's sake, even some butter!"

I put my shirt on.

"Forget it, Mother," I replied, combing my hair. "Everything will wind up in a good place. Now don't make anything of it."

I knew she was waiting for the money. I was eager to give it to her, had wanted to as soon as I came in. But I couldn't rush it, and I knew she would wait for me to hand it over on my own and not ask for it. I had thought about this moment many times. About myself, my mother, the money in my purse, and the buttered bread too. I hung the towel on the nail, rolled up my sleeves, then turned to her. When she saw me reaching into my pocket, she fussed with her kerchief, and seeming to remember something pressing, she turned toward the fire in the stove.

"Wait, Mother. Here is my pay."

She stopped, stepped back, and clasped her hands at her waist. When I began emptying my purse onto the table, she went to it. She held out her hand; I counted the money into it to the last fillér.

"I bought these trifles with the rest."

She looked at the money, immediately touching one piece after the other lightly with her fingers. She sorted them, one here, another there. She tossed a couple to the base of her fingers, others to the bottom of her palm, and one or two to the side of her hand. She was lost in herself, forgetting I was even there. She tilted her head slightly toward her shoulder, and when I looked at her forehead, I suddenly noticed that her forehead, like her palm, ran into wrinkles too. Come to think of it, she was holding our whole life in her hand. That's what she was sorting, one day this way, the next day that, until she had filled all seven days. Death and birth, breakfast, supper—our whole life lay in her hand. It was a wonder her arm didn't break.

She took a pengő and put it on the table.

"Keep this, son," she said, "and don't spend it all at once."

As I was thanking her, the door opened and my brothers and sisters ran into the room. Someone had probably told them I had arrived, and they were searching for the packages I had brought home. Mother had a hard time shutting them up. They got some chairs and climbed up to the table. They calmed down only when mother emptied the water from the pan I'd used, filled it again, and ordered them:

"All right, now wash your hands!"

By then I was sitting beside the stove, pretending to read the newspaper. My mind wasn't in it. The cracklings were fresh and their aroma flew to me. My mother had also opened the package of butter. It bloomed with a nice yellow color, and I could feel its good warm flavor on my tongue. How long I had been preparing for this day! To me, butter, cracklings, and happiness were the same. I'd gone to the butcher the day before and made sure there would be some cracklings available for this day. I wanted to make a holiday out of my first earnings by buying happiness—some cracklings and butter.

My brothers and sisters were seated at the table, and I was getting ready to join them. I waited for my mother to speak and call me to the table. I watched her in vain. She didn't say a word to me. She cut a slice of bread for each of them, spread butter on them generously, and divided some cracklings into even little heaps among them. She wrapped up the remaining cracklings and put them into the window. She also put the left-over butter there. Then, like one who has finished her task, she looked the table over and said gently to the smallest ones:

"Eat, my little ones, eat. My, how good it is. Enjoy it, my dears . . . Good delicious cracklings, tasty bits of butter." She stood watching them as if only they existed in the world and she weren't aware of anything else.

I couldn't believe my eyes. I couldn't understand what she was doing. I thought, maybe she is teasing me. But she never did that with food, nobody would let her. Maybe she has forgotten me. That can't be. After all, she always gives me my share first. My heart ached, and all my feelings of contentment fled me instantly. I looked at my mother. Just then she came to the stove. When she reached it I faced her. My voice struggled, something seemed to be holding it back.

"I . . . am hungry . . . too, Mother."

She paid no attention to me. She was taking the lid off the large pot.

"We shall eat, son, we shall eat too, right away."

And she was already pouring bean soup, which she had just removed from the fire, into clay dishes. Some for me into one, some for herself into the other. She gave me some bread and put a spoon into my dish. Then she sat down on the small stool, placed her dish on her lap, and began blowing on the steaming soup. Before tasting it, she looked at me and asked:

"Shall I slice some onions, son?"

She always gave my father onions when we had bean soup. Now she was offering me some. I looked down at her, and with a sudden heartache I saw she was looking at me the way she did at my father and expecting an answer in exactly the same way. She was seated at my feet just as she did beside my father. Her head reached as high as my hand. Then, as if seeing her for the first time in ages, I noticed how white her hair was. My God, like snow! How old my mother is already. I spoke to her gently, as if kissing her:

"Slice some, Mother. Let's have some onions with it."

While she was slicing the onions, I leaned against the door jamb and took in the table where my brothers and sisters were eating. I looked at the cracklings, the many slices of buttered bread, and I finally understood that none of it belonged to me. My father never got any either. He would sit to one side like this too, and my mother would crouch beside him. It never occurred to me that they didn't even get a taste. It belonged to the children, not the grownups. I barely noticed that I sighed. I had often tried to mimic my father unsuccessfully, but now, without meaning to, I sighed exactly like him. I instantly forgot about everything. I am already sighing like my father! Inside me moved a stronger joy than I had felt at the moment when I was paid. To make sure, I sighed again. Just like the one before! If someone couldn't see me, he would take me for my father. Just then my mother returned, and when she sat down in her place, I touched her arm gently and nodded toward the children.

"I did the right thing, didn't I. Just look how they are eating."

She put her spoon down and looked at the table. She rested her eyes on them, and a soft, lovely smile appeared on her face, sweeping her wrinkles away for an instant.

"The poor little things, they were really very hungry."

Bending over my dish, I began eating the soup again. I put some onions into it with the tip of my knife. They were good red onions, such nice round slices as only my mother could cut, no one else.

When I got up after my afternoon nap, I told my mother I was going for a walk and not to expect me until suppertime. When I reached the gate I put my hands in my pockets and began whistling away. I strolled slowly along the street. When I neared the butcher shop, I combed my hair and straightened my jacket. At the door I pulled my shoulders back and entered the shop. There were many customers and no one noticed me. I headed directly for the cashier's desk. From a distance I beheld the face of the butcher's wife. I looked at her exactly the way she had me at noon. She could've laughed at me now and I'd have given her a snappy answer. After all, I could've spoken up at noon but it wasn't possible for me then. Now it was. No one could deny I was no longer a child. I went up to her, and before she could utter a word I took out the pengő my mother had given me for spending money. As I spoke to her, a smile settled on my face, exactly like the one she gave me when she had looked at me so steadily.

"You gave me a pengő too much in change earlier, if you still remember me."

Before she could move I pressed the money right into her palm as she had done with me. Until then she looked at me; now she quickly snatched her eyes away. I wouldn't let go. I kept my eyes on her until she looked up at me again. Then she glanced around, and seeing that no one was watching us, she smiled. She looked into my face, closed her eyelids a little, and smiled at me. So beautifully my heart pounded . . .

No More Dying Then

To the memory of García Lorca

The guard was walking two or three steps behind his prisoners to keep a vigilant eye on them, and, just in case, to fire his weapon from the right distance—not too far for an accurate aim and not close enough to endanger himself. In short, he was following them at the distance stipulated by regulations.

The prisoners weren't handcuffed—there were two of them, two men not young but not old either, both wearing the same gray trousers and coat, and both barefooted—their legs and arms were also unshackled. They were moving over a changing, rather hilly terrain, and occasionally they had to hang on to keep their footing. At times like that, the guard stayed a little farther behind and kept an especially sharp eye on them.

"Prisoners should be handcuffed!" he swore. "What a hell of a way to do things!"

He crawled forward on the hillside cautiously, holding on with one hand. He braced his machine gun under his armpit and aimed it at the two men. The tight uniform, the many buckles, belt, bindings, heavy boots, tight-fitting cap, rolled-up overcoat, shoulder pack, crossing straps, and the machine gun made his moving about tiring; and though the day wasn't warm—there was even a light breeze blowing—sweat streamed down his back and abdomen and face, where it ran in thin but endless rivulets to his chin or to the tight collar of his fatigue jacket.

"Closer! Move closer together!" he said, gasping for breath and blinking ever faster from the sweat flowing into his eyes.

The two prisoners hastened to move together and climbed on nearly shoulder to shoulder.

When they arrived on a flatland covered with green grass, the guard called out to them again—panting harder, his whole body swimming in sweat, his eyes burning. Remaining a couple of steps farther back than required by regulations, he said:

"Halt! Get closer together!"

He wiped the sweat off his brow with his arm. Bracing one leg against the other, he lifted his heels in his boots slightly, pushed his cap back on his head, took the kink out of his spine by pulling his shoulders back, turned his neck in his tight jacket, emptied the air from his lungs, stretched his arms high to exercise his muscles. Next he glanced at his gun, at the safety catch, which in its off position kept the machine gun ready to fire, and raising the barrel a little, aimed it directly at the backs of the two men.

"It won't be long and you won't be out taking the air," he said, apparently with their light clothing in mind. "Or rather, you'll really be airing yourselves, only you won't know it."

He kneeled down to rest his leg muscles. Keeping his gun aimed at the captives with constant accuracy, he rocked back and forth a few times.

"You rotten bastards, you won't be airing youselves much longer! Get moving!"

He stood up, and delaying a step, followed his captives.

One of the prisoners spoke up—very quietly, gasping for breath slightly:

"In any case, the 1895 retrospective exhibit arranged by Vollard was already up . . . Some Balkan king, maybe the Serbian, actually asked Vollard: 'Didn't this master of yours know how to paint beautiful women at all?' "

The other prisoner, taller and thinner, stepped around a single blue flower in the grass:

"Even though a king, he was right. However, what you say doesn't alter a thing because if my memory serves me correctly or if he finished the painting in '94, then it easily could have been in the Vollard exhibit in '95."

"In any case, it was in the exhibit," his companion said, "but he painted *The Cardplayers* in '92, and the painting was already finished before this one was."

The other raised his hand.

"Wrong! *The Artist's Wife* was finished in '94, but our master started on it in '90, and he isn't the only one to make mention of this fact in several of his letters. Choquet also speaks of it. What may have confused you is the fact that it took him four years from the conception of the subject in '90 to its completion in '94."

"Perhaps . . . Is it possible?"

"I'm absolutely positive."

His companion narrowed his eyes for an instant. "It seems I was wrong . . . Well, getting back to that pail and the stones. He didn't let a day pass—and, you see, that ugly woman, that pursuer of the Muses, who is sitting on the chair as if about to get up and tend to her household duties because, after all, what value is there to art if we don't finish our work in the kitchen. Well, that ugly woman never forgot to have the pail in its place—as if accidentally—always full of water, and—as if miraculously—stones would never run short in the garden croft so the poor man could keep throwing them. In short, the master didn't let a single day pass without going to that enclosure after completing his stroll to pick up stones and throw them one by one, aiming carefully at the pail, counting—apparently anxiously and tremblingly—how many landed in the water and how many missed it, because, my God, how important this is! Why, who can know what the tormented and endlessly surging nervous system managed to surmise or prophesy on the basis of the number of successful hits? And I wonder what could the upright citizens of Aix have thought during their walks when they saw this strange man, uncommunicative, with unsmiling face under his large forehead, throwing stones one at a time with lazy, ponderous motions?"

The tall one laughed.

"When Shelley was spending some time with Byron at Ravenna, he gave the following account of his visit in a letter he wrote to Picot: 'I found Lord Byron's household very pleasant, and disregarding his servants, particularly with respect to his eight dogs, three monkeys, five cats, two eagles, one crow and one falcon . . . ' In his postscript he adds, however: 'I realize that I had not enumerated everything, for I have just now met on the grand staircase five peacocks, two guinea hens, and an Egyptian crane . . . All these roam about the lord's rooms in complete freedom, and he passes his time conversing with them.' "

They both started to laugh heartily. A pure, merry mood settled on their faces. They didn't say anything to each other for a while, and laughter kept returning to their lips in short intervals. The sun, however, was behind a white veil-like cloud. Practically covering the whole sky, the cloud allowed only a faint, opalescent light to reach the earth. The grass was wet under their feet; the air was crisp and clear; the hills, attired in blue on all sides, were quiet; and the nearby valleys burst upon the eyes in green, brown, and delicate yellow colors.

"Getting back to Cézanne," said the taller prisoner, "with respect to the stones and pail, Jean-Jacques' form of diversion wasn't much different from his tossing of those stones . . . "

"Diversion?" said the other, raising his eyebrows. "My God, what kind of diversion is there in that?"

"Jean-Jacques did the following at Madam de Warrens . . . "

"At the gentle and devout, pure-souled woman's—the lamb of God, and the little lady who, with her eyes fixed to the ground, never thought of anything else but God!"

"In that little valley where her villa was situated, or in that house they rented or, I think, leased instead, Jean-Jacques collected stones during his morning walks and deliberately threw them at branches or tree-trunks. If I remember correctly, he told of this habit himself in *The Stroller,* but anyway, Diderot informs us, on the basis of what Rousseau told him, that if he didn't hit the target with the specific number of stones he had decided upon ahead of time, then after each throw he'd move one step closer to the tree or branch, thus telling us that the emphasis was on striking the target. And that's why it happened that sometimes the last stone, which represented victory to Jean-Jacques in case it hit, was a mere step away from the tree trunk. Then, like someone who has done his work well, he was satisfied for that day, for, after all, he had scored more often than not."

"Didn't someone near him ever say: 'Master, heave a whole rock at it and you won't have to do it again for an entire year'?"

He laughed heartily, and his companion accompanied his laughter with a soft chuckle. In the next instant, however, he tumbled forward, threw his arms out wide seeking his balance, and then after two or three clumsy steps, fell flat on the ground, his arms striking the grass well in front of him.

The guard stood behind them. He raised his leg and shoved the taller prisoner with the sole of his boot. The prisoner stumbled and also fell down, and he and his companion struggled to their feet together.

The barrel of the machine gun was aimed at their chests, the opaline light gleamed on the steel.

"Shut up!" said the guard. "Now march close together! If you laugh just once more, I'll flatten your stinking mugs!"

He stretched his neck in the tight jacket. Lifting his free arm, he wiped his nose in the heavy cloth, then spit on the ground.

"Now close up and get going!"

The two prisoners stood next to each other. The shorter one adjusted his coat, then raised his finger to his nose.

"Did you get hurt badly?" the other one asked.

"No, I don't think so. The fear was greater."

He glanced up at his companion.

"For a moment I thought I'd brought Jean-Jacques' wrath down on myself." He smiled, then sniffed through his nose again. "Maybe I struck my nose, I think it might bleed. Did you get hurt?"

"I don't think so . . . but he took me completely by surprise. No preface . . . or words or harangue . . . no swearing at all. This is something new, eh?"

"Yes, it really is . . . By the way, before I forget. Joyce played in the following manner. He tried catching up with strollers ahead of him, singling out one of them, within a certain distance and a fixed number of steps. If he didn't succeed —or didn't succeed exactly as he had decided or accepted within himself, then for the rest of that day he was completely out of sorts—as they used to say, his work didn't go, and all day he feared the unexpected and sudden arrival of some catastrophe."

The taller prisoner smiled. "Really . . . He too?"

The shorter prisoner also smiled and kept his voice even lower: "It must be terrible for that poor fellow in all those things he is loaded down with . . ."

The other one spread his arms out.

"Please," he said, "we, on the other hand, really can't complain. I have been constantly cold ever since we started out."

"I too. However, I still forgot to express something earlier . . . namely, in connection with Cézanne. Stone-throwing, pail, insecurity, doubt, anxiety, loneliness, dejection, sorrow, humiliation? Take a look at the 1894 *Portrait*. The one who is tossing stones outside, his broad forehead bent toward the ground—here in the painting, oh God! isn't he celebrating the festival of his future triumph?

Or if this is more apropos, the triumph of the future in me? That is certain! That I know for sure! That is victory! And then nothing else matters! That's what the painting says—or the painting expresses the greatest argument providing eternal and insuppressible, indestructible and divine strength: Certainty about the future!"

His companion's eyes flashed with gentle joviality: "And imagine all this by the side of a more sexually attractive wife!"

They bowed their heads and smiled. Then, still sniffing through his nose frequently, the shorter prisoner continued: "But try and look at the situation from the woman's point of view. Weariness, common work beside a man who follows bankruptcy with bankruptcy, who travels isolated and obsessed the road that doesn't offer anything in material benefits or recognition. His sullenness is unbearable and so is his eccentricity. He doesn't want to leave the place of his seclusion. He doesn't want to hear a word about Paris. On the other hand, his wife's every thought is in Paris and she detests above all else the dullness of provincial life. Her plans, dreams, longings have all been consumed by the fire of a man's suffering . . . I don't want to be repetitious, but every once in a while ask yourself this question: Actually, is it only the great man who deserves the laurel?"

"The question is a proper one. Especially in connection with such famous men as Galileo, Newton, Adam Smith, Hobbes, Descartes, Locke, Spinoza, Kant, Leibniz, Hume, Gibbon, Macaulay, Leonardo da Vinci, Raffaello, Michelangelo, Händel, Beethoven, Mendelssohn—who, as everybody knows, were every one of them bachelors, and accordingly didn't have the slightest intention of sharing their laurel with any kind of wife. With the exception of these, you are absolutely correct in all the other cases."

Smiling, the other prisoner glanced at him. "For my part, I'll gladly be satisfied with all the other cases."

The guard spoke up behind them:

"Knock off the nonsense and talk intelligently! Before long you won't be saying anything at all!"

They fell silent. They walked beside each other quietly. Then the taller prisoner spoke up:

"Well, what shall we do!"

He didn't say anything for a while. Finally he spoke again: "Look at that tree in front of us, there to the left. That solitary tree with branches spread way out."

"Yes," the other prisoner said. "It's an Austrian oak, isn't it. Or an oak rather?"

"An Austrian oak," said the taller one. "I don't know how familiar you are with it. It's noted for belonging among trees with the heaviest weight. However, the weight of the trees is calculated in the weight ratio of one cubic decimeter. I'm not certain, but I seem to remember that the coco is the heaviest and maybe the ebony . . . ."

"And the mahogany?"

"I myself was surprised to find it much farther down the list. I distinctly remember that the Austrian oak comes before it, the one in front of us there, and before the blue beech as well."

The taller prisoner looked in the direction of the Austrian oak with narrowed eyes. He smiled and sighed:

"How good it would be to be able to remember everything! If I haven't forgotten a great deal, then its organic parts are cellulose . . . "

"Yes, it's mainly that . . . "

"Then lignin, volatile oil, tannin . . . "

"Resin," said the shorter prisoner.

"Of course, resin . . . then starch in generous quantity, pigments, protein."

"You dirty traitors!" the guard spoke up behind them. "In a short time there'll be nothing in you! Get closer together!"

The prisoners looked at the Austrian oak. After a little while, the taller one said very softly:

"What a lovely tree! and it doesn't know it is mortal."

Reaching the end of the flatland, they eased themselves down the side of gully. They descended with their arms outstretched, legs fixed, their weight on their heels. The guard walked at a slant, lowering himself after them, leaning with his left hand occasionally on the ground. In his right hand, held tight under his shoulder, his finger on the trigger, the machine gun was constantly aimed at the two prisoners.

"Closer! Closer together!"

They tried to move closer to each other, and their arms, spread far apart for balance, touched, and for a moment they took hold of each other's hand. Hanging on to each other, they braked their momentum, which would have carried them running farther down into the depths. Then they let go of each other, and bending back all the way, they leaned against the side of the gully and continued their descent, digging their heels deep into the ground.

"To the right, you bastards! Bear to the right!" the guard yelled at them. Because they weren't able to shift direction immediately, to brake their momentum and direct it sideways, he yelled at them again, and because he couldn't move close enough to kick them, he spit at them in helpless anger: "To the right, you bastards! Are you deaf?"

Bearing to the right, traversing the steep gully sideways, they finally left it behind them, and taking a little turn backwards almost in the direction they had come from the top, they continued their way on the nearly perpendicular side of the flatland. At right angle to the gully and then hugging the side of the flatland, a wide river ran swiftly out of the valley and joined the narrow trail on which the three men were cautiously advancing.

The taller prisoner spoke up:

"It was a lovely tree."

"Yes," the other said," and it really doesn't know it is mortal."

"No, it doesn't. Evidently it never read the *Metamorphoses*. If it had, then perhaps it would look more humbly at the world and say to its companions: 'My brothers and sisters, never forget that we know not only that we are mortal singly and individually but also that our civilizations are mortal. They come into existence, they reach a peak, and they pass away!' "

He spoke rather loudly because about four or five meters below them—with a similarly steep but passable trail leading down to it—the river churned and murmured between the gloomy cliffs.

"That's not the only thing it is unaware of," he continued. "By virtue of destiny's special consideration, it is unaware of the fact that even though everything is mortal, human stupidity is endless, indestructible, and eternal!"

"I don't agree," said his companion.

The guard shouted at them: "Aren't you ever going to shut up!"

In that instant, just as he was speaking, he stumbled and his whole body lunged forward. Toppling to the edge of the path, he tried to hang on to the slope. It was all in vain. He tumbled and fell swiftly down to the river bank. Then searching futilely for something to hold on to, lashing about, beating the air, shrieking incoherently, he plunged into the churning water. He held his weapon high above his head; the current grabbed his body, spun him around, and carried him, twisting and turning, between two majestically rising cliffs toward the middle of the stream.

The prisoners turned around simultaneously. Frozen, startled they watched the body fall, then tumble with arms flailing toward the river. Their hands subconsciously searched for each other, and they stepped farther back, almost bending into the cliffside.

"Hang on!" shouted the shorter prisoner, and letting go of his comrade's hand, he started to run back on the path. Then after a few meters, at a point where the bank was less dangerous, he descended toward the river, with his arms spread out wide, as fast as the footing allowed. His companion was running and holding on behind him, grabbing on to roots and rocks.

"Stay here!" he shouted. "For the love of God, stay here! I'm an expert swimmer! Please stay on the bank!"

He went around him, and reaching the water's edge, he threw his coat off, meanwhile repeating, trying to outshout the other:

"Don't do anything foolish! Help by staying right here on the bank. Find a tree branch or something you can hold out to me."

He waded into the stream, and spreading out, cut into the waves with powerful strokes.

The guard continued struggling in the river between the two cliffs. Sometimes the lashing waves tossed him into the middle of the stream, sometimes back in the direction of the bank. His clothing was weighed down with water; his heavy boots were pulling, drawing him down into the depths. All his thrashing about was useless. Besides, he kept gripping the machine gun with his hand ever harder trying to hold it high above the water. His shouting didn't stop, his eyes—whenever his face could be glimpsed for an instant—flared with terror, his wide-open mouth gasped for breath.

"To the right! the right!" shouted the prisoner on the bank when he saw his companion's head rising high in search of the drowning man. "To the right! more to the right! More!"

His voice was lost in the roar of the water. But his companion, struggling against the currents, continued to get closer and closer to the drowning guard. Finally he reached him and grabbed him by the hair. Setting his back against the cliff and treading water high, he lifted above the stream the rattling mouth, the closed eyes, the struggling man's head.

Holding the guard—his machine gun was still in his hand—by the arms, the two prisoners carried him with difficulty and gasping for breath all the way up to the path. They spread him out on the cliff, and the shorter one quickly unbuttoned his jacket and then his shirt until his broad chest was completely exposed. He looked up at his comrade.

"Are you all right? How do you feel?"

Staying on his knees, he reached up and clasped his companion's hand.

"Lie down, you lie down too."

The taller one leaned against the side of the cliff, his chest rising and falling, seeming to strain to the bursting point. Then, sliding down against the side of the cliff, he lowered himself to his knees, and finally leaning back carefully, he stretched himself out full length on the ground.

"I'm all right," he said with heavy, labored breaths. "Try and do . . . something . . . for him!"

The other prisoner came over and kneeled down beside him.

"How do you feel?"

"Just fine . . . I'm just very weak. I have to rest a bit. Go and try to give him artificial respiration."

"Yes," the other prisoner said.

He didn't even get up from his knees. He slid over to the motionless body, and raising the guard's arms, he began moving them with repeated rhythm down, up, down, up . . . The guard's chest rose; then large streams of water began gushing from his mouth.

The tall prisoner spoke up: "He has to be raised, lift him by the legs."

He struggled to his feet and went over to them.

"Help me take hold of his legs . . . But let's take the gun out of his hands first."

The shorter prisoner loosened the guard's fingers from the machine gun.

"He is still gripping it," he said.

"That's the way. Pry his fingers loose."

The shorter prisoner took the weapon into his hands. "It's much lighter than I thought."

Holding it out in front of himself, a little away from himself, he examined the weapon, then put it on the ground.

"Let's lift him up," the taller prisoner said.

They lifted the guard up. They held him by his ankles, the head hung way down, and retching, the mouth emitted water. Then they laid him back on the ground. His head moved, and straining, his eyes opened for an instant.

"Now," said the taller prisoner, "now try artificial respiration again."

The guard's mouth opened, struggled with words. His eyes then became completely visible, his eyeballs looking here, then there, and then, however irregularly, his chest began rising and falling.

"Are you feeling better?" the taller prisoner asked him.

The guard looked at him. Then with an effort he raised himself on his side. He began spitting, then vomiting. After that, he breathed normally, and looked from one prisoner to the other with dim eyes swollen red. Suddenly terror overwhelmed his face. He raised himself higher, and with frightened, horror-stricken face, he looked beside him to the right, then to the left.

"Give him his gun," the taller prisoner said.

His companion picked up the machine gun, and after giving it another close look, he handed it to the guard.

"Are you feeling better?" he asked.

The guard got up. He staggered and leaned against the side of the cliff. Hanging his head, he inhaled, sucking the air in with deep breaths. Then suddenly, in the fraction of a second, he jerked his head up and stared with an alarmed, perplexed expression at the two prisoners. His mouth remained open; he kept snatching his eyes from one to the other. On his face remained the confused, and strange, frightened wonderment, which intermingled with the expression of a deep, almost animal fear.

Completely flattened against the side of the cliff, slowly raising the barrel of the machine gun at the prisoners, and feeling his way along the cliff with his other hand, he moved some three or four short steps away from them. His jacket was open, his hair had fallen into his eyes, his clothing was heavy with water.

The prisoners were standing a few steps from him. The taller one was wringing out his clothing, the pressure forcing water from it in thin streams. The other one was staring at the machine gun; then he raised his eyes, and a strange smile coming to his face, he asked:

"Do you feel better?"

With ever-widening eyes the guard stared at them. His voice came with difficulty.

"What kind of men are you?"

It was the first time he had not used the familiar form of address with them.

The shorter prisoner again looked at the machine gun with curiosity and attention. His companion kept on wringing out his clothes, meanwhile moaning and panting.

"You . . . are going to be . . . hanged tomorrow!" shouted the guard.

He kept looking from one to the other. His face still wore the perplexed, wondering alarm, the deep, profoundly deep and never previously sensed and seemingly maddening bewilderment.

"Don't you know that?"

For an instant the shorter prisoner looked at the ground. Then because his companion didn't say anything, he raised his head and said:

"Of course . . . we know."

The guard's mouth quivered. He searched for words with which he really didn't know what he wanted to express. If possible, his eyes grew even larger. Then, jerking the barrel of his machine gun high and aiming it directly at the prisoners' chests, he stepped back. In an almost inhuman, wild, almost incoherent and an extremely desperate tone and with his eyes fixed on them, he yelled:

"What kind of men are you?"

His whole body was trembling, his face became contorted, his eyes, nearly deranged, grew ever larger and more terrified, and a nearly insane despair moved into his countenance.

The two prisoners looked at each other. Then the taller one, with the other's help, put his coat on. After standing beside each other for a time without speaking a word, the taller prisoner said to the guard, who was just standing there, his entire body still trembling, the muzzle of his gun fixed on them—he said to him, without particularly raising his voice:

"Come . . . let's move on."

He turned around. The other prisoner did also, and they again started off, walking as they had before. Looking back after a few steps, they stopped and waited for the guard to set out as well.

After a little while, the shorter prisoner spoke up:

"He became completely confused, and the poor fellow has fallen into a deep despair."

Glancing back quickly, his companion started to smile. The shorter one quickened his pace and added:

"He got into a completely neurotic state. But no wonder, for if I remember correctly, according to Freud, the beginning point of a neurosis is insecurity and the threat of an inferiority complex . . . "

They laughed, and the taller one, who was still wringing out his coat, said:

"Getting back to Byron, to his animals namely. Walter Scott kept thirty or forty dogs. With a favorite, an apprentice named Thomas Purdie, who understood animals very well, he whiled whole days away together with ten or twenty of his dogs. Carlyle called his horse—his numberless horses—his best friend. Or think of Goya and his many cats. And Cicero writes about how when Lucilius and Scipio went to the country, they tumbled about the length of the Caitean beaches and gardens with dogs and monkeys, and even though the old man makes no mention of it, he himself also behaved in the same way. On the other hand, Bentham dubbed one of his cats a knight and demanded that his servants show it the respect attending the title."

The shorter prisoner laughed—and they continued on their way.

From: Interview, 1967[1]

. . . nothing is more important to human beings and especially to . . . writers than the preservation of their independence of thought against the extremes of alluring and revolting passions and the constant protection of their freedom to strive for the act of rational and correct judgment, accordingly to protect that which is the most difficult to guard in an age when nothing is easier for writers than to falter, to lose their way, precisely because extremes are enchanting and because nothing is more simple and comfortable than to substitute a particular statute based on blind faith for a concept founded on balanced and open-eyed reflection. Writing is tantamount to changing. Every great piece of literature is a metamorphosis, for every literary work is our personal confrontation with the world, and that world is different today from what it was yesterday and it will be something else again tomorrow. We must measure the changing issues of this changing world again and again against the norms we writers personally hold to be true and to render a judgment about our own actions—in the end, to determine what we can shoulder and what we can't, how much we can take in hand according to our own strength, what we must abstain from and what we must, if necessary, cry out to the very last breath. If we don't live and write with flawless attention to this endlessly moving acceptance and rejection, then our talent becomes moldy or devours us, or, at the very best, it turns into mere exhibition.

While thinking about this, I became even more certain that socialism is so great an endeavor in behalf of humanity that it is growing ever more deserving of our assistance. The reason is that, settling and clarifying, it manifests an ever-increasing disposition for patience, for moderation; it increasingly respects thoughtful and objective criticism. The readier it is for this kind of accommodation, the greater the degree to which it becomes even worthier of support by as many individuals as possible. Beyond the indispensable merits it has already obtained, socialism also deserves respect for its capacity to accept responsibility for its crimes and errors, and for its striving to rid itself of the idiots and fanatics in its ranks. An idea capable of this, of reforming itself, and one potentially carrying so many possibilities within itself, deserves our participating in its struggles with vigilant attention and sensitive alertness by deeds and criticisms alike; it also deserves our learning from it that point beyond which we don't know anything additional or anything better. I don't believe that salvation lies in a single idea, but I am certain that in the struggles and endeavors of this age, a part, a *greater* part of the truth lies here; and in its final dénouement, in its final effect, this idea will be one remembered with respect by future centuries. Namely, the basic substance called for by the present age.

[*Interviewer:*] This isn't a socialist profession of faith in socialism. It brings to my mind a thought of Sartre's, according to whom the theme of the great authors of the twentieth century is "The Adventure of Socialism." What is your view of the present mission of literature?

The mission of literature in every age is one and the same. For this reason I don't know how to answer the question on its mission today. Unless I simply say that between its two fundamental functions—to delight and to stir doubt—we are today compelled to consider the latter function to be more important. To awaken doubt most responsibly about the bases for the existence of infatuation, of that most dangerous stupidity of all—fanaticism. More than all preceding ages, our century is filled with exasperating, horribly absurd anachronisms. Half the world is starving, yet weapons are being manufactured at the cost of billions. Shelves are lined with books containing the thoughts of humanists, yet the generation stepping into our place is being taught to shoot down human beings, the mother what to do when her child is incinerated by a radioactive ray. One man or a few can send millions to die, the poor wretches. We can't make pure drinking water gradually available to our children, yet the earth's depth and the oceans are being contaminated.

Our most important responsibility is to curb—while we still can—the opposing animosities. We must find partial truths and force them to be found; we must try to reconcile them and make them bear fruit through mutual endeavors. Our age not only bears the greatest danger of being destroyed; more than all earlier times, it created its own conditions, and it demands a *synthesis*. This is the greatest edict of our age, and anyone who shirks it is guilty. We must stand in the way of the obsessed who don't want to acknowledge this fact; we must pull the rug out from under them; we must discredit the hideous, degenerate, sick logic of the cursed. The light of reason must be shined upon them, for they shall be destroyed by it, even as poisonous vegetation is by the rays of the sun.

[1] Published in *Life and Literature (Élet és Irodalom)*, May 6, 1967.

Ferenc Juhász

Juhász was born on August 16, 1928, in Bia, a small village situated about twenty kilometers from Budapest. His father, a huge man, was a cheerful, convivial person tolerating the routine demands of each day and a detester of books; his mother, on the other hand, a very private person troubled by the circumstances in which the family lived, was anguished and read omniverously. His father spent most of his time with his friends, often participating in the activities of the Choral Society; his mother shut herself away among her dreams and her borrowed books. Juhász often served as a mediator when sharp disagreements developed between them. The family situation was seriously affected by the long illness of his father, whose major lung surgery in 1932 forced him to give up work as a bricklayer and become an office clerk in Budapest. Juhász's memories are full of the shouting and the smell of sweat, as his father sat up in bed vomiting blood into a washbasin. But as a child he always enjoyed sleeping with his father, his head against his back listening to the panting of the half-lung. His father sought escape from his illness and consciousness of death in drinking, and although he never threatened physical harm or endangered financial security, the family lived under great strain and anguish. Juhász had his first inkling that death was fast-approaching when his father asked him for some books and read them all determinedly. He died in 1950, and Juhász memorialized him in a long narrative poem, *My Father* (*Apám*), published in that year.

These trying circumstances forced Juhász to be alone often and made him determined to find a way of life different from his father's. He spent much time wandering in the woods and marshes outside the village, often disappearing for days, to his mother's distress. Highly observant, he used these solitary meanderings to store away detailed images of nature. He still speaks of his hatred of the village, which was set in the middle of what had once been the Metternich estate and kept its feudalistic character until after 1945 despite its proximity to Budapest. The villagers, made up of Catholic Swabians and Protestant Hungarians, also caused him trouble. Noting his odd solitary behavior, particularly his early devotion to reading books of German and Hungarian literature, and, according to Juhász, detesting anyone who rejected the village's way of life, they thought him mad and constantly badgered his mother about him. She herself feared that he would not pursue a vocation acceptable in Bia, perhaps that of a clerk at the village hall, which was, in her view, the highest position a village boy could achieve.

Juhász attended primary school in Bia and then, since unable to meet the Latin requirement for secondary school, senior elementary school in Bicska, twenty kilometers distant, taking the train there with his father, who was commuting to Budapest. When he had finished, his father wanted him to become a mechanic or an electrician or an apprentice at the Hungarian Optical Works, but he and his mother pleaded so determinedly that he was permitted to attend the Lajos Kossuth Business High School in Budapest. By this time he had already worked as, among other things, an hourly laborer on a landed estate and a helper to bricklayers and carpenters, especially enjoying the former. Later, after the war ended, he exhumed corpses from a mass grave, tossing up the remains to the grieving families.

He was drawn into the war in the fall of 1944 by an edict of the Szálasi government, ordering all sixteen-year-old males to military duty. He did not want to obey, but his parents feared the consequences of disobedience; he and twenty-nine other recruits were taken to Budapest in an SS truck. Dropped off to walk to the reporting station, he and a friend deserted, thus becoming the sole survivors of the group. They remained in hiding until Christmas night, when the Russian troops arrived. During the occupation he was bedridden with pleurisy for nine months before returning to complete high school studies, obtaining his diploma in 1946.

After graduation he worked at the French-Hungarian Cotton Factory in Budapest, as did most of his fellow villagers, and then on the night shift in another factory, spending his days with a girl whose parents had been killed in a German concentration camp. At this time he also read widely in art and philosophy, including the Greeks, Kant, Spengler, Nietzsche, Marx, and Engels, Buddhists, saints, religious mysteries, books of death, and ancient epics. Feeling hopelessly locked into the village life he abhorred, he became very despondent.

Fortunately, his life changed in the summer of 1948, when he read an announcement about an opportunity to register for a People's College in Budapest, took the examination in August, and was accepted in September. At the Attila József College, he met László Nagy and István Simon. He also married in 1948. In that same year, to his later regret, he burned a boxful of earlier, very imitative poems. Unable to stand the routines of the College, he never completed his studies, and later also withdrew from the University of Budapest because he found the learning experience meaningless.

Like other young writers of the time, he sought to understand himself in the direct context of the trials his society was undergoing. Also like so many, he believed that poetry must alter painful reality, and although, as he has noted, the world and his life turned out to be much more complex than he had thought, he not only wrote his early works with this specific end in mind, but has since then struggled to hold on to the belief in the value of writing poetry and its power to shape life. His first poems appeared in 1947, and his first book, *Winged Colt* (*Szárnyas csikó*), a collection of poems written from 1946 to 1949, was published in 1949. He was awarded the Kossuth Prize in 1950 for the narrative poem on his father, and in September 1951 he became—and still is—a part-time editor for the Szépirodalmi Publishing House and later an editor for *New Writings* (*Új Írás*), a most influential periodical.

The promising future dimmed for him as the Rákosi years progressed. Eight volumes of his poems had appeared by 1956, and in 1957 his collection for 1946 to 1956, *The Breeding Country* (*A tenyészet ország*), was released. However, he kept encountering difficulties as he deviated from the schematism of the period, even to the point of satirizing current society in "The Rooster of the Frosty Window" ("A jégvirág kakasa"), which drew official criticism. Thinking back to these years, he says that the pressure of numerous perceptions and insights forced him to respond to events in keeping with his personal beliefs. Eventually his depression became deep-seated; it began in 1957 and led to hospitalization in 1958, perhaps his most difficult time, and he did not start to break out of this illness until 1961. He claims that his recovery was made possible by his writing of "At the Grave of Attila József" ("József Attila sírjánál") in 1962, a long poem that produced a great debate when it was published in *New Writings*. *War with the White Lamb* (*Harc a fehér báránnyal*), his first book in nine years, appeared in 1965, to be followed in the same year by a selected edition, *Flowering World Tree* (*Virágzó világfa*). These have been succeeded by ten more volumes through 1977, including collections and editions of essays.

His early poems glowed with joy at the educational and economic opportunities opening to the lower classes. Although he remained a communist, his lyrical accounts of his society gradually moved to the depiction of his personal relations with surrounding reality. As early as 1950, the narrative poem to his father, though it endorsed the changes taking place in the life of the peasantry, revealed a self-absorption and sense of private vision; and when he addressed the 1951 Writers' Congress, he made it abundantly clear that he was establishing his independence.

He told his fellow authors that the flaw of excessive enthusiasm must be excised from poetry "by perceptive, seemingly tangible representations of reality and by boldness of language and form." More pointedly, he stated that "the poet has a make-up, an individuality, a road of development," which clearly, must be expressed and followed. His own path led away from the realism so characteristic of the folk lyric and from purely social themes to the large issues of humanity and by 1953 to intellectual poems characterized by symbolic use of the folktale and by congeries of difficult images making tremendous demands on the reader's imagination. Giving ever broader range to his personal views and emotions, he created a unique blend of description, narration, thought, and emotion —a form of lyrical meditation about human life.

Turning to the depths of human experience in a universal sense—particularly the isolation and mortality of the self—he published two works that mark a new stage in his development: *The Spendthrift Land* (*A tékozló ország*) in 1954 and *The Power of Flowers* (*A virágok hatalma*) in 1955. In the first, an epic treatment of the downfall of György Dózsa, the leader of the Peasant Revolution of 1514, Juhász portrayed the general state of humanity, concluding that the sole value of life rests in living it. In the second, he reduced his feelings of alienation by linking humanity with a cosmic, universal element. Both works also have features that became an indispensable part of his poetry: scientific images in the former and the torrential flow of imagery in the latter. The scientific images serve, he claims, the purpose of exactness, and the torrential imagery opens the door to the universal.

Two books of poetry in 1965, the first in nearly ten years, marked the next stage of his development: *Flowering World Tree*, consisting of previously published selections from 1956 to 1965, and *War with the White Lamb*, all new poems. They express an intensification of his inner struggle to affirm life, to establish order in existence, and to validate the role of poetic expression. "The Boy Turned into a Stag" ("A szarvassá változott fiú") emphasizes the introspective quality of his conflicts and, at the same time, pictures the troubled era, in an archetypal portrayal of a youth who cannot return to the simple life of the past because new principles of existence at work inside him bar the way. From this time on, Juhász wrote increasingly longer epic poems, some as long as 15,000 lines, that departed significantly from the classical epics of, say, Homer and Dante. They are lyrical epics that play down action and plot. Carefully planned and devised with the help of copious notes taken from sources on biology, astronomy, anatomy, indeed any encyclopedic materials making, in his view, existence more tangibly knowable, they are, according to Juhász, "lyrical poems, personal beliefs, original hymns and laments."

His poetry, whether such lyrical epics or lyric poems, searches constantly for the meaning of life. To explain the universe in ways that will sustain the human spirit, Juhász uses every kind of knowledge and experience to create his own universe with the force of chain-reacting images. Convinced that religion provides no triumph over death and that the only hope of redemption for humanity lies in the indestructability of matter, he tries to arm humankind against death's inevitability at a historical time when the entire earth can, as he says, "become a single graveyard"; his horror of the atomic holocaust and his concept of the poet's role are vividly portrayed in "Images of the Night" ("Éjszaka képei"). He uses his poetic art to bring human society into a tighter relationship with the universe, and while doing so, he lays bare the agony and anxiety tormenting him. In the end, he always finds the way to a consoling thought. In *My Mother* (*Anyám*, 1969), breeding redeems humans from death; in *The Epic of the Dead* (*A hallotak eposza*, 1971), humans can accept death only if their life has been full and rich and only if their purpose has been to build the kind of world for the human race that will make the act of suicide avoidable. Eventually, Juhász concludes that death is the completion of life, fitting into the order of nature even as birth does, and that it makes it possible for human beings to develop ethical values and behavior.

Although he is still agonized by the fact of death, his desperate awareness of human loneliness and isolation provides an endless challenge to his thought and role as a poet. In a 1976 television interview he resolutely affirmed that human existence has meaning. This affirmation has permitted him to face, through his poetry, the apparently senseless world in which humans are compelled to live. Declaring in that interview that life is worth living, that it has both meaning and purpose, he added:

> Indeed, I believe that the entire existing universe is not a purposeless swirling for its own sake alone, . . . a building up and a destruction of itself, but that it has a purposeful tendency in some direction. . . . I am not a religious man. But I believe in the intelligibility of human life . . . . I believe that man condemned to this terrestrial sphere is not alone after all. He can't be alone!

He then echoed the adventurous and precarious course of his own poetic quest:

> I think that if man is alone, poets must, with all their poems, plant a belief in life in every man's heart. A single spore or seed in every man's heart planted with a belief in existence. In the worthy human heart must be planted the belief that it is worth living, worth working, that our life is worth continuing and must be continued all the way to natural death.

The Boy Changed into a Stag Cries Out at the Gate of Secrets

Her own son the mother called
from afar crying,
her own son the mother called
from afar crying,
she went before the house from there calling,
her hair's full knot she loosed,
with it the dusk wove a dense quivering
veil, a precious cloak down to her ankles,
wove a stiff mantle, heavy-flaring,
a flag for the wind with ten black tassels
a shroud, the fire-stabbed blood-tainted dusk.
Her fingers she twined in the sharp tendrilled
stars, her face the moon's foam coated,
and on her own son she called shrilly
as once she called him, a small child,
she went before the house and talked to the wind,
with songbirds spoke, sending swiftly
words after the wild pairing geese,
to the shivering bullrushes,
to the potato flower so silvery,
to the clench-balled bulls rooted so firmly,
to the well-shading fragrant sumac tree,

she spoke to the fish leaping at play,
to the mauve oil-rings afloat fleetingly:
    you birds and boughs, hear me
listen as I cry out,
    and listen, you fishes, you flowers
listen, for I speak to be heard,
    listen you glands of expanding soils
        you vibrant fins, astral-seeding parachutes,
    decelerate, you humming motors of the saps
    in the depths of the atom, screw down the whining taps,
        all metal-pelvised virgins, sheep alive under cotton
    listen as I cry out,
    for I'm crying out to my son!

    Her own son the mother called
    her cry ascending in a spiral,
    within the gyre of the universe it rose,
    her limbs flashing in the light rays
    like the back of a fish slippery-scaled
    or a roadside boil of salt or crystal.
    Her own son the mother called:
come back, my own son, come back
    I call you, your own mother!
come back, my own son, come back
    I call you, your mild harbor,
come back, my own son, come back
    I call you, your cool fountain,
come back, my own son, come back
    I call you, your memory's teat,
come back, my own son, come back
    I call you, your withered tent,
come back, my own son, come back
    I call you, your almost sightless lamp.

Come back, my own son, for I'm blind in this world of sharp objects,
within yellow-green bruises my eyes are sinking, my brow contracts,
my thighs—my barked shins,
from all sides things rush at me like crazed wethers,
the gate, the post, the chair try their horns on me
doors slam upon me like drunken brawlers,
the perverse electricity shoots its current at me,

my flaking skin seeps blood—a bird's beak cracked with a stone,
    scissors swim out of reach like spider crabs all metal,
the matches are sparrow's feet, the pail swings back at me with its
                    handle,
come back, my own son, come back
my legs no longer carry me like the young hind,
        vivid tumors pout on my feet
        gnarled tubers penetrate my purpling thighs,
on my toes grow bony structures,
        the fingers on my hands stiffen, already the flesh is shelly
scaling like slate from weathered geologic formations,
every limb has served its time and sickens,
come back, my own son, come back,
        for I am no more as I was,
        I am gaunt with inner visions
        which flare from the stiffening hoary organs
        as on winter mornings an old cock's crowing
rings from a fence of shirts, hanging hard-frozen,
I call you, your own mother,
come back, my own son, come back,
to the unmanageable things bring a new order,
discipline the estranged objects, tame the knife,
        domesticate the comb,
for I am now but two gritty green eyes
glassy and weightless like the *libellula*
whose winged nape and dragon jaws, you know it well
        my son, hold so delicately
two crystal apples in his green-lit skull,
I am two staring eyes without a face
seeing all, now one with unearthly beings.
Come back, my own son, come back,
        with your fresh breath, set all to rights again.

            In the far forest the lad heard,
            at once he jerked up his head,
            with his wide nostrils testing
            the air, soft dewlaps pulsing
            with veined ears pricked, harkening
            alertly to those tones sobbing
            as to a hunter's slimy tread,
            or hot wisps curling from the bed
            of young forest fires, when smoky

high woods start to whimper bluely.
He turned his head, no need to tell
him this was the voice he knew so well,
now by an agony he's seized,
fleece on his buttocks he perceives,
in his lean legs sees the proof
of strange marks left by each cleft hoof,
where lilies shine in forest pools
sees his low hairy-pursed buck-balls.
He pushes his way down to the lake
breasting the brittle willow brake,
rump slicked with foam, at each bound
he slops white froth on the hot ground,
his four black hooves tear out a path
through wild flowers wounded to death,
stamp a lizard into the mold
neck swollen, tail snapped, growing cold.
And when he reached the lake at last
into its moonlit surface glanced:
it holds the moon, beeches shaking,
and back at him a stag staring!
Only now thick hair does he see
covering all his slender body
hair over the knees, thighs, the transverse
tasseled lips of his male purse,
his long skull had sprouted antlers
into bone leaves their bone boughs burst,
his face is furry to the chin
his nostrils are slit and slant in.
Against trees his great antlers knock,
veins knot in ropes along his neck,
madly he strains, prancing he tries
vainly to raise an answering cry,
only a stag's voice bells within
the new throat of this mother's son,
he drops a son's tears, paws the brink
to banish that lake-monster, sink
it down into the vortex sucking
fluid dark, where scintillating
little fish flash their flowery fins,
minute, bubble-eyed diamonds.
The ripples subside at last in the gloom,

but a stag still stands in the foam of that moon.

Now in his turn the boy cries back
    stretching up his belling neck,
now in his turn the boy calls back
    through his stag's throat, through the fog calling:
    mother, my mother
    I cannot go back,
    mother, my mother
    you must not lure me,
    mother, my mother
    my dear breeding nurse,
    mother, my mother
    sweet frothy fountain,
    safe arms that held me
    whose heavy breasts fed me
    my tent, shelter from frosts,
    mother, my mother
    seek not my coming,
    mother, my mother
    my frail silken stalk,
    mother, my mother
    bird with teeth of gold,
    mother, my mother,
    you must not lure me!
    If I should come home
    my horns would fell you,
    from horn to sharp horn
    I'd toss your body,
    if I should come home
    down I would roll you,
    tread your loose veiny
    breasts mangled by hooves,
    I'd stab with unsheathed
    horns, maul with my teeth,
    tread in your womb even.
    If I should come home
    mother, my mother
    I'd spill out your lungs
    for blue flies buzzing round,
    and the stars would stare down
    into your flower-organs

which once did hold me,
with warmth of summer suns,
in shiny peace encased
where warmth never ceased,
as once cattle breathed
gently to warm Jesus.
Mother, my mother
do not summon me,
death would strike you down
in my shape's coming
if this son drew near.
Each branch of my antlers
is a gold filament,
each prong of my antlers
a winged candlestick,
each tine of my antlers
a catafalque candle,
each leaf of my antlers
a gold-laced altar.
Dead surely you'd fall
if you saw my gray antlers
soar into the sky
like the All Soul's Eve
candle-lit graveyard,
my head a stone tree
leafed with growing flame.
Mother, my mother
if I came near you
I would soon singe you
like straw, I would scorch
you to greasy black clay,
you'd flare like a torch
for I would roast you
to charred shreds of flesh.
Mother, my mother
do not summon me
for if I came home
I would devour you,
for if I came home
your bed I would ravage,
the flower garden
with my thousand-pronged

Ferenc Juhász

           horns would I savage,
           I'd chew through the trees
           in the stag-torn groves,
           drink dry the one well
           in a single gulp,
           if I should return
           I'd fire your cottage,
           and then I would run
           to the old graveyard,
           with my pointed soft
           nose, with all four hooves
           I'd root up my father,
           with my teeth wrench off
           his cracked coffin lid
           and snuff his bones over!
           Mother, my mother
           do not lure me,
           I cannot go back,
           for if I came home
           I'd bring your death surely.

In a stag's voice the lad cried,
and in these words his mother answered him:
      come back, my own son, come back
I call you, your mother.
      Come back, my own son, come back
I'll cook you brown broth, and you'll slice onion-rings in it,
they'll crunch between your teeth like quartz splinters in a giant's jaws,
I'll give you warm milk in a clean jug,
from my last keg trickle wine into heron-necked bottles,
and I know how to knead the bread with my rocky fists, I know how you like it,
bread to bake soft-bellied buns for you, sweet bread for the feasts,
      come back, my own son, come back
from the live breasts of the screeching geese for your eiderdown I plucked
                                                      feathers,
weeping I plucked my weeping geese, the spots stripped of feathers turning
      a fierce white on their breasts, like the mouths of the dying,
I shook up your pallet in the clear sunlight, made it fresh for your rest,
the yard has been swept, the table is laid—for your coming.

      O mother, my mother
          for me there's no homecoming,

do not lay out for me twisted white bread
            or sweet goat's milk in my flowered mug foaming,
and do not prepare for me a soft bed,
            for feathers ravage not the breasts of the geese,
spill your wine rather, upon my father's grave let it soak in,
            the sweet onions bind into a garland,
fry up for the little ones that froth-bellying dough.
            The warm milk would turn to vinegar at my tongue's lapping,
            into a stone turtle you'd see the white bread changing,
            your wine within my tumbler like red blood rising,
            the eiderdown would dissolve into little blue flames in silence
            and the brittle-beaked mug splinter into swordgrass.
O mother, O mother, my own good mother
            my step may not sound in the paternal house,
I must live deep in the green wood's underbrush
            no room for my tangled antlers in your shadowy
house, no room in your yard for my cemetery
            antlers; for my foliated horns are a loud world-tree
their leaves displaced by stars, their green moss by the Milky Way,
            sweet-scented herbs must I take in my mouth, only
the first-growth grasses can my spittle liquefy,
            I may no longer drink from the flowered mug you bring
only from a clean spring, ónly from a clean spring!

I do not understand, do not understand your strange tortured words, my son
you speak like a stag, a stag's soul seems to possess you, my unfortunate one.
When the turtle-dove cries, the turtle-dove cries, when the little
                        bird sings, the little bird sings, my son
wherefore am I—in the whole universe am I the last lost
                        soul left, the only one?
Do you remember, do you remember your small once-young
                        mother, my son?
I do not understand, do not understand your sad tortured words,
                        my long-lost son.

Do you remember how you came running, running home to me
                        so happy with your school report,
            you dissected a bull frog, spreading out on the fence his
                        freckled webbed paddle-feet,
and how you pored over the books on aircraft, how you followed
                        me in to help with the washing,
            you loved Irene B., your friends were V.J.

and H.S. the wild orchid-bearded painter,
and do you remember on Saturday nights, when your father came
                    home sober, how happy you were?
O mother, my mother, do not speak of my sweetheart of old nor of my friend,
        like fish they fleet by in cold depths, the vermilion-chinned painter
            who knows now where he has gone his shouting way, who
                    knows mother, where my youth has gone?
Mother, my mother, do not recall my father, out of his flesh
                sorrow has sprouted,
        sorrow blossoms from the dark earth, do not recall
                my father, my father,
            from the grave he'd rise, gathering about him his yellowed bones,
            from the grave stagger, hair and nails growing anew.
Oh, Oh, Uncle Wilhelm came, the coffin-maker, that puppet-faced man,
        he told us to take your feet and drop you neatly in the coffin,
            I retched because I was afraid, I had come straight home
                    from Pest that day;
        you also, my father, went back and forth to Pest, you were
                only an office messenger, the rails twisted up,
            oh, the stabbing knives in my belly then, shadows from the
                    candle ravined your tight cheeks.
Your new son-in-law, Laci the barber, shaved you that day, the
                candle dribbling the while like a silent baby
        regurgitating its glistening entrails, its long luminous nerves like vines,
        the choral society stood round you in their purple hats
                    mourning you at the tops of their voices,
            with one finger I traced the rim of your forehead,
                    your hair was alive still,
        I heard it grow, I saw the bristles sprout from your chin
        blackened by morning; the next day your throat had sunk
                    beneath snake-grass stalks of hair,
            its curve like a soft-furred cantaloupe, the color of a yellow-haired
                    caterpillar upon blue cabbage skin.
Oh, and I thought your hair, your beard, would overgrow
                    the whole room, the yard,
        the entire world, stars nestling like cells in its hiving strands.
Ah! heavy green rain started then to fall, the team of red
                    horses before the hearse neighed in terror,
        one lashing out above your head with a lightning bolt hoof,
                    the other relentlessly pissing
        so that his purple parts passed out with it like a hanged

      man's tongue, while their coachman cursed
and the downpour washed round the huddled brassbandsmen,
      then all those old friends blew with a will,
sobbing as they played, beside the globe-thistle studded chapel wall,
those old friends blew till their lips swelled blue, and the tune
      spiralled out and up,
the old friends blew with cracked lips bleeding now,
      with eyeballs staring,
blew for the card games and booze, the bloated, the withered
      and the trumped women,
played you out for the red-letter day beer-money, the tips
      sent whirling into space after you
they blew, sobbing as they blew sadly down into the
      sedimentary layers of silted sadness,
music pouring from the burnished mouths, from rings of brass
      into putrescent nothingness,
out of it streamed the petrified sweethearts, rotting women,
      and moldy grandfathers in the melody,
with small cottages, cradles, and rolling like onions a generation
      of enamel-swollen, silver-bodied watches,
Easter bells and multifarious saviors came out also on
      wide-spreading wings of sound
that summoned up satchels, railway wheels, and soldiers
      brass-buttoned at the salute,
the old friends played on, teeth reddening behind lips curled
      back and swollen like blackened liver,
and yourself conducting the choir—Well done, boys, that's
      grand, carry it on, don't stop now!—
all the time with hands clasped tight, those gold spiders with
      huge spoke-joint knotted legs, resting on your heart,
in the cupboard your collapsed boots await the relations, white
      socks naked on your bread-crust curling feet,
old friends that day played you out in the crashing rain,
      valves snapping like steel Adam's apples
like fangs of antediluvian birds, teeth of the *carcharodon* looking
      for carrion from out those brass trumpets.

O mother, my mother, do not recall my father,
  let my father be, lest his eyes burst out of the reopening earth.

  Her own son the mother called

           from afar crying:
come back, my own son, come back
           turn away from that stone world,
you stag of the stone woods, industrialized air, electric grids,
chemical lightnings, iron bridges, and streetcars lap up your blood,
day by day they make a hundred assaults on you,
                         yet you never hit back,
it is I calling you, your own mother,
           come back, my own son, come back.

There he stood on the renewing crags of time,
stood on the ringed summit of the sublime
universe, there stood the boy at the gate of secrets,
his antler prongs were playing with the stars,
with a stag's voice down the world's lost paths
he called back to his life-giving mother:
           mother, my mother, I cannot go back,
pure gold seethes in my hundred wounds,
day by day a hundred bullets knock me from my feet
and day by day I rise again, a hundred times more complete,
day by day I die three billion times,
day by day I am born three billion times,
each branch of my antlers is a dual-based pylon,
each prong of my antlers a high-tension wire,
my eyes are ports for ocean-going merchantmen, my veins are
                         tarry cables, these
teeth are iron bridges, and in my heart surge the monster-infested seas,
each vertebra is a teeming metropolis, for a spleen I have a smoke-puffing
                         barge,
each of my cells is a factory, my atoms are solar systems,
sun and moon swing in my testicles, the Milky Way is my bone marrow,
each point in space is one part of my body,
my brain's impulse is out in the curling galaxies.

Lost son of mine, come back for all that,
your *libellula*-eyed mother watches you still.

Only to die will I return, only to die come back,
yes, I will come, will come to die,
and when I have come—but to die—my mother,
then may you lay me in the parental house,

with your marbled hands you may wash my body,
my glandulous eyelids close with a kiss.
    And then, when my flesh falls apart
and lies in its own stench, yet deep in flowers,
    then shall I feed on your blood, be your body's fruit,
then shall I be your own small son again,
and this shall give pain to you alone, mother,
    to you alone, O my mother.

Firelily in the Night

Firelily in the night,
I do not believe in the mockingbird's luring,
do not believe in the worldly-wise wrongdoing,
do not believe in man's sinning,
in this tremendous summer a madness throbbing,
firelily in the night,
I do not believe in the mockingbird's luring,
gray-fur giant moth in electric loneliness wheeling,
its gray star to God's smile adding,
firelily in the night,
plant creatures' green lameness,
green exhalations and plant darkness,
manic worm-sadness spilled from each other's
fibrous silences, giant petal tatters,
green excitement, mare on heat above
with ardor's bloody vulva reflex-love,
mockingbird-lips' fluttered voluptuousness,
firelily, tell me of your aloneness,
firelily in the night,
I believe so much in man's miracle,
in something good, something beautiful,
some purpose man's called to fulfill,
firelily in the night,

moon in the walnut tree's green tangle,
moon in the green method of the walnut's tangle,
firelily at the rim of a lightning-light's circle,
firelily, whore for a night of star-earth,
green thorned stalk-marrow's outward flaring mouth,
from shadowed emptiness prayer ascending,
tiger roar, bloody whitemetal casing,
green palm's erect flame-sexuality, higher
a yellow lizard-comet lashes your brain of fire,
its huge battleaxe lays open the universe,
its winds swish downward to the bowels of hell,
firelily in the night,
in this tremendous summer a madness throbbing,
over my heavy heart licks a comet tail,
like jellyfish tongued-in by a killer whale,
like corona-squids' flaccid tangled tentacles
down on my head loosing its laced light-whorls,
some savage angel is weeping in the night,
in an outer world fluttering out of sight,
some blind devil in blind space stamping,
cornets and cymbals in sin to ashes burning,
world-generating stallion, whinnying, called
his mate, kicking hooves back at the blue eye of God,
from the blue eye of God the flame sheets down,
in heaven's howling storm of sparks I drown,
up there roars the Gilgamesh sky-bull,
no one to slay him, no one upon whom to fall,
moon's fire-rainbowed tumescence rises
pouring into space immense slag fires,
in this tremendous summer a madness throbbing,
firelily in the night,
earth trembles, the sea is crawling to the moon:
glutinous renewal, amoeba maelstrom,
in this tremendous summer a madness throbbing,
firelily in the night,
beneath the contorted walnut tree's stone bark
lilies' fires burn holes in the dark,
overhead the dream completes the age of stone
with the walnut tree's cement Laocoön,
down upon lilies screws its meshed stone-muscled
stone-snake vortex, their wounds blood-marbled,

barbed swordfish lance, evil purpled hydra,
leopard's spot avid for raw flesh she-star;
above foundation root-weave, plant's rib-casing,
plant's green wheel-arms, the bloom-blood sobbing:
firelily in the night,
I do not believe in the mockingbird's luring,
like dragon's eyelashes, darkening bands
of leaf-shadow fall on our tight-clenched hands,
I do not believe in the mockingbird's luring,
firelily in the night,
wakeful silence-shedding catafalque candle
lighting up our watching heart's vigil.
Mankind must not burn up apart
like firelilies in the night.

From: Images of the Night

The day I wrote this the skies were clear,
And green boughs blossomed from the crags of Earth.
                    Vörösmarty[1]

MEN'S CHORUS

Avid, unregretting, bark-scented night!
Green boughs cannot pierce the night.
Roofs cannot pierce the night,
windows cannot pierce the night,
grave-stones cannot pierce the night.
Night of insect's fungus eye, of bird's bloody beak, of profound root world.
Why no glimmer from the stars' deep-sea flowers?
Why won't the consuming soft arms of space pull
open the pulsing corona-mouths of the carnivorous stars'
chiselled teeth-rows of a blind flower-skull?
Night, bear-loin smelling, plant-viscera lining, coal wing-root of a bird.
Solitude cannot pierce the night.

The night cannot pierce the night.
Only the wakeful watch. Twined branches of waking thoughts flower out of
        sight.

. . .

POET

    No!
    I cannot sleep!
    I see images in the night!
    I see images in the night, like a blur of cards shuffled in the devil's hand,
    I see images in the night, like teeth erupting along the dry bones of the dead.
    I see images in the night, like staring eyes of water-animals surfacing,
    I see images in the night, like screens of judgment flickering!
    I see images in the night: a hand leafs through the layered heavens!
    Ah, has judgment overtaken me?
    Ah, is this the tongue of terror licking over me?
    Ah, does the sliding jaw of madness crunch me, like flowers or grass
    in a cow's rosy mouth?

CHORUS

    Fool, say what you see!

. . .

POET

    I can see beneath earth's belly skin:
    in the book of earth I read the future's strewn lettering of bones.
    I see into the high stars' membraneous wombs:
    I can see in unsighing crystals the clustering embryos.
    I see how the future is surging out of the past,
    the blackly billowing past.
    Mankind, I fear for you.

. . .

CHORUS

    Alas, what remained after the destruction?
    After the Atom, Hydrogen, and Neutron?
    Cursing horror? Curses, horrors!
    But who any more can curse? Who is left to be horror-struck?
    Rotted cosmic debris, boiled slime of human blood?
    The dwarf tree, struggling up out of human flesh?
    The rock coated with human bone, like a white rash?
    Or those few who remained?

MEN'S CHORUS

    But who are the ones who remained?

NARRATOR

    Are they the dead or the living? The dead were printed upon seared rock, upon Earth's stellar structure, like fossil creatures' shadow-imaged parchment wings, spinal cords, or downy jellied dot of seed; is the human race only a memory of the globe, like the departed ages of crustaceans, giant mammals, dragons, or vertebrates? And shall existence without man grow ever lonelier, the soundless sadness of a sigh be all from the orphaned few remaining before the final annihilation?

    Why has life labored to give birth to man through the milliard years' ascent from gas, fire, rock, plant, and animal? What did it purpose with its ideals, with purity, goodness, liberty? With ideals worth more than life itself, preconditionings of life's worth and meaning?

    This insect's-heart-sized planet, this Earth, among stars as big as whales' hearts, is it to go on turning *emptily* in solitude, an overgrown, desolate graveyard, Mankind's graveyard? Or shall Man once more teem in torrents from its tortuous, exquisite womb, blessed little primeval mother, tenacious re-bearer of Mankind? Shall Earth tumble on over and over about the sun-star's fire-spouts, like a lonely desert of bone, metal, and rubble, or will there be someone to trim and comb out its straggly green beard, to burnish its dulled and cataracted wandering ocean-glance, to smooth the death-wrinkles of suffering from its Earth-countenance, and shall the deranged Earth-skull ever again conceive meaningful human thought?

    . . .

NARRATOR

    Was anything of Man left on the space-island of death? Anyone left on this earthly afterwards, after dying once, to suffer on through the *other* life of victorious monsterdom, time of derangement, post-Man existence? And the strange, never-before-heard sounds of this monsterhood? Anything of Man left, whose heart dared go on beating?

    . . .

CHORUS

    Then how did Mankind regain faith?
    Were machines to bring Man forth?

Ferenc Juhász

POET

> There live on still, in solitude, the self-mutating machines that have survived; beneath the impenetrable glassy weed-forests in their mole-man mad purple-lit tunnel warrens, in Earth's concrete entrails, in the depopulated cities' wilderness of skeletons and human rottings, in the scrapyards of culture and civilization, on Mankind's rubbish heap swarming with multiple-headed flies, all over this rubbish-dump world, here and there their lamps will glimmer, give off signals, send out messages. Large electronic machine-mice, machine-ladybirds, machine-foxes, machine-monkeys scurry, roll, perambulate, their hard eyes glaring on-off rhythmically, nodding, clacking, hobbling, crackling; photo electric-eyed steel doors open-close in empty underground chambers, monumental electronic brains compute hysterically, confusedly, unable to stop living, electronic translators print out unordered, garbled words, whole languages; in the back of a laboratory looms a man of glass in lilac-pink luminescence, like a glass rose lit from within, his organs and nervous system phosphoresce, arteries and brain outlined in flickering red-blue-yellow-green circuitry like a giant translucent mosquito-larva; centered in a tunnel's star, a machine man clad in rigid light repeats over, ten, a hundred, thousand, million times his recorded text; self-reproducing electronic devices bring forth self-reproducers, and they again more new ones, new hybrid machines tinkling, crackling, whimpering, machine-mothers in labor are whining, drenched in oil sweat; machine horses whinny, machine monkey-mothers clasp to their rubber teats dead decomposing monkey babes, fur falling out, turning to jelly; electronic composing machines orchestrate man-horse whinny symphonies, galactic oratorios, and blast out music into the night of shattered vegetation.

CHORUS

> And what remained after the destruction?
> After Atom, Hydrogen, and Neutron?
> . . .

POET

> The day breaks. Gold tiles are roofing over darkness.
> On my wakeful window I watch ruby-flecks falling.
> Across my room's mauve wall, like X-rayed lungs' veiny lace,
> light has printed the bushy cells of curtaining.
> My lamp, like old soldiers' graveyards, grows fainter.
> It gives no light—why should it?—to the light coming.
> On my wife's neck, fluffy light-fields gleam brighter,
> like star-clusters: shimmering, pulsing, paling.
> Green boughs now falteringly pierce the night:

the joy-drunk nesting birds flutter, hover, raise and dip their heads again,
they keep up a screeching, drink dew, hunt beetles.
And slowly the Sun waves across space his invincible flag of Flame.

FULL CHORUS

The day I wrote this the skies were clear,
And green boughs blossomed from the crags of Earth.

POET

I believe in you, Mankind.
My imagined dead shall not defeat you.

[1] Mihály Vörösmarty (1800-55) was the most important romantic writer in Hungary. His lyric and narrative poems were especially successful. His later works were significant for their somewhat pantheistic view of Hungary and humanity, but his attitude toward both was colored by his pessimism about the possibilities for progress.

Béla Bartók and the Tree Frog

In his last exile years, voluntary tormenting barren bitter time of greater than ever humiliation, of infinite defenselessness of such perfect silence outside, where as in a hermetically sealed glass sphere, vast untooled blue glass globe, Béla Bartók stood meditative forlorn orphan-hearted, in sealed up vast glass-sphere time, in rarefied air inner glass-tear space that oppresses the austere divine creative mood and uncomplaining human heart into rhythmless nervousnesss, ever since almost the last life-giving air was drawn off eagerly sucked out from sealed up glass time by mercilessness and denial of love in the barren last years, flowerless cliff-face barren in the self-consuming self-consumed firehearth barren last years of his anguishing life ruthless with crystal flamings of his searing meteor fate, Béla Bartók used to work and pass the time in a devoted friend's country cottage in the northern part of the United States of America, in a cottage belted with hardy tall forests metallic green flamings, barren and stonestar-eyed mountains beneath the wailing wind and in maelstrom yellowing grass crowns' wailing. There he listened to visible silence walked broad forest paths or broke through trackless flame-tissue in loneliness like Creative Will in loneliness like Creative Suffering. God surely walked thus: at His creating's mid-point in time, in almost universal time because he knew what he had to do though not if in his heart there would be time enough for completing. To have still humility enough grace enough and wrath of his being enough to continue the creating and to complete the creation impossible of completion. God surely walked thus in meditation and thus in loneliness. Because he walked within himself and within the creations of his being, because he walked in his faith in blossoming images of his loneliness in his constraintless sounds of creating. This loneliest most austere man, within whom suffering was growing not only in his body's flesh in his heart's red terror growing also in the blossom-shedding permanence of his being putting forth branches stars' laciness underbrush shootings solidifying compressing into striating splinters like crystal needles: thornily splinterings in lines of force in star-clustering needles as a needle star-rose tumor, in threadings pointings in projections as they mount sprouting and swelling, this man walked with the white crystal needle-bush of suffering in his flesh and in his being, stiffened almost from the needle-bush crystal pain pervading his being. From time to time he would sit on a phosphorous foam-coated fallen trunk on a porous ancient horse's skull-rock, on a star shock-haired grassy hill because the journey hurt him and would be long yet. And the needle crystal knives kept germinating. Suddenly out from the green leaf lacework-fire or perhaps from pure space a little tree frog jumped onto his resting knees. And it was panting there blinking and pulsating like a golden sickle, this sweating little knot of stammering this sticky fright with jelly star hands. And Béla Bartók offered a seat to little green tree frog on the tip of his right thumb and paralyzed it squatted there stuck to the clod rose, a palpitating little four-handed grave mound throbbing and green a heart sprouting the hands of a child, a swollen panting oozing moist silken ball a gluey teardrop with soft gold balled eyes, a gluey green mystery a blinking rubber bud and it embraces the thumb of Man with blue rubbery freckled silk glove hands, little glandulous green Virgin Mary at the Cross, or a terrified child its mother's neck, green teardrop of foliage sitting there tiny green drumming heart's terror on the Creating Thumb sitting there a dumb green gummy imp Stupefied Earth Spirit. Like Little Green Annunciation Angel to a barren pink star. And Béla Bartók gazed at tree frog its yellow silken beat-beating delicate belly bag, its delicate fluttering rubber beat-beating puffed up double chin, its conical stretch throbbing green silken cupped eyelids. He gazed at the anxious terrified stooped crouched and glistening green silence of the glandulous silky angel. And he heard silence. Because Béla Bartók heard tree frog, as he sat in the grief and grace of loneliness. Because he heard the skin's green creasings on its delicate crouching, the wild blossoming life-ferment of particle inner skin, ,the weavy stretch and lacily growing ramification bundles and fibers of muscles, because he heard blood's soft beats blood's bulk blood's particles floating drifting heaving because he heard the wild life thunder of cells molecules atoms nuclear particles, their flowering gluey membraneous breathy feeding exploding and mysterious life-fabric and their blazing ordering, because he heard immense sub-cutaneous life and death thunderings erupting into life of nucleic space-forces affinities bonds explosions and excretions growing through interpenetrating percussions, heard the booming atoms in the frog's skeleton because he heard all the mysteries of matter, all its maladies and conditions Béla Bartók heard all the sub-cutaneous secrets of existence, all its forms and temptations and humiliations just as he heard the explosions the thunderings and shudderings the revolutions the ferment the boiling the groaning the moaning the wild thunder of atoms and elementary particles in the body in the realizing within raw matter of little green tree frog crouching on his thumb. Béla Bartók heard the elementary sounds and states of existence. In the trees' concentrated cells, in their microscopic vessels' system he heard the circulating swishing fluids, lights' green explosions in foliage molecular stirrings in the bosoms of worms, underground flaming of the dead the howling-light highway of arch-stars and heavenly prodigal bodies, tender growing of fluff in birds' armpits, sorrow of soils feeding micro-organisms growing of eggs in the bodies of owls, rose heart-face owls growing of embryo in mother's body, birth of stars and the howling the crying the wailing the madness the pleasure and the tears of silence. Béla Bartók heard with his life all matter's forms of existence heard life and death, the fossilized and the yielding solid and soft, heard condensings into material form and whirlings in loose clouds rolling flames that were to condense and coagulate, and the vast disdainful primordial ball of flame that was to explode into rings of cosmic fog. Béla Bartók heard all the states of being of Existence their torment anxiety dream beauty randomness panic, their creatures terrors triumphs blasphemies, he heard everything material angelic imaginary divine everything that is beyond the human and is unhearable everything cosmic around man. And he heard everything human every human joy and suffering, every human life and death every human terror humiliation absolution, every human loneliness and happy unloneliness, Béla Bartók heard everything humanely human. He heard man and the universe, he heard life and death the blossoming of the universe in man, man's journey in the cosmos in pulsating flashes of light-speck, he heard the mist-speck dissolution of man's beautiful heart glitteringly in the life-blessed death-conceived primordial matter of the universe. This was Bartók's music. Simultaneity of hearing these fateful anguishing happy pure sounds was the music of Béla Bartók, because his music was harmony somber and uplifting stubborn and crystal-mysterious of the sound of Existence, the music of Béla Bartók was at last utterly robustly melodious wild happy pure ensemble of man created on Earth of holy tangle and holy confusion sounding matter enclosing man cast at the universe's peril into infinite primordial space. He heard even the sound of history, sounds of Earth's ever-since-primordial-history's beginnings, the growing of giant prehistoric ferns, the tremendous lurch of prehistoric dragons, the frantic happy surge of peoples thunder barren prehistoric seas, cries and wailing of peoples their women-in-labor shouting, he heard fires whirlings rocks cooling and secret growing, and the pure song of his own nation purifying grace-giving, radiating from history and suffering which blossomed and gurgled from lips dewy or swearviolet. His simultaneous hearing of the universe was creative liberty itself. His all-hearing knowing was unsparing faith in freedom. His free music of the infinite was the greatest affirmation of man's freedom. This is why this Very Lonely Man, this Man Giant hearing and creating with God became and could become example faith and ecstasy of our own fate and life and faith.

From: The Coffin of Zoltán Latinovits[1] Written All Over Inside and Out Like an Egyptian Mummy Dummy

The way you could recite "My Mother"
    —like no one else!
I'm gnawed to the skeleton by sorrow.
    You, by rottenness.

Blind, you were! For Erzsike[2] you were—as now I you—
    schizoidly lamenting.
Fool. Fool. Yielding up yourself to your own self-view!
    Why, with hope remaining?

For there is always hope; how foolish you were,
    conceited, rotten!
And into our hearts you wiped out, like a small people by war,
    that death you had chosen!

And we burn, bleed, small country to barbarians going
    down in defeat!
Who croaks this way is already dead utterly, going
    down in defeat!

You coward! Even your dying is someone else's death, all
    drink-vomit wretching.
Why the Waltz? You had not, even then, grasped the whole,
    Death-Rascal!

Why the Tango, the last, the vagina-penis slavering
    him-her corpse-ball?
Now you know, how through your stiff-stuffed coffin the spade cuts in.
    What death is, but that's all.

You thought you were a hero, with your crazed-leaping snarl,
    because the train came?
Yourself you could never change, for someone else's role.
    Your death least of all!

You, too cowardly to endure yourself defiantly,
    I loved as my own.
Now I shout in vain, for Erzsike too, vainly.
    Child, gray-grown.

Wrong, impossible at forty-five this throat's whimpered
    laughing-sob lump.
Only a slobbering chuckle, because the pint-pot has been filled.
    And, a jump.

Into the noose. Facing the engine. From the gas-pipe hanging,
    under iron wheels laying;
so closed the mouth, knife-thin, blue, neither the woman's tongue protruding.
    Right eye bulging.

As the snailhorn onion-like pushes out from the velvet
    puddingy snailbody,
so was your eye growing out from the right eye socket.
    Swollen blindly.

Wrong, after all, one cannot simply jump like this, as you
> the two of you, did!
If you knew, that I must therefore bear both of you!
> And what was it I did?

What was the sin? What the disgrace? What so unforgivable?
> What was the curse?
To me, if there were such, that I'd thought our beings inseparable
> —your country my existence!

And reversed now, I've become your countryless-existence, you dead,
> each a suicide.
You woman-genius little-depression, and You my schizophrenic diamond
> gallant!
> I've no sobs to hide!
. . .
No! No! No! I don't give myself up. I don't give up easily,
> Curses, both!
Who sunlight-speckledly, gold-dottedly, sun-flame foliagedly
> dissimulate, both!

Even when dead, you dissimulate! Mourning, forebearance
> —demanding it!
He who received existence-power from the begetting parents
> should shoulder it!
. . .
But there will come after this, traitors, will come, Selling-out perjurers,
> will come,
> there will come revolution,
production, defiant plant-breed, will indeed come
> give-and-take of man-woman.

Still, on my billion cells, billion catafalques, lie
> the blind dead.
Flowering world-tree of the dead, am I. But away
> with your whining, you dead!

Death! Death! Death! Death! Death! Death! Death!
> Death! Death! Death!
Death! Death! Death! Death! Death! Death! Death! Death!
> Death! Death! Death!

Death! Death! Death! Death! Death! Death! Death!
    You are not my love!
My cannibal-heart tears out human hearts, rends corpses with its teeth
    —behold, the victory I have!

[1] Latinovits (1931-76?), educated as an architect, became a highly successful actor with a gift for intellectual roles and also for reading poetry, including Juhász's. A very difficult and nonconformist personality, he performed only in the provinces during his last years.

[2] Juhász's life was also tragically affected by the suicide of his lovely and fragile wife, Erzsébet Szeverényi, in 1973.

From: "Notes for an Epic"

Fourth Thesis

Sin is man's! But the Word also is of man! Man's alone! Man, too, is nature. Man is nature, too! Or may not man be nature's consciousness of sin? A man is what I am, with huge developed brain. I am nature, and a man from out of nature because I know nature and I know death. I am burning in transitoriness. As a man I am thus by nature more, humanized. Not just sensing and fulfilling the law, implementing destiny, serving the law through my existing. But Man wanting to want law to become morality. A law-seeker, too. Man. Group-being, in history-being. Conquering, possessing, seeking, searching, recognizing! Transmuting. Mine the word. Mine the ancient word, that of the mother-tongue. And because I am a social being, a historical being—I had to become a moral being, too. And an aesthetic being. Only from existence, from existence with recognized consciousness can morality send forth branches, and only from morality with a universe-consciousness and history-consciousness may there branch forth an aesthetics of creative, thinking existence of the mortal human condition. Conscious art is the property of man. It sings. It constructs epics of the written word. New Poems. From ideas coming from reality and ideas coming from the imagination. Thus is a new reality and ideas coming from the imagination. Thus is a new reality created by conscious man. That he should preserve something of Conscious Horror, of Recognized Nature, of Existence's Law, and of Death in Existence's Law! Because man is immortality desiring. Because man alone desires immortality. Therefore he is the humbled proud mortal. Hence his consciousness of sin!

Sándor Csoóri

Csoóri was born on February 3, 1930 in Zámoly, "right in the middle of a teeth-chattering hard winter and the similarly severe economic crisis." His parents were peasants and Protestants, who were defenseless against the desperate economic situation but stubborn in their faith and convictions. His father was always stirred by historical events and social justice, and picked up every scrap of newspaper to inform himself about such issues; his mother, on the other hand, was, according to Csoóri, a peasant who existed purely within "the world of oral tradition," and it was she who not only ran the household but assigned all the tasks on their small farm, and who distributed the portions at meal times but, in keeping with village custom, never sat at the table to eat with the family. Csoóri often pays tribute to his parents for the hardships they endured throughout his boyhood and youth. His mother, he says, experienced "enough anguish, fear, and apprehensions for five lives," for "whatever [burdens] she couldn't share with others weighed down upon her." He also reports on his father's risking being killed by poachers or soldiers at Christmas of 1945 as he walked the 120 kilometers from Zámoly to Pápa through woods and snow storms to fetch him home from school rather than riding the top of a train.

The family farm of about seven acres and the poverty of the village made it difficult for him to obtain an education past the six years of elementary school. Before Csoóri only one other village inhabitant had managed to go on to high school. Csoóri was fortunate, in 1942, to be included among 600 peasant children recommended for a free secondary education by the National Village Talent

Search Institute, probably begun at the instigation of the populist writers. Surviving a series of screening examinations, he passed the final test at Pápa, and after some administrative delay, entered the famous Protestant College there. It became such a shaping force in his life that he feels its influence to this day, which has made him question the wisdom of the State's dissolution of this ancient school and those at Debrecen and Sárospatak, "like some ruined castle haunted by owls." Until he began his schooling at Pápa, he had, he says, only a peasant's view of the world, "unable to imagine the summer without the crackling of straw, without dusty acacias and sleepy hens." Much later, when standing on the ocean shore in Mexico, he "heard the startled horde of starlings crackling in the froth of the waves striking high." The war initiated him into "adulthood," or "let me say bitterly rather—modernity, universality. I arrived in the vicinity of physical catastrophes from alongside oxen. Within the period of three and one-half months, my village changed hands seventeen times. After the front passed by, we spent two weeks burying human beings and animals. After that came trenches and underground bunkers."

His first poem was published on May 1, 1949, in the *Pápa Popular News* (*Pápai Néplap*). Hired by this newspaper in recognition of his potential even before he graduated from high school, he toured the country for stories and often wrote highly enthusiastic articles about the changes taking place under socialism. After graduation he became the editor of a column for *Veszprém County Popular Newspaper* (*Veszprém Megyei Népújság*). In 1950, growing ever more discontent with village life, he went to Budapest, with which he had first become enamored on a visit with a student delegation in 1948—to study Russian history, Marxism, and, chiefly, the art of translating at the Lenin Institute. He was soon chosen a member of the board of directors of the recently established Young Writers' Association, where in debates he addressed himself to aesthetic problems in literary expression, already taking issue with the application of schematism to poetry, even as he today raises pressing questions about relations between literature and society as a member of the Writers' Federation. He left the institute after "three-fourths of a year of fakery," a time followed by "a fleeing from all kinds of dogmatism and strictly directed pedagogy." Becoming seriously ill in the winter of 1952 from a condition that has troubled him all his life, he returned to Zámoly and spent the spring with his family.

His life and activities, growing increasingly literary, drew him to Budapest, where he served on the staff of *Free Youth* (*Szabad Ifjúság*) in 1952 and of *Literary News* (*Irodalmi Újság*) from 1953 to 1954 and then was the head of the poetry section of *New Voice* (*Új Hang*) from 1955 to 1956. Csoóri considers these early years of the 1950s, especially his familiarity with the hardships of village life, critical to his development. Viewed as a promising young writer by the Literary Foundation, he was awarded an annual stipend to write, but he used the income primarily to support the family. When asked in 1976 what impact the Rákosi years had upon him, he replied that if he can be grateful to Rákosi it can be for one thing only: "he taught me to have faith in myself. In my own desires, in my own experiences." And that emphasis on the need to defend individuality from destruction was more recently stressed in a commitment "to preserve the significance of the individual in the great war against impersonality."

Csoóri won the Attila József Prize for his poetry in 1954, also the year of the publication of *The Bird Takes Wing* (*Felröppen a madár*), a collection of five years of his poems. This early work was inspired by folk poetry and the poems of Sándor Petőfi, still one of the greatest Hungarian poets, though he died at 26 in 1849. They reveal a love of country, a joy of building Hungary along socialist lines, and a feeling of fulfillment at being one with the community. The poems of the early 1950s are not personal in tone but are pitched, rather, at the level of his country's development; however, his peasant origin and personal awareness already had appeared in poems published in the fall of 1952 in *New Voice*. After he encountered some consequences of land reform during his convalescence in Zámoly, his poems, some of them published in *Literary News* and *Star* (*Csillag*) in 1953, took on a critical tone at the economic and psychological suffering experienced in the villages. "Indignation," he says, "gave birth to my first writings. Understandably, they contained more moral than aesthetic value. Occasionally even today, he candidly adds, "the continuing struggle between these two is observable in my poems and in the texts of my lyrically masked prose." He has used other prose genres, including learned essays on literature, folklore, and art history, and he has written in collaboration with others several successful filmscripts, one of which, *Ten Thousand Days* (*Tízezer nap*), won a major award at the Cannes Festival in 1964, and the most recent was concerned with the suicidal trek of a band of Hussars to aid the nation during the Revolution of 1848-49; since 1971 he has been a dramaturge at the Hungarian Film Studio. Some of his most moving prose stems from the establishment of the cooperatives (*Report from the Tower* [*Tudosítás a toronyból*], 1963), and his sociographic writings treat questions of his society. His collection of essays, *Journey While Half-Asleep* (*Utazás, félálomban*, 1974), is considered by critics to contain some of the most important prose writings of the period. His *Cuban Diary* (*Kubai napló*) was published in 1956 and is based on a visit to Cuba during which he also met Che Guevera. In the last ten years or so, he has developed a strong interest in the preservation of every kind of Hungarian folklore, in light of the threat posed to it by changes occurring in the villages, and has contributed to the development of halls for authentic folk dancing, the Folk Art Studio for Youth, and young folk musicians. Despite this wide-ranging activity and his effective, often inspired use of prose genres, it is still his five books of poetry that ensure him a place among the major figures who came onto the literary scene after the war. The eventual development of this corpus of poetry was clearly indicated by the volume of poems published in 1957, *Devil's Moth* (*Ördögpille*), in which he turned from the national community and its political and social issues to the personal world of his anguish and existence; and it is further reflected in the successive titles of other significant collections such as *Flight from Solitude* (*Menekülés a magányból*, 1962), *My Second Birth* (*Második születésem*, 1967), and *Dialogue, in the Dark* (*Párbeszéd, sötétben*, 1973). His latest volume of poetry, *A Visitor's Remembrances* (*A látogató emlékei*), was published in 1977.

Csoóri, who calls himself "an intellectual who never ceased being a peasant," looks upon contemporary civilization and technological advances with a jaundiced eye. To remedy their mistakes and to preserve and restore values that sustain human relationships in the alienating present, he advocates reliance on the ethical values inherent in humankind's past, the human traditions, especially those provided by folklore, and the historicalness of human events, an attitude widely criticized for leading to easy generalizations but earning a grudging respect for the wisdom that often results from it. To him the past is needed to stabilize and correct the invidious effects of knowledge and technology on the inner life of contemporary humans. Civilization, he avers, would gladly destroy human sensitivity to the historical past with its confident belief that technological solutions can be found for all ailments of society. Admittedly, some problems can be solved in this manner, but, he insists, in many instances, even as they are being solved by these means, many other things are being destroyed. In his view the basic flaw is that the laboratory ideas of scientific learning are thought to be capable of solving human problems that have evolved historically. That approach cannot work because what to the mind may seem a perfect solution is very possibly not so to the emotions. His fundamental idea is that "twentieth-century man should cling ever more tightly to a knowledge of history at least to the extent he once did to religion." By doing this, humankind would have an orientation toward existence in this world as it did from religion in the Middle Ages.

Csoóri sees literature as a very special means of linking man to a direct perception of the most ancient and supportive essentials of life. "Look about the world," he urges, "and everywhere you will find confusion and despair, outer or inner,—in the worst instances, degradation. You see that the night of human relationships will arrive sooner than their dawn." He is convinced that human beings have become "social creatures" far too much, that "if long ago the issue was for man to triumph over nature, now it is for him to rule over society." It is poetry, the drama, and the novel that direct human attention to human totality, "whether pointing out our distortions," or mixing "suffering and freedom together," and "the good writer is one who, like history, makes us wiser but doesn't explain. . . . Good works must be as suggestive as reality is suggestive." And to him, poetry—like all the arts—helps humans to create an order in their inner world, restoring them to a direct and primary relationship with the earth that civilization has stripped away from them.

His lyric poems, generally considered to be his most effective form of poetic expression, are distinguished by the candid self-revelation of the innermost, the most personal thoughts and emotions through memories suddenly reviving themselves in verse. In many ways they are extremely complex as he attempts to convey experience by interweaving recollections that touch basic human situations, sometimes unexpectedly, through imagistic rather than conceptual means. He views the lyric as his principal form, not simply "to provide abstract beliefs or even resolute ideas but a zest for life, so that, besides fear, which is as much a part of human culture, say, as the yearning for freedom, it will teach man to love this Earth." In his dedication to this objective, he attempts to understand the most fundamental situations encountered by human beings throughout time. The poems illuminating his personal spiritual torment and revealing his effort to unravel his deep feeling of isolation and loneliness offer a fulcrum for the comprehension of a fundamental and ancient existence, a taste, however slight sometimes, of that happy and natural condition from which technology and civilization have wrenched humankind so tragically since the end of the second world war.

Interrogating Ode to Women

    Am I to look back at you from beneath the earth?
        Out of the irreparable night,
            while stone and flower have at it
            out of some ancestral hatred?
            while out of the ocean's basket the pearl of the deep
            spins itself asunder
            and I no longer have hands to gather up the fragments
            for your sake?
        Out of clayish half-light? Through a curtain of roots?
        From beneath the ruins of the sunken temple of spring?
            Tearing apart the picket-fence of carrion nags and goat-bones
            beneath the yellowing dill and milkweed?

My spyglass would be a submerged tank's snorkel
and your hair, like a swarm of hunters out practicing,
would soar overhead with a defiant whoosh.

Wars and weekdays are the perpetual menace.
Your smiles alone are the cease-fire.
Your hands are the only wall I can lean on:
let the sun roast my face in this end-of-summer stupor!
What I've touched up till now, I've abandoned;
only you remain, the final colony,
which I invade each day and occupy.
I think of your mouths as a boat's wake:
beneath, the deathly waters, and above, the sky.

Farewell to Cuba

I turned to look
and you were already gone. Island = country.
There were bits of your palmleaves stuck there in the sunlight
like birds that swoop to the sea's surface
and your tarred boats
like tired old horses of the waters.

A hand untied the sea from the horizon
I waited for it to come running after me
but its face, turned only toward me, was in flames.

Leaving you, I felt dark and knotted up
like one of your ebony statues.
I knew that a summer as big as the world was kicking me out,
and that Europe awaited me with its 80-degree cold,
with its ten thousand tons of soot,
with its eye-liquefying fog,
with its streets that lead nowhere like tunnels in a cave.
Awaiting me were smiles practiced for 2,000 years,
advertisable principles, soothing words, like:
that's a no-no, like: can't be done;
my friends laid out on café catafalques
draped o'er with shrouds of cigarette smoke . . .

On account of your women and your sunshine
I became a traitor.
And your recklessness made me a child
who imagines he's concluded every struggle for freedom,
who goes around shirt unbuttoned,
no longer preparing for battle, only for love.

Your oranges, cannonballs of summer,
come crashing down right here,
close to me.

When I Touch You

Why should I write poems,
when I can be with you?
Just in order to pretty up time
and to people the universe with words?

Right now I'd most like to take the sun in hand
and roll it to the horizon
bowling down forests one after the other,
just for you,
strike after strike.

Why should I write poems,
when I can be with you?
Your breasts are prettier
than the most unexpected similes,
your mouth,
than the nakedest rhyme.

It's summer: your hand burns like a magnifying glass,
and the lakeshore sand grows hot beneath your body.

Birds come this way, and trains.
Each time the smoke clothes you, my eye, groping,
strips you bare.
I don't even know why I constantly want to see you.
If you were a stretch of reeds, I'd look at that,
if you were earth, I'd look at earth.

Why should I write poems,
when I can be with you?
Words empty out like cottages in autumn,
they die away like people—

but when I touch you,
the touch remains undying: it becomes neither future
      nor memory.
Why should I write poems if all of me can be yours:
    a part of your legs
      of your hands
        your breath.

Just Nowhere

Neither here nor there
neither inside nor outside
barely leaning on the gallery of clouds
from Monday to Tuesday
in a foreign night:

I'd collapse just anywhere if there were room,
into some home for stretching out,
but even the meaningless regions are already floating away,
the stone, the silt want to hit
the road, the dust wants to see the world
and the cities
launch their rocket hearts.

That which lives, scurries. Slyly, one-sidedly,
doesn't want to see what it sees,
this sun, this earth don't want a witness
to their spreading night, but just to be
always in transit,
      just nowhere;
out of the hollows of their bodies
pleasure, stirring, splatters like rainwater,
out of their mouths the oceandeep gall,
they leave, go the long way around,
proud of their hangover;
heavy upon them weighs my regal eye, inward-turned,
my skull fenced-in with ramparts.

But That Water Is Still Flowing Here

When the time comes I will
die and you will also die
Mud will seep in between our teeth
and water into our gums.

But that water is still flowing here,
still giving off steam ahead of us.

Birds alight on it, like aeroplanes
on runways of concrete.
Horses rush into it up to their chests,
jolting along like immortal stagecoaches,
with messages to the farthest sea.
It washes the extremities of cities
as Mary Magdalene washed Christ's.

But are we not that water—
love and perfidy and anger,
sheets of gold devouring lightning,

the fishes' playground, or the
smile which daubs the lips of children,
or the dewy branch of oceans?

But are we not that water—
a summer's letter-box,
the mirror of what flies above
and of celestial wars?

The world can see itself in us
because it will not pass.

Those who live with their backs to death
can behold their faces on earth.

On the Third Day Snow Began to Fall

The first day served
    to make me forget everything;
the second to make me remember it all.
And on the third day snow began to fall
    and the suspicion was born
    that it would not ever stop falling,
    from your brow to your lips,
    from your lips to your loins,
    all the way along your body,
    all the way along my life.
The ceiling will snow, the telephone receiver too
    when I pick it up,
the fuzzy sky of childhood when I look back.
Among the stranded trees and stranded haystacks too,
    only the snow's ghost wanders,
    on the earth plunged into darkness it sits,
    crowning those who are fleeing the war.
And now I knew I would not be alone,

    this snow will come with me wherever I go,
sitting beside me in the train,
crossing with me over the sea,
in the steaming car-tires and airless towns
        of the night
        it calls me in my mother-tongue
        and vanquishes countries for me,
        because vanquishing countries
        is what you wanted—
and when I shall not have even a homeland,
        because I shall not have the strength to write of it,
I shall shut myself up in this falling snow,
as one who puts on a white shirt,
a white shirt on the last day.

And to Step toward the Door

    For years, you and no one else. And afterward, everything that you are not: drought in the throat, in the bones, the nationwide defeat of idling blood. Your leather skirt: a bat sloughing off its skin.

    I can see your face still. I can still follow it. It circles the Earth in a droplet of water. Each new day is the Monday of my outer space period, but I no longer have anything to regret. The weight of my pain and my body is gone.

    And now even my faithfulness may be auctioned off, like the martyrs' shirts. I am allowed even to laugh in front of the mirrors, with a razor in my hand. And to step toward the door, like one approaching himself.

    The threshold rises up before me like the dew, the garden beyond the threshold, the country beyond the garden. And then the maddened dust, like our secret child.

The Other

I can touch her,
I can kill her,
I can burst in on her,
here and now I can drink of her breath,
knotted to her hair I can fly around the globe,
or round myself, at the throbbing of her flesh,
but my words do not reach her,
but my words will never become her blood,
from behind the double hedge of hatchets
her face
desperately calls,
then denies,
avoids,
floats by on a cloud,
her memory is not my flesh,
her shadow not my clothes,
through my eyes
she tumbles down
back into herself,
from her body
back into her body.

Mumbling

Rains, poems. Snows.
In the helpless snow a bird takes his bath.
Your hand. My hand. The signs of your body.
Death's key. The lock whose bolt won't throw.

Silence. Rage. The loneliness of the world.
People's unchanging chances against themselves.
Weapons roused. Thorns.
The ashes of thorns in you and in me.

Sándor Csoóri

Meditative Inventory

well now, were there forests?
and birds iron-shod?
rivers out sunning, like women's legs parting on the sand?
rooms with a view of the apocalypse?
well, and were there brushfires
following me on my walks all the way home?
flames as far as the garden gate?

the dog happily swam
around the yard

well, and were there yards,
dogs,
whimperings in paradise?
whistlings filtering through over the flooded trenches?
comings and goings in summer?
comings and goings in time?
was it I who flew up there
in those flagellant jets? I, the king
of my flesh and bone?
and the enamel of the Caucasus
did it chip off in my eye?

well, and were there hands mutually translucent?
faces burning into one?—just taking a break
over music cheated back from death?
shopping bags filled with shared bread?
weeping with shared tears?
countries with shared footprints?

Eyes

Rips, tears,
narrow windows on my life,
keyholes, door-wounds, slits,
always someone watching, looking in through them,
seeing my wrist, my bed,
and the root of my dreams,
    where even I can't see,
where the very first cherrybud—who knows?—
bleeds under my tooth, and murderous files
lie in my throat athwart
and knock-knock: among the rising walls
my friend's girl steps in
over my scarlet doorstep
    eyes in front of her eyes in back of her
eyes, eyes: diver-eyes, torpedo eyes
ploughing the depths that bind my cells together
eyes, eyes: disc-eyes cleaving
to my back: from whom
    do I take my leave this evening?
and: to whom do I offer my porphyry chalice in the garden?
and: the one who cast curly pig's bristles over the flowers,
    is he my accomplice?

Eyes, speckled idle eyes sliding down
    under the cover of the lamps' light,
Eyes, spackled idle eyes slipping down
    on the windscreen streetcorner

as if I had to sleep in show-windows
    and smooch in butcher shops.

It's Not I Who Sit There Now

I've become gentle, slow and acquiescent,
a stuffed sea-serpent
in an underwater museum,
just staring at the day's bubbles rising,
just staring at what I ought.

Monday comes to me barefoot,
Tuesday comes too, with leafy branch,
Wednesday butterflies arrive: tourists
    at the resettling of Eden
Thursday's, Friday's orators come to speak
of the bloodied sacks that are rushing toward our midst,
women come to love
and informers, their chins flecked with tobacco, to flatter;
we drink up my wine, we look at each other,
and turn inside-out smiling back and forth
but their moonlit teeth remind me of the Arctic Ocean
and the tedious field of snow where I walk
in my dreams until morning
and it's not I who sit there now among them
in a picture-frame big as a room,
I don't turn blue with hairroots clotting—
my eyes and my ears are withdrawing from my body,
leaving behind them walls as obtuse as aspic.

Self-Portrait in a Misty Mirror

I'm getting fat, like someone
regularly fed on
suckling pig by spoon-brandishing
kitchen maids.

I'm getting fat. A tousled and
pink head resting on
my shoulders.

My blood no longer moves timber or rocks
and when the snow melts in the spring
I only know what my eyes tell me.

I hear the corrugated sonnets of
Hungary's longest nights.

I live. I live because I've slipped
into the rut of living on.

Still, sometimes I alertly wait
for the piercing whistle,
for the Sun to cast its rays
on the nape of my neck;
sometimes I wait for someone to
entice the sea away, beyond my ribs.

Then I burst out singing with the
somber lather of seven nights.

Manhood

              Just music,
as if there weren't even
any grass anymore,
any trees, any bugs,
any lying back,
                  just flitting around,
whisking by, rustle of branches,
                        memories of bodiless sounds

    and the sky torn off like a shirtsleeve
        fluttering above the Tisza
            just the lost, the wearisome fields'
       mud smell
    from back home, out of a rainy August,
        kisses that anticipate war
        exchanged in the Gulf of Finland
    and slowmotion shots of departure
        of my son as he leaves me
        his hair flying,
  dissolving in the incomprehensible afternoon
        and of how a woman dressed in a sack
        vanishes into a wall of brick.

In Floodlit Night

She knelt down in the tub and shoved
her long neck under the showerhead's heaven
and the bathroom filled with wild tigerlove
steam and suddenly I thought, it would be better
if I ran out into the hills out into May's
flowers breaking up and drifting out between
drafty cellars where distended vinestalks stretch tumbling
and the earth's nostrils flare like a young stallion's
it would be better to go for a walk or to shout
with much foaming to swap my left
arm for a branch my heart for a walnut-leaf better better than
yawning through some opera written for female voice
in which whetstones and headhunters sing
but I weakened
and stayed
and in silence's echoing globe
I listened to her sighs grow louder
saying nothing, like someone who knows in advance the final judgment
and I stretched out on her horizontal pelvis

    like a spastic side-car racer—
    I raced forward ears buzzing in floodlit night
    floodlit insects burst apart on my brow

Approaching Words

    I have no sharp, clear, reliable memories. Those I have seem only coincidentally to be mine.
    I was four when I first ran away from home. I loved the sudden, explosive crack of the swineherd's whip, his gravel voice, his big hairy dog. More than anything else, I wanted to be a swineherd. I was afraid of the boars, though, because I'd been told they eat children. But when I was four, even that fear was okay.
    After so much time, how can I justify and assess that first escape?
    I escape nowhere now.
    The uncertain roads, too, I set out on sluggishly.
    Without a sense of guilt, never.
    I am not yet forty, yet already I feel tired, burnt-out, broken.

* * *

    Here by my window stands a shaggy chestnut tree. Green, enormous, it seems to separate me from my past. Everything that happened to me happened behind it. Small, shuffling noises filter down through the leaves. I try to piece together the sounds: bicycle bells, the creaking of heavy manorial carts, tanks, church bells—no use. Then, like a sudden splash, comes the noise of the parish feast, accompanied by the sound of paper horns. And out of the deeply lowering night, the terror of Sunday brawls—My God, they're killing Miska Tanarki!—but the greedy chestnut tree flings itself on the cries, the shouts, and soaks them up. And furtively, changes everything to a whisper.
    Some kind of order must have dissolved, some kind of sense must have been lost, that all I see of my past are brief illuminations. There is nowhere a connection that might jolt me; nowhere an organizing principle to comfort me. The birds and birdsong are separate in me. The forests are separate, the woodcutters, the muffled blows of the ax. I see a snow-covered road crowded with war refugees. To one side stands a wounded horse left to die, his back to the crowd. His

flank is wide open, like the window of a butcher shop. I can still see, in separate images, his head, his wobbly legs, the bloody gap between his ribs—and myself, watching, an adolescent boy bundled in a peasant woman's coat. And the planes as they dive down upon us. There they are, the fragmented facts of the war. But where are the reasons and motives that bind them together? Where are the lasting anger, the hatred, the resistance?

And I have traveled all over the world. By plane, by ship, on impossibly long trains. I have seen the volcanic wounds, older than memory, of the Caucasus. I have seen the Bahama Islands with the backward glance of Columbus. Cuba, and Che Guevara only a stone's throw away. I have walked in the largest cemetery in the world—the sovereign nation of the six hundred thousand Leningrad dead. German tourists in short pants whirred their motion picture cameras. Bridges, churches, movie theaters, execution walls, brothels, restaurants—all these flashing images are mine.

And yet, it is as though these images had been seen by someone else. In Rome I spent half a day on the square where Giordano Bruno was burned. That beautiful, attractive man, provocative even with his body, was stripped naked by his executioners as they led him to the stake. My God! What would happen if I were to follow him?

I know now that even my daydreams were dreamed by someone else.

I am sitting in a chair, and I can feel it falling to pieces under me. First the back—softly, quietly; then the legs. I look out the window and watch as the Saint Swithin's Day rain dissolves into strands.

A long time ago, I had a word I liked to toss around. Was the sun shining? The heat deadening? "Irrelevant," I answered. Did the newspapers work hard to conceal the obvious facts, the plain truth? I had a ready response: "Irrelevant." Irrelevant were the books I read, the love affairs in which I became entangled, my complaints and lamentations, the wills people wrote. Irrelevant also the laughter, which hoped for an echo.

Never in all my dreams did I imagine that this carefree grin of mine would some day cloud over.

Mornings, I still can't believe that there's no sense getting up. I protest with my body against the futility of it. I wash to the waist in cold water, run down for milk and the paper, and make the coffee myself.

By afternoon, however, all my efforts become irrelevant. The scribbled sheets of paper head for the waste. This is the only certainty in my day—this pathetic procession. Never mind an actual human figure—I cannot bring even a common snowman to life. He melts before I can press the paper cap on his head.

But, next day, I begin all over again. Perhaps the women, the old loves! If I can bring *them* back to life! Just enough to make their movements visible: their hands, waists, and hips; the way they brush their hair, make the bed, stir the tea. I call to Magda over a distance of twenty years: "Look me up." Alarmed, she steps back, withdrawing into the doorway. Damp posters rustle under her feet. I call to Irene. She runs, happily. We meet on the Margaret Bridge. "Come on up," she says, "you haven't been to my place in fifteen years." I go. She sits me down on her bed. That same plank-hard bed, where one can brood so easily on journeys and death. On the shelves above the bed, medicine bottles. I look at the chalk-white tablets; I look at Irene's dark eyes. They say that whores have this same tirelessly burning gaze. I wait for her to speak—a word, a sentence, anything to which I can reply.

For a long time she says nothing. As if we were cellmates. Then she stands, takes a revolver from the drawer and throws it beside me on the bed. She nods for me to take it. I don't move. She begins to smile. Then, without warning, she rushes out of the room, leaving me to myself. Later, from the street outside, I hear inconsolable weeping.

I don't understand. I don't understand any of it. Everything happened differently, not at all as I've written it here. How is it that I remember those things that never happened, better than those that did?

* * *

Emptiness, everywhere emptiness. The familiar homelessness in words, in the outside world, in my thoughts. Homelessness in writing, in love, in the house I call my own. A small boy lives in this homelessness, and a woman. Each day I greet them, and each day I say goodbye. We laugh, we plan, we eat green onions together, but the transitoriness is there in the clashing of knives, in the rattling of dishes, in our laughter. Though we try, we cannot conceal it: these days we would betray one another without batting an eyelash. Were there three windows in a room, we would each look out in a diffferent direction. One to the north, one to the south, one to the west. Could we speak three languages, we would each choose a different tongue. Like spirits, the old words, the old phrases, still come back. We survive, they say, to show the way home. These words must be forgotten. An impossible desire gave them birth.

To await complete emptiness. Perhaps that's the secret. To prepare one's failure like an assault—that's what must be done first. And one must settle with pain, because pain is compromise. It chains a man to what he cannot finish, alter, or put straight.

I need new memories—which is to say, new truths. A new past, to enable me to step out of my fatigue.

Each day the temptation grows. To spin the world on its axis, to bring what was behind before. Where I once saw only wounds, let me now see the skeleton.

Is that a bee in the room? I jump up and close the window behind it. Wickedly, I have it trapped. Let it bump the wall, the window, the ceiling; let it rage and buzz. Yes, perhaps this will help. Perhaps with this, the bee, I can begin. Perhaps I can summon a swarm. They flew above my head when I was a child, disturbing the silence in the suffocating stable and the wretched loft. Gloomy Isaiahs, they mumbled judgments over my tottering cradle.

Did the summers impress me when I was a child?

The dimensions of the past are of no interest to me. Nor is the memory of sunlight stretched taut over the yards and gardens. All I hear are the voices of judgment saying, "Poverty stinks, kid." The well is next to the dung heap, the kitchen door to the pig sty, God to despair. You clung to that poverty. For many years, it blinded you. Loyalty prevented you . . .

From what?

As though someone had whispered: Travel.

I do.

Down to the Tisza river.

For days, there is no one around me.

The temptation strikes again. To begin here. To abandon childhood, the bees, poverty. The facts are not true, anyway. The kindness and anger that can be made to flow from them are.

But where *are* the kindness, the anger? The world around me is empty, unmarked. There is only a seagull screaming the whole day long. A merganser. I've heard that when a man approaches their nest, they attack, screeching, and bombard him with excrement. I ought to learn wildness from them. Harshness. Aggression. Because behind all my defeats lie the trampled masks of innocence.

Forget the parables. They belong in books. Smoothly worn stairs that lead—not up, but up-and-down, up-and-down.

Rather, again, the sounds. The roaring of water, the beating of waves, the wind's pistol shots in the leaves. The cracking and exploding of branches. To follow this stubbornly, with persistence. To believe that in sounds there is power. Power and enlightenment, as in music.

I fast for three days, in order to hear the sounds more sharply.

On the fourth, great chunks of the river bank tumble into the water.

Meanwhile, the tracks seem to flare up. Tracks of insects, crabs, and earthworms. The tracks in the sand of naked human feet. Let's follow, see where they might have gone. To the ferry? The iron bridge? In under the willow bushes? No. You can't follow.

One must give up the tale that can be pursued. One must give up the stories that can be told. Stories and tales are contrived by affection and wisdom, because affection and wisdom believe in them. They believe that the joy and sorrow of a good story may bring someone comfort. What pious credulity! What fraudulence! In a world where the news of a single morning can overshadow Dante and all his hell, the stories, too, are obscure. One knows neither where they begin, nor where they end. And who, finally, dares to call his story his own? To call it finished, complete? Who dares to oppose the almost universal fate, more oppressive than the ancient tyrannical gods, that hangs over us now? I stir up time and pluck myself out. Stories tumble behind me like rocks down a cliff. January 1944. A Soviet soldier has leveled his pistol at me, because he is saying something I don't understand. I stand there before him, comprehending nothing. Least of all that something irrevocable may happen. He bellows again, then collapses exhausted into a chair and falls asleep sitting up.

Whose story is it that I'm alive? His? Mine? Or does the story belong to us both? Whose story would it be if I were *not* alive? Whose story is the war?

I cannot step twice into the same river; nor can I step twice into the same story. It is not the stories, then, that must be summoned, but the parts. I see faces, the dead, a darkened sea. Houses, women lying in the sand, and intimidated men, the smile forced on their mouths like a muzzle. Their thoughts matter, but what they say is not what they think. They light cigarettes, clink glasses, while every line on the open map of their faces betrays their forty years. How many such snapshots make up our lives! How many nervously stubbed-out cigarettes, outbursts of self-annihilating laughter, moments of passionate feeling, brief attachments to women, mountains, cities! Yet, of the war's millions of shrapnel-like fragments, it may happen that only one represents the entire war to us. That of all the ten thousand small gestures of love, only one backward glance signifies love. To stop the spinning! To stop events and draw out only the chosen moments! These moments are the supporting pillars of time. Describe how you felt after the war, when, mangy as Job, you had to wear black German military gloves. And the girl, your first love, whom you never once touched. You were ashamed you had hands, ashamed of your body, with a shame that was born in exactly that moment when your body became aware of itself. Explain how you felt when you had to slap your father, who understood nothing of his lifelong misery except that your mother had been the cause of it all. Not governments, not hailstorms, not cowardice, the POW camp or the false accusations— only a single human being. And the funeral you witnessed. The martyrs had been disinterred; the unrecognizable remains had been laid out in ornate coffins for public viewing. Why did you stand there silently, stupidly, behind the hired mourners? You were afraid, weren't you? Afraid they would shut you up. Afraid they would tear the clothes off your back, the only dark suit you owned that fit. Yet, had you spoken then, new stories might have begun. If you speak now, new stories may begin even yet. There is around you a concave world crowded with trees, nations and families in aspic; and within you a second world, convex, with voids and unfilled moments, warmed by the constant tension of expectation.

Don't stop! Approach yourself!

I approach.

It can't be. The bushes on the far shore have taken fire. The trees are green, Van Gogh-like flames.

Not those. Common poplars. The fishermen lean their bicycles against them.

Sándor Csoóri

The bicycles are also on fire. Their frames melt; the wind carries across the river the smell of burnt mudguards and leather saddles. Close your eyes, I say to myself. You'll see what I'm talking about.

I close my eyes and see—myself. The Tisza flows beside me, showing off its muscles like a champion fighter. It's cold; I'm beginning to shiver. I must give up the images too. And fantasy. I don't want them to raise the barrier, to force me to escape. Because the world always justifies an image, but it cannot justify me, who sees it. There do exist rose-soldiers, dew-drop foals, invisible trumpets that mosquitoes blow into our ears. There are, indeed, Green Angels that devastate nations, telephone monsters and travelling graveyards; but, for my part, it is the everyday monsters, the everyday graveyards, that will not let me live. What will not leave me is what I was. The man I see with closed eyes, in the most cutting light. What were those words of encouragement? Approach yourself!

I approach.

I smother the images. I smother fantasy. Also hope, so that it will not disturb me. In vain. The words are still there before me! Like uncrossable minefields. In every word a world with mountains, chasms, forests with their roots turned up. I speak the word love—and go astray. I say the words sorrow, going home, arrival. This may be the most dangerous road of all. I say: snow, ice, mud, bomb crater, politics. I fly; I shiver; I plunge. Screaming gull over the Tisza. Rapid change. The gull glides over the mouth of the Kőrös. I say the names in succession: Sebes Kőrös, Fekete Kőrös. What I hear is not the roar of water, but the gnashing of teeth. Ady[1] weeps at the window of the castle at Csucsa. Neurotic, fevered, a burning genius, Ady was the last man able to cry with complete rage. I say . . . the words are endless. Window, furtive, craven, grief, the local courts, the right to speak, freedom of speech, the glass mountain, iron will, iron mask, iron curtain—I am there in every word. History is there, as are my lies, my weakness, the always half-spoken truth. Here, then, is what has been kept silent. Perhaps this is what I am; perhaps this is what I must reach. Words, you are my last chance, my last obstacle. With you must I begin again. Tell me your meanings—water, apple, bread. And you—bomb, mechanized affection, dreams of the space age, the boundaries between nations. What do *you* mean—armed illustrious filth, the ennobling scramble of the world? What do you mean, words—naked, provocative words, stripped of appearances and my abuses—to me, to others, to everyone?

---

[1] Endre Ady (1877-1919), one of Hungary's greatest lyric poets, departed dramatically from the poetic conventions and political ideology of his country. His poems grow out of his emotional and intellectual dilemmas and symbolize the tragic conditions of his times.

István Csurka

Csurka was born on March 27, 1934 in Budapest, where his family had first moved in 1929 from Nagyvárad, Transylvania. His parents, he states, centered all their energies on ensuring the welfare of the children. His father, whose family roots lay in the peasant culture around Békés, also in Transylvania, greatly influenced Csurka's decision to follow a writing career. His father tried various kinds of employment in Budapest and finally secured a post at a credit bank. To supplement his income, he contributed articles and fiction to periodicals in the early 1930s, and he eventually established a large readership with his stories and novels, the latter published serially. Csurka vividly recollects from his earliest years the clatter of his father's typing late in the night. The family remained in Budapest until some two-fifths of Transylvania, including the places of the Csurka family's origins, again became a part of Hungary in August 1940 through the terms of the Vienna Award. As he had long wanted to do, his father took the family back to Nagyvárad and established a rum and liquor distillery. In Békés Csurka continued the schooling he had begun in Budapest.

    In 1944 the course of the war forced the family, after a stay of three years, to enter upon a period of wandering. First they returned to Budapest, then went back to Nagyvárad, from which Csurka and his brother were sent for safety from bombings to Bedő, a small village in Bihar County. Finally the entire family again sought refuge in Békés, only, in the end, to accompany the father to a military assignment in Munich. Encountering difficulties along the way at Kőszeg, which is situated near the Austrian border, Csurka's father bought a horse called Vilma and a wagon, and the family crossed the Alps and settled down in Lichting, a little village near Munich. Csurka spent the summer of 1945 there riding around in the meadows and experiencing the terrors of bombing raids and strafing runs, once so closely that he could make out the "grinning face" of the pilot. His father was captured by the American army; and after his release, finding it impossible to settle in Budapest or Nagyvárad, he took his family to Békés, this time in a coach drawn by the same horse, where they lived for some time in a small room. Csurka completed his high school studies in this village; despite the trying circumstances in which the family lived, he considers these years in Békés with his family and relatives among the happiest he has known, including the summers he spent working as a thresher or construction laborer. He believes that the wide range of experiences during childhood and youth has contributed significantly to his outlook and to the subjects and themes of his writings.

In 1952, he began his studies at the College of Theater Arts in Budapest with his father's encouragement and assistance, and with a reputation of sorts as a discus thrower. He obtained his degree in dramaturgy in 1957, the year he also married and became a father. He has made Budapest his home ever since, and is, at present, living with his own family in a small sublet flat near the cemetery where a brother and his father lie next to each other—his father was killed in 1964 in an automobile accident in Budapest without attending the premiere of Csurka's first play, an event that would have given him "the happiest day of his hard life." Never having actually held down a job to make a living for his own family, Csurka describes his way of life as somewhat resembling that of the bohemians at the beginning of the present century, especially as a result of his involvement with the theater, whether the stage or the cinema. He also enormously enjoys the companionship of persons who, like himself, are addicted to playing the horses and gambling at cards, and both activities often furnish symbolic situations for his writing. Not possessing, as he says, a plot of ground or a house of his own, he frequently escapes the distractions in Budapest and sequesters himself for two or three weeks in a resort provided for authors by the state, particularly when he senses that characters and themes of long-standing have "ripened" inside him. He does not discard any of his writings, not even when he is certain they are bad, believing that "like a screw, they might one day be good for something."

Csurka's literary career began in 1954, when he was twenty and still a student, with the publication of "The Wedding and the Slap in the Face" ("Nász és pofon"), a short story, which was promptly attacked for its cynicism and for its slander of the youth of Hungary but which became the title story of the retrospective collection he published fifteen years later. Ever since then, though troubled by shifts in political climate and by personal anguish and doubt, he has regularly engaged in various writing activities. He has written reports and articles for newspapers, plays for radio, television, screen and stage, two novels, some satirical pieces, and many short stories. He considers himself to be a dramatist foremost—

and his plays show some signs of eventually giving a much-needed lift to the contemporary stage in Hungary—but it is his short stories that are widely accepted as his most forceful genre. Like Hemingway's, his narrative style is spare and economical; he draws characters with quick strokes, and composes intricate dialogue that flows naturally into penetrating revelations of the innermost states of the characters. This is particularly true of his short stories, some of which consist, like "The Two Rheumatics" ("A két reumás"), almost entirely of dialogue.

Generally speaking, the world of Csurka's writings, regardless of genre, has evolved in three closely related phases, all of them formed by his responses at various periods of his life to contemporary Hungary and the complex dialectic of individualism and collectivism that is experienced there. The first phase, represented by a collection of twenty-three short stories published in 1956 under the title *Leaping Over Fire* (*Tűzugratás*), portrays largely the skepticism of young people toward the life about them during the early 1950s as they grapple with their formal education and with the beginnings of their life careers. In these stories Csurka's satirical mode and political bent are already present as he treats the confusions and pressures his characters encounter in accommodating themselves to reality. Some of the best in the collection, like "Main Wall (Főfal)," are based on his years as a student at the College of Theater Arts. The second stage, developed in *Extension 105* (*Százötös mellék*), a collection of thirteen stories written between 1958 and 1964 and published in 1964, only after two years of hesitation on his part, explores the painful circumstances and acute desperation of disenchanted and disillusioned human beings, anti-heroes who seek to break out of their critical situations and meaningless lives through rebellion and such absurd acts as deliberately breaking a leg to obtain solicitude, or who, perhaps even more futilely, simply resign themselves to reality and move about emptily in a meaningless world. This period deepens his depictions of the anguish of being trapped between accommodation and reality. This focus on moments of personal human crisis in such terms brought upon him the charge of existentialism from many critics, which plagued his literary fortunes for many years. The third and most recent phase turns to the fringe world of horse races and touts and the card table and gamblers to intensify unrelentingly his view of the twentieth-century scene as being occupied by human beings who are indolent and indifferent, greedy and full of self-love, and intellectually and emotionally impoverished—a time awash with middle-class values—all to the ultimate end of demonstrating that individual human beings, and therefore humankind, cannot survive without worthwhile beliefs or purposes. In seeming defense of his absorption in such subject matter, he insists that he delineates the absurdities of life not because he is drawn to the peculiar and the exceptional around him, but because his desire to portray everyday life realistically leaves him no alternative.

Csurka's confrontations with this absurd reality make clear that politics and political engagement are at the core of his creativity, without his fearing, he insists, that this commitment will make him "obsolete in the future and unable to create works of lasting validity." He can, he says, imagine that there may exist in the present age a great writer who has turned his or her back on politics, but he cannot do so easily, for politics "is born inside a human being, there is no life without it," and "everything else is humbug." Undoubtedly such singleness of commitment has inherent dangers, especially the deadening of the artistic imagination that narrowness and rigidity invariably impose, especially when supportive of an established political system. Fortunately, Csurka's explorations of contemporary life transcend his attacks on reactionaries who simply want to restore the past or on establishmentarians who think that the ideal society has been achieved. As much as he sets his stories within the social and historical circumstances of his people, his vision still penetrates to factors going beyond particular domestic situations. According to him, the bane of humanity in the second half of the twentieth century is the inability to see life clearly. With so many events occurring at the same time throughout the world and with such vast amounts of information coming from so many different directions and contradicting one another, the human perception of reality has become terribly confused. Even the enormous technological advances do not produce what can confidently be called progress. Instead, they juxtapose "an unprecedented affluence and an unprecedented wretchedness." Having lost their compass, humans, he speculates, cannot create an order in which they can anchor their being.

This interpretation of reality carries tremendous implications for Csurka's analysis of writers' attempts to portray contemporary life wholly, as well as for individuals experiencing a similar sense of fragmentation and dislocation. "It is increasingly harder," he confesses, "to speak, to epitomize . . . increasingly difficult to find the seed." Although his lack of wholeness stems from the complexities that the events of 1956 imposed on him, he believes that this disintegration of focus, this capacity to perceive and record only "tokens" is the fundamental problem of contemporary civilization. He could very well be writing about himself when a character in one of the vignettes in "Arias and Duets by Drunkards" ("Részeg áriák és duettek"), a work written in 1956, expresses his profound frustration and acute desperation at finding himself incapable of carrying out his function as an author. This character, conversing with his sympathetic wife, is distressed by his failures. He evaluates reality, but not what he should; he records the truth, but not the whole truth because, he asserts, he has never yet perceived the Great Totality; he speaks plainly but "never the true great word." All he does is to "steal the thoughts of others one by one," and he is "a stupid, ignorant fellow." Like all other writers, he is a tightrope walker, except that he is probably balancing himself "on a different rope," from which he may plunge at any instant, if "the dull darkness in my brain" should jerk him down and flatten him out, like a pancake.

In each phase of his more than twenty years of literary activity, Csurka presents effectual variations of this character's fearful anguish at his emptiness, at his having been cut adrift in the sea of time:

> I am lost. I no longer have a belief, an old conscience. The Ideal is no longer before me. I, too, am a balloon, only not a red one like the others, and that is why I am so visible in the great redness. . . . Without the Ideal everything is a balloon. These days everyone is becoming a balloon. Man should have an Ideal, so should the world, and especially me [as an author]. But where is it? where shall I get it? Was the Ideal cast out of reality a long time ago? I don't know. . . . You see, I don't know if the ancients cast the Ideal out of reality or if they found it and then clung to it tenaciously, nobly, and believed in it. When I look at life, I find it hard to believe that the Ideal was once present in it in any kind of fundamental state.

Readers who know similar moments of desperation will have no difficulty sharing Csurka's feeling of futility in the face of such a void:

> [Finding the Ideal] requires some kind of jolt. At the very least an impulse, some scraps of conversation, a vision, a dream. But there is none. There is nothing. I see only the object and chaos. No polarization, no crystallizing, no belief.

The Two Rheumatics

"Who slapped you?"
"Somebody."
"Is that all you know?"
"Had large palms."
"That's it?"
Szegyedszky wanted to reply, "That's it," but a large wave covered his mouth. Ignoring warnings against it, a young man leaped into the pool head first and the waves inundated Szegyedszky. When he bobbed up again, he said:

"Mean." But that remark no longer pertained to the person who had slapped him but to the one who had just dived into the water.

The unlawful movement of the water didn't bother Táplán. He was a tall man with a long neck, and the waves that covered the bald Szegyedszky sitting beside him were only licking his Adam's apple.

After a short interval, they resumed their conversation.
"What did you do?"
"I identified myself," said Szegyedszky.
"You get slapped and you identify yourself?"
"Without question. The situation was such."
"What was it?"
"He questioned my identity as a Christian Hungarian."
"Did he call you a pagan Arab?"
"No. Do you know what he said? To me, to a Szegyedszky?"

"A nazi?"
"I?"
"No. The one who slapped you."
"I don't know."
"He had to be if that's what he called you."
"He wasn't the one who said it."
"Well, who did?"
"His wife."
"His wife? How do you know she was his wife?"
"I just think so. They were holding hands."
"On the streetcar?"
"There."
"Do you remember it correctly?"
"Everything, exactly."
"And you didn't hit him back?"
"Who?"
"You."
"It's not my way. But that's not what was important. I had to clear myself of the accusation."
"After all that, what did you do?"
"I got off."
"From shame?"
"No. I had to get off. My wife had sent me to the store."
"You?"
"I was on vacation."
"What did you buy?"
"Bacon. I got a lot of bacon for a pengő."
"How much?"
"One kilo of bacon came to a pengő."
"And that is a lot?"
"For a pengő? Nothing will ever be as cheap again as it was then."
"When?"
"Then. During the last years of peace."
"What about the slap in the face?"

Szegyedszky stretched out on the little bench, lifted his arms out of the water and spread them behind him on the cold tiles.

"My God, one slap. That's not such a big deal. I have been slapped in this political order too, but I can't buy one kilo of bacon for a pengő."

The matter began to interest Táplán. So far he had been of the opinion that Szegyedszky, whom he met only here in the steam and who was an SZTK[1] rheumatic like himself, was stupid. But now it appeared as if some kind of coherency was glimmering in Szegyedszky's thinking. He sank into the water up to his chin so his shoulders could get some of the warmth, and continued questioning Szegyedszky.

"Have you been slapped on the streetcar in this political order too?"

"No, in front of the Millenary."[2]

"What were you doing in front of the Millenary?"

"I wanted to go to a bicycle race."

"And you didn't go?"

"No."

"Because of the slap in the face?"

"Partly."

"Who slapped you in front of the Millenary?"

"A party."

"And you don't know anything about him either?"

"No. Nothing."

"He called you a Jew too?"

"No. Under the present order? The opposite."

"What do you mean, the opposite?"

"He called me a dirty Nazi."

"Then you identified yourself?"

"Yes."

"How were you able to prove that you weren't a Nazi, there in front of the Millenary."

"Just by chance."

"What?"

"I always carry the papers with me."

"Even here?"

"In the locker, of course."

"Well then, you can be insulted only here in the thermal waters, when you are naked."

"Yes. Here one is defenseless."

"What kind of papers did you identify yourself with then? When was it?"

"1949. With the papers from the Seventh District National Committee. In 1945 they identified me immediately, without a single hitch."

"And you showed this in front of the Millenary?"

"Yes."

"The person read it?"

"Yes, and others did too."

"A crowd gathered."

"Of course."

"And you stood in the middle handing the papers to everyone to prove you have never been a Nazi?"

"I didn't let go of them."

"Why not?"
"You just don't let go of such papers."
"A great truth. And you didn't slap the person back?"
"No."
"Why not?"
"The race began."
"But you didn't go in."
"I didn't, but the others did."
"What did you do with your ticket?"
"I sold it."
"For how much?"
"Twelve forints."
"How much did you pay for it?"
"Ten."
"So you made two forints on it."
"If you want to look at it that way."
"What do you mean, if you want to look at it that way. Did you or didn't you?"
"I didn't want to make a profit."
"Tell me, which was the bigger slap, the one in 1938 or the one in 1949?"
"The latter. One can't hit as hard on a streetcar, especially a crowded one, as on solid ground."
"Didn't you ever consider hitting back?"
"Of course. I have hit back a few times. I'm no coward."
"As an example, who did you hit and when."
"My brother-in-law in 1956."
"Where did it happen?"
"At our apartment. We were playing cards."
"And?"
"My brother-in-law was cheating."
"One thing led to another, right?"
"Yes. Then the women separated us."
"And?"
"We continued playing. I couldn't throw my brother-in-law out on the street. At that time."
"It happened then?"
"Then."
"Is your brother-in-law short and fat like yourself?"
"He wasn't so fat then."
"And now?"
"Not now either. He died the year before last."
"Of what?"

"Rubella."
"Don't be ridiculous, that's a childhood disease."
Szegyedszky looked at him innocently.
"My brother-in-law died of rubella," he said.
Táplán took a deep breath. He tried to remain calm.
"How old was your brother-in-law?"
"Sixty-one."
"Well, a sixty-one-year-old man can't get rubella."
"I don't know anything about that, the fact is that he died of rubella."
"Try and think. I'm sure you are confusing it with something else."
"I'm not mistaken."

Táplán nervously struck the water as if it were a table, except that the water splashed and now flooded his eyes and mouth. Szegyedszky was also drying himself and looked up accusingly at him. This made Táplán even angrier.

"Get this straight, rubella is a childhood disease. It's ridiculous to insist that a sixty-one-year-old bloke died of that disease."

"Well, he did die of it," said Szegyedszky with unshakable calm.

"That's absurd," said Táplán, by now very vehemently. "Why are you insisting on the impossible, tell me."

"I?"

"You."

Perfectly calmly, Szegyedszky lowered himself into the water up to his neck.

"I just don't know why some people have to be so smart," he said. "Poor Kálmán was my brother-in-law, so I certainly know what he died of. Rubella."

Táplán shivered in the warm water. He stood up and stepped in front of Szegyedszky.

Szegyedszky smiled very faintly and disappeared into the water as much as possible. He already knew what was coming.

Táplán put his hands on his hips, leaned close to Szegyedszky, quite close to his face. Szegyedszky was only looking at his arm. His right arm. The skin was somewhat loose on Táplán's arm, but even so, it still looked quite sinewy and strong.

"I'm going to ask you for the last time, what did your brother-in-law die of?"

Szegyedszky sank up to his lower lip in the water, and from that position he said:

"Rubella."

Táplán lifted his right arm from the water to strike him, but he didn't. The rhythm of the whole thing wasn't right. With the slap he wanted to say something very insulting and at the same time appropriate. Some sort of two-part statement that would have said "you dirt"—as his arm was cutting across the air toward Szegyedszky's face—and also something more important—exactly as his hand struck Szegyedszky—but he couldn't think of the second part. This way the slap would have been entirely meaningless.

He quickly turned away and crossed to the other side of the pool.

Szegyedszky braved it out of the water and looked after him, smiling. Then after a good five minutes, he swam across and sat down beside him.

"Admit it, you wanted to hit me."

"I admit it," said Táplán.

"I could tell."

Táplán was furious. He decided to avoid Szegyedszky after this. He'd much rather sit in the colder pool, or come in the afternoon when it's terribly crowded. He'd had enough of Szegyedszky.

"What do you think, why didn't you hit me?"

"Surely you don't think I'm afraid of you."

"No, no, of course not," Szegyedszky warmly assured him. "But I saw the situation very clearly," he continued. "You retreated because the word got caught in your throat. You know I am not this or that, not pro or con."

"You are a fat, senile old man."

"You're no Adonis either."

Táplán turned to Szegyedszky once again. They stared into each other's eyes for a few seconds. Szegyedszky was smiling proudly because he felt that the impression he made during these moments was captivating; Táplán, on the other hand, was showing increasing amazement.

"Well, try it. What can you say?"

Táplán was quiet.

"I'm sixty-one now, but so far I've cleared myself of all accusations. I stand innocent in front of history's court."

Táplán shivered once again.

"Where do you stand?"

"Just as I said. If somewhere, sometime an injustice touched me, I immediately cleared myself. Test this. I am curious whether you could say anything to me now that I need to clear myself of. What can be said today of such an innocent man?"

Táplán looked at the water for a moment.

"You queer," he said dryly.

"Today that's no longer a disgrace. It doesn't have any political overtones."

Táplán didn't ask further. His silence was so depressing, rigid, and rejecting that sooner or later Szegyedszky had to evaporate from beside him. He stood up in a little while, but turned to Táplán.

"One thing's sure. I can't be insulted," he said and walked out of the pool.

Only in the rest area did they meet again. Szegyedszky was already lying there, covered up to his chin, when Táplán entered wrapped in his blanket. Only the bed next to Szegyedszky was unoccupied.

Szegyedszky spoke up only after Táplán was finally fumbling about on the bed.

"You're right, my brother-in-law didn't die of rubella."

"Well, I was right."

That was enough of a victory. Táplán softened.

"What did he die of?" he asked after a while in the old friendly tone.

"They hanged him," said Szegyedszky.

Táplán turned white under the cover. He found out whom he had been questioning all afternoon.

"I wonder what drove this unfortunate mad"—then he quickly gained control over himself and turned to Szegyedszky with a final question.

"Tell me, was there a tragedy in your life?"

"Indeed yes. Oh my!"

"What?"

"I don't know that anymore," said Szegyedszky.

"That's straight-out," thought Táplán. "How is it I didn't realize this sooner!"

"But your rheumatism is improving."

"Thank God," said Szegyedszky and knocked on wood.

[1] Trade Union Social Insurance Center (Szakszervezeti Társadalombiztositási Központ), which was founded in 1949 to look after the health and economic well-being of workers and their families.

[2] A monument at the entrance to the City Park of Budapest dedicated on the occasion of the one-thousandth year of Hungary's history as a people. It features the seven chieftains of the original tribes that arrived in 896 A.D., led by Árpád.

The Main Wall

"Say, fellows, aren't we going to decorate?" Pugacsics posed the rhetorical question as he sat down at the table to wolf down the breakfast just brought up from the deli. The question had weight, even in those days, indeed especially in those days: it was September 3, 1952. But that didn't mean the question and the related subject could be ignored. Especially here, in the student dormitory, among the first-year drama students of the Vorosilov Street College of Dramatic Arts. It proved that the questioner, Antal Pugacsics, was more alert and enthusiastic than the rest.

Miklya, a farmer's son from the Alföld, was grinding his teeth, and Róbert, who yesterday, before going to bed, was able to gain distinction through the sad fact that he had walked the hell of concentration camps, approved with an innocent smile. But Lovas, a gentleman's son, who, except for his unnecessarily large muscular physique and creamy complexion, had not been able to distinguish himself in the present circumstances in relation to his future profession, once again could hardly hide his disgust. In a flash, Miklya decided to participate in the action in only the smallest possible way because he wouldn't volunteer for a second-rate job. He knew from his technical college training that now it no longer mattered who nailed the pictures on the wall, the credit would belong to Pugacsics. What's more, whoever would be too eager after this would be suspected of insincerity, and would find himself in a dependent, subordinate relationship. The result of all this was that Róbert had to go to the superintendent for the decorations. Róbert was without suspicion, he was happy to be able to help; he had never done any decorating before in his life and had no idea that through his eagerness to decorate a person might be expressing his political views, advancing himself, or, like Lovas, who would have liked to act gutsy here too, expressing his opposition. Pugacsics told him exactly what to bring.

"Bring four pictures and some letters."

"There aren't any," said Miklya, who already knew everything. "We'll have to cut those out."

"Then paper, scissors, and sprayer." He gave orders like the commander of a pioneer camp to his little charges.

Róbert started to leave, but turned back at the door:

"Sprayer? What kind of sprayer? Are you making fun of me?" Róbert lisped.

"Paint-sprayer," said Miklya disdainfully, instead of Pugacsics. Róbert was standing in the doorway. He was embarrassed. Now he tried to appear even more helpless.

"What kind of pictures shall I get?"

Pugacsics's mouth was full of bologna. He looked up at Lovas, as if to say, what a helpless little kid. He needs someone who is bigger and better informed.

"Please help him. You're a smart kid." And he snickered, feeling that this was the best cut of all. Even Miklya liked it. Lovas, on the other hand, blushed and had nothing to reply; he followed Róbert with his face frozen into a stiff superiority.

Two left and two stayed. Pugacsics felt that he was in good form and the time was ripe to win over his greatest enemy too; so with seeming trust, he turned to Miklya, who was still dressing.

"What kind of slogan shall we write? I think one good slogan is enough."

Miklya immediately realized this was a quiz. "Well, let's see."

"What were you thinking of?"

"I was thinking of a good fighting slogan."

Pugacsics hadn't yet realized that he had jumped into this battle quite unprepared; he couldn't immediately think of even one slogan that Comrade Stalin might voice to four young Hungarian dramatists. His head was full of slogans appropriate for pioneers, but those were useless for the present occasion. Miklya was much better prepared. The experience he had gained during his technical college training was paying handsome dividends.

"There are so many," he said, as if he knew them all. He was already enjoying Pugacsics's visible confusion and struggle. Finally Pugacsics came up with one.

"Learn. Learn. Learn."

"That's Lenin," said Miklya, then added: "That's conventional. It's everywhere."

"For students, it is the best one, believe me," Pugacsics said.

"You can't learn art."

"I don't care. Let's put up another one." Miklya was quiet, he was waiting. When his silence began to indicate that he didn't know anything either, he spoke somewhat superciliously.

"Create masterpieces. J. V. Stalin." He said it like that, complete with signature.

Pugacsics stared as if he were wondering about the meaning or the appropriateness of the sentence. He would have liked to object to it, so that Miklya wouldn't have what he wanted, but the sentence with the signature was beyond attack.

"Good," he said finally, constrained to do so, and if possible, he hated Miklya even more. Then he thought of something.

"Are you sure he said it?"

"Positive," said Miklya.

Pugacsics didn't argue further, partly because he wasn't sure of the slogan's origin and partly because he thought that if Miklya made a mistake and it became clear after it was posted, then he would be all the more embarrassed.

Miklya, on the other hand, seeing that he could now freely kick the tired, dead lion, kept on kicking him:

"But we could use something else. For us the most important among the arts is the film. This fits us too."

Pugacsics was struggling and fuming. He had seen it, even read it. "It is in every movie theater,' he thought to himself.

"That's true, but it belongs in the cinema."

Meanwhile, the other two were looking for Comrade Fóti. Róbert, on Lovas's advice, first rang the bell at the apartment. Comrade Fóti, the caretaker, and his family, lived in the building on the first floor, in the apartment finished just the past summer. The apartment opened into the hall; the name plate on the door read: Richárd Fóti. While Róbert was ringing the bell, Lovas was wondering how

Fóti came to be called Richárd. Only the small window opened in response to the bell, and an uncombed wrinkle-faced woman in a robe peeked out. She immediately understood that the students were not looking for her.

"My husband is in the storage room," she said. As soon as the little window was closed, a judgment, the same judgment, formed in the minds of the two drama students: "Proletar."

Comrade Fóti was, in fact, in the storage room. Because many upperclassmen had just arrived, he was issuing mattresses, blankets, and sheets. Such work, connected with the responsibility for material things, always made him nervous, because the experienced older student is sneaky and choosy, wants more than his share, and has sticky fingers. But when Lovas came in and greeted him, Comrade Fóti smiled anyway.

"Is your blanket good enough, chubby?" he asked, and offered his hand, and of course he had to offer it as well to Róbert, the unfortunate figure next to him.

The sophomores and juniors noticed this unusually enthusiastic reception; they didn't understand it. Comrade Fóti immediately explained it to them.

"We finally have a national champion, that's how you should look at this descendant of Czája." The others were looking, and Lovas blushed. Intense emotions always marked his baby face. Comrade Fóti asked seriously:

"What kind of national champion are you, Comrade Lovas?"

"Weights, the discus," said Lovas. He was never first, except at home in the county competition, but then, "Dénes Lovas, county champion" would have sounded feeble. "They don't read the sports, anyway," he thought.

A junior sporting a moustache and boots looked Lovas over and asked:

"What is your major?"

"Drama," Lovas said.

The one in boots just shook his head.

"You'll really have to throw the discus then. Perhaps you'll go far."

Everyone snickered. Comrade Fóti also laughed. Lovas was standing in front of him and felt that Fóti had already eaten some of the sausages. Let it be known that the two thick rolls of sausages, the side of bacon, and the twenty eggs (all discretely wrapped) that Lovas's father had handed to Fóti only yesterday were responsible for Comrade Fóti's selective kindness. Lovas was admitted to the school, but without a scholarship, and he would have accepted that fact, but his father didn't let it go at that. He knew what strings to pull, and Comrade Fóti promised to look after the matter. He said a national champion must have a decent scholarship. And he did get one. The two Lovases —father and son—agreed that every month the son would receive a package and he would give a certain portion of it to Comrade Fóti. Dénes found this degrading and fought against it, but his father disarmed him:

"Do you want a scholarship? Do you want to finish your studies? Or do you want to get kicked out the first semester?"

"But how? . . . What can I say to them?"

"Do it with style. That's what gets them, you know. Anyway, it doesn't matter how you give it. The sausage counts, not your words, you silly."

Well, it did count. Róbert, on the other hand, didn't know about any of this; he believed it was sports that produced such an effect. "This Lovas is really somebody."

The decorations were in a corner, on a trunk. 50 by 70 cm. pictures of Stalin and Rákosi and a few of Marx and Engels. Together they selected some good ones of Stalin and Rákosi and took what pictures of Marx and Engels they found. All this occurred in silence; no one dared to comment because it was obvious even here, in the darkness of the storage room, that there was no joking about these sacraments. They took them upstairs.

Pugacsics accepted the lot, spread the pictures out on the table, and examined each one with care. Then lifting and holding the picture in front of him, quite awed, he said in a spiritual voice:

"Comrades, I believe I am the oldest in the room, and I had the highest rank in the DISZ[1]—I was local cultural leader—so I think I can insist that Comrade Stalin be above my head."

No one answered, but Róbert immediately grabbed the picture of Rákosi.

"And I'd like the picture of Comrade Rákosi, fellows, if that's possible."

"It's possible," said Lovas, almost coldly. He and Miklya looked at each other. Neither of them said anything. Really, it didn't matter to either of them, they would rather not hang any pictures above their beds. At the same time, it was clear to both of them that here and now the pictures alone did not matter, that much more was at stake.

Pugacsics's choice started a complex spiritual struggle in them. They began the fine and—for those who grew up in different circumstances and under different influences—incomprehensible weighing of almost unmeasurable values and relationships. Poisoned and determined by politics, they were the only youths capable of such weighing. They all felt that this was their most important confrontation since they had been together, and its effect, the consequences of the present choices, would last a long time.

At this moment there were eight beings in the room: four mortals and four Gods, except that—at least in their sick or at best unhealthy and deformed perception—the Gods were not of equal strength and power. Stalin was the GREAT GOD, the Omnipotent. Clearly, the one who got Stalin's picture would stand at the top of the room's hierarchy and the political hierarchy of the entire school. And the same with the Rákosi picture: 99% Omnipotent.

It was beautiful but of no practical value to sleep under the pictures of Marx and Engels, when there were two living and omnipotent Gods in the room as well. And even they, the two dead gods, were not altogether equal. "Marx and his faithful helpmate, Engels"—that was all they knew about the whole matter, that was what they heard most often. Without even reading one line of their works, they judged the two philosophers according to the above formula: Marx was the master, Engels was his assistant. He who prefers Marx prefers a dead God, he who prefers Engels prefers a dead demi-God.

"Engels was much more liberal"—that's what Lovas remembered now. Who had said it? His father? One of the young ministers in the church garden where they often talked after graduation, or a university student home on a visit? All that seemed beside the point now. The sentence, its speaker unidentified, turned up as a real, true, and eternal idea, and brought Lovas to a decision: he accepted Engels. With this he showed resistance, at least seemed less of an eager-beaver, he thought.

He and Miklya didn't divide anything, they didn't even say anything to each other. The picture of Marx was on top, the other underneath. Miklya reached for the picture of Marx slowly, without enthusiasm. Anyone could have interrupted him, stopped him (perhaps that was what he was waiting for), but Lovas held the lower corner of the Engels picture in the same deliberate way and waited until Miklya pulled off the picture of Marx. They looked at each other and said:

"All right?"

"Of course."

Theoretically, with this, the whole matter could have been closed, the pictures could have been hung on the wall, if Pugacsics had not wanted to be celebrated and to celebrate his victory. Pugacsics sat at a victory banquet and announced:

"I think that's fair, guys."

Even Róbert found this objectionable, although he was satisfied with his Rákosi. Not to mention Miklya, who immediately began the counterattack, although he had already accepted defeat: "only Marx." His devious and quick mind immediately produced the steps of the counterattack.

"Maybe, but I don't think so," he said, "and there are other opinions. What'll you see when you step into this room? Directly in front of you, on the wall: Marx and Engels."

He looked around for approval.

"Isn't that right? On the main wall Marx and Engels, and in the back"—he raised his voice—"hidden, Comrade Stalin . . . Well, my boy, if that seems fair to you . . . " He didn't finish the sentence and threw the picture of Marx back on the table.

"What brains," thought Lovas.

"There is something to it," said Róbert, who was not affected by it at all, because his bed stood in front of the side wall, and that could have been a main wall as well. He insured it just the same:

"Comrade Rákosi's place is on this wall, that's without question."

Miklya was looking for an alliance.

"Obviously," he said. "I'm not talking about that."

Pugacsics stopped thinking. He stepped forward, toward Miklya and the table, and began speaking in a voice that indicated that he had seriously considered the matter:

"You are right, Comrade Miklya. Comrade Stalin's place is on the main wall. I insist on Comrade Stalin." Now he was only looking at Miklya. "Let's switch places and I'll take this picture with me."

Miklya retorted:

"Not that."

"Why not?"

"Because."

"Do you have to sleep by the main wall? Or are there numbered beds here, and you were assigned to that one?"

"I came in first, I put my things here, this is my place."

"That's right," chimed in Róbert.

"Why? Because his train arrived first? Let's divide the room again."

Lovas understood that turning away from the swampy ground of political relationships, here in the sphere of practical power relationships, his physical strength could play a decisive role. He interrupted in a voice that expressed with fine shadings only but still expressed his advantage through strength.

"We're not dividing anything."

"Well then," said Róbert.

"Well then, I don't know what will happen . . . " said Pugacsics somewhat forebodingly. Lovas grew even braver.

"Nothing," he said. "The picture of Marx can stay on the main wall. Anyway, I believe, isn't he the father of the whole thing?"

Then he blushed again as he stated this because he felt that he had said it awkwardly and unprofessionally. In an obscure way he expressed his separateness and even his disgust. Then he realized that he shouldn't have said "the whole thing." The others didn't notice this slight blunder. What's more, Miklya, for the first time, looked at him gratefully and somewhat surprised. For the first time he felt he could work with this "gentleman's son," and perhaps he was not such a "gentleman's son," after all.

"Well, that's that," he said.

Róbert approved too, but didn't quite understand exactly what had happened. Pugacsics withdrew.

"You're right. It would be conceited to decide who is the greatest."

He didn't mention the names. He felt he couldn't. It was really enough of this game of sacrilege.

Miklya threw Marx's picture on the bed. Well, that's different—that's what his action expressed. He started for the bathroom with his shoe brush, planning to shine his shoes, but at the door he looked back for a moment at Lovas. The discus thrower understood the look, and after a while he too went outside. Although there were many students washing by the large, round, twenty-fauceted sink, and the noise was enormous, it didn't bother them. They openly laughed at each other.

"We mixed all that up well," said Lovas.

"Thanks. You interrupted at the right moment."

"Main wall, that's the main wall," snickered Lovas. Then he added: "You were very clever."

Miklya spat on the toes of his shoes. The "gentleman's son" didn't disgust him any longer. Unexpectedly and unexplainably, the lines of an alliance began to develop. Lovas felt the same. "This is a good Hungarian boy," he thought.

[1] Union of Working Youth (Dolgozó Ifjuság Szövetsége), an organization founded in June 1950 to guide young people in the fulfillment of socialist responsibilities.

LSD

In September 1969 Fülöp Merész, a trade official in the Vác Box Factory, suddenly acquired a substantial amount of LSD. Or, more accurately, he was given this dangerous drug for safekeeping. It happened this way: a lively group of young workers from the factory had spent a part of the summer in Western Europe on a trip organized by the Express Travel Bureau. It was these long-haired kids who brought back the LSD, but because of their basically healthy upbringing—though they managed to get hold of the stuff (in fact they stole it)—they were afraid to take it. On the other hand, they never stopped talking about their scoop. Their club was full of noises such as "We've got the stuff, we've got it!" Such showing-off was bound to reach the ear of the factory manager and of the city fathers sooner or later, especially since several of their children were involved. Eventually the rumors mobilized the entire community; the leaders of both the town and the factory thought it was time to settle the whole business, once and for all. The only question was how? After all, no trace of LSD was actually found: the youngsters were dancing and kissing with the same abandon, showing the same trance-like absence of mind as before; nor had the intensity of their incapacity for work decreased; in fact, their inflated boasts seemed to lack all material proof. At the same time, it was unnerving to know that there was LSD in the town, and worse: in the factory. When the tension began to reach an unbearable height and it began to be feared that someone at Visegrád or even in Budapest would hear about the existence of LSD at Vác, Lajos Joó, the President of the Union's Executive Committee, called for Fülöp Merész and said:

"Listen, Fülöp. Don't you think we should get to the bottom of this LSD business?"

"Sure, Lajos," replied Fülöp Merész.

Joó raised his finger in a gesture of warning:

"We've got to before it's too late."

"That's exactly what I think."

"Fülöp! You have settled many touchy situations in the course of your long and successful career as a trade unionist and as a party man. Won't you once again bring your well-known efficiency to bear?"

Merész thought for a while and then said:

"If the Union Executive Committee wants me to . . . "

"It does, Fülöp."

This is why Fülöp Merész had to visit the local youth club and stand more than thirty double brandies for the spokesmen of the younger generation, just to learn "the secret of the LSD." It wasn't easy to make the leading personalities of the club speak, but they certainly gulped down the double brandies without any fuss—quite unlike the LSD.

From all these financial outlays Fülöp Merész learned that there was indeed some LSD around, that it was still untouched, and, finally, that it was kept in a plastic bag in the pocket of Fülöp Merész, Jr.'s jeans. In fact, it had been there for the last few months. Merész, Sr. was surprised, especially because his son had not taken part in the Western tour. During that same time he was visiting the U.S.S.R., and so it could be taken for granted that it was not he who got hold of the LSD. The kids explained:

"We gave it to him to avoid suspicion."

"The little stinker," muttered Fülöp Merész under his breath.

Having said this much, he went home, and putting on a very grim look, he addressed his wife, who was busy scraping mold off the top of a jar of plum jam.

"Do you know that it's our kid who got the LSD?"

"Sure I do," his wife said.

"Why didn't you tell me?"

"I like peace and quiet," she said.

Fülöp Merész didn't answer, though he could have said a thing or two; he stood there, knitting his brows. After a while, however, he spoke.

"Where is it?"

"In the clothes closet," said his wife.

This was something beyond Fülöp Merész's comprehension. In the past few years he had only seen his son in jeans and he found it hard to imagine that he wasn't wearing them.

His wife explained:

"Ever since his pay increase, he's been wearing ordinary gray pants."

"I see," said Merész and going to the closet, found the jeans, and after a short search, managed to locate a small plastic bag in the fourth pocket. He took it out, held it up, and showed it to his wife.

"Is this it?"

"Of course. What else could it be?"

Merész heaved a deep and sad sigh, signifying: "I had to live to see this!" For some time he just stared at the bag, looking at it this way and that. He had the impression that he was being taken in, that it was all a silly joke and that this couldn't be LSD. "Well, we'll see," he thought and turned to his wife:

"What's for dinner?"

"Potato stew."

"Again?" and the thought of whether one should take LSD with Hungarian potato stew flickered through his mind. For he had immediately decided to take some right after dinner.

And take it he did. Not much; he just dipped the tip of his pocketknife in the stuff. Then he went out into the yard and looked up, far away, into the starry sky. In the first few minutes he was preoccupied by the same thoughts as on any other day: he was thinking of practical problems, ideological problems, social matters. He was about to wave angrily, to turn and go back to the house with the conclusion "This is no real drug, dammit," when suddenly a lion appeared in the sky on a parachute. It was descending into his yard in a slow and majestic motion.

"Ooops," growled Merész inwardly. "Something's happening after all? Okay, let's see." In the meantime the lion touched down and shook off the colored parachute quite like a dog would a wet rag. It approached with slow, smooth, feline footsteps and stopped in front of him.

"Who sent you?" asked Merész.

"The Trade Unions Congress," the lion answered.

"The Center?"

"Of course."

Merész was nodding briskly; now he knew what it was all about.

"They didn't send a saddle?"

The lion shook his head.

"Typical," said Merész and reluctantly climbed on the lion. "So where's the conference?" he asked the animal.

"In Kisoroszi."

Off they went. It was a short ride. Where the village of Kisoroszi used to be a huge circus top was now standing, as big as the village had been. Its dome reached the sky and it was almost bursting with a radiant light. Merész spurred his lion to a trot and arrived at the center of the arena to thunderous applause. The circus was crammed with imperialists; even the upper galleries were full. Merész not only saw this, but was well aware of who they were, and so he didn't yield to their ovation, or to the applause, or to the ecstatic waving of bowlers and top hats. No, he eyed them sternly and didn't even get off the lion, though the animal urged him with quite unmistakable twitches. When the storm of applause subsided at last, Lajos Joó entered the arena from behind the curtain across the way. He was wearing a richly ornamented gold cloak, and he spoke to the audience:

"And now, I would like to ask Comrade Merész to address the gathering."

At this point, Merész finally slid off the lion and cleared his throat.

His talk was as short as his trip from Vác to Kisoroszi. It was even possible that the whole talk consisted of nothing but clearing his throat. Its effect was beyond question, however. For, thanks to this speech, the victory of world revolution became an accomplished fact. The imperialists rose from their seats in utter dejection and left the circus with bowed heads. Once outside, they all asked for political asylum from Lajos Joó who granted it to some and refused it to others. Then Joó and lots of other people came into the arena, people from Vác, friends and colleagues, and each in turn congratulated Fülöp Merész on the swift and bloodless achievement of the world revolution.

"We should have got him to do it long ago," said someone at the back.

This pleased him best. He turned to Lajos Joó:

"Anything else, Lajos?"

"Not at the moment, Fülöp."

"Well, in that case, I'd better go."

"Fine, Fülöp. You can leave the rest to us."

He just looked at the lion, and the next moment they were back in his yard. Merész patted the lion's neck.

"Do give it a scratch, and my belly, too," the lion said.

"Okay." He scratched it as requested.

"Are you going back to the Center now?" he asked to lion.

"I am, as fast as I can. Last month I put in thirty-five hours of overtime. In the morning I have to take a foreign delegation to Szoboszló. All this traveling is ruining my health."

"That's a fact, one's system gets worn out. Though, I'd say, it happens on every job."

"Well, I could name a few where there isn't so much wear and tear," said the lion, who began to look more and more like an old acquaintance of Merész's, a chauffeur. And when they shook hands over the fence, it was him all right. Balog, the chauffeur from Kisoroszi, his wartime buddy; they had served together with the sappers. No lion or circus or radiance. And when he called back, Balog was already leaving, stepping closer to the fence, asking confidentially.

"Can I ask you something, chum? You are so well informed here in Vác . . . Is there any truth to this LSD business?"

Merész looked straight into his old friend's eyes and, after some thought, said:

"Did you notice anything peculiar about me while we were talking?"

"Not a thing."

"See? And I took the stuff just before you came."

"You don't say. And don't you have any visions?"

"Me?"

"Then it isn't LSD."

"Of course it isn't. Or if it is, then it's gone stale. All its power is gone. You know what I think the naked truth is? These kids were taken for a ride by someone there in the West."

"But if they stole it, as they say they did . . . "

"So what! They'd say anything."

"Well, I must go. See you."

"See you sometime. The best to you!"

Once again they shook hands over the fence.

Next evening Fülöp Merész took another dose, for his conscience was somehow troubled by the whole business, especially because he had lied to his old friend, but also because the question of world revolution intrigued him. He wished to hear his whole speech, all his arguments, and he hoped that the whole thing would not shrink back to local matters. He dipped his knife into the drug twice. He didn't even go outside this time, thinking it better to wait for the lion in his most comfortable armchair. But the lion didn't come. Instead, there was a shower of flowers from heaven; and then he saw vast colored shapes, heard beautiful music, and walked in a brilliantly glittering stalactite cave. Even the chauffeur's forecast came true: female shapes appeared, gliding before his eyes. Finally the Lord himself was walking toward him—with Merész's mother on his arm. His mother was wearing a beautiful wedding dress, with a mile-long veil floating after her.

After that, he took a dose every night as long as the stuff lasted. Unfortunately, the question of world revolution never came up again. When Lajos Joó finally called him in to report on his mission, Fülöp Merész went for the interview as a shadow of his former self. He had lost weight, his hands were trembling.

"What's with the LSD situation, Fülöp?"

"There is no LSD in Vác," Merész stated firmly but sadly.

"Thanks. That's just what I expected of you. And now, let me ask you, what would you like as a reward? I was told that you incurred some expenses, too . . . So, what would you like?"

"A passport," Fülöp Merész said resolutely, looking at Lajos Joó with the dim but stubborn, determined stare of the addict.

The Passengers

Only one of their journeys seemed to be too long, and this was the shorter. The other, which was truly long, their own journey, of which this train journey was only an insignificant, transient, and not unpleasant fraction, of that, they formed no opinion, nor did they consider it in any way overlong. Together, the three were over two hundred and ten years old. Outside, there was sleet and drizzle; here in the compartment it was unbearably hot, well over thirty degrees. The elderly woman sat by the window, with her back to the engine; the man in black sat opposite her; and the third one, in the gray sweater, sat at some distance in a corner by the door. The conversation was begun by the man in black, on the level of generalities, with "Dreadful weather, isn't it?" Then this grew more involved. All three agreed that the weather had turned topsy-turvy because the whole world was turning topsy-turvy. According to the man in black, it was the space probes that had upset the climate, and the one in the sweater blamed it simply on "the atom." The old woman, Róza Nemesvépi-Szakály by name, evidently thought both were likely, seeing that she nodded with approval at both men's views.

The first personal communication, or confession, also came from her.

"That whole bunch of brick-stealing gypsies came from Pozsonyhorpács."

The two old men accepted this. Róza Szakály went on: "The dividing wall is so thin, it's only a partition, it could be pierced by a knitting needle. And they take out the bricks. The bricks are being cut out from most of the dividing wall, and they are sold for three forints a brick to the gypsies of Pozsonyhorpács, even though that's now in Czechoslovakia. The dividing wall could fall down on me any minute."

"I understand," said the man in black. "These days, you can't find an honest man anywhere except in Transylvania, and even there only in the Székely districts. There, no one ever locks their doors, and if one goes in and shouts, then the owner finally turns up. I know of only one instance when a young man went astray and stole a hive of honey, and by the time the police went to look for him, he'd gone out in the woods and hanged himself."

He wiped his eyes. His eyes kept watering, even in the stifling warmth.

"I started out as a bookkeeper," he added later. "When they shut my office down as they did the others, and handed it over to time-servers, I ended up in a cottage industry."

Róza Szakály nodded: she understood. This almost matched her own tragedy, her own sufferings.

The man in the sweater looked at them grimly, almost with hate. And while he was nervously folding and throwing into his briefcase the papers he had spread out on his knees and on the seat next to him, he joined the conversation in a sharp, angry voice.

"Even the BTK,[1] in the socialist workers' society . . ." He choked. He felt that no word order he used could express his feelings, and went on, raising his voice even more: "At the highest level . . ." but he was still dissatisfied, and slamming the firmly strapped case by his side, he drew a little nearer to the other two in order to make himself more intelligible.

"That is, certain official persons simply refused to take any notice." He was cooler now, expounding reason. Then he almost finished with a despairing statement: "Or rather, they didn't take the trouble to acquaint themselves with Marxlenin (He said it like that, as one word) aesthetic. They may even misuse it, and make a joke out of these brick-stealing incidents and similar instances."

Then he realized that he hadn't said anything about himself, though that was what he had wanted to do. He drew nearer, right into the middle, and looked first at the one, then the other straight in the eyes, awaiting appreciation, the little shriek, that "yes, that's quite something, that's a real tragedy."

"I must add as a matter of general interest that I had a friend who'd been divorced several times, at present she's Mrs. Miklós Soványháti. That's the woman I unmasked, I unmasked her vicious perverted tendencies. She robbed me of everything, she even attempted to murder me; with her unbridled temper, she's capable of anything. They locked me up for thirty days, and they still won't let me alone."

After a sympathetic nod, Róza Nemesvépi-Szakály carried on from there.

"It's a large front room. It's sixteen by fifteen, and outside just opposite my door in the passage, there is my kitchen. There is a sink in there, and a gas cooker. But you couldn't put a bed in there. It's too small. And the ceiling fell down there. It keeps falling in chunks over an area of about a square yard. And my bed fits best along the outside wall, so that the brickwork will fall on me when the partition is quite dismantled by those gypsies from Pozsonyhorpács. So I applied for a fair exchange."

She would have gone on, but the man in black interrupted. Róza Nemesvépi-Szakály found it odd that he should be staring with his dribbling eyes at the man in the sweater while he was interrupting her story. By way of protest she snatched her bag into her lap, and she threw the food bundled in a napkin on the little table between her and Dribble Eyes. She didn't undo the bundle but went on scrabbling about in the bag.

Meanwhile Béla Hidvéghy, the man in black, said to Mihály Bakó, in the gray sweater, whose facial expression had not changed during the unexpected twists of the lengthy statement: "Lenin was not only a genius, but a real human being. He carried the photographs of Gercen and Tcherniyivski in his wallet, though both were rich men."

"He died," Róza Nemesvépi-Szakály corrected him. With satisfaction, she untied the cloth, picked up a leg of fried chicken and sniffed audibly at the air sweetened by the smell of fried fat rising from the cloth.

"He died, I know," said Hidvéghy, and tried to draw away from her gobbling. He had a feeling that he ought to educate this blabbering female. So he said: "I am Dózsa's descendant;[2] with my parents, we paid a high price for freedom. In the revolution, in nineteen-eighteen, we stood by the people. My father wasn't a poor man. And I have written fifty-seven religious poems in my time. As far as I know, only Vörösmarty[3] can compare; he wrote almost as many, forty-five to be exact."

This was rather a weighty communication. Róza nearly choked on a mouthful of bread. Mihály, however, drew a little further away, and it was only after a breathing space that he added: "Well, of course we all produce what we can according to our skills and sense of duty."

Róza said: "They enlisted it."

"Who enlisted what?" asked Hidvéghy.

"My petition."

"You mean they listed it," he corrected her, leaning back, a somewhat superior smile spreading over his face.

"Yes," said the old woman, ignoring the superior attitude. She went on eating and continued: "The situation got worse after the floods." She bit into a gherkin. "The housing department is closed. They took down the particulars. They will notify me in writing. And meanwhile these types come and steal from me."

Superiority is catching, though it's possible that it was the fried chicken and its smell which troubled Mihály Bakó, and he too joined in: "Who?"

"The brick thieves." It was all quite clear to her, she couldn't understand how her fellow-travelers couldn't see it. She finished one leg and didn't start on the second; she began to pack it away slowly. "Sándor Tóth has neither hands nor feet. He is totally blind," she continued, evenly and undisturbed. "His wife is ill too. He has two daughters, they are twins, both twenty, and his only son is fourteen. Then Jóska Tóth's one-legged nephew moved in too, and István Tóth and his wife and two daughters. They took the nails from my imported Japanese furniture with a magnet and sold those in the same place."

"Where?" asked Hidvéghy.

"At Pozsonyhorpács."

The eyes of the two men met. Now they understood, and they agreed. Róza, although she noticed it, didn't mind; she was used to this. It had happened to her more than once that when she reached the point in the story of her persecution where the nails were removed by a magnet from her furniture, the attitude of her listeners suddenly changed. They became unsympathetic or, alternately, they smiled and agreed with everything she said but didn't do anything for her. Of course, even those with whom she had omitted this detail didn't do anything for her. No one did anything for her. "These two won't either," she thought. Not that she'd had much hope of them anyway, they didn't look particularly influential when they settled in the compartment, but then, she thought anything is worth trying, any opportunity worth taking—you can never tell, after all. But she went on, for the sake of talking.

"Sándor Tóth is not registered as disabled. When he was ill four years ago, they offered him service quarters, though he had not entitlement as he was on welfare. Very good quarters—a nice apartment, larger and with less rent to pay. But he was too vain to accept it; his twin daughters had something against it."

"You're full of contradictions," Mihály Bakó cut in angrily. Meanwhile Róza had repacked her provisions and put them back in her shopping bag. Even the aroma was gone.

"Oh, of course," said Hidvéghy, and he immediately started on his own communications, but in a tone more elevated than the one he'd used earlier, for he felt it to be necessary and proper after all her confused babble.

"Whenever I have the chance, I polish my ten thousand poems and the three thousand texts suitable for musical setting. Once a publisher called me for an interview to discuss terms, but when they saw me, even though I am still young in outlook, they said they publish only young writers. In other words, it wasn't the spirit of my poems that mattered, but the number of my years. Since then, I write for my own eyes, and that's a good publisher. It accepts everything."

Mihály Bakó fidgeted; he picked up his case and opened it. Hidvéghy felt that Bakó was about to speak, about to trump him, so he quickly added with a bitter emphasis: "My misfortune was that Endre Kóréh died in Vienna; had he come back, I'd be all right. And there was this teacher, she coached actresses, but she died too. I was to have married her."

At this, Róza Nemesvépi-Szakály threw her head back and looked Hidvéghy up and down. The result of her examination remained unknown, for all she said, looking very straight into Bakó's eyes, was: "My pension is 920 forints."[4]

Mihály Bakó started up with the vehemence of someone who has long felt himself to be pushed into the background. His accumulated emotions were making it impossible for him to form clear, whole sentences to express the things he wanted to say, and as he was aware of this while he talked, he was even more heated. He stood up, waved his arms about, occasionally bent right into Hidéghy's face or beat the air in front of Róza, who'd shrunk into the larva of her fright.

He began, still seated: "I admit that I'm a dangerous character, but only for those who ignore the Marxlenin aesthetic and human dignity."

Hidvéghy relaxed and nodded. This wasn't trumping him.

"I am one of the many children of a poor working-class family," he said and took a step toward Hidvéghy, waving his fists. "I bore everything in the bloody war of the vandalhitler." (He said it like that, as one word.)

"While she, to protect her position and avoid a moral scandal . . ."—his anger tossed him back to his earlier train of thought and he tried to finish what he was saying—"I bore everything, just to kill the fascists." And now he could continue with the real matter: "And so she called me a danger to society and God knows what else, or rather she wanted to have me declared dangerous. In her unbridled anger she is capable of anything."

Róza interrupted. "The woman?"

"Yes, of course, that's what I'm talking about, am I not? She's a notorious drunk, though of course she is trying hard to behave properly where she lives now, to stay in the good graces of her idiotdoctor (he spoke this as one word too) husband."

"That's awful," said Róza.

Bakó threw his hand in the air to imply that this was still nothing. "She lifted my three thousand forints," he said proudly, with enjoyment, looking from one to the other to make sure they clearly understood even the smallest detail, "and she did it by smuggling a sleeping pill into my tea so I fell deeply asleep. Obviously. Then she carried out the theft. And now it's she who's offended, and her protectors, because luck is on my side at last."

Both his auditors looked toward him at this, inquiringly. Bakó sat down and placed his hand on his briefcase.

"I have filed my memoirs with the Ministry of Justice. To get protection."

Róza accepted his explanation, but Hidvéghy, whose fears had dissolved by now, didn't. "And the thirty days?"

"I've done them."

"For slander, wasn't it?"

"Yes, of course, but I was surrounded by false witnesses."

"It's likely you'll get an even longer one now."

"Me? Me, an active, in the bloody war . . ." he faltered, he lifted his arm, but all that came to his lips was "bloody war" and he couldn't finish that, so he stopped it. "Me? An honest workingman?"

"Because of your memoirs," said Hidvéghy seriously, meaningfully, as befits an educated and deep-thinking man.

Poor Bakó was shattered by this. He slumped back on his seat; he pushed his briefcase roughly to the corner and covered it with his body. This was as dark and dangerous a point for him as the nails removed by the magnet were for Róza.

His petitions and supporting documents . . . All the same, he was extremely pained by the bull's eye scored by Hidvéghy. "What's that sickly looking old black creep after? He's got one foot in the grave, what's he so uppish about?" But the time was not yet ripe for a retort.

It was growing dark and the rain was beating against the window. Hidvéghy, who didn't really mind the half-dark, remarked after a few minutes' silence: "An express train, and no electricity. That's typical."

"You can switch it on," said Róza, and she pulled herself up, and proudly, drawing herself up as much as she could, she stepped to the switch and clicked it. The light went on. Róza sat back in her place with her head held high, tingling with the pleasant awareness that she had put to shame these two helpless, silly men . . . Hadn't they ever been on an express train before?

The light also cleared in Mihály Bakó's head. "I'd like to see those poems."

"You can't. They're not meant for you."

Bakó turned toward Róza. "Does he look like someone who's written ten thousand poems?"

Róza shrugged, and inclined her head: it could be, though it wasn't all that likely.

"They're numbered," said Hidvéghy.

"Perhaps by the time I get home and open my front door, I'll have nothing left," said Róza.

"And five hundred are religious? That's hard to believe."

"Not five hundred, only fifty-seven, and not so much religious as about God. That's something quite different."

"Don't talk so freely about your clericalized scribblings. Who needs it nowadays? You could be up for breach of the peace."

"I am not afraid. I have the right to put my emotions down on paper. And to make them rhyme."

"That's just the point. I too have the right. Nobody has the right to doubt that, you see? I was cruelly misunderstood, because I will not tolerate injustice. In the battles of the past . . . " His words became heated and tangled. He pointed his finger toward Hidvéghy.

"Fighting to win the liberty we enjoy today . . . in the battle of the past . . . the unbelievable, gigantic . . . the walls and chains against us . . . "

Hidvéghy smiled indulgently. It's a shame to tease this one, he thought.

The door flung open, the conductor came in. He said a polite good evening and asked for their tickets. He was a big man around forty, with a tanned but firm face, radiating strength and health; the lined greatcoat of his uniform made him look even more powerful. His whole towering appearance, his thick deep voice simply squeezed from the compartment the steam, the mood generated by the emotional relationships of the previous hour. Naturally, Róza Nemesvépi-Szakály was the first to find her ticket. It was a reduced-rate ticket, but it was in order.

"To Győr?" asked the conductor.

"To Győr. Home," said Róza.

Bakó managed to get in first. As he handed over his half-price slip he was already naming his destination: "Mosonszentmiklós." The conductor nodded, punched the ticket, and handed it back with thanks. After all this, Hidvéghy placed his own ticket into the conductor's hand like a coin, like some noble's condescending alms. The conductor looked at it at length, turning it this way and that, and with knitted brows, asked heavily:

"Where are you going, sir?"

"To Kunágota," said Hidvéghy.

"You've taken a very large detour, sir. In this direction you could only get to Kunágota by going round the whole world via Japan. This is another line. This is the wrong direction for you."

"Why?" asked Hidvéghy.

"It's the wrong line," said the conductor.

Hidvéghy wouldn't be beaten. "Perhaps it's the train that's going in the wrong direction then," he said, angry and disapproving. The conductor kept his temper, and held the ticket with two fingers, like a piece of criminal evidence.

"It's not impossible, sir; one can never be too sure. But you must get off the train now, the sooner the better, and go back to Budapest, and there you must cross to the Keleti station, there you must take the train eastward to Lökösháza, where you must change to the local line for Dobmiratos—Kunágota—Mezőkovácsháza. It's a narrow-gauge train, but it stops at Kunágota. We don't stop at Kunágota. Never."

One could have expected Bakó to burst out laughing as he heard this, but he didn't even smile. Nor did Róza. She shook her head in mute despair, full of sympathy for the man in trouble. Hidvéghy deduced from this very silence just how big a mess and trouble he was in, and that there was no point in any further display of pride.

"I shall get off," he said darkly.

The conductor was getting hot. He had not anticipated having to spend so much time in one compartment. He took his cap off and put it on his bag.

"Then I won't process this ticket now, because it is perfectly good to Lökösháza, but you must buy one from me to take you to Komárom. With the extra charge."

This started an argument. Hidvéghy refused to admit the propriety of charging him an extra fee; he kept harping on his helplessness. The conductor accepted his innocence, but he could not ignore the facts, according to which Hidvéghy was a passenger traveling without a valid ticket on this particular train, even if he had in his pocket, or at this minute in the conductor's hand, a ticket; it was invalid on this line, but he could make use of it later.

There was further trouble: Hidvéghy had no money. All that his carefully guarded wallet held were two ten-forint coins; he was more aware of this than of any other fact in the whole world.

"Let's go into the corridor, it's too warm in here," he proposed and the conductor agreed with relief. They went out. Hidvéghy went a long way from the compartment, and the conductor followed him, understanding that this blinking old man wanted to tell him something that the other two passengers should not hear. With a begging, pitiful look Hidvéghy confessed the sad truth.

"I have no money, sir. I can't even go to Budapest. My relatives were expecting me at Lökösháza. I was to spend the winter there. Because I can't afford to heat my room. I can no longer carry the coal from the basement, and I can't afford to pay someone to bring it upstairs."

The conductor sighed. "But why did you go to the Nyugati?[5] And where did you buy your ticket?"

"At the Ibusz travel agency. I bought it in advance."

The conductor looked at the ticket. This was true, he had noticed it earlier, but he was pleased to find something he could believe in this confused mess.

"One must go by subway to the Keleti,[6]" said Hidvéghy, gaining a little courage as the conductor seemed to relent, "and the subway is very drafty. It's my eyes . . . I thought the Nyugati was warmer."

He signaled toward his eyes with his right hand, to clarify what he was trying to say.

"Well, it is a bit warmer," said the conductor, and swore at length. He gave Hidvéghy's ticket back, and told him exactly what to do. He must get off at Komárom and catch the train coming the other way; there was no way to miss it, all he had to watch was that it should go in the opposite direction; it was due in half an hour. As he couldn't buy a ticket, if they caught him he must tell the truth, all except that he'd been let off this time. They would fine him. He might have to pay that. There was no other way. Hidvéghy heard it all with his head bent, his teeth chattering. He could hardly mutter his "thank you." The conductor saw him back to the compartment, and opened the door for him.

"That's settled, then. It's all right, we've settled it," he threw after the tottering old man. Then he turned back once more. "Get ready, sir. The next stop is Komárom."

Hidvéghy was so exhausted that he couldn't even budge the suitcase which he'd tossed in the rack earlier with a masculine jerk and no less masculine groan. Bakó, who saw this and felt for him, jumped up with keenness and jerked down the case, which, however, proved a lot heavier than expected and so he landed with it in poor Róza's lap.

"My god! what's in here? Not poems!"

"Only the sonnets," stammered Hidvéghy.

"The main thing is that it should all end well," said Róza, thus obviating the need for an apology which should have followed such a hefty collision.

By now, Hidvéghy couldn't even put on his own coat. First he put on his hat, but only just, and as he was shaking, almost skipping himself into his coat, his hat tipped from his head to the floor. Róza picked it up and held it for him. And she noticed something else too; something was missing.

"Your scarf? Didn't you have a scarf?"

Of course he had, in the sleeve of his coat. Róza stood up and pulled it out, she even tied it for him and patted it nicely into place. She also buttoned the top button of his coat. Hidvéghy bore it all, like a scared child, but he wouldn't look at either of them; he just peered into nothing and blinked.

Mihály Bakó grabbed the suitcase and in one breath took it to the end of the carriage; he put it down in front of the lavatory. Hidvéghy nearly dashed after him, but turned back halfway, as it occurred to him he hadn't taken leave from the lady who was quite nice, after all.

"See you again," he said, pushing half his face back into the compartment.

"All the best!" nodded Róza.

Bakó was carefully guarding his suitcase until he came back. Hidvéghy held out his hand. "Thank you. I'm Hidvéghy. Thank you."

"It's nothing. I'm Bakó."

They shook hands.

"Have a good journey," said Mihály Bakó.

"Oh god . . . " shrugged Hidvéghy.

Bakó went back to the compartment and pulled the door tight after him. He shivered and rubbed his sweater on his chest.

"It's quite cold out," he said.

Róza didn't speak. After all the excitement, she was now very thirsty, but somehow she felt it would not be in good taste to bring out her flask and drink. Somehow not quite . . . She was wondering how long she should wait.

The train braked and slowly, screechingly came to a halt. Róza looked out of the window, to get her bearings: "Is this Komárom?"

Bakó looked out too. It was pitch dark outside, and very quiet. Mihály Bakó stated: "It's open country."

These interruptions seemed sufficient to Róza to venture having a drink. She took the flask from her shopping bag, unscrewed it with some effort, and raised it to her lips. She drank loudly, and long. Bakó swallowed in unison with her. Róza sensed it, and as she took the flask from her lips, she lowered it into her lap, without closing it again; she just held it. She waited a little, and then asked:

"Perhaps you are thirsty yourself?"

"I am, and hungry too. I'm everything."

Róza ignored the hints, and just held the flask toward Bakó. "You can drink from it," she said. And Bakó drank, about half the bottle.

Meanwhile the train started up again.

As they arrived in Komárom, Róza spread her coat on her shoulders and then opened the window, as she wanted to see "the artist" get off. Meanwhile she had decided that even if he didn't have ten thousand poems, he must be some sort of artist, as he was just as absent-minded and as formless as artists tend to be.

But no one got off the train at Komárom.

"Well, he isn't getting out." Róza pulled the window up as the train started.

"He didn't get off? Really?"

They stared at each other in growing fear. They were afraid to speak their fears aloud. Now it was Róza who went out first. Bakó followed her.

The suitcase was no longer in front of the lavatory door where Bakó had put it down but was sticking halfway out of the open carriage door, where Hidvéghy had pushed it, obviously thinking it would be easier for him to reach back for it once he was off the train and on solid ground. Only, after the lowest step there must have been such a deep ditch out there in the open country that he could only fall down. He must have fallen on his face, on wet, sharp stones.

The other two up in the train knew it all exactly. The sharp air whistling through the dangling suitcase hovering on the edge of the darkness told them, quite unmistakably, how it happened.

"Should we pull the emergency brake?" asked Róza.

"The emergency brake? Who's got money for that?"

"They might understand . . ."

"They fined him too, you know. He's sure to stumble across a house or something. Why bother with the emergency rod? The train can't turn back and fetch him."

"That's true," said Róza. She muttered as she went back to the compartment. "Not back." She shook her head. "Never back. Only forward."

Bakó carried the suitcase after her.

[1] The Penal Code (Bünetető Törvénykönyv).

[2] György Dózsa (c. 1470-1514) was the leader of the futile Peasants' Revolt in Hungary in 1514. The victorious feudal nobility executed him by roasting him alive in a red-hot iron chair, and they forced his followers to eat of his flesh.

[3] See note 1 on page 269.

[4] About forty-five dollars at the present rate of exchange.

[5] The West Railroad Station in Budapest.

[6] The East Railroad Station in Budapest.

PART TWO
Authors since 1965

Anna Jókai

Jókai, a native of Budapest, was born on November 24, 1932. Her father had great difficulty supporting the family, and he increasingly felt the weight of the economic Depression during the thirties. After graduating from high school in 1951, Jókai tried to make her own living; she worked as an office clerk, an elocutionist, and head bookkeeper. She eventually entered the Loránd Eötvös University in Budapest, and on completing her studies in Hungarian language and history in 1961, she became a teacher at a small elementary school in Pest for ten years, then at the Mihály Vörösmarty High School of Budapest, and is still employed as a teacher. Until she was sixteen, she constantly felt the compulsion to write, but then, thinking it was just an adolescent's sense of a calling, she ended her literary experimentations. She did not begin writing seriously until about 1965, and her first book, *4447*, a novel, was published in 1968, when she was thirty-six. Since that time, other works have quickly followed: *Without Rope* (*Kötél nélkül*), short stories, 1969; *Assets and Liabilities* (*Tartozik és követel*), a novel, 1970; *The Ball* (*A labda*), a novelette and short stories, 1971; *Days* (*Napok*), a novel, 1972; *Our Loves, Our Lovers* (*Szeretteink, szerelmeink*), short stories, and *Assets and Liabilities*, this time as a drama, 1973; *Until Death* (*Mindhalálig*), a novel, 1974; *The Angel at Reims* (*A reimsi angyal*), short stories, 1975; *The Task* (*A feladat*), a novel, 1977. *Assets and Liabilities* has been performed in the Thalia Theater in Budapest. Her writings have been recognized by two awards: the Attila József Prize in 1970 and the Central Council of Hungarian Trade Unions Prize in 1974.

Anna Jókai

Jókai's short stories and novels are popular. Psychological in approach, they probe mainly the problems of children and youth, and the difficulties found in family situations; their compassionate treatment of the daily lives of women tells much about their roles in contemporary Hungary. Probably her most ambitious effort to date is *Days*, in which she traces the life and times of a typical male figure through all the drastic changes in Hungarian life from the 1930s to the present.

The Angel at Reims

She stands in the doorway, her wings still stretched in travel.

"I'm here," she says to the broken statue of a man standing beside her. She smiles with a flirtatious grimace, as if she had just revealed herself after playing hide-and-seek for a long time.

The man is offended. Three deep wrinkles show on his forehead; he isn't even looking at the angel. Perhaps he doesn't hear her. Lowering his swollen eyelids, he looks at the ground in front of him—the very picture of desperation.

"I can't stand it any longer," he says. Yet he is a saint.

Above them the gothic forms stretch wildly. Fingers taper off in search of receding meaning.

It is already autumn, the bone-yellow of the dry lace-like carvings grows colder.

Hippies shelter there, a tin can rattles, roils down the steps, and tomato-sardines splatter. Jean-Baptiste takes out his pipe, smoke rises into the angel's face. Louise laughs.

Jean-Baptiste approves.

"We'll smoke her out," he says.

He wipes his sticky fingers on the angel's feet. The tomato shines like blood.

"Where were we yesterday?" asks Louise, pulling her black flowered jersey over her ankles, wrapping herself up in it.

"What difference does it make?" Jean-Baptiste sits down beside her, kicks off his sandals, and rubs his naked soles against the edge of a step.

"And where are we going from here?"

"Don't ask," answers the boy, "he who asks is lied to."

The girl shrugs her shoulders, lies down backward on the steps, her head dangling.

"This is our angel," she says suddenly. "Just look at her hair."

It does indeed curl softly on her forehead and by her ear. Jean-Baptiste is unraveling the bottom of his trouser-leg.

"I once cried," says Louise, apparently without logic.

The boy digs around in the threadbare sack. He takes out a bottle of orange soda and drinks. He offers it to the girl, she takes a swig.

It is morning. Jean-Baptiste urinates next to the angel's feet; the stream flows down.

"We too shall die," says Louise.

"We won't notice it." Jean-Baptiste braids his hair into a whip. "We don't manufacture pain. Nothing is pleased by nothing. Do you understand that?"

A closed soot-black Mercedes passes by the church and turns to the left.

"Who is smarter?" asks Louise, "the one who chooses aimlessness or the one who denies it and invents the tin box with four wheels?"

"Pigs!" Jean-Baptiste spits. "But don't ask."

The closed soot-black car returns from the right and brakes to a stop at the steps. The recessed door opens and the head of the family steps out. The blond, well-groomed beard swallows up his mouth. He helps his wife out; her hair is blonde too, long and straight, and every strand reaches the middle of her back with millimeter accuracy. The children, two little girls, are also blonde. On their heads are white canvas hats, brims folded back and ribbons under their chins. Their teeth protrude, giving them the look of the curious.

"This must be it," says Klaus. He begins to walk up; the woman and the children line up behind him; Klaus's beard is waving in front like a shield.

They go around Jean-Baptiste and Louise, the spittle, the sauce, and the urine puddle; they avoid them one by one and sneak a furtive look.

"Sad, how very sad," says Hilde, and she straightens the little white hats.

Jean-Baptiste sticks his tongue out as far as he can, Louise too, and they begin to moo.

"Why are they doing that?" asks Hilde.

"They are expressing their animal nature," says Klaus, "and their disdain of all things that glorify the greatness of the human spirit. The cathedral on whose steps we are walking is a pregnant expression of true gothic forms . . ."

The smaller of the white-hatted girls stares back at Jean-Baptiste and Louise. She trips on the top step. Her father notices it and, as a warning, jabs his thumb without emotion into the little girl's ribs. The child cries out once, but that's all. Thus warned, she steps into the darkness.

"Will we get rid of them all? Every one of them?" asks Louise. She is throwing the sticky papers out of the sack.

"Stupid. Laugh at them. Look"—Jean-Baptiste points up—"she is laughing at it all too."

He reaches for the angel's knees with one hand, feels them; then they pick up the sack and, pulling it behind them, disappear in the dust.

Klaus squints in the bright light and closes the guide book. "The richness of the nave competes with the richness of the transept," he says. "Let's hurry up, Hilde. There are three more left."

"Klaus." The woman stops on the bottom of the step, the two children beside her. She leans on them lightly. "There must be an angel here. Some kind of angel . . ." she continues, hesitating in the quiet, "that's what the books say."

"Conventional statement. Angels swarm here. The characteristic of the Medieval Church," says Klaus, instructively.

"But this is a different angel . . . unusual," says Hilde, and she hangs on to the thin little necks. Klaus looks at her sternly.

"Angels are all alike. Flat decorative element. I just don't understand you, Hilde."

Hilde tries once more, she steps back; the children stop, they do not follow her. Klaus is down by the car; this disintegration, this sliding of the rectangle is frightening.

"I'm coming, Klaus," she says. She sits in the car with smoothed-down skirt. "Where are we going now, do you know?"

"I just don't understand you, Hilde," he says again. He pulls on his gloves and starts the engine. "We came from Metz and we are going, through Paris, straight to Chartres. Is it clear?"

The little girls tighten the ribbons under their chins. Hilde nods, and, as the car starts, her hair falls into her face.

"I'm late," pants Madam Chouchou, and knocks five times on the stone with her stick. "They would have given me something, I can feel it."

Usually she stands next to the side entrance. Foreigners think that she is holding the silver box in the name of the church.

"Dear, good Virgin Mother, help me," she says to the angel. "What a day, my dear Virgin Mother. You can arrange everything. Where should I run now? Maybe to the movie house? Dear Virgin Mother," she says to the angel stubbornly, "I am asking you for two weeks of sunny weather so they will feel like coming. And bring those who have and those who give. What's this to you? You see I have faith in you, and in exchange you could arrange it. Help your faithful, not your enemies; be good, be smart, dear Virgin Mother." She blows a kiss on her fingers held in a bouquet and sends it up the pleats of the angel's dress.

"The smile is not enough," she says with mild reproach. "You too can see that."

She stands leaning on the stick, watching the main street; the sun reaches her, the silver box reflects the rays, Morse code vibrates in the air.

"What?" says the old woman. "Shall I go over to the crown jewels?" She becomes excited. "I can do that, but if you fool me again, I'll get very angry."

Before she starts down, she taps the steps with her stick. An enormous cloud clings to the sky, and it rains for hours. It is like a spring rain, it soaks everything; the church warden closes the door.

Up from the road runs Marcello with his drawing pad; he flattens himself against the wall, underneath the angel. The rain reaches him here too, and the puddle collected on the base drips on the wide brim of his hat.

He would like to run on; he is hiding the drawing pad under his checkered cape. He looks up at the sky, but instead sees the angel unexpectedly, quite close. He is surprised. A thin thread of water flows down the angel's face; from her eyesockets, across the stretched corners of mouth the drops fall with short breaks onto her thin chest.

"Beautiful," Marcello thinks, and watches mesmerized. "The eternal smile beneath the eternal tears."

"I won't ever forget it," he promises himself. He is carrying the pad, squeezing it to his stomach, into the line of cooling trees.

It stops raining, but the sun doesn't return. It only glimmers through the grayness.

A bus shaped like a whale arrives; it has one tiny door at the front. The tiny door opens and the driver gets out. He waves. Then everybody gets out in a straight line; the guide's lips move. He includes the driver in the group too. He takes out a key and carefully locks the door of the bus. The rest wait while he places the key at the bottom of his briefcase.

"You may go in a little farther," the guide says, and they go in a little farther.

A kerchiefed old woman, with heavy braids on top of her head, hesitates at the entrance. She is about to lift her right hand to her forehead. The guide quickly steps beside her, takes her right arm at the elbow, and politely helps her across the threshold.

They stay inside a long time. A young woman wearing sunglasses reads from a mimeographed sheet; at times she looks around, searching, and then, when paper and object are matched, cries out victoriously.

On the way back, they almost miss the angel. The guide shakes his head, whispers something to the woman, and points with the corner of his briefcase to the last item on the sheet.

Embarassed, the woman guides the group back. In a melodious alto voice she tells everything one should know about the statue. Two take notes. The guide hurries to the front and opens the door of the whale-bus. He stands there as they get in one by one, his lips moving. He gaily shoves the driver in and jumps in after him. Some wave from behind the unbreakable glass; they wave to the empty square.

It is dusk, but one can only guess that, for only the gray grows grayer as the light withdraws.

Hriszto carries two stuffed suitcases, a sailcloth bag on his back.

"Just let me get to this church," he prays, "this wretched cheap church. I'll sit on the steps below those archaic mugs, rest and then go on to the railway station."

The packages thud on the stone. Hriszto takes out his handkerchief, spreads it out on the step, lowers himself, and locks his knees. He licks his leathery palms.

He becomes restless and opens his canvas bag and looks for something; he finds it and sighs.

"I took care of everything," he thinks with satisfaction. "I thought I would run out of time, but I made it."

Mária walks slowly up the steps. A green muslin shawl swims behind her; she has tied up her graying hair. The pleated skirt opens like a silent accordian.

She is cold and puts her hand across her neck; it appears as if she were trying to choke herself with her left hand, but her right hand won't let her.

"You always drag everything along with you," she thinks, although she is only carrying a small beaded bag with a nickle clasp. "Always everything, everywhere."

The angel melts into the wall; the woman looks around hesitatingly, but she sees only the hollow darkness.

Hriszto thinks Mária younger; he is fooled by the green muslin and the beaded bag. He moves closer and puts his treasures on the step.

"Technology," he brags. "Radio. Sechs transistor. Verstehen? Six."

"I left home," Mária thinks. "At home my daughter is dyeing her wig. My daughter's daughter is vomiting up the formula. My daughter's father is watching T.V. and drinking beer."

"Magnetofon," says Hriszto, and he begins to pack feverishly. "Made in Japan. First Class." He lights up the tiny elements, thin as a thread.

Mária nods, preoccupied.

"It was a shame," she thinks, "but now it's final. They didn't close up the world, only my window became milk-glass."

Hisztro is showing enormous scissors, clicking them.

"Prima . . . prima . . ." he rolls the 'r', it jumps popping about on the stone.

Mária is about to get up when the floodlights come on.

Hriszto sees her face, he quickly begins to pack.

The angel shines, her smile pours from the shadows.

"Angel," says Mária, with surprise, "*the* angel."

"Ein Engel," waves Hriszto, "nur ein Engel." He points to the 2000 watt floodlight. "Technika . . . ja. Technika ja. Aber Engel." He shakes his head in sympathy. He is in a hurry. The train leaves at 21:20 and then, with one transfer —home.

The woman stays. She tries to look behind the statue. She stands on tiptoe, she tugs at the chipped toes. It is a sly light, it moves from bottom to top.

"What do you know?" she challenges the angel. The incessant smiling irritates her.

László Marsall

Marsall, whose first volume of poetry was published when he was thirty-seven, was born on November 3, 1933 in Szeged, a city on the banks of the Tisza River in southern Hungary. He was, he says, "an uncommunicative child, a solitary and maniacal dreamer," and his "real home was the attic, the lilac path, and the narrow corridor for cats bordered by the fence," where he "drew maps of imaginary continents and countries" and "was occupied with imaginary people." He regarded the outside world in those days only when he could make its messages conform to his own world order. Detesting school, he avoided it whenever possible; he often failed mid-year examinations but always barely managed to pass those given at the end of the year. His experiences with the war in Budapest terrified him and remain vividly etched in his memory. As a ten- to twelve-year-old dreamer, he was totally unprepared for the bombings and for "the terror of pale and nervous adults." Crouching on bedding in an air-raid shelter, he "escaped into a dull, dead state of mind difficult to resolve." He did not "wake" up until he was sixteen and then spent the remaining three years of high school "wide awake, open, and curious," studying art, mathematics, and physics. Meanwhile, he was writing novels and poems, perhaps "searching for my healing, perhaps for the thread of my lost childhood." Graduating in 1952, he studied mathematics and physics at the Loránd Eötvös University with "great energy and agony." Although unaware of the fact, he was by then chiefly interested in writing poetry. Three years later he had to make a choice: he left the university, and, ever since then, he says, literature has been "my bread and my fountain of youth as well."

His works are: *Watermarks* (*Vízjelek*), poems, 1970; and *Alpha Point of Love* (*Szerelem alfapont*), poems, 1977.

A highly distinctive and mature tone characterizes his poems from the beginning. His unornamented poetry aims at developing his individuality, because he is convinced that every human being must constantly shape his or her thoughts and character. The image of holding the watermark up to light symbolizes his concept that the poet's responsibility is to compel "silence" to speak out to assist readers in their quest for their real selves in the existing circumstances.

River and Sun

upside down

a crystal shower comb
a skein of dreamhair
inside
      a thrush sleeps

it cuts it up in pieces with its beak

it's left its every bone behind
dawn is breaking

if you toss it up it's white

up to its knees in clouds
the river wades
its hair
is the earth

startled awake
the river, wounded,
dashes to earth,
    goes sprawling,
        stays there for ever

bleeding river body
heap of river bones
river skull

never will fall

The Depths of Silence

Could it be a dream of wind?
Sing-song of fish tossed ashore?
The psalms of ceaseless come and go
in a shinbone buried away in the ground?

No longer does the ear hear it
the Subcutaneous Someone listens:

> A sheet of paper in the dark
> Watermarks clamoring
> in a potato-sprout

> The microwave beat of the sea
> Breath beaten back from the wall
> into the face of the sleeper

> Lax clang of carbon cycles
> A pinion which grazes
> the hand sewn into the skeleton of the heart

For the angel is not mute
He is more whispering than the whispering
and awesomer

Striptease

elbows bend
two arms
disappear to the elbows
into the dark side
fingers somewhere behind
breast-high

bridge linking
two shimmering hemispheres
sags in the middle
bridge hemispheres fall

eyes
all around
multiplying eyes

elbows bend
two arms
wrists on the hip-bone
belt-high

mirroring belt moves slithers
falls

eyes
all around
round eyes
ever rounder eyes

elbows bend
right arm
in front on the bright side
nail of right forefinger
from chin-tip to pubis
slashes the skin

skin like cast-off overalls
spotlight-blue
in a heap on the stone floor

eyes
all around
narrowing eyes
contracting eyes

elbows bend
left arm
in front on the bright side
nail on left forefinger
from chin-tip to pubis
slashes the flesh

flesh like lilac catsuit
brown entrails smolder
in a heap on the stone floor

eyes
all around
dilating eyes
canal-black eyes

elbows bend
forearm-bones above the skull
knuckles metacarpals wrists
smash down on the skull

bones scattered all over
shattered house of sticks
spotlight-blue on the stone floor

eyes
all around
shivering eyes
bloodshot eyes

barren female voice
above the shimmering hemispheres
above the belt

above the piles of skin
and flesh and bone
barren female voice

here I am
who'll take me from here
who'll take me to his home

eyes no longer
eyes shut
eyes not seeing even within

each takes her home with him

István Császár

Császár, who was born in Budapest on June 23, 1936, recollects observing Miklós Horthy, regent of Hungary from 1920 to 1944, amble up the red-carpeted steps of the Parliament with his official party to open Christmas gift parcels, and feeling quite left out of the proceedings as a member of a poor family. Later he saw a ten-kilometer stretch of the national highway leading into Budapest "stacked on both sides with the bodies of dead Soviet soldiers." It was a sight which, he says, "brought both my callow childhood and the war to an end." His schooling was a frustrating experience. At first, he intentionally sat in the front row, so that he would be forced under the teacher's eye to pay attention. But when he felt "an enormous thirst for learning at fifteen or sixteen," he could no longer "waste the time" and moved to the back row, where he "devoured" as many books of his own choice in class as possible. This way of learning absorbed him so intensely that he could no longer take seriously his formal education. Later he changed jobs so frequently that feelings of inadequacy, he confesses, raised his doubts about what course he would follow, causing him to think his only options were to "become a criminal, a mental case, or a writer." Deciding that he "lacked the talents" for two of these possibilities, he chose to become a writer. According to him, he lives to write his "autobiography" in every literary genre he uses. His works: *Turning of the Head* (*Fejforgás*), short stories, 1971; *Notes from the Last Bench* (*Feljegyzések az utolsó padból*), short stories, and *Sonic Boom* (*Hangrobbanás*), a play, 1973; . . . *and other stories* (. . . *és más történetek*), 1975; *This Is What I Was* (*Én voltam ez*), short stories, and *You*

Won't Last Until Your Death (*Nem érsz halálodig*), a short novel, 1977. He has also contributed to the film and broadcast media: *Journey with Jakab* (*Utazás Jakabal*), a filmscript; *Intentional Homicide* (*Szándékos emberölés*), a radio play; and *Circumstances* (*Körülmények*) and *Murderers* (*Gyilkosok*), both plays for television.

His literary objective is "to relate something that will make both myself and my readers more complete," for, he declares, "literature is, like a can opener, only a tool." The totality of his commitment to reality as a writer is sharply expressed in his insistence that "he would not exchange bleak reality for a thousand invented stories." His prose writings are constructed with a sincerity approaching that of confessional works, but with sufficient aesthetic distance between the events of his own life and the characters and situations he develops; the style is based on the language of the world around him. Ironic in his analyses of the present state of civilization, Császár most often portrays the difficulties, the disenchantments, and the tensions of ordinary human beings, in order to convey instruction applicable to life generally.

A Break in the Film

Hajdú, as was his habit, went home drunk. When his wife heard the noise in the hall, she got up and went out. She watched her husband take off his coat and hang it on the rack. Hajdú lost his balance momentarily, clutched at the coat, and brought the rack crashing down. She didn't say a word. He stood there helplessly holding the coat, then clasped it to his breast with an affectionate hug.

"I'm home," he said to his wife.

"Have you had something to eat?" she asked.

"No."

They went into the kitchen and the woman put a saucepan of potatoes on to heat. Hajdú slumped down on a chair next to the table, still clutching the coat in his lap.

By the time she got back from the hall Hajdú had put the potatoes down in front of him and was eating them out of the pan with a spoon. There he sat, his head craned right over the pan, stuffing the food down.

"It didn't even get warm," his wife said.

Hajdú stopped eating and looked up.

"What are you staring at?" she asked. "You eat like a pig."

"Because the stuff you cook is swill," said Hajdú, with surprising logic. "It's swill what you cook, that's the truth. Your mother doesn't know how to cook and you don't either. You're barbarians, the whole family. You do everything just because you have to. That's not what life's about."

He took a scoop out of the food and thrust the loaded spoon into his mouth. The woman left him there and went off to bed.

They had been married for three years. He was the head of the fitters' section at the Housing Repairs Cooperative. He often went out on jobs to check up on the workmen. The fitters were for the most part old hands at the job. They'd seen quite a few section heads before Hajdú and had learned sooner or later to treat them all in the same way as they treated their tools. They called Hajdú "sir" and listened with exaggerated respect when he told them what to do. They waited for him to finish all his inspections and walked with him down to the corner, where they dragged him off for a glass of beer. Hajdú insisted on paying for his own drink, but by the time he had got to the cashier, the apprentice was already bringing back a little glass of cherry brandy and a mug of beer.

Hajdú could have turned the drink down, but he was only too aware how much younger and inexperienced he was than these old skilled workers he ordered about, and since his father and mother were both working people, he was ashamed of himself, strong and healthy man that he was, for having merely to stroll around or just sit behind a desk. To turn down the invitation would have meant that he was one of those pale bespectacled types who break out in a cold sweat if they ever touch a drop; either that, or the fitters would have thought he looked down on them. So he drank up the stupefying mixture of cherry brandy and beer, and if he didn't make his escape in good time they forced him to down another one as well.

The fitters didn't make out badly, because they pilfered materials and did work on the side during working hours, but this happened in every section head's time and it will go on happening in the future until the fitters themselves break the habit. The reason they forced drinks down Hajdú was not to get him to turn a blind eye to such things; they had no need to. It was just that they felt sorry for him for thinking he was such a terribly clever fellow.

"The rack's fallen down," said Hajdú in the morning, when he got up. He was standing in front of the bathroom mirror, shaving.

"You knocked it down," said his wife.

"I didn't touch it."

"Oh yes you did. You were reeling about drunk."

"I did have a bit to drink yesterday, you're right. But I didn't touch the rack."

"Don't you remember calling the meal I cook for you swill?"

"You're just saying that. I don't remember anything. I don't even remember coming home. Interesting, that. It's the second time something like that has happened. The last thing I remember about yesterday is feeling very drunk and setting off for home. I crossed the street and hailed a taxi. And that's it. After that I woke up here at home."

"You had a conversation with me as well," said his wife.

"I don't remember it," said Hajdú.

Some time later, when he was having a drink or two with the fitters, he told them about the incident, going off into peals of laughter, for they were on their third round by now.

"A touch of amnesia, Feri, my old pal," said Szántó. "That's what they call it. All proper boozers get it. You have a drink, then all of a sudden there's a break in the film."

"At last I've got something," said Hajdú, laughing again, as if he was tickled pink. "I'm at the tender age of twenty-eight, folks, and I've managed to get amnesia. Doctor Ferenc Hajdú, Accredited Amnesiac Extraordinary, Lecturer in the Department of Amnesia!"

The fitters laughed too. They could see he was a promising young fellow, this Hajdú.

In the evenings, when it got late, Hajdú's wife would pull up a chair to the open window and keep an eye on the street. She couldn't get to sleep until her husband came home. She would sit there leaning on the sill, dozing, with her head resting on her arms, but only for short spells. Whenever she heard the sound of footsteps she resumed her watch on the street—the policeman pacing along without a word, hurrying couples, mysterious old women, and drunks crooning raucously or breaking into squabbles. Curious scenes could be witnessed at such times in the herb-like fragrance of the night. Once, on the other side of the street, a gray-haired man was walking, leading a tiny girl and a small boy by the hand. The boy was carrying a violin case and saying something about a coffee pot, even though it was already past midnight. Hajdú's wife didn't take in such scenes; she waited impatiently for them to pass, as though they were the unavoidable preliminaries to her husband's return. She would have been unable to say why she waited up for him. Perhaps their relationship had deteriorated so rapidly that she hadn't had time to change her ways. She still went on waiting as though she believed the truth lay not in what was but in what had been. It was only after some time that she began to quarrel with her husband, and then in a rather strange way.

"What sort of chandelier is that?" asked Hajdú in the sitting room. "Have you gone and traded the place?"

"Eat your meal and go to bed," she said.

"A dazzling chandelier," Hajdú said.

"Sanyi's been here this evening," she said. "He brought it. He also put it up right away. Go to bed now."

"Oh, so you've been having guys over, defiling the sanctity of our home."

"I've told you, it was Sanyi who put it up. Your sister's husband."

"I'll bet you stood on the ladder and he ran his hand up under your skirt."

She looked at her husband, and suddenly it was a stranger she saw in front of her. A strange man with grubby shoes, a badly chosen ready-made suit and sweaty forehead, a puffy-faced fellow grinning stupidly at her, a man for whom she felt a dreadful hatred for forcing his way into her flat and her life.

"Of course he ran his hand up my skirt. And he didn't stop there either. He slid his sensual hand all the way up to my stomach," said Mrs. Hajdú, her lips growing numb with the lie she had invented. Never in all her life had she said anything like "sensual hand" before, but she now remembered that her brother-in-law's hands really were sensual.

"Did you sleep with him?" asked Hajdú, no longer laughing now.

"Yes, I did sleep with him!" shouted the woman. "I got fed up with always having to wait up for you. I hate you! You don't mean a thing to me anymore!"

She would have gone on, but Hajdú burst into tears, unnerved like a child.

"But I love you, I love you."

"I hate you. I detest you," she said.

Hajdú went over to the table and flopped down into a chair, his arms spread out before him on the table.

"Has it come to this?" he mumbled, and then, with a final sob, he let his head sink down on the table and began to snore.

"Go to bed," said the woman wearily. Hajdú looked up.

"Shall I?" he asked, and shuffled off to bed.

"How did I get home?" he asked the next morning.

"The way you always do," said his wife.

"I must have been pretty drunk," said Hajdú. "Don't be angry."

"Why should I be angry? I'm used to it by now," she said. and that was how they went on living.

When Hajdú came home drunk his wife, quivering with rage, would tell him how she had been unfaithful to him, and each time she managed to invent fresh details. Everything was explained with sickening precision. Hajdú wept, called his wife a dirty whore, blamed himself for everything, magnanimously offered to forgive her, flew into a rage, shouted that he would throw himself under a train, and in the morning could not remember a thing. He went on giving the fitters instructions with a sheepish grin on his face, reluctantly went out for drinks with them and watched helplessly as they plied him with round upon round.

Mrs. Hajdú often thought of divorcing her husband, but she was unable to make the decision, because it would have meant divorcing herself from everything, from her own self too, from the person she was and the person she wanted herself to be.

One day she carried out what she had threatened. She derived no pleasure from the miserable escapade, but she felt no sense of guilt either.

Their television set was repaired by a youth with the looks of a cuddly bear. He winked lazily when she began to flirt with him and simply seized her by the waist there and then, with a motion that might have been part of the repair job.

When Mrs. Hajdú gave him a twenty-forint tip in the hall he accepted it just as he always did.

"I've been on a bit of a spree," said Hajdú when he got home late that evening.

His wife was already in bed.

"Your meal's in the kitchen," she said and fell asleep. There were no stories that night, nor ever again.

Dezső Tandori

Tandori was born on December 8, 1938 in Budapest into a family with a long tradition of advanced education. His father was first a doctor of jurisprudence and then a certified public accountant. Tandori obtained a degree from the Loránd Eötvös University in Budapest to teach Hungarian and German in high school, and beginning in 1962, he taught German for nine years. He is now on the staff of the Hungarian People's Republic Art Foundation, as a translator and writer, most of his income coming from translating. Among the most important of his translations are: the poems of Johann Hölderlin, Heinrich Heine, Rainer Rilke, Georg Trakl, Gottfried Benn, and Bertolt Brecht; the dramas of Heinrich von Kleist; the prose of Franz Kafka, Karl Kraus, and Robert Musil (*Der Mann ohne Schatten*); and the treatises of Theodor Adorno, Thomas Mann, and Walter Benjamin. From English and American literature, he has translated the poems of John Keats, Lord Byron, Robert Browning, A. A. Milne, Samuel Beckett, Randall Jarrell, Elizabeth Bishop, and Sylvia Plath, and the prose of Virginia Woolf, Samuel Beckett, William Faulkner, and J. D. Salinger. Chiefly a poet, he has also published fiction and essays. He has received several prizes: the second prize of the International P. E. N. for poets under thirty, in a regional competition for Eastern and Central Europe, 1967; the Kassák Prize awarded by the periodical *Hungarian Workroom* (*Magyar Műhely*), which is being published in Paris, 1974; and the Milán Füst Creative Award in Budapest, 1975. His works are: *A Fragment for Hamlet* (*Töredék Hamletnek*), poems, 1968; *Clarification of Something Found* (*Egy talált tárgy megtisztítása*), poems,

1973; *The Ceiling and the Floor* (*A mennyezet és a padló*), poems, 1976; "*During the Night Koalas Walk Here*" ("*Itt éjszaka koalák járnak*"), short stories, 1977; *Bears in Infinite Numbers* (*Medvék minden mennyiségben*), children's poems, 1977; and *Why Do You Want to Live Forever?* (*Miért élnél örökké?*), a novel, 1977.

Like János Pilinszky, Tandori believes that human existence is bound by an inescapable finitude, and he looks at the limitations of place and time from the perspective of death. His tendencies toward skepticism and pessimism are expressed with linguistic ingenuity and seasoned with self-irony. He charts his inner world with a highly individualized virtuosity in ideas and verse techniques as well as bold experimentations with words and sounds. The exuberant playfulness of spirit and language so widely identified with his poetry—certain of its traits clearly showing the influence of e. e. cummings—first appeared in his second volume, and remains a source of challenging entertainment. In his third volume, he concentrates his craftsmanship on various lyric forms, including the sonnet, never abandoning his characteristic self-mockery.

Irreducibility
(Sketch for a Competition)

(Deletable auxiliary line)

    ALL DISTANCE IS *INFINITE*, IF THERE IS BETWEEN WHAT.

(Geometry)

    ALL *IS DISTANCE*, IF THERE IS BETWEEN WHAT.

(Paradox)

    ALL, IF THERE IS BETWEEN WHAT

(Correction)

    ALL IS *BETWEEN WHAT*.

(   )

    ALL *IS*

(

    *

*Omit *is* at this point

The Interview

"BATHOMORPHIC? PATHOMORPHIC? ALLOMORPHIC?
ALGOMORPHIC? ANDROMORPHIC? ACROMORPHIC?
ARCHIMORPHIC? BIOMORPHIC?
                                            MYOMORPHIC?
ENDOMORPHIC? EXOMORPHIC? ERGOMORPHIC?
HYDROMORPHIC? HYGROMORPHIC? HYMNOMORPHIC?
HYPNOMORPHIC? HYPSOMORPHIC?
                                        XENOMORPHIC?
ZOOMORPHIC?"
"Not so orphic. (Who fears Morpheus?)"

Cerebral Inions

A loathsome, frightening opinion
is forming, taking shape within one:
A pinion in the train is turn- (well—As a)
propelled by myosin (muscular plasma).

To love thy nearest neighbor as thyself
Take stock of your surroundings and Yourself.
To keep your head above rising waters.
Try to find Permanently Dry Quarters.

But no, but no, but no, but no.
I know, I know, I know, I know.
Oh yes, oh yes, oh yes, oh yes.
Certainly, really, nevertheless.

And that opinion, what is that? Just this:
Simply that our little friends'
lark, more than ever now, is not amiss.
Thus: myo-pinion.

The Belated Halt, or Dr. Jekyll's Dream

Mersault, then Murphy. These are important stations.
We clackety-clack right through them. Now Oran,
and now, Hyde Park. We throw cold water on
some lively arms waving at their relations,

(a daring image) or friends trapped on the train.
Then they depart, the people at the turnstile:
they know what's transient, and what remains.
It is quite clear, their guests coming by rail

have not arrived. Precisely: the train didn't stop.
Our boring expectations turn to nameless
excitements: But what about *me*? . . . my home? . . . my shop?

Which aren't the questions. Soon we cease to fault
our insulation from the "factual" world.
(With squealing brakes the train begins to halt!)

For the Klee-Milne Sketchbook

Let us set out into a charming landscape.
We're pleased enough; we don't want other kinds.
A rhyme is coming shortly, and a shape
(or shapes) not novel: often on our minds.

Where are we going. Do I have to say?
We've had a jolt already, at the ford
across the river, or the waterway—
that dull white strip dividing words from words.

We amble onwards with our gentle friends.
Signposts emerge: we note them as we pass—
our bears beside us on the road that wends

. . . where to? We've just begun, and round this bend
now turned, we see our pleasant journey was
a rambling preparation for *The End*.

Anna Kiss

Anna Kiss was born on January 26, 1939 in Gyula and grew up in Zsadány, both in Békés County, which borders on Rumania. All her ancestors were peasants and artisans, and she maintains that the character of her poetry and verse plays is dependent on and derives from this ancestry. While studying at the Debrecen Medical School, she frequently worked as an auxiliary nurse in several hospitals. After a successful two and a half years in her medical program, she decided to become a teacher and secured a diploma from the Szeged Teachers College in Hungarian and Russian. For a time she was a tutor in a school for children whose families lived on farms in the Hortobágy area of the Great Plains. Since 1963 she has taught in Budapest, living before "the judgmental eyes of children," which she considers "a natural state of affairs." She looks at many aspects of existence through their eyes, happy that she had "the courage to seek out my place in the world." She does not lead two lives, for "one must teach only the way one must write poetry. Only the agony of creating can elevate an individual to his fate." Gyula, Zsadány, and Debrecen are the places of her early meditations; Orosháza, also in Békés County, the place of her mature thought. Debrecen and the Hortobágy, she states, made her into a writer. Unable to list the names of all who have helped her with her life and problems, she thanks them with "every one of my writings, every year of my life." The fact that her life has never been easy has taught her many things, including the beliefs that "only a person with a conscience can have faith in anything," that "inhumanity is a boomerang," and that "the truth of poetry serves some kind of purpose." Her "closeness to the earth and the justice found in the folk tale," she maintains, give her "faith and a sense of security." Her works are: *Wooden Puppet* (*Fabábú*), poems, 1971; *Black Ring* (*Feketegyűrű*), poems, 1974; *Hauntings* (*Kísértenek*), poems, and *The Two Oxen* (*A két ökör*) and *The Fortress* (*A vár*), two verse dramas, 1976.

These three books of poetry are clearly rooted in the village and city life of the Great Plains. Her early poems show an ambivalence toward her existence in that setting, as, for example, in the metaphor of the "Wooden Puppet," which weeps because it would like to become a human being. Eventually, however, she seeks an understanding of life not by communing with nature but by inventing a mythology from that world and populating it with such images of medieval superstition and magic as sorcerers, witches, and ghosts, among whom she herself sometimes appears. The folk song and ballad dominate her early poetry, the prose poem her recent work.

The Birth of the Tale

Moon changes in the blind mirror,
A shiny thread catches on my fingers,
Three elders on the edge of my bed
Weave, spin,
Select the years.
I hear that only the lean years
Yield such seeds . . .
It is dawn. It is quiet.
Where are they?
To the maimed tree they have tethered
Three stars to shine.

In the Vineyard

Finally, the colors are together
In the vintage light,
I sit at the base
Of plundered-happy vines,
Rust-colored, rattling yellow
Iron sulphate
Turns on me;
Black vines chased me so far,
I listen to the leaves,
At whose edges
The fire, the stain of my burned days
Trickles into my lap,
The wild oat, too,
Leans on me
Its empty head,
"Do not fear," it says,
"Do not fear."

Silence

Farmstead, close to the sky and far from the roads.

The colts are dreaming of salt bread and they paw the flooring, the shade of sleeping ricks is blue, the sparsely foliaged trees are wan, the third cock-crow dies away.

Early summer cool from rains.

The Sunday fields are quiet, the young animal steps into foxholes, looks in through the window: On the shelf a copper coffee roaster, on the table bread and an almanac.

A peacock preens.

The soldier walks around the house and goes to the well. He drinks. His beard reaches into the water.

With a single motion, he reaches for his key; inside, he finds clothes; he buries what he has on in the hay ricks.

A broken pencil in the almanac.

"Do not mourn, I am alive."

Then he takes the bread, puts the key in its place, leaves.

He is ponderous, like the earth itself.

He melts easily into the silence.

Gentian, full-grown, everywhere

Gentian, full-grown, everywhere,
gentian everywhere, grown full.
Densely lettered stones.

Dark-blue gentian, darker winds
rushing through the gentian.
And the haunting stars.

Hearts and hearts. The fall's red trees.
Letters and firm stones erode.

The water's back is stronger.

Two Little Snakes

Two little snakes
walk in my wake
on their own legs
two little snakes.

My many ills
proliferatin'

out to the world
my heart they straighten.

My many troubles
vindicatin'

in secret gardens
liberatin'

my heels for travel
acceleratin'.

József Utassy

Utassy was born on March 23, 1941 in Ózd, near the Czechoslovakian border, where his father lived in a barracks as a laborer and on Saturdays traveled by bicycle to his home in Bükkszenterzsébet. Forced to change jobs frequently, his father worked in a mine and a quarry, and was a seasonal contract worker in Germany for three years. About him Utassy writes: "Then came the draft, the Don River Bend, and that moment when a German private valued oat fodder more than the lives of my father and his brothers-in-arms—in three-degree weather somewhere in the vicinity of Minsk. (Through the good graces of a military doctor we received all his belongings from Minsk; even his ring had been filed off his finger.) He was buried on February 19, 1943." Utassy was not quite two years old at the time. His mother made their living as a day-worker and seamstress. He completed elementary school in Bükkszenterzsébet and Tarnalelesz, both towns in Heves County, and received his high school diploma in 1959 in Eger, in the center of a famous wine-growing area. He then worked for three years as a clerk in the National Savings Bank, a share-thresher, and an elocutionist in Pétervásár, also in Heves county. In 1961 he was admitted to Loránd Eötvös University in Budapest, but because he was frequently absent, he was not permitted to take his examinations. He wound up for a time as a laborer at the sheet iron works in Borsodnádasd, in Borsod County, and then returned to the university. On graduation in 1967, he worked in the library of the Hungarian Ship and Crane Factory (Magyar Hajó- és Darugyár), but after a short while, he took a position as a teacher in the student dormitory of a vocational school associated with the building industry. After five years, in August 1972, he freed himself from such occupations because he had to "give myself body, soul, and spirit to my calling as a writer: otherwise, nothing doing!" In 1973 he participated in the International Festival of Poets at Struga, and in 1974 he was a Zsigmond Móricz Fellow. His works are: *My Fire, My Flag!* (*Tüzem, lobogom!*), poems, 1969; and *Orphan of the Stars* (*Csillagok árvája*), poems, 1977.

Utassy strongly identifies with the social order of present-day Hungary as he searches for his own and his country's role in the world. His poems are full of both rhythmic and imagistic tensions, in ways suggesting the influence of Ferenc Juhász and László Nagy. Although the jaunty air of his youthful verses is occasionally present, his thoughts have deepened. His responses to the burdens of life affirm his belief in the integrity of the human spirit and his deep commitment to the common people.

Illegal Honeymoon

It's dark here now,
like in a can of sandwich-spread.

I lie on my back on the bed.
You lie on your back on the bed.

Outside, under the concrete sill,
a cricket, hallucinating, trills.

Burned down to a lacquer between your fingers
the flickering end of a cigarette lingers.

You take a drag. I see your breasts.
Beneath them, two large shadow-scythes.

We do not speak. Our quilt's a mist.
The bed takes slow and vigilant strides.

Illegal honeymoon, undercover!
Your hair is the halo round the face of your lover.

On our bodies stars burst into flower.

"Good?"
"Oh very!"
"Love me?"
"I love you!"

Moonlight, and bedspread of dust.
Hungary snores out loud.

Trains' lonesome whistles.
You sleep. I kiss your mouth.

Quiet. The bell peeps.
Yawning, with iambic step
the old housekeeper goes to open the gate.

And you grumble, still half-asleep:
"Set the alarm ahead for eight."

Envious

A tiny cricket
has built his home
here in my room.
That's him singing right now,
just to the right,
just out of sight.

After Harvest

Wine press at rest.
Deafening smell of must.
In my ears, music
     plays without sound.

In the yard, grapes
and drunken wasps
     stagger around.

Your Pennies

Here, for example, we have this beggar.
But where, I wonder, can his left leg be?
For the beggar, the beggar is here, you see.
And his homeland is mine!

That little bowl there simply's got to go.
Let it wobble up to heaven and become a moon!
Night is cawing, winter's coming soon.
Your pennies are twinkling.

Gábor Czakó

Czakó was born on September 14, 1942 in Decs, a town of about 5000 inhabitants in southern Hungary. His father, who was a toolmaker, electrician, and photographer, disappeared during the battle at the Don River Bend in 1943; his mother, the daughter of a carpenter, raised him and an older brother by operating his father's photographic shop. He completed high school in 1960 in Szekszárd, a few kilometers north of Decs. After studying art for a year in Budapest, he went to Pécs and completed law studies at the university there in 1965. He then served for a year as an instructor to inmates at the Prison for Juveniles at Tököl, in the County of Pest on Csepel Island in the Danube. From 1966 to 1972 he was employed as a legal adviser, first by a business firm, next by a cooperative farm, and finally by the Central Corporation of Banking Companies. Since 1972 he has supported himself entirely by writing, mainly short stories and novels but also sociographic studies, plays, and some poetry. His first book, *The Room (A szoba)*, a short novel concerned with the connection between living conditions and the development of human character, appeared in 1970. It was followed by: *Human Garden (Emberkert)*, short stories and tales, 1971; *Passionate Reports (Indulatos jelentések)*, a collection of his sociographic writings, 1973; *The Savior (Megváltó)*, a novel, 1974; *A Fight Every Blessed Day (Csata minden áldott nap)*, a novel for children, 1975; *School Fortress (Iskolavár)*, a novel attacking the traditional modes of education and, at the same time, exploring the major points of the existing social order in Hungary, 1976; and *A Tragic Play about a Villainous Mangalicz Pig, who . . . Received his Deserved Punishment*

(*Tragikus játék egy hitvány Mangalicza sertésről, aki . . . elnyerte méltó büntetését*), a comedy, 1976.

Czakó experiments with different techniques, indicating, perhaps, his search for that harmony between narrative mode and theme essential to the unique expression of his personal intellectual perspective. For example, in "The Cat," as in all the tales published in *Human Garden*, he turns, for a model, to the classical animal fable—a not uncommon practice among Hungarian authors—in *The Savior* to the parable, and in *School Fortress* to realism. Regardless of the particular narrative mode, Czakó always focuses on moral issues, not by analyzing thoroughly the set of circumstances in which behavior occurs but by portraying the innermost traits of a character's personality, to suggest not societal but individual responsibility for the inescapable ethical act.

The Cat

The cat didn't like sitting at home in her old age. Although it was winter and bitter cold, she still preferred to loiter about or in gardens. She didn't miss the warmth very much and she didn't have young anymore that she needed to play with at home. So she would rather loaf and see the world.

About two springs ago she ran into an old lacy-eared tom: from habit they tortured each other in the attic, but nothing came of it. But she liked kittens. Every year she brought three or four and sometimes five into the world. Now that there weren't any more, she didn't miss them. It's the order of things.

She walked slowly on the trampled-down sidewalk. The snow was deep. People didn't bother to clean all the sidewalk but only a shovel-wide path in the middle that was marked like a wall by the high snow. Small streets broke off it to the left, leading to the entrance of houses—at the threshold they widened to small squares.

Slowly she was nearing the end of the street. Here, between the houses, was the old cemetery. They weren't using it anymore; the cemetery was small, and the living outgrew it. When she was young, she often came hunting here. The wide branches of the linden trees surrounding the large cross provided an excellent place for hiding, and birds also liked to build their nests in the thick foliage. That's where she was heading.

In front of the last house, a dog was sitting on the small square. An iron-gray sheep dog. She knew only that during the summer he accompanied the shepherd and lived with the sheep in the meadow. His eyes did not match. Gray-brown.

Steel-gray with a warm brown. She looked at him. She tried to sneak by; she hadn't heard anything good about sheepdogs. After the meadows, the street and yard are too small for them, and they have an inferiority complex in relation to the village animals. They are quarrelsome because they always want to prove something.

The dog was peacefully sitting on his hind legs. He moved his paws forward a bit. He didn't say anything. The cat, holding her head sideways, took a step forward and was measuring the dog with uncertain glances. Long ago she wouldn't even have noticed such a meeting. She would spit once, and if it was necessary, scratch, and then be out of sight. Now it's not so easy. There is snow. Deep snow, and the fence is far away. But anyway, one can only walk past here; nicely, with dignity, without excitement. No running. This is a sheep dog. He is in shape, quick, and there is the snow, deep snow, and she wouldn't be able to touch the ground.

"I'll try talking to him." She stopped and looked at the dog, but he was sitting on the threshold, relaxed, superior. He didn't seem inclined to converse.

"I'm lost!" Terror started jumping in her heart. "I shouldn't have stopped." Moaning, she tried to say something, but the dog with a single look, silenced her. She was terribly afraid.

"If I go on, nothing will happen, maybe he won't even notice me. I can only run now." She calmed down a bit. "Which shall it be?"

She took off; gathering up all her energy, she ran. That's what the dog was waiting for.

"Where are you going?" he yelled and threw himself after her. With an unusual side canter, like after sheep.

The cat had a head start, and she felt she was running as never before. The icy air rushed into her lungs; it seemed to burn. Soon her ears began to ring and flaming circles began to dance in front of her eyes, but she kept running.

"Don't let the road end, don't let the road end!" she was imploring silently. She felt the dog nearer and nearer. "Forward! Forward!" The fence fell behind and the path turned to the right, toward the highway.

She came to a sudden stop. An enormous snow pile blocked the road. She threw herself over it. Snow! Snow everywhere! Deep snow! She kneaded desperately, she sank up to her chest, she pulled her legs out and crawled on. The resumption of the path appeared a good two jumps away.

"If I could just get there!" The sharp powdery snow blew into her eyes, melted there, weighed down her fur, but she drove on.

Then she stopped. She could tell the end had come. In front of her stood the dog, towering above her high and dark. He snickered. White teeth flashed from his blood-red mouth.

He grabbed her by the neck, but in such a way that her head, slightly askew, looked down his throat. Stinking hot air and flapping tongue slapped her in the face. The dog slowly, almost considerately, carried her to the top of the snow mound, but because of the bad grip, her neck ached horribly.

They returned to the road. She calmed down. She remembered the linden trees, the spring miaows, and her kittens. Beautiful gay kittens. White, black, red, dun, mottled, depending on who the father was. Then she remembered that she too, with a similar grip, but ever more gently, used to carry them from one den to another.

Miklós Veress

Veress was born in Barcs, a small town on the Drava River in Somogy County, on January 13, 1942 in house number 13, which led him to observe that he could not have started life with "a better poetical prognosis," since "a poet reaps when hail has destroyed the wheat." His mother was a native of the province, which is inhabited by Croatians as well as Hungarians. His father's family, all artisans, had moved from Kiskundorozsma in Csongrád County to Arad in Transylvania, when impoverished by the famous Szeged flood in 1879. From there his father had gone to Budapest first as a student, then as an actor. Later, traveling in the country as a civil servant, he found himself in Barcs. Veress makes special mention of two childhood memories: a bombed-out home in Budapest from which the family barely managed to escape and a ruined marriage followed by his parents' divorce. His mother and her relatives raised him in Barcs until he became seriously ill with meningitis, which left him with chronic pneumonia. He completed school in Kaposvár, the largest city in Somogy County, and then specialized in Hungarian and Russian studies at the University of Szeged from 1960 to 1965. After receiving his degree and teaching in a high school for a time, he became a journalist with a small newspaper in Szeged, and then, from 1969 to 1974, he worked on the staff of *Southern Hungary* (*Délmagyarország*), the city's long-established newspaper. He has lived in Budapest since 1974, where he first worked on the staff of *Life and Literature* (*Élet és Irodalom*), and then, asked to do so, he established and is now managing editor of *Moving World* (*Mozgó Világ*), a literary, fine arts, and critical journal featuring the most current authors. He began to write and translate poetry during his school days in Kaposvár. During his time at the university, he was already know as someone who frequently published poems. His first book of poetry, *Forest for the Beasts* (*Erdő a vadnak*), appeared in 1972, after he had experienced serious lung surgery and an unfortunate marriage. He translates frequently, mainly from Russian literature. His remaining works are: *King of Sheet Iron* (*Bádogkirály*), poems, 1975; and *Snowy Morning* (*Hóreggel*), poems for children, 1977.

Veress uses verse forms ranging from the sonnet to the ancient forms of Hungarian poetry to the sayings of children in his attempt to synthesize the clashes he finds between traditional and modern ideas, the mind and the heart, and belief and skepticism. His long history of illness has resulted in a troubled and philosophical relationship with life, his views often reflecting the influence of Kierkegaard and Sergei Bulgakov. His own confrontations of a vast Nothingness confirm his belief that the possibilities of human action are tragically limited, that no one can escape from the prison of his body, and that the elements of love, history, faith, and destiny are condensed in the human condition. Veress finds a measure of consolation in the death of a star: ". . . nothing weeps amid such beauty/with such struggling bitterness/ as a star plunging into the void." A highly regarded critic, the late Géza Féja, insists that "there is no trace of pessimism, the escape of weaklings, in his poetry," that "a renewed strength, hence an escape, springs out of his tormented feeling toward the tragic in life."

Mothers

      nothing can hurt the way mothers are hurt by age
      when they hunt after snapshots in worn-down drawers
      and in the stove lonesomely the evenings blaze
      nothing can hurt more

            somewhere the woodworm scratches ever
            yellow ships are on the rug
            once per month the dear boy's letter
            asks for cash and grub

      nothing can hurt the way holidays hurt mothers
      when in twilit windows they wait in vain
      for noisy children to come running from the rain
      nothing can hurt more

            their ancient dresses then loom dark
            a letter comes and cuts to the quick
            the neighbors go inside to prate
            and words hurt mothers' hearts

      for nothing can hurt the way mothers are hurt by sympathy
      when a shadow sits on the creaking corner chair
      and the cups grow dusty listlessly
      nothing can hurt more

            for themselves alone then they make their tea
            and their shadows reach out wide
            mothers then do softly sleep
            and the wrinkles on their face subside

Death of Planets

The fog has fallen on winter night
and night will be white once again
Locked fist-deep in stone a star's ablaze
and inside the death of planets spins

An arm to heaven: a puny stalk of weed
leans and entreats with the shifting wind
The grass shudders the muddy sick yellow
stoops in spite And with it time swings

January blue northern blue like pines
that glimmer by day through ruddy fires:
frozen galaxies with needly leaves

On their bony boughs a tiny silence sings
like a blind bird: and out from under hoarfrost life
an upward-thrust and curdling world

Ballad

There's a window without a house. It sways.
Its pane is celluloid.

Behind it suicided planets blaze
and a face weeps to the void.

Elsewhere not here or merely set away
from each other are the place and time.

It pains its mother and in shudderingly joyful fever the infant whines.

There is white mourning in my smile
in your star-eyes, midnight.

We are but birds in a house that flies
and not a window in it.

Benedek Kiss

Kiss was born on March 19, 1943 in Akasztó, in Bács-Kiskun County. Having known only village life and culture until he was fourteen, he definitely is tied to the people and land between the Danube and Tisza rivers, a fact attested to by the subject matter, imagery, and diction of his poetry. Both sides of his family came from that level of the peasantry from which there had been considerable movement into industrial and professional occupations. Unfortunately for him, his parents' marriage dissolved very quickly. His mother, who raised him and a younger brother, is still employed as a seamstress. His father, with whom Kiss constantly quarreled even after the separation, was educated for the priesthood by his Greek Orthodox family, but abandoned this career before his ordination and worked with a road construction company until he retired. Kiss attended high school in Kalocsa in 1943 and received a degree in Hungarian and adult education from the Loránd Eötvös University in Budapest, where he has lived ever since. He wanted to become a journalist and actually served as an apprentice at some newspapers while a university student. But he took a position as a resident teacher at a vocational institute. Before long, however, he decided to become independently employed, and for the last ten years he has, despite some periods of hardship, devoted his energies entirely to writing, chiefly poems, which first began appearing in journals and anthologies in 1967. Recently he started to translate from the works of Bulgarian poets, some of whom he became acquainted with during a two-month fellowship in Bulgaria, and he has begun to write poetry for children. His works are:

Derelict Season (*Gazdatlan évszak*), poems, 1970; *Paths, Peace be with You!* (*Békesség nektek, utak!*), poems, 1973; and *Top, Top, Wooden Top* (*Csiga, csiga, facsiga*), children's verses, 1976. He was awarded the Attila József Prize in 1979.

His poems, linked somewhat to the tradition represented by László Nagy, are preoccupied with the relationship between humankind and nature, with love between men and women, and with the world of human emotions. They are original and energetic in their use of wide-ranging imagery. Totally devoted to the expression of beauty, his lyrics, especially those in his first volume, vibrate with lively concreteness and association of images, usually developed cohesively in short lines; and they convey an incorruptibility of the human spirit and a feeling of human community.

White Field

A slim white fountain pen
on a white field.

Where will it go next?

In the darkness of blood
in the dark bloody night
where will it go next?

A scrawny hunting dog
carries a dead rabbit,
a partridge.

The hunter gorges himself on these
and moves on
sickening nicotine nausea in his knapsack
with holy futility.

And ahead
the darkness of blood
the dark bloody night
and in the sleeping night
a white field.

Unmarked, the white field.

The Winter Moon

Winter moon
I love the winter moon!
Blazen horses charging at midnight
neighing at the winter moon.
A stallion bites at the snow, aflame—
a mare glows white hot in the fire of her teeth.
At midnight fevered slush
is foaming noisily
on soft pastures.

By the time morning stumbles over the children's sleds
in the bushy darkness,
gray and proud and prancing, they halt:
hoofprints, a few ragged dreams
torn apart in front of our bloody eyes
and the land grows numb
with cautious enamel.

An Old Stag

The fire of his hooves crackles the dry grass
and fallen leaves—
the red eyes of the old stag
shine out through the smoke,
swirling, as at daybreak.

Decrepit and beaten, a dog bares his jaws
and grinds his teeth.
What kind of stag has red eyes?
Links of chain, a hunter,
the jaws of a trap.

What Do I Want?

I don't want anything
that isn't on my mother's lap.

I don't want anything—
the moon is bloody against the sky.
A knife tossed aside,
in among the violets—
someone threw it there.
Who planted it
there among the violets in the meadow?

My life falls apart into fibers
Shame sends out roots to surround me
So what can I want out of this?

Only what is in my mother's lap!

György Petri

Petri was born on December 22, 1943 in Budapest into a family of civil servants. He has, since boyhood, wanted to be "a poet and something more than just a poet." After graduation from high school, he worked at various jobs for four years, including occupational therapy at a mental hospital; having developed an interest in psychology in late adolescence, he found this job the most interesting. His desire to become a psychiatrist lasted until he learned that psychology contained "more playful fantasy than authoritative knowledge." He finally discovered in philosophy the sphere, in addition to poetry, in which his interests meet, he hopes, his potentialities. In 1966, when twenty-three, he undertook the study of philosophy at the Loránd Eötvös University. A few of his poems appeared in periodicals between 1960 and 1965, including the important *Contemporary* (*Kortárs*) and *Life and Literature* (*Élet és Irodalom*). But his productivity increased substantially during the second half of the decade, especially during 1968-1969. His works are: *Explanations for M* (*Magyarázatok M. számára*), poems, 1971; and *Circumscribed Tumble* (*Körülírt zuhanás*), poems, 1974. The main intent of the first was "to evoke a tangible individual through the real motives of my life and not some sort of generality scattered among visions." The second has, he believes, attained "a more rudimentary and thus a more suitably aesthetic communication" and also reduced his "dictatorial demands regarding the interpretation of the verses"—a change not implying regret about having published the first volume, for "many kinds of poetry are possible and necessary. (Though, perhaps, not all kinds.)"

György Petri

Petri's sense of the fragmentary nature of life and the agonizing impotence of human beings in the face of that reality is stylistically expressed in ways more commonly found in the lyric poetry of the West, particularly that of T. S. Eliot, whose methods of composition, Petri acknowledges, have helped him to relax the traditional boundaries of the lyric. His lyric style is intellectual, detached, and ironic. Usually connecting daily problems with philosophical and historical considerations, he voices a deep pessimism about the human prospect, a pessimism which István Vas calls "a certain vigorous and honest pessimism . . . that must carry out its own faith, its own harmony."

Once Again

        Once again
        the solitary swimming pools.
        The beach chairs.
        Lavish sunshine
        spraying tired bodies.
        Soon the wind
        will peck away
        at my body-long watery imprint.
        The shower is a stupor
        of heat and vapor.
        Booming on the nape of my neck:
                        a fragmented ray.

Only a Person

If I could be
only a person to you,
definitive but incidental
like a bent rusty nail
in the warm dust,
like a lonely gleam
atop the shaded stairs.

Only one person's immersion
haphazard, in the flow of time.

If for one single moment I could be
timeless
as time evaporates; if I could be
your frozen property.

If I could be—until
the rung lies in the shade, until
the nail crumbles away—

only a person to you.

Xenia

Light, water, salt, bread,
dill and mustard seed:

Our cucumber has gingerly
matured into a pickle.

It has absorbed the elements.
The child of nature and of art.

Meeting

You come toward me across the room
in endless approach—feet treading space,
getting nowhere,
dressed in the same impossible colors
you wore in the coffin:
green cardigan, calf-length flannel skirt,
dull gray woolen stockings.
You come across the room
(I hear my mother puttering in the kitchen)
with your childlike, trustful, toothy smile,
and I stand up with a nervous smile.
My God, how can I say
it's hopeless! I can't live with you,
You've risen from the dead in vain.

Lovers

On the honey-ooze split-
open plum, a bee is dying.
Together
they are scorching, rotting
goldened, blackened
in the abandoned garden.

Inscription

The era of cactus and sand is coming upon us
—friendship's end.
An end, all you dear ones, to loving.
Love
encapsulated,
wind-born,
will harden like quartz.
Present—it withholds its presence.

Grace

    he with whom fate toys graciously
    will find himself light suddenly
        serene empty
    teetered by death on a fingertip
        eggshell upon a waterjet

Géza Bereményi

Bereményi, who was born on January 25, 1946 in Budapest, was as a child raised by his aged maternal grandparents, who operated a small vegetable and fruit store. Later he went to live with his mother and foster father, a physician. He spent his childhood on Teleki Square, in a building in which retired elderly ladies and small shopkeepers lived. He was about four years old, when he listened to freight handlers and idlers, warming themselves there in his grandparents' kitchen, reading aloud stories about Tarzan and the Wild West, for which his grandfather gave them a few coins. On some Sundays a disabled soldier would take Bereményi to the Kerepesi Cemetery, next to Teleki Square, to spit on the grave of Artúr Görgey, a general during the 1848-1849 Revolution who surrendered his forces to the invading Russian army in 1849. He grew up among individuals who did not understand very much about life but who, according to him, maintained themselves in their own distinctive, even heroic way. He completed high school at a small provincial college. He obtained a teaching diploma from the faculty of philosophy at the Loránd Eötvös University in Budapest, and afterward worked for one year at a book-distributing agency.

By the time of his graduation, his writings had begun to appear in provincial periodicals and anthologies, and a volume of his short stories, *The Swedish King* (*A svéd kiraly*), was published in 1970. His writings continue to appear in anthologies and journals, including *A Legendary* (*Legendarium*), a serialized novel, completed in the spring of 1979 and consisting of juxtaposed past and present historical situations. Besides fiction, Bereményi has written a musical called *I Am Thirty* (*Harmincéves vagyok*), four plays, and numerous songs, some of which have been set to music in the films of a noted director, Miklós Jancsó, and others on a popular record entitled *Letter to my Sister* (*Level nővéremnek*). A film, *Romance* (*Romantika*), based on his scenario, appeared in 1972, and his newest play, *A Cubic Centimeter of Air* (*Légköbméter*), was premiered at the Comedy Theater (Vígszínház) in Budapest during the 1978-79 season.

His fiction is directed not at exploring the metaphysical implications of individual actions but at enriching the understanding of moral behavior and human choice, often in situations from the historical past. His writing skill and his erudition are, in the opinion of many critics, equaled by very few authors of his generation.

Last Spin on the Water

Responding to the bell, Márta opened the door. Her eyes took my measure, and when her look settled on my face, she clapped her hands together.
"Well!"
"What's wrong with you?" I asked.
"How ugly a man is when he's drunk."
"Don't be crazy," I said. "I'm cold sober."
She shook her head scornfully.
"Of course, you always say that."
"Because you are always silly about this thing."
"I'm ashamed of myself, Miklós."
"In my place, right?"
"Yes, in your place, Miklós."
"Since when is my name Miklós?"
"Since you became a drunkard. All drunks are called Miklós."
I squeezed her against the wall, gently hit her head against it a few times, and whispered in her ears:
"Tell me about your sister; you and your opinion don't interest me."
"Let go." She tried to escape my grip.
"You dummy," I said, "I'm stronger than you."
"I'm stronger," she panted.
"Then beat me up."
I pressed her shoulders against the wall because I didn't want to touch her

breasts; her hands, which were free, struggled to no avail, trying to push my arms away. Finally she pushed my chin back. I laughed, looking at the hall ceiling.

"You are stronger?"

"Yes." Again she tried to escape from my arms.

"Then how do you explain this failure?"

"You drunken animal!" she raged.

"Enough," I said. "Well, who is stronger?"

"I am."

"All right, you are," I agreed, because I was already bored by it all. "But then I have better technique."

I wanted to knock her head against the wall again, but I became too cocksure and Márta escaped. I grabbed her and threw her into the corner, and grinding my teeth, I approached her threateningly.

"Who has a better technique?"

"You do."

I pulled her ear repeatedly.

"Who is the only one in the world leading a moral life in the present moment?"

"You are," Márta said.

"Who is the most beautiful?"

"You are."

I grabbed her arms, and she could sense from my voice that I was ready for anything.

"Who is drunk?"

"I am," she whispered.

I patted her on the shoulder and lit a cigarette. This was how I gained victory over Márta.

"Are you coming to the Danube?" I asked.

"Now?"

"If you like, we can leave fifteen minutes from now."

"The weather is bad."

"Then I'll go alone."

The frig. stood by the door. Márta took out a bottle of wine and went into the kitchen. I followed.

"Well, will you come? You don't have to swim, if you don't want. We'll go see Csaba."

"Does he live there now?"

"He's renting a cottage. We'll buy something to drink and have dinner there. It's not far on the bus."

She filled a glass with wine and gave it to me.

"Mari is here," she said.

"Don't be silly." I stared out of the kitchen window. It was possible to see the hallways of two floors, windows, doors, a woman leaning on the railing looking at the rain-laden, unpredictable sky.

"Did she decide to come home?" I asked, still gazing out, and only then did I turn my face toward Márta. She was shrugging her shoulders.

"Well then?" I asked. "What's with her?"

I drank the wine.

"You recommend I leave now, right?"

She shrugged her shoulders, and I put down the glass.

"You dirty drunkard," she said. "You drunken beast."

But I had already passed through the kitchen door and crossed the hallway. I only knew that Márta remained propped against the kitchen cabinet as if I were still pushing her by the shoulders. I stopped at the door. I would never have believed this about myself.

"Hello, Mari," I said.

She snatched the book to her face and peeked out from behind it. Then, as if she were playing, she hid her face once again. By then I realized it was hopeless.

Their room was large and a mess; there were two beds, one Mari's and the other Márta's. Poor reproductions hung on the wall. There were a few on the shelves propped against the books that were somewhat better.

I pulled a chair up to the bed and lit a cigarette. She peeked out from behind the book, then held it up to her face again. I remember that written on its jacket in large letters was: Angyal Gigi. And a female head with thin lines. I knocked on the jacket.

"Hello!"

I repeated this game with the book a third time; she quietly laughed. I knocked again.

"Hello!"

Then she lowered the book and we looked at each other.

"Home again?" I asked. "A fine thing, I can say. Circles under your eyes."

"And your face is swollen," I heard her say.

"Home for a visit?" The cigarette was shaking in my hands as if I had been arm-wrestling with Csaba for several hours. Then I lit it.

"I have a few clothes here. Only for that."

"Don't you have enough there?"

"We're going on a trip."

"You're going on a trip?" I asked.

"Will you give me a cigarette?" I took one out of the pack and put it between her lips.

"Will he marry you?"

"He wants to get married but I'm not sure yet."

"Why didn't you give me a call?"

She shrugged her shoulders and made a funny face.

"Are you sorry we're meeting now?" I asked further.

"I didn't think it could be avoided. Márta said you have been coming up often and were questioning her."

"Are you sorry we met?"

"Well, yes and no."

"Why yes and no?"

"Because I want to know how things are going with you. It's awful not to know what you are doing."

"Why?"

"Because I can see that you still can't believe I've left you."

"What shall I do?" I asked. "I want to do what's best for you. What shall I do? Tell me."

"I don't know."

"Don't shrug your shoulders or I'll hit you in the mouth," I said. I could tell she was really frightened.

"Let's go to the movies," I invited her.

"Not possible," she shook her head.

"It's not allowed? Have they forbidden it?"

"I don't have time, I have to pack."

"Are you leaving tomorrow?"

"Yes."

"Have a pleasant trip." I stood up. I stood there at a loss and looked into her eyes. Lines like the spokes of a wheel ran in them.

"Don't go yet," she said. "Say something. What are you doing these days?"

"Nothing."

"What about Bodor?"

"He's getting married."

"Who to?"

"You don't know her. She's new."

"And you. Are you getting married?"

"Later," I said. "Come out to the Danube."

"In this weather? And anyway, I said I didn't have time."

"Must you pack?"

"Yes."

"Too bad."

I really wanted to leave now.

"Say something, what's up?"

"Nothing." I thought for a moment. "Unless . . ."

"What?"

"Well, what do you think?"

"You got someone pregnant."

"No."

"Does it have anything to do with me?" she asked.
"No."
"Just with you?"
"Yes."
"Something important?"
"Very important."
"Serious?"
"Most serious."
"Are you getting married?"
"No."
"Then I don't know."
"Try," I egged her on.
"You are going on a trip?"
"Maybe."
"It's connected with the trip?"
"Yes."
"You got a car?"
"Something better. Anyway, I don't have that much money."
"You've bought a lot?"
"Something better."
"A scholarship to Lebanon?"
"No."
"Tell me!"
"A yacht," I said finally.
"What is a yacht?"
"A double cabin on a motorboat, with an English motor. Up to Bratislava, Vienna, down to the Iron Gate."
"It's not true!"
"Good," I shook my head. "It's not true."
"What's it called?" she asked quickly.
"Péter I."
"When did you buy it?"
"Last Friday."
"Where do you keep it?"
"In a marina. In the Habselyem resort marina. The boatkeeper is called Károly. His bathing trunks are blue denim and he wears a necktie."
"Why don't you ask me to see it?"
"You were the one who said you had to pack."
Now I sat down. "I'll get over her," I thought. "Let her go on the trip, at least I'll get over her."
"How much did it cost?"
"It's used. Nineteen hundred forints. Csaba and I went halves. We got an ad-

vance for a movie script we're writing. I have a typewriter as well." Not an exceptional one, I thought meanwhile.

"Are you glad?" I asked.

"About the boat? Very. But only if you are."

"I'm glad," I said.

"Then I am too. You finally have something. We still have your tent. Now I'll return it, and at night you can set it up on the bank."

"I can set it up on top of the cabin too," I said. "Then four can sleep on the boat. It consumes six liters, we can stand that. Are you glad mostly because you can leave freely?"

"Yes, and no, too."

"Does he have a car?" I asked.

"No, only a wife and kids."

"I know," I said. "But he was able to rent an apartment."

"Why, where should we live?"

"Where did we live?"

"That was different."

"Do you love him?" I asked.

"It's possible. Aren't we going to look at the boat?"

"If you wish. It's full of gas, we can take a spin on the water. Csaba is out there."

"Good, but only a spin. Let's hurry."

The rain was already pouring in thick threads on the roof and into the four corners of the courtyard. When we passed the kitchen window in the passage, I didn't look in. You little dummy, I thought of Márta as she gazed after us leaning against the kitchen cabinet.

"A summer shower," I said to Mari. "You'll hide in the cabin, you'll be able to see from there too. Only a narrow strip of rushing water will be visible, but it will be interesting as the raindrops dig small funnels on the river and we dash between them. It's useless for you to shout down there because the noise of the motor drowns out your voice, the wind is strong, and the air cuts your face. We'll buy a bottle of wine and take it along too. You'll see, the Danube is wonderful even in the rain."

"Only one spin," said Mari. "Then I'll have to go."

The bus rushed on.

"Have you ever been on a motor boat in the rain?" I asked.

"No. And you? Have you?"

"Yes, I have. It was raining last Friday when we first went out with Csaba."

"It was really raining," she said.

"A summer shower. It will probably stop by the time we get out there."

But it was still raining when we got off the bus. We ran between summer cottages, their windows and doors shut tight. The street was deserted, only a man wearing a hooded raincoat was walking barefoot, stepping slowly into the water on the asphalt.

We stopped in front of an imposing family house with a fence.

"Csaba!" I yelled.

"He lives here?" Mari asked.

"There." I pointed to a cottage beside the house. It must have been a summer kitchen or maybe a toolshed at one time; its chimney was a long metal tube topped off with something that looked like a tilted helmet. When the sun was shining, chickens scratched around in front of the cottage's open door. All closed now, it was quiet.

"Csaba!" I yelled.

Finally he crawled out with a key. He greeted us with a wave, then ran to open the gate.

"Did you come to sunbathe?" he asked and sniggered.

"We'll go out on the water," I answered as we ran in.

Only a table, a washstand, and an iron bed could fit into the room. On the bed sat a girl in Csaba's pajamas.

"They call her 'Four-flies,' " said Csaba to Mari.

"Hello!" Four-flies greeted us. We sat down beside her on the bed. If I remember rightly, Mari and I went dancing a year ago. We danced in a small, crowded and smoky room; the band was too large, so the noise was deafening. We whirled. I tightly embraced her familiar body and rubbed my chin against her sweaty forehead. Perhaps I remembered this as we sat down on the bed because Csaba's room was small and crowded too.

"They call her Four-flies," Csaba was explaining to Mari, "because she once found four flies in her soup."

Meanwhile he put water on the stove for tea, then sat on the table and looked at us.

"Do you want to swim?"

"No," I said. "I want to show our boat to Mari. We'll go down to the resort and I'll ask for it, so we can take a spin on the water."

"You want to use it?" asked Csaba.

"Can I go too?" interrupted Four-flies.

"You can't," said Csaba. "We'll go tomorrow if the weather improves." He turned to Mari and looked at her carefully.

"I haven't seen you for a long time, Mari. How are you?"

"Why can't I go with them?" asked Four-flies.

"Because they want to make out and you'd only disturb them." Csaba was pouring the tea through a sieve into a beer mug. After a search, he found the mustard cup and poured the rest into it. He gave the mug to Mari and the cup to me.

"I think it's ridiculous to go boating in such rain."

"Mari is going on a trip tomorrow. Who knows when we'll have another chance."

"Even so, it's ridiculous. Mari can go without boating. Right, Mari?"

"Yes," said Mari, "I can go without it."

"I don't know why you have to get into it," said Four-flies. "If they want to to so much, let them."

"You shut up." Csaba was sitting on the table again, smoking.

"Is something wrong with the motor?" I asked.

"There's nothing wrong," Csaba waved. "The motor's perfect, but you are dumb. Drink the tea and go."

He had been living in the cottage for a month; his face was brown from the sun. He sat on the table in a light blue warm-up suit, with cheap sandals on his feet. At times his ability to understand things without explanations was depressing, and in that moment he had already formed a one-sided opinion.

"It's nice you don't kick them out," said Four-flies.

"You only want to kick me out," said Mari, looking at Csaba. "Right, Csaba?"

"I've never had any problems with you," said Csaba. "You know I've always liked you."

"Then what's the matter?" asked Four-flies.

"Shut up." Csaba sat on the table grinning and dangling his legs.

"Do you still play poker?" asked Mari.

"They play poker day and night," said Four-flies.

"You've talked enough."

Csaba bent his arm at the elbow, made a fist, and with his eyes invited me to play. I put the mustard cup down. We each put our right elbows on the table, and with the motions of experienced players we smacked our palms together. I knew I would win, sometimes one can sense that. My wrist was quite a bit weaker than Csaba's. That's why I knew he wanted to win by breaking my wrist. I, on the other hand, trusted in the muscles of my upper arm, so endurance was my advantage. In the battle of the wrists, Csaba was a quick type. Luckily, our builds were so complementary that the outcome of each round was uncertain and depended mostly on either's situation at the moment. That's why my quick victory was unusual. And also because I won by bending Csaba's thick wrist. We were both panting.

"That was lovely," said Four-flies. Mari didn't say anything.

"Come, let's have another go." Csaba bent his arm again.

"I don't want to," I said. "That's enough."

We sat in Csaba's little cabin. Outside the rain was pouring, and when we looked out of the window, we could tell it wouldn't be stopping soon. We smoked another cigarette.

Finally Mari and I were standing on the bank. The wind was striking our face, the raindrops were cutting small funnels in the river, and then I told her:

"I brought you here for nothing, Mari. I don't have a motorboat."

Vilmos Csaplár

Csaplár was born on June 29, 1947 in Újpest, a little town which was incorporated by Budapest a few years after his birth. His father is a technician, still employed in a workshop as a refrigeration specialist; his mother worked throughout her life at various jobs and retired as a store clerk. After graduating from high school, Csaplár studied law at the Loránd Eötvös University, but after a year he changed to the study of Hungarian language and literature and received a teaching diploma in 1972. He has, for years, made his living as an author. In the spring of 1976 he became assistant editor of the literary section of a newly founded cultural weekly, New Mirror (*Új Tükör*) and is, at present, also working on feature films with directors.

His first collection of short stories, *The Age of Chivalry* (*Lovagkor*, 1971), really a cycle, was characterized by an opulent language and abundant sentiment, but in subsequent writings he achieves his effects with spare and detached expressions of his thought and feeling. He says that he despises sentimentalizing and strives to purge lyricism and word-play from his works. He even calls on his readers to eradicate without hesitation, "if possible with a broad pen," any such elements that have eluded his vigilance. His other works: *Two Days When We Quarreled, or the Difficulties of Historiography* (*Két nap, amikor összevesztünk, vagyis a történetírás nehézségei*), a novel, 1972; *The Princess's Sponge Coat* (*A királylány szivacskabátya*), a novel for youth, 1974; *Our Customer's Attention is Drawn to the Model 968 Zaporzsec Automobile* (*Vásárlóink figyelmébe ajánljuk a Zaporozsec 968-as tipusú gépkocsit*), short stories, 1975.

Our Customers' Attention Is Drawn to the Model 968 Zaporozsec Automobile

Mr. and Mrs. Pósa—they are the ones who once cowered in trees, clutching clubs and nibbling at roots, who huddled in the recesses of caves, chewed raw meat (and, later, roasted it), bored holes in stones, paring shafts to fit into them; who crept out of their hiding places to hunt, gather berries, spike fishes with the tips of spears in rivers whose waters gushed forth at the behest of mysterious forces, and in which, when they looked into them, the tireless teeming, crawling and darting exerted on them an age-old, familiar attraction. "This is where we were once," they would have said, if they had been able to speak. In those days no one troubled about them yet. Now and then they would appear on the wall of a cave, leaping around some bison or mammoth with their stick-figure companions; nothing more. Time passed. They smelted copper, bronze and iron, herded animals, pressed seeds into the earth. By this time they had long been "protected" by "kinsmen" on horseback brandishing swords, but still no word was heard of them. Then, from time to time, they began to be mentioned in certain documents as "the army of serfs mown down by arrows," as "souls" who were bought and sold or put to the sword in their burned-down villages. Now records began to be kept of their religious persuasion; they were flogged, maimed, beheaded, burned; scythes rose high, flails whirled, sticks and hoes cleft the air, redolent with the reek of burning lords. Then all grew quiet again; they went on digging the soil, and no one in the meantime had any inkling of what they thought.

But now eyes began to turn directly toward them: "the people" was the watchword, "the nation" even; they were called upon to take up the struggle, rights were demanded for them, some of them granted and some not; later on those granted were withdrawn, only to be granted again, then once again withdrawn. Meanwhile interest began to be shown in their lives, no longer in general terms but also in their particular lives. Commiseration, disdain, fine words and abuse followed by turns. And speculations continued: what do they want, what do they think about? Are their lives worth living? Will they indeed survive?

And now they are standing here in Budapest in front of the new multi-story car park in Martinelli Square, clutching hands and gazing about them. Behind the sheets of glass, on the various levels, rows of cars are lined up; their mysterious shadows seep through the glass, and as the Pósa's gaze passes upward over the facade, they themselves grow smaller and smaller; Pósa's hat and gray overcoat and Mrs. Pósa's two-piece suit of rough check are old and familiar items from a doll's wardrobe; Pósa's briefcase (he's come straight from the factory) swings about like the tuft on the end of the tails of toy lions. A bus moves away from the stop and merges with the stream of traffic beside the reinforced concrete skeleton of the telephone-exchange-to-be; pigeons land on the ledge of the stuccoed baroque parish church with its spider-web windows; an airplane crosses the sky, the afternoon is invalid, it'll soon be evening; the dachshund of a dear, fat colleague (fellow worker, comrade, workmate) leaves a trail running across the pavement next to a street sign. Mr. and Mrs. Pósa cross over, take an awkward glance behind them (perhaps, from the ocean-like depths of their ruminations, there has surfaced the admonishment "In our society a car is not a measure of value, it is never an end in itself"), and set off toward the car showroom which is situated on the ground floor of the offices that have been built into the car park.

"Do you know what I'm thinking?" says Mrs. Pósa.

Listen carefully, we're at last going to hear what up to now has only been guessed at.

"What?"

"That a Zaporozsec could be nice for us as well. We'd get it quickly and our share from the vineyard'll cover the cost, so we won't have to borrow anything."

Pósa's glance, darting ahead, takes in the dark glassy body of the showroom—"Let's have a closer look," he says, "then we'll see"—which is filled with cars standing in rows and people sitting about in red armchairs staring out from the poured mold. At a table one of the blue-coated staff holds a telephone receiver to his ear.

"They're all white," Mrs. Pósa points out, disappointed.

Pósa grips the handle of his briefcase. "What should they be?"

"Pardon?"

"What should they be?" His grip tightens.

"But why do they all have to be white?"

He is standing in their hotel room during their honeymoon at Lake Balaton, looking out the window at a car some people are just getting into. His wife has just awakened; he can hear her moving in bed. "Ooh, how white your bottom is!" "You've got a thing about white," he says.

"A thing about it? Me?"

"Yes, you have." He grips his briefcase more tightly.

"Hey, you're squashing my hand!" squeals his wife. "What's the matter with you?"

Now they are hovering in the doorway of the showroom. "After you." He wants her to go in first.

"No, you go first," says Mrs. Pósa, hanging back.

"Oh, go on!"

"Why me?"

No one turns in their direction when they enter, no one asks them what they want. Just as the man in the blue coat puts down the receiver, the telephone rings again. He picks it up. He pushes back the chair in which he is sitting and runs his fingers through his hair. "Second half of 1974, sir. Good-bye." He slams the receiver down. Another blue-coated assistant heaves his behind up onto the table and surveys the customers lingering around the display models; the two halves of his coat fly open like fins. Some people come up and talk to his colleague, who leaves his hand on the telephone and drums with his fingers on the dial. A third assistant in blue is leafing through a book with a spiral binding. There is a fourth, too. He is on his way upstairs, his bald pate playing a scale on the head-sized letters of a sign above which is fixed a metal arrow. SPARE PARTS, it says. "I'd like a part for my car," imagines Pósa. "What kind is it?" "A Zaporozsec." "Oh really, sir?" says the salesman with a grimace. "This way, please."—"Come on, there it is over there." His wife is tugging at his arm.

Inside everything is black: the instrument panel, the steering wheel, the seats, and the lining of the doors. "It's a bit small."

"What do you mean, small? It isn't small at all."

"Go on, get in."

He stares at his wife's legs as she gets in. Her shin bones curve outward like croissants. And she has no calves. "Good god," he thinks, "I *am* hungry." His glance falls on the turned up tips of his own shoes. Even now his shoes are always muddy, just as in those far-off days when, as a youth, he walked the streets and fields of the village delivering the mail. He is on his way home from the vineyard, the quarter share of which, falling to him, will provide the money for the car they want to buy. "Lanky, lanky! Daddy-long-legs!" the children shout. And now he is an engineer; the shoes he wears should be gleaming—"Try the back seat. You never know where to put your feet." Mrs. Pósa presses her foot down on the accelerator and at the same time grips the steering wheel tightly, turning it from side to side. She'd love to head out through the plate-glass windows into the square. You can just see the church—"Do you remember my nephew's car?" he asks through the window. "The one they took us to the church and the photographer's in? That was some car, that." He feels warm, and shifts his briefcase to his other hand. "What kind is the Patakis'?" asks his wife. "A Wartburg. I'm going to have a look at the trunk." He goes to the front. "It's stable all right," he thinks. "Rear engine." Will it hug the road? He bumps into a placard. What's this? OUR CUSTOMERS' ATTENTION IS DRAWN TO THE MODEL 968 ZAPOROZSEC AUTOMOBILE. Underneath are the technical details and the price. Delivery within two months, and orders can be placed at savings bank branches. While he is struggling with the trunk lid, his wife comes around to join him; she too trips over the sign. "Why on earth do they have to put this thing here? There isn't room for it. I'll put it behind this pillar." "Don't you touch it!" Pósa hisses, glancing warily toward the table where the men in coats are sitting. "All right," his wife says soothingly. "Don't shout." "I'm not shouting."

The acid smell of rubber comes from the trunk. "What a nice new smell," Mrs. Pósa says, taking several long sniffs. Her husband turns up his nose. "Just try smelling it the whole day." He thinks of the factory, but, strangely enough, it is not he himself, the chemical engineer, that his mind's eye conjures up, but some workers in aprons slopping around in high boots. "I've done a fair bit in my time. And I've learned something along the way as well. You've got to study, it's the only way"—"The Patakis' is smaller than this," says Mrs. Pósa, sizing up the inside of the recess with its lining of rubber matting. "Of course it's not smaller." "It is." "Look, how could a Wartburg's be smaller than this?"

Now his wife was upset again, because he is "shouting." "Have you tried the back seat as well?" he asks, to conciliate her.

Mrs. Pósa draws back. "No."

"Well, go and try it then." He slams the trunk lid shut. "Go on, sit in the back a bit."

"They could have put four doors in it," he growls, ramming the driver's seat forward. There's his wife's croissant leg again. "Aren't you hungry?" he asks, pushing the seat back. "No. There, you see." She runs her hands over her knees. "What are you all worked up about?" "Can't you see how small it is? I've told you, it's too small!" "It isn't small." His wife sits squeezed up in the back seat, almost doubled up, her thighs stuck somewhere under her chin. "They're asking all that money for it, and it's as small as this. Come on, let's get out of here!" He jerks forward the seat, which his wife has been gripping with one hand, so that her knees plunge forward and she nearly falls out the door. "What are you doing?" "I'm telling you to get out. Why do you keep sitting there? It's too small. How many more times do I have to tell you?" Mrs. Pósa makes one last attempt. "But mightn't the front seats be too far back, dear?" Pósa snorts. He shifts his briefcase to his other hand again, pushes his hat back and rubs his forehead, which makes his fingers dripping wet. He'd very much like to smear them over the Zaporozsec, but he doesn't dare, because when the browsing customers see them opening and shutting the doors three of them come over and gather around them.

"They're supposed to have fitted the first batch with special Volkswagen engines," one of the men says. "It was a gift at the price."

"Look, dear." Mrs. Pósa hasn't got out. She's made some adjustment under the seat, pulled it back in front of her and, her knees slightly to one side, is now sitting in perfect comfort.

She has always had problems with her enormous hands and feet "Lali, have you found a girl to marry up there in Pest?" his grandfather would ask at holiday times when he went home, after he'd started working in the rubber factory. "Get yourself a wife as small as my little finger here. That's the secret of a happy life, you'll see. Your poor grandmother was as tiny as that when she was alive." Then this wife came along, who can only walk about in low-heeled shoes, so as not to seem taller than he. "My children, I would like you to give our poor orphaned country sons as great as our own St. László," the priest murmured after the service. But what had come of all those fine hopes? Last month his wife had her second miscarriage. Whose fault is it?

He goes up to the open door of the car again. His wife is laughing. She fingers the tubular metal base of the seat, explaining something. As she bends down she puts one foot outside on the floor. Again that croissant leg. He feels hungry and full at the same time. The feeling of fullness remains, overcoming his hunger, and grows stronger and stronger, as if he had crammed himself full of food and the food wanted to come out. "I've sinned against the laws of nature." He stares fixedly at his wife's leg. And that shovel of a foot. It might even be bigger than his; they ought to measure them some day. What's she saying? "Look, I've pushed this forward here." She leans back and draws in her legs, trying to make herself comfortable. "It's all right now. Aren't I clever?"

"Not a bad job, this," says one of the men, patting the back of the car.

The other man, the one who spoke first when they strolled over, repeats his comment. "A gift at the price."

"Anyway, the kids'll sit in the back, won't they?" remarks the third one to Mrs. Pósa with a leer. "There'll be room enough for them."

The expression of happiness fades immediately from her face. "Yes, that's right," she nods.

Pósa jerks the seat forward roughly. "Come on out of there, for God's sake! Do you want to spend the rest of your life here or something!" He grabs at her arm, ready to drag her out if need be. She lifts her hands and presses them against her breast, just staring at him, as defenseless as someone whose clothes have been torn off. *Those men* are having a good look at all this. Pósa steps back, and as he swings back his left hand, which is holding his briefcase, he bangs his elbow against the window. He quickly hunches up his shoulders, anxious to free himself from the door's embrace, but now the door handle gets caught in the grip of his briefcase. There is a cracking, snapping sound, and when he has disentangled the handle it just hangs down limply. His wife sits there, not moving. Pósa feels like hitting something, slashing at it, smashing it to pieces; his head is about to split apart. At last she moves her legs and gets out.

They carefully push the door to, leaving it unfastened, and avoid looking at the three men who, in any case, as luck would have it, are strolling away to size up the Zsiguli. "What can people like that be doing for a living?" Pósa thinks, boiling with rage, and mentally shooting a contemptuous glance in their direction. "To think they can spare all that time!" As the Pósas pass the sales desk they keep their eyes on the ground. The telephone rings. "Hello, Martinelli Square Car Showrooms. Can I help you?" "This lot are stuck to their desk as well, instead of helping people. They could at least show you things. I wish we were outside."

"All white," grumbles Mrs. Pósa. "They don't know how to make them in any other color."

A cool breeze fans his face at last on the corner of Bécsi Street. He stops and lets his wife catch up with him. When she reaches him she stares in front of her, waiting for him to say which way they should go. Pósa grasps her by the shoulder, but since she pretends not to notice, he soon lets go. Slowly the tightness of his grip relaxes; his briefcase hangs loosely from his curled-up fingers. The breeze blows on his face again, and he shoves his hat back to let his forehead dry. He sets off, not caring which way he is going. "Let's walk a bit before we go home." He is conscious that his wife does not move for a moment, but then she is there again, trailing along beside him. The street broadens out; cars line the sidewalk. *"Evening News!"* shouts the vendor. He sits at the corner on a campstool under a canvas shelter. "Now that's like the Patakis'," says Pósa, pointing to a Wartburg.

"Except theirs isn't white, it's lemon-colored," says his wife.

"There you are on that white again. What have you got against white all the time?"

"Nothing. It's all right," Mrs. Pósa says, walking on. "Don't shout!"

"Come here," says her husband, gesticulating. "Just look how much bigger this one's trunk is."

His wife turns around and trudges back.

"There you are. See for yourself, with your own eyes."

"How can I?" asks Mrs. Pósa, shrugging her shoulders. "It's shut."

"You can still see when it's closed. You'd have to be blind not to. Come over here."

"Do you want to buy a car? It's for sale." A man stands there on the sidewalk. He thrusts a jingling bunch of keys toward the lock and opens the door.

Pósa looks at Mrs. Pósa. "Yes, we do actually. We've just made inquiries, but there's such a long wait, for the kind we'd like, I mean, and we were just coming to the conclusion that this is the trunk size we'd need, because we've got things on the outskirts of town, you know."

While Pósa is speaking the man takes a good look at him. His glance lingers hesitantly on the muddy shoes; then he makes up his mind—why not? "Well, you won't have to wait for this one." He reaches in his pocket and holds out a sheaf of visiting cards. "The other day I thought of driving over to the Exchange with it, but who's got time for that?" He hands Pósa a card. IMRE ZSIBÓI, GENTS' FASHION DESIGNER. "You can call me at this number, sir. The car is two years old in May and it's in first-class shape. I'm only selling it because I'm getting a bigger one which some of my relatives in the West have sent over. It's already in the country, and I'd like to make a quick sale because of the customs and the tax, know what I mean?" He glances at his watch and plays with the cuffs of his jacket, which sits snugly on his plump body. "So when can I expect to hear from you?" Pósa is still turning the card between his fingers. "How much are you asking for it?" "We're reasonable people, we'll come to some arrangement. Good-bye." The gents' fashion designer holds out his hand. "Lajos Pósa. Good-bye." "Good-bye, madam." "Mrs. Lajos Pósa. Good-bye."

A thought strikes Zsibói, and he looks at his watch again. "Which one of you is the driver?"

"My wife's taking her test next week. I didn't want to start till then. I'm like you, you know. I don't have a great deal of time to spare and . . ." "Don't worry," the gents' fashion designer interrupts him. "I'll give you a ride around the block, so you'll be able to make up your minds more easily. The lady can sit in the back." He flings the rear door open. "There we are, take a seat." He ushers the hesitant woman into the back seat, which is covered in sheepskin. "And if you would care to sit here, sir, next to me." As Mrs. Pósa climbs in, there is again the sudden flash of her croissant leg. The doors slam. "After this we'll go and have a bite to eat somewhere," thinks Pósa, putting his elbow out of the window.

Zsibói starts the engine and puts it into gear. The car leaps forward. A boy runs across the road in front of them. He stumbles and falls, and his satchel thumps against the back of his head. "You little brat, why don't you look where you're going?" bawls Pósa, thrusting his head out of the window. The sudden braking has made his pulse race, and his hand tingles from the pressure of the window frame. "You know what I'd do? I'd pass a law so that if anybody dashed across the road like that and got run over, the driver wouldn't be held responsible." He clenches his fist, opens it, and clenches it again. "Little brat! You're not hurt, are you, dear?" Mrs. Pósa runs her hands over her legs. "No."

The gents' fashion designer drives on. "Comfortable there in back, isn't it, madam?" he asks. "Yes, very." "Comfortable, dear?" inquires Pósa, twisting his neck around. He is smiling.

Szilveszter Ördögh

Ördögh was born on October 28, 1948 in Szeged. His parents, as well as his remote ancestors, were peasants in that area, and his experiences with village life through his family are the principal source of his early short stories. He completed elementary and high school studies in Szeged and Hódmezővásárhely, a city about twenty kilometers from Szeged. Then, after service in the army, he entered the Loránd Eötvös University in Budapest and in 1973 obtained a teaching diploma in Hungarian and French. At the university, he chose Péter Veres, the chronicler of village life, to direct his thesis work; he did so in the belief that "I must face this world with the greatest possible severity and the greatest possible love, to be able to continue myself. Not the world but myself—it is very important to note—because I knew and sensed that a greater part of this world is within me as well." He attended the College of Theater and Fine Arts on a fellowship for two years. He is now an editor with the Magvető Publishing House in Budapest, and is serving as the secretary of the Attila József Circle of Young Writers. Since 1966 his short fiction and critical articles have been appearing regularly in various important literary periodicals published in Budapest and the provinces as well as in a number of weekly and daily newspapers. His works are: *The Colt (A csikó)*, short stories, 1973; and *Mountain of Skulls (Koponyák hegye)*, a short-story cycle concerned with Jesus Christ, 1976. In 1974 he was awarded the Attila József Prize for *The Colt*.

His stories delineate the changing life in Hungarian villages and the thoughts and emotions of a young man who has left that world to live in the city, looking back on the former without nostalgia and viewing the latter realistically but with a sense of the future. Concluding that history cannot be altered, Ördögh believes that escape from it depends on resolution of the dialectic between the past and present within the individual self linked to humankind.

The Elephant

"Been to the vet's, have you?" The little red-haired boy picked his nose, then gave his bare leg a rub.

Ambruska gave a start and blushed.

"How did you know?" he asked, embarrassed, and threw an instinctive glance around him to see if anyone else had heard.

"Oh, because I happened to be watching you," the other boy laughed, showing his ugly, crooked teeth. "Is your pig sick, eh?"

Ambruska was overcome with shame. He didn't even know the boy; this was the first time he had set eyes on him.

"No, that's not true!" he retorted quickly, lowering his head involuntarily. "We haven't got a pig!"

"Well, what have you been to the vet's for then? Don't give me that stuff about not having a pig." The red-haired boy brandished his fist and clicked his tongue, then scratched his skinny thigh again. "I'll bet your dad's a peasant! I'll bet he is—that's why you've been to the vet's, you're pig's sick. Want a bet, kid?"

Ambruska only wanted to get away, to run off somewhere where this boy couldn't catch up with him, but he didn't dare move. Elegantly dressed elderly ladies were walking along the street, net shopping bags in their hands and lipstick on their mouths. Ambruska looked at the boy's trousers and saw they were made of buckskin, with an antler pattern embroidered on the straps. He cautiously moved his hand behind his back to cover the patches on the seat of his pants.

"We haven't got a pig! And my dad's not a peasant, so there!"

"Well, what is he then? Just tell me, kid, what is he? Why were you at the vet's if your dad isn't a peasant, eh?"

Ambruska, covered in confusion, started walking away.

"My dad's not a peasant, he's . . . he's a train engineer! You don't have to believe it if you don't want to, but my dad's an engine driver," he blurted out in a gabble.

"You don't think anyone'd believe that, do you? So why have you been to the vet's?" The boy with red hair wouldn't be shaken off. There were his nice leather sandals pattering along the pavement beside Ambruska's worn-out gym shoes, a pair of grimy ankles visible alongside.

"If you must know, I've been to the vet's because . . . because there's something wrong with . . . with our elephant!"

"Ha, ha, ha! What a story!" jeered the boy, tapping the end of his nose. "You're a liar! There aren't any elephants for anybody to keep. They only live in zoos. And in Africa. I've seen them in a picture book. My dad showed them to me."

"Well, I don't care, we *have* got an elephant. Just because nobody else's got one, that doesn't mean we haven't," said Ambruska angrily. "He's at home in the stable, and if you must know there's something wrong with his eyes. They're bleeding. The blood is just pouring out of them!"

"I'll believe it if I like, I'll believe it if I like," the other boy laughed.

"Well, if you don't believe it, come on over to our house, and I'll show him to you." Ambruska said this so loudly that he startled himself.

"All right, I don't mind if you do show him to me, I'll believe you then," the boy agreed, scratching his nose and thrusting his hands into his pockets.

They walked along slowly side by side, without a word. Ambruska, tense with worry, looked at the pavement.

Red and red-white-and-green flags fluttered from the houses in the spring breeze, and over a shop door, between flags, a photograph was fixed. There were few people about in the street. A street sweeper was making his leisurely way along in the shade; then a street sprinkler came by, and as the water squirted down it churned into mud the rubbish he had so carefully scraped together. The street sweeper swore.

The red-haired boy let out a hoot of laughter.

"That guy really got it, didn't he?"

Ambruska did not reply.

They turned another corner. The boy picked his nose.

"Have you just got an elephant?" he asked inquisitively.

"No." Ambruska didn't look up. He kept his eyes fixed on the pavement and on the tips of his gym shoes where his toes stuck out.

"Well, what other kinds of animals have you got then?"

"We've also got a giraffe."

"A giraffe! Ooh, that's great!" said the boy, nodding his head in amazement. He smacked his lips admiringly.

"And we've got six lions too. Two of them have got those long manes, do you know what I mean?" Ambruska's hands traced the outlines of a mane; then he quickly put them back over the patches.

"Hey, that's really great! Six lions! That must be just fantastic for you, pal!"

"And we've got a tiger too and lots of birds."

"What sort of birds?" The boy craned his neck.

"Oh, all sorts. There's ostriches, there's eagles. Eagles are the ones we've got the most of. And we've got vultures too."

"Have you got all these at home?" The red-haired boy's eyes opened wide.

"Of course we have. You'll see!"

"Hey, that's terrific! Really great! Seeing lions all the time, and a giraffe too! Do you play with them?"

"Of course I do." Ambruska blushed and smiled. "It's always me who feeds them. The elephant, the giraffe, the tiger and the lions. My mom feeds the birds. I let her. I get a bit bored with the birds."

"Of course you would, when there's lions!"

They ambled along in silence until they came to the square. There were flags on the House of Culture too, and large photographs and slogans, but the square was deserted. An old woman was puttering about in front of the statue of St. Francis with his broken hand. She was arranging flowers in a jar.

"Silly old bag, isn't she? Nuts!" sniggered the red-haired boy again. Ambruska didn't say anything, and the boy stopped sniggering, picked his nose and stuck his hands back into his pockets.

"Too bad we haven't got any wild animals. We live on the third floor, you know, and you can't keep them there." He thought about this for a while, then spoke again. "My dad's a lecturer at the university, you know. He's got a room all to himself there. He's even got his name up outside!"

"And my dad drives big railway engines. He goes abroad too," Ambruska put in quickly.

"He goes abroad?"

"Yes, of course. Over to Russia too."

"My dad's been abroad too. He's even been to Germany. And I've been to Pest and the Balaton and Sopron. Does your dad take you with him when he drives his engines?"

"Of course. Whenever I feel like it. But I've had so many rides on engines they bore me now."

"That's something." The boy nodded despondently and took his hands out of his pockets.

"Right now, if I wanted to, I could go anywhere I liked, because I know all the engineers and they take me with them. But I just don't want to right now."

"Why don't you want to?" asked the red-haired boy eagerly.

"Because . . . because I haven't got the time. I've got to feed the animals."

"Oh yes, of course. I'd forgotten that. Is it far now?"

Ambruska's heart gave a leap. They were turning into the street where he lived.

"No, its not far now . . . it's just down here . . . " Now he was reaching into his pocket and fingering the key to the gate.

"Can I help you feed the lions?" He looked at Ambruska with pleading eyes.

"I wouldn't mind, but I'm afraid they might attack you. You know, they don't know you yet . . . "

"But if I come around a lot they'll get to know me, won't they?"

"Well, I don't mind then. All right, you can feed them if you want to."

"Of course I want to!" The red-haired boy rubbed his hands in delight and gave a little skip of pleasure.

The pavement was surfaced with bricks, some of them missing here and there. In the dust of the roadway there were the tracks of wagon wheels and dried-up horse droppings. The sun blazed down, and you could see that the acacia leaves were covered with dust.

"This is where we live," said Ambruska, pointing to a house.

"You've got a nice big house!"

Ambruska tried the door. He felt his hand trembling.

"It's locked." He suddenly relaxed. He quickly slipped his hand back in his pocket and clutched the key tightly.

"It looks as if dad had to go off somewhere."

"What about your mom?"

"Mom's . . . mom's away on a holiday . . . Didn't I tell you?" Ambruska's cheeks burned.

"Who'll feed the animals? They'll starve." The boy looked despairingly at Ambruska.

"I'll have to wait for my dad, he's got the key."

They stood there at a loss. Ambruska glanced around anxiously, in case one of the neighbors might notice them.

"Well, what'll we do now?" The boy picked at his nose.

"I'm going to my grand-dad's until dad gets back; I know they'll give me something to eat. When something like this happens I always have my dinner there."

"Oh, I see." The other boy nodded and scratched his head. "Okay then. So you'll show me the lions some other time, right?"

"Of course," said Ambruska. "Well, I better get going to my grand-dad's now."

"Yes, I'll be getting back home. Too bad it's locked."

"Yes, too bad I can't show them to you now."

"Still, it doesn't matter. You'll show them to me some other time."

"Well, so long then." Ambruska set off in the opposite direction. Occasionally he stole a look back to see whether the red-haired boy had turned the corner yet. When he saw that he had, he was back in a flash. He closed the gate quickly behind him.

His father came back from the fields with the others at dusk. They had been hoeing, and the water can clanked against the bicycle.

"The vet said he'd come tomorrow morning at six."

His father said nothing. He was running water into a bucket and plunging the hoes into it. His mother was getting things ready for cooking. She sat down on a stool. In front of her stood a basket without any handles, with potatoes in it.

"Did you feed the chickens at noon?"

"Yes." Ambruska squatted in the kitchen doorway.

"Have you gathered some beet leaves for the pigs?"

"Yes."

Out in back the pigs began to squeal. His father was pouring the swill into the trough.

"Have you collected the eggs?"

"Yes, there were six. I put them in the basket."

"Did anyone call?"

"No."

Then there was silence. The fat began to sizzle on the stove. The pigs could still be heard impatiently gulping their food down. The stars twinkled drowsily in the sky.

Miklós Vámos

Vámos was born on January 29, 1950 in Budapest. His father, a lawyer, worked in the Ministry of the Interior after World War II until the Rajk dispute, after which he became a millworker and then, for a long time, as a semi-skilled worker at a typographical factory. From 1958 to his death in 1969 he was a legal adviser at a leather factory. His mother was, until her retirement in 1973, an administrator in a factory manufacturing agricultural machines. Under the influence of his father, Vámos developed an early interest in literature, establishing at the age of ten a school newspaper named *Bugle Call* (*Kürtszó*) with some friends. While reading literary histories in high school, he concluded that he could not become a poet, "for poets are invariably skinny, dreamy-eyed, possibly consumptive," while he was "stockily built and in the pink of condition," and besides there was already a poet in his class. After his application for admission to the faculty of philosophy at the Loránd Eötvös University in Budapest was denied, he worked for a year as a printer at the Egyetem Publishing House; then he applied for admission to the law faculty. Accepted this time, he first served his year in the army and began his studies in September 1970. While a student he received a monthly stipend from the government and worked as a journalist for *Hungarian News* (*Magyar Hírlap*) and also as a television critic for several periodicals. After obtaining his law degree in 1975, he "took life easy" for a year. He is now on contract as a literary adviser at a film studio. His works are: *Preface to the ABC's* (*Előszó az ábécéhez*), short stories and sketches, 1972; *At Present Thirteenth on the List* (*Jelenleg tizenharmadik a listán*), short stories, 1973; *Borgis* (*Borgisz*), a novel, 1976; and *Exchange (P and M)* (*Váltás [Pé és Em]*), a short-story cycle, 1977. Six of his radio plays were produced from 1970 to 1976, and two of his plays were staged, one in 1975 and the other in 1976.

Vámos writes about contemporary Hungarian life critically and tendentiously, with the clear intent of influencing readers' attitudes and values. His stories usually involve the activities of schoolboys, the problems of loneliness and isolation, and the many complexities troubling average human beings. He does not analyze characters in depth. Instead, he reduces their traits and situations to barest essentials to achieve pace and dramatic impact.

Keresztes

He noticed the others were looking at him strangely. "What in the hell can be wrong?"

During recess they whispered together in groups. Then suddenly Bors was standing in front of him, with Károly and János B. lined up behind him, and he said:

"Hoffman, you're a Jew!"

"You're one! I'm not a Jew! No way!" Hoffman defended himself. The truth was, he had quite hazy notions about what a Jew really is. Someone bad, he sensed. Maybe someone like an idiot, only much more mysterious.

And so he protested with a reddening face.

"Don't you deny you're a Jew!" said Bors, twisting his mouth. "Just look at that curly hair. It's already starting to spread over his face. By the time he's grown up it'll cover his whole face. Jews' faces are hairy, like monkeys'."

"It won't grow over my face!" He reached for his curly hair. "I just haven't got to the barber for a long time . . ."

"That's a lot of bullshit, kid," Bors checked him with a gesture.

The bell rang. The teacher entered. The hour passed slowly. When it ended Bors and his two buddies again stood in front of Hoffman.

"Well, what's up, you little Jew?" asked Bors.

"Leave me alone! I've told you I'm not a Jew," Hoffman sputtered nervously.

"Don't get jumpy!" Bors grinned. "Jews are always jumpy. My father told me so. If you keep jumping around, we'll give you a real licking!"

That very night he anxiously waited for his mother to come into his room and sit down on his bed.

"Momma, what is a Jew?"

"A religious belief."

"Is it bad for somebody if he's a Jew?"

His mother didn't reply. She looked deep into her son's eyes. She was thinking of her husband, who had died at Buchenwald on the day the camp was liberated. Then she gave a sigh.

"No, my son, it's not bad for somebody to be a Jew anymore. A long time ago, during the war, it was bad, very bad."

"And I . . . Am I a Jew?"

After a short silence she replied: "Yes."

"But I don't want to be a Jew! Nobody's a Jew in the class, only me! Bors told me. He made fun of me!"

His mother was silent. Then she kissed him on the forehead.

"Don't listen to Bors," she said and left.

The next day in school, the teacher returned the birth certificates the students had been asked some time ago to bring in. (For some administrative reason.)

Hoffman placed his before him and looked at it. His name, his mother's name, his year of birth. Then he found a heading: Religion. He tried reading it. In their third year, they could already read without breaking words into syllables, properly, but he had never read this kind of grown-up handwriting before. No matter how hard he tried, he couldn't make it out.

"Oh well, so what," he said. "It must say I'm a Jew."

During recess Bors came over to him and snatched the birth certificate out of his hands.

He peered at it for a long time (sweat streaming from Hoffman all the while), and then suddenly, he raised his eyebrows in admiration:

"You really aren't a Jew! It says here: keresztény!"[1]

He shook hands with Hoffman. The others looked at them in amazement.

Hoffman went out into the corridor.

The next class was on Hungarian grammar. Hoffman spent the entire hour staring fixedly at the document lying before him.

"No matter how things stand," he muttered, "Keresztény isn't written here. After all, that would have ten letters, and this doesn't have six even."

He couldn't understand what was going on. Then suddenly it dawned on him. What Bors had read as "Keresztény" was actually "Keresztes." That's where he was born. And the heading "Birthplace" was directly above the heading "Religion." Bors probably hadn't noticed this.

Suddenly he sensed he was being observed. He looked behind him. His eyes met János B.'s. János B. occupied the seat directly in back of him. Now raising himself completely out of his seat, he looked at Hoffman's fingers, which were still fixed to the document at the heading "Birthplace." (The third-graders still followed the place with their fingers as they were reading.)

János B. curled his lips. He too understood Bors's mistake.

Reddening, Hoffman jerked his head forward. János B. tapped him on the shoulder.

"Don't shit in your pants, you little Jew!" he said (in the same accents as he'd heard Bors using). "I won't squeal on you."

Hoffman snapped his head around. János B. nodded his head at him tolerantly.

Hoffman straightened up. During recess he went over to Bors.

"I'm a Jew," he said calmly.

[1] The Hungarian word for "Christian."

Little Boys and Big Boys

The building was being remodeled at the time. Inside and out. The ceiling in each classroom was shored up with beams fastened together by enormous cramp irons.

Eight columns stood in every classroom. In two colonnades, four columns to each. The two colonnades stood on two long beams, and they supported two other beams (parallel with those forming the bases) that actually held up the ceiling.

The big boys enjoyed all this very much. The beams made the class (VII/A) spirited and, I could say, very romantic.

During the twenty-minute recess, Big János B. (János B.'s big brother) remained in his seat and began to shake.

"Is something wrong?" asked Big Bors (Bors's big brother), looking at him with concern.

Big János B. didn't reply. Then he stopped shaking.

"The inside of the train in that Russian film was just like this," he said. "Columns just like this in the middle of the coach."

"But without the cramp irons," nodded Big Bors, and the two of them continued riding the train.

Before long the whole row of seats knows that this is the Siberian train and that they are soldiers traveling on the train to Siberia.

"We're going to the front," said a Big Boy (who had a scar under his nose), and he grinned.

The boy with glasses was chewing his nails.

"Are we Hungarian or Russian soldiers?" he asked.

"Hungarian, of course," the Big Boy retorted.

"But the Hungarians are going to lose the war," the boy with spectacles objected.

"Then . . . then we're Russians," the Big Boy.

"But I'm Hungarian," Big Bors proclaimed. "The Russians are like gypsies!"

"How do you know that?" The boy with glasses wrinkled his forehead.

"My father told me!" Big Bors came back triumphantly.

They shut up. The seats were creaking. (Because meanwhile the train is progressing, and they are all shaking diligently.)

"Let's be partisans, Hungarian partisans," the bespectacled boy recommended.

"Then we won't lose the war?" asked the Big Boy. The one with the glasses scratched his head.

"The partisans fought on the side of the Russians," he said uncertainly.

"Against Hungarians?" Big Bors raised his voice.

"No, no, against the Germans," the bespectacled boy answered.

"They didn't fight the Germans," Big Bors shook his head. "My father said that if the Germans had won the war, Transylvania would still belong to us."

They were silent again.

"I'm a partisan anyway," said the Big Boy, "and I'm fighting the Germans!"

But within himself he said: "Transylvania or no Transylvania, the Germans are going to lose the war. So it's better for us to be against them."

"Are you fighting against the East Germans or West Germans?" Big Bors asked. The Big Boy licked the side of his mouth hesitatingly.

"Well . . . wherever the right is!"

"Hm . . . , " said the boy with glasses.

"Let's be on the home front," spoke up Big Károly (Károly's big brother).

"What's that?" asked Big Bors.

"The home front is the area"—he pulled his sleeve protector higher—"where the war isn't going on."

"Then what use is there for a soldier there?"

"To run things," said Big Károly instructively.

"And so which home front should we be on?" asked the boy with glasses.

"What do you mean which?"

"Well, every country has a home front. Shall we be on the Russian or Hungarian home front?"

"That doesn't matter," said Big Károly.

"How can't it matter?" The boy with glasses spread his arms out wide.

"What's important is that they don't do any shooting at all," Big Károly cautioned them with a wave of his hand.

"That's simple," said the boy with glasses. "We won't shoot and they won't shoot either!"

"Aw"—Big Károly shook his head—"the main thing is that we don't die. Partisan or not partisan, that makes no difference. What counts is that we squeak through. My father can also tell you that," he finally said irresistibly.

"Just exactly why are we going to the front?" said a boy in short pants in a tearful voice. "The Ten Commandments say 'Thou shalt not kill,' " he shouted. "German, Russian, Hungarian—it's a sin to kill any of them. God punishes you for it!"

"And what if somebody wants to kill you? Then what? Are you going to let him kill you because if you kill him God will punish you? What do the Ten Commandments have to say about that, huh?"

"I . . . nobody wants to kill me!"

"How can you be so sure about that?" The boy with glasses put his hands on his hips.

"Oh, come on, why are you guys fighting? Cut it out." Big Károly shoved his way between them.

"Mind your own business!" said the Big Boy.

"Don't push me!" snapped Big Károly.

"Shut up!" said Big Bors, striking him on the back.

A melee broke out. Everybody against everybody else, everybody in the row was at it.

They fought each other for two or three minutes. Then suddenly the teacher appeared at the doorway.

"What's going on in here?" she roared threateningly.

Silence descended. Blood dripped from the nose of the boy in short pants.

"We were just playing," said Big Boy, gasping for breath.

(Trains and warships started moving again, munition factories were producing —world politics was taking shape.)

Bibliography

Anthologies of Twentieth-Century Hungarian Literature and Writings of the Authors in the Present Work in English, French, and German Translation

Compiled by
Kathy Elaine Tezla
   and
Ilona Kováks

Bibliography

The purpose of this bibliography is to provide readers with the opportunity to enlarge their view of twentieth-century Hungarian literature by drawing their attention to English, French, and German translations of the writings of authors from the present century included in anthologies devoted solely to Hungarian literature and to those of the twenty-four authors in this anthology that have been published in individual editions, anthologies, and selected periodicals. To assist readers in obtaining anthologies and editions of individual author's works through interlibrary loan services or, perhaps, in duplicating particular selections from such publications, location symbols in the *National union catalog* (Ann Arbor, Washington, D.C., and London, 1956+) are recorded at the end of the content description of each available publication. To secure the same information for translations available in periodicals, readers should consult *the Union list of serials* (New York, 1965), *New serials titles* (Washington, D.C., 1950+), and *Minnesota union list of serials* (Minneapolis, 1976).[1]

The compilation is based primarily on the holdings of the Hungarian National Széchényi Library and the Library of the Hungarian Academy of Science's Institute of Literary History in Budapest, both of which make a special effort to collect translations of Hungarian literature in the major languages. In addition to these resources, the following indispensable bibliographies, all of which report translations in English, French, German, and other languages, were searched: Tibor Demeter, *Magyar szépirodalom idegen nyelven* (Budapest, 1957+), *Index translationum* (Paris, 1949+), and *Magyarországi irodalom idegen nyelven 1945-1968. Bibliográfia* (Budapest, 1975). The information recorded for each of the items is based on direct examination, and the closing date of the search for materials was September 1, 1978.

1. A bibliography of union lists for various geographical regions similar to the one for Minnesota can be found in Ruth S. Freitag's *Union lists of serials. A bibliography* (Washington, D.C., 1964).

Anthologies. The anthologies, including a few special issues of periodicals devoted entirely to translations of Hungarian literature and numbered for cross-referencing from the section on individual authors, are arranged according to language and date of publication. A revised or enlarged edition was used for an entry whenever it was available for examination; a first edition was cited in brackets whenever it was not and the compilers were able to confirm its existence.

The scope of an anthology is described whenever its title does not make the content clear or, as often happens, when the anthology covers more than the twentieth century. The content of each anthology is arranged alphabetically by names of the authors, and gives inclusive page numbers. The names of the authors appearing in this text are italicized and, in their case only, the titles of their works are listed. In view of the lack of information about twentieth-century Hungarian literature in foreign languages, such ancillary materials as prefaces, introductions, and biographical notes are also cited.

Works of Authors Appearing in the Text. Translations of the work of these authors are listed chronologically under *Individual Editions* and *Periodical(s)* respectively, but only translations in periodicals reported by the three union lists mentioned above as available in United States libraries are cited. When an author's works have appeared in more than one number of a periodical, they are listed together in chronological order paralleling the sequence of the listed translations and followed by the title of the periodical and then the volume, number, date, and inclusive pagination. In such instances, the date of the first work so recorded determines the chronological place of the entry under the heading.

ANTHOLOGIES

ENGLISH

See also no. 33.

1. *Modern Magyar lyrics.* Selected gems from Alexander (Sándor) Petőfi and other modern Hungarian poets. William N. Loew (translator). Budapest: Wodianer, 1926. 103p.

   With the exception of Petőfi, the authors are from the twentieth century: Endre Ady, 13-19; Mihály Babits, 19-23; Elek Benedek, 23-24; László Bródy, 24-25; Lajos Csáktornyai, 26; Imre Farkas, 27; Oszkár Gellért, 27-29; Ignotus (Hugó Veigelsberg), 32-33; Gyula Juhász, 33; György Kemény, 34-38; József Kiss, 38-39; Ede Kisteleki, 39-47; Andor Kozma, 47-49; Géza Lampérth, 50; Emil Makai, 51; Árpád Pásztor, 54-57; József Patai, 51-54; Antal Radó, 57-60; Tivadar Rédey, 60-61; István Rónay, 61-62; Ede Sas, 62-67; Zoltán Somlyó, 67-68; Mihály Szabolcska, 68-70; Gyula Szávay, 71-73; György Szécskay, 73-74; Árpád Zempléni, 75.

2. *The Magyar muse.* An anthology of Hungarian poetry 1400-1932. Edited and translated, together with specimens from Ostiak and Vogul by Watson Kirkconell. Foreword by Francis (Ferenc) Herczeg of the Hungarian Academy. Winnipeg: Canadian Hungarian News, 1933. 222p.

   The authors from the twentieth century are: Emil Ábrányi, 121; Endre Ady, 164; Lajos Áprily, 193; Mihály Babits, 180; Aladár Bán, 152; Lajos Bartók, 126; Aladár Bodor, 172; Minka Czóbel, 137; Sándor Endrődi, 123; Géza Gárdonyi, 145; Jenő Gáspár, 201; Géza Gyóni (Achim), 184; Kálmán Harsányi, 162; Lajos Harsányi, 179; Jenő Heltai, 154; Ödön Jakab, 129; Gyula Juhász, 174; György Kemény, 158; József Kiss, 117; Jenő Komjáthy, 136; Dezső Kosztolányi, 191; Andor Kozma, 138; Géza Lampérth, 156; Elek Londesz, 160; László Mécs, 208; László Ölvedi, 211; Lajos Palágyi, 149; Lajos Pósa, 124; Antal Radó, 144; Sándor Reményik, 203; Gyula Reviczky, 131; Sándor Sajó, 151; Sandor Sík, 201; Mihály Szabolcska, 142; Gyula Szávay, 141; Ernő Szép, 186; László Tompa, 176; Árpád Tóth, 195; Antal Váradi, 130; Gyula Vargha, 128; Gyula Wlassics, 188; Árpád Zempléni, 147.

Also: Hungaria, 9-12; foreword, 13-14; introduction, 15-26. CtY, WU, CLU, NIC, OO, OCl, OCU, OU, MiU, ViU, PP, PU, DLC, CU, TxU, CoU, CaBVaU, CaOK, NjP, NN, CaBVa.

3. *Modern Magyar lyrics.* The first selected English edition of present-day Hungarian poems. Translated from the Hungarian by Barna Balogh. With an introduction by Gyula de Pekár, member of the Hungarian Academy of Sciences, President of the Petőfi Academy. Formerly Hungarian secretary of state for education. London: Central European Literary Products, 1934. 47p.

Endre Ady, 19-23; Mihály Babits, 25; Barna Balogh, 7, 38, 40-46 (specimen translations of a Barna Balogh poem in Hungarian, French, German, Italian, Spanish, Portuguese, Danish, Swedish, Dutch, Norwegian, and Esperanto); Tamás Falu, 24; Imre Farkas, 18, 30; Sándor Feleki, 8; Jenő Gáspár, 14; Endre Györkössy, 18; István Havas, 15; Jenő Heltai, 28; Menyhért Kiss, 17; Dezső Kosztolányi, 9; György Kula, 37; Sándor Márai, 26; László Mécs, 10-12; Ferenc Móra, 17; Zoltán Nadányi, 13; István Nemes, 32-33; Eszter Osváth, 27; Sándor Reményik, 34-36; Sándor Sík, 33; Zoltán Zomlyó, 27; Zoltán Szathmáry, 16; Anna Szederkényi, 29; Árpád Tóth, 31; Lajos Zilahy, 12.

4. *Hungaria.* An anthology of thirty short stories by contemporary Hungarian authors. Introduction by Alexander Korda. Translated by Lawrence Wolfe. London-Budapest: Nicholson-Watson-Athenaeum, 1936. 302p.

Mihály Babits, 1-12; Lajos Bíbó, 13-19; Lajos Bíró, 20-26; Sándor Dallos, 27-34; Mihály Földi, 35-46; Andor Endre Gelléri, 47-59; Jenő Heltai, 60-69; Ferenc Herczeg, 70-80; Sándor Hunyady, 81-88; Frigyes Karinthy, 89-97; Aurél Kárpáti, 98-112; Lajos Kassák, 113-121; János Kodolányi, 122-134; János Komáromi, 135-142; Ferenc Körmendi, 143-161; Dezső Kosztolányi, 162-171; Sándor Márai, 172-177; Ferenc Molnár, 178-187; Zsigmond Móricz, 188-197; József Nyírő, 198-208; Károly Pap, 209-217; Béla Révész, 218-229; György Sárközi, 230-236; Ernő Szép, 237-245; Antal Szerb, 246-260; Zoltán Szitnyai, 261-268; Dezső Szomory, 269-272; Áron Tamási, 273-284; József (Józsi) Jenő Tersánsky, 285-297; Lajos Zilahy, 298-302. Also: Translator's foreword, vii-x; introduction, xi-xiv. LC.

5. *A Little treasury of Hungarian verse.* Edited by Watson Kirkconell. Washington, D.C.: American-Hungarian Foundation, 1947. 55p.

Beginning with Ferenc Kazinczy, the authors are primarily from the nineteenth century with the following from the early twentieth century: *The Hungarian Tradition*: Endre Ady, 35-36; Géza Gyóni (Achim), 33-34; *The Hungarian Scene*: Lajos Áprily, 42; Mihály Babits, 45; István Havas, 44; Lőrinc Szabó, 41; *The Hungarian Soul*: Endre Ady, 54. Also: foreword by Béla Báchkai, 3-5; a little treasury of Hungarian verse, 6-7. DLC, CaBVaU, WaS, ViU, MiU, NN, InU, MH, NcU.

6. *Hungarian poetry.* Selected and edited by Egon F. Kunz. Sydney: Pannonia, 1955. 158p.

The anthology includes primarily nineteenth-century authors. Those from the twentieth century are: Endre Ady, 95-113; Mihály Babits, 122-128; Pál Gyulai, 87; Attila József, 116-119; Gyula Juhász, 114-115; Dezső Kosztolányi, 129-134; Árpád Tóth, 120-121. DLC, PBm, PLF, ICU, MtBC, MH, NcD, OClW, NjN, OU.

7. *Flashes in the night.* A collection of stories from contemporary Hungary. Edited by William (Vilmós) Juhász and Abraham Rothberg. New York: Random House, 1958. 87p.

Tibor Déry, 11-25, 54-68; Miklós Gyárfás, 37-46; Gyula Illyés, 8-9; *Ferenc Sánta*: "Straw bliss," 32-36; Pál Szabó, 47-53; Áron Tamási, 26-31, 69-84. Also: introduction by William (Vilmós) Juhász and Abraham Rothberg, 1-9; biographical notes, 85-87. NjR, ScU, NcU, WU, NIC, FU, ViU, OrU, MB, MoU, NN, AAP, KU, NbU, OCl, CU, InU, MiU, CLSU, IU, MH, CtY, NcD.

8. *Hungarian Short Stories. XIX and XX centuries.* Edited by László Pődör. Introduction by István Sőtér. Budapest: Corvina, 1962. 391p.

With the exception of Mór Jókai and Károly Eötvös, the authors are from the twentieth century. They are: Sándor Bródy, 141-150; Géza Csáth, 345-358; Andor Gábor, 307-334; Andor Endre Gelléri, 383-391; Jenő Heltai, 165-172; Sándor Hunyady, 367-382; Margit Kaffka, 257-280; Frigyes Karinthy, 359-366; Dezső Kosztolányi, 335-344; Gyula Krúdy, 173-204; Kálmán Mikszáth, 57-140; Ferenc Molnár, 205-220; Ferenc Móra, 221-232; Zsigmond Móricz, 233-256; Lajos Nagy, 281-306; István Tömörkény, 151-164. Also: introduction by István Sőtér, 7-18. CNoS, PPULC, InU, CU, NN, OkS, RP, CoU, MiEM, NIC, TxDaM, NbU, KyU, ICU, NcD, KU, CaAE, MiU, OCl, IU, AAP, TxU, IaU, CLU, WaU, NhD, NcU, IEdS.

9. *The plough and the pen.* Writings from Hungary 1930-1956. Edited by Ilona Duczyńska and Karl Polanyi. With a foreword by W. H. Auden. London: Peter Owen, 1963. 231p. (Also: Toronto: McClelland and Stewart, 1968. 231p.)

Part I – *Wasteland:* Gyula Illyés, 50-64; Zsigmond Móricz, 33-49; Áron Tamási, 65-79; *Pinions of Poverty:* Tibor Déry, 115-127; Pál Szabó, 92-104; Áron Tamási, 83-91; Péter Veres, 105-114; *Pledge:* Tibor Déry, 131-141; László Németh, 142-165; Part II – *Attila József and Gyula Illyés*: Attila József, 169-172; Gyula Illyés, 173-180; *The Communist Poets:* László Benjámin, 183-184; *Ferenc Juhász:* "The foaling time," "Song of the tractor," "Your ribbed, peasant hand," "Farm, at dark, on the Great Plain," "At twenty-six," "Man imposes his pattern upon a dream," "The boy changed into a stag cries out at the gate of secrets," "Season," 197-220; Péter Kuczka, 194; Lajos Tamási, 190-193; Zoltán Zelk, 185-189. Also: foreword by W. H. Auden, 9-11; preface, 13-15; "The Hungarian populists," an introduction by Ilona Duczyńska, 17-29; notes on the authors, 221-232. CLU, CU-S, MiD, ICU, MH, KU, NjP, RPB, ViU, OrPS, OU, NcD, CSt, IU, PSt, MdB, CaBVi, CaBVa, NNC, OKS, NbU, LU, CU, WU, IEdS. *Toronto edition:* NN, CaOTU, CtY, InU, CaBVa, NIC, FTaSU, NjR.

10. *Landmark.* Hungarian writers on thirty years of history. Edited by Miklós Szabolcsi, assisted by Zoltán Kenyeres. Budapest: Corvina, 1965. 358p.

I. Historical Background, 17-19; György Bálint, 63-64; Tibor Déry, 46-53; Andor Endre Gelléri, 43-45; Belá Illés, 66-74; Attila József, 21-23, 54-55; Ferenc Karinthy, 81-85; Zsigmond Móricz, 24-35; Lajos Nagy, 36-42; Miklós Radnóti, 65; Imre Sarkadi, 75-80; Mihály Váci, 56-62; *II. Historical Background*, 89-92; László Benjámin, 157-158, 235-237; József Darvas, 138-142; Tibor Déry, 195-202; Imre Dobozy, 210-214; Endre Fejes, 205-209; Gábor Garai, 176-184; Gyula Illyés, 124-135; *Ferenc Juhász:* "Granny," 136-137; Lajos Mesterházi, 93-98; György Moldova, 185-194; Zoltán Molnár, 151-156; Boris (Barbara) Palotai, 159-163; Kálmán Sándor, 215-229; István Sőtér, 102-113; Pál Szabó, 114-123; Lehel Szeberényi, 173-175; Judit Sziráky, 230-234; András Tabák, 143-150; Józsi Jenő Tersánszky, 99-101; Péter Veres, 164-172; Zoltán Zelk, 203-204; *III. Historical Background*, 241-242; *Sándor Csoóri:* "Report from the tower" (excerpts), 277-291; Ferenc Erdei, 317-329; Lajos Galambos, 265-276; Gábor Garai, 342-343; Endre Gerelyes, 300-307; Lajos Kassák, 247; Géza Molnár, 292-299; László Németh, 243-246; *Ferenc Sánta:* "Land," 248-255; György Szabó, 330-341; Károly Szakonyi, 256-264; Endre Vészi, 308-316. Also: introduction, 9-13; chronological guide, 351-354; the writers in the volume, 355-358. MtU, FU, ViU, NSyU, IEdS, PPULC, KyU, IEN, IaU, CaOTP, CtY, NNC, DeU, KyLoU, CaQMM, OrPS, OKentU.

11. *Hungarian anthology.* A collection of poems. Second edition revised and enlarged. Translated by Joseph Grosz and W. Arthur Boggs. Toronto: Pannonia Books, 1966. 315p. (First edition: Munich: Greiff-Druck, 1963. 251p.)

Some nineteenth-century poets and some even earlier ones but the poets included are primarily from the twentieth century. These are: Endre Ady, 100-135; Lajos Áprily, 185-

187; Mihály Babits, 148-156; József Bakucz, 294; Ferenc Baranyi, 310-311; Anna Bede, 291-293; László Benjámin, 283-284; Sándor Bihari, 312-313; György Borshy Kerekes, 201; Imre Csanádi, 286; *Sándor Csoóri*: "Vineyards before the war," "Neither death nor stonetiles," 302-303; Ottó Demény, 295; Jenő Dsida, 251; Tamás Emőd, 193; József Erdélyi, 205; Tibor Flórián, 259; András Fodor, 297-298; József Fodor, 206-207; Milán Füst, 194-196; Gábor Garai, 299-301; Géza Gárdonyi, 92; Oszkár Gellért, 140; Imre Györe, 306-307; Jenő Heltai, 95-99; Béla Horváth, 253-258; Ignotus (Hugó Veigelsberg), 93-94; Gyula Illyés, 217-224; László Jávor, 225-226; Károly Jobbágy, 288; Attila József, 227-248; *Ferenc Juhász*: "The wastrels' country," "Milk-drunken," 296; Gyula Juhász, 143-147; Margit Kaffka, 136-138; Frigyes Karinthy, 190-192; Lajos Kassák, 188-189; Simon Kemény, 141-142; Dénes Kiss, 308; László Könnyű, 281-282; Dezső Kosztolányi, 172-180; Mihály Ladányi, 304-305; Anna Lesznai, 164-171; László Mécs, 202-204; Zoltán Nagy, 161-162; Ottó Orbán, 309; *János Pilinszky*: "Apocalypse," 287; Miklós Radnóti, 260-274; Sándor Reményik, 200; György Sárközi, 208; Sándor Sík, 197; Zoltán Somlyó, 139; Lőrinc Szabó, 209-216; Mihály Szabolcska, 91; Ernő Szép, 157-160; Pál Tábori, 252; Árpád Tarnócy, 163; Árpád Tóth, 181-184; Tamás Tűz, 285; Mihály Váci, 289-290; Zseni Várnai, 198-199; István Vas, 275; Sándor Weöres, 276-280; Zoltán Zelk, 249-250. *Second edition*: IU, CLU, MH, NBuU, NcP, WU, NbU, RPB, OLSU, OrCS, IdU, CtY, OrPS, TxFTC, CaOTP, OClW, NjP, ICU, CSf, NjR, MB, KEmT, NN, MiD, CtW, WaU, MdBJ, RP, MoSW, NuU, IaU, NNC. *First edition*: CU, CLU, CoU, NN, ICU, MiD, MH, PSt, PSU, OU, OkU, MdBJ, NbU.

12. *The Literary Review*. Hungary number, IX, no. 3 (Spring, 1966). 493p.

All the authors are from the twentieth century. The authors of the stories are: *István Csurka*: "The barge pilot," 347-352; Tibor Déry, 352-366; Endre Fejes, 368-373; Ferenc Karinthy, 400-403; *Iván Mándy*: "An ordinary member," 413-420; *István Örkény*: "There is no pardon," 439-441; Géza Ottlik, 432-438; László Cs. Szabó, 443-454; Áron Tamási, 473-480; Szabolcs Vajay, 481-486. The authors of the poems are: László Benjámin, 346; György Faludy, 367-368; Milán Füst, 374-377; Gyula Illyés, 391-396; *Ferenc Juhász*: "The prodigal country," 397-399; Lajos Kassák, 404-405; Géza Képes, 406-408; Zoltán Keszthelyi, 409-412; *Ágnes Nemes Nagy*: "Ice," "Toward springtime," 421; *János Pilinszky*: "Harbach 1944," 442; Lőrinc Szabó, 455-456; István Vas, 487-489; Sándor Weöres, 490-491; Zoltán Zelk, 492-493. The authors of the plays are: Gyula Háy, 378-390; László Németh, 422-431; Magda Szabó, 457-472. Also: Paul (Pál) Tabori: "In spite of it all; a brief survey of contemporary Hungarian literature," 341-345.

13. *Twenty-two Hungarian short stories*. From the middle of the last century to the present day. Introduction by Alfred Alvarez. Budapest: Corvina, 1967. 432p. (Also: London: Oxford University Press, 1967, as *Hungarian short stories*. 432p.)

With the exception of Mór Jókai, the authors are from the twentieth century: Sándor Bródy, 75-87; Géza Csáth, 194-202; Tibor Déry, 242-262; Géza Gárdonyi, 88-96; Andor Endre Gelléri, 344-357; Jenő Heltai, 106-114; Sándor Hunyadi, 214-241; Endre Illés, 308-326; Gyula Illyés, 327-343; Ferenc Karinthy, 390-417; Frigyes Karinthy, 203-213; Dezső Kosztolányi, 185-193; Gyula Krúdy, 115-141; József Lengyel, 263-271; Kálmán Mikszáth, 11-74; Zsigmond Móricz, 142-152; Lajos Nagy, 153-184; Károly Pap, 272-297; Magda Szabó, 358-389; Antal Szerb, 298-307; Dezső Szomory, 97-105. Also: introduction, ix-xvi; bibliographical notes, 417-432. *Budapest edition*: ViU, CSt, CLU, OkU. *Oxford edition*: WU, NjP, IU, KU, MnU, CLU, FU, MiEM, WaU, NNC, AU, IEN, OOxM, IaAS, IaU, OrU, InU, NBuU, ViU, MB, NSyU, MdU, NcD, GU, CSt, CtU, CU, N, NCU, TxU, NH, CLSU, NIC, KyU, NBuU, AAP.

14. *Hungarian poetry. Poésie hongroise. 1848, 1919, 1945*. Budapest: Youth Publishing House, 1968. 214p.

Except for Sándor Petőfi, the authors are from the twentieth century, but only English and French translations of these authors are shown: Endre Ady, 33-53; Ferenc Baranyi, 203-205; Gábor Garai, 197-199; Gyula Illyés, 65-87; Attila József, 97-123; *Ferenc Juhász*: "The boy changed into a stag cries out at the gate of secrets" (extracts), "Imploration pour trouver le juste milieu pendant la composition d'une épopée," 183-189; Lajos Kassák, 57-59; Miklós Radnóti, 129-141; Mihály Váci, 159-164.

15. *New writing of Eastern Europe.* Edited by George Gömöri and Charles Newman. Chicago: Quadrangle Books, 1968. 263p.

The Hungarian authors included are from the twentieth century: Endre Bálint, 268; Miklós Boros, 237; Tivadar Csontváry, 269; Tibor Déry, 25-40; Gyula Háy, 129-140; Attila József, 161-166; Jenő Medveczky, 267; *László Nagy*: "Cloud with a woman's face," "Squared by walls," "Advancing through soot and snow," 259-261; *János Pilinszky*: "The desert of love," 150; Miklós Radnóti, 243; András Sándor, 151-160; Pál Veres, 68; Sándor Weöres, 55-67. Also: Charles Newman: Introduction, 9-12; George Gömöri: "Literature deprophetized: new trends in Eastern European literature," 13-24. OU, NjP, ViU, MB, CSt-H, MnU, IaU, KEmT, RpB, LU, TxU, CaBVaU, OrU, MU, AU, OkU, CoU, TU, NcRS, WaU, IU, MH, GAT, TNJ, CSt, NNC, IEN, NjR, WU, NBuU, GU, MoSW, NbU, NbuC, ICU, InU, FU, KU, CtY, LN, MiU, NmLcU, NN.

16. *Hundred Hungarian poems.* Edited by Thomas Kabdebo. Manchester, England: Albion Editions, 1976. 125p.

Selections begin with the Middle Ages, but more extensive coverage commences with the nineteenth century. The poets from the twentieth century are: Endre Ady, 44-46; Lajos Áprily, 57; Mihály Babits, 47-49; Károly Bari, 109; László Benjámin, 87-88; József Berda, 68; Gábor Devecseri, 88-89; Jenő Dsida, 77; György Faludy, 81-83; Ferenc Fáy, 91; Ferenc Fehér, 103; József Fodor, 58-59; Milán Füst, 57-58; Gábor Garai, 103-104; Ágnes Gergely, 104; György Gömöri, 105; Dezső György, 60; Victor Határ, 87; Ignotus (Hugó Veigelsberg), 44; Gyula Illyés, 61-67; Attila József, 68-75; *Ferenc Juhász*: "The day of superstitions," 97-101; Gyula Juhász, 46-47; Frigyes Karinthy, 55-56; Lajos Kassák, 56-57; László Kemenes Géfin, 107-108; Dezső Kosztolányi, 51-53; Ádám Makkai, 106; Imre Máté, 106; *László Nagy*: "The love of the scorching wind," 93-95; *Ágnes Nemes Nagy*: "To liberty," 91-92; Géza Páskándi, 104; *János Pilinszky*: "Introitus," "Fish in the net," 90-91; Miklós Radnóti, 78-79; György Rónay, 83-84; András Sándor, 105; György Sárközi, 59-60; István Siklós, 107; László Cs. Szabó, 76; Lőrinc Szabó, 60; Margit Szécsi, 101-102; Ernő Szép, 49-50; Imre Takács, 96-97; *Dezső Tandori*: "The two handles of the funerary urn from the private collection of E. E. Cummings," 108; Tibor Tollas, 89-90; Árpád Tóth, 54-55; István Vas, 79-80; Sándor Weöres, 85-86. Also: introduction, 3-6; notes on the poets, 110-118; selected bibliography, 119; index to English titles, 122-123; index to Hungarian titles, 124-125.

17. *Micromegas*, IV, no. 2 (1970). 40p.

Sándor Csoóri: "Village silhouettes," 34-35; Milán Füst, 12; Gábor Garai, 31-33; Ágnes Gergely, 36; Gyula Illyés, 13; Amy Károly, 29-30; Lajos Kassák, 5-11; Ágnes Keresztes, 37; *Ágnes Nemes Nagy*: "Trees," "The geysir," "Night oak," "Storm," 24-28; Imre Oravecz, 39-40; István Vas, 14-16; Sándor Weöres, 17-23. Also: introduction, by Frederic Will, 2-4.

18. *Modern Hungarian poetry.* Edited, and with an introduction, by Miklós Vajda. Foreword by William Jay Smith. Budapest: Corvina, 1977. 286p.

The poets included are entirely from the period from World War I to the present: István Ágh, 268-269; László Benjámin, 122-125; Imre Csanádi, 130-135; *Sándor Csoóri*: "Golden pheasants flying," "Barbarian prayer," "Ague," "Whispers for two voices," "I would rather run back," 233-237; István Csukás, 263-264; Gábor Devecseri, 126-129; István Eörsi, 238-

239; Milán Füst, 5-6; Gábor Garai, 229-232; Ágnes Gergely, 240-243; Gábor György, 225-228; Anna Hajnal, 47-51; Gyula Illyés, 14-40; Zoltán Jékely, 118-121; Ferenc Juhász: "Gold," "Silver," "Power of the flowers," "The boy changed into a stag cries out at the gate of secrets," "Crown of hatred and love," 196-220; Márton Kalász, 244-245; László Kálnoky, 84-86; Amy Károly, 52-82; Lajos Kassák, 1-4; István Kormos, 161-164; Mihály Ladányi, 246-250; László Nagy: "Frosts are coming," "The coalmen," "The bliss of Sunday," "Fair and frosty May," "The ferryman," "Prayer to the white lady," "Squared by walls," "Without mercy," "The break-up," "The peacock woman," "Love of the scorching wind," 168-187; Ágnes Nemes Nagy: "Statues," "I carried statues," "Between," "Defend it," "A comparison," "The shapelessness," 156-160; Ottó Orbán, 251-257; György Petri: "You usually come in the morning," "With the thin girl," "Song," 271-274; János Pilinszky: "Under the winter sky," "Sin," "Passion of Ravensbrück," "The desert of love," "Apocrypha," "Postscript," "Fable, detail from 'Kz-Oratorio'," "As I was," "Celebration of the Nadir," "I shall be watching," "Metronome," "Exhortation," "Every breath," "The rest is grace," "Meetings," "Cattle brand," 142-155; Sándor Rákos, 140-141; György Rónay, 87-117; István Simon, 188-194; György Somlyó, 136-139; Lőrinc Szabó, 8-13; Margit Szécsi, 221-224; Dezső Tandori: "And brief good mother? For I am in haste? Whither??", "Homage," "Details," "Sadness of the bare copula," 265-267; Judit Tóth, 258-262; Mihály Váci, 165-167; Szabolcs Várady, 275-276; Miklós Veress: "Self-portrait at thirty," 270; Zoltán Zelk, 41-46. Also: William Jay Smith, foreword, xv-xviii; biographical notes, 279-286. LC.

FRENCH

See also number 14.

19. *Échos français de la lyre hongroise.* Traductions du hongrois. Volume I. Budapest: Bárd, 1921. 56p.

The volume begins with Mihály Vörösmarty. Authors from the twentieth century are: Endre Ady, 42; Mihály Babits, 43; Jenő Heltai, 44; Ignotus (Hugó Veigelsberg), 45; Gyula Juhász, 47; Dezső Kosztolányi, 48; Emma Ritoók, 50; Mihály Szabolcska, 41; Ernő Szép, 52. Also: au lecteur, 5; avant-propos, 6.

20. *Anthologie de la poésie hongroise contemporaine.* Établie et traduite par Léon Bazalgette, Géo. Charles, etc. Sous la direction de Béla Pogány. Révision de Géo. Charles. 2ème édition. Paris: Union, 1927. 218p.

Endre Ady, 13-20; Mihály Babits, 21-32; Béla Balázs, 33-36; Kornél Bányai, 37-40; Sándor Barta, 41-46; Tibor Déry, 47-52; József Erdélyi, 53-56; László Fenyő, 57-58; Imre Forbáth, 59-62; János Fóthy, 63-66; Milán Füst, 67-70; Oszkár Gellért, 71-76; Jenő Heltai, 77-80; Ignotus (Hugó Veigelsberg), 81-84; Gyula Illyés, 85-89; Gyula Juhász, 89-94; Margit Kaffka, 95-98; Lajos Kassák, 99-108; Simon Kemény, 109-112; Aladár Komjáthy, 119-122; Aladár Komlós, 123-125; András Komor, 113-118; Dezső Kosztolányi, 127-136; Sándor Márai, 137-140; László Mécs, 141-144; Sándor Nádas, 145-148; Zoltán Nagy, 149-154; Tivadar Raith, 155-160; Vilmos Rozványi, 161-168; György Sárközi, 169-172; István Strém, 173-178; Lőrinc Szabó, 179-186; Ernő Szép, 187-190; Aladár Tamás, 191-192; István Tamás, 193-196; Sophie (Zsófi) Török, 197-208; Nándor Várkonyi, 209-210; Béla Zsolt, 211-218. Also: préface, 7-12.

21. *Anthologie des conteurs hongrois d'aujourd'hui.* Établie et traduite par Ladislas Gara et Marcel Largeaud. Notes biobibliographiques par Béla Pogány. Paris: Rieder, 1927. 261p.

All authors are from the period before World War II: Mihály Babits, 11-58; Sándor Barta, 59-88; Lajos Bíró, 89-100; Jenő Heltai, 101-108; Frigyes Karinthy, 109-120; Lajos Kassák, 121-136; Dezső Kosztolányi, 137-144; Ákos Molnár, 145-158; Ferenc Molnár, 159-180; Zsigmond Móricz, 181-192; Tivadar Raith, 193-200; István Strém, 201-214; Dezső Szabó,

215-230; Dezső Szomory, 231-240; József (Józsi) Jenő Tersánszky, 241-260. Also, avant-propos, 7-11. MWelC, CtY.

22. *Les maîtres conteurs hongrois.* Traduit par Louis J. (József Lajos) Fóti et Georges Délaquys. Budapest: Librairie Française, 1928. 171p.

All authors are from the twentieth century: Zoltán Ambrus, 119; Lajos Bíró, 97-109; Géza Gárdonyi, 36-61; Ferenc Herczeg, 73-84; Dezső Kosztolányi, 110-118; Kálmán Mikszáth, 7-25; Zsigmond Móricz, 85-96; Béla Révész, 26-35; István Tömörkény, 62-72. NN, CoU.

23. *Poèmes hongrois.* Traduits par Georges Philippe Dhas. Budapest: Springer, 1935. 79p.

Except for Sándor Petőfi and János Arany, the authors are from the twentieth century: Endre Ady, 49-60; Mihály Babits, 71-74; Sándor Endrődy, 79; Géza Gyóni (Achim), 61-64; Dezső Kosztolányi, 75-78; Gyula Wlassics, 65-70. CtY, CU, NjP, DLC-P4, OCl.

24. *Anthologie de la poésie hongroise.* Par Jean (Jenő) Hankiss et L. Molnos-Miller. Traductions de Eugène Bencze, Alexandre Eckhardt, etc. Paris: Sagittaire, 1936. 240p.

Except for Bálint Balassa, Miklós Zrínyi, the Kuruc poems, and Ferenc Faludi, the poets are from the nineteenth and twentieth centuries. Those from the twentieth century are: *Between Two Centuries*: Miklós Bárd, 105-106; Géza Gárdonyi, 110; József Kiss, 100-101; Jenő Komjáthy, 98-99; Endre Kozma, 104; Gyula Reviczky, 93-97; Mihály Szabolcska, 107-108; Gyula Vargha, 102-103; Árpád Zempléni, 109; *The Triade of 1910*: Endre Ady, 111-115; Mihály Babits, 116-122; Dezső Kosztolányi, 123-127; *Contemporary Poetry*: Lajos Áprily, 128-129; János Bartalis, 130-131; Mária Berde, 132-133; Aladár Bodor, 134-135; Jenő Dsida, 136; József Erdélyi, 137-138; Tamás Falu, 139; Lajos Fekete, 140-141; József Fodor, 142; Milán Füst, 143; Jenő Gáspár, 144; Oszkár Gellért, 145-146; Pál Gulyás, 147-149; Géza Gyóni (Achim), 150-151; Kálmán Harsányi, 153-154; Lajos Harsányi, 155; István Havas, 156; Ignotus (Hugó Veigelsberg), 157-158; Gyula Illyés, 159-160; Attila József, 161; Gyula Juhász, 162; Margit Kaffka, 163-164; Frigyes Karinthy, 165; Lajos Kassák, 166-167; Simon Kemény, 168-169; István Lendvai, 170-171; Anna Lesznai, 172; Tibor Marconnay, 173-174; László Mécs, 175-180; Jenő Miklós, 181-182; Zoltán Nadányi, 183-184; Zoltán Nagy, 185-186; Gábor Oláh, 187-188; Lajos Olosz, 189; Sándor Reményik, 191-192; György Sárközi, 193-194; Sándor Sík, 195-196; Andor Simon, 197; Domokos Sípos, 198-199; Gyula Somogyváry, 200-201; Lőrinc Szabó, 202; Kornél Szenteleky, 203-205; Jenő Szentimrei, 206-208; Ernő Szép, 209-212; István Szombati-Szabó, 213-214; László Tompa, 215-216; Árpád Tóth, 217-219; Géza Vályi-Nagy, 220; Végvári (Sándor Reményik), 221-223; Gyula Wlassics, 224. Also: poésie populaire, 225-228; ballades populaires, 229-240; and avant-propos, 1-2. IEN, InU, NBuU, NNC, DLC-P4.

25. *Anthologie de la prose hongroise.* Par Jean (Jenő) Hankiss et Léopold Molnos. Traductions de Pierre Barkan, Albert Gourseaud, etc. Paris: Sagittaire, 1938. 364p.

Selections begin with the eighteenth century, but more extensive coverage commences with the nineteenth century. The authors from the twentieth century are: Zoltán Ambrus, 119-122; Mihály Babits, 204-207; Boris Balla, 342-346; Mária Berde, 246-253; Margit Bethlen, 196-198; Lajos Bíbó, 257-259; János Bókay, 275-280; Imre Cziráky, 306-313; Sándor Dallos, 321-326; István Darkó, 338-341; Mihály Földi, 289-293; Géza Gárdonyi, 123-127; Irén Gulácsy, 281-288; Zsolt Harsányi, 221-225; Jenő Heltai, 142-147; Ferenc Herczeg, 128-136; Margit Kaffka, 180-184; Frigyes Karinthy, 226-230; János Kodolányi, 314-316; János Komáromi, 260-264; Ferenc Körmendi, 327-330; Dezső Kosztolányi, 208-215; Gyula Krúdy, 158-162; Aladár Kuncz, 215-220; Sándor Makkai, 265-267; Sándor Márai, 317-320; Ödön Mariay, 199-203; Jenő Maróthy, 294-299; Kálmán Mikszáth, 97-109; Ferenc Molnár, 153-157; Ferenc Móra, 171-179; Zsigmond Móricz, 164-170; László Németh, 331-337; József Nyírő, 238-245; Ottokár Prohászka, 110-113; Viktor Rákosi, 114-118; László Ravasz, 185-189; Miklós Surányi, 190-195; Dezső Szabó, 163-164; László Cs. Szabó, 351-358; Mária Szabó, 231-237; Áron Tamási, 300-305; György Terescsenyi, 253-256; Cecil Tormay, 145-152; István Tömörkény, 137-141; Sándor Török, 347-350; Lajos Zilahy, 268-274. Also: avant-propos, 9-10. NNC, DLC, MH, OCl, IaU, NPurMC.

26. *Terre hongroise. 11 poètes hongrois de 1848 à 1948*. Traduction et commentaire de Montarier H. Kallus. Boudry: Édition de la Baconnière, 1948. 32p.

With the exception of Sándor Petőfi and János Arany, the authors are from the twentieth century: Endre Ady, 10-13; Mihály Babits, 14-15; Milán Füst, 24-25; Gyula Illyés, 28-29; Attila József, 20-21; Dezső Kosztolányi, 18-19; Miklós Radnóti, 22-23; Árpád Tóth, 16-17; Sándor Weöres, 26-27. Also: note du traducteur, 30-32.

27. *Nouvelles hongroises. Anthologie des XIXe et XXe siècles*. Présentation d'Aurélien Sauvageot. Préface d'András Diószegi. Paris: Seghers, 1961. 382p.

The authors from the twentieth century are: Endre Ady, 151-156; Zoltán Ambrus, 77-86; Sándor Bródy, 87-94; Géza Csáth, 309-320; Andor Gábor, 273-298; Géza Gárdonyi, 95-104; Andor Endre Gelléri, 375-382; Jenő Heltai, 131-138; Sándor Hunyady, 347-362; Margit Kaffka, 229-250; Frigyes Karinthy, 321-328; Dezső Kosztolányi, 308; Gyula Krúdy, 157-186; Kálmán Mikszáth, 63-76; Ferenc Molnár, 187-200; Ferenc Móra, 201-212; Zsigmond Móricz, 213-228; Lajos Nagy, 251-272; Károly Pap, 363-374; Béla Révész, 139-150; Zoltán Thury, 117-130; István Tömörkény, 105-116; Gyula Török, 329-346. Also: avant-propos, 9-16; introduction: la nouvelle en Hongrie par András Diószegi, 17-28. IEN, ICU, CU, WU.

28. *Anthologie de la poésie hongroise du XIIe siècle à nos jours*. Rédacteur, épilogue par Ladislas Gara. Préface de László Cs. Szabó. Paris: Éditions du Seuil, 1962. 501p.

More than half of the text is devoted to the poems of twentieth-century authors: *II. Romanticism and Post Romanticism*: Lajos Bartók, 204; Minka Czóbel, 201-202; Jenő Heltai, 205-206; Ignotus (Hugó Veigelsberg), 203; József Kiss, 194-196; Jenő Komjáthy, 190-191; Andor Kozma, 200; Lajos Palágyi, 199; Gyula Reviczky, 192-194; Géza Szilágyi, 207; Gyula Vargha, 197-198; *III. The Nyugat Generation and Their Heirs*: Endre Ady, 212-223; Lajos Áprily, 270-271; Mihály Babits, 231-243; Béla Balázs, 247-248; Sándor Barta, 305; József Berda, 335-336; Jenő Dsida, 354-355; József Erdélyi, 299-303; György Faludy, 393-397; József Fodor, 306-308; Milán Füst, 282-286; Andor Gábor, 249; Oszkár Gellért, 225-226; Pál Gulyás, 311-312; Anna Hajnal, 357-358; Győző Határ, 389-392; Gyula Illyés, 323-334; Ferenc Jankovich, 355-356; Zoltán Jékely, 385-386; Attila József 337-351; Gyula Juhász, 244-246; Simon Kemény, 229-230; Margit Kaffka, 223; László Kálnoky, 374-375; Frigyes Karinthy, 279-281; Lajos Kassák, 272-278; Géza Képes, 359-360; Aladár Komját, 290; Aladár Komjáthy, 294; Lajos Kónya, 399; Dezső Kosztolányi, 254-263; Sarolta Lányi, 291; Anna Lesznai, 263; László Mécs, 297-298; Zoltán Nadányi, 292-293; Zoltán Nagy, 250; Miklós Radnóti, 361-365; Sándor Reményik, 288-289; György Rónay, 387-388; György Sárközi, 309-310; Sándor Sík, 287; István Sinka, 303-304; Zoltán Somlyó, 226-228; Lőrinc Szabó, 313-322; Ernő Szép, 251-253; Gyula Takáts, 372-373; Pál Toldalagi, 398; Sophie (Zsófi) Török, 295-296; Árpád Tóth, 264-269; István Vas, 366-371; Sándor Weöres, 376-384; Zoltán Zelk, 352-353; *IV. New Voices*: László Benjámin, 405-407; Gábor Bikich, 427-429; Imre Csanádi, 413; János Csokits, 451-453; *Sándor Csoóri*: "Cette femme est une fleur," "Temps à soulever les vallées," 457-458; Gábor Devecseri, 409-410; András Fodor, 455; Gábor Garai, 454; Erzsébet Gyarmati, 425-426; *Ferenc Juhász*: "La baleine irisée," "Tristesse en culture," "La fleur du silence," 445-450; Áron Kibédi-Varga, 443-444; István Kormos, 431-433; Péter Kuczka, 430; László Lator, 442; *László Nagy*: "Crépuscule, aurore," "Les amants," "Dangers des fleurs," 438-439; Ágnes Nemes Nagy: "Octobre," "Le tramway," "Notes sur la peur," 420-424; János Pilinszky: "Trapeze et barres," "Un P. G. français," "Apocryphe," 415-419; György Rába, 435-437; Sándor Rákos, 414; István Simon, 440; György Somlyó, 411-412; Magda Szabó, 408; Margit Szécsi, 456; Imre Takács, 441; Miklós Vidor, 434. Also: la poésie hongroise par László Cs. Szabó, 9-34; la traduction de la poésie hongroise et ses problèmes par Ladislas Gara, 459. NN, NjP, NNC, NjR, MdU, InU, IEN, NBuU, IU, CoU, MH.

29. *Europe*. Revue mensuelle. Littérature hongroise, XLI, no. 411-412 (Juillet-Août, 1963). 329p.

László Benjámin, 91-94; *Sándor Csoóri*: "J'ai volé ton visage," 108-109; István Csukás, 114-115; József Fodor, 79-80; Gábor Garai, 107-108; Imre Györe, 111-112; Gyula Illyés, 80-83; *Ferenc Juhász*: "Devant la tombe d'Árpád Tóth," 105-107; Márton Kalász, 112-113; Lajos Kassák, 77-79; Zoltán Keszthelyi, 85-86; Ferenc Kiss, 84-85; Lajos Kónya, 90-91; Mihály Ladányi, 113-114; András Mezei, 109-110; *László Nagy*: "Mon amour, ô vie qui nous brises," 101-102; *Ágnes Nemes Nagy*: "Le geyser," 100-101; Ottó Orbán, 110-111; *János Pilinszky*: "Épilogue," 99-100; György Rónay, 88; István Simon, 104-105; György Somlyó, 94-99; Mihály Váci, 103-104; István Vas, 86-88; Sándor Weöres, 89-90; Zoltán Zelk, 83-84. Also: fourteen articles discussing various aspects of Hungarian literature, 3-76.

30. *Les lettres nouvelles*. Numéro special. Écrivains hongrois d'aujourd'hui, XII (Septembre-Octobre, 1964). 317p.

László Benjámin, 127-128; Gyula Csák, 252-266; *Sándor Csoóri*: "Ma main," "Fuite de la solitude," 243-244, 289-290; *István Csurka*: "Le timonier de péniche," 282-288; Tibor Déry, 19-34; Milán Füst, 13-17, 42-43; Gábor Garai, 267; György Gera, 173-181; László Gyurkó, 291-298; Gyula Háy, 62-75; Gyula Illyés, 45-49; *Ferenc Juhász*: "Jeudi, jour de superstition," 299-302; Ferenc Karinthy, 215-231; Lajos Kassák, 15, 60-61; János Kodolányi, 36-41; E. (Emil) Kolozsvári-Grandpierre, 159-171; György Konrád, 268-281; István Kormos, 250-251; József Lengyel, 101-109; Georges (György) Lukács, 76-100; *Iván Mándy*: "Un simple militant," 194-205; Lajos Mesterházi, 232-242; *Miklós Mészöly*: "Cinq souris," 134-145; György Moldova, 245-249; *Ágnes Nemes Nagy*: "Le tramway," 212-214; László Németh, 110-117; *István Örkény*: "Mort sans crédit," 154-157; *János Pilinszky*: "Paradis obscur," 182-193; György Rába, 119-120, 158; György Somlyó, 129-133; István Sőtér, 206-211; Tibor Tardos, 121-124; István Vas, 125-126; Sándor Weöres, 146-153. Also: Georges (György) Kassai: "Traduire du hongrois," 303-306; actualités, 307-317.

31. *Milliaire*. Trente années d'un pays à travers sa littérature. Sous la direction de Miklós Szabolcsi avec la collaboration de Zoltán Kenyeres. Budapest: Corvina, 1965. 332p.

The contents are same as number 10. MH, CLU.

32. *Panorama de la littérature hongroise du XXe siècle*. Choix, biographies et portraits d'auteurs par György Bodnár. Collaborateurs Béla Pomogáts et Csaba Sík. Introduction István Sőtér. Budapest: Corvina, 1965. Volume 1, 414p.; Volume 2, 355p.

Volume 1: I.: Endre Ady, 21-41; Zsigmond Móricz, 42-112; *II.*: Mihály Babits, 113-133; Gyula Juhász, 167-172; Dezső Kosztolányi, 134-166; Árpád Tóth, 173-179; *III.*: Sándor Bródy, 180-200; Ferenc Móra, 214-222; Zoltán Thury, 201-206; István Tömörkény, 207-213; *IV.*: Zoltán Ambrus, 223-230; Viktor Cholnoky, 289-298; Géza Csáth, 299-307; Sándor Hunyady, 338-348; Margit Kaffka, 279-288; Frigyes Karinthy, 318-337; Gyula Krúdy, 248-278; Károly Lovik, 231-239; Ferenc Molnár, 240-247; Dezső Szomory, 308-317; *V.*: Milán Füst, 349-365; Lajos Kassák, 398-414; Dezső Szabó, 392-397; József (Józsi) Jenő Tersánszky, 366-391. Also: avant-propos de l'éditeur, 5-6; de la littérature hongroise par István Sőtér, 7-20. *Volume 2: I.*: Attila József, 5-33; Lajos Nagy, 33-74; *II.*: Andor Endre

Gelléri, 99-110; Aladár Kuncz, 75-85; Károly Pap, 86-98; Antal Szerb, 110-118; *III.*: Gyula Illyés, 119-159; János Kodolányi, 185-211; László Németh, 159-185; Áron Tamási, 240-273; Pál Szabó, 226-240; Péter Veres, 211-225; *IV.*: Béla Balázs, 307-319; Tibor Déry, 319-340; Andor Gábor, 294-298; Béla Illés, 299-306; Frigyes Karikás, 283-294; Miklós Radnóti, 274-282; Lőrinc Szabó, 340-351. CLU, ViU, CaOTP, NNC.

33. *Humana Hungarica.* Poètes et écrivains hongrois au service de l'homme. Choix de textes établi par László Pődör. Préface de Máté Kovács, Président de la Société des Bibliophiles Hongrois. Budapest: La Société des Bibliophiles Hongrois, 1969. 97p.

The volume begins with Janus Pannonius. Authors from the twentieth century are: Endre Ady (one poem in English), 32-33; Mihály Babits, 34-35; Béla Bartók, 41; László Benjámin, 54-57; Milán Füst, 42-43; Gábor Garai, 67-68; Gyula Illyés, 48-51; Attila József (in English), 44-45; *Ferenc Juhász*: "Man imposes his pattern upon a dream," 64-66; Lajos Kassák, 38-39; Zoltán Kodály, 41; Dezső Kosztolányi, 36-37; *László Nagy*: "Hurlement," 62-63; *János Pilinszky*: "Le troisième jour," 61; Miklós Radnóti, 46-47; István Vas, 52-53; Sándor Weöres, 58-60. Also: préface, 9, 11; selected bibliography, 69-70.

34. *Marginales.* Revue bimestrielle des idées et des lettres. Visages de Hongrie, XXIV, no. 127-128 (Septembre, 1969). 176p.

Iván Boldizsár, 50-52, 109-113; Milán Füst, 27-46; Gábor Garai, 161-163; László Gereblyés, 47-49; Gábor Goda, 67-72; Gyula Illyés, 18-26; Zoltán Jékely, 73-74; *Ferenc Juhász*: "En marge de mes années de léthargie," "Imploration pour trouver le juste milieu pendant la composition d'une épopée," "Bonheur," "Anna Keleti ou l'exorcisme," "L'heure du silence," "Notes de fin d'hiver," 154-160; László Kéry, 119-131; *Iván Mándy*: "Cinéma du bon vieux temps: La Mort de Laurel," 136-146; *László Nagy*: "Paysage avec moi-même," 147; *Ágnes Nemes Nagy*: "L'étang," "A mon métier," "Le sans-forme," "Fenêtres: statues, lazare, arbres," "Tempête," "En revenant," 114-118; *István Örkény*: "Le dernier train," 79-90; Géza Ottlik, 94-101; *János Pilinszky*: "Francfort 1945" (extract), "Harback 1944," "Passion de Ravensbrück," "Poissons dans un filet," 105-108; György Rába, 134-135; Miklós Radnóti, 53-54; György Rónay, 75-78; István Simon, 148-149; György Somlyó, 102-104; István Sőtér, 55-62; Mihály Váci, 132-133; István Vas, 65-66; Sándor Weöres, 91-93; Zoltán Zelk, 63-64; László Zolnay, 164-174. Also: avant-propos, 3-4; la littérature hongroise moderne vue à vol d'oiseau par Péter Nagy, 5-18; Géza Perneczky: "Les beaux-arts de nos jours en Hongrie," 150-153; bibliographie, 175.

35. *Le cahiers du groupe,* les hongrois, no. 5 (1971). 104p.

István Csurka: "Le lustre," 77-84; Zoltán Fábian, 94-104; Endre Fejes, 37-43; Endre Illés, 85-93; László Kamondy, 59-76; József Lengyel, 16-26; *Iván Mándy*: "La mort de Pat," 5-15; György Moldova, 51-58; *Ferenc Sánta*: "Souvenir d'Italie," 44-50; András Simonffy, 27-36. Also: introduction par David Scheinert, 3-4.

36. *Mes poètes hongrois.* Deuxiéme édition augmentée (par) Guillevic. Budapest: Corvina, 1977. 360p. (First edition: Budapest: Corvina, 1967. 273p.)

Except for János Arany and János Vajda, the authors are from the twentieth century: Endre Ady, 51-63; Mihály Babits, 71-79; Béla Balázs, 93-94; László Benjámin, 263-269; József Berda, 153; *Sándor Csoóri*: "Cette femme est une fleur," "Temps conditionnel," 331-334; Gábor Devecseri, 271-275; Jenő Dsida, 201; Milán Füst, 119-131; Gábor Garai, 327-328; Oszkár Gellért, 69; László Gereblyés, 229-232; Anna Hajnal, 203-204; Gyula Illyés, 141-152; Zoltán Jékely, 235-236; Attila József, 155-189; *Ferenc Juhász*: "La fleur du silence," "En marge des mes années de léthargie," "Imploration pour trouver le juste milieu pendant la composition d'une épopée," 315-319; Gyula Juhász, 81-92; Amy Károlyi, 233; Lajos Kassák, 115-117; Géza Képes, 205; Lajos Kónya, 261; Dezső Kosztolányi, 95-108;

László Nagy: "Paysage avec moi-même," "Qui portera l'amour?", "Attila József," 305-309; *Agnes Nemes Nagy*: "Dans le quartier Krisztina," "Glace," "Nuit," "Quatre carreaux," 299-304; Anna Pardi, 337-338; *János Pilinszky*: "La passion de Ravensbrück," "Le troisième jour," "Vent froid," "Sur un astre interdit," "Damnation," "Attentat," "In memoriam F. M. Dostoievski," "Final," "Détronisation," 289-294; Miklós Radnóti, 207-218; Sándor Rákos, 295-298; György Rónay, 255-260; István Simon, 311-312; György Somlyó, 279-288; Zoltán Somlyó, 65-68; Lőrinc Szabó, 133-139; Imre Takács, 313; György Timár, 329-330; Árpád Tóth, 109-114; Judit Tóth, 335-336; Mihály Váci, 321-325; István Vas, 219-228; György Végh, 277; Sándor Weöres, 237-254; Zoltán Zelk, 191-199. Also: préface à la première édition, 17-27; préface à la deuxième édition, 29-30; notices bibliographiques, 339-360. *First edition*: NjP.

37. *Poésie hongroise*. Anthologie. Poèmes choisis et adaptés par Marc Delouze. Budapest: Corvina, 1978. 261p.

The anthology begins with Janus Pannonius. Authors are primarily from the twentieth century: *Introduction*: Endre Ady, 33-34; chansons populaires, 37-41; *Anthologie*: Károly Bari, 45-47; László Benjámin, 48-51; Attila Béres, 52-55; Sándor Bihari, 56-58; Imre Csanádi, 59-62; *Sándor Csoóri*: "Le temps sous un masque de rat," "Grommellement," "Dans un lent imparfait," 63-65; György Czigány, 66-69; Péter Fábri, 70-72; Zoltán Gábor, 73-75; Gábor Garai, 76-80; Imre Györe, 81-85; Tibor Hajas, 86-91; Anna Hajnal, 92-94; Gyula Illyés, 95-99; Zoltán Jékely, 100-104; Attila József, 35-36; *Ferenc Juhász*: "L'homme se dérobant," "Un feuille sur le catafalque abandonné du château des roses," 105-109; László Károly, 110-113; Judit Kemenczky, 114-119; *Anna Kiss*: "Utopie," "Autel-quadriptyque: Le spectre, Kristian et le Renard, Désordre, Jeu," "Dani-les-marionettes," "L'art de la vieille," 120-125; István Kormos, 126-129; Mihály Ladányi, 130-132; László Lator, 133-136; *László Marsall*: "Les profondeurs du silence," "Imploration," "Palissades," "Je le crois à ta main," "Monnaie," 137-140; Katalin Mezey, 141-143; Péter Müller, 144-146; *László Nagy*: "Crépuscule, aube," "Gels, l'un après l'autre," "Je jure qu'elle est éternelle," "Madone sacrilège," "Le rayonnement d'Egry," "Les souliers-de-fer d'Hölderlin," 147-152; *Agnes Nemes Nagy*: "La vision," "Méditation," "Chêne de nuit," 153-156; Imre Oravecz, 157-161; Ottó Orbán, 162-166; Lajos Pass, 167-173; *György Petri*: "Escalier," "L'oignon parle," "Reproche," "Synopsis de Beckett," "Si rare . . . ," "J'aime bien," 174-177; *János Pilinszky*: "Vent froid," "Quatrain," "Agonia Christiana," "Sur la plage," "Le troisième," "Au troisième jour," "La passion de Ravensbrück," "Question," "Tel que j'ai commencé," "Un beau jour," "Je crois," "Autoportrait, 1944," "Jugement d'exception," "Comme la terre," "Vers où? Comment?" 178-183; György Rába, 184-187; Sándor Rákos, 188-192; György Somlyó, 193-198; Margit Szécsi, 199-201; Magda Székely, 202-205; *Dezső Tandori*: "The heart of the matter," "Koan bel canto," "Tous les détails," "Le prodigue," "Koan II," "Gargouilles," "La route de damas," "(Dison:) Koan 1970," "Collection privée," "La tristesse du seul verbe d'existence," "Salon; l'année," 206-213; György Timár, 214-218; József Tornai, 219-222; Judit Tóth, 223-226; Szabolcs Várady, 227-229; István Vas, 230-237; Sándor Weöres, 238-247; Zoltán Zelk, 248-253. Also: traduire c'est entre-prendre par Marc Delouze, 7-11.

GERMAN

38. *Ungarn*. Ein Novellenbuch. Herausgegeben und übertragen von Stefan J. Klein. München-Berlin: Georg Müller, n.d. 289p.

All authors are from the twentieth century: Zoltán Ambrus, 7-17; Lajos Barta, 19-47; Lajos Bíró, 49-59; Sándor Bródy, 61-80; Géza Gárdonyi, 81-85; Ferenc Herczeg, 87-94; Ignotus (Hugó Veigelsberg), 95-110; Daniel Jób, 111-120; Frigyes Karinthy, 121-129; Miklós Kisbán, 131-150; Tamás Kóber, 151-156; Dezső Kosztolányi, 157-168; Gyula Krúdy,

169-175; Géza Laczkó, 177-197; Ferenc Molnár, 199-208; Tamás Moly, 209-224; Zsigmond Móricz, 225-233; Lajos Nagy, 235-244; Béla Révész, 245-262; Ernő Szép, 263-270; Gyula Szini, 271-281; István Tömörkény, 283-289.

39. *Moderne ungarische Dichter.* Ins Deutsche übertragen von Lajos Brájjer. Nagybecskerek: Fr. Paul Pleitz, 1914. 100p.

All authors are from the twentieth century: Emil Ábrányi, 9-11; Endre Ady, 12-18; Mihály Babits, 21-24; Ignác Balla, 25; Miklós Bárd, 26-27; Ferenc Benjámin, 28-31; Ákos Dutka, 32-37; Renée Erdős, 38-40; Imre Farkas, 41; Milán Füst, 42; Géza Gárdonyi, 43-44; Oszkár Gellért, 45-46; Jenő Heltai, 47-49; Ignotus (Hugó Veigelsberg), 50-52; Ilma Jörg-Draskóczy, 53-56; Margit Kaffka, 62-63; Simon Kemény, 57-58; Dezső Kosztolányi, 64-66; Andor Kozma, 59-61; Sarolta Lányi, 68-69; Anna Lesznai, 70-71; Alba Naevis, 19-20; Árpád Pásztor, 72-73; Ferenc Ráskai, 74-75; Zoltán Somlyó, 76; Mihály Szabolcska, 77-78; Zoltán Szász, 79-80; Gyula Szávay, 81-84; Aladár Székács, 84-85; Ernő Szép, 86-90; Géza Szilágyi, 91-96; Antal Szirbik, 96-100. Also: Vorwort, 3-4; moderne ungarische Lyrik, 4-8.

40. *Ungarische Erzählungen.* Band 1. Übersetzt und herausgegeben von Stefan J. Klein. Konstanz am Bodensee: Reuss und Itta, 1916. 75p.

All authors are from the twentieth century: Lajos Bíró, 45-54; Sándor Bródy, 27-36; Jenő Heltai, 5-11; Ferenc Herczeg, 19-26; Károly Lovik, 67-75; Ferenc Molnár, 12-18; Zsigmond Móricz, 37-44; Gyula Szini, 55-66. MnU.

41. *Neue ungarische Lyrik.* In Nachdichtungen von Heinrich Horvát. München: Georg Müller, 1918. 251p.

With the exception of Imre Madách and János Vajda, the authors are from the twentieth century: Endre Ady, 3-16; Mihály Babits, 19-36; Béla Balázs, 39-44; Ákos Dutka, 47; Tamás Emőd, 51; Renée Erdős, 55-56; Zoltán Franyó, 59-60; Milán Füst, 63-64; Oszkár Gellért, 67; Géza Gyóni (Achim), 71-73; Ignotus (Hugó Veigelsberg), 77; Gyula Juhász, 81-89; Margit Kaffka, 93; Artur Keleti, 97-100; József Kiss, 103-120; Jenő Komjáthy, 123; Dezső Kosztolányi, 127-142; Sarolta Lányi, 145-150; Anna Lesznai, 153-154; Sándor Mezey, 161-164; Jutka Miklós, 171-172; Aladár Mohácsi, 167-168; Zoltán Nagy, 175-176; Lajos Palágyi, 179-185; Piroska Reichard, 189-193; Zoltán Somlyó, 197; Malvin Schack, 201; Lajos Szabolcsi, 205-207; Euphrosyne (Fruzsina) Szalay, 211; Ernő Szép, 215; Géza Szilágyi, 219-225; Árpád Tóth, 229-232; Gyula Vargha, 241; Gyula Wlassics, 245-247.

42. *Ungarische Lieder.* Ein Reigen von Gedichten zeitgenössischer ungarischer Dichter. Aus dem Ungarischen ins Deutsche übertragen von Karl Somló. Vorwort von Leo Heller (Berlin). Leipzig: Xenien Verlag, 1918. 78p.

With the exception of János Vajda and four minor figures the poets are from the twentieth century: *Songs from the War:* Ákos Dutka, 31-32; Tamás Emőd, 27-28, 30-31; Géza Gyóni (Achim), 14-18, 23-27; József Kiss, 18-22, 29-30; Menyhért Kiss, 32-33; Mihály Szabolcska, 30; Zoltán Szávay, 28-29; *Songs from Peace:* Endre Ady, 53-54; Mihály Babits, 44-45; Géza Gyóni (Achim), 41-43; Jenő Heltai, 75; Ignotus (Hugó Veigelsberg), 76; Károly Somló, 51; Simon Kemény, 79; Dezső Kosztolányi, 76-77; Ferenc Móra, 70; Mihály Szabolcska, 37-40, 46-58, 60-75, 77-79; Gyula Szávay, 48; Zoltán Szávay, 50-51; Ernő Szép, 55; Géza Szilágyi, 56, 62-63; Árpád Tóth, 59-60; József Turéczi, 60-61; Gyula Vértessy, 43. Also: zum Geleit von Leo Heller, 7-10; Vorwort von Mihály Szabolcska, 13.

43. *Das junge Ungarn.* Novellen. Übertragen von Stefan J. Klein. Potsdam-Berlin: Kiepenheuer, 1920(?). 226p.

All authors are from the twentieth century: Lajos Barta, 37-58; Artur Elek, 59-74; Frigyes Karinthy, 89-110; Miklós Kisbán, 111-154; Gyula Krúdy, 23-36; Sándor Márai, 155-226.

454 Bibliography

44. *Ausgewählte ungarische Dichtungen und Volkslieder in deutscher Übertragung von Christian Kraft.* Berlin: n.p., 1922. 41p.

There are only four authors from the twentieth century: *IV.*: Endre Ady, 35; Sándor Endrődy, 40; Sándor Sík, 36-37; István Szomory, 41.

45. *Ungarische Lyrik.* Übertragen von Ladislaus (László) Szemere. Budapest: Johann Hollóssy, 1933. 80p.

With the exception of Sándor Petőfi, János Arany and János Vajda, the authors are from the twentieth century: Endre Ady, 50-52; Mihály Babits, 53-64; Gyula Juhász, 74-75; József Kiss, 46-49; Dezső Kosztolányi, 65-73; Lajos Palágyi, 43; Gyula Reviczky, 44-45; Árpád Tóth, 76-80. Also: Vorwort, 3.

46. *Ungarische Dichtung.* Übertragen von Ladislaus (László) Szemere. Budapest: Gergely, 1935. 399p.

The volume begins with Sándor Petőfi. Some attention is given to the nineteenth century, but most of contents is devoted to the twentieth century with concentration on: Endre Ady, 35-41; Lajos Áprily, 87; Mihály Babits, 42-59; Sándor Csizmadia, 90-92; József Erdélyi, 83-84; Tamás Falu, 95; Imre Farkas, 93-94; Sándor Forbáth, 98; Oszkár Gellért, 72-78; Jenő Heltai, 79; Gyula Juhász, 64-68; József Kiss, 28-34; Dezső Kosztolányi, 60-63, 225-270; Henrik Lenkei, 88-89; László Mécs, 81-82; Zoltán Nadányi, 95; Alba Naevis, 97; Lajos Palágyi, 25, 271-332; Sándor Reményik, 85-86; Gyula Reviczky, 26-27; Lőrinc Szabó, 80; Károly Szalay, 333-399; Sándor Szőke, 100; Árpád Tóth, 69-71; Zseni Várnai, 96; Eszter Urbán, 99.

47. *Ungarische Lyrik 1914-1936.* Ins Deutsche übertragen von Lajos Brájjer. Budapest: R. Gergely, 1936(?). 111p.

András Adorján, 3; Endre Ady, 4-5; István Agyagfalvi-Hegyi, 5-6; Gyula Andor, 6; Gr. Cz. Ilona Andrássy, 6-7; Mihály Babits, 8-9; Ambrus Balázs, 10; Ignác Balla, 10-11; Miklós Bárd, 11-12; János Bartalis, 12-13; Jenő Bán, 13; Ferenc Borsodi, 13-14; Hugó Csergő, 14; Zoltán Csuka, 14-15; Minka Czóbel, 16; Gyula Debreceni, 16; József Debreceni, 17; Ilma Draskoczy-Jörg, 17-18; Kálmán Dudás, 18-19; Ákos Dutka, 19-20; Tamás Emőd, 20-21; Béla Endrődi, 21; József Erdélyi, 21-22; Renée Erdős, 23-24; Tamás Falu, 24; József Faragó, 25; Imre Farkas, 25-27; Jenő Fehér, 27-28; Lajos Fekete, 28-29; Sándor Feleki, 30; Milán Füst, 30-31; Döme Gács, 31-32; Margit F. Galambos, 33-34; Oszkár Gellért, 34-35; Boriska Gergely, 35; István Gergely, 36-37; Pál Gulyás, 37; Géza Gyóni (Achim), 37-40; Samu Halmágyi, 40; Sándor Hangay, 41; Zsolt Harsányi, 41; Jenő Heltai, 42; József Holder, 43; Zoltán Horvát, 43-44; Sándor Huszár, 44-45; Ignotus (Hugó Veigelsberg), 45-46; Ödön Jakab, 46-48; Elemér Jászai-Horváth, 48; Zoltán Jékely, 49; Attila József, 50; Gyula Juhász, 50-51; Lajos Kassák, 51; János A. Kató, 52; Simon Kemény, 52-54; Arnold Kiss, 56; Menyhért Kiss, 54-56; Róbert Koványi, 56; Aladár Komjáthy, 57; László Koosz, 61-63; Aranka M. Kornis, 57-58; Lajos Korvin, 58; Dezső Kosztolányi, 59-61; Erzsébet Kövér, 59; Frigyes Kreska, 63-64; István Kristály, 64-65; József Kürti, 65; Ferenc Lanátor-Pogány, 66; István Laták, 66-67; Henrik Lenkei, 67-68; Anna Lesznai, 68; Tibor Marconnay, 69; Lia Marschalko, 70; László Mécs, 71-74; Jenő Miklós, 74; János Miskolci Simon, 75; Zoltán Nadányi, 75-76; Alba Naevis, 78; Endre Nagy, 76-77; Gustav (Gusztáv) Nagy, 77; Lajos Nechansky, 77-78; Irén Oelbey, 79; Gábor Oláh, 80; Gyula Ortutay, 81; Margit Pálföldy, 81-82; Károly Páljános, 82; Árpád Pásztor, 83; Ilona Péry, 84; Andor Peterdi, 84; Móricz Petri, 85; Andor Pünkösti, 85-86; Miklós Radnóti, 86-87; György Sárközi, 87-88; Ede Sas, 88; György Sas, 89; Zoltán Somlyó, 89-90; Lőrinc Szabó, 90; Géza Szilágyi, 90-91; Menyhért Szász, 91; István Szatmári, 92; Franciska Szemő, 92-93; Kornél Szenteleki, 93-95; Antal Szirbik, 96; József Tass, 96-97; Béla Telekes, 97; Ferenc Timár, 97-98; Pál Toldalagi, 99; László Tompa, 100; Zsófi

Török, 98; Árpád Tóth, 101; István Váczy, 102; Gyula Vargha, 102-103; Jenny Várnai, 103-104; Ede Véssey, Junger, 104; Gyula Wlassics, Junger, 105; Tibor Wlassics, 105; Eta Zórád, 106. Also: Vorwort von Lajos Brájjer, 1-2.

48. *Ungarn.* Ein Novellenbuch. Herausgegeben von Dezső von Keresztury. Breslau: Wilh. Gottl. Korn, 1937. 346p.

All authors are from the twentieth century: *Part I. Nation*: Lajos Bibó, 33-40; Zsigmond Móricz, 1-32; József Nyírő, 56-63; Áron Tamási, 41-55; *Part II. Poverty*: Sándor Dallos, 81-94; Andor Endre Gelléri, 95-111; Lajos Kassák, 69-80; *Part III. Form*: Ferenc Herczeg, 117-129; Frigyes Karinthy, 137-147; Dezső Kosztolányi, 130-136; László Németh, 163-178; László Cs. Szabó, 148-162; *Part IV. Disorder*: Mihály Babits, 183-199; Sándor Márai, 212-223; Sophie (Zsófi) Török, 200-211; *Part V. Turning Point*: János Kodolányi, 247-272; Károly Kós, 308-329; Cecil Tornay, 229-246; Sándor Török, 273-307. Also: Nachwort, 330-341; Anhang, 342-346.

49. *Stimmen für Europa.* Ein Chor ungarischer freier Rhythmen. Jenő Kerpel-Claudius. Neuauflage. Basel: Aeterna, 1941. 49p. (First edition: Berlin: Aeterna, 1927. 49p.)

All authors are from the twentieth century: Mihály Babits, 25-34; Milán Füst, 11-18; Margit Kaffka, 19-24; Lajos Kassák, 43-49; Dezső Kosztolányi, 35-42. NN, PU, IEN.

50. *Neue ungarische Lyrik.* Übersetzung von Friedrich (Frigyes) Lám. Budapest: Ruszkabányai, 1942. 93p.

Authors are from the first four decades of the twentieth century: Endre Ady, 3-9; Lajos Áprily, 10-11; Mihály Babits, 12-22; Miklós Bárd, 23-26; Irma Barsy, 27-28; József Berda, 29; János Bódás, 30; Ákos Dutka, 32; József Erdélyi, 33-34; Tamás Falu, 35-36; József Fodor, 37-38; Andor Endre Gelléri, 38-40; Pál Gulyás, 41; Kálmán Harsányi, 42; Lajos Harsányi, 43-44; István Havas, 46-47; Gyula Illyés, 48; Zoltán Jékely, 49; Attila József, 50-51; Gyula Juhász, 52-54; Dezső Keresztury, 54; Dezső Kosztolányi, 55-57; Tibor Marconnay, 58-60; László Mécs, 61-62; Lajos Missuray-Krug, 63-64; Zoltán Nadányi, 65-66; Sándor Reményik, 67-69; Elemér Ruszkabányai, 70; György Sárközi, 71-72; Kálmán Sértő, 72-77; Lőrinc Szabó, 78-82; Béla Telekes, 82-84; Pál Toldalagi, 84; Ernő Träger, 85-97; Sándor Weöres, 88; Lajos Zilahy, 89-90. NNC.

51. *Würze des Lebens.* Zusammengestellt und herausgegeben von der Ungarischen Paprika Propagandastelle im Verlag für Wirtschaft und Kultur, Payer und Co. in Wien. Wien-Berlin-Zürich: Für Wirtschaft und Kultur, Payer und Co., 1943. 255p.

All the authors are from the twentieth century: Sándor Dallos, 192-196, 233-237; Zoltán Gesztélyi-Nagy, 92-178; Ferenc Ilosvay, 211-216; Ferenc Jankovich, 227-233; Miklós Kállay, 179-186; Dezső Kosztolányi, 237-244; Lajos Nagy, 217-221; László Németh, 206-211; József Péczely, 197-201, 249-252; Margit Simonffy, 245-249; Áron Tamási, 202-205; Sándor Tatay, 222-226; Jenő (Józsi) Tersánszky, 5-91; Gábor Thurzó, 186-191. Also: Würze des Lebens, 253-255.

52. *Stimmen der Gefährten.* Ein ungarischer Chor aus dem anbrechenden zwanzigsten Jahrhundert. Herausgegeben von Eugen (Jenő) Kerpel-Claudius. Budapest: n.p., 1946. 49p.

Endre Ady, 7-8; Mihály Babits, 11-19; Milán Füst, 31-40; Lajos Kassák, 43-49; Dezső Kosztolányi, 23-28.

53. *Was einem Siege gleichkommt . . .* Ungarische Erzählungen. Übersetzung von H. Csongár. Berlin: Volk und Welt, Rütten-Loening, 1950. 345p.

All the authors are from the twentieth century: István Asztalos, 105-124; Tibor Déry, 79-86; Béla Illés, 23-38, 125-134; István Karczag, 55-78, 319-345; Ferenc Karinthy, 209-258; Zsigmond Móricz, 5-22; István Nagy I, 39-54, 301-318; István Nagy II, 193-208; Lajos Nagy, 291-300; Imre Sarkadi, 87-104; Péter Veres, 135-192.

54. *Die eroberte Heimat.* Hundert Jahre ungarischer Dichtung. Eine kleine Anthologie mit erstmaligen Nachdichtungen ungarischer Lyrik der jüngsten Zeit. Zweite Auflage. Wien: Globus, 1952. 45p.

With the exception of Ferenc Kölcsey and Sándor Petőfi, the authors are from the twentieth century: Tamás Aczél, 45; Endre Ady, 31-33; László Benjámin, 40-42; Attila József, 34-36; Lajos Kónya, 43-44; Zoltán Zelk, 37-39. Also: Hundert Jahre ungarischer Dichtung, 7-18. NN.

55. *Ungarn erzählt.* Ein Einblick in die ungarische Literatur. Ausgewählt und Standfest Hilde-Kühn Heinz unter Mitwirkung von Álmos Csongári und Horst Görsch. Berlin: Volk und Wissen, 1954. 200p.

The collection begins with Mihály Vörösmarty. The authors from the twentieth century are: Endre Ady, 50-51, 112-114; Magda Aranyossi, 70-79; László Benjámin, 147-149, 183-186; Tibor Déry, 125-134; Andor Gábor, 137-138; Gyula Háy, 61-69; Béla Illés, 90-101, 115-123; Gyula Illyés, 52-60; Attila József, 135-136; Gyula Juhász, 165; Lajos Kónya, 156-157; Kálmán Mikszáth, 80-83; Zsigmond Móricz, 102-111; István Nagy, 166-176; Sándor Nagy, 139-146, 158-164; Boris Palotai, 177-182; Pál Szabó, 150-155. Also: Álmos Csongári: "Kurzer Überblick über die Epochen der ungarischen Literatur," 9-14; biographische Anmerkungen, 187-195; zur Aussprache der ungarischen Wörter, 196; Verzeichnis der Abbildungen, 197; Quellennachweis, 198-200. DLC-P4, MH.

56. *Ungarische Erzählungen von gestern und heute.* Eine Anthologie ungarischer Prosa aus fünfzig Jahren. Übersetzung von Géza Angyal, Imre Roboz, H. Csongári. Wien: Globus, 1955. 151p.

All the authors are from the twentieth century: Tibor Déry, 41-53; Sándor Gergely, 84-110; Miklós Gyárfás, 147-151; Jenő Heltai, 33-40; Béla Illés, 111-122; Ferenc Karinthy, 141-146; Zsigmond Móricz, 9-32; Lajos Nagy, 77-83; Sándor Rideg, 129-140; Pál Szabó, 123-128; Péter Veres, 54-76. Also: Vorwort, 7-8.

57. *Ungarische Meistererzähler.* Eine Auswahl der schönsten Geschichten von Jókai bis Mikes. Eingeleitet von Georg (György) Mikes. Übertragung aus dem Ungarischen von Stefan J. Klein. Zürich: Werner Classen, 1957. 112p.

With the exception of Mór Jókai, the authors are from the twentieth century: Jenő Heltai, 71-76; Ferenc Herczeg, 44-53; Sándor Hunyady, 36-43; Frigyes Karinthy, 101-104; Dezső Kosztolányi, 93-100; György Mikes, 105-112; Kálmán Mikszáth, 54-58; Ferenc Molnár, 77-85; Zsigmond Móricz, 59-63; Viktor Rákosi, 22-27; Ernő Szép, 64-70; Pál Tábori, 11-15; István Tömörkény, 86-92; Julianna Zsigray, 16-21.

58. *Der Hase und der Kater, Knüppelchen, schlag zu!, Täschlein, öffne dich!* Drei ungarische Puppenspiele. Leipzig: Friedrich Hofmeister, 1957. 72p.

"Der Hase und der Kater," ein Märchenspiel in 2 Akten und 6 Bildern (no author), 3-24; László Hárs, 25-46; *Miklós Mészöly*: "Täschlein, öffne dich!" 47-72.

59. *Ungarische Geisteswelt von der Landnahme bis Babits.* Herausgegeben von Johann Andritsch. Baden-Baden: Holle, 1960. 324p.

Selections begin with the Middle Ages, with an extensive number from the nineteenth century and a few from the twentieth century. The twentieth-century authors are: *V. The World and a Small People*: Mihály Babits, 288-304; Béla Bartók, 273-280; Gyula Illyés, 281-287; Gyula Kornis, 264-272; Ottokár Prohászka, 249-263. Also: Vorwort, 9-12; Einleitung, 13-32; Anhang, 305-306; Anmerkungen, 307-311; Literaturverzeichnis, 312-316; Die Autoren dieses Bandes, 317-321; Quellennachweis, 322-324. CU, NN, MH, ICU, NjP, InU.

60. *Ungarische Erzählungen aus drei Jahrzehnten.* Herausgegeben von Antal Mádl. Übersetzung von Heinrich Weissling. Leipzig: Reclam, 1961. 215p.

Three decades of twentieth-century authors are included: Imre Dobozy, 162-193; Sándor Gergely, 71-96; Béla Illés, 152-161; Lajos Nagy, 29-70; Sándor Sásdi, 18-28; Áron Tamási, 3-17; Gábor Thurzó, 97-129; Péter Veres, 130-151. Also: Nachwort, 194-205; biographische Angaben, 206-213; Anmerkungen, 214-215.

61. *Das junge Europa.* Erzählungen junger Autoren. Mit einem Geleitwort von Joachim Maass. Wien-München-Basel: Verlag Kurt Desch, 1962. 623p.

The Hungarian authors included are from the twentieth century: *István Csurka*: "Die Komödianten kommen," 512-522; György Moldova, 523-538; György Sebestyén, 539-543; István Szabó, 544-557. Also: Geleitwort von Joachim Maass, 9-15; biographische Notizen über die Autoren, 611-623. MiDW, IU, NN, DLC.

62. *Sonne über der Donau.* Moderne ungarische Erzählungen. Ausgewählt von András Diószegi. Berlin-Budapest: Verlag der Nation-Corvina, 1962. 401p.

Imre Dobozy, 364-367; János Földeák, 112-128; Sándor Gergely, 5-11; Gábor Goda, 241-267; Béla Illés, 297-314; Endre Illés, 223-240; Lajos Mesterházi, 145-169; Sándor Rideg, 170-190; Kálmán Sándor, 315-320; István Szabó, 345-363; Magda Szabó, 321-344; Pál Szabó, 99-111; Áron Tamási, 12-21; Józsi Jenő Tersánszky, 90-98; Zsuzsa Thury, 191-205; Gábor Thurzó, 66-89; Máté Timár, 22-65; László Tóth, 206-222; Ernő Urbán, 268-296; Péter Veres, 129-144. Also: Nachwort von Álmos Csongári, 389-396; biographischer Anhang, 397-401.

63. *Nur ein Strauss Kornblumen.* Erzählungen aus Ungarn. Herausgegeben von László Zay. Deutsch von Heinrich Weissling. Berlin: Union, 1963. 125p.

All the authors are from the twentieth century: Ágoston Karner, 45-50, 82-88; László Possonyi, 35-42, 91-102, 121-126; István Szamosközi, 5-24, 50-58, 72-82, 88-91, 117-121; József Vámos, 62-64, 102-105, 109-113; Lajos Várady, 64-68, 105-109; László Zay, 24-35, 42-45, 58-62, 68-72, 113-117. Also: Autoren, 127.

64. *Wort in der Zeit.* Ungarische Gegenwartsliteratur, nr. 12 (Dezember, 1963). 64p.

István Csurka: "Die Komödianten kommen," 30-36; Lajos Galambos, 42-44; Gyula Háy, 16-17; Attila József, 18-20; *Ferenc Juhász*: "Die Nacht des Zauberers," 41; *Iván Mándy*: "Die rote Kulijacke," 37-40; *László Nagy*: "Transdanubischer Friede," 41; László Németh, 20-24; Géza Ottlik, 24-30; *János Pilinszky*: "Harbach 1944," "Fragment vom Goldenen Zeitalter," "Apokryph," 45-47; György Sebestyén, 48-50; Tamás Tasnády, 50-55. Also: Paul Hernadi: "Ungarische Dichtung im 20. Jahrhundert," 3-9; János Vajda: "Die Suche nach dem eigenen Gesicht. Erzählung und Roman der Gegenwart in Ungarn," 9-16; biographische Angaben zu den Autoren, 56-57.

65. *Exkursionen.* Erzählungen unserer Zeit. Ausgewählt von Leonore Germann. München: Carl Hanser, 1964, 326p.

The Hungarian authors included are from the twentieth century: *Iván Mándy*: "Das Mädchen aus dem Schwimmbad," 180-186; Károly Szakonyi, 187-205. Ou, NNC, MiDW, MoU, IU, VtU, IEN, TxHR, OrPS.

66. *Ungarische Meistererzählungen.* Zweite Auflage. Budapest-Berlin: Corvina-Aufbau, 1964. Volume 1, 366p.; Volume 2, 514p. (First edition: Budapest: Corvina, 1960. 327p.)

Volume 1: With the exception of Mór Jókai, the authors are from the twentieth century: Sándor Bródy, 120-127; Géza Gárdonyi, 110-119; Andor Endre Gelléri, 332-354; Jenő Heltai, 162-167; Sándor Hunyady, 297-313; Margit Kaffka, 135-161; Frigyes Karinthy, 289-

296; Dezső Kosztolányi, 168-175; Gyula Krúdy, 252-288; Kálmán Mikszáth, 41-109; Ferenc Molnár, 176-190; Ferenc Móra, 247-251; Zsigmond Móricz, 191-246; Lajos Nagy, 314-331; István Tömörkény, 128-134. Also: Nachwort, 355-357; Biographien, 358-366. *Volume 2*: All authors are from the twentieth century: Lajos Barta, 5-13; József Darvas, 401-410; Imre Dobozy, 437-445; Milán Füst, 23-54; Sándor Gergely, 100-105; Gábor Goda, 411-422; Béla Illés, 79-99; Endre Illés, 342-354; Gyula Illyés, 222-341; Jenő (Józsi) Tersánsky, 55-68; Lajos Kassák, 14-22; József Lengyel, 106-141; Lajos Mesterházi, 423-436; László Németh, 182-221; Sándor Rideg, 390-400; Kálmán Sándor, 355-389; Magda Szabó, 446-475; Pál Szabó, 69-78; Áron Tamási, 161-181; Ernő Urbán, 476-500; Péter Veres, 142-160. Also: Nachwort, 501-506; Biographien, 507-515; Ausspracheregeln, 516. *Second edition*: CLU. *First edition*: DLC-P4.

67. *Meilenstein.* Drei Jahrzehnte im Spiegel der ungarischen Literatur. Herausgegeben von Miklós Szabolcsi, unter Mitwirkung von Zoltán Kenyeres. Budapest: Corvina, 1965. 335p.

Contents same as number 10. MnU, NIC, MB, IEN, MU, WU, TxHR.

68. *Ungarische Erzähler der Gegenwart.* Herausgegeben und eingeleitet von Friederka Schag. Stuttgart: Philipp Reclam, 1965. 296p.

All authors are from the twentieth century: Endre Ady, 9-16; Mihály Babits, 79-93; *István Csurka*: "Wir kommen vom Rundfunk," 269-283; Sándor Dallos, 142-154; Tibor Déry, 255-268; Andor Endre Gelléri, 120-124; Ferenc Herczeg, 46-57; Gyula Illyés, 165-173; Margit Kaffka, 25-36; Frigyes Karinthy, 103-113; Lajos Kassák, 67-72; János Kodolányi, 132-142; Dezső Kosztolányi, 94-103; Gyula Krúdy, 17-24; *Iván Mándy*: "Eisverkäufer," 238-248; Sándor Márai, 113-120; *Miklós Mészöly*: "Unter dem Felsen," 248-254; Ferenc Móra, 72-79; Zsigmond Móricz, 124-131; László Németh, 174-185; György Rónay, 203-217; Imre Sarkadi, 218-230; Desző Szabó, 57-67; Magda Szabó, 231-237; Áron Tamási, 155-164; Gábor Thurzó, 186-202. Also: Einleitung, 3-8; über die Autoren, 284-294. IaU, Cty.

69. *Konturen 1956-1966.* Moderne ungarische Prosa. Herausgegeben von Vera Thies, aus dem Ungarischen übersetzt. Berlin: Aufbau, 1966. 408p.

Bulcsú Bertha, 9-20; *István Csurka*: "Apparat einhundertfünf," "Mieter und Komödianten," 23-58; Endre Fejes, 61-86; Zoltán Galabárdi, 89-101; Lajos Galambos, 105-110; Erzsébet Galgóczi, 113-148; Endre Gerelyes, 151-161; László Kamondy, 165-192; Gábor Mocsár, 195-226; György Moldova, 229-255; Pál Salamon, 259-280; *Ferenc Sánta*: "Wir waren zu viel," "Acht Joch Land," 283-306; István Szabó, 309-329; Károly Szakonyi, 333-363; András Tabák, 367-393; Mihály Várkonyi, 397-406. Also: Vorbemerkung, 5-6; biographical sketches precede each author. MH, IEN.

70. *Ungarn erzählt.* Herausgegeben von Ivan Nagel mit einem Vorwort von Mario Szenessy. Frankfurt am Main: Fischer Bücherei, 1967. 159p.

All authors are from the twentieth century: *István Csurka*: "Apparat hundertfünf," 140-156; Tibor Déry, 58-75; Lajos Galambos, 101-110; Andor Endre Gelléri, 39-48; Endre Illés, 82-92; László Kamondy, 131-139; Virág Móricz, 93-100; Lajos Nagy, 20-23; *Ferenc Sánta*: "Nazis," 76-81; Imre Sarkadi, 49-57; Magda Szabó, 111-130; Áron Tamási, 24-38. Also: Vorwort, 7-19; Bibliographie, 157-159. NBuU.

71. *Ungarns Dichtung in deutscher Sprache.* Herausgegeben von László Abaffy. Frankfurt am Main-Huttenheim: Aurora-BBdA, 1967. 28p.

With the exception of Ferenc Kölcsey, Mihály Vörösmarty, Sándor Petőfi and János Arany, all the authors are from the twentieth century: *Modern Hungary*: Endre Ady, 13-14;

Gyula Illyés, 20-28; Attila József, 15-19. Also: Vorwort: Ungarns Dichtung in deutscher Sprache von László Abaffy, 1-5.

72. *Almanach.* Das zweiundachtzigste Jahr. Redaktion von J. Helmut Freund und Gerda Niedieck. Frankfurt am Main: S. Fischer, 1968. 199p.

Contains only one Hungarian author's work: *István Örkény:* "Richtung Salzfuss," 96-100.

73. *Festbeleuchtung auf dem Holzmarkt und andere ungarische Erzählungen.* Herausgegeben und Nachwort von Dezső Keresztury. Budapest: Corvina, 1968. 319p.

All the authors are from the twentieth century: Mihály Babits, 66-78; Géza Csáth, 95-98; Tibor Déry, 135-178; Milán Füst, 99-118; Andor Endre Gelléri, 267-276; Sándor Hunyady, 119-136; Endre Illés, 258-266; Gyula Illyés, 245-257; Erzsébet Kádár, 210-220; Margit Kaffka, 54-60; Frigyes Karinthy, 87-94; János Kodolányi, 191-209; Desző Kosztolányi, 79-86; Gyula Krúdy, 25-38; Kálmán Mikszáth, 7-11; Ferenc Molnár, 12-24; Ferenc Móra, 50-53; Zsigmond Móricz, 39-49; Lajos Nagy, 61-65; László Németh, 234-244; Károly Pap, 186-190; Imre Sarkadi, 292-301; Magda Szabó, 277-291; Antal Szerb, 221-233; Áron Tamási, 179-185. Also: Nachwort, 302-309; die Autoren, 310-319. LC.

74. *Ungarische Dramen.* Herausgegeben und Nachwort von Georgina Baum. Berlin: Volk und Welt, 1968. 456p.

The authors are from the twentieth century: Miklós Hubay, 213-238; Endre Illés, 343-434; Gyula Illyés, 123-212; Lajos Mesterházi, 239-270; László Németh, 5-122; Imre Sarkadi, 271-342. Also: Nachwort, 435-450; über die Autoren, 451-452; Anmerkungen, 453-456. WU, NbU, IEN.

75. *Literatur und Kritik.* Anthologie ungarischer Lyrik von Sándor Weöres, Sándor Csoóri, Gábor Hajnal, u.a. nr. 35 (Juni, 1969). 315p.

Sándor Csoóri: "Niemandsland," 270; Gábor Hajnal, 271-272; Gyula Illyés, 273-277; *Ferenc Juhász:* "Mein mit Visionen gesegnetes Leben," 277-279; Amy Károlyi, 280-282; József Lengyel, 294-312; *Ágnes Nemes Nagy:* "Statuen," "Bäume," "Geysir," "Rückkehr," 283-286; *János Pilinszky:* "Grosstadt-Ikonen," "Harbach 1944," "Fragment vom Goldenen Zeitalter," "Passion," "Karfreitag," "Van Gogh," 287-290; György Rónay, 290-291; György Somlyó, 293; István Vas, 292; Sándor Weöres, 261-270. Also: Rezension, 313-314; Hinweise, 315.

76. *Rosoka bläst Trompete.* Eine Anthologie ungarischer Erzählungen vom XVIII. Jahrhundert bis zum Beginn des XX. Jahrhunderts. Herausgegeben von Vera Thies. Leipzig: List, 1970. 367p.

The authors from the twentieth century are: Endre Ady, 365-367; Zoltán Ambrus, 274-289; Sándor Bródy, 290-296; Géza Gárdonyi, 297-302; Elek Gozsdu, 254-265; Jenő Heltai, 332-339; Károly Lovik, 340-346; Kálmán Mikszáth, 237-253; Dániel Papp, 303-309; István Petelei, 266-273; Béla Révész, 356-364; Gyula Szini, 347-355; Dezső Szomory, 317-324; Zoltán Thury, 325-331; István Tömörkény, 310-316. Also: Vorwort von Vera Thies, 7-18. WU, InU.

77. *Ungarische Dichtung aus fünf Jahrhunderten.* Ausgewählt von György Mihály Vajda. Vorwort von Stephan Hermlin. Nachwort von György Mihály Vajda. Das Nachwort übersetzt von Jörg Büschmann. Die Autorenkommentare verfasste István Tálasi. Budapest: Corvina, 1970. 346p.

The anthology begins with Janus Pannonius. The authors from the twentieth century are: Endre Ady, 158-181; Mihály Babits, 187-196; Béla Balázs, 201-205; Milán Füst, 225-227; Andor Gábor, 197-200; Géza Gárdonyi, 157; Gyula Illyés, 278-282; Attila József, 236-

269; Gyula Juhász, 182-186; Lajos Kassák, 221-224; József Kiss, 154-156; Aladár Komját, 228-229; Jenő Komjáthy, 151-153; Dezső Kosztolányi, 206-214; Miklós Radnóti, 270-277; Gyula Reviczky, 150; Lőrinc Szabó, 230-235; Árpád Tóth, 215-220. Also: Vorwort, 5-8; Nachwort, 283-314; zu den Autoren, 315-346. ICU.

78. *Neue ungarische Lyrik.* Ausgewählt von Gerhard Fritsch. Vorwort von György Rónay. Salzburg: Otto Müller, 1971. 100p.

The authors are entirely from the twentieth century: László Benjámin, 55; *Sándor Csoóri*: "Niemandsland," 89; Gábor Devecseri, 58-60; József Fodor, 26; Milán Füst, 11-12; Gábor Garai, 83-88; Ágnes Gergely, 93-94; Anna Hajnal, 35-36; Gábor Hajnal, 43-46; Gyula Illyés, 27-32; *Ferenc Juhász*: "Dein gequältes, trauriges Gesicht," 80-82; Márton Kalász, 97-98; Amy Károlyi, 38-39; Lajos Kassák, 8-10; Géza Képes, 37; Mihály Ladányi, 95-96; László Lator, 78-79; András Mezei, 90-91; *László Nagy*: "Das Feuer," "Die Tage der Untreue," "Osterlegende," 73-75; *Ágnes Nemes Nagy*: "Dazwischen," "Rückkehr," "Sturm," 68-72; *János Pilinszky*: "Apokryph," 64-67; Miklós Radnóti, 17-20; Sándor Rákos, 61-63; György Rónay, 51-54; István Simon, 76-77; Lőrinc Szabó, 13-16; Margit Szécsi, 92; Mihály Váci, 21-25; István Vas, 40-42; Endre Vészi, 51-57; Sándor Weöres, 47-50; Zoltán Zelk, 33-34. Also: Vorwort, 5-7; biographische Daten, 99-100. MH, NjP, NIC.

79. *Wie könnte ich dich nennen?* Ungarische Liebesgedichte aus alter und neuer Zeit. Herausgegeben von Géza Engl und István Kerékgyártó. Budapest: Corvina, 1971. 142p.

Anthology begins with Bálint Balassi. Some attention is given to seventeenth, eighteenth, and nineteenth centuries, but most of the contents are devoted to the twentieth century. The twentieth-century authors are: Endre Ady, 41-47; Mihály Babits, 52; László Benjámin, 111-112; József Berda, 72; Jenő Dsida, 95-96; Anna Hajnal, 104-105; Jenő Heltai, 40; Gyula Illyés, 73-78; Attila József, 79-93; *Ferenc Juhász*: "Die Liebe des Alls," 127-131; Gyula Juhász, 50-51; Margit Kaffka, 48-49; Lajos Kassák, 59-60; Dezső Kosztolányi, 53-55; Zoltán Nadányi, 61-65; *László Nagy*: "Regenbogen auf Schnee," "Blutbellende Fee," "Wer bringt die Liebe hinüber?" 120-126; *Ágnes Nemes Nagy*: "Durst," 119; Miklós Radnóti, 97-103; Sándor Rákos, 117-118; György Sárközi, 46; György Somlyó, 113-116; Lőrinc Szabó, 67-71; Árpád Tóth, 56-58; István Vas, 106-107; Sándor Weöres, 108-110; Zoltán Zelk, 94. Also: Geleitwort, 133-137.

80. *Erkundungen.* Zwanzig ungarische Erzähler. Herausgegeben und mit einem Nachwort versehen von Georgina Baum. Berlin: Volk und Welt, 1973. 349p.

All the authors are from the period after World War II: Lajos Baráth, 54-80; *Géza Bereményi*, 190-205; Bulcsú Bertha, 125-138; *István Csurka*: "Die letzte Adresse," 111-124; Klára Fehér, 206-208; Erzsébet Galgóczi, 19-40; Endre Illés, 231-239; *Anna Jókai*: "Die Pyramide," 257-289; G. György Kardos, 41-53; Ferenc Karinthy, 240-256; Ákos Kertész, 299-335; Emil Kolozsvári-Grandpierre, 139-155; József Lengyel, 290-298; *Iván Mándy*: "Das einfache Mitglied," 81-90; Gyula Marosi, 156-166; Géza Molnár, 167-175; Miklós Munkácsi, 5-18; Barna Sipkay, 176-189; Károly Szakonyi, 209-230; Erika Szántó, 91-110. Also: Nachwort, 336-341; bibliographische Notizen, 342-348; Quellenangaben, 349.

81. *Es geschah bei Tagesanbruch.* Ungarische Erzählungen. Leipzig: St. Benno-Verlag, 1973. 207p.

All the authors are from the period after World War II: Péter Árva, 128-130; István Fekete, 79-83; Antal Ijjas, 115-121; Gyula Kinszery, 44-55; *Iván Mándy*: "Morgenwind," 13-24; *János Pilinszky*: "Es geschah bei Tagesanbruch," 7-12; Pál Pitroff, 25-34; László Possonyi, 69-78; György Rónay, 131-144; Sándor Sík, 84-114; Géza Szarka, 122-127; Béla Szira, 56-68; Gábor Thurzó, 145-191; György Újházi, 39-43; Gyula Zaymus, 35-38. Also:

Beobachtungen, Erlebnisse, Erfahrungen, 192-205; Literaturangaben zum Nachwort, 206; Quellenangaben, 207.

82. *Der Kuss der Anna Szegi.* Eine Anthologie ungarischer Erzählungen aus der Zeit zwischen den beiden Weltkriegen. Herausgegeben von Vera Thies. Leipzig: List, 1973. 452p.

Mihály Babits, 117-123; György Bálint, 406-410; Tibor Déry, 239-245; Milán Füst, 188-208; Andor Gábor, 124-138; Andor Endre Gelléri, 411-416; Gábor Goda, 417-452; Sándor Hunyady, 209-224; Béla Illés, 270-278; Endre Illés, 387-394; Gyula Illyés, 395-405; Margit Kaffka, 91-99; Frigyes Karikás, 246-269; Frigyes Karinthy, 181-187; Lajos Kassák, 148-180; János Kodolányi, 348-368; Dezső Kosztolányi, 139-147; Gyula Krúdy, 35-47; József Lengyel, 279-293; Ferenc Molnár, 21-34; Ferenc Móra, 48-55; Zsigmond Móricz, 56-90; Lajos Nagy, 100-116; László Németh, 369-386; Károly Pap, 324-347; Pál Szabó, 231-238; Áron Tamási, 312-323; Jenő (Józsi) Tersánszky, 225-230; Péter Veres, 294-311. Also: Vorwort von Vera Thies, 7-20.

83. *Ungarische Erzähler.* Übersetzung aus dem Ungarischen und Nachwort von Andreas Oplatka. Zürich: Manesse, 1974. 455p.

Authors from the twentieth century are: Lajos Baráth, 387-438; Tibor Déry, 336-361; Jenő Heltai, 204-214; Attila József, 380-386; Dezső Kosztolányi, 284-335; Ferenc Móra, 274-283; Zsigmond Móricz, 215-273; Antal Szerb, 362-379. Also: Nachwort, 439-455.

84. *Ungarn/mit 8 Graphiken ungarischer Künstler.* Moderne Erzähler in der Welt. Auswahl und Redaktion von Mátyás Domokos und Hildegard Grosche. Tübingen-Basel: Horst Erdmann, 1975. 431p.

The authors are mainly from the period after World War II: *István Császár*: "Nichts als Einbildung, oder?" 387-409; *István Csurka*: "Happening," 353-374; Tibor Déry, 242-255; Erzsébet Galgóczi, 282-293; Gyula Hernádi, 344-348; Endre Illés, 256-274; Gyula Illyés, 164-177; *Anna Jókai*: "Ungarische Stunde," 349-351; László Kamondy, 66-89; G. György Kardos, 107-118; Ákos Kertész, 335-343; József Lengyel, 227-241; *Iván Mándy*: "Biller war hier!" 199-226; *Miklós Mészöly*: "Bericht auf fünf Mäuse," 294-303; György Moldova, 304-311; Péter Nádas, 375-386; Lajos Nagy, 17-23; László Németh, 24-51; *István Örkény*: "Mini-Novellen: Budapest, Meinungsforschung, Der Juckreiz," 410-414; Géza Ottlik, 119-144; *Ferenc Sánta*: "Nazis," 90-96; Imre Sarkadi, 275-281; István Szabó, 178-198; Magda Szabó, 312-334; Pál Szabó, 145-163; Áron Tamási, 97-106; Péter Veres, 52-65. Also: Vorwort, 7-8; Einführung, 9-15; die Autoren und ihre Werke, 419-431. LC.

85. *Sprachgekreuzt.* Ungarische Lyrik im deutschen Sprachraum. Ágnes Mária Csiky, Gábor Kocsis, Imre Máté, Dezső Monoszlóy, Éva Saáry, Tibor Tollas. Redaktion von Charlotte Újlaky. Einführung von Hans Bender. Duisberg: Gilles & Francke, 1975. 82p.

Ágnes Mária Csiky, 17-24; Gábor Kocsis, 27-34; Imre Máté, 37-44; Dezső Monoszlóy, 47-54; Éva Saáry, 57-64; Tibor Tollas, 67-74. Also: Hans Bender: "Vom Reichtum der ungarischen Lyrik," 9-14; biographische Daten, die Autoren, 77-79; die Übersetzer, 79.

86. *Der entschlossene Löwe.* Ungarische Satiren. Herausgegeben von Hans Skirecki. Aus dem Ungarischen übersetzt von Jörg Büschmann. Berlin: Volk und Welt, 1976. 221p.

The authors are from 1940 on: *István Csurka*: "Óvári und Sóvári," "Warum die ungarischen Filme schlecht sind," 25-67; Tibor Déry, 5-18; Miklós Gyárfás, 19-24; Ferenc Karinthy, 156-161; Lajos Mesterházi, 68-106; György Moldova, 162-202; *István Örkény*: "Mini-Novellen: Nichts neues, Wir werden alt, Unsere kühnsten Träume sind realisierbar, Der neue Mieter, Harem, Die Óbudaer Drillinge, Ungarische Mondrakete zur Erde zurückgekehrt, Hinweise und Verkehrseinschränkungen in Verbindung mit dem Ereignissen am 1. Februar, Budapest," 125-141; Gergely Rákosy, 107-117; András Simonffy, 142-151; Sándor Somogyi Tóth, 203-208; Károly Szakonyi, 118-124; Tibor Szántó, 152-155; *Miklós Vámos*: "Abendgesellschaft," "Vorworte: Vorworte zum Alphabet, Vorwort zur Speisekarte eines sehr teueren Restaurants, Vorworte zu einem Märchenbuch," 209-219. Also: biographische Notizen, 220-221.

87. *Das elfte Gebot*. Moderne ungarische Dramen. Aus dem Ungarischen übersetzt von Barbara Frischmuth, Vera Thies und Ita Szent-Iványi. Leipzig: Philipp Reclam, Junger, 1977. 414p.

All the authors are from the twentieth century: Klára Fehér, 145-223; Tibor Gyurkovics, 315-398; Lajos Mesterházi, 225-313; *István Örkény*: "Familie Tót," "Katzen-Spiel," 5-144. Also: Anhang: "Aus einem Gespräch mit István Örkény," 401-408; Lajos Mesterházi zu seinem Stück "Das elfte Gebot," 409-412; Lajos Mesterházi: "Brief an das deutsche Publikum," 413-414.

88. *Heckenrossen*. Erzählungen aus Ungarn. Herausgegeben von Vera Thies. Berlin: Der Kinderbuchverlag, 1977. 304p.

All the authors are from the twentieth century: Tibor Déry, 91-99; Imre Dobozy, 105-115; Endre Fejes, 39-55; Tibor Gyurkovics, 214-217; Éva Janikovszky, 164-174; Zsuzsa Kántor, 285-295; József László, 243-260; *Iván Mándy*: "Csutak und das graue Pferd," 272-284; *Miklós Mészöly*: "Die Rache," 5-12; Zsigmond Móricz, 13-20; Paula Oravecz, 100-104; Boris Palotai, 175-196; Judith G. Szabó, 197-200; Magda Szabó, 201-213; Lenke Szalay, 261-271; Imre Szász, 56-70; Judit Sziráky, 139-152; Sándor Tatay, 116-138; Zsuzsa Thury, 71-90; László Trencsényi, 153-163; Antal Végh, 218-242; Péter Veres, 21-38. Also: zu den Autoren, 296-305; Quellennachweis, 306-307.

AUTHORS IN PRESENT WORK

Géza Bereményi

ENGLISH

Periodical: "The last lap on the water," *Hungarian Review*, no. 2 (1972), 14-16.

FRENCH

Periodicals: "Un tour sur l'eau," *Revue Hongroise*, no. 2 (1972), 14-16. §§ "Lettre à madame Z . . . ," *Arion* 7 (1974), 121-131.

GERMAN

See number 80.

Vilmos Csaplár

ENGLISH

Periodical: "The boy turned into a pebble," *Hungarian Review*, no. 4 (1973), 14-16.

FRENCH

Periodical: "L'histoire du petit garçon changé en caillou," *Revue Hongroise*, no. 4 (1973), 14-16.

István Császár

ENGLISH

Periodicals: "Stalemate," *The Hungarian P.E.N.*, no. 15 (1974), 73-76. §§ "An easy job for beginners," *Hungarian Review*, no. 4 (1974), 14-16.

FRENCH

Periodicals: "Un boulot facile pour débutants," *Revue Hongroise*, no. 4 (1971), 14-16. §§ "Comment j'ai tenté de tuer notre ami," *Arion 5* (1972), 91-96.

GERMAN

See number 84.

Sándor Csoóri

ENGLISH

See numbers 11, 17, and 18.

Periodicals: "Barbarian prayer," "Ague," *The New Hungarian Quarterly*, VIII, no. 27 (Autumn, 1967), 84-85; "Golden pheasants flying," "The dreamers of my dream," "I stole your face," XII, no. 43 (Autumn, 1971), 131-133; "Whispers, for two voices," "I would rather run back," XVII, no. 64 (Winter, 1976), 63-65. §§ "Elegy for horses," *Hungarian Review*, no. 5 (1969), 14-16. §§ "The sentence" (a film story done with Ferenc Kósa), *The Hungarian P.E.N.*, no. 13 (1972), 52-72; "For encouragement," "Dry storm," no. 15 (1974), 84-85; "Light music," "Conditional," "The other," "White, whiteness," no. 18 (1977), 39-42. §§ "Approaching words," *Arion 7* (1974), 35-39; "Afternoon of grand old men," "By the time it dawns," *Arion 9* (1976), 140-141. §§ "I stole your face," "The dreamers of my dream," *The New Republic*, 176, no. 13 (March, 1977), 29. §§ "I would rather run back," "Whispers, for two voices," *American Poetry Review*, VI, no. 3 (May-June, 1977), 24-25.

FRENCH

See numbers 28, 29, 30, 31, 36, and 37.

Periodicals: "Temps à soulever les vallées," *Synthèses*, XVIII, no. 213 (Février, 1964), 145-146. §§ "Crépuscule banal," "Poème irrégulier sur la mort d'un professeur de géographie," *Action Poétique*, no. 30 (Mai, 1966), 5-7. §§ "Elégie chevaline," *Revue Hongroise*, no. 5 (1969), 14-16. §§ "Prière barbare," *Esprit*, IV, no. 391 (Avril, 1970), 754. §§ "Passages," *The Hungarian P.E.N.*, no. 12 (1971), 14-15; "Temps conditionnel," "Anciens battements," "Consolant squelette," no. 17 (1976), 56-58. §§ "Écrit sur le mur d'une église," "Souvenir d'une ancienne rue," *Arion 5* (1972), 115-116; "Adieu à Guevara," "Quelqu'un te chuchote," *Arion 8* (1975), 83-85; "Souvenir d'une ancienne rue," "Passages," "Écrit sur le mur d'une église," *Arion 9* (1976), 141-142. §§ "Pour qu'il ne fasse pas nuit," *Alif*, no. 4-5 (1974), 155. §§ "Marcher vers la porte," *La Barbacane, Revue des Pierres et des Hommes*, no. 15-16 (1974-1975), 72. §§ "Vers la porte," *Le Temps Parallèle*, no. 6 (Septembre, 1975), 22.

GERMAN

See numbers 67, 75, and 78.

Periodical: "Abschied von Che Guevara," *Arion 3* (1970), 184-185.

István Csurka

ENGLISH

See number 12.

Periodicals: "We're from the radio," *Hungarian Review*, no. 1 (1964), 14-17; "Till lunch," no. 6 (1969), 14-15. §§ "The phone calls of a palmist," *The Hungarian P.E.N.*, no. 11 (1970), 17-21; "The passengers," no. 17 (1976), 34-43. §§ "The wanderer of the

464   Bibliography

deep," *The New Hungarian Quarterly*, III, no. 7 (July-September, 1962), 175-181; "Fall guy for tonight" (fragments), XI, no. 39 (Autumn, 1970), 76-91; "Nothing simple," XIII, no. 45 (Spring, 1972), 149-165; "Bottles and women," XVIII, no. 62 (Summer, 1976), 110-117. §§ "Kerbside," *Arion 5* (1972), 86-90. §§ "Happening," *New Letters*, XL, no. 2 (Winter, 1973), 31-49. §§ "LSD," *Webster Review*, no. 2 (1974), 3-8.

FRENCH

See numbers 30 and 35.

Periodicals: "Nous sommes de la radio," *Revue Hongroise*, no. 1 (1964), 14-17; "En attendant midi," no. 6 (1969), 14-15.

GERMAN

See numbers 61, 64, 68, 69, 70, 80, 84, and 86.

Periodical: "Wir sind vom Rundfunk," *Ungarische Rundschau*, no. 1 (1946), 14-17.

Anna Jókai

ENGLISH

Periodicals: "Hungarian lesson," *The New Hungarian Quarterly*, X, no. 33 (Spring, 1969), 64-65. §§ "Mimosa," *Hungarian Review*, no. 5 (1970), 14-17.

FRENCH

Periodicals: "Mimosa," *Revue Hongroise*, no. 5 (1970), 14-17.

GERMAN

See numbers 80 and 84.

Individual Edition: Gleichung mit zwei Unbekannten. Berlin: Verlag Neues Lebens, 1977. 279p.

Ferenc Juhász

ENGLISH

See numbers 9, 10, 11, 12, 14, 16, 18, and 33.

Individual Editions: The boy changed into a stag. Selected poems 1949-1967. Translated by Kenneth McRobbie and Ilona Duczyńska. Toronto, New York, London: Oxford University Press, 1970. 158p.

    Contents: "Brief confessions about myself," 21-32; "Violet-eyed little sister," 33-34; "The foaling time," 35-36; "Song of the tractor," 37-38; "Farm, at dark, on the Great Plain," 39-45; "Black peacock," 46-47; "At twenty-six," 48-49; "Crown of hatred and love," 50-53; "The boy changed into a stag cries out at the gate of secrets," 54-68; "Sorrow bred to perfection," 69-72; "Seasons," 73-74; "Four voices: Non-maledictory, in lament and supplication," 78-88; "Man imposes his pattern upon a dream," 89-92; "On the margin of my years is suspended animation," 93; "Firelily in the night," 94-96; "Gold twig past time," 97-99; "At childhood's table," 100-113; "Images of the night," 114-128; "Power of the flowers," 129-140; "The grave of Attila József," 141-158. Also: introduction, 8-19; the works of Ferenc Juhász, 159. LC, LN, TxDaM, OrPS, WaO.

Selected poems: Sándor Weöres. Translated with an introduction by Edwin Morgan. *Ferenc Juhász.* Translated with an introduction by David Wevill. Harmondsworth, England: Penguin Books, 1970. 136p.

    Contents: Part I: "Silver," 83; "Gold," 84; "Birth of the foal," 85-86; "Then there are fish," 87; "Comet-watchers," 88-89; "Mary," 90; "The tower of Rezi," 91-92; "November elegy," 93-94; *Part 2*: "The boy changed into a stag clamours at the gate of of secrets," 97-110; *Part 3*: "Hunger and hate," 113; "Four seasons," 114-115; "The flower of silence," 116; "A church in Bulgaria," 117-121; "A message too late," 122; "Black peacock," 123-124; "The rainbow-coloured whale," 125-129; "Thursday, day of superstition," 130-136. Also: introduction by David Wevill, 75-80. DeU, OCI, CaQMM, PPiU, CStm, IU, CoGUW, CtY, NIC, NN, WU, CaBVaU, CLU, MoSW, MdU, UU.

Periodicals: "Granny," *Books from Hungary*, VII, no. 1 (January-March, 1965), 7. §§ "Thursday, the day of superstition: When it's most difficult," *The New Hungarian Quarterly*, VII, no. 21 (Spring, 1966), 102-106; "The force of flowers," VII, no. 23 (Autumn, 1966), 136-137; "Crown of hatred and love," XI, no. 38 (Summer, 1970), 67-69. §§ "The grave of Attila József," *Arion 2* (1968), 130-138; "Four voices: Nonmaledictory, in lament and supplication," *Arion 3* (1970), 169-177; "To his fellow poets," *Arion 4* (1971), 39; "Béla Bartók and the tree frog," *Arion 5* (1972), 32-34. §§ "Silver," "Gold," "Mary," "November elegy," "Four seasons," "The rainbow-colored wheat," *DELOS*, no. 4 (1970), 137-145. §§ "Your ribbed, peasant hand," "The foaling time," "At twenty-six," *Chapman*, II, no. 4 (1973), 17-19.

FRENCH

See numbers 14, 28, 29, 30, 31, 33, 34, 36, and 37.

Periodicals: "Jeunes Mariés, arbres en fleurs," *France-Hongrie*, no. 55 (1956), 43. §§ "La baleine irisée," *Synthèse*, XVIII, no. 213 (Février, 1964), 141-144. §§ "La fleur du silence," "En marge de mes années de léthargie," "Imploration pour trouver le juste milieu pendant la composition d'une épopée," *Action Poétique*, no. 30 (Mai, 1966), 13-16; "Mère," no. 51-52 (1972), 191-192. §§ "Imploration pour trouver le juste milieu pendant la composition d'une épopée," *Arion 1* (1967), 207-208; "Le miel du Christ," *Arion 8* (1975), 73-81. §§ "Lettre sur le catafalque abandonné de Château-rose," *Esprit*, IV, no. 391 (Avril, 1970), 752. §§ "Ma mère," *The Hungarian P.E.N.*, no. 13 (1972), 12-14. §§ "Chants d'enfants" (extracts), *Alif*, no. 4-5 (1974), 160-164.

GERMAN

See numbers 64, 67, 75, 78, and 79.

Individual edition: Gedichte. Nachwort von Paul Kruntorad. Frankfurt am Main: Suhrkamp, 1966. 50p.

Contents: "Mein Dorf," 8; "Flüchtling," 8-9; "Tag Aberglaubens Donnerstag, wenn es am schwersten ist," 10-16; "Am Grab Árpád Tóths," 17-19; "Ruf des in einem Hirsch verwandelten Jünglings aus dem Tor der Geheimnisse," 20-30; "Letzte Fotographie Endre Adys," 31; "Warum heult die Nacht?" 32; "Hunger und Hass," 33; "Verspätete Nachricht," 34; "Sechsundzwanzigjährig," 35-36; "November," 37. Also: Anmerkung zu den Gedichten, 41; Nachwort von Paul Kruntorad, 45-50. IEN.

Periodical: "Feuerlilie in der Nacht," *Arion 3* (1970), 167-168.

Anna Kiss

FRENCH

See number 37.

Benedek Kiss

ENGLISH

Periodical: "Sea," "Inside timeless fall," "Glassblowers," "My mother," "Sacrificed a pigeon," *Lake Superior Journal*, no. 2 (1977), 8-11.

Iván Mándy

ENGLISH

See number 12.

Periodicals: "Morning at the cinema," *The New Hungarian Quarterly*, II, no. 4 (October-December, 1961), 157-162; "Private lives," VIII, no. 26 (Summer, 1967), 140-155; "Girl from the swimming pool," X, no. 36 (Winter, 1969), 90-95; "The kitchen wall," XIV, no. 51 (Autumn, 1973), 111-116. §§ "The death of Zoro," *Hungarian Review*, no. 4 (1968), 14-16. §§ "Mother," *Books from Hungary*, XIV, no. 4 (October-December, 1972), 12-14. §§ "To see father," *The Hungarian P.E.N.*, no. 13 (1972), 15-26.

FRENCH

See numbers 30, 34, and 35.

Periodicals: "Mort de Pat," *Revue Hongroise*, no. 4 (1968), 14-16. §§ "Maman," *Le Livre Hongrois*, XIV, no. 4 (1972), 12-14. §§ "Le cinéma des souvenirs," *The Hungarian P.E.N.*, no. 17 (1976), 66-80.

GERMAN

See numbers 64, 65, 68, 80, 81, 84, and 88.

Individual Editions: Die Frauen des Fabulya. Roman. Stuttgart: Deutsches Verlags-Anstalt, 1966. 139p. MB.

Erzählungen. Frankfurt am Main: Suhrkamp, 1966. 132p.
    Contents: "Urlaub," 7-13; "Die Hochzeit," 14-41; "Melonenmesser," 42-50; "Im dritten Stock," 51-74; "Die Jacke," 74-83; "Der Mitläufer," 84-96; "Der Handlungsreisende im Krankenhaus," 97-131. CoU.

Stoppel und das graue Pferd. Stuttgart: Franckh'sche Verlag, 1967. 160p. LC.

Am Rande des Spielfeldes. Roman. Stuttgart: Deutsches Verlags-Anstalt, 1971. 213p.

Kino alter Zeiten. Was gibt's, Alter? Berlin: Volk und Welt, 1975. 198p.

Periodicals: "Schularbeit," *Neues Forum*, no. 162-163 (Juni-Juli, 1967), 523-525. §§ "Mutter," *Bücher aus Ungarn*, XIV, no. 4 (1972), 12-14. §§ "Mutter," *Literatur und Kritik*, no. 64 (Mai, 1972), 226-230.

László Marsall

FRENCH

See number 37.

Periodicals: "Tram," *Esprit*, IV, no. 391 (Mai, 1970), 756. §§ "La dernière fois," "Entretien en bas rouges," *Arion 5* (1972), 117; "Solstice," "Tram," *Arion 9* (1976), 146.

GERMAN

Periodical: "Artist des Tierkreises," *Literatur und Kritik*, no. 64 (Mai, 1972), 207.

Miklós Mészöly

ENGLISH

Periodicals: "Report on five mice," *The New Hungarian Quarterly*, IX, no. 31 (Autumn, 1968), 131-137; "The falcons," XI, no. 40 (Winter, 1970), 83-111. §§ "Balcony and poplars," *Hungarian Review*, no. 9 (1969), 14-17; "At the state cattle dealers," no. 10 (1972), 14-17. §§ "Investigation," *Books from Hungary*, XV, no. 3 (July-September, 1973), 16-19. §§ "Quest," *Arion 7* (1974), 28-35. §§ "Quest," *Fiction* (1975), 3-9.

FRENCH

See number 30.

Individual Editions: Mort d'un athlète. Roman. Traduit du hongrois par Georges (György) Kassai et Marcel Courault. Paris: Éditions du Seuil, 1965. 186p. IEN.

Saul ou la porte des brebis. Roman. Traduit par Anne-Marie de Backer et Georges (György) Kassai. Paris: Éditions du Seuil, 1971. 170p. LC, WU.

Periodicals: "Le balcon et les peupliers," *Revue Hongroise*, no. 9 (1969), 14-17; "A l'office du cheptel," no. 10 (1972), 14-17. §§ "Enquête," *Le Livre Hongrois*, XV, no. 3 (1973), 16-19. §§ "Des vieillards et des morts" (fragment), *Cahiers de L'est*, no. 4 (Décembre, 1975), 31-48.

GERMAN

See numbers 58, 68, 84, and 88.

Individual Editions: Gestaltungen. Aus dem Ungarischen von Barbara Frischmuth. Literarisches Colloquium. Berlin: Berliner Künstlerprogram des DAD, 1963. 64p.

Contents: Number 38 of the series, it is entirely devoted to two works of Mészöly: "Gestaltungen," 7-42; "Reise," 43-64.

Der Tod des Athleten. Roman. München: Carl Hanser, 1966. 262p. MB, InNd.

Saul. Roman. München: Carl Hanser, 1970. 184p. LC.

Saulus. Leipzig: St. Benno-Verlag, 1970. 179p.

Landkarte mit Rissen. Erzählungen aus dem Ungarischen von Hildegard Grosche. Mit einem Porträt des Autors von Walter Höllerer. München-Wien: Carl Hanser, 1976. 165p.

Contents: "Hohe Schule," 7-60; "Die Alten und die Toten," 61-137; "Bettlertanz," 138-145; "Spurensicherung," 146-150; "Landkarte mit Rissen," 151-164. Also: Miklós Mészöly, 165.

Periodicals: "Eine herausfordernde Gegenwart," *Akzente*, XIV, no. 3 (Juni, 1967), 201-206; "Briefe aus dem Tal," XV, no. 2 (April, 1968), 160-168; "Recherche," XXII, no. 6 (Dezember, 1975), 498-506. §§ "Recherche," *Bücher aus Ungarn*, XV, no. 3 (1973), 16-19. §§ "Ana Kamphos," *Europäische Ideen*, no. 7 (1974), 23-24. §§ "Landkarte mit Rissen," *Neue Rundschau*, LXXXVI, no. 4 (1975), 595-604.

László Nagy

ENGLISH

See numbers 15, 16, and 18.

Individual Edition: Love of the scorching wind. Selected poems 1953-1971. Translated by Tony Connor and Kenneth McRobbie with a foreword by George (György) Gömöri. Budapest: Corvina, 1973. 84p. (Also: Oxford University Press, 1973.)

Contents: "Lovers," 1; "The coalmen," 2; "Have a good rest," 3; "On faery-beautiful faces you fed," 4-5; "Fair and frosty May," 6; "Whom does it hurt," 7-8; "Carrying Love," 9; "Squared by walls," 10; "Hymn for anytime," 11-12; "Dreamlike speech," 13; "Without mercy," 14; "The faces of our kin," 15-16; "Cloud with a woman's face," 17-18; "Howls," 19-20; "Easter legend," 21; "Day of unfaithfulness," 22; "Csontváry," 23-24; "The visitors," 25-26; "My mother approaching," 27-28; "The hawk-nosed one's funeral," 29-30; "A present," 31; "Grasshoppers on the bell," 32; "Threats," 33-34; "Viola," 35-36; "Pleasuring Sunday," 37-46; "Love of the scorching wind," 47-52; "Wedding," 53-60; "Bear psalm," 61-63; "Sky and earth," 64-78. Also: Foreword by George (György) Gömöri, vii-xiii; Bibliography, 79; notes, 80-83; index of titles, 84. LC, WaU, OCU, MiEM, NcU, TNJ, IaU, OrU, NsyU, VtU, NjP, UU, OkU, NjR, TxU, PSt,

AzU, CoU, OrPS, MoU, MB, WU, NIC, InU, CU, NcGU, CtY, OOxM, NWM, NmU, IaAS, IU, NcRS, ViU, CtW, NbU, LN, CoFS, FU, TU, CaBVaU, NN, MnU, NNC, IcarbS, NBu.
Periodicals: "Bartók and the beasts of prey," *The New Hungarian Quarterly*, VII, no. 23 (Autumn, 1966), 134; "The ferryman," "The prayer to the white lady," "The break-up," "The peacock woman," VIII, no. 27 (Autumn, 1967), 42-49; "The bliss of Sunday," XI, no. 37 (Spring, 1970), 106-113; "Fair in frosty May," "Without mercy," "Coalman," XI, no. 40 (Winter, 1970), 112-114; "Frosts are coming," XII, no. 41 (Spring, 1971), 96; "Csontváry," XII, no. 42 (Summer, 1971), 55-56; "Love of the scorching wind," XIII, no. 48 (Winter, 1972), 111-115. §§ "The tenement house," *The Hungarian P.E.N.*, no. 9 (1968), 7-16; "All the stars from my face," "Funerals of his hawk's features," "The present," no. 11 (1970), 67-69. §§ "Easter legend," *Modern Poetry Studies*, II, no. 5 (1971), 206. §§ "Coalman," *Books from Hungary*, XIV, no. 1 (January-March, 1972), 13; "Without mercy," XVI, no. 1 (April-June, 1974), 30. §§ "My mother approaching," "Sky and earth," *Arion 6* (1973), 76-86; "The sadness of resurrection," *Arion 10* (1977), 161-162. §§ "Fair and frosty May," "Bartók and the beasts of prey," *Chapman*, II, no. 4 (1973), 15-16. §§ "The break-up," "Squared by walls," *American Poetry Review*, VI, no. 3 (May-June, 1977), 24.

FRENCH

See numbers 28, 29, 33, 34, 36, and 37.

Periodicals: "Dangers et fleurs," *Synthèses*, XVIII, no. 213 (Juillet-Août, 1963), 140-141. §§ "Paysage avec moi-même," *Arion 1* (1966), 182; "Le jour de l'infidélité," "Csontváry," *Arion 3* (1970), 164-165; "Pour le héros des roses sur la colline des roses," "S'approche une nouvelle saison," "Les arbres fondent," *Arion 8* (1975), 81-83; "Deux crinifères," "Un loup parle," "Cadeau," *Arion 9* (1976), 126-127. §§ "Qui portera l'amour?" *The Hungarian P.E.N.*, no. 9 (1968), 40; "Soir," no. 14 (1973), 38. §§ "Absente, la pitié," *Esprit*, IV, no. 391 (Mai, 1970), 748-749. §§ "L'ange vert" (fragments), *Alif*, no. 4-5 (1974), 153-154. §§ "Le jour de l'infidélité," *Le Livre Hongrois*, XVI, no. 1 (1974), 32. §§ "Chimère," "Ta splendeur infernale ô mer," "Tremble l'occident . . .," "Qui fera passer?" *La Barbacane, Revue des Pierres et des Hommes*, no. 15-16 (1974-1975), 69-71. §§ "Pour le héros des roses sur la colline des roses," *Action Poétique*, no. 64 (1975), 166. §§ "Deux crinifères," *Le Temps Parallèle*, no. 6 (Septembre, 1975), 21.

GERMAN

See numbers 64, 78, and 79.

Individual Edition: Poesiealbum 45. László Nagy. Berlin: Verlag Neues Leben, 1971. 31p.

Contents: "Anflehung," 3; "An die Aschenbrödel," 4; "Frühlingslied," 5; "Die Zukunft zu Bahn," 6; "Bulgarien," 7; "Brief von der Messe in Plowdiw," 8-9; "Sommerlied," 10; "Ein Schmied," 11; "Wer bringt die Liebe hinüber?" 12; "Lass mich nicht auf den Gebeinen stehen," 13-14; "Osterlegende," 15; "Blutbellende Fee," 18-20; "Der schwarze Dichter," 21-22; "Bartók und die Bestien," 23-24; "Attila József," 25-26; "Wenn die Erde dröhnt," 27-28; "Anbetung des heissen Windes," 29-30; "Im Verwald versteckt," 31-32.

Periodicals: "Osterlegende," *Akzente*, XIV, no. 3 (Juni, 1967), 254; "Das Feuer," "Milchzähne hab' ich nicht mehr," "An die Aschenbrödel," "Sommerlied," "Hymnus zu allen Zeiten," XXI, no. 1 (Februar, 1974), 8-12. §§ "Das Feuer," *Sinn und Form*, XXI, no. 1 (1969), 96; "Der Durst," "Die Bäume," XXV, no. 1 (1973), 113-114.

Ágnes Nemes Nagy

ENGLISH

See numbers 12, 16, 17, and 18.

Periodicals: "Storm," *The New Hungarian Quarterly*, VII, no. 23 (Autumn, 1966), 132; "Statues," "I carried statues," X, no. 35 (Autumn, 1969), 75-76; "Between," "Comparison," "Defend it," "The shapelessness," XVII, no. 62 (Summer, 1976), 30-33; "Night oaktree," "The proportions of the street," "The courage of cats," "The ghost," XVIII, no. 68 (Winter, 1977), 85-88. §§ "The geysir," *The Hungarian P.E.N.*, no. 11 (1970), 16; "Four squares," no. 17 (1976), 64-65; "Without bison," no. 18 (1977), 46-51. §§ "Lazarus," *Modern Poetry Studies*, II, no. 5 (1971), 207. §§ "The trees," "Storm," *Arion 6* (1973), 135-136; "The trees," "Between," "Lazarus," *Arion 9* (1976), 123. §§ "Storm," "Lazarus," "Simile," *Modern Poetry in Translation*, no. 19-20 (Spring, 1974), 24. §§ "Bird," "But to look," "Words to a song," "Like someone," *Green House*, I, no. 2 (Winter, 1977), 49-52.

FRENCH

See numbers 28, 29, 30, 34, 36, and 37.

Periodicals: "Dans le quartier Krisztina," *Arion 1* (1966), 181; "Ekhnaton au ciel," "Les objets," "Arbres," "Au-dessus de l'objet," *Arion 3* (1970), 159-161; "Orage," *Arion 4* (1971), 87. §§ "Entre-deux," *Esprit*, IV, no. 391 (Avril, 1970), 745-746; "Arbres," XII, no. 398 (Decembre, 1970), 872. §§ "Fidélité à la forme, choix des mots," *The Hungarian P.E.N.*, no. 11 (1970), 48-49; "Le sans-forme," no. 14 (1973), 39. §§ "Statues," *Alif*, no. 4-5 (1974), 156-157. §§ "Oiseau," "Le sans-forme," "La nuit d'Ekhnaton," *La Barbacane, Revue des Pierres et des Hommes*, no. 15-16 (1974-1975), 61-66. §§ "Les proportions de la rue," "Le courage des chats," *Le Temps Parallèle*, no. 6 (Septembre, 1975), 18-20.

GERMAN

See numbers 75, 78, and 79.

Periodicals: "Dazwischen," *Akzente*, XIV, no. 3 (Juni, 1967), 249-251. §§ "Vogel," *Arion 7* (1974), 115.

Szilveszter Ördögh

ENGLISH

Periodicals: "The colt," *Hungarian Review*, no. 9 (1974), 14.

FRENCH

Periodical: "Le poulain," *Revue Hongroise*, no. 9 (1974), 14.

István Örkény

ENGLISH

See number 12.

Periodicals: "The 'Silly Season' in Budapest," *Hungarian Review*, no. 9 (1956), 25; "It's nice to be warm," no. 8 (1967), 14-16; "One minute stories: 'No news,' 'Confession,' 'A few minutes foreign policy,' 'Satan Füred,' " no. 2 (1973), 14-16. §§ "A few minutes foreign policy," *The Hungarian P.E.N.*, no. 8 (1967), 23-25; "Pebbles," no. 15 (1974), 48-58. §§ "The hundred and thirty-seventh Psalm," *The New Hungarian Quarterly*, VIII, no. 26 (Summer, 1967), 131-139; "The Tót family" (fragment), VIII, no. 28 (Winter, 1967), 125-132; "One minute stories: 'Art history,' 'There is always hope,' 'The great march,' 'The actor's death,' 'Climacteric,' 'Portrait of a man,' 'Honeymooners on flypaper,' 'Savior,' " IX, no. 29 (Spring, 1968), 58-65; "One minute stories: 'Thoughts in a cellar,' 'Art and the illuminating experience,' 'Self-fulfillment,' 'On my health,' 'Introspection,' 'To the salt cellar,' 'Dial 170-100,' 'Death of a spectator,' " X, no. 35 (Autumn, 1969), 64-74; "Catsplay" (excerpt), XII, no. 44 (Winter, 1971), 69-106; "Memoirs of a puddle," XIV, no. 59 (Autumn, 1975), 82-119. §§ "Instant stories: 'The harem,' 'Inventory,' 'Citizens,' 'One desperate tulip,' 'Opinion poll,' 'The meaning of life,' 'A classified ad,' 'New proverb,' " *Arion 4* (1971), 32-36; "Catsplay" (excerpt), *Arion 7* (1974), 20-26. §§ "One Wednesday," *Books from Hungary*, XV, no. 2 (April-June, (1973), 12-13. §§ "Snowy landscape with two onion domes," *Tri-Quarterly*, no. 31 (Winter, 1976), 14-15.

FRENCH
See numbers 30 and 34.

Individual Editions: La famille Tót. Adapté du hongrois par Claude Roy. Paris: Gallimard, 1968. 114p. LC, ICRL.

Minimythes. Textes choisis, adaptés du hongrois et préfacés par Tibor Tardos. Paris: Gallimard, 1970. 216p.

Contents: "Rien de neuf," 13-16; "Budapest," 17-18; "Une critique constructive," 19-23; "Page blanche," 24; "Sport," 25-29; "L'écho," 30-31; "Le temps passe," 32-35; "Recette," 36; "Bulletin de l'étranger," 37-40; "Avis divers," 41-42; "Tant qu'il y a de la vie . . .," 43-44; "Une tulipe aux abois," 45-46; "Deuil," 47; "D'une méprise à l'autre," 48; Jeunes mariés dans la glu," 49-52; "Qu'est-ce que c'est? Mais qu'est-ce que c'est?," 53-56; "Café Niagara," 57-68; "Climax," 69; "La Longue Marche," 70-71; "Fringale," 72-73; "Paysage de Russie," 74-75; "Extase," 76-80; "Nos rêves les plus hardis," 81-83; " 'In memoriam K. H. G.,' " 84; "Le harem," 85-88; "Renseignements," 89-90; "La société protectrice," 91; "Dans le bureau du directeur," 92-93; "Lied," 94-95; "Le cambrioleur de l'express de Liverpool sous les verrous," 96-98; "La mort du comédien," 99-100; "La pesanteur," 101-103; "Moeurs d'une époque," 104-105; "Simple comme bonjour," 106-109; "S.V.P. BU-DA," 110-114; "Il faut que ça change," 115; "Réflexion du païen Sutto au cours de son écartelément (1072)," 116-117; "Envisageons l'avenir avec optimisme," 118-120; "Portrait d'homme," 121-125; "Exercices de style," 126; "Dédicaces," 127-132; "Le Rédempteur," 133-134; "Dernières paroles," 135; "Impressions du Cosmos," 136-137; "Le module lunaire hongrois," 138-142; "Gallup," 143-145; "Le conducteur," 146-147; "Lève-toi et marche," 148-154; "Grande vente annuelle," 155-158; "Le Juif errant," 159; "Le Moucheté," 160-161; "Les triplés de Budapest," 162-166; "Cachet," 167; "Dans la cave," 168-169; "Raison de vivre," 170-172; " 'Home sweet home,' " 173; "Ce que client veut . . .," 174-186; " 'Bello bambino,' " 187-189; "Le choix," 190-191; "L'approche du printemps," 192-193; "Déclaration," 194; "Communique le 1er février," 195-196; "Rivalité," 197-201; "Un souci de moins," 202; "Le temps des noyaux," 203-206; "La santé," 207; "Bricolage," 208-209; "Dans le sablier," 210-213. Also: Örkényland par Tibor Tardos, 7-12. LC, CU-S.

Chat! Tragi-comédie en deux parties adaptée du hongrois par Vercors. Paris: Éditions Gallimard, 1974. 100p. LC, MiDW, WU.

Periodicals: "La morte saison à Budapest," *Revue Hongroise*, no. 9 (1956), 26; "L' homme a besoin de chaleur," no. 8 (1967), 14-16; "Minimythes: 'Rien de nouveau,' 'Tendres aveux,' 'Commentaire de politique internationale,' 'Satan à Balatonfüred,' " no. 2 (1973), 14-16. §§ "A propos d'objets," *Europe*, LI, no. 526 (Février, 1973), 115-118. §§ "Un mercredi," *Le Livre Hongrois*, XV, no. 2 (1973), 12-13. §§ "Chat!" (excerpt), *Arion 7* (1974), 20.

GERMAN

See numbers 72 and 86.

Individual Editions: Eheleute. Berlin: Tribune, 1953. 595p. (Also: Wien: Stern, 1953. 595p.) *Berlin Edition*: DLC-P4.

Der letzte Zug. Erzählungen. Berlin: Volk und Welt, 1973. 436p.

Contents: "Ringelreihen . . .," 5-16; "Die Herzogin von Jerusalem," 17-63; "Der letzte Zug," 64-83; "Die Familie Tót," 85-224; "Budaer Fasten," 225-250; "Bubu," 251-286; "Gerstenkorn," 287-307; "Du Liebes, Liebes . . .," 308-348; "Briefe ins Kollegium," 349-385; "Die Angelegen Frau Hanák," 386-406; *Inserat*, 407; "In our time," 408-411; "Der Stammgast," 412-415; "Hochzeitsreisende auf dem Fliegenfänger," 416-419; "Ins Poesiealbum" (poem), 420; "Geduldspiel" (poem), 421-422; "Erscheinung," 423; "Was verkündet der Lautsprecher?" 424-426; "Ein Zimmer, Lehmziegelmauern, Strohdach," 427-429. Also: Nachwort, 430-436.

Familie Tót. Katzenspiel. Zwei Stücke. Übersetzer Barbara Frischmuth und Vera Thies. Berlin: Hensch-Verlag, 1975. 141p.

Periodicals: "Gedanken bei der Arbeit" (excerpt from *Eheleute*), *Neues aus Ungarn*, no. 3 (Januar, 1954), 22-23. §§ "Bekenntnis zur Groteske," *Literatur und Kritik*, no. 64 (Mai, 1972), 231-235. §§ "An einem Mittwoch," *Bücher aus Ungarn*, XV, no. 2 (1973), 12-13.

György Petri

ENGLISH

See number 18.

Periodical: "The thin girl," "You usually come in the morning," "Song," *The New Hungarian Quarterly*, XII, no. 44 (Winter, 1971), 117-120.

FRENCH

See number 37.

Periodicals; "Poème d'un poète est-européen inconnu, en 1955," "Tu viens toujours le matin," *Arion 5* (1972), 100-101; "Une de mes méditations," "D'un poète inconnu d'Europe centrale en 1955," "Tu as l'habitude de venir le matin . . .," *Arion 9* (1976), 161-163.

GERMAN

Periodical: "Nur eine Person," *Literatur und Kritik*, no. 64 (Mai, 1972), 208.

János Pilinszky

ENGLISH

See numbers 11, 12, 15, 16, and 18.

Individual Edition: Selected poems. Translated by Ted Hughes and János Csokits. Manchester, England: Carcanet New Press, 1976. 67p.

Contents: From *"Trapeze and Parallel Bars," 1940-46*: "Fish in the net," 17; "Trapeze and parallel bars," 18; "Under the winter sky," 19; "Harbach 1944," 20; "You have had to suffer rain and cold," 21; "What underground struggle," 22-23; *from "On the Third Day," 1946-58*: "Sin," 24-25; "World grown old," 26; "Complaint," 27; "By the time you come," 28; "The French prisoner," 29-30; "On the wall of a KZ-lager," 31; "Passion of Ravensbrück," 32; "Frankfurt 1945," 33-34; "Impromptu," 35; "The desert of love," 36; "Revelations VIII.7," 37; "Apocrypha," 38-40; "Quatrain," 41; "Under the portrait," 42; "Cold wind," 43; "Unfinished past," 44; "November elysium," 45; *from "Requiem," 1959-64*: "Epilogue," 46-47; "Fable" (detail from 'Kz-oratorio' entitled 'Dark heaven'), 48; *from "Big City Icons," 1964-70*: "Big city icons," 49; "Introitus," 50; "Van Gogh," 51; "The passion," 52; *from "Splinters," 1971*: "As I was," 53; "Crime and punishment," 54; "Exhortation," 55; "The prayer of Van Gogh," 56; "My coat of arms," 57; "Gradually," 58; "Enough," 59; "Straight labyrinth," 60; *from "Denouement," 1971-74*: "Meditation," 61; "Jewel," 62; "Stavrogin takes his leave," 63; "Stavrogin returns," 64; *from "Space and Relationship," 1975*: "Aquarium," 65; "Pathography and swansong," 66; "Crater," 67. Also: introduction, 7-14.

Crater, poems 1974-75. Translated by Peter Jay. London: Anvil Press, 1978. 63p.
    Contents: "Homage to Isaac Newton," 13; "And yet," 14; "Self-portrait 1974," 15; "Pascal," 15; "Auschwitz," 16; "Spaces," 17; "Good news," 18; "Pathogeny and swansong," 19; "Dream," 20; "Two," 21; "Depression," 22; "Differences," 23; "Confusion," 24; "On the back of a photograph," 25; "Letter," 26; "Homage to Paul Verlaine," 27; "Posthumous passion," 28; "Waltz," 29; "Eternity," 30; "A beating," 31; "Hölderlin," 32; "Green," 32; "Stoneware," 33; "Aquarium," 34; "Relationship,"35; "Gothic," 36; "Backwards," 37; "Crater," 38; "Gérard de Nerval," 41; "Pupil," 42; "The flies," 43; "Stunning tongs," 44; "Sum," 45; "Temptation," 45; "Homage to Sheryl Sutton I," 46; "Homage to Sheryl Sutton II," 47; "Definition of your attraction," 48; "We and they," 49; "Transformations," 50; "14 October, 1970," 51; "22 December, 1970," 52; "Veil," 53; "Life sentence," 54; "Breaking up," 55; "Here and now," 56; "Arms and neck," 57; "The prodigals," 58; "Knocking," 59; "These things happen," 60; "Miss I. B.," 61; "Sketch," 62; "Release," 63. Also: preface by Peter Jay, 7-9.

Periodicals: "Postscript," *The New Hungarian Quarterly*, VII, no. 23 (Autumn, 1966), 130-131; "Apocrypha," IX, no. 30 (Summer, 1968), 103; "Cattle brand," "All that is needed," "I shall be watching," "Metronome," "Every breath," "The rest is grace," "Celebration of the nadir," "Meetings," XIV, no. 50 (Summer, 1973), 154-158; "Under the winter sky," "Sin," "Passion of Ravensbrück," "The desert of love," "Apocrypha," "Fable" (detail from 'KZ-oratorio' entitled 'Dark heaven'), "As I was," "Exhortation," XVIII, no. 62 (Summer, 1976), 33-40. §§ "Cattle brand," "All that is needed," "I shall be watching," "Metronome," "Every breath," "The rest is grace," "Celebration of the nadir," "Meetings," *Chapman*, II, no. 4 (1973), 12-15. §§ "Agonia Christiana," "Van Gogh," "Eine kleine Nachtmusik," "The passion," "Like earth," "In memoriam N. N.," *Modern Poetry in Translation*, no. 19-20 (Spring, 1974), 23-24; "Fable: From 'KZ-oratorio,' " "Straight labyrinth," "Enough," "Searching for the prodigal son," "Your hand, my hand," "Now," "Nothing but," "Van Gogh's prayer," "My only reading," no. 25 (Summer, 1975), 15-16; "Self-portrait 1974," "Dreams," "Depression," "Difference," "On the back of a photograph," "Eternity," "Hölderlin," "Aquarium," "Relationship," "Knocking," "Sketch," no. 30 (Spring, 1977), i-ii. §§ "From the diary of the executioner," "Like earth," "Van Gogh," *Arion 9* (1976), 118-119. §§ "Under the winter sky," "The desert of love," *American Poetry Review*, VI, no. 3 (May-June, 1977), 23-24.

FRENCH

See numbers 28, 29, 30, 33, 34, 36, and 37.

Periodicals: "Apocryphe," *Synthèses*, XVIII, no. 213 (Février, 1964), 137-140. §§ "Le troisième jour," *Arion 1* (1966), 182; "Passé simple," *Arion 3* (1970), 155; "Quatrain," "Sans témoin," "Sous le ciel d'hiver," "Monde refroidi," "En marge d'une passion," *Arion 9* (1976), 117-118. §§ "Passé simple," "Passion," *Esprit*, IV, no. 391 (Mai, 1970), 743. §§ "Passion," "Crime et châtiment," "Parabole," "Échafaud en hiver," "Ma seule lecture," "Moi, je ne compte pas," *The Hungarian P.E.N.*, no. 14 (1973), 95-97. §§ "Le désert de l'amour," *Alif*, no. 4-5 (1974), 152.

GERMAN

See numbers 64, 65, 75, 78, and 81.

Individual Edition: Grosstadt-Ikonen. Ausgewählte Dichtungen und Essays. Salzburg: Otto Müller, 1971. 97p.

Contents: "Bad um Mitternacht," 5-6; "Trapez und Barren," 7-8; "Du, besiege mich," 9; "Weil ihr durchnässt wart und froret," 10; "Harbach 1944," 11-12; "Französischer Gefangener," 13-14; "Grabspruch," 15; "Klage," 16-17; "Niemandsland," 18-20; "Fragment vom Goldenen Zeitalter," 21; "Bis du ankommst," 22-23; "Impromptu," 24-25; "Odland der Liebe," 26; "Zwei Vierzeiler," 27; "Offenbarungen," 28; "Apokryph," 29-32; "Vierzeiler," 33; "Agonia Christiana," 34; "Halbvergangen," 35; "Elysium in November," 36; "Am dritten Tag," 37; "Ravensbrücker Passion," 38; "Kalter Wind," 39; "Under ein Bildnis," 40; "Epilog," 41-42; "Introitus," 43; "Das Meer," 44; "Kleine Nachtmusik," 45-46; "Grosstadt-Ikonen," 47-48; "Van Gogh," 49; "Passion," 50; "Auf dem Grabstein-Überhitzter Blumenstrauss," 51; "Sonderurteil," 52; "Selbstbildnis 1940," 53; "Aus dem Tagebuch des Henkers," 54; "Wohin, wie?" 55; Auf verbotenem Stern," 56; "Wie die Erde," 57; "Der heilige Schächer," 58; "Das dunkle Himmelreich KZ-Oratorium," 59-74; "Die Geschichte meines Engagements" (essay), 75-82; "Das Los der schöpferischen Imagination in unserer Zeit" (essay), 83-93. Also: Nachwort, 95-97. LC.

Periodicals: "In einigen Worten," "Wie nur," "Gerades Labyrinth," "Gleichnis," "Das Fest des Tiefpunktes," *Literatur und Kritik*, no. 64 (Mai, 1972), 200-202; "Aus dem Tagebuch eines Lyrikers," no. 75 (Juni, 1973), 265-268. §§ "Die Geschichte meines Engagements," "Kalter Wind," "Agonia Christiana," "Vierzeiler," "Am dritten Tag," *Akzente*, XIV, no. 3 (Juni, 1967), 216-221, 251-252. §§ "Ravensbrücker Passion," *Sinn und Form*, XXI, no. 1 (1969), 105. §§ "Aus dem Tagebuch eines Lyrikers," "Lebende Bilder," *Ensemble, Lyrik, Prosa, Essay*, 5, (1974), 101-113.

Ferenc Sánta

ENGLISH

See number 10.

Periodicals: "An Italian story," *Hungarian Review*, no. 3 (1964), 14-16. §§ "Twenty hours," *The New Hungarian Quarterly*, VI, no. 17 (Spring, 1965), 65-74; "God in the wagon," XII, no. 42 (Summer, 1971), 66-75; "The initiation," XIX, no. 69 (Spring, 1978), 48-54. §§ "Nazis," *Books from Hungary*, XIV, no. 2 (May-August, 1972), 17-19.

FRENCH

See numbers 31 and 35.

Individual Edition: Le cinquième sceau. Traduit du hongrois par Anne-Marie de Becker, Georges Kassai et Jean Rousselot. Paris: Gallimard, 1971. 223p. LC.

Periodicals: "Nazis," *The Hungarian P.E.N.*, no. 2 (1961), 4-9; "Du bien au soleil," no. 15 (1974), 28-36. §§ "Souvenir d'Italie," *Revue Hongroise*, no. 3 (1964), 14-16; "Nazis," "Des soudards," no. 4 (1966), 14-16. §§ "Nazis," *Le Livre Hongrois*, XIV, no. 4 (1972), 17-19.

GERMAN

See numbers 67, 69, 70, and 84.

Individual Edition: Zwanzig Stunden. Roman. München: Bogen, 1970. 190p.
Periodicals: "Italienische Geschichte," *Ungarische Rundschau,* no. 3 (1964), 14-16; "Bewaffnete 1944," no. 4 (1966), 14-16. §§ "Nazis," *Bücher aus Ungarn,* XIV, no. 2 (1972), 17-19.

Dezső Tandori

ENGLISH
See numbers 16 and 18.
Periodicals: "Fragment to Hamlet," "Koan bel canto?" *The New Hungarian Quarterly,* X, no. 33 (Spring, 1969), 60-61; "Homage," "Details," "How everything's enlarged," "A bush flown away," XII, no. 47 (Autumn, 1972), 198-200; "And brief, good mother, for I am in haste," XIV, no. 49 (Spring, 1973), 94-95; "Loss of amateurhood," "Private collection," "Sadness of the bare cupola," XVI, no. 57 (Spring, 1975), 108-113. §§ "And brief, good mother, for I am in haste," *Arion 6* (1973), 112-113; "Entering," "Self-portrait, 1965," "So this is," *Arion 7* (1974), 132-133. §§ "Self-portrait," *The Hungarian P.E.N.,* no. 14 (1973), 58; "(Maybe!): St. Severin-corner," "St. Severin dies out of context," "It goes on," no. 18 (1977), 71-73. §§ "A separation," *Modern Poetry in Translation,* no. 19-20 (Spring, 1974), 25.

FRENCH
See number 37.
Periodicals: "Koan I, Koan II, Koan III," "Sur la carte J.P.," "Baignade," *Esprit,* IV, no. 391 (Avril, 1970), 760. §§ "Hommage," "Le prince H. devant beau-père," "Maintenant et à l'heure de notre mort," *Arion 9* (1976), 156-157.

GERMAN
Periodical: "Fortwährend," *Literatur und Kritik,* no. 64 (Mai, 1972), 208.

Miklós Vámos

ENGLISH
Periodicals: "Prefaces," *Hungarian Review,* no. 9 (1970), 14-16; "Notes," no. 6 (1974), 15-17. §§ "The dance," *The New Hungarian Quarterly,* XVII, no. 61 (Spring, 1967), 112.

FRENCH
Periodical: "Préfaces," *Revue Hongroise,* no. 9 (1970), 14-16; "Messages," no. 6 (1974), 15-17.

GERMAN
See number 86.

Miklós Veress

ENGLISH
See number 18.
Periodical: "Self-portrait at thirty," *The New Hungarian Quarterly,* XVII, no. 61 (Spring, 1976), 111.

Contributors

Contributors

Translators

Daniel Abondolo is a native of Connecticut. After early concentration on French and German in public school, he received a B.A. in Ancient Greek language and literature at Yale College in 1974 and an M.A. in linguistics at Columbia University in 1977. Now a doctoral candidate in the Subcommittee on Uralic Studies at Columbia, he also teaches the first two years of the Hungarian language there. He has been translating from French, Italian, German, Swedish, Classical Chinese, Hungarian, and Finnish poetry since the mid-1960s, and has also participated in poetry readings in New Haven, New York, and Boston, and at Smith College. His work has appeared in *The Weekly Appendix*, an occasional journal published in Cambridge, Massachusetts.

Robert Austerlitz, who was born in Bucharest, Rumania, of Austrian and Hungarian parents, has resided in New York since 1938. He obtained a B.A. in philosophy in 1949 at the New School of Social Research, and an M.A. in general and comparative linguistics in 1950 and a Ph.D. in Uralic and Altaic languages in 1955 at Columbia University. He has been a professor of linguistics and Uralic studies at Columbia since 1958 and also a visiting professor at several universities, including Yale, the University of California at Berkeley, the University of Cologne, and recently the University of Hawaii. He has edited a Finnish reader and published numerous articles in scholarly periodicals and translations of Portuguese, Spanish, Rumanian, and Hungarian poems in such magazines as *Poetry Northwest* and *Mele*.

Contributors

Enikő Molnár Basa, a native of Hungary, became a United States citizen in 1956. She received a B.A. in English at Trinity College, Washington, D.C., in 1962, and an M.A. in comparative literature in 1965 and a Ph.D. in the same discipline in 1972 at the University of North Carolina, Chapel Hill. She taught at The American University and Hood College before joining the staff of the Library of Congress. She is President of the American Hungarian Educators' Association and an editor of the Hungarian section of the Twayne World Authors Series, for which she is preparing a monograph on Sándor Petőfi, the eminent mid-nineteenth-century Hungarian poet. Her articles on Hungarian literature have appeared in the *Yearbook of Comparative and General Literature* and *Books Abroad*, and her translations of Hungarian poetry and prose in the *Canadian-American Review of Hungarian Studies*.

Tony Connor was born in Salford, Lancashire, England. He obtained an M.A. from the University of Manchester and taught at Technical College, Bolton, Lancashire, from 1961 to 1964. He is currently professor of literature at Wesleyan University, Middletown, Connecticut. He has published many successful books of poetry, including *With Love Somehow, Lodgers, In the Happy Valley, The Memoirs of Uncle Harry*, and *Seven Last Poems*, most of them by Oxford University Press. His numerous translations of contemporary Hungarian poetry have appeared most often in *The New Hungarian Quarterly* and *Bulletin: Hungarian P. E. N.* He has also published an edition of selected poems by László Nagy with Kenneth McRobbie.

The late **Ilona Duczynska** assisted Kenneth McRobbie in making his final versions of the Ferenc Juhász poems published by Oxford University Press. She edited with her husband an anthology of Hungarian literature, *The Plough and the Pen* (1963), and she translated some of the fiction of József Lengyel.

Carl R. Erickson is a native of Philadelphia. He received a B.A. in English at the University of Chicago and his M.A. in Uralic and Altaic studies with concentration on Hungarian at Indiana University. He spent 1972-74 in Hungary on a grant from the Hungarian Institute for Cultural Relations, studying Hungarian literature of the period between the two world wars. He taught Hungarian for several years and at present is working and living in California. His translations of Hungarian prose have appeared in *The New Hungarian Quarterly* and *Bulletin: Hungarian P. E. N.*

John Freeman was born at Tipton, Straffordshire, England. He was educated at Dudley Grammar School and at Jesus College, Cambridge University, where he obtained a B.A. in German and French in 1969 and an M.A. in 1973. After teaching modern languages, he became a trainee librarian at the University of London's Institute of Germanic Studies, and after receiving a diploma in librarianship at University College, London, in 1973, he joined the library staff of the

School of Slavonic and East European Studies, University of London, where he also undertook the study of Hungarian. He spent time in Hungary in 1974 working on the language. He has translated works of a miscellaneous character, mainly from German, but has recently turned to the translation of Hungarian short stories and novellas.

George Gömöri, a native of Hungary, teaches history at Cambridge University. He assisted both Tony Connor and Kenneth McRobbie in their final versions of László Nagy's poems published by Oxford University Press, a role he frequently performs. He has written a study of Hungarian and Polish literature from 1945 to the mid-1950s, also published by Oxford University Press.

Georgia Lenart Greist, who was born in Pápa, Hungary, came to the United States with her parents in 1957 and became a naturalized citizen in 1962. After completing work on a B.A. in comparative literature at Indiana University, she continued her graduate studies in the same discipline at the University of Wisconsin, Madison, where she was awarded an M.A. in 1967 and a Ph.D. in 1975. The title of her thesis was *The Reception of French Naturalism in the Hungarian Novel*. Her translations appear for the first time in the present work.

Timothy Kachinske is a native of Duluth, Minnesota. He received a B.A. in 1971 and an M.A. in 1977 in English at the University of Minnesota, Duluth. He spent a year in Hungary on a University of Minnesota Fellowship, studying Hungarian language and literature. At present he is a student in the Hungarian program at the School of Slavonic and East European Studies, University of London, where he is writing a thesis on the poetry of Miklós Radnoti, whose life was cut short in a forced-labor camp near the end of World War II. Kachinske's translations of Polish and Hungarian poems have appeared in little magazines.

Mari Kuttna, a native of Hungary, emigrated with her family to Australia after World War II. She graduated from Sydney University with first-class honors and the University Medal for English, and also won a scholarship for postgraduate research at Oxford University. After leaving Oxford, she first worked in publishing, then in journalism, and she is still a free-lance film critic. On one occasion she served six months as English subeditor for *The New Hungarian Quarterly*. She began translating prose writings for Corvina Press in Budapest in 1964, including major works by Áron Tamási and Kálmán Mikszáth. In recent years, besides translating short pieces for *The New Hungarian Quarterly* and *Bulletin: Hungarian P. E. N.*, she has translated plays by István Örkény, Gyula Hernádi, and István Eörsi.

Kenneth McRobbie, a professor of history at the University of Manitoba, Winnipeg, Canada, specializing in European cultural and intellectual history, has published two collections of poems, *Eyes without a Face* and *What Is on Fire Is Happening*, and his poetry has appeared in many anthologies and periodicals, including *Poetry* (Chicago), *Canadian Forum, Poetry: Glasgow, Cave International: New Zealand, Combustion: Toronto,* and *The Far Point.* He has also written several articles on Hungarian literature and translated extensively from Hungarian poetry, including editions of the selected poems of Ferenc Juhász and László Nagy, the edition of the latter with Tony Connor. His numerous contributions to the knowledge of Hungarian literature abroad have been acknowledged by several awards: the "Pro Litteris Hungaricis" Medal in 1968, the Sándor Petőfi Medal in 1970, and the Special Prize of the Board of Hungarian Publishers in 1974.

Edwin Morgan, Titular Professor of English at the University of Glasgow, has published many books of poetry since his first volume in 1952, the latest being *Star Gate* (1979). He has brought out a collection of his essays (1974) and edited several anthologies of American, English, and Scottish poetry, including *Scottish Satirical Verse* (1980). He has written several opera librettos and recently accepted a commission for another. Translation has engaged him throughout his career. He has translated Brecht, Neruda, Pasternak, Mayakowsky, and Yevtushenko, and has published four collections of his translations since 1975. He has translated more than twenty Hungarian poets, principally Lajos Kassák, István Vas, and Sándor Weöres, and his contributions earned him the P. E. N. Memorial Award in 1972. He took early retirement in 1980 to devote himself entirely to his own work.

Peter Sherwood left Hungary with his parents in 1956, settling in Selford, England, near Manchester. He obtained a B.A., first-class honors, in Hungarian language and literature in 1970 at the School of Slavonic and European Studies, University of London, and then spent 1970-71 as a postgraduate student at the Institute of Linguistics, Hungarian Academy of Sciences. On his return to London, he served as a teaching assistant at the School of Slavonic and East European Studies, and he has been a lecturer in Hungarian language and literature at the school since 1973. Often called upon to write articles and book reviews on Hungarian literature, he has also translated many poems and prose pieces for *Arion, The New Hungarian Quarterly*, and several little magazines in England.

Maxim Tabory, a native Hungarian and now a United States citizen, is director of the Learning Resource Center Library of Cherry Hospital, Goldsboro and lives in Kinston, North Carolina. He is a poet and a translator of both poetry and prose. His translations and book reviews have been published mainly in United States periodicals. He is a member of the Goldwayne Writers' Guild and the North Carolina Poetry Society. He assisted the late Watson Kirkconnell with the preparation of his still unpublished anthology, *The Hungarian Helikon*, containing poetry in English translation from five hundred years of

Hungarian literature, including many contemporary poets living in Hungary and abroad. Tabory frequently reads his poems and translations at colleges and at meetings of reading and book clubs in North Carolina.

Others

Ilona Kovács is the head of the Cataloging Division, the National Széchényi Library (Országos Széchényi Könyvtár), Budapest. She received a B.A. and M.A. at the Loránd Eötvös University in that city and an M.A. in library science at Kent State University, where she spent 1974-75 on a fellowship. In the fall of 1979 she carried on research at the Immigration History Research Center, University of Minnesota, on the subject of books in the lives of Hungarian immigrants in the United States. She has chiefly published articles on library matters.

László Országh is especially known as a linguist and lexicographer and as a teacher and scholar of English and American literature in Hungary. Until his recent retirement, he headed the Department of English at the Lajos Kossuth University in Debrecen. A prolific scholar, he has published numerous articles on literary and linguistic questions in noted periodicals, and his book-length works on the same subjects are widely used. English-speaking students attempting to learn Hungarian are especially indebted to him for his monumental Hungarian-English and English-Hungarian dictionaries. He was recently named Commander of the British Empire by Queen Elizabeth.

Kathy Elaine Tezla, who was born in Chicago, Illinois, has resided in Minnesota since 1949. She received a B.A. in history and library science at the University of Minnesota, Minneapolis, in 1970. She spent 1972-73 in Budapest on a grant from the Hungarian Institute for Cultural Relations, studying Hungarian language and literature at the Loránd Eötvös University. Since 1973 she has been employed as a library assistant in the Special Collections and Rare Books Department of Wilson Library, University of Minnesota, and she is also working on an M.A. in history at the university, with a concentration on nineteenth-century Hungary.

LIBRARY OF DAVIDSON C

Books on regular loan may be che